Caspar Morris

Letters of Travel From Caspar Morris, M. D. 1871-1872 to his family

Volume II.

Caspar Morris

Letters of Travel From Caspar Morris, M. D. 1871-1872 to his family
Volume II.

ISBN/EAN: 9783337021238

Printed in Europe, USA, Canada, Australia, Japan

Cover: Foto ©Andreas Hilbeck / pixelio.de

More available books at **www.hansebooks.com**

Letters of Travel

from

Caspar Morris, M. D.

1871-1872

To His Family

Volume II.

Printed for Private Distribution
1896

TIMES PRINTING HOUSE
PHILADELPHIA

THEBES, Feby. 4, 1872.

My Dear Son:

I enclose the sheets of my journalizing letter written day by day, hoping it might possibly repay my children for the labour of deciphering its shamefully illegible characters, and with the hope that you may extract from it some equivalent for the toil (made such an equivalent by your love) now while your mother and I are separated from you. I cannot think anyone, unless it may be myself, will ever take the necessary trouble, if I keep it till our return. I write under some difficulty, in my own room, which does not admit of a table, though amply large for comfort; often while still lying in bed, so soon as the light is strong enough to enable me to see the lines on the paper. Then both my pens "have come to grief" through my carelessly leaving them lying on the writing desk, which the servants close when I am out of the way.

Your note on Mrs. Cope's letter was most grateful. I am sorry you are so oppressed with professional duty, but would only pray that you may have the strength given you to endure, and wisdom to acquire and apply properly the knowledge of disease and remedy, and thus serve God in your generation in the most godly of all callings, except that for which He only can qualify man—the ministry of the gospel of His son.

I am sorry to be obliged to say that your mother is laid by with the pleuro-pneumonia. I hope it may prove slight and yield to treatment. Her cough has annoyed me for a month or more, and to my great disappointment the Egyptian winter, though not inclement, is not adapted to invalids. The nights are cold and the winds high; and neuralgia and rheumatic pains are common. I have cupped your mother and to-night will apply a blister if she is not more relieved. Her pulse is soft and does not rise over 80 per minute, but her head aches and her eyes feel badly. There is slight subcrepitant râle at the old spot. The cups covered the old marks of scarification. I gave her paregoric and nitre last night, and have prepared morphia for to-night. It is now too dark to see without light and I shall leave the rest of this sheet for to-morrow's report. The sun has just set, but there is no transition stage of twilight.

Monday, 8 A. M.

Your mother was quieter last night from the influence of the morphia, but at 5 I found the vesicating fluid had not yet produced any effect and renewed the application. She is still drowsy, but has the constant desire to inflate the lung always attended by pain.

The family will soon get away for the Tombs of the Kings, which will keep them all day, and I shall keep her perfectly still. They are *anxiously solicitous* to do everything for us which love can dictate, but so many in a small space with only *thin board partitions*, and windows which cannot be moved without rattling, and floors which creak under every foot, and doors which will creak whenever moved, are not adapted to the comfort of the sick, and are things which *cannot* be altered or modified, even by their loving care.

8.30.

Your mother's pulse is only 76 and soft and skin cool. She now reports the blister taking effect and will take some coffee and a light boiled egg. I quite hope the attack will prove a slight one.

I find your Uncle is about sending his letters, and, therefore, dispatch this and shall retain my larger journal and send it down by some of our friends who may reach Cairo before us or keep it till we get there, which will we trust be about 3 weeks from this time.

Which way we shall then journey is wholly *unsettled;* we feel as though we had set our faces *homeward*, but may go to Jerusalem if we find proper conveyance. There is said to be no cholera to interfere. I have seen a gentleman just arrived here by steamer who reports all well on that score.

I have just read my letter to your mother, who desires me to add her love to you *all* and says the morphia brought you *personally* to her side last night and she enjoyed the privilege of a long talk with you. I do not think you need have any anxiety about her attack, but act on the principle we have always recognized that entire truthfulness in our communications is better than the distrust which is caused by the concealment of that which is unpleasant. The mails are uncertain from these up country places, but I will write by the next one and beg you all to rest assured I will keep back nothing.

I am glad to learn from Mrs. Cope she thinks she had improved a little. I do not touch on such subjects in my letters to her, though my anxious desire for her recovery is such that I beg you will adopt any change you may think promises advantage or consult any one who may be able to assist you in understanding the mysteries of the case, or applying remedies for her relief.

Were it not for your mother's sickness I should be enjoying myself to the full amid these ruins of past glory and wonders of Divine power. The sources of pleasure and the subjects for research are alike inexhaustible. The power which broke and overthrew these massive statues and columns is only less extraordinary than that by which they were first brought here; 800 tons is the weight of one statue brought several hundred miles. When brought, how were they raised to their bases? How again thrown down and broken? How strange that men possessed of such power and knowledge should have worshipped and served the creature rather than the Creator! I hope to bring photographs of some of the more imposing. I cannot express our love to dear Mellie and your children and all our other children and grandchildren as though named.

Your loving father,

CASPAR MORRIS.

LUXOR, UPPER EGYPT, February 11, 1872.

My Dear Children:

Having already dispatched large and heavy instalments of my journal letters, I shall spare you any more until we arrive at Cairo at least, and perhaps may keep the remaining sheets till I return home, as I think you must have had enough of Egypt, its ruins, its people, its river, its sun risings and settings, to satisfy if not to disgust you. Yet I know your love craves further information of how we are and what we are doing, and your anxiety for us will have been stimulated by the report of your mother's indisposition which the last two letters conveyed. I am thankful to be able to report improvement, though she is still not well. The catch in her side has not gone and she is weak, keeping her room most of the day, but joining the family in the saloon at tea time. She is obliged to have recourse to morphia nightly, and even with the aid of that she does not sleep well, and her appetite is poor.

This attack has decided the Syrian question for us, which we had kept open till she was taken sick, thinking it possible she might be carried in a palanquin between mules the 40 miles from Jaffa to Jerusalem or if she was not fit for that I might leave her there while I went to the Holy City and returned. We shall not attempt either. Your Uncle and Aunts will pursue their original plan and entering Palestine at Jaffa go to Jerusalem and the sea of Galilee and Jordan and so to Damascus and Beyroot. Your mother and I propose to go directly on by steamboat from Jaffa, where they land, to Beyroot and there wait for them when they have made their tour. I do not think it would be proper for her to undergo the fatigue and exposure, and she thinks I should not, so we agree entirely in the result, and though it is somewhat tantalizing to be so near such sacred scenes it is but a trifling sacrifice to make; so trifling that it costs me nothing and my only prayer is that we may be kept peacefully in the hollow of the hand of Him who chose Mount Sion as His Holy Mount, and abide in Him who, leaving the glory which he had with the Father before the foundation of the world, took upon Him our nature, and as man walked among men 1800 years ago amid those hills of Judea and plains of Galilee. He is not now to be found there, He is risen. We may not find Him there any more than Mary in the tomb. He is nigh all that call upon Him, yea, all that call upon Him faithfully, even looking to that man that is of contrite heart and trembles at His word, though he dwell in the Isles of the Sea or afar off among the gentiles. We are seeking for grace to live one day at a time and to commit you and your concerns to His loving care, asking for you that you may one and all seek His kingdom and its righteousness and trust that He will provide all things needful.

The weather has been very cold. Dr. Kingsley, who is here with the Earl of Pembroke and has spent four winters on the Nile, called on us last evening with the Earl and said he had never experienced such cold here. The last three days have been pleasant. The wind not so boisterous; but we are able to take long walks at midday without finding the sun oppressive.

Day before yesterday your mother was so much more comfortable than she had been that I went with your Uncle and Aunts to see the ruins of the Rameseum, the Colossal statues of Rameses and Amunopth, which stand near it, and the fragments of the great granite figure weighing 800 tons which lies broken near them. One of those still standing was the "Vocal Memnon," and has inscribed on its foot in Greek characters the record of the visits of Emperors and Consuls of Rome and travellers from Greece, and the assertion that they heard its melody when the sun's rays first fell upon it at the time of their visit. The ages which have rolled like floods around them have destroyed their features and spoiled the song. Yet they do stand grandly out to speak yet of the power and lofty imagination of man's heart so long time ago. And they do yet speak to our hearts, if not with the soft notes of song, with the trumpet tones of valuable truth.

Just behind them, crumbling like themselves, are the walls on which Rameses caused to be sculptured the record of his triumphs over his enemies, who fly before him as he drives his triumphal chariot over their smitten hosts and batters down their fortified towers.

Behind these the mountain rises like a honey-comb so perforated with tombs on which are painted similar stories of the might of his successors and great men. Between them lie scattered at the mouths of the pits truly "as when one cutteth wood" the fragments of the bodies of the actors in these very scenes. The Sarcophagi in which they had been deposited have been violated for the sake of the spoil they were supposed to contain, long ages since. They are like other men returning to the earth that which they had taken from its products, and the story of their greatness and their littleness serves us "to point a moral and adorn a tale."

The beauty of the morning is wonderful. An English artist has pitched his tent near the figures that he might catch and fix on canvas the wonderful tints with which the fronts of the figures, and those of the mountains, are bathed in glory each morning. I see them from my cabin window and am overwhelmed with the spectacle as it is renewed day by day. He has made a good picture which he will take to London for exhibition. He was highly gratified by my simple criticism, "It must sing!"

We visited some of the tombs running hundreds of feet into the mountain with stair ways in the interior by which you go from one stage of descent to another till you get some two hundred feet below the surface. The extent of the excavation of this one tomb is not less than 23,000 square feet, all of course in total darkness. Yet every inch of the walls is covered with sculpture or painting, or both, executed 3000 years ago yet retaining its freshness, where it has not been smoked by the lights of visitors. How were they lighted while the work of excavation was being accomplished? How while the decorations were being laid on? We burned candles and tried Magnesium lights without much success. In one of the halls of a small temple among the tombs was a scene representing the god Osiris sitting in judgment on the character of one who was being brought before his throne by Chem, and other minor gods, one of whom was weighing in a balance the merits of the candidate. In the one scale was an urn containing them, and in the other the emblem of truth. The beam stands even; but a movable pea hangs on the side of that emblem, indicating that the character of the man was above the standard. Another god stands reading the record of his deeds.

The desolation of these scenes is indescribable, nothing but disintegrating rocks. Yet standing there we see the ruins of no less than five temples, any one of which impresses one with an idea of the wonderful riches and power of the people by whom they were constructed. The immediate plain watered by the river still teems with fertility and is luxuriantly green with beans, lentils, barley, wheat, flax, cotton and cane.

The people of to-day live in houses built of unburned bricks with only one room and that not sufficiently high to permit a man to stand within. They build within these rooms circular receptacles of the same material, in which they store their grain and other goods. On the ground, those who can afford it, spread Turkey and Persian rugs; those who are not able to purchase such luxuries, mats made of palm leaves, and these compose the entire furniture. I have been prescribing for one of the most affluent, and entered the house through a court yard in which pigeons, chickens, donkeys, cows and calves clustered around the door to the room in which the sick woman lay. She was carefully and lovingly watched and tended by her friends, and is recovering.

This house, with others, was built on the *debris* of those of past generations which has accumulated till it has so filled the temple of Luxor that the capitals of the columns stand in the rooms and court yards which cluster around them, while broken and mutilated statues of the ancient gods lie about the doors. In one part is the granary of the Khedive where the wheat is piled up, and I yesterday saw there repeated such a scene as is represented on the walls of one of the tombs 3000 years old, which we had visited the day before. Men were carrying bags of grain and emptying it on the top, while a clerk was standing taking note of the amounts. There was on another a representation of the bringing of tribute from some foreign land. Trees in tubs were slung on poles borne by men; and baboons and giraffes were among the animals. A monkey was represented climbing the giraffe's neck. The taste for caricature is often shown in such little matters. In one place where water is represented it is evidently meant for an ocean, as the skate fish and lobster and sword fish are very well drawn.

One unpleasant incident quite troubled us yesterday. As we left one of the tombs an Arab demanded backsheesh as a right due to him as sheik of the tombs. The dragoman had contracted to meet this expense, and refused. The man then came to your Uncle and myself, and had a violent altercation with the dragoman. On our return Joseph complained to the governor, and this morning told us the poor fellow was to receive 100 lashes. This troubled us greatly. We could not enter into the merits of the man's right, but only into the terrible suffering of his punishment. Your uncle and I went at once to the consular agent, and, by earnest intercession, procured a remission of the sentence. I think this was the cause of your dear mother's increased indisposition. We have been very quiet to-day, and she is better now, having eaten more dinner than I have known her to do for several days.

There have been no fewer than thirteen dahabeyahs lying here during this week. Several left yesterday and day before and some came, so that to-day we have only six, and all are keeping the day quietly on board their boats. The natives have learned that we never move and do not come near us.

I went this morning to the Coptic service. It consisted in chants and incense and reading lessons in Arabic, which the people understand and speak. The Coptic itself is a dead language to them. The officiating priest wore an ecclesiastical garment ornamented with crosses. Lights were burned on the altar, but there was no crucifix nor other image. The people appeared to unite in the prayers, uttering responses as we do. Much of the service was chanted by boys accompanied at times by cymbals. Your mother desires her love to all. I shall not write again till we reach Cairo, which will be in about three weeks.

Your loving father,

CASPAR MORRIS.

LUXOR, UPPER EGYPT, February 13, 1872.

We are having again an illustration of the uncertainty of the climate. The wind cold and penetrating, and loaded with impalpable dust of sand. During the night two boats came in to the shore from the Upper Nile. One of them moving past my window at an early hour attracted my attention by having two crocodiles fastened to the boom. I supposed they had been shot by the party, but am told they are dried skins purchased from the natives; rather cumbrous and inelegant articles to carry home.

We are all confined to the boat by the disagreeable weather and dependent on our internal resources for our pastime and enjoyment. Your mother has been arranging her knitted pieces in her quilt while I read to her from Wilkinson's Ancient Egyptians. The wealth he reports in the possession of the Kings and some few wealthy families was enormous. But evidently then, as now, the masses were slaves and laboured not for their own profit, but that of their masters. It was thus these great buildings were erected. Then, as now, for instance, they were obliged to pay a tax even on the fish they caught in the river or canal. I find the poor fellows whose incessant labour I have noticed in watering the fields by the shadoof are themselves the proprietors of the crops which they produce.

The habit is still the same as that of the land of Judea in the days of our Lord. As we walk through the fields the traveller has no hesitation at helping himself to whatever amount he chooses to pluck, whether of beans, onions or other crop. It is a recognized right which in those places through which travellers pass to objects of interest, attended by a large retinue, must make an inconvenient draught on the crop.

February 14.

The chapter of Romance is closed ! The climax of our voyage has been reached ! I am drinking in the last draught of delight from the glory of the rising sun on the mountain of Thebes. Your mother and myself have abandoned the thought of " going up to Jerusalem "; so that for us there remains nothing but the prosaic coming down from the height we have reached ; and as we start from here to-night, on our return, there is the day by day striking off one after another, the notches that remain for us before we find ourselves in the dusty path of every day duty. God grant we may there find the light of His countenance, and the joy of domestic happiness ; the two richest joys of existence.

The other members of the party spent the morning at Karnac. Your mother, Aunt Jane and myself visited Mustapha Aga, Mourad Ali, and my patients. I wished your mother to see them and shall leave to her the pleasure of description. It afforded her the opportunity to see the mills and dwellings and some of the ruins of Luxor, and also the beauty of the wheat fields and palm groves from the top of the bank. It was the first time she had been ashore since we left here on our way up. We visited the place of deposit of the grain which is received in payment of taxes ; and saw the great heaps of wheat and beans and lentils. The mill was being turned by a cow, the meal received in a basket. The stones lying at an angle which caused it to fall to the one side where a pit was sunk in the earthen floor to hold the basket. The oil mill was locked and we had an opportunity of seeing the wooden key. It is constructed on the same principle as our most approved safety locks, a curved wooden stick, having on the face of the shorter end a number of short projecting pieces, set at special distances and of different lengths in each key, adapting it to move in the wards which it fits and in them only. One of these little points was broken, and though they made many attempts to introduce a substitute they could not get one which would move the lock.

The friends of my patient presented your mother with some very choice scarabei ; " not as payment for services, but as a token of the grateful feeling." It was done very prettily.

February 16th.

The sun in his glory is now just emerging above the horizon. It is a glory worth a voyage to Egypt to enjoy, so calm in the majesty of its power. One realizes, as no where else that I have ever been, the immensity of the space in which he swings with his attendant system; and its cloudless expanse gives higher ideas of purity than I have ever before realized. There is a feeling of deep regret associated with the conviction that we cannot, many days longer, enjoy the splendor. But what is it in comparison of the rising to the eyes of the redeemed of the Sun of Righteousness? To see Him as He is and be meet for that inheritance is a destiny for which one may gladly drop these glories which shall pass away.

Our ride to Medeenet Haboo yesterday was a pleasant one. It led us more than a mile across a sand-bank, which was entirely covered by the Nile during the inundation, and doura stalks still standing at certain points show where the shallows then were, having been placed to stake out the channel for the guidance of the steamboats. A part of it is now planted with watermelons. Leaving this we ascended the bank and crossed a canal and passed the telegraph office at which we entered on a tract planted with beans and lentils and wheat. The donkey road lay through this, and the men and boys indulged the oriental usage which now, as in the days of our Lord's wanderings through Galilee, recognizes the right of the traveler to pluck and eat as he passes through the fields. The green beans were plucked and eaten freely. Camels, donkeys, buffaloes, cattle, were being fed with the vetches which are pulled and carried to them. The Camel gathers its feet under it as it does to receive or be relieved of its burden, and then lays its long neck on the ground and feeds lazily. It is certainly a most ungainly attitude. One of them was attended by a calf or foal, only a few days old, looking like a white sheep mounted on stilts.

Passing the Colossi, we rode across the edge of the desert at the foot of the hill of tombs, and reached the heaps of bricks half buried, in which rise the columns of the Temple erected by the Third Rameses. His palace was immediately adjoining. His reign was contemporaneous with the early Judges of Israel. In one of the upper chambers of his palace I found an American gentleman seated amid the sculptures which record the triumph of his arms over his enemies, with a pile of piastres lying before him, bargaining with the descendants of the subjects of the Conqueror for antiquities dug up from the ruins of his palace, and Miss Harris bought from one of the labourers a little charm of white stone he had just picked from the dust he was preparing to scatter on his wheat field.

On one wall we see the Conqueror driving his chariot into the discomfited ranks of his enemies. On another he is represented presenting his captives to Amun Ra. On another scribes are enumerating and recording the thousands of hands of the slain which are piled in three heaps before him, while on another the King, attended by his patron god, is carried in procession on the shoulders of priests, while a canopy screens his head and flabellæ or fans are borne before and behind him by the youthful princes. The gods are seated on thrones waiting to welcome him, and in some places they are pouring over his head showers of the symbols of life and power. It is supposed that Rameses the Third overcame the Philistines of Canaan, and thus became the involuntary agent in preparing the land for the occupation of David by delivering the Jews from the terrible bondage in which they were held during the days of the Judges and Saul, and it is not an improbable conjecture that these prisoners are Philistines. They were evidently a Northern race, well clothed, and the colors still remain on their flowing robes in alternate stripes of red and green.

The reference to Egyptians in Canaan in the books of Samuel prove at least that in some way they found themselves in Palestine.

The walls of some of the rooms at Medeenet Haboo are covered with hieroglyphic inscriptions. The columns in some of the halls of this palace and temple are very beautiful as well as massive. Plain round columns of granite of a much smaller size lie strewn on the area of one of the great halls which is surrounded by cloisters with grand sculptures on the walls. These smaller columns are the remains of a *Christian* church which was erected within the enclosure.

To-day we have been passing through a very wide and fertile plain on which are the mounds which mark the site of ancient Coptos from which the caravans started for Kossayr on the Red Sea during the days of the Ptolemies; but the entire district is stamped with a sacred character by the fact that it was the scene of terrible suffering on account of their faith on the part of Christians during the fearful ten years' persecution under the Emperor Diocletian. We have seen nothing on the Nile equal to the fertility of the soil and beauty of the scene. Wild mountain ranges scarped and bare enclosing * * * *

(*Nothing missing here. He evidently dropped his pen for some reason, and did not resume it until the next morning.* ED.)

February 17th.

We find ourselves this morning staked under a high mud bank at the river port of Keneh, a town which lies about one mile inland, celebrated as the place of manufacture of the porous water jars, called "goolahs," and also for a better quality of dates.

DENDERAH, ON THE NILE, February 18, 1872.

My Dear Children:

My last was sent while I was sick. You will I know now rejoice with us at my recovery. I have been able to be about again for a week, after spending ten or twelve days in bed with pluero-pneumonia (my old friend), which required three blisters this time. I was more troubled for your father than myself, as he had not only the nursing, but no one to share the responsibility, tho' I frequently enjoyed Cheston's visits and long talks, in fact you each one flitted in and out as is your habit when I am sick, for being under the effect of morphia, I was in a very happy state. Even it, however, did not give me all the comforts of home. No airy room; no ice water. The state room is 5 feet 7 inches long and 5 feet wide, berth 27 inches wide. So you can see 'twas cramped to be ill in, and the only window, *at my elbow*, made it difficult under the circumstances to ventilate; no quiet. But we are very thankful 'tis all over and trust there will be no repetition. 'Twas not the result of imprudence. We could not account for it. The weather has been so cool and often so cold that I have been very much wrapped up all the time and tried to avoid the drafts, having a constant apprehension of this before me. As I was so sick all the time we were at Thebes (2 weeks) I saw nothing and your father but little, as he very seldom left me; even missed an Arab dinner given to the party by the American Consul, which I regret. He was very pressing in his invitation to have me moved to his house, into an airy room, but by that time I was rather revelling in the ability to reach everything from my bed, and the Arab houses I have been in are not very tempting.

Our present intention is to stop at all the points of interest on our way to Cairo, where I suppose we will be by the 10th or 12th of March, remain about a week. From thence we, *your father and I*, go to Beyrout and will be pretty quiet. *Perhaps get* to Damascus, while the rest go further, *where*, I don't think anybody knows as they change their plans all the time. The truth is *neither* of *us* are able to undertake what they are thinking of and we learn we can be very comfortable at Beyrout. I am very sorry your father cannot go to Jerusalem, &c., &c., and would not let him stay with me if I thought him able to go, but unless he is much better than he has been for the last month or six weeks he could not do it. 'Twould be madness to undertake it. I cannot account for his condition. He is knocked up by exertion, either walking or riding; and has fainty turns.

While we were at Thebes he was much sought by the natives and had the satisfaction of relieving several. I walked with him to see one of his convalescent ones, the sister of the Austrian Consul. She was very grateful and her family also. They gave me some scarabei, and just as we sailed a large basket of very nice fresh Arab bread came on board, and a most acceptable offering it was.

To-morrow is a great feast day with the Mohammedans, so we are to remain here at Kench where there is a mosque. The town is quite a large one, built of mud however, like all the rest. Houses or huts all stuck together like wasps' nests, only occasionally about 3 or 4 feet wide streets. All flat roofs, of mud also; no windows, and the doors very low. Little or no furniture is required, as they sit on the ground, eat off the ground, and sleep there also. They do have a sort of mud closet to put their valuables in.

We are now tied under a steep bank, the town overlooking us and the whole day the women and girls are coming down for water, with earthen jars on their heads, each holding a bushel, and 'tis wonderful to see them climb up with this load, balancing it so nicely, without raising a hand; and this we see all the time. Some children of five or six years.

We saw Mellie's name on Mustapha Aga's book at Thebes. We took quite a fancy to the old man and feel sorry his office has been taken from him. He begged us if any of our children ever come here to write him a letter, and we surely will.

February 22nd.

Here is a lovely day and all except your father and I are off to Abydus, a recently excavated Temple. We are really sorry not to go, but 8 hours on donkeys and feet we thought too much for either of us, tho' we are both much better than we have been for some time. I better than since we left Cairo. I have never recovered from pneumonia as promptly before. I had quite a long donkey ride a few days since, the latter part of which I quite enjoyed, tho' I was wondering if any one of you could recognize us, if suddenly placed before you in our riding costume, mounted, and with the innumerable attendants of Arabs. We start with two or three to each donkey, and as with our courier and dragoman we are 11, you see 'tis quite a cavalcade. The donkeys are very small and some very indifferent. The donkey men are very attentive, aiding you in every way; push or almost lift you, and the donkey too, up the hills and support them in going down; carry umbrellas over us if we wish it and entertain us with their "leetel English," and anxiously repeated any words or names for things that we give them. I do pity the poor Egyptians, they are a poor down-trodden people, but industrious, and I do think as far as their knowledge goes, anxious to do right.

Yesterday we stopped to allow the crew to visit a Sheik whom they say has maintained the same posture for 120 years, without moving. They all went and our gentlemen also. They saw an old man, perhaps 90, sitting in a hole in the ground without clothing or covering of any kind. He moved his head and hands and received the offerings our crew took him, with pleasure, and in return pronounced some blessing on them and any articles which they took for the purpose.

I am sorry we can have no communication with any of them. Our dragoman speaks English so imperfectly that his interpretations don't amount to much, and Freizier don't understand Arabic at all. Your father is going to send you his account of the Arab dinner, which we all have enjoyed. I am only sorry I did not go too.

February 25th.

Another little chat with you all, my dear children, hoping, *as the Browns say*, this will find you all well. We are, and happy too; getting a little impatient now to hear from you, which however we cannot do until we reach Cairo. I think we are all becoming reconciled to this loafing life. We ladies sew or knit and the gentlemen read and write, tho' I think your father does the most of both. The evenings we always spend together, but in the days each acts independently, consequently we pass much of them in our little staterooms, changing from one to the other to get out of the sun. I sit up on the bed and that gives him the chair and room on the bed for the writing desk Mrs. Cope gave him. The sun is too hot and exhausts us too much to be on deck except early in the morning and late in the afternoon, and at those times 'tis so cool and the wind so strong that we have to wrap as tho' 'twas mid Winter, and the changes are so sudden that 'tis difficult to regulate your clothing. I look at the natives with amazement and sympathy too, and only wonder at their living through it, for the *most* clothed of them wear but very little, many children nothing—that is the boys. Girls always have a veil which covers the whole figure. I shall bring you some carte-de-visite to show you the costumes.

February 28th.

Siout is in sight, where the last letters from the Nile are to be mailed, so each are engaged with their pens and I have laid aside my cushion and needle too, but do find it very difficult to write at all to go so far, as nothing seems worth relating, but knowing the assurance of our health and happiness will be acceptable. We think and talk much of you, in our own little apartments. I do wish you could each see all we have been seeing and *that* with your father. He does so enjoy everything and sees so intelligently that I often regret his grandchildren have not the advantage to go over all this ground we have been traversing, with him. To poor old me 'tis all thrown away as I don't *see* much and remember less, so don't expect me to recount to you.

We shall remain at Siout two days to allow the crew to bake bread and we visit the missionary, &c., and try to find something in the bazaars to take home of Egyptian manufacture, and that involves another donkey ride, which I assure you I don't look forward with any pleasure to, but as I am well I have no excuse for withdrawing.

I expect in our next, which will be from Cairo, we shall be able to tell you our plans, as we know you will want to know. I do feel very thankful to each and all of you for your letters. They have been most acceptable, and tell the grand-children if I could, each of theirs should be acknowledged. I have only one fault to find with them. I requested each would express his or her desire as to what they would like us to take them and we would then have some guide and yet not feel obliged to comply if inconvenient. There is yet time for it. Indeed I often wish I knew what the old ones would like, both men and women. 'Twould be a great help. Remembered you all are, but we want to have some token of it. I must say farewell as the envelope is now to be closed.

With much love to each ; I remain as devoted as ever to my children and grand-children.

    Yours truly and affectionately,

                    A. C. MORRIS.

                February 21st.

The breaks and irregularities in these notes are inevitable. The interruptions are constant. The objects to be seen demand instant attention or they are passed. The assistance required must be given at the moment it is demanded and there is none other to render it. I have abandoned all attempt at continuity.

Yesterday the wind blew so strongly that we were cold in the shade, while the sun was oppressively hot. To-day there is a very pleasant breeze and your mother and I have been seated on deck, she knitting while I protected her from the sun by my umbrella. The direct rays of the sun were very hot, but thus shaded, she sat dressed with her usual winter garments over which were two wadded sacks, a flannel sack and her waterproof cloak. The terrible wilderness bounded our view with its heaps of yellow sand drifting over the hills, against whose precipitous cliffs it rested like snow banks. The valley of the river smiled in all the luxuriance of our June. Wheat fields in full head of living green, varied by tobacco, sugar cane and beans, and the whole dotted with palm and acacia groves.

We landed at one spot to see our crew pay their respects to Sheik Selim, a Santon, who has sat in one spot on the bank, they say for 120 years. He is a wretched object. Just like one of our imbecile lunatics, with red eyes and matted gray hair and beard. His obesity proves that his admirers keep him well fed. The climate demands no clothing, and he has never troubled himself with any. Offerings of bread and dates abound. We saw him eat and drink like an animal. Our Reis says his uncle saw him where he now is when Napoleon was here.

                February 18th.

A lovely morning finds us still staked to the bank at the shore near Keneh, a town on the Arabian side of the river. The sunset last evening was grand ; its parting rays illuminating the rugged faces of "the everlasting hills," and gilding the tops of the towering palms which give such beauty to the plains.

One cannot avoid contrasting the present with the past when this was a point in the great line of traffic with the East, and the "wealth of Ind" was poured through this channel to Alexandria. the great centre of the commerce of the world. Then as now the mass of the people dwelt in houses of unbaked brick, and were mere slaves of the Greek conquerors who held the country from the day of its conquest by Alexander till the luxury and vice, which were the natural offspring of wealth and power, produced a degenerate race from whose grasp that wealth and power were transmitted to Roman hands. These savage hills and desert plains, and fertile shores and groves of palms and acacia and tamarisk, remain unchanged through all these vicissitudes of natural things.

As I gazed on the glow of the parting day, and sat musing on these changing scenes in the drama, I found my thoughts turning to the spiritual rise and fall which had been accomplished here. Some herald of the Cross had found his way to the humble homes of the oppressed felaheen of those days, and the "glad tidings of great joy" for all people had been whispered softly from one to another till these palm groves had resounded with the "songs of peace for them that love peace" and the sorrows of their lot were forgotten, while they found in the majesty of their river and the splendor of the morning and evening, grand symbols of the glory which shall be revealed even for them, and in the towering palms emblems of the victory which had been achieved in their behalf and for their benefit by "Jesus of Nazareth," who was thus preached to them. And as I looked upon the lovely scene, bathed in a soft moonlight, and raised my eyes to the overspreading arch of heaven with its countless stars glowing there, the feeling of sympathy with the Christian multitude who once peopled these plains and "worked out their salvation with fear and trembling, knowing that it was God who worked in them to will and to do of His good pleasure," became so strong that I could follow them with the eye of faith to the banks of the River of Life, whose glories are so faintly shadowed by these, impressive as they are, and seek with renewed earnestness for grace to follow them "who through faith and patience have inherited the promises."

It was a more pleasing association of feeling than that with the court of the Ptolemies with the luxury and license of which history has transmitted so imposing an account. More ennobling than that with the intellectual splendor of the Museum even with its galaxy of philosophers and physicians and poets there collected, though there they achieved an eminence in science which has never been surpassed. The names of Euclid and Conon and Hipparchus and Eratosthenes are still honored as those of men whose patient industry penetrated the mysteries of nature, determined the shape and measured the circumference of the earth; calculated the extent of its orbit, and fixed the latitude and longitude of its noted cities; and determined the courses of the stars. Egypt was the home of these men, and her monarchs the patrons by whom they were nurtured. But such men looked no higher than to their earthly friends. To them they ascribed all honor and power ; and clothing them with the robes and insignia of the gods they have inscribed on the walls of majestic temples, built to their honor, the names we still read in mysterious characters, and when Berenice, the sister and wife of Ptolemy, in fulfilment of a vow made to the gods when her "brother and husband" went forth to meet Antiochus, cut off her tresses, astronomer and poet, with united flattery transferred them to the stars as a constellation which still bears her name, and celebrated their "reluctance to leave her head even for the glory of the skies." The figures of "Ptolemy and Berenice" stand on the walls multilated and defaced. The Museum, with its treasures of science and art and literary stores, has long since become a heap of dust indistinguishable from that of the hovels which have accumulated over it for ages ; but who can properly appreciate the glory and honor and immortality of the humblest follower of Christ, who amid these shades so walked as He walked? That is a glory "which excelleth." I find myself very prone to covet the honor of the philosopher and poet; my imagination constantly runs away with them and their greatness, but this morning I am happy to have it peopling this valley with witnesses for Jesus and summoning them to the house of prayer, and listening to their songs of praise, and thinking of the glory of "that day" when from these tombs shall arise those who counted not their lives dear unto themselves, but sealed their testimony with their blood, and as I read the Holy Scripture which has been handed down to us I think how precious to them were the same gracious words, and how wonderful the wisdom and power of God who has preserved them " for our learning upon whom the ends of the world are come."

On the walls of one part of the temple at Karnac, which was then the library, Herodotus tells us was inscribed more than 3000 years ago the famous sentence which taught that " knowledge is the medicine of the mind." To know Jesus "is the life of the Soul." *That* knowledge passeth away ; this endureth forever. *That* is not to be despised but cultivated with assiduous toil. *This* to be sought as His gift "whom to know is life eternal." So long as I live on earth I would be found labouring to acquire more and more of that knowledge which enlarges the intellect and nourishes the mind. Forever may I grow in that knowledge which is the gift of grace through Jesus Christ our Lord. Forever I shall grow in all the gifts and graces of the Spirit, nor would I undervalue the conviction of my judgment that amid the blessings of eternal life He who has taught us as regards earthly comforts that our Father " knoweth we have need of them " ; and having freely given us His Son will freely with Him give us all things, "caring for us," will also provide for the growth of that intellectual part of our being with which He has endowed us, and that while our spiritual being will be more and more conformed to His holiness, our intellectual nature will find food for its support and delight, and will expand amid the larger lessons and wider spheres of observation which will open to it when the trammels of the flesh and the fetters of corruption shall be laid aside and dropped, and with bodies changed and made like unto His glorious body, we shall know more than our first father lost. How can it be otherwise? If the second Adam is the Lord from Heaven, His children must be like Him, for "as we have borne the image of the earthly, we shall also bear the image of the heavenly." This is a wide digression, but these monuments of human glory, decaying and crumbling (though they have resisted the power of destruction of so many ages) and the calm majesty of the glorious river illuminated by the splendor of the setting sun, and the moon softly sailing in the star enamelled firmament "changing not," transport me to higher and more lasting glories.

February 19th.

At an early hour this morning our dahabeyah was moved to a point nearer to the temple of Denderah, and soon after breakfast we started to visit it, "none missing." It was a delightful morning. A warm sun was rendered pleasant by a soft, cool breeze. Your mother was wonderfully well and strong, but the first step cost her much; indeed, it almost overcame her. A very steep bank was to be climbed, as the river has now reached almost its lowest point. This was effected with the assistance of two Egyptians, but not without exhausting her breath and causing great palpitation of heart. This was a poor preparation for the next more formidable step of mounting the donkey. Many were collected, and a crowd of lookers-on with their unintelligible clamor did not add to her equanimity. It was a *mite* of an animal, yet it must be mounted, and that was a difficulty which was more formidable in appearance than reality. A chair put her almost on a level with the seat, but no sooner was that accomplished than a really serious obstacle was presented in the necessity to ride down the steep side of a canal and climb the other. It was enough to appal even myself, accustomed as I have become to the facility with which men and donkeys go over these places. Two men embraced each of us, and might be said to have carried us, donkeys and all, down and up again. It was some minutes before your mother recovered her breath, or I the courage to ask her how she was doing, and we rode some mile or more before she recovered her breath and power to speak.

Our road lay through a plain planted with wheat and beans, *both most luxuriant*. The wheat in full head. The roadside was gemmed with daisies and dandelions, here and there a many-coloured pea-vine showed its beautiful flower among the green wheat or bean-stalks and the air was perfumed by the odor of a very beautiful plant which looks to me like an Oboranche. It has no leaves, but shoots up from the ground a succulent stalk covered with ringent flowers of lilac colour, striped with brown and shaded with rose. They are equal in beauty to the Dendrobrium, though not so large. The spikes were many of them a foot—some even two feet—high, and clothed with flowers to at least half the height. I wish much for the power to depict its exquisite beauty. At Heliopolis we saw a smaller species of the same plant of deeper color, and both there and here have attempted to save the seeds, and here have put some small specimens in press, but fear they are too succulent to be dried in that way.

The ride was over three miles across this beautiful plain, dotted with clumps of green Tamarisk trees, with here and there a grove of palms of both varieties, and bounded on our left by the yellow sand heaps of the desert, rising gradually to the harsh outlines of the hills. We passed several hamlets, in one of which the wail for the dead sounded plaintively on our ears, while far in the distance the Cemetery, with its many smaller tombs, and domes of half a dozen tombs of the Sheiks, seemed close at hand but ever receded as we advanced. Distances are very deceptive where there are no objects to divide them. We saw the Pylon of the temple soon after we reached the plain, but after riding half an hour it seemed still as distant as when first it met our view.

Your mother gradually recovered her breath and the tumultuous action of her heart ceased and she became accustomed to her seat and the support of the arms of her two attendants, and the easy motion of the donkey, and began talking to her attendants, and by the time we reached the temple was compensated for her suffering in the first part of the ride by the pleasure of the last.

We were obliged to ride up the great mound composed of the usual *debris* of baked brick and broken pottery, near the summit of which we passed through a pylon with its sculptured sides and architrave, and saw before us the massive front of the temple. The interior has been cleared out, but the rubbish rises before it to nearly half its height, so that we stood and looked down into the first court with its grand columns. This portico was erected by Tiberius, and has not less than twenty massive columns covered with sculpture, more raised than common bas-relief. The ceiling is covered with winged globes and figures of the goddess Athor are found in each corner of the ceiling, extending gigantic limbs on either side. The ceiling has also a Zodiac which has great celebrity from having been supposed to exhibit proof of an antiquity which was used by philosophers a few years ago as furnishing proof that it had existed ages before the received epoch of the creation. In this instance science—falsely so-called—may find a lesson of humility. Believers in Revelation were snubbed and scoffed at till it was found from an inscription on the temple itself that the ancient Zodiac, instead of being antediluvian, as it had been wisely decided it was, was not more than 1800 years old, being at the oldest Ptolemaic in its date.

To the portico of twenty-four massive columns with capitals ornamented by heads of Athor and palm branches and papyrus buds, and covered with figures of the gods, succeeds a court or hall with six columns, behind which is a central hall, or adytum, like a small temple itself, with a well lighted passage passing around it, on which nine smaller chambers open. All these walls are covered with sculptured figures of the gods and goddesses, and in the central one are portraits of the celebrated Cleopatra and her son Cæsarion, so named for his father Julius Cæsar. They are well sculptured but do not give us the idea of beauty generally associated with that infamous but captivating woman, who held in her captivity so many of the great men of her age. The roof of this temple remains entire. One of the stones is not less than twenty feet square by at least four in thickness. The entire ceiling was sculptured with stars and winged figures, and the deep blue with which it was coloured may still be discovered through the soot which has blackened it during the ages in which it covered the hovels of the Arabs, who found shelter beneath it. Much colour may still be detected on many of the figures and when the whole was perfect it must have been a very imposing edifice. A flight of easy stairs leads through one of the walls to the roof, each wall covered with sculpture and hieroglyphics. The entire length of the temple is over 200 feet and its front 100 feet and though, as it stands at present, no part dates further back than the Ptolemies, and most of it is of the date of Tiberius, yet it stands on the site of one built by Cheops and rebuilt by Tothmes III.; the first about 2500 years before the birth of Our Lord and the last 1000 years later.

February 20th.

It is almost as difficult to write connectedly here as it would be in the market place or amid the distractions of business. Some beauty to be gazed at for the last time, some novel object, or some remnant of past ages is constantly claiming attention and rendering continued thought impossible.

Feby. 20, 1872.

As we are now slowly dropping down the stream, not designing to stop long enough to land, and with only the perpetual repetition of beautiful green sloping wheat fields, palm groves and clumps of Acacia and Tamarisk trees alternating with stretches of desert sand, now coming quite down to the river and then receding some miles from the shore, I have taken the occasion to look over the very crude, hasty, disjointed and imperfect notes I have made during the last two or three weeks.

Egyptian History is an intricate problem which has exercised the powers of the profoundest scholars and deepest thinkers of modern time. It is not to be supposed that it can be taken up and solved by one so unlearned as myself in general history and unaccustomed to labourious investigation. There appear to have been then, as in more recent periods, epochs in which power manifested itself simultaneously in the action of the conqueror and the development of art ; such as, for example, in the Elizabethan era in English story, when the energy of the nation displayed itself in military power and literary growth. Such undoubtedly was the era of Rameses the Second whose reign dates about 1300 years before the birth of our Lord ; and such, though not to the same degree, had been that of Amunoph, more than a century earlier. Or perhaps it would be more correct to speak of this one era beginning with the first and culminating in the second. Certain it is that while tombs and pyramids and obelisks of an earlier day attest the civilization of the people and prove that their manners and customs and religion had undergone no change, nearly all the great temples from Abydos to Aboo Simbel belong to the period between 1500 and 1200 years before our era and none were built at a later day until the Ptolomies, when Arts and Philosophy and Letters again flourished, and again the temples either in the form of additions to those of the earlier period or on new foundations.

Through all these ages the condition of the masses appears to have been unchanged. They must have been as they still are mere slaves of the priestly and royal and military cast, which was one. Weak monarchs were governed by the priests, who controlled the soldiers. Wise and strong monarchs became conquerors and brought back from the conquered people the spoil. This became the possession of the priesthood either in the shape of temples in honor of the gods, ornamental work on those already erected, or was stored under their care in those temples, which were all strongholds of defence, in which they were protected from every danger except that of foreign conquest, and in which these treasures accumulated until they became the prey of the Persian and the Greek and Roman. The massive buildings with secret passages and dark chambers in the walls and surrounded by extensive lofty and solid walls of unbaked brick were so many fortresses.

The earliest notice we have of Egypt is that in Genesis when Abram went down into that land to escape the famine of Canaan, and then it was undoubtedly a rich country, with princes as well as a king. This was, according to our received chronology, more than 2000 years before the coming of Christ ; about the date usually given to the pyramids of Gizeh. Earlier than that of any obelisk or temple or tomb. From that time not only through all vicissitudes of the life of the patriarch and his descendants, not only during the time of their sojourn, first as honored guests of the king and then as slaves, not only during their national existence, but down to the present time, when the sculptured temples and tombs of Egypt afford so much light upon scriptural narrative, Egypt and Canaan have been associated either as typical of the world and its enmity against God, on the one side, and the glory which remaineth, and the rest of His people, on the other—or in actual historic connection. The Pharoah who is mentioned in connection with Joseph and the going down into Egypt of Jacob and his sons, was probably ruler only over the lower kingdom, the capital of which was at Memphis, near Cairo, though the obelisk at Heliopolis, which is of granite, came from Syene, nearly 1000 miles further South, and bears on it the names of Osirtasem, who reigned over upper Egypt and built the earliest portion still remaining of the great temple of Karnac at Thebes. Such is the difficult entanglement of the records of those ages.

The best solution of the enigma is found in the supposition that there were many minor kingdoms, to a certain degree independent at times, and at others held in subjection by some one dominant power. Thus Memphis in lower Egypt appears about the time at which Joseph lived, to have been the residence of the Pharoah who governed upper Egypt also, and some centuries later when the time appointed of God for the liberation of His chosen people drew near "another king who knew not Joseph arose" in the Pharoah of Upper Egypt, whose seat of government was transferred for the time from Thebes to Memphis. It is certain that Memphis

(*This breaks off suddenly here.*—ED.)

ABYDOS, Feby. 22, 1872.

My Dear Children:

I am profoundly thankful to be able to report your dear mother quite restored. Indeed for the last week she has been really stronger and has enjoyed herself more than at any time since we left home. She was even able to ride to the temple at Denderah without being greatly fatigued. To-day she and I are *alone*.

This is the seat of one of the oldest Capitals of Egypt—Originally called "This"; by the Greeks, Abydus; and a colony exiled from here settled at Abydos before the days of the Trojan war. The priests told Herodotus it was the birth place of Perseus, and that he visited it on his way to get the head of Medusa in Ethiopia.

Nothing now remains but the tombs in the hill sides, and the temple of Osiris, and palace of Rameses the Great, on the border of the desert eight miles from the nearest point to it on the river shore. To visit it will require not less than six perhaps eight hours on donkeys and on foot. Your mother could not endure it and I think it better not to do it myself, tho' it requires strong effort of self denial as the ride over the plain, which is said to be very fertile and highly cultivated in wheat and beans, would be delightful, and the temple and palace have been only lately excavated by Mons. Mariette under the auspices of the Khedive.

Dating from the time at which the then civilized world was under the sway of Egypt, they are among the most perfect remains of the splendor of its glory. The whole interior was once lined with alabaster; and Strabo, who visited it a few years before the birth of Our Lord describes it as sparkling with gems and resplendent with gold, its recesses veiled by richly embroidered curtains, behind which were placed the sacred animals worshipped as gods; pampered during their lives and made into mummies when they cast contempt on their worshippers by proving their weakness by yielding to the power of death. I had a great desire to visit it, but surrender to the control of circumstances.

The weather is now delightful and while we sit in the saloon with all the windows closed and the sun shining around us, dressed in winter habiliments it is true, but feeling the advantage of fresh air with the thermometer at 60° F., we think of you celebrating the birth day of a greater than Rameses; the founder of an empire wider than his and destined to extend the area of freedom for man, while the Egyptian kingdom was one of slavery and oppression; and we fancy you surrounded by ice and snow and rejoicing that the reign of winter draws to a close. We have known nothing of its rigor, though we have felt the cold more than we had anticipated, and we hope as our course now tends northward we may continue to escape both extremes.

Whether the other members of the party will persevere in their purpose of visiting Jerusalem and Galilee, while we wait for them at Beyrout, and then enter Europe by Constantinople and so up the Danube to Vienna; or sail to Brindisi and thence to Vienna by Trieste, will remain undecided until we reach Cairo and learn more than we now know of the quarantine arrangements. We have not the time to spare for Lazarettos, nor do we wish to encounter the certain ennui and disgust, and the probable sickness, which would be our lot in those gloomy abodes.

I must refer you to my very imperfect daily notes for the record of our acts and feelings among the ruins of Thebes and the Thebaid, where we have spent the last month. Sharpe in his History of Egypt says: "The wide acres of Theban ruin prove alike the greatness of the city and the force with which it was overthrown." The buildings which retain their perfectness when contrasted with the fragments of those of equal solidity, by which they are surrounded, prove that the mad application of man's power is more destructive than the lapse of ages. The color and sculpture remains, defying time, the imperishable granite lies in fragments, split by the determined effort to destroy of the same power at whose bidding it had first been wrested from its bed in the solid rock, and fashioned into the shape and features of the conqueror, who defied the influence of time, yet was obliged to yield to the mightier arm of a puny creature of the day like himself.

"These temples and statues have seen the *whole portion* of time of which history keeps the reckoning-roll before them; they have seen kingdoms and nations rise and fall; the Babylonians, the Jews, the Persians, the Greeks, the Romans. They have seen the *childhood* of all that we call ancient; and they still seem likely to stand to tell their tale to those who will hereafter call us ancient." The only traces of decay are those which owe their beginning to the wanton destructive agency of human spite or envy or vengeance. Time has made no entrance where man has not opened the avenue to his destructive influence. The same Rameses who added to the older temples at Karnac and built the Ramessium at Thebes built the Ramessium and temple of Osiris here; *before* it entered into the heart of David to build a temple for the true and only God, or of Soloman to build himself a house, by *three centuries*. The mode of building arches was then but little known though some still remain built of unburned brick having on each the stamp of the monarch in whose reign they were made, of still older date than the temple. In it the roof is formed by laying immense blocks of stone from the architrave which runs along one range of columns to that which runs along another parallel range, and then cutting out the under side to form a vaulted roof. This is covered with hieroglyphics and sculptures richly coloured. While I look at the description given of it I cannot but feel deep regret that I am not able to ride to it, though within two hours. I have seen so many equally grand that I can well imagine how much I lose in missing this.

Even Friezier (an old Courier making his first trip on the Nile) has become enthusiastic on the subject of Egyptian Temples, though for weeks he declared himself "*Absolutely disgusted*, and totally unable to comprehend how people should be such fools as to allow themselves to be betrayed by the enthusiasm of a few learned Egyptologists, who fancy themselves wiser than everybody besides, and spend so much money to make themselves uncomfortable here when they might enjoy so much beauty in Roman and Greek remains with less trouble and cost."

I have thus quoted one of his deliberate utterances, but you should have seen his disconsolate face and the shrug of his shoulders to appreciate its force. The change in his views contributes to our comfort as well as our amusement. A few evenings since he volunteered to read us some pages of his Diary in which he has recorded the account of the Dinner given by the American Consular Agent at Thebes to our party. It was while your mother was too ill for me to leave her. I asked Friezier's permission to copy the account and send it for your amusement.

THEBES, NILE, February 8, 1872.

"In consequence of yesterday's excursion we all felt rather tired this morning and a day of rest was decreed. Shortly after breakfast Ali Mourad, the American Consul, came on board and invited Mr. Morris and family to dinner, served in Arab style, which is to come off at six o'clock. In courtesy to him the invitation was accepted. He also asked the Dragoman and myself to come so that we might extend a helping hand to his servants."

"I was highly delighted with the opportunity afforded me to witness such an interesting and mysterious ceremony. All the enchantment and wonder we read of in Arabian Nights took hold of my imagination and ran riot in my head all day long. I pictured to myself a grand array of black slaves richly and curiously clad in Eastern fashion, receiving us at the door with slavish humility and proceeding with us to the presence of their dreaded master, who received us most graciously, and after a great many Salaams and repetitions of meaningless and empty phrases, bade his guests to sit down near him on richly covered Ottomans which ran round three sides of the room. I thought the floor should be covered with soft and beautiful Persian carpets, wrought in exquisite Oriental patterns and imagined the gentleman to be dressed in Damascus Silk habiliments, with a few inestimable India shawls wound round his loins and turban, and curiously wrought Oriental Arms studded with precious stones stuck in his girdle."

"I imagined the Hall to be beautifully illuminated with a subdued and mysterious light proceeding from a number of variegated lamps suspended in all directions, filled with fragrant oil which in burning dissolved a delicious perfume which was very pleasing to the senses."

"In this way I went on picturing and imagining most extravagant Oriental scenes to myself, to beguile the time which I found proceeded but slowly. At last the wished for hour arrived and we started for the Consul's house, two gentlemen, three ladies, Joseph and myself."

"After having mounted two flights of *brick paved* stairs, and traversed part of a *brick paved* terrace we came to the door of the entrance hall, which opened at once as if by magic."

"I found this *entrance* hall had been turned into a dining saloon on this occasion. It is a long narrow passage which gives entrance to two rooms on each side of the walls, but not in juxtaposition to each other. In the four *corners* hung as many very ordinary looking lanterns having each a very ordinary looking European lighted candle in it. The brick paved floor was partly covered with small pieces of carpet, of various designs and colors, in the midst of which stood a pretty large round table made of Zinc, the border of which was turned up half an inch, which gave it the appearance of a huge Tea tray. It was raised about one foot and a half from the floor. Around it, on the carpet, lay six long narrow pillows in white cases. On the table stood a real blue Willow Pattern *Staffordshire* Soup tureen with six soup plates to match, a large plated soup ladle, not *scrupulously* clean. Each plate had a spoon of the same material and hue lying beside it, with a piece of good bread and clean napkin. Nothing else was visible on the table."

"Dinner was announced and each guest sat down *A l' Orientale*, that is cross-legged or tailor fashion, on a pillow as near the table as possible they could get."

"Now the host began to ladle out the soup, and hand it round with a certain grace quite Eastern. Meanwhile I was asked to carve a boiled fowl, which was boiled to rags, with an English carving knife that *would not cut* and took me consequently a long time to accomplish. When I put it on the table I was quite dismayed when I found that every bit of table furniture had disappeared. The host had a large roasted turkey before him, the fleshy parts of which he was lustily digging into with his fingers and nails, and tearing off nice little bits, which he presented to his guests in succession, who of course not only accepted them but ate them with their fingers."

"At this stage of the proceedings I became rather perplexed and wondered whether they were also to drink with their fingers or whether each in turn were to have a pull at the bottle. I remained not long in this suspense, for real European tumblers and wine were brought in after the turkey was removed, and a great many different dishes were brought in and taken away in quick succession. For the life of me I could not tell what they were composed of. Some were solid and some were liquid. I did not count them, but I believe without exaggeration that at least a dozen courses must have been served, all of which the guests ate from *without the use of plates, knives or forks*. The host served them round with his *fingers* and they were arrested and eaten in the same way, seemingly with the greatest *gusto*. In fact Mr. M. and party seemed to enjoy it immensely."

"All through the dinner I observed the host closely, to see whether he would not suck his fingers now and then. I should have liked to see him do it. But, No! he quite disappointed me. I did not see him attempt it, but I cannot say as much for one of the guests whom I observed several times furtively licking the digits, which served as knife and fork, and which I believe constituted a great breach of etiquette in Eastern society."

"The meats and vegetables were all disposed of. The sweets were served up. First came a dish which looked to me very much like pan cakes; served simultaneously with a dish of boiled rice. The former were torn in pieces and served out as the meats had been, with the fingers. Then came two dishes of a brown substance in a semi-liquid state. Its component parts have remained a mystery to me; followed by three dishes of a white solid substance which looked much like paperhanger's paste. The guests partook of all these, always with the fingers, and seemed to enjoy them very much."

"These were removed and now came the last and most interesting dish of the whole dinner. It was an ordinary slop basin full of a brown colored liquor, accompanied by six wooden spoons. The host distributed the spoons, one to each guest. They all held their spoons within their hands looking at one another with alarm, and a certain misgiving depicted on their faces, of what was to come next. The Consul observed the embarrasment and as an intrepid Amphitrite he showed the way. He plunged his spoon into the basin, stirred it up well, brought a dried rasin to the surface, caught it along with a spoonful of the liquid, conveyed it to his mouth and swallowed it—of course not the spoon but the contents—altho' the spoon went so deep that I thought I should never see it again."

"The guests followed his example and plunged their spoons boldly into the basin and did as the Consul had done. Wa! thought I, first spoonful is very well, because they are clean and have not touched any other lips, but the second must be a bold undertaking. I could see very plainly that Mr. M. and party would have gladly cried 'quits' here, but the host urged them on with gestures and entreaties not to abandon him in the last efforts at hospitality. Of course they felt themselves bound by courtesy to continue, altho' I could see it was quite against their inclination. Here again the French proverb is verified, '*Ce n' est que le premier pas qui coûte.*' So they dived in one after another until the basin was nearly empty, and herewith the dinner was finished."

"Now came a black servant with a ewer and basin, of very graceful and antique shape, but like the table made of zinc, and poured water over the guests' hands so that they could wash them clean, after having usurped the functions of knives and forks. Now they all rose to their feet, which is not so easy to be done by one not used to such a cramped position, and retired to an improvised saloon to take coffee and to smoke (in which the ladies showed their courteous breeding by graceful acquiescence). I thought what a comfortable arrangement it would have been in England some forty or fifty years ago amongst the highest classes (who were wont after meals to drink until they rolled helplessly under the table) if they had been seated in Arabian manner. They might then have reclined with the greatest ease and have a pillow to lay their aching heads on until the fumes of the wine had evaporated."

"The table with its stand and pillows was removed and stowed away. Now Joseph and I were invited to dine off the remains of the feast. *We sat* down in real European style, on real European chairs, before a four legged deal table of European make, and which was covered with a mass of very ill assorted and curious objects, which I took the liberty to examine while they brought in the dishes. First of all there was a pair of very greasy snuffers, an Egyptian wooden lock and key, which is a very funny piece of mechanism—some onions—Morocco slippers—some pipe bowls—a rusty carving knife and fork—an imitation antique statue of Osiris of glazed terra cotta—a red skull cap with a blue tassel—a complete Nubian ladies costume, consisting of a brown leather belt about a foot wide cut into small strips like shoe strings to within an inch of the top, which was ornamented with glass beads of different colors, and sheep's claws alternately. This is worn around the loins and is the only garment which constitutes a Nubian woman's toilette, with the addition of a profuse quantity of iron or brass and sometimes silver rings which adorn the nose, ears, neck, arms and ankles. Then there was a palm leaf fly whisk, a most necessary piece of furniture, a bottle of Henessey's Cognac—two bottles of Claret and a bottle of Vermouth from Turin. Now all the dishes came in at once. All the articles above mentioned were swept into a heap to make room for the viands to be put on the table. There was such a quantity that I was rather puzzled to know where to begin first. Soup we did not want. While I was hesitating Joseph had attacked the turkey most vigorously. I plunged my fingers into a dish containing a brown composition of lumps and liquid which I found to be mutton stewed with dry raisins, which I did not like at all. I tried another which looked much like small pieces of sponge fried in oil, which turned out to be very nice. Close to my elbow stood a plate which I thought had some tempting looking sausages on it. I took one and found it also to be nice. Rice mixed with minced meat and rolled up in lettuce leaves that certainly was not bad. Then I tried some more dishes but could not tell of what they were composed, but they were all very nice and savory, if they only had adopted the Chinese fashion of providing us with chop sticks instead of compelling us to eat with our fingers."

"Mr. M. and party were by this time ready to return to the boat, so we moved on, preceeded by two sailors carrying huge lanterns before us, without which we never could have found the road, for it was pitch dark by this time, and there was no moon. It really requires a stout heart to move about in the dark in an Egyptian village for the streets are full of pits and ridges where people would risk the breaking of their legs or necks, independently of the attacks of furious dogs who are howling about all night long, and who would not in the least scruple to take a bite out of a Christian leg but never attack their own countrymen."

I thought Friezier's sketch—the work of an impartial looker on, might amuse you. It requires his German accent and emphasis and mispronunciation to give the true tone to the picture. With those it is very good.

February 28th.

We are now near Siout about 200 miles above Cairo. All well. We hope to reach Cairo this day two weeks. It is long, very long, since we heard of you and we have you each individually always in our hearts, in our thoughts, and often on our lips; and pray for your preservation. I have some thirty sheets of letter which I shall probably send from Cairo. I have already sent as much since we came up the Nile, in several packages; and hope some of them may have reached you to amuse your winter evenings which are now waning as the days increase. Mr. Greble passed us again a few days since on his way back, in the same boat with a Mr. and Mrs. Reeves from Ohio who are cousins of Mr. Samuel Reeves. I hope Miss R. did not captivate the Russian officer who did the honors of the Alexis ball for her. Much love to all.

    Your loving father,

CASPAR MORRIS.

February 23, 1872.

The excursionists returned yesterday delighted with their ride of sixteen miles through fields of barley, wheat, oats and beans; all most luxuriant. Camels, cattle, sheep and goats tethered amid rich clover fields, and the people looking happy, living in temporary booths of doura stalks, busily engaged in gathering the barley and tending their flocks. They speak of it as the most beautiful picture of eastern life they have yet seen.

The temple and palace were reached by a straight and level road of at least twenty feet wide which has been made recently for the accommodation of some member of the Khedive's family. A royal road, a King's highway. They speak of the sculpture on the walls as being very fine and the colours fresher than any we have seen. Joseph very kindly brought me a fragment. The buildings are of limestone, with ornaments of granite and some parts still retain the alabaster coat with which the interior was lined.

Mr. Longstreth climbed to a projecting hinge in one of the door jambs and found it a block of wood with a hole, in which the pivot on the door had turned. If the giant oaks which guard the homes of the Percy's high born race could utter tales were they furnished with tongues, what lessons would come from that "cardinal point" on which has turned the valve which admitted into these walls the grand processions in honor of Osiris, when Rameses returned from the conquest of Ethiopia or Scythia? What changes in the fate of empire and destiny of man have been wrought since the carpenter fashioned that block and the mason fastened it in the hole it has filled during those long ages, in each of which the great ones have fretted their little hour on the stage; while the pictured wall below reveals to us that the land is tilled and the crops gathered in the same manner now as then, and these masses have undergone as little change in manners and customs as the wood or stone. Yet generation after generation has felt the anxieties and suffered the sorrows which wring the soul, in its individual existence, and rejoiced in the sunshine and sported in the joys of their little hour, with the same intensity of delight we do now; and amid all these changing scenes there is One who changeth not, whose mercy is over all His works and who has dispensed His blessings to each generation with equal hand.

We are now passing a grove of palms so beautiful that I cannot refrain from the expression of delight even if it be a thrice told tale.

The temple and palace at Abydus are the last we shall visit. The tombs at Beni Hassan and the pyramids, and sphynx, and museum at Boulac, will fill up the chapter. Three weeks more and our home on the Nile will be broken up. It is a pleasant home to which we shall look back with gratitude for its privileges and blessings when we return to the more familiar home born joys and obscure destiny of the dusty path of daily toil from which we have thus been permitted to turn aside.

GIRGEH, February 24th.

We arrived at this place about eight last evening. A brilliant moon, about the full, lighted it up, throwing its soft veil over all deformities and exhibiting the ruins of a mosque of Saracenic architecture, whose pointed arches stand on the bank, which is being washed away by the encroachment of the river. The tall white minarets gleamed picturesquely above the town, which is of more substantial structure than any we have seen since we left it on our way up. It was formerly the capital of this part of Egypt, and in the days of the Christian Eastern Roman Empire, an important place.

The name Girges, or Georges, is in honor of St. George, the patron saint of Egypt, and there is still a convent here with an European monk at its head. There is another near the edge of the desert, which claims to have been founded by the Empress Helena in the days of Constantine. This part of Egypt was then a Christian nation, and until the conquest by the Saracens continued such, and was the seat of a wealthy Christian population. It is the most beautiful and fertile part of Egypt even now.

The strong north wind yesterday retarded our progress so that we did not accomplish more than ten miles during the whole day. We rolled as though at sea, so rough was the stream, and waltzed around with the "Zingara," a boat having on board Lord Howard de Walden and the artist McCollum. Several times we were in immediate contact and obliged to push each other off. We drifted like logs on the stream. For a time the river was so rough and the head wind so strong that oars and current combined were unable to resist its power on our bare deck and poles, and we came to a bank. This gave me an opportunity for a walk among the beautiful green wheat and bean fields, dotted with duora houses, and flocks and herds and busy fellaheen.

I was amused at two boys of some fourteen years, who had been sent to pull vetches and lettuce from the wheat—among which they grow as cockle in our fields. They had filled their bag and had a large bundle, which they endeavored to carry loose on the back on their donkey. The wind was too strong and blew the loose parcel off. They promptly stripped off, converting their garments into receptacles for their greens, loaded them on their donkey and trotted off.

Last night was cold; this morning is fresh, but with a fine sunshine. The day will be pleasant unless the wind should rise. When it does, the dust is sadly distressing. You can form no idea of the appearance of the party on their return from Abydus. The boat was filled with fine sand, though so soon as it began to blow, a close canvas envelope was dropped all around the windward side.

We have now on one side of the river limestone cliffs, perforated with tombs—some with the entrance still dressed and sculptured; others have been reduced to mere holes in the rock by the crumbling of the surface. The Pasha is gathering limestone at the bottom of the cliffs without the cost of quarrying.

Girgeh, which we left an hour since, is the place from which we saw the departure of so many of the conscripts as we passed up. Your mother and I are obliged to keep our cabin, well wrapped up. About noon we were called to look at a beautiful stretch of green cultivated flat land, with noble palm groves. sheltering pretty villages and a very extensive, handsome, solidly-built house, the residence, our Reis says, of "one of the rich" who owns the land and villages. It is really a beautiful spectacle, the more so from contrast with the sterile mountain and desert sand opposite.

EKHMIN, February 25th.

This is the site of one of the most ancient cities of Egypt, and one which, under the Romans, enjoyed great privileges. Strabo mentions it as, at the time of his visit, "an ancient city," and famous for its linen and workers in stone. Before him Herodotus had found it less prejudiced against the manners of the Greeks, and he describes a temple here dedicated to Perseus, so famous in the Greek mythology, whom they claimed as a native of this place, and that Danaus emigrated from here; and the priests showed Herodotus the genealogy of

Perseus and Danaus. The Mahometans also claim for it great antiquity, asserting that it was founded by a son of Misraim, and grandson of Ham. The Saracens destroyed the city and temples. Of none of these are any traces to be found except a few imperfect inscriptions. The confident conviction of the absurdity of all these legendary tales does not preclude the possibility of the injurious influence the constant dwelling among them has on our own faith. Great cause have we for thankfulness that God has set apart a day on which we are invited to seek His favor only, laying aside all other pursuits and entering more closely into communion with Him. These gods many and lords many, who once held in thraldom such minds as those of Herodotus and Strabo, bowed before the power of the Lord Jesus, and those fields have drank in the blood of the noble army of martyrs.

This was once the seat of prosperous Christian churches. Anasthasius certainly ruled here with that stern, uncompromising will which defied emperors and crushed out the charity which is more precious than faith.

As I look at these poor fellaheen, toiling ceaselessly at their shadoofs or tending their flocks and herds, themselves with scarce a garment, and yielding the sweat of their brow to the rapacity of the tax-gatherer now, as they have done in every generation during all these ages since the first record which has been transmitted to our day, it comforts me to think that the Son of God is not ashamed to be called their brother; for them Christ died. He took not on Him the nature of angel, of emperor, or of priest, but "took upon Him the form of a servant" when He was found in likeness as a man. What wondrous power is contained in those words—"It became Him by whom are all things, and for whom are all things in bringing many sons unto glory to make the Captain of their salvation perfect through suffering!" The greatest sufferer, the most down-trodden and despised may say: "He is my brother," and have hope through Him.

February 26th.

Yesterday was cold, with a sunless, cheerless leaden sky; very much like one of our N. E. equinoctials. We spent the day, as is our wont, quietly moored beneath the bank. Wistar and Jane walked ashore and reported a large town with houses much better than any we have been in, having *jalousies* to the windows and good lattices. There are many mills, one of which is driven by a steam engine of good construction made in Paris. The fuel is chopped doura stalks. The population is a mixed one, with a large proportion of Copts and Roman Catholics whose shops in the bazaar were closed for the Sabbath. In the afternoon our Reis got under way as they are fearful their bread will not last them till they reach Siout, which cannot be earlier than the night of the 28th. We made but little progress before the force of the wind jammed us under a high hard bank where we were obliged to lay by, exposed to the high wind which raised wave enough to beat us against the bank very unpleasantly, during much of the night. The morning is clear and we are now rowing down stream an hour before sunrise.

10 A. M.

We have made but little progress and that with much toil against a strong wind which has whirled us round again and again, being more powerful than the current. For a time the men towed us along a sand bank and when we reached a high mud bank, they stopped to breakfast and I clambered to the top assisted by one of the crew. The sight was an ample compensation. Wheat fields of the deepest green I ever beheld were waiving their heavily laden bearded heads in the gale; while radishes with blue and purple flowers and turnips with golden blossoms, and convolvuli with their pink bells, were laughing in the sunshine. Villages, palm sheltered, were dotted on the plain, high roads leading from one to the other, along which camels and asses were driven by men in brown burnouses, while women, children, and dogs clustered around the temporary booths of doura which were studded here and there amid the fields. Walking in the sunshine was pleasant; though we feel the cold on board more than is agreeable or safe. We yesterday witnessed some of those touches of nature which "make all mankind kin"; in the shape of parental and filial affection. A poor water carrier loaded with two heavy skins of water, helped his little child down the steep bank to see the monkey on our boat and lifted her back again with every manifestation of patient love; and when we sailed we were distressed by the disconsolate shrieks of a little boy, son of one of our crew who lives here. He was torn from his father and placed on the bank where he stood screaming "my father, my father," threw his cap on the ground, and "rent his raiment," throwing it from him in the intensity of his distress.

Before midday the power of the wind became irresistible, and we were compelled to come to, a little above Soohag. A fisherman had just drawn his net, so we had an opportunity to examine its contents. Carp, mullet, catfish and one Lepidotus, the sacred electric fish worshipped by the ancient Egyptians. It is an ugly looking creature with smooth skin of a light yellowish brown color with spots of dark brown. The head is large, shaped much like that of the catfish but it is without the sharp spiny fins of that fish. The mouth is smaller and beneath the head. The eye is a prominent feature, with an ill expression. As the fisherman placed it in the basket with the others caught I presume it is eaten. Wistar tested its electric power quite to his satisfaction.

When we climbed to the top of the bank we saw large wheat, bean, and tobacco fields, and the commencement of a canal which carries the water of the river to the back of the cultivated land and so to Siout. The town of Soohag is large and substantially built, and has a very jail like looking Police Station—Voltaire's emblem of civilization—and, great as is the libel on humanity, it is a proof of the justice of the legal axiom "the greater the truth the greater the libel." It is but the assent of human experience to the truth of the Divine teaching that "there is none that doeth good, no not one," uttered as the description of those who were the chosen people. During my walk this morning I saw many cucumber and melon vines planted along the banks of the canal, in the midst of which was a booth of doura stalks set on end and wattled together at the top; quite a pretty lodge in a garden of cucumbers.

February 27th.

We lay at our moorings all yesterday, starting this morning at about 3 A. M., quietly dropping down by moonlight. The wind has entirely subsided, but the temperature is lower than it has yet been. We have no out of door thermometer but that in the saloon was 52. Every one covets the warmth of the sun. The banks are verdant with wheat and tobacco and for some days passed we have occasionally seen poppies which have been cultivated here since the days of Herodotus.

I was much interested in reading in Sharpe's History a letter from the Emperor Hadrian, written to one of his intimate friends from Egypt during his second visit. The allusion he makes to the "worshippers of Christ" confirms the impression I had already received that the Gospel had penetrated the masses here. That letter must have been written before the close of the Second Century and speaks of the Christians in the same terms as it does of other inhabitants. Then the term "worshippers of Christ" speaks volumes as to the view then held by Christians of Our Lord. An object of worship to them, as their gods Serapis and Isis were to the unconverted Egyptians; and Jupiter, Poseidon and others were to the Romans. This was before philosophical speculation had beguiled them of their simplicity. Jesus was the Son of God, thinking it not robbery to be equal with God and that all men should honor Him even as they honor the Father.

Feby. 28th.

This has been a most genial day. We were aroused about 3 A. M. by the starting for the day but before five we came to grief, finding ourselves firmly impacted on a sand bank in the midst of the stream. The moon was gibbous, about two thirds illuminated and shed a flood of soft light on the wide spread stream and I amused myself with the thought that we were converting a "*planet*" into a "*fixed* star" and for some time with little hope of a remedy (our pennon carries aloft a single star). After much grinding of the bottom of the boat and many grunts and groans and choral songs of the crew, we floated off just as the sun lifted his golden crown over the brow of the savage cliff which limited our view toward the Arabian desert. Our progress since has been smoother and pleasanter than for any day of our downward voyage.

The palm groves have been very frequent; the acacia trees very beautiful, the wheat crop most luxuriant, and lifting heavy heads on strong straw to rejoice in the ripening influence of the genial sunshine; beans, vetches, tobacco, cummin, and other plants have given variety to the green; poppies, scarlet and white, have lent colour to the picture, which has been framed by frowning cliffs of limestone perforated in their fronts by the tombs of past generations of "our brethren," and savage deserts of yellow sand. Through all these the rapid current of the meandering stream has borne us swiftly on, to the measured stroke of the splashing oar, whirling us amid the changing objects which have been like dissolving and mingling pictures of some colossal kaleidoscope. Flocks of wild geese have screamed over our heads. Pelicans and herons line the edges of the sand banks like so many sentries on guard, never moving at our approach. Sparrows and other little birds settle fearlessly on our deck. Everything is Arcadian. In ancient times some part of this valley rejoiced in that very name.

It is a strange feeling which creeps over one when we reflect that the *Father of History* was here taught the legends of what was *then* mythical lore and learned from the priests, who then taught the immortality of the human soul, the certainty of a judgment to come, and the need of a godlike advocate who had somewhat to offer; that the Perseus of Greek Mythic story had been born in this very vicinity, and exhibited his sandal as a relic left by him on his expedition into Ethiopia to procure the Head of Medusa. Through all these ages before and since, this mysterious river has given fertility to these spreading plains and supported myriads of human beings by the product. This very fertility enabled Rameses to hire his mercenary hosts and sweep over the known world, and in later ages—distant future to his contemporaries, distant past to us;—fed the armies of the Ptolemies and Cæsars and supported in indolence and kept in subjection to their tyrants, the idle and turbulent mobs of Alexandria and Rome. Still the inexhaustible fountain pours forth its riches, and barge after barge goes down the Alexandria laden as of old with the golden treasure.

February 29th.

About four P. M. yesterday we reached Siout and having sealed and directed letters home I went immediately to learn from Dr. Johnson, the American Medical Missionary resident here, the proper hour etc. for mailing them. I walked through rich fields of wheat and clover about a mile and a half, to the town, which is walled and well-built. The domes and lofty minarets gave it an imposing appearance. It stands on a mound raised by the debris of the old Egyptian town of Lycopolis, devoted to the worship of Anubis, the wolf headed god ; and wolves as his sacred animal were pampered here. We entered one of the gates and found ourselves at once in a crowd on an open square, buying and selling country produce in the shape of forage for cattle; and onions, sugar cane, and turnips, and radishes for men. Passing across this we came on the smithies with the little anvils on which the red hot iron was being forged, two hammers working as with us, in regular strokes and scattering the heated scales. Shoemakers, pipemakers and turners were passed successively and we saw masons building with burned brick and mortar. We soon entered the main bazaar with its little closets of goods of many varieties, many of them of Manchester and Staffordshire manufacture.

Siout has great repute for its own pottery in the shape of ewers and pipe bowls of red and black glazed ware of very pretty shapes, which was tastefully displayed at the doors of the shops. Groups were seated at the doors of the coffee shops or stood around the cook shops. All well clothed in graceful flowing robes and heavy turbans. The figures of the men are imposing and their countenances very dignified, with regular features and oval shaped face and a light brown complexion. There were many Greeks and some Italians among the crowd.

The bazaar is covered by a wooden roof at the top of the houses, which are two stories in height. Many side passages led to other bazaars and some apparently to large magazines of merchandise. The town is divided into sections which are separated by walls with massive gates. Large quantities of almonds, filberts and Madeira nuts were exposed for sale as well as cotton, doura, lentils and other products of Egypt. It was a busy animating scene. The light bread in round thin loaves looked really tempting.

I made my way to the residence of Dr. Johnson and was glad to find him and Mrs. J. at home. I sat talking about their mission an hour or more and was about leaving when I met Wistar and Sisters at the door and we returned and remained until the waning light reminded us it was time to seek the boat. The sun set soon after we left the town and we met at the gate numerous flocks and herds coming in from the pastures in which we had seen them tethered on our way. They were in fine condition. Many of the cattle fine looking and the asses double the size of any we have yet seen. They were all gay, even the buffaloes and camels caracoling and kicking as they passed each other.

The setting sun threw a rich glow over the western sky against which the tapered minarets and crowned palms elevated their lofty columns, while groves of acacia and clusters of young palms lent a soft grace to the scene. It was a lovely evening. Crowds of well dressed, happy looking people thronged the road and several wheeled carts loaded with lime and drawn by horses belonging to the Khedive, presented a novel feature to us, so long accustomed to see nothing but camels and donkeys bearing stones and burdens of every kind on their backs.

The mission here is a very successful effort. The converts support their own teachers and schools and two of them have built a Protestant Church at the cost of several thousand dollars. They have adopted the habit of systematic setting aside a percentage of their profits for the service of the Lord and send teachers to out stations to promulgate the glad tidings of redemption through the blood of Jesus.

Your mother has really *enjoyed* a ride on a donkey. The animals here are larger and stronger, and she got herself well seated without being fatigued before starting; and had the experience of her ride at Denderah. She trotted along gaily, looking at the various objects of interest. We followed the highway to the main gate of the city, the same as I have described on our way up the river. We crossed a canal by a stone bridge of several arches and through a lofty gate, under the shade of which were collected several highly respectable looking men. The space within was shaded by large trees of the of the fig sycamore, and beneath them were stands for the sale of coffee. Passing by these we entered the winding streets and passed through the same bazaars as yesterday afternoon, to the house of Dr. Johnson, who gratified us by reading the interesting report of their year's labours which he had just prepared.

Leaving your mother and the other members of the party, I went with the dragoman to attend to the posting of our letters, which led us through the entire length of the City. When we reached the office at one of the gates we were told the Postmaster was at the Prison, which took us again a long round. We passed under the gloomy portal, with arms standing against the walls, and were told there were often two or three hundred prisoners, very many of them for non-payment of taxes or other offences against the government. We found a knot of men seated on the ground with books and money bags about them, and scribes writing and reading accounts. Some of the books were forms of receipts, handsomely engraved. On mentioning our object one of them took the package, studied out the Arabic superscription, pronouncing the name Tod Rathbun & Co., turned it all about, examining it carefully, talked much about it to our dragoman and the bye *sitters*, and then endorsed on it the name Morris *hakim*, which he enquired of Joseph. He then took his scales and ascertained its weight. It was large and his metal weights were not sufficient so he supplemented them by adding first a stone and then a piece of broken cup. These being too heavy he put another fragment of pottery in the scale with the package and having examined them all carefully, proceeded to add and subtract on a fragment of paper. The figures were set and the lines drawn from right to left just as he had written his endorsement. He then requested one of his assistants to calculate the postage. He declined; and he was obliged to do it himself. After which he turned to Jopeph and asked how much backsheesh he designed to give him. Joseph refused entirely. He laughed and receiving the Napoleon handed it to another official who unlocked his safe and drew forth his bag to make change, which he gave without any further reference to bribery. Whether the package will go safely is the question which I shall be interested in making when we reach Cairo.

While I was absent your mother had made some purchases of Ivory work. We then mounted our donkeys and rode out of the town to visit the Church built at the sole expense of the Protestant Copts at a cost of several thousand dollars. We saw in one of the Courts adjoining one of the schools of little children, bright happy little faces; after which we rode back having occupied three hours most pleasantly.

March 1st.

A most beautiful day. Temperature perfectly genial, just enough movement in the air to give a feeling of freshness.

We left Siout soon after sunrise and have been advancing steadily by current and oar through scenes of Arcadian beauty. Unbroken stretches of green fields, the only variation being from one shade of green to another as we passed from one crop to another. Herds of cattle pasturing; each tethered till every blade that can be reached by stretching to the utmost and assuming the posture which gives the greatest scope.

It is the very perfection of luxurious travel. We parted from the missionaries with regret and with the highest estimate of the value of their services, the faithfulness of their effort and their personal worth and adaptation to their task.

As your mother and I came out of Siout our way was blocked at the gate by an immense collection of camels. We wondered what could have been the object of gathering so many as they were without burden. We find they were for the Khedive who gets them at his own price for his sugar works. Yet with it all the people appear happy.

Dr. Johnson tells us that the greater part of the vast plain over which our party rode to Abydus, whose richness impressed them so strongly, belongs to one owner residing in Girgeh. It was undoubtedly the tomb of some such landed proprietor on the walls of which the habits and customs of ancient days have been transmitted to ours.

Great fields of Rape in flower give a rich and lively yellow tint to the soft green of its foliage; and poppies rear their crimson, white and purple flowers in vast patches, as they did in the days of Dioscorides or even of Herodotus, while one ever welcomes afresh each successive grove of lofty palms, many of which bear the notches of a century of Summers on their brown and rugged shafts, which have each year borne the solitary crown of the single season during as many revolutions of the changing yet changeless earth; ever decaying and ever renewing its annual glory. The wheat which was just growing when we went up the river, is now in full head and the tobacco has grown to a good size and is putting out its blossom.

March 2d.

Another indication of the unadaptability of Egypt as a sanitarium. The genial weather of yesterday, crowned by a soft and clear sunset, is followed this morning by cloudy skies, cold wind and great dampness. We were lying all night at one spot so that the change is not attributable to change of place, nor have we made any change of latitude within a day or two as the river here runs a most tortuous course. Much of yesterday was through scenes of Arcadian beauty. Toward evening we skirted a cliff of limestone, but passed again into a plain. We got under way this morning about 6 A. M. and now have on the one shore a wide stretch of cultivated plain and on the other immense drifts of yellow sand. We passed Manfaloot yesterday morning; a large town which a few years since was threatened with entire destruction by the encroachments of the river. Now the channel has changed and it stands quite half a mile from the water, but the crumbling houses on the top of the bank tell how narrowly it escaped destruction.

March 3, 1872.

About 4 P. M. yesterday the wind abated sufficiently to permit us to leave the place at which we had been compelled to stop before noon. The clouds of sand drifted about us, so dense as to obscure the view, and one puff which swept over us would certainly have overturned us had we encountered it on our way up with our immense spread of canvass. While lying still we all mounted the bank and strolled along the edge of the wheat field, which extended far inland. It was much poorer than we have lately seen. There was much of the same green knotted grass which takes possession of the land with us; and also an ambrosia or rag weed. I saw a beautiful little portulacca, and pulled several plants I had not met with before.

As we walked an old kindly looking man approached us, and offered us some of the cherry-like fruit which we have seen sold in the bazaars; for which we paid him. It has but little taste and a very large stony seed.

Towards evening the wind subsided so that your mother and I enjoyed an hour or two on deck after we started. We passed no objects of special interest; cultivated plains, skirted by cliffs perforated by the tombs of the *myriads* who once peopled them, are constantly present objects of interest. The mountain about Siout is *thoroughly honeycombed*. These tombs were the refuge of Christians in the days of persecution; and the resort of ascetics when it became the custom to seek peace for the soul in abandoning the duty man owes to God through sympathy with his fellow man. The desert of the Thebaid then, for a time, became more populous than its fertile plains; and Gibbon, with his usual disposition to scoff at everything which has any religious aspect, says that the Emperor Theodosious during the war he waged with his rival, finding the oracles of Delphi and Dodona had been silenced, sent to consult a hermit of special sanctity who had withdrawn into one of these tombs on the side of a lofty mountain where he secluded himself from all association with his fellow men, never admitting them to any intercourse except through a grated window, through which he received his scant supply of food weekly. At the same time he healed their diseases and replied to their questions; and in the case of the Emperor sent him an answer that he should succeed though at much cost of blood.

We drifted on through these scenes during the entire night; so that we saw nothing until the morning found us approaching Rhoda, where we now lie immediately beneath the bank on which stand very extensive sugar works of the Pasha. We have passed through the district which yields the supply of cane on which these works depend. It has always been noted for its fertility; and for the intelligence of its labouring population. In the first three centuries of the Christian Era it was the seat of many Christian Churches, and possessed of great influence; contemporary ecclesiastical historians who inform us that the faith was held here in more purity, and with greater earnestness than in other parts of the Roman Empire. This is also the spot at which Antinous, the favourite of Hadrian, sacrificed himself to his Imperial friend by drowning himself in the river, in order to secure prosperity to the Emperor, which an oracle had declared depended on the loss of something most highly prized. In commemoration of this self-sacrificing act of friendship Hadrian built here a temple dedicated to Antinous as a god; and erected a triumphal arch and hippodrome for games, in honor of his memory, and made it the capital of a nome or district, and it became under the Romans one of the most important towns in this province of the Empire.

We kept quietly to our boat all day. Lord Bulwer has been spending some weeks here and left by special railroad train to return to Cairo, soon after we arrived.

On Monday we visited the sugar manufactory, which is on a magnificent scale. Six thousand acres of land are cultivated in cane which is crushed here in rollers, the juice evaporated, the sugar refined, and the waste manufactured into alcohol and Rum. More than two thousand men are employed in the culture of the cane and in the mills and refining. The land is ploughed by steam ploughs; irrigated by steam pumps, and the syrup is boiled, under vacuum, in steam-heated pans; purified by animal charcoal, and dried by revolving hydro-extractors. The machinery and apparatus is of the costliest kind; and the buildings most extensive and solid. Near them stands a palace built by the Khedive at the enormous cost of £100,000. It is an imposing building surrounded by extensive gardens. It has never been furnished and no one has ever occupied it but the man who has charge. The garden is fine and the custodian presented Miss Harris with a very pretty little bouquet of roses, etc. An Englishman lives here with his wife. He formerly resided in Cuba and Louisiana, and there acquired the practical knowledge which qualifies him for the superintendence of these extensive operations. He admitted without hesitation the oppression of the people who receive, *nominally*, three piastres a day; but are obliged to feed and clothe themselves out of that sum, which is about equivalent to six cents with us. Even that is not always paid them. Their food consists exclusively of coarse bread and onions; and they wear but little clothing. Much of the labour is performed by children; boys and girls. This is the period of the year in which the cane is cut and crushed. It only lasts two years after which time the land requires a rest, during which they plant it in doura or beans. The cane is not so rich in saccharine matter as in Louisiana and Cuba and is rendered still less valuable by being set too closely on the land. This is manured by the guano collected from the pigeon houses I have described so often. When the crop is all out the hands are employed in setting fresh canes. This begins in April, at which time the steam pumps are set in operation. Six of them, each of 120 horse power, are required for the six thousand acres in cultivation.

At what a cost of human sorrow our luxuries are produced! I felt ashamed of the paltry coppers which I distributed among the poor creatures as we passed around. One of them drew my attention to a cross tatooed on his arm as the token of brotherhood in Christ. I would gladly have given him more than I had with me, and yet it would probably have drawn on him envy and ill-will.

The superintendent and his wife are obliged to send their children to England and to live here in perfect isolation except as they are visited by travellers during the Winter. This is sometimes as much of an annoyance as gratification to them, as they expect more attention than it is convenient to extend. Lord B. for example, had taken possession of the entire house during eight weeks; occupying every room in it for himself and servants, except one small apartment; and to this the only access was through a hall in which his servants slept.

Though in the last stages of pulmonary consumption, Lord Bulwer is diligently engaged in preparing the life of Lord Palmerston; writing or reading without the least intermission.

The Pasha's superintendent here is a purely practical man. He told us the story of Antinous, without knowing his name or that of the Emperor; and said there were formerly ruins of temples and palaces on the opposite side of the river, but he had found the stones were very well adapted for foundations of his buildings, and had used them as such without any regard to the sculpture and hierogliphics. He said there were some tombs not more than a mile or two distant, but he had never seen them.

After visiting the works we started in the afternoon and about nine P. M. reached our stopping point from which to visit the tombs of Beni Hassan. These are very celebrated having furnished most of the illustrations of ancient Egyptian life which have become familiar to us in the descriptions of writers and tourists. They are of the earliest date, bearing inscriptions of a century before Abrams first visit to Egypt.

Your loving father,

CASPAR MORRIS.

BENI HASSAN, ON THE NILE, March 5, 1872.

My Very Dear Children:

I just learn that we shall stop in less than an hour at Minieh, and our last letters from the Nile will be mailed there, so altho' I know I can tell you but very little, I feel as if I would like to say a few words, if 'tis only to tell you we are all well.

Some of the party have been to-day to the tombs here, but as it not only involved a donkey ride but a long, hard climb up the mountain, your Aunts Hannah, Jane and I remained home and occupied ourselves in mending, etc. The donkey ride I could have taken, but the climb would have been too much for me.

Since my last to you I went with your father into Siout and really enjoyed the ride, owing in a measure to being more comfortably fixed than heretofore. I was disappointed in the purchases I had hoped to have made there; the things had been bought up by other travellers; but we were much interested in the Missionaries whom we saw there and their work and to find the natives themselves making such efforts to spread the Gospel. They deserve great credit, for doing anything more than sustain life here must require great self-denial. A man's wages are three Piastres a day, equal to six cents of our money and out of that they must find themselves.

Yesterday we were at Roda where there is a large sugar manufactory belonging to the Pasha. We went through the works and had a long conversation with the gentleman in charge, but it only made me deplore more than ever the condition of the people here, and I am almost sorry to know so much about them and yet in all the degradation they are cheerful. Children of all ages at work, and all are controlled by the whip. We often see the scars on the backs of the men, for many have but little clothing on, and at all the places where we stop, men, women and children flock to the shore to look at us and we have had some difficulty with our men to prevent their using the whip to drive them off; the sight of it is often sufficient to make them scamper.

This day week is the extent of the time this boat was taken for, so by then we must be in Cairo, wind permitting, where we hope to get our letters for which we are getting more anxious and yet fearful. Occasionally we get an English paper from some Dahabeyah and see the smallpox is still very prevalent in Philadelphia. We try to trust you will all escape. I saw in a dream Richard, and Murray C. very busy in the Chestnut Street house last night and it made us think of what may be its condition. I hope Israel understands we are willing he should do what he thinks best with it and we will be satisfied. I feel for him, as I would not like myself to have either the responsibility or the trouble we have laid on him.

I suppose our next will tell you what our plans are, as on reaching Cairo they will be decided on positively. We do not desire to tarry there long as 'tis a dirty disagreeable place. Fleas abound there and they don't seem to mind the powder, which however is efficacious here. We have not been much incommoded by things of the kind, in our journeyings. I fear I shall miss the quiet Nile life when we are again travelling, as sitting with my work, while your father reads, suits me; which is the way in which we spend nearly all our time. Our evenings are always spent together in the saloon, and one reads aloud; but in the day each acts independently and of course all take an interest in the passing objects, and scarce a day passes without speaking one or more vessels and the American flags are always hailed with most interest. Some of the boats have mixed companies, and there will be several flags. We carry three ourselves, American, English and Maltese. The two latter are Friezier's and the Dragoman's.

Farewell, with much, very much love to one and all of you and our brothers and sisters.

    Yours truly and affectionately,

           A. C. MORRIS.

As these lettters are carried by runners from one station to another and we hear are not entirely to be relied on, your father will keep the sheets containing his journal until he can mail them.

March 6th.

We yesterday explored the grottos of Beni Hassan, probably, with the exception of the Pyramids, the oldest works of human power and exhibition of human art now extant. The only other exception being perhaps the cave temple of Ellora or Elephanta in India. There are several testimonies of their antiquity which confirm the record of the Hieroglyphic inscriptions. There are no references in them to the minor deities, nor representation of the judgment of the dead as found in tombs at Thebes, boats are of less elaborate structure, and tho' the figures of cattle and other animals are numerous there are no horses, which abound in the sculptures of the age of Rameses. We are therefore justified in receiving the testimony of the inscriptions which tell us that the elaborately ornamented chambers in the rock are the anti-chambers of the tombs of Monarchs or governors of Nomes or Districts of Egypt under Osirtasen, whose reign preceeded that of Rameses by 500 years, being placed about 2000 years before the coming of our Lord. They are therefore older by a century at least than the first notice in the word of God of burial places; the Cave of Macphelah, bought by Abraham of Ephron, the Hittite, as the burial place of Sarah.

The valley of the Nile is here as everywhere in its whole extent, bounded on either side by cliffs which are sometimes, as here, quite near and at others more remote, but rarely out of sight, and wherever they approach near enough are used as the places of sepulture of the mummified bodies of the myriads who in the long succession of generations have peopled this valley and in the ages so long past had reached an elevation in art and power which is still the wonder of the present age. These cliffs are composed of strata of rocks of various composition and degrees of hardness and very generally lie in horizontal strata. Here we rode about one mile—less than two, certainly—before we reached the base which is formed by the debris of the rock above. A great slope of sand and gravel, destitute of the slightest vegetation.

While passing across the lower margin of this slope our attention was arrested by numerous shallow pits spotting its surface, with here and there dark heaps lying between them. On inquiry we found that some German speculator has acquired the right to disinter the remains of these long gone fellow men and that they are transported to Europe for fertilizers of the soil, so that the people of the present day are fed with the corn of Egypt of 4000 years ago on which these, their predecessors in mortality, were nourished.

This sandy slope is filled with nodules and fossils from the decomposed hills beyond it, and in many places dotted with large black boulders of a silicious rock composed of masses of shells. These boulders differ materially from the limestone of the stratum which is perforated by the caves and pits and come from a looser stratum which overlies it, from the edge of which they project above. They are the deposit of the bottom of a sea which rolled over it, animate with marine life—When? and how were they thus first agglomerated and consolidated, and by what cataclysm were they broken into masses and then rolled into boulders and deposited here amid the smaller detritus in which they are imbedded? Such questions force themselves on our minds as we ride among them.

Clambering, or rather struggling, up this ascent we reached the level of the tombs, which are all excavated in one limestone strata and lie like so many residences along a road or street, the entrances of some still square and smooth, of some still bearing the sculptured name of the occupant and the age at which it was prepared for him, while of many time and weather have destroyed the front and they gape their open mouthed unadorned entrance to the chamber of the dead.

We rode or walked along in front of this street in the great Necropolis turning in to examine the dwellings now bereft of their occupants. All have pits in them, square and well cut, descending perpendicularly into depths below. Into these the bodies were lowered. Many—most—of the walls were plain and bear on them still the marks of the tool of the workmen. They are plumb and square and of uniform height, even where there is no ornament, and as those on which the pictures remain are coated with a preparation of lime, like our finest coat of plaster, it is possible that those which are now naked may when finished have been plastered and painted also. Many of those which are without paintings contain columns which have been left while excavating them and dressed into graceful shafts with basses and capitals. Some are polygonal, having sixteen squared faces and some are lighter and more graceful, though less imposing, cut as though they were formed of four shafts bound together at the top by a fillet with a capital similarly divided and projecting. These are undoubtedly designed to represent four stalks of the papyrus reed with the swollen bud at the top. These columns are arranged in regular rows at uniform distances, sometimes transverse, dividing an inner recess from the main body of the chamber, and in others dividing this longitudinally into a central body with side aisles. The architrave is well cut, as though to represent an artificial architrave of stone, from which springs the roof, which is vaulted. It is therefore not unreasonable to suppose that these caves were cut in imitation of buildings with columns and arched roofs already erected. From many of the tombs the columns have been carefully removed. The bases are there still and the squarely cut cavity in the architrave above shows that the shaft and capital has been carefully taken away to adorn some more modern building. The size of these chambers varies greatly, some being not less than fifty feet square and all are from ten to twenty feet in height.

The great attraction however is found in the pictured representations of the habits and customs and arts and costumes of the times, represented on the walls of the larger. They are more or less faded and defaced, but some parts are as fresh as though but recently executed and with a little patience all may be traced so as to give us a correct idea of the whole. There are birds there so well represented that they would serve as plates of a volume of some Wilson or Audubon of that distant age; fish gracefully sporting in the water; cattle which might well excite the envy of the most fastidious breeder of choice stock at the present day. Antelopes and wild oxen, with hunters in the chase, some with drawn bows and poised arrows, some running on foot with a speed which would at least equal the most expert runner of the Volunteer Fire Department of our Western cities. The beauty of the birds and animals and the perfection of their proportions was wonderful.

It is supposed that these pictures represent the occupations of the inhabitants of the district of which the tenant of the tomb was governor, or perhaps those of his personal dependants. There are glass-blowers diligently forming vessels of various forms and patterns, some of exquisitely graceful shape; potters with vases and urns, which are even now the models on which our modern artists delight to dwell and reproduce as the perfection of form. Vines are being dressed, grapes gathered and pressed, and wine stored in jars. Flax is planted, watered, rolled, beaten, spun, woven and fulled and bleached. Cattle are fed and fields are plowed. Nets are drawn; birds are trapped; animals are chased by dogs of graceful form and various breeds. Athletic sports are represented—wrestling, boxing, tumbling, ball-playing. Various plants and flowers are offered to the master of the whole, and fruits are brought in baskets. On one is a procession of captives, clothed in garments of many colours, bringing with them offerings of different kinds. The proprietor is represented seated on a chair of great beauty, clothed in robes of which the figures convey the idea of rich brocade or some other costly stuff, elaborately and heavily embroidered. Punishment is being inflicted on some delinquents, male and female; the former stretched on the ground, the latter kneeling to receive the stripes.

Around the base of the room runs a long inscription in hieroglyphic characters cut into the stone, and around the cornice another is painted; the former telling the name and occupation of the deceased, and the incidents of his life; the latter giving the names of the birds and beasts painted below them. This is surmounted by a rich, many-coloured border, and the arched or vaulted roofs are divided in regular squares of alternate blue and red colour, or ornamented with stars on a blue ground.

It is an interesting fact that while on the walls of these tombs there is no representation of a god or of anything connected with another life, at a short distance is an unfinished small temple in the rock, known as the Speos Artimidis, with the date of Rameses, and having tablets of the Ptolemies, in which the cat-headed deity is represented receiving offerings. Does this indicate a change in worship in the intervening centuries?

March 6th.

Minieh, at which we lay over night, is connected with Cairo by a railroad, cars running there daily in a few hours.

Our boat lay just in front of a palace of the Pasha with frescoed balconies, plate-glass windows, and surrounded by an extensive garden, enclosed by a high wall. An esplanade or wide walk, shaded by mimosa trees, runs in front. A stone stairway descends to the water, with landing places at various heights to suit the stages of inundation, and arches to allow the water to flow through. The Pasha has extensive sugar works here, as at Roda, and as we passed the house of the superintendent, who is a Frenchman, we saw winding stairways covered with handsome floorcloth, while the windows were hung with lace curtains. All this presents an imposing European-looking front on the river.

160 Miles above Cairo, MINIEH, ON THE NILE,
March 5th, 1872.

My Dear Children:

We have just returned from a visit to the tombs of Beni Hassan, which bear upon their fronts, sculptured in hieroglyphic characters in the indestructible rock, the date of their age—more than two thousand years before the birth of our Lord. They were prepared for the bodies of their owners more than a century before Abraham bought the cave of Macphelah from the children of Hamor, the son of Heth; and the owner of each had pictured upon them the description of his wealth, his habits of life, and the occupations of his servants and dependants. And though somewhat effaced by the influence of forty centuries, we can still understand what is designed; and on many portions of the walls the colours, green and yellow and red and blue, are as fresh as though laid on but yesterday.

When any of you youngsters play at ball, or wrestle, or perform tumbling, or turn somersaults, or any other acrobatic feats, you are but repeating the acts of the men, women and boys of that remote age; and when you take a pigeon by the wings to carry it without fluttering or struggling, you are but using the same means as are here represented Servant after servant brings geese, ducks and fowls to their master, held in the same manner. Hunters pursue their game with bows and arrows, running with the same movement as one of the turbulent mob of the old volunteer fire department of Philadelphia; and if they deserve thrashing, they may be thankful that they will not receive it as the administration of such discipline to both sexes is represented then and there.

Many of the birds are so well executed, that they would serve for the work of a Wilson or Audubon. The fish were equally well executed and cne can easily distinguish the different animals which are being pursued and the different kind of dog used in the chase. The flocks and herds are of such animals as would excite the envy of our modern breeders of choice stock, the furniture of the apartments would rival that of our most sumptuous drawing-rooms and the clothing of some is represented of patterns which convey the idea of rich stuffs and costly workmanship. Vases and pitchers are there of forms which our modern artists are content to copy as the highest symmetry, and everything combines to confirm the impression that at that day Egypt was without a rival the "head of Nations" and had already attained a degree of refinement of manners and luxury of habits which have never been exceeded. Which of us when we have read of Abraham's going down to Egypt, has thought of the contrast it must have presented to his own country and his nomadic life, or even properly estimated the sacrifice made by Moses five centuries later when he chose rather "to suffer affliction with the people of God than to be called the son of Pharoah's daughter," and possible heir to the crown of such a kingdom.

Your mother of course remained on board. We rode some mile or more across a cultivated plain and then reached the edge of the desert, along which we rode, skirting cliffs of limestone rock which here as everywhere along the valley, is perforated everywhere by openings into great galleries of tombs. We passed across mounds which have been excavated within the last few years. They cover countless myriads of bodies of the undistinguished dead. These are now *lying in heaps* on the surface, waiting for transportation to Europe where they are used as fertilizers of the soil; so that when we buy grain from the Baltic it has probably been nurtured by the decomposing remains of some subject of the Pharoahs who, in those days long past, had himself been fed by the grain from the fields over which we have just trodden. We climbed up the slope of sand which is the result of the disintegration of the rock and then rode along in front of the tombs for miles just as one would ride by the doors of houses opening on a street. Some still have the square door frames with lintels and jambs covered with hieroglyphic inscription; some are perfectly plain; some have crumbled under the influence of time.

Looking in, in most cases we saw nothing but square chambers hewn in the rock ; with deep square wells in the floors by which the bodies of the dead were lowered into chambers below these, which appear to have been designed as temples or places in which sacrifices should be offered to or for the dead. On stamping on the floor, or throwing forcibly down on it a heavy stone, the resonance proved that all below was hollow. We entered many of these upper chambers in which were niches which had held the statues of gods and in some these statues were still to be seen, though much defaced. In one which was larger than the others there was a central seated figure, and on either side a standing statue having the usual attitude of Osiris.

One most interesting feature in these tombs is the vaulted or arched roof which is supported by columns of various styles and proportions. One chamber has ten columns composed of three shafts bound together, with each a capital also divided into three parts, apparently designed to represent papyrus stalks and flowers. These columns are so arranged as to divide the space into a central nave and side aisles, each with a vaulted roof. The cornice around is formed of a rich pattern of green and yellow, and the roof is divided into squares of alternate colours. In some of the other tombs the vault is covered with stars. Some have columns of large size and dressed with many sides as though it was the first step toward forming fluted columns. In many cases these columns have been carefully removed, evidently for use as monolithic shafts elsewhere. The base remains square and clean and the marks of the stonemason's chisel above shews the pains taken to cut it free without injury either to the part taken or that left.

But the chief interest is found in the pictures which adorn the walls. Glass blowing is plainly represented and the articles which have been manufactured stand in heaps. Flax is sown, watered, pulled, spun and woven. Cattle are fed, land is plowed, harvests are gathered, grain is stored in magazines, and these are built with circular arched roofs, which proves that at that early period they knew how to form an arch. Grapes are gathered and pressed and the wine is stored away in jars. We see nets dragged, filled with fishes, and rivers with aquatic plants are found. Women knead bread and prepare it for the oven.

The owner of this tomb is described in hieroglyphics as Governor of this part of the country. Many asses are seen among the animals but no horses, which is one evidence of the antiquity of these pictures, as horses were introduced so early of 1500 years before the Christian era.

Immense black boulders of masses of shells mingled with silex lie scattered about and are seen projecting from the surface of one of the horizontal strata of which these cliffs are formed. Other strata are composed of limestone with fossil shells in it. The boulders were too hard to be broken and too large to be carried away. The shells resemble those on our own mountains.

We are hungering for news, especially since we hear rumors of trouble between England and America.

Your loving father,

CASPAR MORRIS.

March 7th.

A cold windy morning finds us slowly drifting away from the present beauty, and remains of past glory, of Egypt. Barren sand banks and rugged cliffs, have taken the place of wide-spread fertile plains and groves of palms and bouquets of acacia. Before us on the Arabian side rises the line of cliffs on which the Convent of our Lady the Virgin stands, from which the monks swim off to passing boats, soliciting alms on the ground of their being Christians.

Wilkinson notices ancient quarries in this neighbourhood and some sculptures of the days of Rameses, and also others with Greek inscriptions of Roman times.

Every point at which the desert recedes from the river is marked by the lofty chimney of a pumping station, indicating that the Pasha has sugar plantations in the neighbourhood.

March 8, 1872.

We have been steadily advancing night and day. The crew have now been at their oars 30 hours out of 36. We have left the region of cliffs; have passed through much desert and some fertile plain and are now at five P. M. approaching Benisooef, which is a large town only 80 miles south of Grand Cairo. Till we reach the pyramids of Sakkarah, Dendoor, and the mounds which are the only traces of Memphis, the ancient capital of Lower Egypt as Thebes was of Upper, we shall have no object of interest. To-day the wind has been but light, and from a southwesterly quarter, when it has blown, and the sky has been overcast and the weather warm and relaxing. The fellaheen have been busy planting the margins of the river with some summer crop, we cannot learn what. They set it in deep trenches running at right angles with the river. We have seen more horses; and the houses for the pigeons have been many and peculiar; built of jars laid on the side with their mouths turned inward, so as to afford a nest for each pair. They surmount the stables of the camels and donkeys, which are solid structures about 8 feet high, without any exterior opening, surrounding an inner court entered by a gateway. The pigeon houses are arranged like domes above and have a very picturesque appearance. There are fewer trees of any kind; very few palm trees, and the villages stand without the groves which have given them a home-like look in the Thebaid. The river swarms with boats laden with grain and pulse and sheep and poultry on the way to Cairo.

The romance of the Nile has disappeared, and I feel saddened by the thought that one of the greatest enjoyments of my existence is drawing to a close. When I think of the tombs with their paintings and sculpture of 4000 years ago, and how little time in that long lapse has impaired them, and then of the cliffs in which they stand, I cannot avoid the question, how much longer have those bare brows been fronting the storm and yielding slowly and silently to the destructive power. And what token of the existence of the present generations of man shall be as imperishable as the records of the triumphs of the heroes of 3000 years ago, which exhibit not only the features of conquerors and conquered, but the character of the products of conquered kingdoms, even to the trees and plants, in boxes slung on men's shoulders, and brought to adorn the halls of the conqueror with their beauty, render them odorous with their fragrance or refresh them with their fruit? Man's nature has not changed any more than the everlasting hills.

Thank God for the assurance that He changes not, and that His mercy and love abide, and we enjoy privileges which were not enjoyed by them, and blessings of which they were ignorant.

March 9th.

Though we are rapidly approaching the close of our voyage and have now been nearly twelve weeks conversant with the peculiarities of the Nile, it has lost none of its majesty; and the mystery which has so long hung over it is still unsolved. We have now ascended and descended, passing over five hundred miles of its course, during all of which it has received no addition from any tributary, while it has flowed on, on! on!! moment after moment pouring away its stream to the sea, while solar evaporation and constant draught for irrigation by steam-pump, sakkia and shadoof have absorbed millions of gallons, and yet it flows as full here as at Assouan, and though the increased height of the bank proves that the volume is less, it yet spreads itself with little or no perceptible diminution except on here and there a sand bank, where its waters flowed two months since. What must Egypt have been when seven millions of souls dwelt on these shores; not only themselves supported on the produce of the soil, but able to supply the millions of Rome and Constantinople with food; the tax amounting to twenty millions of bushels annually!

The heat of the weather to-day has been very oppressive, and no breeze has mitigated its power. Men and animals have sought relief in the stream, which has spread its bosom to the sun unruffled even by the ripple of a current—its sluggish appearance concealing a rapid current.

We passed an enormous mass of stone known as the *false* pyramid, which stands on the western side of the river about fifty miles above Cairo. The remains of pyramids of various sizes and heights extend from this point to the mounds which mark the site of Memphis.

March 10th.

This morning our crew started early, but not till I had recognized the pale, ghost-like forms of the Pyramids of Ghizeh in the uncertain light. It is now noon, and we have been slowly advancing, having passed Memphis and the scene of the finding of the infant Moses ; the powder magazine of the Khedive, with the encampment of the Nubian army, with their close jackets and loose scarlet lower garments. The mosque in the citadel lifts its grand dome and slender minarets grandly, on the one side ; and the Pyramids sit solemnly on the other. The bosom of the river is enlivened by countless sails and the shore skirted by extended groves of palms. The atmosphere is thickened by dust or fog, and a high wind renders the heat, which would otherwise be oppressive, endurable. It is now past mid-day, and we are still short of our point of debarkation, and shall not reach it probably for some hours. We have had our meeting for Scripture reading and a sermon, and shall quietly wait our arrival. Our letters cannot be had, of course, until to-morrow, even if we had arrived last evening.

Evening.

The wind became so strong that after vain and prolonged efforts to reach the bridge we were compelled to anchor opposite the Nilometer on the Island of Roda, directly beneath a large building, much dilapidated, which appears to be the resort, or dwelling, of Greeks, whose children in gay and elegant *Parisian* costumes contrast strangely with the surrounding objects, and still more strongly with the population to which we have so long been accustomed. The young folk sport on the bank and find *amusement*, a thing which does not exist in the habits of the present inhabitants of the country, nor is it represented among the pictures of those of their predecessors, except on the most ancient tombs. Music of flutes and voices floated from the boats in which they pulled around us, and loud laughter bespoke minds not under the thraldom of oppression such as grinds to the earth the serfs of the rural districts and the towns on the river. We lay there until one, when the Reis availed himself of a calm, and we rowed some three hours.

When I waked this morning (March 11th), the first object which presented itself was the iron railroad bridge which, yet incomplete when we left here, had interposed a barrier to our sailing. It is a graceful and beautiful structure on solid piers. At the one end is what looks like a range of dwellings on the bridge, but is the *draw*, which I suppose slides on rollers, the one part into the other, thus opening a way for the passage of boats. It is closed till noon, so that we are obliged to use our patience and "strengthen it by reason of use," as we cannot get through before that hour and must wait till afternoon for our letters. Meanwhile a perfect calm has succeeded the blow of yesterday, and a dense fog rises from the surface of the river so as to obscure the bridge on the one side and make the palm trees on the other like ghostly troops guarding the shore. We were yesterday tormented by countless swarms of flies which would not be repelled, and our nights and days have lately been disturbed by fleas, of which your mother caught one in either hand at the same moment, and your Aunt Jane counted the prey of one night and found she had killed no fewer than thirty.

The rising sun is just penetrating the fog, and gilds the palms which wave their towering heads as though to welcome his return and restore them to their natural comeliness and glory. A few hours more and we shall descend from our princely estate and the luxury of our recent experience, which not even the plagues just noticed can rob of its attraction; and find ourselves once more mingling on a footing of equality, if not of inferiority, among those who speak our own language and have our own habits and manners.

The holiday has been perfect, almost as much so as that sought by Segid, the king of Ethiopia.

CAIRO, March 11, 1872.

My Dear Children :

We have just risen from a sitting of several hours over the glorious large package of letters which we received this morning at the banker's. So full of everything adapted to stimulate into still greater activity the thankfulness, which was the dominant feeling in our hearts even before we opened them.

That you should have all escaped the terrible epidemic which was even then still so rife among your fellow-citizens, was an equal mercy; and that dear Hannah's case should have terminated so happily was yet more so. If I had been asked who of all human beings I knew was least liable to such an assault, I should have named her, so gentle, so loving, so true, so full of all that can draw out love from others, and so free from any trace of those infirmities of temper which excite hatred or revenge. I am at a loss to conceive that it is possible there can exist a human being so heartless and fiend-like, as he or she must be who has been guilty of the attempt. Our only feeling must be pity for such an one, and thankfulness that the size of the dose, designed to make it more deadly, was such as to defeat the object by causing the prompt ejection of it from the stomach. It is another and loud call to us one and all, older and younger, to "live each day as 'twere our last," that, whether by the wrath of man or the providence of God, whenever the summons to lay aside our bodies shall meet us, it may find us in the full assurance of faith, having the testimony of a good conscience, at peace with God and with the world.

The several letters from our grandchildren, from Tyson and Effingham down to Henry Johns and dear little "Grandma" at Ivy Neck, were much enjoyed, and we count it among our greatest blessings that our Heavenly Father has given us children and children's children whom we can commend to his grace, and for whose good report we can be thankful; and we daily pray that one and all may "grow in grace as they grow in age," and that on our return we may find nothing to mar our delight or diminish the pleasure with which we shall be welcomed.

I have sent several small *volumes* of my Nile journal, and still have some thirty sheets on hand which I shall forward soon; though I fear you may find it a miserable repetition of sentimental twaddle. We have been nearly thirteen weeks on the Nile without any one incident to mar our pleasure. The boat has been all that the most luxurious Sybarite could desire. I wish you could look into the large saloon with its silk damask divans, and curtains and hangings to the doors, and peep into my stateroom, with your mother seated on one end of my bed writing (as she chooses to do, with her paper on a box-lid), while I am seated on a chair using the remaining surface of the bed to support my portfolio, your letters lying strewn between us. We write thus hastily because we learn that a letter mailed to-night will go by the French mail, and we would not prolong your anxiety on our account by one hour that can be avoided.

We are still in the enjoyment of health, and have been so during the voyage, with the exception of your mother's illness, from which she is quite recovered. Your uncle has not gained as much as I had hoped he would, and is still easily overcome by fatigue, which gives him headache lasting a day or two. I hope they will abandon the trip to the Holy Land. Much as I have desired to walk over the Mount of Olives and stand on the site of Bethany, I am sure none of the party is strong enough to encounter the fatigue which is unavoidable. Your mother and I are very careful not to say anything which will influence them to abandon it on *our account*. We have *decided not* to accompany them, but to wait their return (if they do go) at Beyroot. Friezier throws every possible impediment in the way, and even the dragoman does not encourage it. Your aunt Mary and Mr. Longstreth are very unwilling to give it up. I have expressed my doubt about little Mary being able to go, and something is said of leaving her with us.

Your mother's thumb has recovered so that you will find her needle has been as busy on the Nile as at home. She has worked two beautiful cushions, and is far advanced toward the completion of her quilt. Annie's patterns reached her in time to enable her to add to its beauty by borders. You need none of you think to possess either of them. I cannot give them up. They are inwrought with glorious golden threads (to my heart), though others may not see them.

In one of Israel's letters he mentions having received *notice* of a box from Venice containing a Megalithoscope, and now says a box of engravings and olive wood has arrived. The Megalithoscope is your Uncle Wistar's. I have not felt justified in taking so large an amount from the comfort of the family for the gratification of my taste. I allude to it only to beg you that if by an error in the directions you should have received your uncle's box, you will be very careful of it and the engravings. They did not wish their boxes opened until their return, but Mr. Bacon reports it was wet, and he had taken the package out. I hope there has been no error.

There are few things would give as great pleasure as to meet dear Hannah and Galloway if it is right for them to come, though we would regret the ill health which it would indicate, and are as yet utterly unable to say what will be our route and when we shall reach any part of Europe.

It is very pleasant to return even to this mongrel city. Your uncle and I went in for our letters, and met so many horses and carriages, and people in the costume of the West that we felt almost at home. Then the quarter through which we rode is filled with noble dwellings built in the villa style and surrounded by beautiful shrubberries and gardens.

At the banker's I was told that much anxiety had been expressed to know when we would get down, as my counsel was wished in the case of Mrs. Lansing; and on my meeting Dr. Grant he told me that he and Dr. Worlabet had been looking anxiously for me. Dr. Worlabet (Cheston knows him) was here superintending the publication of a medical work in Arabic, but has left, so that Dr. Grant and I shall lose the benefit of his counsel.

The weather is warm, but windy and dusty. It is the first time we have felt the heat since we left here in December. Each child and grandchild may take the whole of my love, as it is one of those affections which multiplies and grows as fast as it is distributed.

    Your loving father,

                      CASPAR MORRIS.

Israel's pamphlet has not come to hand. Thanks for the slip. We have not opened our newspapers.

                    CAIRO, March 11, 1872.

My Dear Children:

I find your father is going to try to get a letter off in great haste, hoping to reach England in time for the mail, and I must add a line to express our thankfulness at the preservation of dear Han. We feel stunned at the account, and are at a loss to conjecture the reason for such an *attempt*, especially on her. What could have provoked such feelings? And I always thought both Louisa and Edward so attached to them both, Gall. and Han.

We reached here at daylight, and immediately after breakfast your father and uncle took donkeys and rode into Cairo, a few miles, to get our letters and engage rooms at "Shepheard's Hotel." They returned with, oh! such a nice package, which has now occupied several hours to read, and we shall with equal pleasure re-read. Some from all of you, except dear Han., and she is very excusable. (I don't know that Harry is, however. I am looking for his, crossed.)

Well, we have made the Nile trip, and enjoyed it too, even *I*, and will leave our little palace with regret, though, as you well know, I have some cares and anxieties here, so it is not Paradise, and don't let any ever persuade you into thinking it *is*. No people could have been more favoured than we have been, in all outer surroundings; we have had no heat to complain of, but some cold.

I do most heartily thank each and every grandchild for their letters, down to little Annie, and we will try to execute the commissions. I wish I could tell you what our next step would be, but, like me, you must be patient; a few days will now settle it. We should be delighted to have Gall. and Han. join us, if it is right for him to do so; it would be most acceptable to all the party. It is very uncertain *when* we shall return. August, Sep., and even Oct. are talked of; but our next letters will give more definite accounts.

The accounts from West River of the Christmas enjoyment, which only reached us to-day, are very pleasant, and we feel very grateful to our Phila. friends for thinking of and doing so much for them. I can hardly imagine *Fanny* a *grandmother*, but think I know a little *how* she feels. Remember me to her, and the Dr. also, and to all at the Ridge. I was glad to note that Sam is better.

I think we shall have to send a box of odds and ends from here. Am afraid Is. and Annie will be burdened, but hope they'll excuse it. Open and look, though there's not much worth looking at either, and please don't let them be in your way; but we are so full we must thin out, and yet are afraid to send the *little* nice things I have picked up.

We have a dog and monkey on board, and their gambols have afforded much amusement sometimes, but occasionally the latter gets loose, and then he is an annoyance. To my discomfort this morning, while packing my trunk on the deck (for there they have all been all the time), he sprang on my head, and for a while I could get no assistance. From my head he went into the trunk and unceremoniously helped himself. Farewell, with oh so much love to each and all.

Yours truly and affectionately,

A. C. M.

CAIRO, March 12, 1872.

My Dear Son:

We have only now left our Dahabeyah and taken possession of our rooms at Shepheard's Hotel, having been detained on board yesterday by the curious combination of progress and ancient retentiveness which marks this place probably more strongly than any other at present existing. A new iron bridge on handsome solid, well-built stone piers strides the Nile. It has a draw which, being placed at one end, makes it so difficult to pass except when the wind is in a certain direction that, you may remember, we were a week in our departure, waiting for a favorable opportunity. Then the draw was not completed so that it stood always open. Now it is completed, and we found a crowd of vessels lying there, and were told that it is opened only from 12 to 2 P. M. daily, and that when the wind is very high they keep it shut even at those hours. That was the case yesterday; so your uncle and I mounted donkeys and got our letters in the morning, and spent the afternoon in reading them, and I wrote a hasty letter to forward by the French mail to announce our safe arrival. This morning we packed our effects and bade adieu to the boat and the accomplished and worthy officers and crew, who have not only given us no ground for complaint, but have earned our hearty commendation for their energetic and faithful and cordial deportment. Never was a better boat better served.

The same strange association of the new and old met our view on every side. Elegant new villa residences by the score lined either side of the avenue; the dust laid by iron water carts. These residences stand in handsome and large enclosures, and are planted with ornamental flowering shrubs and beds of scarlet geraniums, verbena, etc., with pumping machines in the corner of each enclosure, worked by horse power, to keep the gardens watered. The avenue and crossways are planted on either side with young trees of a species of acacia which attains a great size, has a profusion of dark green foliage, does not appear to be liable to the attack of insects, and judging from the great number of seed vessels which now hang upon the trees, must have very many flowers in the season, which are said to be very sweet-scented. I have secured seeds enough to try how far it will bear the climate of Ivy Neck. It flourishes well here, but the greatest degree of cold never reaches freezing point.

Though winter does not kill plants here, it evidently checks vegetable life. The public square or Usbekêêh is very nearly opposite the hotel, and we notice a very decided change since we left here. Many plants are putting forth fresh foliage and flower buds which, when we were here before, looked dull and decaying, and some have already thrown out their flowers. They are kept watered (and the grass also) by a novel arrangement. There is a central reservoir supplied by steam power, and hose or tube is laid from this to every part of the grounds, perforated at stated intervals with holes through which the pressure forces out a fine jet, like rain, which falls on the grass and flower beds. It is open to the public at all hours except certain ones during each day when a band performs there; at those hours there is a small charge. The Pasha is expending large sums in promoting the improvement of the city, and many others, Italians, Frenchmen and Greeks, are imitating him by building handsome—really elegant—residences and shops on European plans.

Your eye constantly meets German, and French, and Italian, and Greek signs. It does look very strange to see those characters which we have been wont to associate only with Plato, and Xenophon, and Homer and the Holy Scriptures, inviting custom for the various wares of every-day consumption, and to see the book-binders with the term "Relieur" in large letters over the doors, while "Chambers a louer" and "Menuisier," etc., tell how many sons of France have expatriated themselves for the sake of gain; while "Bier Braueries" announce that the Teuton does not leave his national tastes behind him; and good Roman letters greet us with the homely English announcements of confectionery and Manchester and Birmingham wares.

The Turkish bazaar has its tiny closets and stocks in trade adapted to the size of the place of sale, which are so small that they admit no occupant but the vendor, who, as he sits cross-legged at the door, fills entirely all the space not occupied by the goods arranged on shelves, so that he can reach every piece of every article without rising from his seat.

Except the dealer in dry goods each shop sells but one kind of goods, and the making of shoes, and caps, and each several article of wear or consumption, is carried on by the street side, with open door, so that everything each makes or sells is seen by the competitor for trade in the same article. These remarks are applicable to all the Egyptian towns. At Siout I walked through the length and breadth of it. The bazaars there are very extensive, and are much better shaded from the sun. They are all covered and made cool by having roofs at considerable height. Many are here similarly screened, but they are more thronged, and cannot be kept so clean as were those of Siout.

Your mother and myself have become more familiar with the strange looks and habits of the people, so that I shall venture more freely into the bazaar than I did when we were here three months since, and I hope she will be able to go with me, though we see nothing we wish to purchase unless it be some articles of need for present service. We find Mr. E. T. Greble is here, and also Mr. Mark Reeves, of Cincinnati, Ohio, a cousin of Mr. Samuel Reeves. His wife has been quite ill on her way down the Nile and since her arrival here, but is now improving under the judicious care of Dr. Grant, a Scotch physician who married a daughter of Mr. Torry, Member of Congress from Honesdale, I believe, or some of those coal places. He wishes me to join him in attendance on Mrs. Lansing (a sister of the Rev. Dr. Dales, of the church at 16th and Race Sts.), who is suffering from some chronic malady which has defied the efforts of some of the most eminent medical men of Great Britain, to whom she was sent.

SHEPHEARD'S HOTEL, CAIRO, March 13, 1872.

My Dear Children:

We find ourselves so much more comfortably accommodated in this hotel than we were in the more extensive and pretentious one, to which Friezier was beguiled on our way up, that we may be obliged to change our record of this place then made. Every apartment comfortably furnished, good servants, and well cooked food, contribute as much to the mental composure as to the sensuous gratification of the bodily appetite. We have no ground of complaint about our fare on the boat, but to sit to a clean, well-ironed table cloth with fresh napkins, well washed and polished with the iron, for each meal and to have that meal terminate as the Romans did (*ab ovo usque ad malum*) with a perfect "Brown Betty" (rejoicing though it did in the more aristocratic style of Charlotte des Pommes) was certainly no small contribution to our welcome to this outpost of modern civilization. And now your mother is just moving from a sweet repose on a good mattress on a spring foundation, not having had either flight from fleas, or fights with them because they would not flee, nor have we either of us any wounds to count received in involuntary conflicts with autochthonous occupants.

The fatigue of packing and leaving the boat and the disquiet attendant upon parting from our Arabs, whose kindness and devotion to us have been such that we cannot leave them without emotion, indisposed us yesterday to any out-door observations. Our windows open on a beautiful garden animated by flocks of birds, and when we had settled ourselves and got out the apparel necessary for association with civilized people we were ready "to take our ease in our inn" with a mingled feeling of regret that we should no longer have days without toil, but must at once enter on the discussion of plans and arrangements to accomplish the most that can be done, and to suit the strength and taste of a party combining so many varieties in both aspects, and rejoicing that once more we are brought within comparatively easy access to you and our home. We saw yesterday a Boston gentleman who had reached here two days within three weeks of the time he left his home.

There are crowds here of Americans and Europeans on their way to Syria. One party we had met several times up the river, left yesterday to cross the desert. There were father and mother and son, three only, but besides the horses they were to ride, they required thirty camels to transport their luggage and tents and provisions. The steamboats are all crowded with pilgrims and travellers anxious to reach Jerusalem for Easter, so that there is difficulty about getting passage to Jaffa and Beyroot, and this, with the other hindrances, leads us to hesitate greatly about pursuing our proposed plan. My own judgment is very positive that it is inexpedient, and your Uncle Wistar's is the same. Your Aunt Mary says Wistar's state is, that he does not yet see his way clear and will not go unless he does. Your

Aunt Mary is very desirous to go to the scene of the earthly life of our Lord. But the more I hear and read and think on the subject the more I incline to the opinion that it is not without a providential purpose that Jerusalem is trodden down of the Gentiles; and the Holy Land stripped of the influences it might have had if it had been held in the uninterrupted possession of professed followers of Christ, who would make its sacred scenes, like the Brazen Serpent of the wilderness, an object of idolatry; which justified and called for its destruction. With only traditional accounts and the great uncertainty of the verity of the locations, there is, and has ever been, superstitious exaltation of the sacred character of these spots, and I know from the tendency of my own imagination and feelings that there is a snare in such things which renders it necessary to be on the watch.

No trace of "the place where He dwelt," nor of that "where the Lord lay" can be found. Even the location of the towns of Nazareth and Capernaum and Bethany, those which are most surely the places in which His human nature abode during His ministry—Diaconate as the original has it—has been matter of much doubt and the occasion of voluminous discussion ; and the house of Martha and Mary and Lazarus, the only dwelling in which He ever had a place to lay His head after entering on that active mission of three years which immediately preceded the great sacrifice by which it was *finished*, no longer opens its door to enable His redeemed ones to look upon those things on which He looked and feel they are within the walls which sheltered Him from the malice of His enemies, and afforded Him the consolation of companionship with those He loved. No prayer offered in the Garden of Gethsemane would be more sanctified by the blood of His agony than is that of the humblest and feeblest believer in the most remote Isle of the Sea, or amid the tumult and confusion of the most populous mart, and the Calvary and Sepulchre of modern superstition and contention are certainly not the altar on which the victim bled for us.

Nothing material remains to usurp the place of the Universal Temple in which they who worship in spirit and in truth find Him, ever and everywhere present, as the High Priest touched with a feeling of our infirmities, who, though He once died for all, is risen to the right hand of the Father, and there liveth to make intercession for us ; and now that I stand upon the shore almost of that land, and in that into which He was taken to avoid the power of Herod, I am satisfied that it is better to have my heart open to receive that Holy Ghost whose blessed influences are confined to no land, or city, or dwelling, than to tread the soil He trod and gaze upon the mountains He walked over or even the one most certainly fixed of all points connected with His history, that road over Olivet by which He was carried in triumphant procession as He entered the city, or that on which He stood when He beheld the city and wept over it.

He Himself said it was expedient that He should go away ; and the angel told His sorrowing followers, "He is not here, He is risen." And He has said to every one who will open the door of the heart at which He stands and knocks, "If any man open the door I will come in and sup with him, and he shall sup with me."

Noon.—Immediately after breakfast your mother and aunts and myself set out together to go into the Mooskee, the street of shops, as she needed some new bonnet strings. etc. They decided that they could attend to such little matters better without the assistance of even a husband and brother, than with the bother of his interference. I will not venture to suggest a stronger word. So I was content to wait on them to the door of Madame Cecille, Modiste, etc., where we had dealt on our previous visit—to think of being able to refer to the experience of a former visit to Cairo—and left them there.

We had walked by the Usbekëëh with its beautiful grassy lawns, and grottos of artificial rock work, and varied clumps of flowering shrubs, and in front of the Circus and the American Mission residence; which two intruders into this foreign land stand fronting each other at the entrance to the Mooskee. I was glad to be their attendant as far as the door, and when they entered I sauntered along, though with no object of pursuit, certainly not an idler, as all one's wits are in active exercise to avoid being run down by carriages, trodden under foot of camels, jostled by donkeys, or elbowed by the crowd of human beings, of every shade, from the black Nubian, with his tattooed face, to the blue-eyed, fair-haired, ruddy Teuton; of every form of feature, from the straight profile and oval face of the Greek, to the short round negro, of whom it is difficult to determine what is the latitude and which the longitude of the countenance, with every sound that gave to Babel its name of confusion, uttered in as many languages as led then to the dispersion of the "one family" of "the one blood" to people all the regions of the habitable globe.

As for costume it is the proper place for the moulders of fashion to study the diversity of form that may satisfy the taste for variety, which demands that unceasing change of modern civilization which strikes one so forcibly when one has been for many months accustomed only to that of our first parents with the slighest possible change during 4000 years. It is absolutely bewildering to look at. Tight pants which display the spindle shank and curved leg of some Frank dandy, are all the more unbecoming beside the solid fluted column of brown or green silk or stuff, made of I know not how many yards, carefully plaited in at the waist, and falling in regular folds to within an inch or two of the ground, where it is again gathered in and fastened between the ankles so as merely to permit the feet to protrude and prove that this man is also a *bi*ped and moves by stepping one foot before the other as other men do; a point about which otherwise there might be room for doubt, so entirely is the bifurcation of the genus concealed. Flowing robes with graceful drapery, topped by full turbans of white, intertwined with yellow silk shawls, mingle with red skull caps, having long black silk tassels dangling behind, stove-pipe black hats and soft felt ones with wide soft rims, the crown covered with white muslin gathered in folds around it and hanging down to the shoulders, or enveloped in parti-colored silk similarly arranged. I met one Englishman with lilac veil intertwined with white muslin around his hat.

Water carriers pushed through the throng with their skin of a goat so carefully arranged that the neck and feet and tail all stand out stiffly, filled with the water they contain, slung over the shoulder, and holding with one hand the neck, and in the other, two or more bright brass cups which they clatter, like our boys do the "bones" of the Ethiopian serenaders, while they add to this noise the perpetual cry, "Mōieh," "Mōieh;" water, water. Venders of candies and fruits and vegetables and clover, tied up in little parcels for the donkeys and horses, add their cries to the ever-increasing discord. Boys with boxes and brushes, are as thickly seen as about that resort of the sovereigns of our city who lounge on the pavement of Independence Hall, and solicit you in the same words to "black boots."

Gentlemen drive through the crowd in their Landaus and Phaetons; preceded by the runner in full white surplice, crying loudly to clear the way, while, with no curbstone to shut off a *trottoir* from the carriage-way, loungers sit smoking and drinking coffee in front of the restaurants, which are as frequent as beer and wine shops on our streets. I saw many with large Greek uncial letters on the signs, side by side with the crooked cursive lines of Arabic. Other crowds collect around venders of various wares. I saw one in the midst of which stood a man who was describing, with the most voluble Arabic, the advantages of a manifold letter-writter, and moving his stile from right to left, exhibiting the perfect copy made in the letter-book by the use of the black sheet interposed between the two white ones. Money changers sit at short intervals with their tables filled with gold, silver and copper coins, chucking handfuls of the latter with a peculiar dexterity, the result of incessant practice, to invite attention. Is there not variety enough in the objects to demand all one's eyes and occupy one's mind so that a walk of an hour was no idle stroll?

In all this I have only alluded to the crowd, without making any reference to the contents of the shops. The Mooskee is the street in which the shops are mostly kept by Greeks, Italians, Frenchmen and Germans, and they sell various articles; differing in this from the regular Turkish and Egyptian bazaars, which are further in the heart of the town, and where, as I have told you before, each trade or occupation is found grouped together. Very many of the shops in the Mooskee are filled with groceries, some with dry goods of every kind, some with Paris-made shoes and ready-made clothing. "Macchina da Cucire" are advertised on the corners, and the various kinds of Walcot; Wheeler & Wilson, etc., compete with each other for the favour of Arab *men*. Women do not sew here. Among the most attractive articles exposed for sale are the contents of the Fruiterers' stalls. Golden oranges, blushing apples, their ruddy cheeks tinting their straw-colored skins, purple olives, luscious pears, are all piled abundantly on every side.

While I sauntered amid all this profusion of objects of interest and listened to the mingled jargon which distracts one's thoughts, I saw a movement in the crowd before me, which swayed as it opened to permit a passage to a procession of some twenty or thirty men in uniform, who preceded and followed a fine-countenanced corpulent Turk in rich attire, with much gold lace about his robes and a tiara on his head fastened by a gold band around his forehead, mounted on a horse richly caparisoned with crimson and gold, and led by two grooms. I inquired who it was, and was informed it was the Grand Mollah of Egypt, the head of the Moslem priests. (*Judiciary.*—Eds.) A new one is appointed annually by the Sultan and resides here during his official year. I followed him on my way back to Mme. Cecille's, where I found your mother and aunts, who had just completed their purchases, and as the day was advancing and the sun getting hot we walked slowly back to our rooms where I have beguiled the hour in thus giving you a rough sketch of our morning.

March 15th.

After much anxious and earnest discussion about the propriety of our going to Jerusalem, in which I took the part of opposition on every account and for the sake of all the members of the party, your uncle has yielded to your Aunt Mary's desire and decided to make the effort. A reported outbreak of Mohammedan violence, in which some Christians were murdered at Beyroot, of which we heard the report last evening, does not move your Aunt, whose heart appears strongly set on accomplishing this part of the tour. We shall leave here by rail for the Suez Canal on the 21st and take the Austrian Lloyd steamer at Port Said for Beyroot, and have secured passages from Beyroot to Constantinople for the 7th of April; the interval to be spent at Jerusalem and its environs.

Your loving father,

CASPAR MORRIS.

CAIRO, March 14, 1872.

My Dear Brother (Galloway Cheston):

Among the many letters that awaited us on our return here, was yours of Feby. 9th, for which we thank you, though the report of dear Margaret and yourself was so sad that we cannot but wish we could be with you; and the relapse of Mary Ellen is very disappointing, but should not be allowed to discourage us. I have no hesitation that your purpose to send her back to the situation in which she found so much benefit is judicious. I feared that she had not been there long enough to have the restoration established. Tell her from me that I am sanguine in my expectation of her recovery, and that she must not allow her present suffering to depress her.

Your letter is the latest date received by any of the party, and the latest intelligence from home any of us are likely to receive for a month at least. Our movements when we leave here, and the time at which we shall leave, are both so uncertain that Wistar has decided to leave our letters still in London, and the last order to Brown, Shipley & Co. was not to forward any to this place after the 26th of Feby., so that we do not expect any more here.

The question whether we shall go to Syria is anxiously discussed. Anne's illness on the boat decided for her and myself that we would not attempt the journey to Jerusalem, but if they go await their return at Beyroot. I do not think we should be justified in encountering the fatigue and exposure of two weeks in tents, merely to see the Jerusalem of *to-day*, which, though it stands on the mound formed by the debris of that over whose destruction our Lord wept, contains nothing which can be associated with His presence, any more certainly than is the whole earth He has redeemed, unless, perhaps, it be the road over the Mount of Olives, by which He descended in the one procession with which He was honored. But even that, how changed! No palms wave now their feathery crowns to furnish branches to strew in His way, and one may see in the *mental* picture more that is grand and solemn, than when walking or riding wearily over the desolate brow of the weather-beaten mount standing naked and forlorn.

Few if any of the places which are supposed to represent those mentioned in the sacred Scriptures are beyond dispute; and even if we admit the claim of any one to the exclusion of another, it has no material substantial thing (even in ruins) to give it association with scenes enacted there. Old as are the trees supposed to mark the site of the Garden of Gethsemane, it is scarcely possible that they should be those which witnessed His agony, and even if they were, the High and Mighty One who inhabiteth eternity, has *not* told us that He will be found *there* of those who seek Him, though He has said that He will "look upon him that is of a contrite heart and trembles at His word," wherever that man is found on the face of the whole earth, every inch of which has been redeemed by the blood which there fell from Jesus in His agony. No one would find His advocacy more potent there than in the most remote isle of the sea, or corner of the earth to which that spirit of adoption and fellowship has been sent, which our Lord promised to His people when He cheered the sorrowful hearts of His disciples by telling them it was "expedient that He should go to the Father" and send "the Comforter to take of His and show them unto us," wherever we may be.

I am, perhaps, as subject to the influence of imagination as most, and it is a trial to me to be on the shore of the land in which He dwelt and not cross the boundary to enter. But I have not the slightest feeling of the kind which would attach more sanctity to Judea than to any other portion of the ransomed world, and would not expose Anne to the slightest discomfort, much less to any peril, for the gratification of those feelings if I had.

I had written thus before breakfast. After dinner, at the table, Wistar informed us that he was making arrangements for palanquins to convey the party, and to arrange the travel so that there should be no exposure to the weather in tents till they reached Jerusalem, where there is a good hotel, at which those who are not able to go to the more remote points, may be as comfortable as at any other hotel; from which we infer that he has decided to go to Syria. Under such circumstances it is possible we may find it *most expedient* to accompany them.

I have expressed my opinion in the clearest and most decided terms, that it is not right to go. Wistar's wife is equally decided that it is right, and her conviction that we shall be cared for, and get through safely.

(After tea.)

At tea table Brother Wistar announced that our passages for Syria have been taken to leave Port Said on the 23d of this month. Thus our indecision is concluded, and we shall endeavor to commit ourselves to the good providence of our Heavenly Father. So far as sisters and Anne and myself are concerned, we are going against our judgment, which would lead us to turn our steps toward Italy, France and Germany, and so return to our homes in August. This will detain us in Europe till October.

March 15th.

We have been much distressed by the sad account of the illness of dear Margaret's nephew, James Carey, which Cheston and Mary Yarnall mention. It is a fearful addition to the claims on your sympathy. Certainly we are taught by sore lessons that there is no rest on earth; and I find the only hope of rest hereafter in the advocacy and atonement of Him who died for us, and has told us He has compassion on our infirmities and pardoneth our iniquity, great as it may be. I left home to escape the responsibility of my profession, and I am here obliged to consult in several cases of serious disease. This morning am to visit Col. Rhett, of S. Carolina, who is in the service of the Pasha and has had a paralytic attack. He is under the treatment of an able Scotch physician with whom I am attending an Englishman, and who has requested me to see the Colonel.

A Mr. Lee from Baltimore is here, making costly purchases of Oriental articles. We met at Luxor. I suppose him to be a son of your banker. He is with young Sherman, of Duncan, Sherman & Co., of New York.

Friday, P.M.

I believe the long and earnest discussion of plans has resulted in the decision to spend six weeks of travel to accomplish one week in Jerusalem. We shall be cut off from our advices from home till we reach Constantinople, about the first of May. It appears to Anne and myself a large expenditure in every way for the smallest gratification. We may pick up some gratification by the way. I am very sorry for the decision. With much love to Margaret.

Your afft. brother,

CASPAR MORRIS.

CAIRO, March 18, 1872, 5 P.M.

My Dear Children:

No language adequate to the description, and no power of the imagination to the conception of the disgusting character of such a day as this is. Yesterday was hot and oppressive. Your dear mother and I attended Divine service twice, greatly to our comfort notwithstanding the heat, and after service in the evening took a carriage and drove to the Protestant Cemetery, that I might relieve Mrs. Betts by writing to inform her that the vault was properly arranged in which she had left the remains of her husband. To our surprise the clouds gathered, looking as though we should have a heavy gust, but it resulted in only enough to allow us to say that we had been caught in a shower at Cairo.

The night was very windy, but this morning a clear sky and fine air tempted us to carry out our plan for the day and start for the Pyramids of Ghizeh. The road led us first through the quarter of Cairo in which the Khedive is himself building, and encouraging others to erect fine mansions surrounded by large gardens filled with shrubbery and flower beds. We then crossed the Nile by the new bridge, which is a very fine wide iron structure on good stone piers. Immediately on reaching the west bank of the Nile we entered on a wide avenue which has been raised at very heavy cost and is lined on either side by Acacia trees. There is one of the Pasha's palaces on the road, and until we reached it the trees are already so large that the branches meet overhead, forming a delightful shade. The palace is now undergoing repair and extension. It is already large and encloses numerous courts with fountains, and shrubbery which overtopped the wall in some places, and in others was seen through iron railing or open arches. Crowds of workmen were busy—masons and carpenters—and hundreds of children, boys and girls, many of them of very tender age, carrying out the rubbish or taking in materials to the workmen in little boxes or baskets on their heads. Overseers with long sticks kept them very busy, but the cheerful temper of the people, on which I have so frequently remarked, was displayed in the merry tones of song with which they kept time as they ran to and fro. From the palace to the pyramids, a distance of quite five miles, the same raised avenue runs in a direct line. The trees have been more recently planted, and do not yet afford shade; but as they grow rapidly they soon will, especially as they bear to be removed of a large size. The top is cut off, and the branches shoot out vigorously and soon form a large crown of foliage. When in flower the odour must be very fine and the whole effect beautiful. Each tree here requires daily to be watered. Think of the toil, a double row about 20 feet apart, and seven miles in length! A canal for irrigation runs parallel to the road the entire distance, and the eye wanders over a perfect level of varied verdure, with here and there a patch of beans with the blue flower, or rape seed with its yellow blossom, or ripe wheat or barley, or white clover to relieve the monotony of green. Cattle tethered, with children leading them, give animation to the picture; but no houses are to be seen, except one miserable little village near the edge of the desert on which the pyramids stand.

Our ride out was very pleasant, but when we reached the base the wind was blowing so furiously that it was difficult to stand while looking at the wondrous pile of which Pliny at the Christian era remarked, that it was "a vain expenditure of money and toil." Just think of a *solid mass* of squared stone blocks, each one not less than four feet thick, by eight or ten in length, laid with cement, covering a square area of eleven acres and rising to the height of 500 feet! As we see it the surfaces are irregular; each row of stones as it rose receded in regular steps, into which were fitted angular blocks, which made the surface smooth when it was complete. They began this outer covering from the top, wedging each lower block under that above. From the larger pyramid all this outer covering has been removed and used by the Saracens and Turks. On what is known as the second pyramid, which is close at hand, the upper third still remains, enabling us to see what was the appearance of them all. About one-third way up, on one side, an opening was discovered many years since over which an imperfect arch of stone is arranged. This had been carefully concealed. This leads to the passage to the chamber in the interior, in which the body of the monarch by whom it was built was to await the return of the soul. All the care taken to conceal the entrance proved useless, as the body had been removed before the chamber was re-entered some years ago; and even the empty sarcophagus was then taken away to gratify the curiosity of our own times.

We saw several parties ascending to the top and descending, assisted by Arab guides. Mr. Longstreth and Miss Harris had intended doing so, but Mr. Longstreth has been sick, and I advised him not to make the exertion. Nothing would have been gained except the empty reputation of having done it. Before they could have reached the summit the atmosphere was so filled with fine sand that we could not see more than a few feet, and so it has continued until this time.

The wind blows a perfect hurricane from the southwest, and everything is densely coated with an almost impalpable powder. The sun is totally concealed by it. No one can say which is east or which is west by any sign of his presence. Happily the wind was on our back as we returned. I do not see how the coachmen could have induced their horses to face it. Fine as it is, the force of the wind is such that it stings our faces. The natives all envelope their heads and eyes in their turbans or some other cloth. It is like a heavy, driving, fine snow at home. No one knows how long it may continue, but *one such day* in the year is enough to deter any one from coming here, much more from making it his abode. The knowledge that one was liable to it would deter the neatest housekeeper from any efforts to be cleanly. It is simply impossible. No measures of precaution have any power, and even after having enjoyed a bath, I feel as though I was dust already and thoroughly, and never could be "dusted." Eyes and nose and mouth all burn with the irritation, and no labour with the brush will ever take it out of the texture of the clothing. It interfered greatly with our examination of the pyramids and sphynx and tombs. We did as much as was in our power before the time for luncheon, which we carried with us, but by the time we had recruited our strength, exhausted by the power of the wind, further exploration was absolutely impossible, and a party of French and Germans who had made their plans to take their lunch before making the examination must have returned satisfied with devouring a lamb roasted whole in the village and brought to table by two men on their shoulders on the long iron spit. They washed it down with copious draughts of champagne and other wines, and became as heady as the champagne itself.

We walked around the sphynx, or the remains of the monstrous Chimera cut upon the rock. You are all familiar with the photographs. As you first see it you cannot imagine that it has any form derived from human art. It looks like some great boulder very much eroded by the weather. The strata of which the mass is composed are of different composition and power to resist the influence of the wind and the corrosion of time. No other influence is felt here. But when you reach the front the ears are still nearly perfect, and so are the plaits of the Coiffure. The crown is gone, and the projection of the nose and chin, but enough remains to give a very good idea of the character of the face, which is very expressive of simple, dignified repose. On the cheeks the reddish brown paint with which the entire face was once covered still remains. It stands about 60 feet in height as it rises from the base; and the feet, which are buried in the sand, project 50 feet in front, while the body has entirely lost the shape it originally had.

It was without doubt a sepulchral monument. The entire plain around is excavated; and tombs and sepulchral temples are buried in the sand on every side. Some have been partially cleared, and at a depth of 50 feet are found Sarcophagi and mummy cases of basalt, some of them covered with costly sculptures, proving that they are the places of deposit of Royalty or great wealth.

We looked down some of the pits and went through one of the Temples built of immense blocks of red granite perfectly squared. I measured some of them with my umbrella, the only measure I could use, and found them six times its length, and the breadth two lengths of it. These massive blocks had been brought from Assouan, five hundred miles south of this, at a period certainly anterior to the visit of Abraham.

The more we inspect these sepulchral remains the more we are convinced that they indicate the belief of the most ancient Egyptians in a future life. The houses of the common people were, as now, of unburned brick and wood, perishable and transient like the present state of being. The tombs which were to receive the bodies and retain them for resurrection were made as solid as human art and skill could render them. The same idea led to the adoption of the Scarabeus as an emblem of immortality deposited with the mummy. The insect commits the germ of future life to the mass of ordure which it has carefully rolled up and deposited at the bottom of a deep hole which it bores out to receive it, and keep it safely till the time comes when it shall be hatched and emerge into a new life.

Their elegantly adorned chambers cut in the rock, and covered with pictures which have transmitted to our day the record of the possessions and habits of the owners, were mortuary chapels in which services commemorative of the departed were annually celebrated. In one corner of each we find deep square pits cut in the rock, or, it is said, in cases where the rock was too soft, lined with stone or brick. These were the receptacles of the bodies of the dead, coffined in stone or wood, or merely enveloped in wrappings saturated with bitumen, according to the wealth of the deceased or the surviving friends.

On the walls of the chapels we frequently find the representation of the trial of the character of the deceased, and the mediation in his behalf of the minor deities, designed to represent the attributes of the great Supreme Being to whom man is responsible for the use of the life received from Him. We thus see the idea of immortality and responsibility lying at the foundation of the whole system. Who would exchange the simple teaching of the word of God, that God is "I am"; and that One "in the form of God and thinking it no robbery to be equal with God, made himself of no reputation and took on him our nature," and dying for us, rose again; thus bringing "life and immortality to light," and prepared a way by which God is reconciled to us, and we to a justly angry God, for all this cumbrous symbolism which, however it was known to the priesthood and the learned, degenerated into a base idolatry among the ignorant masses?

The desert here at Ghizeh consists of sand and pebbles and nodules of flint and broken fragments of fossil shells, the disintegrated material of the rock which underlies it. In this rock are the tombs. Higher up the river these cliffs rise above the level of the valley and bound it on either side. Both here and there the rock is chosen as the place of deposit of the dead, out of reach of the water of the annual inundation; and whether in the cavities of the pyramids, or the wells opening out of the chapels of the tombs, the entrance was always blocked up by masses of rubble mingled with mortar, and made thus impervious to water, and almost as much so by human effort.

The character of the day rendered it impossible for us to investigate the chambers of the tombs near the pyramids, but they are adorned just as those at Tel Amarna and Beni Hassan, which we did examine, and are more difficult of access. We shall probably be obliged to leave without going to Memphis and Sakkarah, which I greatly regret. The tombs there are very ancient, and those of the sacred bulls especially interesting. We could not have stopped on our way down except on the Sabbath day, and the difficulty of access from here is such as renders it improper to attempt it. We must be content with what we have seen, and with what we can still see, in the museum here and in the collections at Berlin, Paris and London, which have been enriched by the spoils of these tombs. I omitted to mention that the stone for building the pyramids was all brought from quarries on the other side of the Nile, carried on a causeway constructed for the purpose at an expense of toil and money equal to that of the pyramid itself, and requiring ten years to make it. We leave for Port Said, where we take the Austrian Lloyd steamer for Jaffa, on Saturday. On Monday leave for Jerusalem, hoping to reach there on Tuesday evening.

Your loving father,

CASPAR MORRIS.

5.30 A. M., CAIRO, March 18, 1872.

My Dear Children:

This is a very poor place to do anything at. We have now been here a week this morning, and received, read and answered our letters and discussed our future movements; this occupied our time until Saturday, which we spent at the museum of Egyptian antiquities belonging to the Khedive, collected by M. Mariette, and now at Boulac until suitable buildings can be constructed in this part of the capital, which the Khedive is making every effort to render as attractive to Europeans as Paris or Brussels. M. Mariette is making explorations among the temples and tombs, and has accumulated a large number of most interesting relics, many more than are yet exhibited. Those which are already displayed are of overwhelming interest. In one room is the gilded cover of the case which contained the mummy of Queen Aah-Hotep, who lived some 1500 years before the coming of our Lord (say 3000 years ago, by way of being modest about dates). It is large enough to receive not only the body, with all its wrappings, but another interior case also. The gilding is untarnished, and covered with delicate tracing of a vulture with outspread wings and other emblems of royalty, proving that the occupant was Queen of Upper and Lower Egypt. An inscription which gives the name of the occupant, chief wife of the king, runs down the front, which is adorned with mourning figures kneeling.

When the case was opened it was found to contain two boats of gold and silver, with images of rowers seated on the benches,—bronze hatchets of elegant shape, with large gold bracelets. Among the linen clothes were found a gold axe and poignards; a heavy gold chain, to which were hung three gold flies, each three inches square; while around the neck was suspended a beautiful heavy gold chain of fine links, intertwined, to which was attached a scarabeus of gold and enamel of most beautiful workmanship; while a diadem of gold and enamel was fixed among the hair so as to rise above the brow; and bracelets of gold and enamel to match the diadem were upon the arms. All these jewels are exhibited in a glass case in one of the rooms of the museum, together with a large collection from various other sources. Some of the bracelets are made of very fine stone beads of various colors, mingled with gold beads in beautiful patterns. These are strung on gold wire. In the same case are found enormous gold ear-rings, and other articles of jewelry from various other sources, all proving the advance made in the art of female adorning at that early period, and giving us an idea of the bracelets and rings and chains which are noticed in the lives of the patriarchs. The description of them would be tedious and unintelligible. They must be seen to be appreciated. In the same room is an alabaster statue of a Queen who lived about the time of Solomon. The countenance is attractive and the features fine.

April 16th.

I find this half sheet in my portfolio, to which I have access to-day for the first time in many weeks, not since we left Cairo, now nearly a month. Since that time we have been living in "bundles," and kicked about at that. You can put together the sheets in Cheston's, Israel's and Galloway's letters, and will find they are a connected series.

ISMAILEH, SUEZ CANAL, March 21, 1872.

My Dear Children:

Little did we dream a few years since, when reading about the difficulty encountered in the construction of the canal which appears destined to bring back to its old channels the commerce of the East, so long diverted from its ancient course, that I should ever address you from its margin in the desert; much less that I should trace the course of the children of Israel from the land of Goshen to the point at which, "entangled in the land," shut in between the sea and the mountains, the Divine power was manifested in their deliverance, and the Divine judgment exhibited in the destruction of their oppressors. Yet here I am, your mother and myself, comfortably accommodated in a plain but neat apartment, looking out on the broad canal, with its deep blue water contrasting most strongly with the yellow margin of sand by which it is bounded.

Your Aunt Mary is quite sick; I hope only a temporary trouble. She has kept out and active up to bed-time last night. She was out all day yesterday, visiting her friends in Cairo last evening, and going to the school of Miss Whately. I heard nothing of her being unwell till we met for breakfast this morning; passages taken and accommodation telegraphed for all the way through to Jerusalem by your uncle. Our trunks had gone to the R.R. depot when I was first told that she had been unwell during the night and had taken opium by your uncle's direction, and he assumed the responsibility of travelling. She has been very uncomfortable all day and has gone at once to bed. We must go on to-morrow and next day, as our rooms here and at Port Said are only taken for the two nights, and the crowd of passengers and the demand for accommodation is very great. It is a painful position in which to be placed. It was the apprehension of the possibility we should meet with this very difficulty which influenced me in my opposition to the tour in Palestine. When once it is entered on, there is no withdrawing or escape; we must go through without stopping anywhere. I am very thankful it is not on the way to Sinai.

The first part of our journey to-day was through a most fertile plain, well watered and highly cultivated. It was well described by Pharaoh to Joseph, "the good of all the land is before you." It is a perfectly level plain, intersected in every direction by canals from the Nile, and every foot of it watered by little channels leading through it at regular distances. The aspect of the country was singularly attractive, diversified by palm and acacia trees lining both sides of the roads which intersected each other at short distances, giving a park-like air to the landscape. Flocks of cranes flew about in the air, wheeling as though with the design to display themselves, their white bodies and dark wings changing as they changed their position. The Pyramids of Ghizeh loomed up in their ghostly majesty, growing smaller and smaller as we left them in the distance.

Wheat was the predominant crop, but flax, in various stages of progress up to ripeness, cotton, tobacco and beans, lent their varied green shades. Ploughs, drawn by camels and buffaloes yoked together, or oxen, were busily engaged in turning up the soil. It was the primitive plough represented in the painting in the tombs of Beni Hassan, and fellaheen were stooping over the same hoes as their predecessors had bent over. We passed several railroad stations with modern names and French houses; at one a carriage and pair of horses were waiting for the arrival of the train.

Many large mounds marked the site of old towns, one of which was Bubastis, once one of the capitals of lower Egypt, and the place at which special honor was paid to the Goddess Pasht, represented with the head of a cat. At one of the stations where we changed cars and were detained an hour or two, a prisoner, manacled by having his hands confined in two pieces of wood locked together around his wrists, keeping his hands at least two feet apart and the arms extended from the body, loaded also with a heavy chain around his neck, sat under the portico with a soldier on each side to guard him. He was not only indifferent to the exposure, but had an expression of recklessness and malignant cunning which gave me the impression that he may have been the leader of a gang of murderous marauders. I never saw a human face more repulsive.

The productiveness of the land over which we passed is entirely dependent on the water from the Nile, carried in every direction by canals of various sizes. The last forty miles of the journey was through arid desert. The surface, swept by the wind, looked as though it were a great gravel bank, but wherever railroad excavations displayed the strata below, we saw the same character of soil as that whose fertility had elicited our admiration. The Khedive is now engaged with a large force extending the Nile canal, and wherever it spreads its life-giving stream, beauty and wealth follow the track; surrounded on every side by the apparently hopeless sterility of the desert.

Just before sunset we reached Ismaileh and saw the head-lands which jut into the Red Sea to the south and east.

March 22d.

Ismaileh is the point at which the railroad for Alexandria and Cairo and a canal from the Nile reach the Suez Canal, which here has the appearance of a lake; the water very light and blue. We were too weary last night to do anything beyond the needful ablution, take our suppers and go to bed, thankful to have reached there without your aunt being worse, and to find a clean, new, hotel with a good meal and better beds.

We were refreshed by a good night's sleep, and I turned out about sunrise this morning to inspect the place. There are not many dwellings, but they are good, enclosed by walls surrounding gardens. The streets are wide, laid out at right angles, well-paved and clean. There is a large public garden, handsomely planted with a great variety of shrubbery, and large beds of scarlet geraniums, wall-flowers, stock-gillies and other familiar sweets. A Christian church stands prominently on the square, and the bell summoned worshippers at that early hour. A bronze bust of the Count Sala, the President of the Canal Company, adorns a niche at one corner of the garden, dedicated to his memory by his fellow-employees.

I met a bright little boy of some twelve years old, with his books, with whom I entered into conversation in French, and found he was on his way to school. He seemed as gay as a bird, and talked away in French as though he thought I was a born Frenchman. He told me his father and mother were in Syria, and all his friends, but he was here going to school. He understood me much better than I did him.

His fluency quite went ahead of my sluggish capacity. A large French flour mill attracted my attention, seeming so out of place here in the desert. The canal having been proposed by Napoleon I. and completed by French engineers, the French influence is seen on every side, and the French language is the medium of communication with foreigners.

The water in the lake and canal is salt, and there are bathing arrangements as though they hope to make it a seaside resort.

PORT SAID ; ON THE MEDITERRANEAN, March 23, 1872.

My Dear Children :

I will send a few lines, though they will be hurried and perhaps very unsatisfactory; having packed, hands are unsteady and head also (but not the heart for you all), I write at your father's bedside; he is right sick, diarrhœa and some nausea (was fainty again last evening), previous to this feature. Also had another fainty spell in Cairo, and I consulted Dr. Grant about him; he directed brandy and iron three times a day and generous diet. Of course you will understand I can't help feeling anxious, and was very sorry this Syrian trip was decided on, and your Uncle Wistar was also, and did what he could to avoid it, and not being able to carry that point, has done all he can to make it easy. Your father's judgment led him to speak very freely in opposition, for the which he is now thankful, as he has not the responsibility to bear. Mary decided it on the ground of her duty; well, she is now right sick herself, and our getting further than Jaffa or Beyroot is doubtful. We are not sufficiently comfortable here to think it best to stay here, but will go on board the steamer in a couple of hours for Jaffa. We have decided to make the best of this, and are really taking pleasure in the journey so far. If all were well it would be very nice. The ride through the land of Goshen, and then the trip yesterday on the Suez canal was very nice, notwithstanding the size of the tug we came in; it was like a baby house, twelve passengers being what they calculated on, and they must be accommodating, two of whom were "nobility" from England, mother and daughter, "Lady Howard." I was in high spirits and somewhat mischievous, as I had heard, pretty direct, she would not speak to Americans ; I was determined to bring it about. The daughter and I were quite sociable; the mother was decidedly haughty to the end of the eight hours, but did speak several times.

Your father says I must stop chatting and let this go, after telling you that in the box of nothings from Cairo, there is a tin box, small, of Turkish tobacco, also a paste-board box with Senna, and separate in soft paper some very valuable specimens of the Senna plant in bloom (this Senna is all for Dr. Carson, and gum arabic plant also).

There is a long roll of a very beautiful plant; undo carefully, as the seed is very fine and we want Gally to try to raise it. These plants are low down in the box, and can't be too carefully handled. The stones are agates we picked up while walking, and some we think will cut prettily. Your father and aunt both are more comfortable, and I hope will soon be relieved entirely.

    Your loving mother,

                  A. C. M.

           PORT SAID, March 22, 1872.

My Dear Children :

At 8 A.M. we took our places on board the nice little steam yacht of the Egyptian Postal service bound from Ismaileh to this place by the Suez canal. The cabin forward was light and airy, with comfortable divans around it, able to seat about twenty-six persons, and we found it filled by Mr. and Mrs. Reeves, of Indiana, with their son and daughter, and Mr. Baker, a German, who travels with them, an English lady and her daughter, and our own party. Other travellers who had come over from Cairo with us were obliged to take a second boat. The air was fresh, the morning bright, the water blue, and we danced off gaily, crossing the lake to the entrance of the excavated canal, on the bank above which stands a handsome Kiosk belonging to the Khedive.

From that point our course lay along the straight canal, with nothing to be seen but the banks, in some places sand drifts, and in others soil which only needs the application of water to render it fertile, though now as destitute of verdure as the yard of a brick-maker's establishment.

We met six first-class steamships during the morning, *two of them aground*, though only drawing 16½ feet of water. The drifting sand which blows over everything, renders the constant operation of dredging machines essential, and we saw several at work. There is an incredible amount of abandoned, rejected and worn-out machinery strewn along the banks, and accumulated at either end of the canal. So much that it would pay to establish some rolling works and use up the waste material, which has cost much to bring it here, but is not worth carrying away again. There are station houses along the line, at one of which we procured a very good lunch, much to our invigoration and refreshment. Much of the distance the canal embankments run through shallow lakes of salt water, and we had a curious excitement among us. Your mother and I were summoned suddenly to the deck by the crying, "Mirage!" "Mirage!" "Come quick." And sure enough there spread out the appearance of a wide sheet of blue water with margins tufted with coarse reeds. I gave one good look and returned below, convinced that it was water. Nothing could so closely imitate it.

Soon after we were called again, and on my expressing my doubt of its being mirage, I was laughed at and told the pilot of the boat had assured them there could be no water there. Three or four times the same thing was repeated, and I began to yield my scepticism, and perhaps should have done so if the English lady had not sneered at the story as perfectly absurd. This rather put me on the defensive. But when we stopped for lunch your Uncle Wistar strayed off a little way and found they had all been imposed upon, and that there was a succession of little lakes running along at a short distance from the embankment.

As we approached Port Said the masts of vessels of all nations lying within the breakwater presented an attractive sight, and the beautiful flag of our country waved from a lofty flag-staff over the house of the consulate. It is a dingy-looking place with its French stores and Frank population. We find ourselves at the Hotel du Louvre, and the sound of a rehearsal of a company of actors in one wing of the house was more noisy than agreeable. A fine breeze blows through our chamber, but the heat of the sun outside forbids any exposure or exertion.

Sat. morning, March 23d.

The Austrian steamer has arrived; your uncle has gone to arrange our rooms; your aunt is reported better. I am myself disordered, with some nausea, compelling me to lie quiet instead of finishing my letters. Your dear mother seems well. They report Mrs. Reeves quite ill. Have told your uncle to go on. Anything better than staying here. If your aunt is not better we must either continue on to Beyroot or stop at Jaffa while those who can go to Jerusalem.

JAFFA, March 24, 1872.

My Dear Children:

We have accomplished one step; we have landed. It is something of which you can form no idea; something which I have always dreaded, and from which I most earnestly desired to escape, and which has been worse even than my worst imagination; worse than I can describe. But we are here in the midst of comfort greater than we have known since we left Naples; a perfectly clean house, table cloths, napkins, knives and forks, glasses, tea-pots and china, small and plain but really sweet, with an air as invigorating and refreshing as the finest October weather at Newport or some such sea-side resort.

We are at the settlement formed some years since by a company of Americans from Maine, who came here under the guidance of a leader to establish a Colony with American enterprise and prepare the way for the introduction of modern influence into this country of the chosen people of God and cradle of Christianity. Many of them perished miserably; others were sent home by the charity of strangers, and the houses they brought with them from Maine are now occupied by Germans. It is an oasis in the wide, wide desert of Egypt, Syria, and I might say Africa and Asia, generally. Orange groves are our surroundings, and the atmosphere is loaded with the fragrance of the blossoms; while oranges such as you never dreamed of in size, lusciousness and odour, are literally as plenteous as potatoes at the time at which they are gathered in the autumn. Camels loaded with them crowded the passages as we left the shore, and we clambered over and among boxes of them as we landed.

But that landing! What shall I say about it which you will believe as having been accomplished by your mother? It was a feat I had not thought she could accomplish to get on board the "Austria" at Port Said. There, there is a breakwater making the harbor as still as Rhode River, but the only way to get on board was by a little boat and then to climb the lofty sides of an iron steamer of some 3000 tons. That was done nicely, and we found ourselves in a good saloon on the upper deck, and our state-rooms all that we could desire; quite equal to Cunard accommodation. I betook myself at once to the berth and lay there, in the same room with your mother and aunts, until daylight this morning. The sea had been smooth; the moon had shed its light upon the waters, not the waves, and when I came on deck at 5 A. M. we were just in sight of the shore. We gradually neared the land.

What associations crowded into our thoughts and filled our souls at the name of Carmel, given to a head-land projecting into the sea far away before us to the north; of Gaza, of Askelon, of Joppa, as one after another became visible in our progress! Elijah in the cave looking out to the sea. Samson with the city gates on his matchless shoulders. The daughters of Philistia triumphing over the death of Saul and Jonathan; the whole district—the Philistia which scourged Israel; the Phenicia which sent its fleets into all waters with its merchandise, and its armies into Egypt as conquerors to establish there the dynasty of the Hyksos or shepherd kings; and when we cast anchor, some three miles from land, on the point before us rose tier above tier the stone houses of Joppa, from which Jonah fled from duty to encounter the storm on that very sea over which we had just passed so safely.

The base of the houses is washed by the waters of the sea, and it was in such a house in this very place dwelt Simon the Tanner, literally by the seaside, on the roof of which the vision of the clean and unclean animals taught Peter the lesson so precious to us, that God looks with equal eye on every member of the human family.

It was well to have such thoughts to occupy the mind and divert the feelings from the fearful ordeal of that landing for your mother. She went to it as she would have gone to any duty. But can you imagine a little boat dancing like a cork on the waves twenty feet below the platform projecting from the deck just large enough for her and me to stand on, with a narrow stair running down on which we were to descend, and from which we were to drop into that boat, sometimes touching the foot of the gangway; sometimes, without a moment's warning, falling eight or ten feet below and as many away? That would be enough, you think? Well, crowd the gangway with Jews, Armenians, Syrians, in every variety of costume; uttering all manner of violent words, in all manner of language which has descended from the confusion of Babel; while sticks, and canes, and Korbashes (or whips of hippopotamus hide), are lavishly bestowed on the shoulders of the struggling throng; and put at the foot of the ladder a dozen boats, knocking against each other, each with its crew of vociferous claimants that you should employ this boat and not the other; and you will feel as thankful as I do that after it all your mother is able to be seated here waiting serenely till the next step is determined on, from the responsibility of which we are happily freed.

Outside all is confusion. A party is about departing for Ramleh, the first stage toward Jerusalem; and the clamor is deafening. Rival dragomen presenting their horses and equipments and tents, are struggling for employment; while venders of worthless curiosities are soliciting custom for strings of shells and beads. One nice little fellow comes up to your mother and myself and begs to be allowed to guide us to an orange orchard. He was born in Maine, is about ten years old, has been here about six years, and only remembers the waves which separate him from his home in America. As genteel-looking, well-behaved, intelligent boy as any of my precious grandchildren; asking if we have any washing to be done, as his mother will gladly do it for us. She will do it in an hour if we cannot wait. Amid all this interest and excitement the eyes will fill with tears as we think over all that is involved in that history! And the question will present itself, "What shall I render to my God for all His gifts to me" and mine? and the prayer that you may all be kept from the trials and sorrows of life so far as may be consistent with the plans of a Father's love and wisdom for bringing us at last to our home.

Afternoon.

Soon after I had written the last line, your mother and I went under the guidance of poor little Willie to visit his mother first, and then to the orange orchard. It was a sad visit to her. She is one of one hundred and sixty Americans who, under the delusion that the time had come at which the Holy Land was to be redeemed from the curse which has rested so long on it, and that they were the agents called and appointed to commence the work, came here six years since and settled. They sold all they possessed and brought with them frames of houses which they built. Only thirteen of them are now here, including the children. Some thirty rest in their graves. The largest number, disappointed in their unreasonable expectations, have made shipwreck of their faith altogether. This poor woman's husband has returned to America and married another wife. She is here dependent on the little recompense of her toil in washing and ironing, and on the charity of strangers. She says she has lived on the orange skins she had found in the streets. It was a sad interview.

The little boy then took us both to the orange orchard. The trees stand so thick that it is difficult to walk among them; are covered with bunches of blossoms as large and fragrant as tuberose stems; and at the same time the yellow fruit is so abundant that the boughs are bent to the ground by its weight, and you will scarce believe that I measured the circumference of several and found them 16 inches in one way and from that to 18 in the other, and so heavy with juice that we were filled with astonishment. The whole atmosphere is perfumed with the odor.

Our present plans are to leave here in the morning for Ramleh on our way to Jerusalem. Our prayer that we may be kept from sickness and brought back safely to you all; more earnest still the prayer that you and we may each be kept by the power of God through faith unto salvation. We have been mercifully preserved thus far and pray for grace to hold fast our confidence to the end. With love to all,
    Your affectionate father,
                                        CASPAR MORRIS.

JAFFA, March 24, 1872.
My Dear Children:

I hope this letter and the one we mailed you yesterday at Port Said will reach you at the same time; as this one from your father will show you he is relieved, and that we are on our way, with all, to Jerusalem; but oh! my children, what we endured in coming *ashore here* baffles description, but we are safely through it, and I cannot imagine I can have anything worse to bear. It was most frightful, but I will try to forget it and tell you how perfectly delightful the air is, and so invigorating; we have not felt anything like it before; and the walk through a grove of orange trees, the most delicious fragrance I ever smelt, and the trees loaded with bloom, in every stage, and fruit; and such fruit as you never saw. We were allowed to pluck what we wanted both to eat and to take away for 20 cents. I have several on the table at my side 16 by 18 inches.

There was no quiet in the house, as it is surrounded by dragomen and horses arranging with different parties for the various trips, all talking in the loudest key, so we walked off to get rid of it all. Our arrangements are all made, and to-morrow morning we start with 12 horses and 24 mules and 3 Palanquins, each of which is carried by two mules. All our luggage is strapped on the mules' or horses' backs. We have seen several companies start to-day, as this is the starting house, and an odd sight it is. As we take no tents from here we want no camels. Our first ride is to Ramleh, only three hours; there we'll stay a night, and the next day six hours will bring us to Jerusalem. Of course I go in a Palanquin, and your father also, generally. On our return here two weeks hence we are to be taken sight-seeing. Among the other places, the house of Dorcas, and Simon the Tanner. The town is built of stone, and although the streets are narrow and dirty, they are not so bad as the Egyptian ones are. There are no vehicles here of any kind. All our heavy luggage was brought up on the backs of men. The costumes are oriental, but different from Cairo and Alexandria, and here there are a number of Germans and some Americans settled. The native women are all veiled, even more completely than at Cairo. We had four hundred steerage passengers, many pilgrims, on board the steamer. They lay all night on the deck on Persian rugs, and this morning we saw them bundling up beds to walk. But the man waits, and I have to say farewell; with much love to all.

    Yours most truly indeed,

              A. C. MORRIS.

            JAFFA, March 25, 1872.

My Dear Children:

  A cool morning—the moisture of our breath condensed on the glass of our windows—finds us stirring at 5.30 A. M., after a night in which your mother suffered from cold with my heavy blanket shawl and her waterproof cloak added to the blanket on the bed. It looks dreary, as we see the heavy, leaden clouds, and already the bustle of preparation for departure is heard, and horses and mules are being saddled and picketed before the house. As I am dressed and have nothing to do before we actually start, I will occupy my time in following my feelings toward you, and endeavor to fill up the gap in my hasty letter, mailed last evening, which announced our arrival and gave a sketch of the manner of our landing.

  The Austrian steamers are noble ships, and we were very comfortably accommodated. A raised deck is reserved for first-class passengers connected by a bridge with a similar deck forward passing over and above the deck occupied by deck passengers. When I went on the upper deck early in the morning and walked over this bridge to look at the land before me, I saw what I have often read of in books on the East, but never could realize, and I suppose no one can without seeing. The entire deck below me was covered with human beings of various nations, covered with German, many-coloured, spreads and quilts and rugs.

2 P. M.

At this point I was interrupted by the summons to give up all baggage to be packed. I must therefore postpone further description of the past for that of the present. I am now seated on one stone step with my paper on another in a paved courtyard connected with the Latin convent of Franciscan monks at Ramleh, four hours' ride from Joppa, on the road to Jerusalem. We have crossed the plain of Sharon and passed Beth Dagon, the seat of the temple of Dagon, where the Fish Idol fell and was dismembered before the Ark of the Covenant of the God of Israel; and Lydda, at which St. Peter, having healed Æneas, was sojourning, when the sorrowing disciples at Joppa sent to inform him of the death of that Tabitha, who, under the name of Dorcas, has been commemorated by the good works of so many faithful women in so many distant lands, and whom he restored to a longer service of her friends on earth, and thus detained from the full possession of the crown of righteousness in heaven.

It is a wondrous ride. We left Jaffa and the sounding sea beating against the base of the house where that same Peter "lodged with one Simon a Tanner," and where he was prepared to receive the revelation of the mystery of "God made manifest for the Gentiles as well as the Jews," and rode through miles of orange groves such as I described in my letter of yesterday, perfuming the atmosphere with the odor of the abundant and beautiful blossom, shining among the polished dark green foliage. Each orchard is enclosed by an *impervious* hedge of prickly pear, adorned by the graceful tracing of the Fumitory vine, which hangs everywhere with its delicate pink blossom. The trees are larger than the largest peach trees with us, and loaded with golden fruit, at the same time that the new white blossom gives promise that next year shall produce a crop as abundant as that which now rejoices the eye of the passing traveller, and still more the heart of the joyful owner.

Our road after leaving these orchards lay across a vale like the great valley of Virginia, and soon "the mountains round about Jerusalem" raised their blue forms in the distance. The soil is fertile, so fertile that it may well be described as "the glory of all lands," and as well adapted to sustain the sons of Anak, and the giant race of which Goliath was the champion. Wheat, lentils, lupins and barley were cultivated in large patches without fence, as soon as we had left the orange groves; as our road lay through a settlement of German Templars. *Ploughs* of European make were drawn by well-yoked oxen, and fine flocks and herds grazed in the pastures. Water stations, erected by the piety of Moslems and adorned with texts from the Koran in Arabic characters, stood at the roadside at short distances, with troughs for the horses and cattle, and shaded seats for the weary traveller. The road was wide and well made, the result of the enterprise of the American colony at Jaffa, while telegraph wires leading to Jerusalem testified to the invasion by modern science of even this deserted land.

About an hour from Jaffa the land ceased to be cultivated, and the soil was covered with the greatest profusion of the most beautiful flowers. Venus Fly-trap displayed its crimson and orange petals among its delicate green foliage Phlox, purple and white; the rose of Sharon, white and pink; with hyacinths and daisies, scarlet anemonies and cyclamen, so exquisitely graceful; and genista, and a multitude of others I cannot name, but each of unequalled beauty, literally made a variegated carpet for the surface of the valley as far as the eye could catch the color. Crimson poppies, white daisies and a bright yellow flower like marigold, were most profusely spread as we approached Ramleh, the ancient Arimathæa and the home of the Joseph who was not ashamed, rich and great though he was, to beg the body of the crucified Jesus from the philosophical Pilate. The cultivation of fields was renewed, but now with the old wooden plough which merely stirs the soil without turning it, such as was used in the days of the Judges of Israel when the Israelites were not allowed any *smith* lest they should forge *swords and spears;* and the crops were much lighter.

Many things which met our eyes afforded strong illustrations of Scripture teaching. The house-tops are all covered with short green grass to which David alludes as of no value " wherewith the mower turneth not his scythe, and wherewith he that gathereth sheaves filleth not his bosom." It is a perfect simile the Psalmist uses. So these cactus hedges which line the narrow roads give additional force to the description of the Lord hedging in the way of His people between them. None can turn to the right hand nor the left, and it not only points out the way and protects the crop of the garden or field from intrusion, but guards the passer-by from assaults. In a narrow way it requires careful walking to avoid feeling the sharpness of its thorns as well. The roughness is veiled beautifully by the drapery of delicate vines with pretty little flowers which the Lord has planted to clothe it with grace not its own, and the prickly cactus does provide a fruit which our little Yankee lad at Jaffa assured was " very good and made very good molasses."

March 26, '72. " Mount Sion," " the joy of the whole earth."
See Psalm 48, verse 2.

My Dear Children:

Thanks be to our God that "our feet stand within Jerusalem, the city of our God," and your hearts must overflow with thanksgiving and your mouths burst forth with praise that we are here among the living; and I unite earnest prayer that your dear mother may survive the terrible ordeal through which we have reached it, with heartfelt thanksgiving for our preservation from the perils of the way, as well as for the ability to endure the fearful fatigue.

When the city gladdened our eyes we could not but feel the natural influence of the excitement every Christian soul must experience when it realizes that it enjoys the privilege of looking on the spot selected from the foundation of the world for the transaction of the great events connected with its redemption. May I feel justified in going further, so far as to express my belief that in the wisdom which formed and developed the scheme of salvation it was fashioned and formed to be specially adapted to the purpose.

But I fear that excitement will only add to the depth which the exhaustion and fatigue must inevitably bring to your mother. The landing at Jaffa and the excitement of arrangements for the journey were nothing compared with the fatigue and danger of the way, great as I thought those were before we started. Yesterday, after four hours' hard riding, we had the greatest difficulty in procuring admission for our party into the Latin Convent at Ramleh ; and then it was only into an open court-yard with a damp cave opening on to one side and containing five beds, standing close side by side, for the six ladies ; leaving only a few inches of space at the foot by which to get into them. There they passed the few hours between the meal furnished (that meal was a most comfortable one—wholesome, well-cooked, warm and nourishing—just what many pilgrims require) and 2 A. M., at which hour we started and reached here at 2 P. M., during all which time we had been in the saddle or the palanquin, hung on the backs of mules, and your mother, Aunts Hannah and Jane, and myself, each several times in the most imminent danger of instant death. Out of them all our God has delivered us, and we will seek for grace to praise Him for the past and trust Him with the future.

The door of your mother's palanquin, which was selected on account of its having sliding glass windows and a covered top, opened directly at the heels of the forward mule, so that, to enter it at all, she was obliged to stoop under one of the rails and be lifted to the height of the floor, and pushed into the carriage.

This process was difficult enough in daylight ; but when it was to be done in the night, with the exhaustion and fatigue of the previous day to contend with, it was a more formidable affair still. With great difficulty she was raised and, putting her hands behind her, sat on the floor till she could be lifted to the seat. What was my horror at hearing the crash of glass, and finding that one of the side windows had been laid on the floor and she was on it ! Is there not reason to be thankful that neither hands nor person were either scratched by the numberless fragments into which it was reduced ; and that the mule neither kicked nor stirred with all the agitation and disturbance at his heels? We finally succeeded in placing her on the seat, and started.

It would be out of place to attempt to describe the beauty of the scenery, the loveliness of the plain of Sharon, carpeted with flowers of every variety, from the white and pink roses and cyclamen to the glorious golden Pyrethrum. Equally out of place would be any indulgence of the flights of imagination, or gushes of feeling which were irrepressible amid such scenes, even by the deadening weight of responsibility and anxiety. The beauty of the morning ride toward the east, with the sun rising over the mountains, is indescribable.

We were a strange caravan; mules loaded with our luggage (reduced to the smallest possible compass and packed in coarse sacks strapped on their backs) preceded us; then followed your mother, seated in the indescribable machine which, while it allowed her to see out in front and on either side, shut her entirely from our sight and hearing. This was supported on shafts with a large mule in front, his back well padded with bags stuffed with cut straw, over which passed the ropes like the back-straps of our horse cart; another mule with her head toward hers was similarly harnessed in the shafts behind, and a man appointed to manage each, though he was rarely or never at his post. Then followed my riding machine, without top, mounted in the same way on a horse and mule; and another with sister Hannah. The other members of the party followed mounted, some on horses, some on donkeys.

It was impossible for any of us to communicate with our attendants except by first calling Friezier, and using him as our interpreter to Joseph, the Dragoman. They were often at opposite ends of the cavalcade, as far as possible from us, and when brought together could not always understand each other or us. Joseph's final reply always was, "My head for getting you safe." The cumbrous machinery was continually getting jammed. It was with the greatest difficulty I could get Joseph to comprehend that my palanquin must be kept directly behind your mother's. In despite of all remonstrances her men would get too far in advance, and I could not stimulate mine to keep up. Then the baggage mules had no driver, and would push themselves with their unwieldy packages in the way of the palanquins, and before very long I found mine whirling around; the two animals going different ways, jerking and kicking, while the screams of the men added to the confusion. Very thankful was I, as I held on to the sides, that it was built as strong and heavy as a farm cart, and that your mother could not see that I was in peril, or indeed that it was any one. A second time the same thing was repeated, when, to add to the horror (for that is not an expression too strong), I found my vehicle dashed violently against your Aunt Jane's horse. How she kept her seat it is impossible to say, but she was kept upon it, and my refractory animals were subdued, not by miraculous interposition, but by Divine providence; and the same good providence which had saved your dear mother from harm by the broken glass watched over her by the way. I was as powerless to aid her, even in case of extremity, as though I had been manacled. I could not even know whether she was faint; that she must be sadly wearied I knew well enough.

Yet with all these saddening influences there was a wondrous fascination in thus traversing a plain spreading widely on every side, covered with wheat and barley and beans where the hand of man cultivated it, and the virgin soil everywhere glowing with the richest flowers, while the larks in countless thousands raised their morning chorus of praise as the dawn gradually yielded to the rosy glow of the advancing day, and the sun sprang from behind the mountains which separate the vale of Sharon from the Dead Sea. This vale was the great seat of Philistine power, from which they made incursions upon the people of God.

After passing it we entered the defiles of the mountains of Judea, passing through the valley of Ajalon and the vicinity of Gibeon. It was on some of these mountains David encountered Goliath, and they point out the brook from which was taken the pebble with which he slew the champion. I have no credulity about special spots. There is nothing to mark them, and a superstitious determination to find as many as possible within reach of pilgrims has guided the location of them in many cases. But no one can look at the plain over which we passed and "the valleys running among the hills" upon which we entered here, and doubt the truth of the Scripture history. The places correspond with the incidents of the narrative so closely that they furnish the strongest confirmation of it.

The gorges of the valley were like winding streams of molten gold with the brilliant flowers of the Pyrethrum, while superb bushes of Genista stood like golden statues among the rocks. It was while we were in the midst of these scenes we came to a castle-like structure at the wayside, near which sat an Arab with a book before him, to whom the "Captain of our horses," as the dragoman styles the man to whom they belong, delivered a paper covered with Arabic characters; and at a booth by the road we drew up for the first meal.

Before I could alight myself I saw your Aunt Hannah roll head foremost to the ground, while the mules of her palanquin dragged it, as I thought, right upon her. Most providentially she had fallen in such a position that a low stone wall guarded her body, and it passed *over* her. She was on her feet again before I could get to her, and on careful investigation we could not find she had incurred the slightest damage except to her dress, on which it is probable a mule had trodden.

We took our lunch and got under way as soon as possible, and not long after were startled by a cry from her, and looking back I saw her palanquin dragging by one animal, the other having been loosened by the breaking of one of the ropes. Happily it was stopped; and she then mounted again with true heroism, and we went on our weary way along an excellent road up zigzags, rising ever higher and higher till we got quite among the tops of the mountains, wild and rocky, and covered with short bushes just putting out their leaves.

Here and there an olive tree or Carab stood; and Joseph informed me we were passing through the territory of an Arab chief who had formerly levied blackmail on all passengers. Some twenty or thirty years since the Pasha of Syria, determined to reduce him to subjection, invaded the district and cut down all the trees and made it the scene of desolation we now find it. The rebel Sheik was killed, but so imperfect was the conquest that the Pasha of Jerusalem now pays his son a large annual stipend, in consideration of which he allows travellers to pass unmolested, and the paper we delivered to his agent, at our stopping-place, was a letter from the Pasha of Jerusalem. Another was brought to us from the Sheik, while we lunched, which was our authority to go to Jerusalem.

I had hoped the perils of the day were passed. But when we came to the brow of the hill to descend, the dragoman came to your mother and told her she must get out and walk; the road was too steep to ride. I remonstrated and told him he had said we could ride all the way in Palanquins. He only shook his head and said, "too steep." I asked how far, "Oh, only little way." There was no alternative—we were compelled to take to our feet. Your uncle most kindly left your Aunt Mary and came to our assistance; and we walked on, on, on, certainly quite a mile, and when we got to the level at the foot, the palanquin was nowhere to be seen; the drivers had gone on. A horse was dispatched to bring it back, and when at length it returned we again set off.

Our road lay amid a scene of desolation which is unparalleled, I must think. Limestone rocks about the color of this sheet were heaped one upon another in parallel strata till I said to an English gentleman, a Canon of the Cathedral of Gloucester, who had joined our party (a most acceptable acquisition), that I thought a more appropriate rendering of the verse, "as the mountains are round about Jerusalem," etc., would be, 'As the indestructible ramparts built by Omnipotence,' etc., so much do the hills here resemble colossal fortifications. There are artificial terraces still on the sides of the mountains built of old to support the ground, and wherever any soil can lodge amid the rocks it is scratched and barley sown upon it. But how it could ever have supported the thousands of Israel and ten thousands of Judah, how the hundreds of thousands of Jews of Jerusalem could have been fed from such rocks is a problem which cannot be solved without admitting a direct Divine judgment destroying the source of supply of food and water then so ample; and all attempts of fanaticism to restore its ancient glory must be futile till Divine power opens the way. I do not mean to incur the punishment of the sceptic officer of the King of Israel who, when the prophet foretold plenty on the morrow in the midst of the straightness of the siege, drew down on himself the just punishment of an insulted God by his sneering reply that "if the windows of heaven were opened this might be." It is only by Divine power it can be done, and that power must be put forth in miraculous energy and not by mere human agency, and so it *will be*, I know—how soon "knoweth no man."

Jerusalem is *hidden* among the mountains. Even after climbing to the top of the ridge from which looking back you see the Great Sea, and Jaffa on its shore, turning again you see nothing of "the city of the Great King." Winding along among the rounded hill tops covered with the grey rocks, your eye at last catches the sight of a small grey fortress-like structure enclosing a few domes and minarets;

and the instincts of the heart assure you that is the Holy City, and my soul was bowed with a deep awe as the thought of all that is involved in beholding Jerusalem, with the perils by the way, out of which we had been so graciously delivered, mingled with the deeper awe of the mystical symbolism with which the Spirit of God has clothed it; and the feeling has deepened hour by hour as the exhaustion and weariness which at first oppressed the springs of thought and feeling, have gradually removed.

I have seized every opportunity at which I have been undisturbed by other duties since our arrival on Tuesday evening (and it is now Thursday morning) to write these sheets, and the solemn feeling deepens hour by hour, while every hour's report of those who are looking around at the places shown as sacred, confirms the view expressed in some of my letters, written when I *hoped* we should *not* come here, that it is like looking into the empty tomb for Him who has risen.

The terrace of our hotel, on which our chamber opens, looks down upon the pool of Hezekiah, and just beyond it the gilded dome of the church of the Holy Sepulchre arises; and beyond that Pilate's house; and still beyond, the sacred enclosure which marks the site of the Temple of Solomon and of Herod, with its green sward and trees surrounding the Mosque of Omar, and el Aksa marking, beyond a rational doubt, the spot to which the Lord guided Abraham that he might exhibit his faith in the offering of Isaac, his "only son" (Gen. xxii.), four thousand years ago—on which David made his offering of atonement on the threshing-floor of Araunah the Jebusite.

2 P. M.

I had written thus far when I was summoned to attend you mother and aunts in a visit to the church of the Holy Sepulchre. This we found closed in preparation for the afternoon service of the church of Rome; washing the feet of the pilgrims. As I stood gazing on the front I saw a balcony above the door on which was sitting a monk. Another soon came from within and evidently wished him to go in. He refused until the other, seizing him, forcibly dragged him in. Unable to enter the church we then passed on to the Via Dolorosa, which superstition has assumed, contrary to all probability, to be the way by which our blessed Lord bore the cross; and the same superstition has marked sixteen points as specially sac ed, at which the devout believers utter special prayers. At one they point to a hole in the stone wall made by the end of the cross when the fainting victim fell and it struck the stone; at another they point out the spot at which Simon the Cyrenian, coming out of the country, met Him, and they laid on him the cross; another is connected with the beautiful legend of Veronica running out in defiance of the rude soldiery and wiping the sweating, bleeding, brow with a napkin; on which was imprinted a likeness of our Lord.

At length we reached the new Romish building called Ecce Homo, and entered in a frame of feeling more inclined to reject all testimony and deny credence to anything that might be presented, than to do homage to any claim of sanctity for the place. All such scepticism vanished the moment we saw the old Roman wall and arched doorway over which the modern chapel is built. There is certainly no reason why it should not be the spot at which the Roman Procurator said, "I find no fault in Him;" at which Jesus stood "like a lamb, dumb before His shearers," at which He replied to the question of Pilate, "thou sayest that I am King;" at which the Governor washed his hands and said, "I am innocent of the blood of this just man, see ye to it;" at which the infuriated priests and people cried out, "Crucify him," "His blood be on us and our children," and demanded that a murderer should be released to them. I envy not the man who can speak on such a spot; who does not realize that it is the most sacred spot on the surface of the globe; who is not so overwhelmed that he would like Peter say, "It is good for us to be here," not knowing what he says; and I pray that the deep impression of that hour may ever grow deeper and deeper till I shall see that despised and rejected Son of Man "coming in the clouds with great glory and all His holy angels with Him," and find my refuge in an atoning Saviour, delivering from the power of the justly condemning Judge. It was a source of comfort to me then and there to remember that all the disciples forsook Him and fled. Terrible desertion of the sorrowing *man*. Christ Jesus! The loving *Lord* Jesus Christ looked upon and pardoned their cowardly desertion. Has He *changed?* Oh, no! Then will He not still look with the same compassion on our unrighteousness and unworthiness; and may *we* not have peace with God through this, our Lord Jesus Christ, by whom we have now received the atonement? Did He not here as at *this* time pray even for those who thus crucified Him; and does He not even now "live to make intercession for us?" There is a fearfully naked simplicity in the worn stone wall. Even Romish fondness for ceremonial and gorgeous display is awed in this sacred spot, and the rough stone wall and simple archway have a sublimity which can never attach itself to any other work of man. I feel attracted to it as by a spell which I do not desire to resist.

But I must close my letter with calling on you to unite with me in thanksgiving that your dear mother seems quite well and enters into all this with as much sacred enjoyment as I do myself. Your uncle, and Aunt Mary and Miss Harris and Mr. Longstreth, have left for Jordan and the Dead Sea, to be absent till Saturday.

Your loving father,

CASPAR MORRIS.

JERUSALEM, March 29, 1872.

My Dear Brother:

I almost shrink from writing to you from this place, knowing how strongly your judgment was opposed to our coming here and how great will be your anxiety until you learn that we are favoured to be once more out of this land, once so highly favoured in temporal and spiritual blessings, now a by-word and reproach and hissing among all peoples. I am here most reluctantly, and left no effort untried to escape coming to the East at all. Before leaving Italy I strove to induce those in whom the direction of our course has settled to abandon the voyage across the Mediterranean and spend the winter in Southern Europe; and again at Cairo (on our return from the Nile) I set before them all the difficulties, dangers and risk of sickness with which we had become familiar from the reports of those who had suffered, and hoped to the last moment that the Syrian trip would be given up for the sake of others as well as Anne and myself.

Mary had set her heart upon it, and my sisters would not abandon Wistar, and I felt that I should not be justified in withdrawing after having done all in my power to prevent the exposure, but must take my share of the peril for the sake of others. I felt all the fearful weight of the responsibility, and looked back with deep regret upon the steps I had taken to promote the voyage, and the longing desire for it which was the originating cause of the whole enterprise. But the purpose for which Wistar had entered on it would have been defeated had he not complied with his wife's earnest wishes. Indeed she took on herself the entire responsibility, and she has now carried him, accompanied by her cousin and Mr. Longstreth, on a three days' excursion to Jericho, Jordan and the Dead Sea, of which an American gentleman who just returned reports that he would not repeat it for $500. We tarry here until they return, in a very comfortable hotel and with enough to occupy our time and thoughts.

The perils of the way by which we came here, from the time we left the Austrian Lloyds steamship, I have described in my letter to the children, to which I must refer you, as I do not wish to bring them back in all their fearful nakedness as they will present themselves if I attempt to write them over; and no power of description in my possession can convey any idea of them. I thank God that we were brought safely through them and pray for increased faith to enable me to trust that He will carry us safely through them on our return. My anxiety is not, however, limited to these. Our party is a large one, and if one is taken sick and detains us there is no foreseeing how long we may be detained. I made this a strong point in my argument against coming, endeavoring to bring it to bear on Mary's maternal anxiety as well as her love for her husband. But she appears to have a strong faith, founded in her belief that she shall better appreciate and understand the truths of religion after exploring the land in which our Lord dwelt, and she moves under the conviction that we shall be cared for and brought safely through whatever perils and dangers may environ us.

I can enter into this also, but think all that is *needful* is given to each one everywhere, and if they believe not Moses and the prophets and apostles and evangelists, coming here will no more convert the soul than the rising of one from the dead.

After all this, it is a wondrous privilege to have our feet stand within Jerusalem, and look upon the Mount of Olives, so wondrously associated with the ascension and coming again of our Lord; and while I have failed to see the slightest token of religious feeling on the part of the pilgrims who crowd the avenues to the church of the Holy Sepulchre, and think there is nothing calculated to confirm and enlighten faith in the absurd superstition which has determined the place at which our Lord fainted under the burden of the cross; and even points to a depression in a stone of the wall caused by the falling against it of the foot of the cross as Jesus fell beneath its weight, and the equally intelligent location of the house of Dives; and the seat of Lazarus; and the shop of the reviling Jew, who is doomed to wander the earth till our Lord's return, I have yet found enough to stimulate warm emotions of holy feeling in gazing on Olivet, crossed by the road to and from Bethany on the last day before Jesus was betrayed; and on the brook Kedron; and the garden beyond it rendered so sacred by the agony and prayer of that last night, and the scene of betrayal by one disciple and the desertion by all.

I had been disposed to treat with contempt the superstition which points out the house of Pilate and the spot on which our Lord was rejected by the high priest and the people, following the lead of the chief priests, and preferring to have Barabbas released to them. But when I entered the church erected by modern piety over the arch and wall so manifestly old as the days of the Roman possession, I found my heart carrying my reason, not a captive but a glad associate, in the belief that there is more reason to think it may be the ruin of the house of the Roman Governor than that it is not. It is in the part of the town in which that would have stood; rests on the solid rock and not on the debris which has filled up other parts, and has all the massive solidity of stone work and peculiar style of masonry belonging to that period.

By a strange coincidence, without any purpose of ours, we find ourselves here at the most sacred and solemn period. To-day is Good Friday and the time at which of all others the associations of Jerusalem are most awfully impressive; too much so for expression. The heat of the sun at mid-day is very great, the nights cool, the winter is just past, and the plains are glowing with a perfect carpet of lovely flowers, while the fig tree is just putting forth its leaves, and the spots where soil rests amid the abounding grey rocks, are taking on them the verdure of spring.

Anne is wonderfully sustained in mind and body amid the fatigues of both incident to our position, and I trust that whether we be permitted to rejoice together on earth or be called to lay down our lives among strangers we shall find the trial of our faith working "patience, and patience, experience, and experience, hope," and that we shall grow in grace and the knowledge and love of God through Jesus Christ our Lord. You have your trials, many great and peculiar. May they all be sanctified to you and to us. We have as a travelling companion a most lovable English clergyman from Gloucester, who knows all the Cheston family intimately, and promises if we accept his *earnest* invitation to go to his house, to invite the Cannings, who are the only representatives, to meet us. He is a most charming old gentleman. Love to Margaret and kindest regards to Mary Ellen.

    Your loving and grateful brother,

                CASPAR MORRIS.

            JERUSALEM, March 27, 1872.

My Dear Children:

Here you will see we are, notwithstanding our determination *not* to come. Well, we have reached it through *many* difficulties, but I think with thankful hearts for our preservation, and we try to trust we will be strengthened to get back, though we all feel it has been a *much* greater undertaking than we anticipated. *I* think our difficulty has been much increased by the inefficiency of our Dragoman, though I don't know that all the party are ready to say that; though they all feel that four different times we were in *imminent* peril by the road. Weary to-day all are, but I am the only one who don't go out to look around. I am too stiff and sore to walk, and there is not a carriage in this city, and the streets are so narrow that it is difficult to ride a donkey through them. I believe your father has given you a description of our caravan; it did present a strange appearance strung along the road, moving very slowly, rarely out of a walk. The road was wide and good, though much of the latter part mountainous. At one time Joseph (after the wonderful escapes of your aunts and father, all three occurring at intervals, just as we began to get over the last a little) came and told me I had better get out and walk a while. Of course I did not hesitate, though to get out of my palanquin and in again was no trifling effort. I found the road would be very precipitous, and although the sun was intensely hot and *'twas a very rough walk*, I was glad to take it, with your father and uncle. The latter is so greatly disturbed at all that has occurred in the last few days, that *we* try to make the best of it and keep him up. I very much fear it will make him sick; the rest are all well.

I have tried to give you some idea of my palanquin. You may imagine the motion is very unsteady as the animals move; and you feel very insecure. Your father's and aunts' were open chairs, very rudely made, but resting on the backs of the mules in the same way. Mine belongs to the Russian Consul and was considered very superior.

28th.

Uncle Wistar, Mary, Miss Harris and Tom went this morning off on a three days' trip on horseback to Bethlehem, Jordan and the Dead Sea. The rest of us concluded we would rather be quiet. Indeed I do not think your father and I will make much exertion while here, but husband our strength for the return, which we are both rather dreading. We have walked about the town and seen some spots that were pointed out; as the Garden of Gethsemane, "The Pool of Bethesda," the house of Pilate, the road where our Saviour carried the cross, the stones on which He rested it, the shop of the wandering Jew. We could not get into the church which is built on the spot on which our Saviour was crucified, but we will go again. To-morrow being Good Friday we shall attend the English service in the morning and leave sight-seeing for the afternoon.

We are delightfully accommodated here and look out on the Mount of Olives, the valley of Jehoshaphat, the Mosque of Omar, and it is a beautiful view from the upper court. We meet with Americans and English people all the time, and are now thrown a good deal with an old English clergyman who seems to want to be with us. He is travelling with his servant only; a Dr. Lysons from near Gloucester. He knew Dr. Cheston well. He was his father's family physician and says there are but 3 descendants left: Mrs. Canning and her two daughters. One of the latter is about to be married. They are his neighbours, and they are on intimate terms. He gives us most pressing invitations to pay him a visit when we reach England. He has a large house and will gladly receive the *whole party*, and then invite medical men to meet your father and the Cannings to see me and talk over our connections. He says Mr. Canning was a Roman Catholic, and these daughters were brought up in that faith, but the mother belongs to the Church of England. I think if we can make it convenient to stop at Gloucester I would like to see them, though of course we have no intentions to intrude on this old gentleman's hospitality. He is a very intelligent man, and we are glad to have him with us in our parlour. He joined us in Jaffa and rode all the way in company with us and will return with us. He says he saw us in Cairo, at Church, but we were not then at the same hotel.

Good Friday.

I am just told the letters must be mailed while we are at church, so I can't do much more than close. I think much of you all; hoping all are well and happy. We shall leave here this day week for Jaffa, and you shall hear again from there. I do not think your father and I will land at Beyroot, but keep on the steamer to Constantinople and let the rest do as they like. But farewell, with much love to all, from

Your affectionate mother and grand-mother,

A. C. MORRIS.

Most affectionate remembrances to uncles and aunts. I don't recommend this trip to any of them, though I admit, there is great solemnity in being here, and after we have endured the conflict, should we be permitted to return, we may not regret having accomplished it, though it is a hard dose to take.

While waiting for the rest to go to church I will chat on. Your aunts and little Holly, with ourselves, are getting on very nicely. Our only trouble is the apprehension that the others are suffering from both heat and fatigue. The former is *very great*, except at night, then it is cool. As regards the latter we saw a gentleman (Mr. Greble of Phila.) yesterday, who has just returned from the trip they have taken, and he gives a sad picture of his distress, and says he would not for $500 repeat it. But we will have to hope they will fare better, they have their tents and *can* loiter, except that from the fear of our anxiety they may hurry back to-morrow evening. Wistar was so troubled that we cannot help fearing for him. He yielded to Mary's earnest desire to come, indeed she put it in such a way before us that, after all opposing as far as we could, there was nothing left for us to do but come. He can't say no, to her.

     Farewell again, yours most lovingly,
          A. C. MORRIS.

I fear we will not have time to write to Uncle G. Let him see your letters.

          1 o'clock.

We have returned from a most delightful service, which has greatly refreshed us all. The church was built and is supported by the Queen of England and the King of Prussia. English service in English always in the morning, and in German or Hebrew in the evening. To-day there were 6 Jews baptized. Bishop Gobat is here in charge. They have a nice-looking set of children in their schools, both boys and girls.

Farewell again.

       JERUSALEM, March 31, 1872.

My Dear Children:

While your mother makes ready for church I turn to you, still slumbering I hope peacefully, waiting the coming of the morn, which here has already advanced toward the midday of the anniversary of the Resurrection of our Lord; that wondrous event which sealed the acceptance of the propitiation here made by that one sacrifice once offered for the sins of many on this chosen spot.

Before my eyes rises the tower of David, on what is thought to be, and in all probability is, the site of the dwelling of that "man after God's own heart," from whose royal line "as concerning the flesh, Christ came," and whose penitential psalms still furnish the language with which we seek for pardon of our sins, as he did of his; while his songs of joyful triumph animate our souls to persevere, that we too may rejoice as he rejoiced.

The days are too short to suffice for all the associations of memory and feeling which throng upon us, without giving any attention to the superstitious observances and locations which are so numerous. Your mother and I try to limit our pilgrimages to those points which are of unquestionable authenticity; but we are compelled to surrender ourselves, to some extent, to the guides, as we cannot know to what we are going until we find ourselves brought face to face with something as absurd (for example) as a hole left by a fossil in a limestone rock in the wall of one of the streets which is kissed by devout passers-by as one of the stones which *would have cried out* if the children had not hailed our Lord with "hosanna," on the occasion of His triumphal entry as the King of Zion, "meek and lowly, on an ass;" or a ruined-looking shop in a corner as that of the Jew whose want of sympathy with our suffering Lord (fainting under His cross) caused him to be condemned to wander an outcast till our Lord shall return to Zion in glorious majesty. Such things are but like the motes floating in the glorious light which beams around us.

Yesterday afternoon in company with Canon Lysons, a most intelligent and highly cultivated clergyman of the church of England, and a loving humble Christian man, I walked over the Mount of Olives by the Garden of Gethsemane and the house of Mary and her sister, and the tomb of Lazarus; returning by the pool of Siloam and across the Brook Kedron, through the valleys of Jehoshaphat and Hinnom.

As we stood on the summit of Olivet looking eastward across the desolate valley which extends from the Holy City to the Dead Sea and Jordan, we thought of the time when that desolate region had been so lovely that in the eyes of Lot it had appeared "as the garden of the Lord." Now the barrenness and aridity are such that nothing grows there. There were driving clouds with occasional showers. Through a rift in the cloud the sunlight illumined the City of David as we turned a moment to gaze upon it; and the next moment a glorious rainbow spanned the desolate valley, beneath which we saw the Dead Sea and Jordan; and beyond, the mountains of Moab, with Pisgah from which (looking westward) Moses had gazed upon the land to which he had led the people, but which he was not permitted himself to enter. It was a solemn and wondrous view. The Valley of Jordan and the Dead Sea, spanned by the bow of hope, while Jerusalem shone in the glory of the sunlight!

We remained long inspecting the several points and resting ourselves after the labour of the climb; and then turning along the east side of the mountain, walked toward Bethany. As we reached the point from which we could look down into the vale of Kedron, our eyes were feasted with the soft green slopes and terraces which cover the sides of the hill beyond the valley through which the Kedron flows. This is the only cultivated spot near Jerusalem, watered from the pool of Siloam. The exquisitely varied flora, of which I have spoken, abounds here also, and at every step we were tempted to stop and pluck some beautiful plant. The showers of the day had refreshed everything. The fig trees were putting forth their leaves and young figs. The almond trees were filled with new leaves and fruit. The Pomegranate twigs were clothed with the peculiar rich foliage of the spring; hawthorn trees were just bursting with flowers; and before us the evening sun was brightening the verdure of the mountain sides. Who could do otherwise than think that He who made all things so beautiful and fair had Himself, in His humiliation as man, found delight in looking upon it? This was the way to the house in which those dwelt of whom it is recorded, "Jesus loved Martha, and her sister, and Lazarus"; and that same human nature which could so love as to weep from sympathy with their sorrows, certainly could find pleasure in these works of His own hand, which, when at His word they came into being, He had pronounced good. The contrast between the calm beauty of the one view and the sterile repulsiveness of the other was perfect. We descended by some twenty winding steps into the vault which is shown as the tomb of Lazarus. It may be. The hill sides have many openings into tombs, and this is a simple one.

Emerging from this and merely giving a passing glance at the house shown as that of Mary, we passed around the Mount and stopped at the pools of Siloam and saw far below us En Rogel. After which we crossed the Kedron and, passing under the wall which supports the site of the Temple of Solomon, entered the city by the gate of David, and so returned to our hotel.

On our way to Bethany we had stopped at Gethsemane. I have not examined the arguments on the subject of the location of these places for many years, though I have carefully read the works of Dr. Robinson and Thomson and Dr. Barclay, as well as the more superficial works of mere travellers like myself. I am therefore not competent to the formation of an opinion on the subject, and can only accept the probabilities, and these seem to me to be greatly in favor of the traditional garden. It is true that this has in it none of the solemn awful solitude and shade with which one always associated the hours of our Saviour's agony. But it must have been near to the city, for "Jesus ofttimes resorted thither," and Judas therefore knew the place. It was across Kedron, and thus we have two important elements of agreement, and no place could have been better adapted to a frequent resort of our Lord. It is now divided into plots distributed among the contending churches. That of the Latins is planted with flower borders and neatly cultivated, and enclosed by a well-built wall on which are marked stations for prayer. That of the Greeks has a loose wall and no culture, and one old olive tree is walled around and pointed out as the place of the agony, and another part is appropriated to the tomb of the blessed Virgin. There are eight of these trees bearing on them the most indubitable marks of very great age. There is no place for quiet solitary reflection and prayer. The most perfect power of abstraction would fail in the effort, and I returned to the Gethsemane *in my own soul*, thankful to have walked over the sacred soil and feasted my eyes on the glorious views from the Mount of Olives, and to have looked upon the once peaceful shades of Bethany, and to have seen the unquestionable location of that Garden of Agony; but with a deeper conviction in my heart that the utterance of the angel was an enduring truth : " He is not here, He is risen " from the dead, and yet I appreciate more highly every hour the privilege of being here.

Evening.

We have enjoyed the privilege of worship greatly. Our blessed Easter services have been delightfully performed; winding up this evening with an infant baptism and a most excellent sermon, from one of the assistants of Bishop Gobat, on the practical value of the doctrine of Christ's resurrection by which we are begotten again to a lively hope. He dwelt especially on the importance of its influence in raising us *now* from the death of sin into newness of life, without which we could never have any hope of a future rising to the life which is immortal.

Monday morning, April 1st.

We find ourselves here at the period of the latter rain. Your uncle and aunt returned on Saturday from the excursion to the Dead Sea and Jericho pretty thoroughly wetted, and it has been showery ever since. This interferes somewhat with the comfort of visits to the various objects of interest, as the streets are sloppy and dirty, and the stones very slippery. Notwithstanding the rain I went on Saturday in company with Oliver Cromwell Morse (brother of Mrs. J. Aspinwall Hodge) on an exploring expedition. We were to meet at the Damascus gate at 8½ A.M., he coming from his tent on the Mount of Olives. The guide and I waited an hour for him. When he came he had an ample apology in the account of his night's adventures. The wind had carried his tent from over him, scattered his clothing, overturned a bowl of stewed prunes into his bed, and put everything generally into a state of confusion. I had occupied the time while waiting not unprofitably in examining the cave said to be that in which Jeremiah wrote his Lamentations, and learning something of the bearings of the different objects of interest, and gazing on the desolation generally. Over the gate are lions carved; I suppose the arms of some of the Crusaders, perhaps of Godfrey of Boulogne, the king of Jerusalem. The walls and gates are evidently of that or Saracenic time.

When Mr. Morse arrived we lighted our candles and entered the quarries under Jerusalem, from which it is supposed the stones used in building the temple were taken. Whether this be the case or no cannot now be determined. But the extent of the excavations and the size of the stones still lying there, and the marks of the cuttings from which others have been removed, prove sufficiently that they were worked for great structures, and the immense piles of cuttings prove that the stones were hammered and dressed and fitted here prior to their removal, as we are told was done by the builders of the temple, so that no sound of the hammer was heard as it rose in its majesty on the lofty platform from which it overlooked the valleys below. There are many openings into these quarries and one, which is now obstructed, was so near the temple that it is supposed the dressed stones were taken out by it. We wandered in every direction, through upper and lower levels of the quarries, everywhere seeing the same traces of the work of the labourer in the marks of the chisel and the deep cuttings by which the blocks were hewn out in massive oblong squares, by the same process as was employed at the still older quarries on the Nile at Silsilis. The quantity of stone taken out must have been very great, and there is a great accumulation of chippings made in dressing the stones. At one place we saw the basin in the rock still filled with water from which the labourers derived their supply. It is strongly impregnated with lime, though beautifully clear. Mr. Morse recognized the names of some of his family who had preceded him in this exploration and placed his own beside theirs, and at his urgent request I allowed him to add mine. Thus I consented to my name being buried where it will not deface any monument, though perhaps at some future day it may startle some descendant as he treads the way his father trod in the hollow caverns under the sacred city.

After spending some hours there we visited what is called the Well of St. Helena, because it was repaired by the mother of Constantine at the time of the visit she made in search of sacred places and relics. It is a very large and deep well, into which you descend by a winding stone stairway with a stone balustrade. I neglected to count the steps before we reached the water, but it was very far down, and our guide assured us that in dry time we might descend as much further in the same manner and still find water below. There are numerous and extensive cisterns of the same kind under the city.

April 1st, P.M.

We have spent the morning in a most interesting exploration of the area of the temple of Solomon, with the mosques of Omar and El Aksa, which last was a Christian church built by the Emperor Justinian in the 6th century. Every part of the Haram enclosure is of the highest interest. There is no room for doubt of its being the Mount

Moriah to which Abraham was led by Jehovah, there to offer Isaac, his only son, in whom the promise was made; and there, on the floor of Ornan the Jebusite, David made his offering and stayed the progress of the plague which was devastating his people; and there, though convinced that the heaven of heavens could not contain the Lord, Solomon accomplished the purpose of his father and built the house to the Lord of Hosts, who condescended to fill it with His glory; and there "the greater glory" filled the second temple built by Nehemiah and Ezra and beautified by Herod; and there still projects the top of the rock of Moriah, on which it is supposed stood the altar of sacrifice.

Mahometan superstition has overlaid all these sacred spots with absurd legends. Not more absurd, however, than those with which the same principle would have inlaid it had it not been driven away by the false prophet. If the Moslem pilgrim recognizes a spot in this rock as the print made by the foot of the Prophet when he sprang up to make the visit to paradise, the neighbouring Christian church has the impress of the feet of our Lord left on the Mount of Olives when He ascended into Heaven. Nor is the fraud which here builds up plaster walls around an excavation made below the rock, that by its resonance, on being tapped, it may convey the idea that there is no solid support to the mass overhead, which it is asserted had such a desire to follow the Prophet to paradise that it split itself off from the rock beneath and was arrested in its flight and is still kept suspended by the angel Gabriel (the mark of whose fingers may still be seen impressed on its edge), one whit more shameless than many a similar lie told in behalf of the truth. They point out also a hole in the ceiling of this cave which receded from the head of the Prophet as he rose from his prayers suddenly, forgetting that it was not lofty enough to permit him to rise to his full height. This rock and cave under it, enclosed in the Mosque of Omar, are next to that at Mecca in sanctity in the esteem of good Mussulmen; and the bodies of all believers in Islam, dying at Jerusalem, are brought into the sacred enclosure before they are interred, that the souls may be at once admitted to Paradise.

The rock of Moriah is protected by an elaborate screen of gilded iron work and a canopy of silk is hung over. We saw the opening into the conduit which, running down below the foundations of the temple, carried the blood and offal of the Jewish sacrifices, into the Tyropean valley; which Mahometan superstition has converted into the entrance to Paradise.

The dome which covers the Mosque is a very noble structure and has, around the tympanum, windows of very beautifully stained glass of the richest colours, in small pieces arranged in arabesque. They appear like precious stones, so rich and gorgeous is the colour—carbuncles and topazes and emeralds. The interior walls are covered with highly coloured and glazed tiles and much gilding, and at various places are introduced marble fragments of sculpture of exquisitely graceful design and execution, which have evidently belonged to some older structure and are reasonably thought to be portions of the Jewish temple. Some of the pillars are of very rare workmanship and most extraordinary design; the marble being so cut as to resemble the intertwining of cords of great flexibility, while the capitols are richly sculptured. There is also the frequent repetition, in bas relief, of the peculiar symbol which is known as the sign of the House of David. Something akin to the true lover's knot. It is only within a few years that Christians have been permitted to enter this Mosque, and now it can only be done under consular protection and with the attendance of a cawass or officer of the consulate. It is requiring repair, and we picked up some fragments of tile which have fallen from the walls.

There are here, as at the Mosque of Tooloon at Cairo, columns standing close together through the space between which true believers of whatever corporeal proportions may press themselves, and have their sins squeezed out in the passage. At one place in the corridor is a sacred stone on one side, and another of a black colour in the wall opposite. Whoever kisses the stone and with closed eyes turns round and without opening the lids walks direct to the black stone and lays his hand on it, before looking, is certain of admission to Paradise. Greatly to the amusement of the Mussulman guide several of our party made the experiment without success. Your mother was the first to accomplish the feat, and I happily was not left behind, marching to it very fairly. Devout Moslems were loudly reciting the Koran in the Mosque at the time of our visit without being in the least disturbed.

This Mosque of Omar stands near the middle of the space which was once included within the enclosure of the Temple, and the dome is supported by *ancient* marble pillars assumed to have been those of the Jewish temple. There can be no reasonable doubt that the smaller columns and ornaments I have described did belong to it.

From the Mosque of Omar we went to that of El Aksa which stands at the end of the enclosure and was a Christian church dedicated to the blessed Virgin, erected by Emperor Justinian in the 6th century. It has been a grand structure, with double aisles and a transept. Some pictures around the tympanum of the dome, which crowns the intersection of the nave and transept, have been spared, contrary to Mahometan custom. At the side at which we entered an old gate is pointed out as the Beautiful Gate, at which the lame man was healed by Peter and John. But though some parts of it are old, the whole is decidedly Saracenic. Not so the Golden Gate on the opposite side. As we sat within it and gazed with awe-struck admiration on its two monolithic pillars of marble, said to have been presented to Solomon by the Queen of Sheba, we felt satisfied even that might be so; but whether or no, they support capitols so elaborately sculptured and so gracefully proportioned and yet so corroded by time, even in their sheltered position, that the coldest scepticism would hesitate to reject the tradition. The whole interior of the chamber of the gateway is certainly older than the Christian era and richly adorned with sculpture. The stones in its walls are of great size, and though the domes themselves may be modern the arches and corners on which they rest bear all the evidences of great antiquity.

A bridge once sprang across the valley from this gate-way which is now destroyed, and the gate-way is walled up on both the exterior and interior. Out of this gate and over the bridge which spanned the valley were led the red heifer of the atonement, and the scape goat of the Levitical ritual, and it was beyond a doubt by this bridge and through this gate that our blessed Lord entered the Temple on the occasion when "seated on an ass and a colt the foal of an ass." He was preceded and followed by the multitude singing "Hosanna to the Son of David, blessed be He that cometh in the name of the Lord, Hosanna in the highest." The Moslem tradition is that through it the Lord shall enter again when He comes, and as that will involve the overthrow of Islam they have walled up the gate to prevent His entering there. It was a very solemn thought that we were thus standing beside the very columns which supported the roof and arches beneath which Jesus thus rode "meek and lowly" and as we looked at the grooves in the wall in which the doors had fitted and the holes in the lintel which had received the pivots on which the doors turned, or through which the chains of the portcullis had passed, the quotation by our guide of the language of the Psalm "lift up your heads ye everlasting gates, and be ye lifted up ye everlasting doors and the King of Glory shall come in," revived in our hearts the expectation of His coming again "without sin unto salvation," and entering by this very gate once more into His Father's House.

It was here he drove out the oxen, and bade them that sold doves to "take these things hence," and overthrew the tables of the money changers. This House of His Father shall yet be "the house of prayer for many nations." Only yesterday the blessed sacrament of the Lord's supper was administered, to show forth His death till He comes, in the church on Mount Zion to a large number; German, English and Hebrew being used in the addresses to the communicants; and Americans, Englishmen, Germans, Jews and Syrians gathered together at the table of the Lord. That golden gate is truly a sacred spot.

From there we descended to the most wonderful of all the antiquities of the Holy City the *substructions* of the temple. They are called, most absurdly, the stables of Solomon. Down, down, we went until we found ourselves in an immense, almost limitless hall, with rows of massive pillars, supporting well turned arches, running row after row as far as the eye can reach; the vaulted roof being at least twenty fee above the bases of the columns, which are built of well dressed stones with the rebatement at the joints peculiar to the ancient Hebrews. It is directly beneath the temple area and the huge stones which we see here below the ground are beneath a part of the temple area opposite to those, of which we saw the outer side, at the place where the Jews assemble weekly to lament and wail over the desolations of the city of their fathers' glory. We felt deeply for their distress when we saw them sobbing and weeping on the outer side, but as we stood here within and realized by the solidity of the structure and the costliness of these arches, thus buried under the mass on which the temple stood, how magnificent must have been the structure itself, we sympathized still more deeply with them and realized more than I had before done, that it was not only to the eyes of the humble fishermen of Galilee that it appeared to be adorned with goodly stones, and to be so massive that they naturally associated the end of all things with the destruction and overthrow of the Temple buildings, announced by our Lord, but that it was truly one of the great structures of the world; grand and glorious and imposing in itself. The appearance of the crowd of descendants of Abraham, old men and women, young men and maidens, bearing on their faces and in their mein and attire the evidence of long ages of oppression under which they have been crushed, yet still retaining the noble features which indicate that they belong to one of the highest types of the human family, presents a solemn illustration of the lesson of the apostle "Behold therefore the goodness and severity of God: on them which fell severity; but toward thee, goodness, if thou continue in his goodness"; and God grant that we may profit by the lesson "Otherwise thou also shalt be cut off." Solid buildings and costly ritual observances did not save the chosen people from being scattered as they now are "until the fulness of the Gentiles be come in"; and still God, changing not, looks upon the heart, and values more highly the heart offering than the costly tribute which does not come thence.

Such thoughts and feelings belong to these scenes. These stones laid, and arches turned to afford space to construct a temple to the Lord of Hosts, on the mount which He showed to Abraham and David as the chosen seat of His glory, now support the Mosque of the false prophet and the superstition, which would supplant the simple worship, struggles with Islam for the possession; while we daily learn more and more clearly that neither "in Jerusalem nor on mount Gerizim" is the Father worshipped but worshippers who worship "in spirit and in truth" find acceptance through the one Messiah, not at one sacred place, but wherever they are placed by His appointment ordering their lot.

In the afternoon we went to the Church of the Holy Sepulchre and saw the struggling crowds of Russian pilgrims lighting their tapers at the Holy Fire presented by the priests, and rushing in procession to the various stations which are covered by the lofty dome which has recently been erected by France and Russia over them. They prostrate themselves and kiss the stone on which the body of our Lord was laid by the loving hands of Joseph and Nicodemus and the women who had followed Him out of Galillee; at the stone on which the angel sat after he had rolled it away from the sepulchre; on the marble slab which covers the tomb; and at the holes in the rock which received the cross; and the fissure in the rock said to have been made by the earthquake. The faces of the pilgrims are those which repel you by their want of intellect, their heads uncombed and their attire not only strange in form, but soiled and tattered by the toil and wear and tear of their long pilgrimage. We may not glory in our greater intelligence and our freedom from the thraldom of superstition; but be humbled by our failure to use more profitably our superior advantages, remembering who hath made us to differ and who has said that He will ask from us according as we have received.

While I dwell amid these scenes I pray for more faith; not the mere belief on these things as historical truths, which everything around me confirms, but more of that living faith which realizes that if one died for all then were all dead—myself among them—and that Jesus died and rose again that they that live "should not live to themselves but to Him who died for them." I find it quite possible that the "belief unto righteousness" which is *of the heart* may be very low, while that of intellect may be strengthened by every moment's observation of the scenes in which Jesus lived and suffered. Faith must be contended for we must *fight the fight of faith* with an unwearied enemy and amid treasonable treacherous foes within.

The city still swarms with pilgrims though some have already gone down to Jordan, and the large company of German, English and Americans is daily diminishing, and we shall probably be among the last to leave.

April 2nd, Evening.

What do you think of your mother and I having just returned from a social party in Jerusalem. A very pleasant evening, too. I had paid my respects to Bishop Gobat immediately on our arrival and last evening received an invitation for your mother and myself to spend this evening there. We met the Pasha of Jerusalem and several members of the Church, with the Dr Chaplin who had taken me this morning to see his hospital, Canon Lysons with whom we have been daily associated here, and a few other travellers. What was my surprise to be addressed by name by one of the guests who said "I have met you before and consulted you in Philadelphia," and on his mentioning the circumstances I remembered clearly his having been sent to consult me about the propriety of his going as a missionary to China. He was a student in the Divinity School at West Philadelphia. Bishop and Mrs. Gobat are simple-hearted worthy people. Yesterday the landlord of the hotel had begged for the use of our parlour during our absence at the Haram al Shereef for the purpose of holding a meeting of the Consuls and gentlemen resident here, to present to the Bishop, on the twenty-fifth anniversary of his Episcopate, on behalf of the Emperor of Germany a model in silver of the church; a splendid porcelain vase with the portraits of the Emperor, and Empress in medallions on it; and a bust of the *late* Emperor, the friend of Chevalier Bunsen, by whom the church had been built, and the Episcopate (in conjunction with the British Government) endowed. These were standing in the drawing-room. But rich and beautiful as they were they had not in our eyes half the value of a picture which greeted us as we reached the head of the staircase—" Wait for Me "—hung there, drawing up her stocking and looking so earnestly after those who had gone on before. *Dear little Annie;* she did look very sweet here in Jerusalem. Who would have thought of such a reminescence of home; while a child's cane-seated rocking-chair (the counterpart of that given by her uncle Wistar to Annie's Mother, now at Ivy Neck) added to the scene. Then Mrs. Gobat handed your mother a volume of photographs of her children and grandchildren, and you all know how that gratified her. Then too the poor good doctor had asked me this morning to see his child suffering with whooping cough and reminding me sadly of our precious Cornelia, so that everything combined to soften our hearts and make us feel a happiness which is not often our lot anywhere, and which we little looked for when we most reluctantly accepted the invitation.

We shall leave here God willing early on Thursday morning for Jaffa. A perilous journey and very fatiguing. We have bought a few olive wood memorials of Jerusalem which will be sent in a box by Mr. Bergheim here, to the care of Austin Baldwin & Co., New York. If it arrives before we do Israel will please pay expenses. I suppose it will go enclosed in a larger one from your uncle Wistar. But we have not decided that yet. I will thank Israel to have the photographs he has received, and these also, mounted and to get a Portfolio to hold them safely. Your mother is a-bed.

    Your loving father,

            CASPAR MORRIS.

         JERUSALEM, April 3, 1872.
My Dear Children:

This is a wondrous age in which we live, and at the risk of wearying you with the repetition of the same thoughts, I must repeat that this is a most wonderful place; the place at which dwelt Melchizedek, King of Righteousness and King of Peace, without father and without mother and without descent; greater than Abraham; the type of the Messiah; and which from that day to the present, though it is less than all lands, has been the focus toward which has been gathered the interests of the world. This morning we have seen it in its two aspects of past and present. Just as we were preparing to go out the clergyman called to invite us to visit the school for Jewish children, and the house for Orphans, and the house of Employment for Jewish women. They are all under the same roof and conducted by the same superintendent. The women are employed on needle work for which they receive pay, and while they sew or make lace for sale, lessons from the New Testament in Hebrew are read to them. Your mother and aunts made some purchases and then we listened to the reading and address. This is the dawn of the future of Jerusalem.

From there we went to the store of Shaphira, a learned Hebrew, who is deeply interested in antiquities. He shewed us fragments of the Moabite stone with the inscriptions deeply cut in its surface. It is of very hard close grain and black color and has been broken into fragments by the jealous Arab Sheiks when they found it was thought valuable by Europeans. They advanced in the price demanded for it from a few pounds to as many thousands; always adding as the sum asked was acceded to. He yesterday received from an agent who is in his employ a cinerary urn, from a Moabitic tomb, covered with inscriptions in Phœnician letters. In the same tomb were found terra cotta rings and other articles; one in shape of a hand, one a perfect Lingam as worshipped by the Hindoos, and others of various shapes all covered with inscriptions in Phœnician characters and raised letters. Mr. Shaphira is endeavouring to secure the possession of a sufficient number of these articles to enable him to frame a reasonable system by which to decipher the inscriptions in the old Hebrew or Phœncian characters which are inscribed upon them.

JAFFA, April 5, 1872.

We are all familiar with the effect of light and shade on the landscape and that that which seen as the shadows are thrown one way may be unattractive or even repulsive, when the shadows fall differently is filled with beauty. Faith always sees things illuminated by Divine love. Therefore faith finds beauty, always, everywhere, even in dry and barren lands. So if we had but had faith in living exercise when we left here and when at Ramleh on our way up to Jerusalem, things and events might not have looked so badly as they must have appeared to you from my letters from those places. God has been very gracious to us and has brought us thus far through many trials and some dangers and we desire to praise Him for His goodness and to manifest our gratitude for the past by trusting the future to His Fatherly care.

The journey back to this place has been without any incident to mar our enjoyment and has been filled with attraction. We had one palanquin less, your Aunt Hannah riding on horseback and your mother occupying her chair, and the arrangements for the charge of the burden-mules were better; and your mother and I had learned to have more confidence in the vehicles and mules and drivers, and these last had been drilled into more watchful attention. Yesterday we rode twelve hours and were very much fatigued, but we reached the Latin Convent at Ramleh at an early hour and had the selection of accommodations and found them very choice; instead of being turned into a court with a cave with six beds for seven ladies filling it entirely (and being told the gentlemen must take what they could get), we had nice apartments for all parties, some with embroidered curtains, and some with green gauze, and the "Frater" who received us instead of the wearied heartless look he had presented (a look which spoke plainly "I do not know what I can do for you"), looked happy to welcome us and confident he could make us comfortable. In due season a delightful meal of soup, chicken, and lamb contributed greatly to our refreshment and a good night's rest completed the happiness. Your aunts needed it; they were obliged to lie down before they could eat. It had been a day of severe exertion, though one also of high enjoyment.

We all felt we had turned the goal, and that however long the time might be and whatever incidents might mark its progress, our way was from thence forward *Homeward*. We had for companions of the way our good English Clergyman, a very typical illustration of a humble cheerful faithful servant of Christ, and his servant who served his master with the same cheerful goodwill as that master serves his Lord; and also an English old bachelor morose and morbid, who has spent his life in foreign parts and never having cultivated family affections wonders there are none to welcome him to their hearts. We got away from the Jaffa gate about 7 A. M. and rode till noon through the wild mountain passes and rugged defiles of the portion of the tribe of Judah. We saw the glorious sun rise in all his splendour over the Mount of Olives and turning our backs on the dreary desolation of the Vale of the Dead Sea and the savage ranges of the more distant mountains of Moab we wound along the highway passing the village which still marks the site of that Emmaus which is associated in every Christian soul with that sweet walk of Jesus with Cleophas and his friend, in which the wondrous words of the Lord made their hearts burn within them by the way, and where He was manifested to them in the breaking of bread. Though the way was desert it yet "blossomed as the rose." The wondrous beauty and inexhaustable abundance of the flowers of the field surpasses imagination. Yellow in all its various shades, crimson, scarlet and pink in all their numerous hues were scattered with profusion amid the rocks and stones and on the soft green sward. The genista, the phlox, the rose of Sharon, clovers of various colours, white, red, pink and purple; some of the varieties so diminutive as almost to escape observation yet with the peculiar sweet odour of our purple clover.

As we got lower down in the valleys we came to gardens and orchards. Quince and pear and cherry trees were in blossom, fig trees were putting forth their leaves, and the young figs were advancing with the leaves, thus relieving me of an embarrassment I had always felt in reading the history of our Lord's looking for figs on the tree on the side of Olivet on the day when he came at the time of the Passover from Bethany to Jerusalem. Here and there orange trees were found in these enclosures and some vineyards were to be seen still destitute of foliage. The mountain sides were still terraced to the very top showing how they had once been cultivated, and proving that these valleys had once resounded with the songs of a numerous population. As we came still lower down wheat fields spread themselves out into the plain and numerous flocks of sheep and goats were to be seen feeding on the short sweet grass amid the widely disseminated flowers. These were often set as thickly as though they had been planted by skill, in beds or borders. But no parterre could rival their elegance. I wish some skilled botanist could visit these valleys and plains and give the world an illustrated work on the flora of the Holy Land. J. Mason Good's exquisite poem on the daisy was welling up in my heart continually.

> "Not worlds on worlds in phalanx deep,
> Need we to prove a God is here;
> The daisy, waked from winter's sleep,
> Tells of his hand in tones as clear."

The valley of Ajalon opened out into the plain of Sharon with its pink and white Cytisus (called the Rose of Sharon), its profusion of Cyclamens, its crimson Anemonies, and its golden plant whose name I have not learned, but which literally was poured along the ravines like a golden stream bursting its banks and overflowing the meadows. The wild chamomile spread white sheets over large spaces, and Salvias of pink and blue, and Melissas were met with constantly. The attention was beguiled at every turn by some variety of these beauties. At the place where we stopped to lunch we were shaded by an oak hanging out its catkins. I looked for an acorn but could find none but those which had been bored by an insect or eaten by mice. Your uncle Wistar got a fern and I dug up the tuber of a Cyclamen and found a Holly bush and a Kalmia. There were many blue Pimpernels (our chickweed) with large flowers of the deepest blue I ever saw, and in the few minutes while the lunch was being spread I gathered an armful of beauties with some of which I am familiar; while others, some beautiful and some curious, were unknown to me.

At Ramleh this morning we were waked first by the Muezzins call to prayer; followed by the bells of the Greek convent and these by those of the Latin at which we were, and when they were hushed a sweet little bird took up its matin song. Our good father provided us with coffee, bread and eggs, and the brother who waited on us did so with a pleasant happy face. The good Canon was able to communicate with him in Italian, and at sister Mary's request expressed our thanks for his kindness and our hope that we might meet in the New Jerusalem, though it was certain we never should on earth. He replied with a very grave look and a shrug of the shoulder that he was kept so busy waiting on people on earth that indeed he had but little time to think of Heaven. When we were alone I slipped a Napoleon into his hands for the convent, with a sign that it was done for love to Jesus; and we kissed each other and embraced. He followed your mother and myself, to the moment we left, with manifestation of reciprocation of kind feeling. The institution is certainly beneficent. It provides a resting place for pilgrims on their way to Jerusalem. Ramleh is the only one between Jaffa, their landing place, and the Holy City. The monks make no charge and all may go without making any recompense. We met there Germans, Protestant deaconesses, and Romish nuns. Of course none who have the ability fail to give at least an equivalent for their food and lodging and your uncle did so for our party. The first night we were there it was crowded to excess. This time there were many beside ourselves of various nations and some evidently without any means.

One venerable looking old man arrived soon after us and sat in the same waiting room. We fell into conversation, he speaking English with a German accent. He inquired where I came from, and on being told said "I am an American and a Pennsylvanian." I told him I should have supposed he belonged to Faderland. He smiled and said his parents were German. He had lived in Port Carbon and in Union County and at other places in Pennsylvania, and knew the Rev. Dr. Seiss, of Philadelphia. We found he was a Homœopathic doctor named Simbal, living at Jaffa, and on his way to Jerusalem. He very soon inquired our plans and told us it was all very well if we should only be in time to get through Germany. He then asked what were our views about the coming of our Lord, and on my giving him mine, which you know are that we should be always watching and longing for the time when "that same Jesus, which is taken up from you into Heaven, shall so come in like manner as ye have seen Him go into Heaven." He said "that is all right, but do you not see plainly the signs of the times" you must look for Him in a few days. "Who is the greatest man now in the world?" he asked me very abruptly. I hesitated a moment and replied "William Emperor of Germany." He laughed very scornfully and said "No indeed, Louis Napoleon. He will very soon be recalled to the throne of France and then will make himself at once Emperor of Rome. He will hold that place but a few days; he is anti-Christ. The Jews will then all immediately come to Palestine and then will be the end." Canon Lysons and I had much earnest conversation with him. We were greatly interested by his earnest affectionate manner and evident sincerity of faith. He has been making great efforts to induce the Pasha of Jerusalem, and the Sultan, to permit the construction of a breakwater at Jaffa and a Railroad to the Holy City, and it is only within a few weeks that he has despaired of success. He says the Turks and Druses are the most moral people in these parts, and that they do not desire the introduction of Europeans. He was told that the Prime Vizier said, after an interview with him, that the Sultan would never grant permission for a railroad. "Jerusalem now a mad house for Christians; I (the Sultan) do not know what it would become then." The old man appeared to be on the most familiar terms with the monks, stopping here frequently on his way to and fro. He is now bound to the land of Moab. I asked if he was interested about the antiquities there. He said yes, but those were trifles connected with history; his interests were in higher things. He gave a poor account of the American colonists who were most of them mere adventurers in search of gain. The German Templars he says are prospering, though he does not agree with them in their views and they do not cooperate with him in his. We parted evidently pleased with each other and he had started on his way to Jerusalem before we rose this morning.

Our ride down here across the plain of Sharon was very pleasant. The sun was not too warm, the air fresh and invigorating, the nightingales and larks sung melodiously the flowers were as beautiful as when we went up ten days ago; orchids, of great beauty, Orobancheæ, and Cyclamens, and Anemones. Miles before we reached Jaffa, before even the town was in sight, the scent of its orange groves was borne on the breeze. They are not only immediately around the city but are planted some distance into the country.

There is a Prussian colony which is introducing improved implements and modes of culture. The primitive plough here is only a hoe, like one of those on the hoe harrows of West River about three times the size of that, perhaps I might say one-third the size of a long handled shovel and shaped something like it. A light handle rises perpendicularly, and another is attached to it by a curved pole to which a yoke of oxen is attached. The whole plough is not much heavier than a common shovel and is carried over the shoulder, as that is. The oxen are small, and I have seen a camel before a yoke of oxen drawing one of these little ploughs. Yet they do stir the earth nicely, and though there are neither trees or fences, nor any other land marks, the lands are laid out and the furrows run as straight as the lines on this paper. The barley is now nearly ripe, the wheat shooting its head, and the people are all busy preparing the ground for melons. Some are already growing. They are said to be very fine and like the oranges are shipped to Egypt and Greece and Constantinople in large quantities.

In strong contrast with the busy scenes of agriculture and the flower-clad and fertile plain, we had in view the desert with its heaps of yellow sand stretching away toward Mount Sinai. It was across this the Ethiopian Eunuch was travelling when Philip was directed by the Spirit to go the desert way from Jerusalem to Gaza, and fell in with him and explained to him the words of Isaiah. No chariots are seen here now.

The Prussians have introduced farm wagons and as we approached two of them were standing by the road side with well fed horses well harnessed. Our muleteers and dragoman immediately went to the head of our mules, who are as much afraid of these strange carriages as our horses are at home of dummy engines. Just before reaching the hotel we passed through the market which was crowded with buyers and sellers. It is held in the Mohammedan Cemetery, and the tomb stones are used as seats for the living. There were large booths fitted up as coffee houses in which scores of men sat with pipes and coffee. The contrast between the living and the dead generations was as strong as that between the flowery plain of Sharon and the yellow desert of Gaza. Here, at Ramleh, and at Jerusalem, the wayside as you approach the towns is thronged by beggars, lepers, and blind, who greet every passer with most piteous and heart rending cries for assistance. It is impossible to give to all, and if we bestow alms upon one the whole throng rise and follow the travellers in hope of sharing in the beneficence.

Though in the irregularity with which I write, and the many interruptions to which I am subject I may repeat the same things, I am sure I omit more. I have just remembered that the land here is infested with squills as that at West River is with Onion. Great tufts of large leaves like those of lilies are seen every where, covered with snail shells as a log in the water would be with barnacles. When they plough they turn out the bulbs as large as my double fists, and throw them out on the road side. We saw but one in flower and Wistar secured that. The land of the plain of Sharon is free from stones and a light and easily worked loam, amply compensating the toil of the tiller.

Evening.

Your dear mother has felt very much the fatigue of the two days' ride coming down. She had been compelled to omit very many of the interesting spots in the vicinity of Jerusalem as there is no way of going about but on foot or on donkeys, and the streets and roads are so steep and stony and slippery that this is perilous. She has, however, enjoyed highly the privilege of seeing what she has been able to visit, especially the sight of Solomon's temple; from which she could look down on Gethesemane, and across to the Mount of Olives and toward Bethany on the one side, and the Mount of Ascension. She went also to that most interesting of all places on the face of the earth, where Jesus stood like a lamb dumb before His shearers, not opening His mouth though reviled and spitted on and rejected; the place where priests and people cried crucify Him. The more I think upon it the more satisfied I am of the great probability that the spot shown is the true one.

She spent an evening also at the Bishop's and called there in the morning the day before we left.

We are now here among the orange groves; and the sounding surf as it breaks against the shore reminds us that it is the same sound as lulled the Apostle Peter when he dwelt with Simon the Tanner by the sea side here. A chorus of frogs reminds us of the sounds of our April evenings at home, and we are relieved by your uncle having telegraphed to Alexandria to endeavor to procure passages from this direct to Constantinople without calling at Beyroot, or going to Damascus. If he should not be able to do this your mother and I will even take second class passage from Beyroot rather than land there. You all know how nervous she is about getting into little boats anywhere, and under these circumstances there is real danger in doing it.

However great has been the fatigue and peril of our trip to the Holy City we feel thankful that we have been allowed to make it. It has been the most blessed part of our journey and voyaging on many accounts, and we have been favoured to feel it so, and thus far there has been no injury to our health notwithstanding the fatigue and exposure.

I enclose a few seeds of the scarlet Anemone which renders the mountains about Jerusalem and the plains of Sharon so splendid in colour. The lesson about the clothing as drawn from the flowers of the field by our blessed Lord was in all probability elicited by this very plant; and as we saw the dry bunches of grass burning under the pots and in the little ovens, we realized how literal was the lesson which spoke of the "to-day is and to-morrow is cast into the oven." It is in such little trifling coincidences may be found the most striking and positive proof of the truth of the Gospel. They are so natural and truthful and are so wrought into the very texture of the sacred narrative that they confirm it and give force and value to its teaching.

The last evening we were in Jerusalem I went with Bishop Gobat to a missionary meeting held in an upper chamber, certainly just such an one as that in which the apostles were assembled for fear of the Jews when, the doors being shut, our Lord entered and breathed upon them and bestowed on them that Peace which the world cannot give; or like that in which they were assembled when the house was shaken and they were all filled with the Holy Ghost. They had an admirable address on the history of Moravian Mission among our Indians and at the request of the Bishop I gave some little account of Bishop Whipple's Mission at Yankton. Bishop Whipple was here a few years ago and was taken ill in the very house in which we met and was carried to Bishop Gobat's to be nursed. The people remembered his visit.

The guide who took us about is a converted Jew and made a most favourable impression on us all. I cannot remember what I have written but when I look over my letters on my return will endeavor to fill up the gaps which I know there must be. It is now nearly ten o'clock and your mother sits knitting while I write, but I will close and we will retire, first commending you one and all as well as ourselves to God and the word of His Grace which only can keep either you or us.

Your loving father,

CASPAR MORRIS.

(NOTE.—*The following remarks regarding the trip in the Holy Land were undoubtedly written when he arranged his letters after his return home.*—EDS.)

The circumstances under which the letters were written which were addressed to my children from the Holy Land rendered impracticable every attempt to give them a connected current. Every opportunity to write was availed of and of course the incidents of the moment assumed the most importance in the mind since if they were passed over, in order to retrace the record to the point at which the previous narrative was broken off, many things would be overlooked and forgotten, and the simplicity of daily impressions would be lost irrecoverably. Any attempt now to reduce these fragmentary utterances of emotion, and description of scenes, and narrative of events into regularity, would render the whole tame, and uninteresting. Yet some retrospect, even after this lapse of time, may give cohesion to the preceeding letters, and be valuable even at the expense of some repetition.

Our landing at Jaffa was affected, as may be inferred from the letters, with some difficulty and danger, and no little distress to those who like your mother have a great dread of boats at all times. It *was* a difficult thing to balance oneself so as to drop into the boat which lay bobbing at the foot of the gangway, and this difficulty was not exaggerated in the description given at the moment of the disturbing accidents. When the wind is high it is impossible to land.

The scramble up the nearly precipitious shore over great piles of boxes filled with oranges was especially difficult for your mother unaccustomed to any other motion than driving, or walking very short distances upon chosen footpaths. The ascent accomplished we found ourselves surrounded by a motley group of Syrians, Arabs of most forbidding aspect, all talking rapidly and loudly, in unknown tongues;

while camels and men jostled each other in the narrow, filthy, streets running between cold stone walls with few or no windows to break the uniformity of their forbidding fronts. We were dragged along as prisoners might be, with no volition of our own, except that we had voluntarily surrendered our freedom, and were not a little pleased when we found that our masters for the time being, the Syrian Dragoman and our Courier, were taking us out of the closely built town to an attractive modern looking settlement on the top of a hill some little distance from Jaffa proper; and though the house was small, the cleanliness and freshness of everything contrasted most charmingly with the filth and orientalism of Jaffa proper.

To describe the various incidents crowded into the time occupied in making arrangements for our trip would be simply impossible. They overlaid each other so deeply that one must of necessity conceal another, and to disentangle them and to spread them out in regular narrative, would be to deprive them of the natural connection which is essential to their interest.

The duty of making the necessary arrangements fell wholly on Wistar, and an irksome, onerous, task it was. The mode in which we were to travel was first to be determined, and then the means provided; and each was to be furnished with that best suited to their several powers and tastes. I look back with amazement and ever increasing gratitude on the patience and skill manifested by my brother. It certainly had a Divine source of supply. Friezier had never been there before and therefore could give neither counsel or assistance in execution. Joseph was embarrassed by Friezier's presence and interference.

It is impossible to describe the scene when, the mode of travel decided, palanquins for three of us and the others mounted on horses and donkeys, the next step was to select from those offered such as were supposed most suitable. Chaffering for prices was mingled with uncertainity about fitness, and the interferences of other parties seeking similar accommodations. Here, as everywhere else during our journey, I kept sedulously aloof from consultations, fearing to add to confusion, and left your uncle to act independently.

A palanquin belonging to the American Consul at Jerusalem was at Jaffa to be returned to Jerusalem. It had been made for his wife and was supposed to be specially desirable. There is something in a name certainly. To myself who had known the eastern vehicle, carried on men's shoulders, the word carried no idea of the cumbrous vehicles which bore the same name here. They have been made by native carpenters, from such material as the country affords, and by mechanics destitute of skill, and ignorant of what is required. I have seen light horse cart bodies which weigh less than the chair; and the poles on which it is borne are more cumbrous than common cart shafts. They are in truth shafts, projecting both before and behind the heavy chair on which the person to be carried is seated. In these shafts are placed two horses or mules, their only connection with it or each other being ropes passing over the back of the animal, like the back straps of cart gears, with a bag of straw interposed between the back of the animal and the rope to prevent the chafing. The rider has no connection with either animal, but sits immediately behind the tail of the foremost, and at the nose of that behind, above the level of their backs, swaying with every movement, yet obliged to keep an even balance. The understanding is that a driver is to be at the head of each beast. But it is of course difficult to establish good understanding where there is no medium of communication in a common language, and the interests of the two contracting parties are as opposite as the shafts of the vehicle. and one finds oneself very often seated aloft between two beasts with no control over them by oneself or any one else. The consular vehicle differed from the others only in having a covered top, with glass in front and at the sides, thus protecting the rider from sun or rain. This, the only vehicle of the kind, your uncle secured for your mother at an increased cost. Much time was consumed in selecting and bargaining for these conveyances for her, your aunt Hannah, and myself; as they would not allow me to follow my own course, which would have put me on horse back.

This arrangement being effected the next step was to hire the necessary horses for the riders, as well as two for each palanquin, and baggage mules to carry our equipments, which, though reduced to the smallest quantity possible for each, made a large amount for so numerous a party. The horses were to be tried by each one, and the best selected. Amid much confusion it was at last effected, and we were stowed in our seats, and each attempted to mount their respective beasts. The scene which ensued baffles description, every element of discord and excitement which it is possible to collect amid beasts and men, was turned loose at that hour. Horses and mules plunged and kicked and screamed. Ladies found themselves on animals they could not possibly ride, and were compelled to dismount, standing helpless and almost defenceless amid the hurly burly, Arabs and Syrians scolded and shouted. Clubs were used to restrain the beasts who could be controlled in no other way. To say all Bedlam was turned loose were to afford a very feeble idea of the confusion. I look back still with a feeling of veneration on the composure of your uncle, on whose shoulders rested the weight of the responsibility, and who stood calmly as Homer represents Jupiter amid the wranglings of Olympus. Thanks to his firmness and coolness all was at length reduced to order. New animals were brought in place of those found unfit for the use of the ladies, and we set off. A strange cavalcade it was.

Your mother's palanquin was to have an attendant at the head of each horse and one to walk beside her and steady the vehicle. Mine with an attendant to each horse was to follow closely; and behind it that of sister Hannah. The other members of the party, including Canon Lysons and his servant man, rode as they pleased, while the baggage mules were driven higgledy-piggledy, or left to follow the bent of their own wills. It was soon found impossible to keep the men at their posts, or to prevent the baggage mules from wandering from the road; and when in it they were constantly crowding upon each other and getting in the way of riders or carriages. I found my only comfort was in seeking for an increase in faith which would enable me to realize the protecting power and love of our Heavenly Father.

I have mentioned the incidents of the way and have endeavored to give some idea of the natural scenery in the letters written at that time. The difficulties to be overcome in starting had made us later than we designed, and though it was only March the mid-day sun was hot; and we found the way weary and reached Ramleh in the afternoon exhausted by fatigue. This is the site of the Arimathea of the New Testament history, and is the station of rest between Jaffa and Jerusalem, about fifteen English miles from the former. There is a small Mohammedan population and a large collection of lepers, begging from pilgrims. Two or three convents of monks are established there to afford accommodation to pilgrims to the Holy City.

We had designed to seek rest in that of the Greek Church, which is supposed to be more liberal toward Western Christians, and to furnish better accommodations. Our detention in the morning had allowed those who proceeded us, together with others returning from Jerusalem, to absorb all their space and we were obliged to turn to that of the Latin. It is like a fortress enclosed with high walls and entered only by one gateway, under arches.

Long we knocked and when at length the door was opened it was to assure us that the delay in responding to our knocking was caused by the fact that every place was full, and all the fathers busy in waiting on guests who arrived before us. What arguments prevailed to open the door for our admission I cannot say, but reluctantly it was done, and we were carried into a paved court-yard about twenty feet square, enclosed by high walls with no windows, and two doors opening into it. Here we were told we must be contented, and seated on a stone step I used the second as my desk and wrote the account of our morning's adventures. In due process of time the two doors were opened and we found them the entrances to the cells I have there described, in which we were to be allowed to pass the night as best we might. We found one great difficulty in our way was the rule of the order excluding women from the penetration of the convent, and that the Canon and his servant were received into much better quarters in the interior of the building; where monkish cells opened on a quadrangular court planted neatly with trees and vines.

After the parties which preceded us had been satisfied we were summoned to a supper of chicken soup and bread, and plentiful draughts of luscious wine which did literally comfort those who felt ready to perish, and made us of cheerful countenance.

But little sleep was found; and the summons to horse at 2 A. M. was gladly responded to. The chief incidents of the day's journey are described in the letter written on our arrival at Jerusalem. The thoughts and feelings which spring spontaneously in the heart and mind of those who have been made familiar with the history of God's chosen people recorded in the Holy Scripture, cannot be recorded. They flow in perpetual freshness and yield each to its successor, leaving only a sense of satisfaction which cannot be analyzed or arranged in order for inspection of others. But I shall never lose the impression of the early dawn as it increased into day, and the glow of the eastern horizon, toward which we rode as the sun climbed over the mountains of Moab, and shed his glorious lustre on the hills of Judea; while larks rose around us at every step "swinging at heaven's gate" and the dewy sward was like some richly illuminated manuscript dotted everywhere with beautiful flowers. The distant ravines were filled with gorgeous yellow bloom, literally like streams of molten gold.

The road by which we travelled had been made by the American colonists at Jaffa with the design to open communication between Jerusalem and the sea-coast at that point, and on its completion one wagon made the single trip to and fro. It was well constructed and its grade is generally good but from neglect it has become quite impassable for any wheel carriage.

At a projecting point of a lofty hill on the right of the road is perched a small village which bears the name of Neby Samwil, and is reported by tradition to be the Ramah at the high place of which the prophet Samuel received Saul and gave him "The shoulder and that which was upon it" (1 Sam. 9 : 24) which had been set apart for the unknown guest at the sacrifice, whose coming had been announced to the seer. The name and sight of the place brought most vividly before one the sad story of the first king, head and shoulders taller than the people and royal in all his personal attributes; while association of ideas carried us a little further forward on the same line we were travelling to the scenes amid which his ruddy cheeked successor tended the flocks of his father Jesse the Bethlehemite, yet innocent of the great offence.

What a calamity it would be were our childhood and youth robbed of the enobling influence of sacred story, whose stirring incidents thronged around us as we rode, filling all space with their glorious images. As I sit here now, quietly writing, the whole comes before me again as in a dramatic view, the sights and sounds of which move livingly around me.

With what reluctant effort your mother and I took to our feet to descend that rugged hill down which the dragoman decided it was impossible we should ride! How heartless and faint was our feeling when on reaching the bottom, we found the planaquins had gone and were out of sight! Well it is all over now, and we have got through and are at home, once more. It was a dark hour then, truly, and made more intensely so by looking down instead of upward. The desolation of all around us became more and more marked the further we advanced. The hill sides stripped of their trees, and the valleys without flocks or culture told of the exterminating war which had swept off even the feeble tokens of human habitation which predatory hords of wandering Bedawin had permitted to rest here a century ago. The ruins of a Christian church, in the last stage of decay, aroused associations with the horrible scenes of the crusades; when savage ignorance clothed itself in the robes of a gorgeous superstition, and brought tens of thousands of ferocious combatants from the West to contest with the equally savage conquering Moslems, the possession of the sacred soil. The hillsides were surrounded to the very top by parallel lines which marked the old terraces which had held the soil for the vines and figs and olive trees, which once clothed with fertility these now desolate regions: and when we knew, as by an instinct, that we must be approaching the goal of our course of pilgrimage, the cliffs of grey limestone, lying one strata above another in horizontal lines, aroused strongly the remembrance of the Psalmist's description of the mountains round about Jerusalem; and one felt as though one was scaling the ruined ramparts of the grandest and loftiest of all works of defence; such as should surround the city of the Great King; the abode of Peace; and the dwelling place of Righteousness; the home of Melchizideck and the place out of which it was impossible a prophet should perish though it was the city which God had chosen to place His name there; and when from the summit we looked at the domes and battlemented walls of Jerusalem, we could not but share in the emotions of the enthusiastic hosts who knelt and worshipped, and appreciate the feeling which is attributed to Godfrey, and led him to hesitate to accept the crown of Jerusalem. But, weary with the journey we were glad to recognize as we approached, the signs of invasion of these romantic scenes by the genius of modern improvement. Along the road from Jaffa houses are being built outside the walls and the "Talitha cumi" house of the Prussian Deaconesses, and the grand structure erected by the Russian Government for the accommodation of the pilgrims of the Greek church, who crowd here at Easter annually, stand most attractive objects by the way side just before one reaches the gate. They are very fine buildings and very imposing in appearance and from the upper stories and flat roof of the latter one may see spread out around, almost the whole territory of the kingdom of Judea.

We gladly entered the Jaffa gate and found ourselves in a small open square at one side of which rises the tower of Hippicus on the site (it is said), of that of David; and on another the English Cathedral church and Episcopal residence; and on another a descent of a few steps brought us to the street of David on which stands the Hotel Mediterranean, at which Wistar had secured rooms for our accommodation. Dismounting at the end of a small alleyway we found ourselves in the inner court surrounded on every side by walls of grey limestone with stair ways on the outside and entrances at flats to the several stories. A good parlour, the largest room in the house, on the ground floor with groined arched ceilings, had been appropriated to our private use; and a flight of stone stairs took us to our chambers on the floor above. From the windows of our room we looked out on the tower of David, now a guard house surmounted by the flag of the Pasha of Jerusalem; while from the flat roof above we could see the Mount of Olives and the more distant mountains of Moab, and at our feet lay the pool of Hezekiah, and just beyond it the twin domes which surmount the Church of the Holy Sepulchre, covering the putative site of Calvary. Our arrival filled the hotel; and the rooms adjoining ours were occupied by the Prince and Princess of Lichtenstein, while our good friend the English Canon was made welcome to share our parlour and added greatly to our pleasure by his cheerful submission to the discomfort of a small chamber in a less pleasant part of the Hotel. Many travellers come from Jaffa with camp equipage and still remain in tents outside the walls, while visiting Jerusalem.

I will not attempt after this lapse of time to take up a continuous account of our daily proceedings. Wistar and Mary and Miss Harris and Mr. Longstreth made an excursion to the Jordan. Sisters sometimes went off with Friezier on explorations of their own. Your mother was not able to go about at all. The streets of Jerusalem are but narrow alleys running in every possible direction and over piles of rubbish, the debris of its former greatness; they can scarcely be said to be paved though they are covered with stones of irregular size and very various colour, some of them of a bright crimson and polished by the wear of the long continued tread of the feet of the donkeys and camels as well as of man. Of course it was impossible to ride and she was unable to walk. The houses are built exclusively of grey limestone with but little wood, and the roofs are stone arches. Hence the groined ceilings of the room within, and the dome like rotundity of the roofs outside. There are but few windows looking to the streets and those are guarded by iron gratings. The gloominess of the streets is most forbidding. That on which fronts the hotel is lined by small shops filled with groceries and other European goods and another which opens from it at right angles has many jewellers shops, the windows of which display articles of little value; some book stores; and one or two which exhibit quite a large assortment of goods. That kept by the Messrs. Bergheim, who are also the bankers of Jerusalem, was well supplied with almost everything one could suppose necessary for the comfort of the small but select company of English and German residents who are most of them in some way in the employ of the various missionary and educational and philanthropic societies established for the purpose of promoting the Christianization of the Jews. Some of these have costly establishments and a considerable number of persons in their employ.

One of the most profitable scources of revenue for the people of Jerusalem is the traffic in the various articles which are made here and purchased by visitors as mementos of the Holy City; serving like the scallop of other ages as tokens of a pilgrimage to the Holy Land having been accomplished. At the door of the hotel you find Jewish dealers in stones and seals and rings, blood stones and carnelian especially, having graven on them the word Jerusalem or some other Hebrew characters, and on the steps of the square in front of the Church of the Holy Sepulchre a crowd of venders of carved scallop shells and beads and images, makes it almost impossible to approach it. Each one as you pass presses on you rudely carved shells or beads of sandalwood; or the nut of the Dhom Palm; and it is only by determination, verging on harshness, that one can overcome their importunity.

In looking for a guide to the places of interest we were happy in securing the services of a Christian Jew, Paul Weintraub who was himself a turner and had a small shop in which we secured such articles of turned olive wood as would serve our purpose for memorials of our visit to the Holy City and presents to our friends, and thus we were at liberty to pass without stopping among the motley crew of venders, as we were compelled almost every time we left the hotel to go through this crowd. Paul was familiar with the usual objects of interest and took pleasure in explaining them though he did not profess his own confidence in many.

In the letters I have described some of the objects to which he took us. Among them the cistern of Helena. There are many other reservoirs of water under the present surface of the city; some of them very large and supposed to be connected with the temple area by under ground conduits. Several of them have been partially explored by Dr. Bartlett and Dr. Barclay, who were residents here many years, near the cistern of Helena. Weintraub shewed us some ancient brass lavers or vases so large that they might contain a barrel of water each, and of very fine proportions, which it is suggested were once appropriated to the temple service. They have been recently discovered.

Immediately adjoining the north wall of the Haran enclosure and the Tower of Antonia is an oblong space walled in, and closely resembling the pool of Hezekiah on Mount Zion, near our Hotel, which is the traditional Pool of Bethesda. All traces of porticos or colonades or porches have disappeared and it is now merely the place of reception for the filth and garbage of the city. By some it is thought to be only the dry moat of the Tower of Antonia and the Temple. The principal claim it has to be the pool of Bethesda rests upon the conviction that the sheep market, at which were kept the supplies of lambs and kids for sacrifice, must have been in this vicinity not only for convenience but also because it is difficult to place it any where else. When one thinks of the multitude who sacrificed "a lamb for every household" at the temple on every annual recurrence of the Passover, it is certain not only that the flocks of Judea must have been numerous to supply the demand, but that there must have been some large space to receive the numbers which were required at that time; and those familiar with the localities think the ground now occupied for cemeteries by Jews and Mohammedans on the East of the city, was most appropriate to this purpose from its extent and isolation. The number of dwellers in Judea under the Roman Emperors was determined by that of the lambs sacrificed. I think Josephus gives it over 250,000 at each feast. The sheep market was therefore an important point. Bethesda, as now shewn, has certainly no healing waters, but it may have been the outlet of some of the great Cisterns to which I have alluded and the stoppage of the conduits by the falling into them of buildings above has cut off its supply.

What fearful scenes have been enacted around these walls of the Temple. The Roman army encamped on the opposing height. The fanatic Jews, given over to madness, defending the temple to the last, and casting into the deep gorge lying between the wall and Kedron no less than 600,000 dead bodies during the seige. What an amount of dust was added to dust there; filling up the chasm down into which Josephus tells us it made one giddy to look from the battlements above! If the great work of man's redemption was accomplished on Calvary the most fearful climax of human misery was reached within and around those temple walls. Well may the outcasts of Zion wail at the sight of the massive stones which stand where Solomon placed them to support the embankment on which was built the glorious structure which, even in the diminished glory of its later day, could excite not only the wonder of the Fisherman of Galilee, but of the Roman General familiar as he was with the grand temples of Rome and Athens and Ephesus.

Even now as I dwell in memory on the successive tiers of masonry composed of stones five feet square and twenty or thirty long, with their "rebated" edges, such as one sees nowhere but in the substructions within this temple space, and in the lower courses of the tower of David, I am filled with awe at the thought of the grand building which rose above them, and *if* the conviction that they are the remains of the work of the son of David be a *delusion*, I do not desire it should be dispelled.

There are few wishes I indulge so gladly as that we may have some speedy development by the explorations now in progress in the Holy Land. In the rooms at the Damascus Gate are found several courses of Masonry of stones of similar size and with the same peculiar "rebatement" looking as though the stones had been placed the one on the other and then a channel an inch or more in depth and about two inches wide cut over the point of junction, and similar characteristics are found in some other of the more ancient walls and tombs, though nowhere so perfect as in the columns supporting the arches under the temple space and in the stones at the "Wailing Place" and in the solid lower part of the tower of David.

The work of exploration was suspended at the period of our visit, but when one thinks of the vast accumulation of stone and mortar and other debris which is piled up covering the remains of this once populous city so often sacked and pillaged, there can be no room to question the valuable results which must follow its faithful execution; and though imposture may seek to profit by credulity and make merchandise of fraud still there remains much to be unearthed, even if the sacred vessels of the temple were not restored to Jerusalem by the Emperor Justinian (as tradition asserts) after having been in the hands Gothic and Vandal Conquerors of Rome itself. Enough has been effected by the imperfect and ill directed attempts to stimulate our curiosity, and impel us to more regularly conducted observations.

The ten days of our stay were insufficient for the most superficial visits to the most obvious objects of interest, and they were made less available by the rain. Our visit to the shop of Shaphira in David's street was very interesting. He shewed us fragments of the Moabite stone and copies of the impression of the inscription which were taken by what are called "squeezes," before it was broken. The process is simply to press forcibly on the object, softened sheets of thick paper while wet, and press them, so that they receive the impressions of the figures, and retain them when dry. It is from these impressions the inscription was deciphered. The sheik of Kerak determined the stone should not be carried away and built a fire around it and when it was heated intensely suddenly cooled it by the affusion of water on it, and thus reduced it to fragments, most of which were afterward gathered up and are in the collections of the curious. We saw there the various articles which have since become subjects of discussion among those who are interested in relics of Jewish Antiquity. I believe Shaphira was himself deceived if they be spurious. He certainly made upon me the impression of honest confidence in their genuine character, and manifested no disposition to induce us to purchase any of the smaller articles which, he could readily have done if he had not thought them what he asserted they were. It would have been easy for him to have sold them at good prices to visitors if he could procure an unlimited supply at the house of the Potter who is accused of making them for him. I believe he bought them under the impression they were genuine and he told us he had an agent in the land of Moab seeking for more.

BEYROOT, SYRIA, April 8, 1872.

My Dear Children:

If ever any one had cause to thank God and take courage, surely we have. The embarkation at Jaffa was made under the most favourable circumstances possible. Not a ripple, even, on the surface of the water. Your mother and I were favoured by having a boat to ourselves with the brother of the dragoman, and Friezier to wait upon us alone. Your dear mother was most signally favoured in the calm, passive, submissive feeling which pervaded our souls during the entire morning.

We had attended the religious services of the German Templars, and were most pleasantly impressed by the solid, intelligent appearance of the congregation. Men and women sat apart, and I have never been in an assembly in which the deportment of the people was more calculated to impress one with their honest, sincere and intelligent devotion. One man presided and led the services, and six others sat near him, and two of them participated by prayer and preaching. The name of "Jesus" and "the blood of Jesus," and "the power of the Holy Ghost," were so often invoked in prayer and referred to in the teaching that I have no hesitation in receiving the conviction that, whatever aberrations there may be from what we think the way, they "build on the Apostles and Prophets, Jesus Christ himself being the chief corner-stone." They evidently sang with the spirit and understanding, and though I could not understand the preaching, I could follow in some degree the chapter in Corinthians which was read, and could hear from time to time words which were "of the truth." Nor was there any manifestation of fanatical enthusiasm; all was done decently and in order.

So soon as we returned from this meeting we were summoned to embark, and on our way met the Reverend Dr. Adams, of Andover, on his way from his encampment outside the gate to conduct a religious service at the American Consul's. The party had just arrived and were on their way up to Jerusalem. We would gladly have participated, but could not tarry. Your mother and I were carried into the boat and rowed out to the steamer. All was calm, and there was no difficulty nor excitement; yet so disturbed was the action of your dear mother's heart that I was *terribly* alarmed lest it should not recover, and most thankful to find that after a time it became quiet under the influence of some aromatic spirits of ammonia, so that before the others arrived on board, she was able to speak to them. We had been favoured to receive good cabins so far as Constantinople, so that the anxiety lest we should be compelled to land here was removed, and we were able to enjoy some Sabbath stillness on board.

We found among our fellow passengers to this place a Reverend Mr. Wynkoop and his wife, formerly of Wilmington, Delaware, who have been around the world, having come to India by San Francisco and Japan and China, to visit a son who is a missionary at Allahabad, and are now on their way home across Europe and the Atlantic—very nice people, and knowing the Lattimers and Halls and Merediths, so that we had a pleasant afternoon and evening of Christian social intercourse. Our state-rooms are very comfortable—the ladies all *in one*; your uncle and Holly, Mr. Longstreth and myself in that adjoining.

Our fellow passengers have not been so happy, and are compelled here to give way to one of the great travelling parties (nearly fifty in number), which has secured the possession of all the accommodation from this place (beyond that we occupy), which had been taken for us from Alexandria. We do not anticipate any pleasure from the addition, as one party (who came from Jaffa here) had left London with that company, and found it so unpleasant that they preferred to forfeit their share and travel on their own account, and say that nothing would induce them to stay on board with that party. The comfort of not being obliged to land and embark again will reconcile your mother and myself to *much*.

Our voyage here was very smooth. At about midnight we stopped at Haifa, at the foot of Mt. Carmel, where we landed some German Templars who have a settlement there, and took on board the Prince and Princess of Lichtenstein, who had occupied the chambers adjoining ours at Jerusalem, and had come overland by Carmel to take the boat here. I was on deck as we arrived, but nothing was to be seen but the lights and the dim outline of Mr. Carmel, though much was to be heard in the noise of the boatmen. I went to bed again and betook myself to slumber till the dawning day awakened me in time to see the sun rise over Lebanon and Hermon as we passed the sites of Tyre and Sidon. Our vessel coasted along within sight of the shore and soon the snowy range of Hermon came in view; and at about 9 A. M. we saw Beyroot lying beautifully on the sloping shore, with its Consulates and Consular flags greeting the eyes of the travellers of various nations, each rejoicing at the sight of his own bunting. A strong sirocco (or south wind) blew, *stifling with its heat* and carrying the sand of the desert in clouds before it.

By 10 A. M. all who were to land had gone ashore and the through passengers sat down to an European *déjeuner a la fourchette* with its meat and wine, instead of good tea and coffee and hot cakes. The other members of our party have disposed of themselves till dinner time, 4 P. M., some ashore; some asleep; your mother at her knitting; and I writing to you. The snow clad heights of Lebanon look tantalizing, not refreshing. I told Friezier if he saw any ice to bring a fragment for your mother, but she countermanded the order, saying she had learned to do without, and would rather not know how good it is till she can indulge not once only but continually.

We are more than ever thankful that we are not compelled to land and wait here a fortnight *at least*, perhaps more, before we could advance further, and I hope your aunt Mary herself is reconciled to the abandonment of the trip to Damascus, which offers no compensation for a *fifteen hours continuous ride* there, and the same back, beyond the empty gratification of saying one has visited the city which was the scene of the conversion of the Apostle to the Gentiles; and was the birthplace of the favourite servant of the patriarch Abraham. Good as are the waters of Abana and Pharpar, and beautiful as are the almond and apricot groves and vineyards of Damascus, they present nothing to compensate for the fatigue. We could not go safely to Palmyra. Antioch and Aleppo have recently suffered from an earthquake and we trust we shall be favoured to get safely to Constantinople, there to be brought once more into communication with you.

The coast as we approach Beyroot is beautiful. The lower slopes green, the mountain heights sublime, the snowy ranges beautiful. The town itself stands amid pleasant looking gardens with its massive structures connected with the modern missionary enterprize, chiefly American colleges, hospitals, schools and private residences, presenting the appearance of great comfort and even some pretension to elegance and solidity. These of course are trifling compared to what they were when Tyre and Sidon were the commercial emporia of the world, and Asiatic Greeks controlled the destinies of mankind. Desolation has brooded over the land and obliterated the cities. This is now the new focus from which the light of the everlasting gospel is to be shed abroad once more in these later days in this its cradle land.

CYPRUS, ISLE OF CYPRUS, Tuesday, April 9, 1872.

I found it impossible to continue my letter as the public cabin was the only place at which one could write, with all the disturbances incident to the coming and going and irregular conversation. Your uncle Wistar and aunt Mary, etc., went ashore at Beyroot leaving your aunts Hannah and Jane, and your mother and myself. They found nothing of special interest and returned oppressed with the heat and dust of the Sirocco, which blew violently. They report the buildings solid and the gardens and trees about the houses very attractive.

Toward evening the Cook's excursion party, numbering nearly fifty persons, came on board and everything was in a bustle till they were settled in their several apartments; which was effected much more readily than I had supposed possible. Among them are some Americans and I fell in with a Rev. Dr. Patterson of Chicago, who knows many of my acquaintances and friends, Mr. Stuart (of course) and dear Mellie; and the McMillans and C. Stuart Patterson. So it is, go where one will one finds evidences that the world is too small to escape from the responsibility of one's actions. At Jerusalem one claims my acquaintance as having been a patient; at Jaffa I caught Friezier giving advice to a young man to wash with rose water an eye which had been wounded by a stone, thrown out of the foot of a horse cantering before him, which had broken his glasses and cut the conjunctiva, and, on interposing with the advice of a physician, was told that I was not unknown having attended his friends in Philadelphia, and found him related to Mr. Ingham who married Miss Hall. Then there came on board at Jaffa and sailed with us to Beyrott the Mr. W. to whom I believe I referred before.

Our voyage from Beyroot to this place was made during the night. The wind was high and this morning all who attempted to move became very seasick, your mother and myself among the number. She is now dressing and will come on deck. The Cook party has gone ashore. I see nothing to attract one. The mountains are very repulsive looking. Some palm trees indicate that the climate is warm as they will not grow where there is winter. There are some other trees, apparently olive, but no indication of culture, though as wine is exported there must be vine culture some where. The dim shadows of its past greatness float into my memory. In the days of the Ptolemies it was a kingdom subsidiary to that of Egypt, and the place of safety to which they sent their treasures and to which they escaped each from the cruelty and treachery of the other. It was the landing place of Roman armies and the scene of plots of Roman generals. In the days of the crusades it was the scene of actions which made it celebrated, and it was one of the possessions of Venice in the days of her glory. Like every other possession of the Turk it is now in decay. The Cook party has landed, so when they return we may learn from some of them what they see.

The boys will think I have forgotten my little store of classic lore if I say nothing of the Paphian Queen who was fabled to be here born from the foam of the sea, and to have found here her first resting place on earth. However brilliant may be the influence of Apollo or beautiful the fabled Venus, seasickness casts a dark pall over the imagination and deadens the power of memory.

A more interesting association with the island is the visit of Barnabas and Paul, who landing at Salamis, then a great city, and passing through the island to Paphos, found there a Roman Deputy who was converted to the faith after Elymas the Sorcerer had been stricken with blindness.

The beauty of the voyage in fine weather must be enchanting. No one can appreciate the Grecian history, poetry, or mythology, without having made it. Highly as the verbal descriptions may be wrought they do not reach the reality even now, in the absence of all that art once added to the glory of the natural scenery. As we passed one island after another, the entire company of passengers expressing their delight at the varied outlines of the mountains jutting out into the blue sea, sometimes clothed with green and at others grey or brown, a gleam of sunshine would burst through the clouds and light up scenes of exquisite loveliness. In one instance a green plain lay at the foot of the sloping hills, terraced to the top, while on the shore rose a square well-built fortress of great extent, and fine houses dotted the environs, surrounded by rich gardens of olives, figs, and vines. Every one was thrilled with delight at the attractiveness of the island. What was mine on finding I was gazing at Cos the birth place of the healing art; the home of Æsculapius and the Asclepiadæ, and Hippocrates. Certainly no position on the face of the earth could be more appropriate for the location of those temples in which were welcomed the numerous invalids who sought relief from the healing powers of the learned priests, which would be greatly aided by the balmy and yet invigorating atmosphere and the wondrous beauty of earth and sky.

It has other claims to historic fame but I will not draw at second hand on such materials. A young Greek on board was enthusiastic in praises of the present products with which we are ourselves so familiar as the sultana raisin, and the best of the figs which reach us from Smyrna. I was not a little surprised to be told by one of our fellow passengers who had been attempting to converse with this Greek, that he received a "*magazine*" from New York and one also from Boston." I thought it strange as he could not talk any English and I was not aware of the publication in either city of a periodical in modern Greek. All at once it flashed across my mind that he meant to say he was partner in a firm which has warehouses, "*magasins*" in French, in those cities.

If you take the map of the Ægean sea you will realize how thickly strewn are the islands along our route, while the headlands of the coast of Anatolia are never out of view. Then recall the fact that these shores of Asia Minor were the seat of Dorian Grecian culture and art, and of the kingdoms of Coria and Mileteus and Lydia (this latter so famed as that of Crœsus) and you will appreciate the gratification which must be experienced by an intelligent mind well versed in classic lore.

Nor is the rich association of Christian interest wanting. Patmos lies by our way (after passing Cos); the place of banishment of that disciple whom Jesus loved and in which he was favoured with that Apocalypse which contains some of the most precious truths of revelation as well at some of the deep mysteries which have exercised the skill of learned and ignorant alike; though thus far neither has found the key by which satisfactorily to unlock and expose the treasures, hidden till the time appointed.

My seasickness interrupted my notice of the island of Rhodes. Till I saw Cos I thought it might be said to be of peerless beauty. We anchored off the modern town which lies on the side of a hill at the foot of which is the old harbour with its narrow entrance guarded by projecting rocks, on which we are told stood the colossal bronze statue of Apollo, more than 100 feet in height, striding from the one side to the other of the entrance. It was overthrown by an earthquake and the fact is sure that the materials loaded 900 camels.

This island was long held by the knights of St. John and their fortresses and the walls of the town still attest the strength of their establishment, which resisted long the attacks of the Moslem power, and when it was compelled to surrender did so on terms which proved the power it still retained, as the knights were allowed to transport to Malta all their arms and equipments of every kind. The houses still bear sculptured on their fronts the armorial bearings of the knights.

One of our fellow passeners landed to endeavor to procure some specimens of a peculiar pottery (like Majolica) which is to be had here, supposed to have been introduced by the knights. He has some he had purchased from collectors but wished to be able to say he had bought some on the spot. He could find but two broken ones, and was told 11,000 specimens had been shipped. How many of them were genuine the number at once renders doubtful, but when you learn that those of our fellow passengers who purchased coins from traders who came aboard might be seen *shaving them up* in a short time as proof that they were mere imitations (casts in soft metal) buried to give them the necessary appearance of antiquity, you may conclude there is much reason to think that some of the plates may have been modern also, even if cracked. The peasants are said to value the genuine ware as heir-looms ; and hang them on the walls of their houses not parting with them except of necessity.

In ancient times the city of Rhodes was said to have been more beautiful than any other in the world, having being built under the directions of one of the most distinguished architects, and its public edifices were enriched with pictures and statues. Pindar celebrates its grandeur and Caspar and Eff. can turn at least to the ode of Horace which begins, if I remember, with the line " *Claram Rhodon et Mytilenen* " * thus proving that in the days of Augustus it was considered a Newport, or something of that kind. I have learned to have greater respect for the descriptions of the poets than I once had, since I came myself under the spell of the same scenes they describe.

3 A. M. Friday morning, April 12th.

Seasickness obliged me to suspend writing in the midst of the sentence about Majolica ware, and I have resumed it in the harbor of Scio in which we have just cast anchor after a stormy voyage through intricate channels among the islands, often illuminated by the flashes

* *Carmen Vii. Laudabunt alii claram Rhodon aut Mytilenen.*—Eps.

of lightning. Thankful to the good providence of our Father in Heaven who watched over us and guided our pilot. This is a large island about seven miles from the coast of Asia Minor and is associated in my memory with the fearful massacre of its inhabitants by the Turks in my boyhood, in the year 1822. Some of the poor refugees found their way even to our country, and the sad story did much to excite the interest in the revolution which finally resulted in the establishment of the modern kingdom of Greece, which appears to be unable now, after the lapse of nearly half a century, to maintain order even in Athens, its capital. Some of our fellow passengers who had ordered their letters to that city (as we have done ours to Constantinople) are afraid to venture there on account of the stories of brigandage under the very walls of the town, and we know a party of English travellers was murdered within two years. Whether the Greek Republic would have done better, if it had been consonant with the wise politics of European monarchies to support that instead of forcing on the Greeks the maintainence of a foreign monarch, is a question unsettled.

To return to Scio. It is one of the places claiming to be the birth place of Homer, and plays an important part in history from the days of Herodotus to our own. Its people were intelligent, and in modern times given to commerce and literature. They had colleges, hospitals and libraries; and the Greek merchants of India and Europe and our own cities were Sciotes. From some cause it had enjoyed the favor of the Turkish conqueror as it had formerly done of the Roman, and was a sort of apanage of the mother of the reigning Sultan, paying a small tribute in Gum Mastich, which the Turkish ladies chew. It was enticed into the insurrection by the influence of the neighbouring island of Samos, and not by any grievance of its own. It had at the time a population of more than 100,000, enervated by long continued prosperity, and really indifferent to the cause they had embraced, and with no memory of wrongs of their own to avenge. The Turks sent a fleet to the principal town while a large army was carried across the narrow strait from the mainland, and in a short time but 2000 Greeks were left in the ill fated island; 45,000 women and children were sold as slaves.

It is still dark, so that we see nothing but the mountainous outline and the lights of the port; yet our ship is landing and receiving cargo, and in an hour or so we shall start for Smyrna, where we shall stop some twenty-four hours at least, and from which some of us will visit Ephesus, so dear to every Christian soul as the scene of the long and loving labours of the great Apostle to the Gentiles and the seat of the church to which he addressed that epitome of the faith, his Epistle, and to which John sent the warning message from "Him that walketh amid the golden candlesticks," which we so often read and may well lay to heart ourselves.

In coming hither from Rhodes we have passed in the night Icaria (the boys will remember the poor fellow who would fly higher than his father and whose wax-joined wings were loosened by the heat of the sun and he fell into the sea giving his name to this island), and Samos which they will also remember from its having been the kingdom of that Polycrates whose prosperity was so great that Amasis, the King of Egypt, renounced his friendship because he was selfish enough not to wish to share in the misfortune which must befall one so universally successful. You remember he tried to cheat fate by throwing a costly ring into the sea, and was shocked to have it brought to him by his cook, who took it from the mouth of a fish he was preparing for the royal dinner. His riches made him like Croesus, the prey of the Persian conqueror, who treacherously slew the Samian while he took the Lydian king to his court where he held him in an honorable captivity which, if I mistake not, Croesus adorned by his wisdom and virtue. I remember meeting him at the Court of Amasis as the companion of the son of the Persian, Cambyses.

8 A. M. Friday.

We are now with a strong *cold* east wind leaving Scio and Mytilene behind us, and winding our way up the Gulf of Smyrna between a long promontory, projecting ninety miles from the mainland, and numerous islets which fill the gulf. The morning is unpropitious, but we can see how beautiful it must be in sunshine.

11 A. M.

We now have the city in sight and are passing highly cultivated hillsides alternating with granite cliffs, while white tents covering pans for the evaporation of sea water, and little pyramids of salt, line the shore. Many sails give animation to the scene, and but that the rain and cold drive us from the deck, we should find it interesting. Smyrna has as large a place in history, sacred and profane, as any other spot, and is still a place of very active commerce; with a population of mixed nationalities of over 100,000. Rain drives us from the deck and permits only glimpses through the windows, but they reveal mountains of granite with deep dells of varied verdure, and clumps of Genista in full bloom, with its golden color tipping cliffs and flowing down into glades, and forests of pine alternating with cultivated plains and sweet looking villages. Smyrna itself is hid in the clouds at the head of the gulf in which ships are riding, while snow clad mountains rise behind.

Saturday, April 13th.

We arrived at Smyrna yesterday about 11 A. M. in the midst of showers of rain which continued at short intervals during the day. The bay is very beautiful. A perfect harbour, surrounded on every side by hills and mountain ranges with gentle slopes, and green plains nicely cultivated and studded with residences which have all the attractiveness of our own homesteads, as we see them from the water. Square well built houses with gardens, orchards and shrubbery. There is a railroad from this point to Ephesus, fifty miles south on the coast, at the mouth of the river Kayster or rather at what was once its debouchement but now a marsh two miles from the shore. This Railroad runs through a beautiful village, which we passed coming up the bay, at which the British residents here spend their summer months, and where there is an English church and resident clergyman and school. The Salines or salt works on the shore of the bay present a curious appearance, the cones of white salt resembling tents of an encampment.

Soon after our arrival most of us went ashore and under the guidance of a Greek, who speaks some English and French, we sauntered through the town which is divided into several quarters occupied respectively by Greeks, Armenians, Franks, and Musselmen. The streets are narrow, ill paved and muddy, though not defiled as the eastern towns with which we have been so long familiar are; and Jerusalem and Jaffa beyond competition the most foul of all. The bazaars are the same as those of Cairo, divided between the various nations into various trades. The houses in those streets on which the people live are of two stories and have glass windows with lace curtains; and at the doors and on the streets were many white children with European costume and satchels of books, returning from school, while dogs instead of snarling or running away sneakingly, were playing about them. As we passed one open door we caught sight of a court yard in the rear with white spirea and a large glycine hanging its numberless lilac flowers, just as with you it may be doing at this very season, while a large elder bush was covered with a perfect veil of white flowers, more welcome to our eyes here than it would have been in the fence rows at Ivy Neck.

The guide took us to the shop of a dealer in Turkey and Persian rugs and carpets. We saw not one equal to those we have at home and the prices asked were higher than in America even without the freight charges and duties, which would have to be added. As we sauntered along the way we priced other articles of oriental manufacture, slippers embroidered with colored silks and gold thread; and gaudy jackets covered with gold lace, and glaring silk scarfs destitute of beauty. None of them possessed of any value except as specimens of the dress and manufactures of this land so celebrated in story, sacred and profane. But the prices of all were so absurd that we did not for a moment think of purchase. It was evident that our guide took no interest in getting them for us except on terms that would enable him to share in a good bargain with the shop keepers with whom he was in collusion to get all they could from the strangers. Even for the sponges, which are the product of these seas, they asked higher prices than we pay for them in our retail drug stores.

There are a few mosques, some of them built of the broken ruins of Roman and even Grecian temples, but none have any attractions, much less splendour. In front of each is a full flowing fountain fed by mountain streams, brought into the town by the piety of the Moslems, to provide not only drink for the thirsty but the means of ablution before entering the place of prayer.

Many sights strange to our eyes met them at every turn, but none more imposing than the long strings of camels in caravans passing in and out of the customs, laden some with sugar and coffee, going into the interior; and others with cotton, galls, figs, acorns and gums and dye stuffs, coming from the country for shipment to the ports of Europe and America, by steamers which lay in the harbour waiting for their freights. It is the last farewell to these animals, and those we saw here are very superior to the wretched, forbidding, scare-crows with which we have been hitherto familiar. They are larger, better fed, have an entirely different expression of face, and their long necks are clothed with curly hair or wool. The burdens they carry are enormous, but there is none of the terrible growling, snarling and snapping which have been the uniform expression of those of Egypt and Syria whose emaciated forms and scarred and galled backs have rendered them objects of disgust.

11 A. M.

At this point we were summoned to the breakfast table an hour since. You would be amazed to see us partaking in three or four courses of meats, with rice and tomatoes and potatoes; winding up with coffee without cream or sugar. Some Germans who sit across the table add an intermediate course consisting of uncooked salt fish, bologna sausage, oil, lemon juice and Caviare, all mussed together with a knife. Caviare looks like a good rich raspberry jam, and consists of the roe of the sturgeon cooked with syrup and looks very attractive—but oh—the disappointment of the taste! tongue cannot express.

SMYRNA, April 14, 1872.

I was interrupted just now by the summons to breakfast, and now attempt to take up the severed thread of my most discursive story. The camels were passing and repassing, as we wandered through the streets of Smyrna, in long lines, and mingled with them human beasts of burden in the shape of porters, bent forward till they resembled quadrupeds in their posture, the arms hanging down like fore-legs just raised from the ground, while huge packs were piled on saddles on their backs and shoulders. Camels and men seem to be the principal bearers of burdens. Donkeys there were none, and but few horses. Burdens too heavy for one man are slung by ropes to two long poles and borne by four men. Large pipes of wine and bales of cotton were thus swung along, and in the narrow ways it required perpetual watchfulness to avoid the one or the other. The doors and window-shutters of the houses are all sheathed with iron plates, thus mutely giving testimony to the reign of violence rather than of law. But our eyes were gladdened by the sight to which they have been long unused; of the door-knockers and handles and bell-pulls, western substitutes for the clapping of hands of Orientals.

Large as is the predominance of white faces—Greek and Armenian as well as Italian—some of our fellow-passengers had alarming proof that they were not under the protection of Christian law. Some of them, wandering off, were pelted with stones by boys, and on one of them striking a boy with his umbrella he was assailed by a shower of stones, and a man seized him by the throat and drew his dagger on him, demanding "backsheesh." Firmness and coolness and the access of some of his friends saved him, and he was allowed to return to the ship, having learned practically that it is safer not to mind a few stones or curses in lands where the crescent rules over the cross. The only point in which he could suppose he had violated their prejudices was in walking through a Mohammedan Cemetery.

We returned to the ship to dinner at 5 P. M., thoroughly wearied, so that I went from the table to bed and slept till this morning, when we were all disturbed at an early hour to prepare for an excursion by railroad to Ephesus. The day is so wet and cold that despite my earnest desire to visit the seat of one of the oldest towns in historic period, the scene of some of the most interesting legends of heathen mythology and profane history, as well as one of the spots most endeared to the Christian soul by the occurrence here of events second only in importance to those occurring at Jerusalem, I exercise sufficient self-control to remain with your mother.

I enjoy greatly an occasional outlook on the town, much more attractive as it rises on the hillside before the eye than it is to the feet of the visitor. Just behind it a noble grove of Oriental cypress raises its black green spires over the Mohammedan Cemetery, and still higher a ruined fortress commands the harbour; while the sunlight, breaking here and there through rifts in the black drizzling clouds, casts its life-giving splendour on the distant hillsides, revealing the varied shades of their cultured slopes and forest-crowned tops. It is a magnificent panorama, and must have been still more so when from Patmos St. John addressed the angel of the church; or Polycarp ruled in its councils, comforted its confessors and martyrs with the words he had himself heard from the lips of the loved and loving Apostle, and finally sealed here himself his Faith by the sufferings of Martyrdom.

The ruined fortress to which I have just alluded contains still on its walls portions supposed to be of Cyclopean work, and its most modern portion certainly was built by the Byzantine Emperors. In it they show the church and grave of Polycarp. The walls, as we see them from the deck, present very much the appearance, and have about the same height, and enclose the same area as those of Cherry Hill prison.

The harbour presents an animated scene. Sailing vessels with the Greek striped flag, and steamers, Austrian, French and Turkish, lie at short distances from each other; while heavy lighters, carrying coal and merchandise, are mingled with light and graceful boats gliding from ship to ship. Much cotton is shipped from here still, and before it was so largely grown in the United States this was the largest cotton port in the world.

I have derived great gratification from learning the direct relations to each other of various points of interest in Grecian, Roman and Sacred history. We sailed past Miletus, to which St. Paul summoned the elders of the church of Ephesus, and where he delivered to them the address which is more replete with pathetic eloquence than any on record. Cæsarea, Ptolemais, Tyre and Sidon, Antioch, Seleucia, Salamis, Paphos, Patara, Coos, Rhodes, are all names familiar as household words, yet giving no idea of the relation of these places; points of interest in Apostolic journeys. Now they stand to me the representatives of places, and will call up hereafter associations with the spots, and to-morrow we leave for Troas, where St. Paul left his cloak and parchments, and Tenedos, to which the Greek fleet withdrew, while their guileful horse was drawn through the battered wall of Troy. This very town of Smyrna had its Homerion and boasted of its connection with the father of poetry, claiming to be his birthplace. Athens is but a few hours distant across the Ægean. Some of our fellow-voyagers have left for its classic soil this morning, notwithstanding the report of the disturbed condition of the neighbourhood, making it unsafe even to visit the Acropolis.

As I could not make the excursion with our party to that sacred spot I have taken the opportunity of looking over the notice of Ephesus in Murray's handbook. The ruins found there are very scarce and widely scattered without any interest in their present condition, but just enough to confirm the statements we have of the riches and grandeur of the place.

Effingham will remember it as the place where his friend Hannibal, after his reverses of fortune, met Antiochus; and where Cicero reports that the citizens honored him with games in the theatre. That theatre has been exhumed lately and has proved capable of seating 76,000 spectators of such games. Temples without number to every god in the Greek and Roman mythology, adorned its area with their columns of sixty feet high, some of them monolithic; and one lying, the solitary representative of some forty others with which it was associated, has flutes large enough to allow a man to walk in one of them without difficulty. The great temple of Diana, seven times burned; and the eighth, 200 years in building, having 120 columns, considered the wonder of the world, burned finally by Herostratus (to procure immortality for his name as the consumer of so much wealth and splendour), has left not a wreck behind ; nor of all the statues of gods and emperors, which must have been accumulated in these glorious temples, is there a fragment left.

Ephesus was one of the many spots claiming to be the birth-place of Apollo and Latona, and the special abode of Diana or Artemis, "whose statue fell down from Jupiter out of heaven." It was represented as covered with breasts to convey the idea of the source of life and nourishment to man ; and the priests are reported to have murdered the sculptors by whom it was made to prevent them claiming the honor of the work.

At Ephesus was born Apelles, who painted a portrait of Alexander the Great for the temple of Diana, and who has left a name which none may challenge as *the painter*. There was a school of painting and sculpture at Ephesus which had no rival, and it claimed to be the birth-place of Homer.

I shall wait the return of your uncle to hear from him what he saw. From the description of books, I infer that nothing has yet been discovered beyond the seats of the Theatre and Stadium, and some tombs, and stones of a cyclopean wall, all scattered over an area of many miles ; thus testifying to the extent, as history does to the riches, of the city.

It was here St. Paul, during more than two years, supported himself by working at his trade as tent-maker, and where he displayed his apostolic power by his miracles. It was also the seat of a school of magic, and the accounts given by profane authors of its riches confirm the truth of the statement made by St. Paul of the value of the books of magic burned there by those who abandoned their magic rites and became followers of the Apostle, working with his own hands that he might have to give to him that needed, instead of using his miraculous gifts to impose upon the credulous and rob the deluded.

Timothy was bishop of Ephesus, and tradition associates the beloved disciple with it as his place of abode after his return from banishment at Patmos. It is here that the legend of the young man who turned robber, after having been a disciple of St. John, is located, and they show still the cavern in which the seven young Christians slept safely during two hundred years of persecution, and waked only to die the same day that they entered the once pagan, then Christian, city. Mahomet adopted this legend, which has a still earlier pagan germ— and the name of the sleepers are even now graven on stones and set in rings and sold as amulets in Smyrna.

PERGAMOS, Lord's Day, April 14, 1872.

Assos, Mytilene, Troas, such are the places (names how familiar to our ears and dear to our hearts from the earliest dawn of intelligence) by which we have been passing this morning. Yesterday was wet and cold, and we were obliged, after leaving Smyrna, to keep within the saloon. About midnight we reached the port of Lesbos or Mytilene, and lay there in the dark, taking in and discharging freight and passengers, with a noise of tongues which was louder and more penetrating than that of winds and waves. About 3 A. M. we got under way again, and at dawn I took my solitary walk on the upper deck watching the advancing day and the progress of our noble ship through this beauteous sea.

The loftiest attainment of poetry can reach no higher than to clothe in appropriate words the description of the simple facts of nature; and while one feels the spell of poetry more strongly *here*, amid scenes made familiar by the words of the most gifted of uninspired poets, and would wash with bitter tears the shame of having failed to treasure in one's memory his sounding lines and melodious words when in youth the opportunity was wasted which the sighs of age cannot now recall; yet even this mortification yields place to the delight of watching the glowing work of the great Alchemist as the rising sun converts into streams of molten gold the dull, leaden clouds which rest above the dark forms of the mountains of Mysia, and empurples them, as one by one they emerge from the darkness in which they have been shrouded, while the green slopes of Lesbos laugh under the softer influence of his silvery rays. And then comes the thought that this promontory is that across which St. Paul was "minded to go a-foot" from Troas, on his memorable journey back from Macedonia and Achaia bound in spirit to be at Jerusalem at the feast.

The waters of the Ægean are blue indeed; and the gentle waves this morning literally kiss the smiling shores, and *we* are highly favoured thus at the even tide of life to enjoy the privilege of visiting the lands made familiar by song to the ears of our youth, and still more precious as sacred to our hearts from their association with that Faith which is the anchor of our souls; the *comfort* of our present; the hope of our future life.

The report of the party who went yesterday to Ephesus reconciled us to the disappointment I have felt in not being able to stand in the temple of Diana, or the Theatre in which was assembled the furious crowd of worshippers of the many-breasted Goddess. The excavations being made have as yet not developed any *standing* ruins. Mr. Wood, who is conducting them, pointed out a pool of water, collected by the recent rains, which covers *seven feet deep* the capitals of a row of columns which he has uncovered, and which he believes to be a part of the great temple; and they saw the two theatres, in one of which undoubtedly was held the tumultuous meeting which "by the space of two hours" expended its force in vain vociferations: "Great is Diana of the Ephesians." Beyond this they saw nothing but broken fragments of columns and statues, some of white and some of many-coloured marbles—enough and widely-scattered, to prove the opulence and size of the place was not exaggerated by Greek and Roman writers, and yet nothing to exhibit any remaining traces of that greatness.

We are now passing the Troad or site of Troy; and Tenedos raises its cone-like summit amid the blue waters of the sea on the left, while beautiful white sails give animation to the scene and make one think of the day when the fleets of Greece floated over it like a flock of gulls, wearied with the ten years' siege in which they must have worn out their cordage and sails and rotted their hulls so that one need not wonder at the mis-adventures of their return.

3 P. M.

Soon after our breakfast we had worship and a sermon in the saloon, conducted by a Scotch Presbyterian clergyman. During that time we entered the Dardanelles, and are now steering rapidly toward the sea of Marmora, which we hope to cross during the night and reach Constantinople early in the morning. The sails in the strait are very numerous. I think as many as thirty large vessels were in sight at one time. The hillsides are stony but cultivated. Snowy peaks rise in the distance, and the wind is cold. I shall leave this room just to add a line on our arrival. Only now uttering the blessed prayer, "*Peace be with you all*"; that peace which Jesus gives and He only can give.

CONSTANTINOPLE, April 15th.

We arrived safely here this morning, and have only room to express our grateful acknowledgment to you all for your letters down to the 19th ult., and pray you to unite with us in thanks to our merciful God for His goodness to us, as we do for His great mercy to you in the preservation of dear Hannah and the restoration of dear Mellie. Wm. Stuart will be a welcome addition to the sweet circle of our loved grandchildren. Much love to one and all.

CASPAR MORRIS.
(But not signed.—EDS.)

CONSTANTINOPLE, April 16, 1872.

My Dear Children:

I find your father has filled his sheet, and so I will write independently and tell you how thankful we feel to be on European soil again, and so within more ready access to you all. We have been most wonderfully cared for in our travels, and we all feel it.

Yesterday after the Doctor had written to you, and we were comfortably housed, having had some difficulty in procuring accommodations, he left me to take a bath. As he stayed longer than I thought it necessary I was getting a little anxious, when he came into the room and *fell on the bed, greatly oppressed*—it had come on suddenly after dressing; no pain, but difficulty of breathing, stricture across the chest, unable to use the arms. I applied mustard which was at hand, gave brandy, sent for the best English physician, but his distress was so great that he told me to give him morphia by injecting it. He was entirely himself, which was a great comfort, and directed all that was to be done and was quite relieved before the doctor got here, which was three hours. Slept well last night, and is this morning *quite well*, and oh! I do feel so thankful; but I can't be as much so as I ought. While the attack lasted 'twas very alarming. The old doctor's visit was a great relief when he did get here, and he is to see us again to-day; he *said* to make a further acquaintance and give some general directions.

We could not account at all for this attack unless it was exhaustion. He had not slept much the week we were on board the steamer and had taken very little food. We shall be here a week now, and then travel slowly and will try to trust all will be well with us. Of course we have *everything* that love or money can procure.

I am sorry to have to be the bearer of this kind of intelligence, but I must tell all or not write at all, and now, my dear children, our hearts are overflowing with thankfulness for the preservation of both Han. and Mellie.

We found here a nice parcel of letters from you, and wish I could answer each; but cannot, so I know you will each take your full portion of love as though this was to each separately. I have not words to express my feeling that the Syrian trip is over, but am beginning to see that I shall hereafter look back at it with pleasure. It has been a *great* real enjoyment to your father, mingled with so much *feeling* and anxiety also that perhaps that has helped too to exhaust him.

It is so cold here in the house that it is almost impossible to keep warm with wraps; no fire, and the house is like a vault, so will take carriages and see what the sun will do. Of course your father goes with us, for I would not leave him, but I am admonished it is time to close for the mail, so farewell. A most hearty welcome for little W. Stuart from us all. We like his name too; and love to his mother and thanks for her letter; though I would not have let her write if I had been by.

Yours most truly and affy.,
A. C. MORRIS.

I sometimes think you will think I give a dark picture. I *try* to give it as *it is*, and am supported through my trials and anxieties. We think it right to remain with the party. We are very glad to hear Han. will have Mrs. Hill with her this summer; the arrangement looks to us just the thing for them. The trial of the servants must have been very trying to Han. Our next will tell of the sentence.

CONSTANTINOPLE, April 15, 1872.

My Dear Brother (Galloway Cheston.—Eds.) :

Your two letters met us here this morning, and though we have not yet got a room to rest in, I am so happy to be able to relieve your anxiety about us by reporting our safe arrival in Europe, and our preservation from the perils of the way thus far, and deliverance from our fears, that I lose no time in addressing you, having merely added a P. S. to my journal letters to my children.

You will have gathered from the tone of our last letters that the eastern part of our tour was not entered on without much anxiety and discussion, and some feeling of trial. God has been better to us than our fears, and though we have suffered enough to justify them we can now look back with thankfulness to Sister Mary that her determination carried the point, and with regret that my anxiety should have betrayed me into the earnest opposition I offered which added to the trouble of the others. It is certainly one of those privileges for which I feel deeply thankful that my feet have stood "within thy walls, oh Jerusalem!" Our strong aversion to landing at Beyroot led Anne and myself to determine at all events to come on to this place, even if it must have been by second-class passage. We urged that the others should carry out their proposed plan and go to Damascus. But they decided on their own account to omit that trip, as it would, of necessity, involve two days' travel in *diligence*, each trip of 14 hours without stopping, and the risk of detention at Beyroot on their return from Damascus, on account of the great crowd of travellers at this season. (There were 70 first-class passengers on the Austrian Lloyds this trip, and they would not engage to take us next trip.) All this would be incurred for the mere gratification of looking at the valley of the Abana and Pharpar, and saying we had seen the oldest city mentioned in history, and the hole in the wall through which tradition reports St. Paul to have been lowered when he escaped from persecution in that city. It brings us two weeks too early here, where the peach trees are just putting out their bloom, and will take us into the wintry cold of Germany.

We are all well, and that is call for profound thankfulness, and still more should that feeling abound for good news from home. Your last letter gives us reason to hope that dear Margaret may improve, though we have felt for some months past great anxiety for both her and you, and even now cannot divest ourselves of the feeling that there still remain many weeks of weather, not doubtful but surely unpleasant and treacherous, before it settles into that genial spring which will enable her to derive pleasure and advantage from driving. We cannot shut out the conviction which daily stares us in the face that our days on earth are rapidly drawing to a close; and our earnest prayer is that we may be kept in our travels, and you, amid anxieties and sicknesses, and permitted once more to exchange on earth those personal expressions of love which are so precious to us in our mortality, and I am warned daily by my infirmities of the need of seeking for the influences of Divine grace that I may be kept from falling, and grow in meekness for that heavenly home into which none can enter except those who have washed their robes and made them white in the blood of the Lamb and who, dwelling in Him by Faith, have His Spirit dwelling in them and bringing everything into captivity to the law of Christ.

Much love to dear Margaret from Anne and myself. We sympathize deeply with her in the trial of her patience—that crowning grace. The message to the church of Ephesus which applies itself with special power to us just now promises great blessing to those that *overcome*. To overcome we must have difficulty with which to contend, and I know of nothing but Divine power which can enable her to overcome in the long, weary conflict she is called to carry on with weakened frame and nervous exhaustion. But it is a blessed thing to *know* that all is measured out by a Father's love and the wisdom of God, and that the strength of omnipotence is ours to call on, and ever ready at our faintest appeal.

Our voyage here through the Isles of the Ægean sea would have been most delightful had it not been rainy and cold. In fine weather the beauty of the shores and the sacred and classic association of the various places at which we stopped, or by which we sailed, must render it a trip of great enjoyment. The passage through the Dardanelles into the sea of Marmora was very attractive, and at day dawn this morning we found ourselves approaching the mouth of the Bosphorus, and the rising sun shed its first rays on the domes and minarets of this city, which rises grandly from the shores of the Golden Horn; houses standing tier upon tier, not, as I had supposed, with gardens and flat roofs and terraces, but in solid blocks and squares with only enough arcades and projecting windows to give an Oriental tone to the European body. We have yet, of course, seen nothing, and shall rest to-day without attempting anything.

You will have sympathized strongly with our children in the trying circumstances through which they have passed, both Cheston and Galloway. It is certainly one of the most mysterious affairs I have ever known. How any one could imperil the life of such a woman as Hannah and the happiness of such a master as Galloway, I cannot conceive; and for dear Cheston and his children to have suffered a second bereavement would have been a terrible blow. We can only take up songs of thanksgiving and find new incentives to faithful and diligent and earnest devotion of heart and life to the service of so loving a Lord.

We learn by our letters from London that our passages are taken for the Scotia (the same vessel by which we crossed this way) on the 12th of October. This will prolong our detention beyond *our* desire, especially as I care nothing for Paris and London, and not much for any other place on this side of the Atlantic, and our hearts yearn over our children and our home.

We have come north rather early, and must linger a few weeks without going further into the cold. June will find us in England probably, and July and August in Scotland. The return is postponed till October in order to avoid the September gales. Thus, if Wistar's present programme is adhered to, a long weary period of exile is still before us. But we will not make it longer by any indulgence in murmuring by the way, but hope and trust that in October we shall be permitted to unite in thanksgiving for mercies.

Make my affectionate regards to Mr. John B. Morris. We both feel deeply for his severe distress, and pray that he may find grace to help in his time of need.

With love to dear Margaret, on behalf of Anne and myself, and kindest regards to Dr. Thomas and the various friends around you, and an especial message of kindest affection to Mary Ellen, with earnest prayers for her restoration. We will do our best to execute your commissions.

    Your affectionate brother,

                        CASPAR MORRIS.

                    CONSTANTINOPLE, April 16, 1872.

My Dear Children:

We have at length reached a point where we can endeavor to gather up the odds and ends of the skein which has been tangled and knotted for some weeks past, and has required to be cut at several points, as no skill could wind it off. Now this will account for the irregular and uncertain current of our letters. I have written and mailed from time to time—often very hurriedly—the most connected record I could frame of our proceedings; having, as I now do, distributed the sheets in envelopes directed to the one or the other (indiscriminately), believing that we "have all things in common," and that each would take to himself or herself the *whole love*, allowing the other to do the same, and wishing each to do so. There is no *share* for any *one*—each has all my heart is capable of producing or containing.

The time in travel is so imperatively occupied every moment in the demands of that moment, that there is no opportunity for indulgence in any thought beyond or behind. Therefore you will find no expression of feelings not attached to the scenes and incidents passing at the time. This does not justify the apprehension that there is no other. The little things which float show only the drift of the surface current. The deep body of waters is unmoved beneath. In that deep bosom you one and all abide in our love.

We have been much moved by the accounts of dear Hannah's illness, and dear Mellie's danger, and thank them both for their precious letters which have confirmed our faith in the precious conviction that God has been very gracious to us. So with dear Mary's letters which have reached us in due order and regularity. We feel much for the isolation of herself and Harry, and address our common letters to those of you who reside in town only because there are more of you collected there.

Our dear grandchildren will please believe us that no letters are more acceptable than theirs, which, one and all, from those of Tyson and Effingham and Cornelia, down to those of Henry J. and Sallie and Annie (including between these extremes of age all the intermediate ones) have been great gratifications to us. We have them in our hearts, but have not the time to answer them. They must take their share of the common letters. We will have separate accounts to settle when we get home, and are meanwhile happy in the belief they are all improving. We feel that we are very rich in such a family to love and who love us.

I hope all my Nile letters have reached you safely; I have no idea of what they contain, beyond the knowledge that they are the continued series of photographs of my passing impressions, and I shall hope to review them with you some day. Your letters are all treasured as the "obverse," to use the language of numismatists, so that if it please our Heavenly Father that we meet on earth we can put them together. The great benefit of coin-collecting is the light they throw on history. These two impressions will be (when combined) our history as a family for this year; one thus far marked by signal mercies. Let us confide in the same wisdom, love and power for the time before us.

As regards our business concerns, we leave them as we did at parting, and pray that God may bless you each in your personal relations, and believe that you will do what is best for our general interests. We could not advise you. It was a relief to us to learn that Galloway has made no change, and we hope by this time that he and dear Hannah are again in their sweet home. We have seen none to be coveted for them in comparison.

Your dear mother is writing to some of you, and the time has come to close, so with much love to one and all—children and grandchildren—from No. 1 to No. 16, inclusive,

       Your loving father,

                      CASPAR MORRIS.

                      CONSTANTINOPLE, April 17, 1872.
My Dear Children :

I wrote you hastily soon after our arrival, giving you the impression made by the approach from the sea of Marmora. The sun rose beautifully over the hills of Bithynia, and illuminated the spires and domes of the imperial city as it rose tier above tier, from the margin of the flood, while on either side stretched out the quietly swelling hills with their kiosks and gardens.

We have not yet settled the topographical relations of the several parts of the city, though we spent yesterday morning driving in the environs, which is the best method of accomplishing this. Stamboul is the Turkish quarter. Pera Galata, Top-hanch and Buyukdereh are several suburbs which surround an inlet from the Bosphorus called the Golden Horn, while Scutari spreads itself over the projecting hill on the other side of the strait. From the heights above Pera the view is very wide and very imposing. The Bosphorus winds among dark hills toward the Black Sea on the one hand, while on the other the port of Constantinople opens out into the sea of Marmora, with its seven islands (called the islands of the princes) in the distance, and countless ships and steamers, either lying in the harbor or giving animation to the sea as they enter or depart.

The hill-sides were covered with the *exquisite little daisy*, known with us as the English daisy, but which certainly is here in its native home and its original purity and loveliness; and J. Mason Good's poem burst spontaneously from my lips as, at my request, the driver brought me a handful that I might be assured the white covering of the hills was not the crystals of snow, but the petals of flowers. The "green cup," the "wiry stem," the "*purple* bud," the "gold embossed gem," "that set in silver gleams within," are all true to nature, and while each flower is not much larger than a small gold dollar, the myriads in which it is scattered "o'er hill and dale" literally make them white as snow in the distance. While our eyes and hearts feasted on their loveliness, we are not unmindful of other attractions, artificial as well as natural.

The environs are hilly, and every hill-side presents some extensive building, to our inquiries about each of which we heard the unvarying reply, "an artillery barrack" a "cavalry barrack," a "military school" or a "military hospital," or some other of the numberless tokens of the military despotism which rules the Ottoman Empire, supported as it is *only* by the mutual jealousies of other nations, neither of which is willing that this seat of ancient empire and *actual power* should fall into the hands of any rival. Public gardens and promenades are planned and in process of planting, and many fine drives are laid out, on which Greeks and Armenians, as well as Europeans, are erecting fine residences on points which command extensive views. Neither Naples nor New York can boast of more beautiful environs. But when we get into the narrow streets and amid the miserable dwellings the glory is all tarnished; and if this is true as regards Pera, the residence of Europeans and of foreign ambassadors, which is the only quarter we have yet seen, what shall we find the Turkish quarter? Friezier had engaged rooms for us in the hotel of Mr. Messiri, which is the only one here of much repute. But on our arrival we found the Grand Duke of Mecklenburg-Schweringen was as large as his name is long and ugly and hard to pronounce, and had made it still more repulsive to us by monopolizing the apartments we had engaged. Mr. Messiri kindly gave us the use of one of his rooms in which to read our letters (which he handed to us), while Friezier sought other apartments, and then gave us a breakfast which aggravated our disappointment by its delicacy and elegance. There was, however, no help; for we of the sovereign people were compelled to give way to them, sovereign by right of birth; and right happy were we when Friezier returned with the welcome information that he had secured good apartments in the Hotel de Ville de Pesthe, which, though less elegant, gives us very good meals, comfortable beds, and tolerable attendance. It is on the main street of Pera, and our windows open out with projecting balconies, so that we have a fine opportunity to notice all that passes by when we are within. Pera is, as I have already mentioned, the quarter occupied by Europeans.

We landed on the shore, and were at once surrounded by porters ready to transport our luggage. Those of you who have not seen the size of our trunks will not be able to appreciate our astonishment at finding they were to be carried by men on their backs up the steep and long ascent from the shore to the top of the lofty hill. Each porter has on his hips a saddle fastened by straps around the shoulders, and when his load is placed on it he appears more like a quadruped than a biped. His body is bent forward until it forms a *right* angle with his legs, and his hands and arms hang down. I have seen three empty tierces piled on one man, three large, thick-panelled pine doors on another, a large lot of undressed lumber on a third, and our twelve porters had something like two dozen packages, large travelling trunks well packed, and bags and bundles heaped upon them.

We certainly formed a strange procession as we struggled wearily up the ascent. The houses through which we passed are of wood, with projecting balconies nearly touching each other from the opposite sides of the street, so that the extension of fires, by which, year after year, this quarter of Constantinople has been visited, is not to be wondered at. The new houses on main streets are of marble and stone, and many of them very elegant, but in other places they are of wood and very slight. In some places they remind me of the shanties on the grand avenues at Galesville, and we have all been struck by the resemblance some of the old ones have to those which, when we left home, deformed the western squares of Market Street, which were slowly disappearing, and we hope may have entirely disappeared by this time.

I have been led away from the porters by the houses. The muscular development of their legs is very disproportioned to that of the rest of their bodies. They stand out large and strong like those of our draught horses. These we do not see at all. Some few oxen and buffaloes are occasionally met. Pack horses are used to remove earth and rubbish.

Private carriages are numerous and elegant. Fiacres, or Turkish hacks, are frequent—round bodies, tube like looking affairs, hung on jacks, with low wheels and creaking axles, their tops often gilded and ornamented; they lumber along over the rough pavement shaking well whoever is unfortunate enough to get into them. European ladies drive themselves in elegant little phaetons with a liveried servant seated behind with folded arms, as in our fashionable drives, while Oriental ladies, Greek and Circassian beauties, very richly dressed, ride in broughams or coupés, exhibiting the white muslin veils carefully folded above and below, so that only the eyes are uncovered; but the perfect white and brilliant rose color seen through the delicate folds of muslin impresses me with the conviction that the complexions are renewed each time before they take the air, and not due to *its renovating power*, but rather to pink saucers and *émail de Paris*. However this may be, they are truly beautiful, and the little children are like cherubs.

7.30 A. M.

You would certainly laugh at the interruption which here created a hiatus in my letter. Your mother had been, as she always is, very successful in her *sporting* expeditions night and morning (not to mention occasional diversions during the day), and I had congratulated her on the good night and the hope for the day. I had achieved my toilet, and was writing while she was making hers, when the torment became too great to be endured with silence, and at her suggestion I laid aside my pen and deliberately laid open the spot which indicated the last repast, when she pounced on the marauder with a shout of exultation equal to that with which a good shot at canvas-backs might be signalized off Long Neck, and safely deposited an enormous *flea* in the basin for my satisfaction. They are much less numerous than on the Nile or in the Holy Land, but we do not hope to become accustomed to the torture or exempt from the torture till we get home.

I may now return to the streets. Nothing attracts me more than the splendid horses, full-blooded, perfectly broken, and groomed so carefully that their silken coats are like mirrors. They stand for hire ready saddled at almost every corner. Their clean, strong limbs and sound little feet supporting bodies of perfect symmetry, with graceful necks and delicate heads, and eyes quick but gentle, and perfect ears. They are black, white and sorrel in color, occasionally a bright bay. Their movements have all the grace of the most accomplished master of ceremonies in a ball room, and as in our drives we have seen the young ladies and gentlemen riding, I have not been able to restrain my enthusiasm. There is a spring and elasticity in their motion and a beauty in their form which money cannot procure for our riders at home. Those standing for hire at the wayside would command large prices from our most perfect judges. The servant who lets them runs with them till the rider dismounts, when they are used only in the city. The animals move as though delighted to bear the rider.

We yesterday drove across the bridge of boats which crosses the Golden Horn to Stamboul. As we were being driven along the wide macadamized road which winds around the hills we observed some commotion among the people, and soon found we were on the way to the Bureau of the Minister of War, which occupies the top of the hill on which that quarter is built and is surrounded by a very extensive parade ground, and that there was to be a review of troops for the Grand Duke of Mecklenburg-Schweringen. We drove into the enclosure, and there found artillery, cavalry and infantry waiting his arrival, which was momentarily expected. Though the ladies had left the hotel with the intention of spending the morning in the Bazaar, the temptation to see a military review was too strong to be resisted by them; so we sat a half hour in the carriage amid the crowd. Better thoughts then prevailed, and we drove out after having feasted our eyes on the horses, which stood like so many bronze models waiting for the signal to move. The entrance to the Bazaar was close at hand, so we drove there, and I kept my seat in the carriage while the ladies and your Uncle Wistar inspected the goods. They describe the Bazaar as a town in itself, composed of vaulted passages lighted by windows in the roof, with small shops in interminable vistas, filled with every variety of European and Oriental goods. They spent two hours in sauntering from shop to shop.

Your mother was surprised by a cordial greeting from one of the shop-keepers, who rushed out of his stall and carried her into it, begging her to be seated and telling her he was "*Two Piastre*," asking if she did not remember him. He had brought a large display of embroidered table covers to sell at Cairo. Your aunts had bought several of him; your mother had admired one, but did not think it was good economy to pay the price for what would have no real value, and laughingly said she would give him "two Piastres" for it. After they had all settled their purchases he offered to let her have it for whatever she chose to offer, even two Piastres if she chose. She of course declined it. He recognized her here and proved he had not been distressed by her refusal to buy, and laughingly offered some other costly article to her for the same price, and, on one of the party saying to Friezier, "Offer to give him that sum," he bowed gravely and said, "Two hundred francs, my lady:" so you see your mother is a favorite wherever she lights.

Some time after we had left the parade ground, as I sat in the carriage, I saw the nephew of the Sultan drive in, escorted by a troop of horse, seated in an elegant barouche, much gilded. He is a youth of some sixteen years, the heir of the Empire. It was not till nearly two hours after that the Grand Duke arrived, so that if they had waited for the review they certainly would have wasted the morning. Mr. Longstreth and Miss Harris did, as they were obliged to leave for dinner soon after the manœuvering commenced.

In the afternoon your uncle took carriages for us, and we drove out the fashionable course along a fine macadamized road, over breezy hills without a tree or shrub anywhere in view. Glimpses of the sea and port, and various mosques and public buildings, were to be had continually. Elegant equipages drove by us. We met the Grand Duke with his outriders, and four-horse coaches; passed by public gardens grouped with men and women genteelly dressed seated drinking lemonade and coffee, and finally reached the top of a hill from which we looked down into the "valley of sweet waters," in which the Sultan has a garden house surrounded by canals and lakes and shrubbery, to which picnic parties resort in the summer afternoons. It was a beautiful quiet vale.

We alighted and roamed over the hillsides, amusing ourselves by gathering numberless *fairy flowers*, the most diminutive beauties of the floral world I ever saw. The hill was shale, with a very thin coating of soil. There were "forget-me-not," with flowers not larger than a pin's head, and clover thickly matted on the ground, but requiring to be shaved off with a knife, it was so small; blue-bottles, the whole head not larger than little Annie's thimble, and countless other plants equally diminutive. We were compelled to get down on our knees to see them. The views around were fine, the atmosphere clear, the air fresh, the temperature genial; the valley at our feet wound round toward the Golden Horn, with golden flowers adorning the banks of the canal, meandering like a silver thread through the soft meadows. Later in the season the nooks in the hillsides would have been swarming with parties of pleasure.

But I must close this sheet and this mail. Your dear mother finds her duties among the party have *engrossed* her time *almost to the exclusion* of other things. She is *invaluable* to them. She had tried again and again to sit down and write, and hopes to be able to put a few lines in this envelope. With the greatest love to all at Hawthorne Ridge, Cedar Park, Tulip Hill, and especially the dear little ones and Miss Alice.

Your loving father,

CASPAR MORRIS.

CONSTANTINOPLE, April 18, 1872.

My Dear Children:

We reached here safely, and with thankful hearts for many mercies in our Syrian trip, four days ago. Found a package of upwards of thirty letters waiting for us, not having had any since we left Cairo. Such a treat you can hardly imagine; and to have favourable accounts in each, for although Hannah and Mellie had both been so ill, they were both so far recovered as to write themselves. Indeed, you are all very good to us in this way. I often regret I can't do better myself, but you know, at best, I am a very poor scribe, and now I find it almost impossible to get a quiet half hour; now, for instance, this is the fifth time

I have seated myself to this sheet. Your father is able to manage better, and his facility for doing it (and doing it well) I think sometimes makes me lazy. But wait until I get home, and then I shall be able to *tell* you all some things, but *not* that I have found any place that I would like to make my home. I do try very hard to be happy and take pleasure in my surroundings and wanderings, and very often am favoured to be so, though at others I am not. Often I can account for it by over-fatigue.

We are undoubtedly the weak ones of the party. They *now* all begin to realize that fact and are considerate, so that will be a relief from this time. You will have learned that I have *twice*—once up the Nile and again in Cairo—been much alarmed about your father, he having each time a sudden alarming attack. Neither lasted long, but we could not account for them. I tried not to be over-anxious, but do not like him to be long away from observation; he had a sudden and *very alarming* attack the day we reached here, though not like the previous ones. He says it was Angina; just difficulty of breathing and feeling as though bound with iron. Could not use his arms; his consciousness was perfect, giving directions as to what remedies we should apply, and others in case he should not be relieved; knowing such cases often terminate fatally. The English physician here came to us in about three hours; by that time he was relieved and has continued *well* since, though he looks badly, and is obliged to avoid much exertion. Now you will understand I have my cares even here. They are all very kind, and anxious to do what they can for us, and although our passages are taken for the 12th of October, they will change their plans if we find in the meantime it is best on his account. I do not think they would let us return without them, and of course we would not like them to return on our account, unless it is really necessary. Dr. Dickerson here assures me, there is no reason now that we should. I can only account for this last by fatigue, loss of rest on board the steamer and four weeks of anxiety on my account during the Syrian trip, and deep feeling at visiting Jerusalem and the surroundings. I do not want to give you gloomy pictures, but think you ought all to know exactly the state of things, and I wish you all to treat us in the same way. He is cheerful and enjoying all he sees and hears, and perhaps these changing scenes are the best for him.

Tell *all* the girls their letters are heartily welcomed; although not acknowledged personally, I think of you all very often, and only wish you could see or I could describe some of these strange sights. This is a most extraordinary city, very large, built on seven hills, and several other cities so immediately adjacent, and they all on hills too, overlooking the Bosphorus and Golden Horn and Sea of Marmora, that they form one city. Many very fine houses and fine wide streets, much cleaner than any of the Oriental towns we have been in. Many of the houses are frame, but as fires for some years have been very destructive here, they are now using stone and brick, and widening streets; so now in many places we can use carriages, and oh, so very fine horses, and elegantly kept. Riding horses, elegantly caparisoned, are in waiting every few squares for hire. Then the owner runs behind at any speed you wish to go in.

There are no carts here, but all the labour of moving building material, etc., etc., is done on men's backs. They have a saddle on them, and they carry enormous weights. We met a man to-day with three barrels of flour on his back; they were lashed together. As they approached you they looked like an animal. Then remember they have *long*, steep hills to climb and be jostled in the crowd. Even the fire engines are carried by men. The women are very handsome—all veiled, but with very thin muslin and differently arranged from the Egyptians; so when I get home I will show the girls how to fix themselves a la Turk.

19th.

I had a hard day yesterday, and so will rest to-day. We were four hours in the *Bazaar*. It is literally a town; all the streets are arched over, and small stores on either side, the vender seated cross-legged on a bench in front, on which he turns round and hands down his goods, every variety of which are there exposed. Most of them English and French. All commanding high prices, even their own manufactures, so I have not been tempted, and even when I did feel so, the recollection of the duties deterred me; so I bought nothing. From there we had a row of three miles in a Kaïk. Sent carriages by ferry boat to meet us on the other side. Then a long, rough, steep ride to see and hear the "Howling Dervishes." The "Grand Duke" was expected, and his honour, of course, kept all waiting an hour for him. Most gladly would I have left in five minutes after the performance commenced. It was disgusting. They did howl, and did twist and rock themselves in every conceivable way. By degrees the excitement increased, and finally one and all were satisfied, and we left them at work still. I believe they continue until some faint from exhaustion. Only men and boys perform; some only a few years old. It being very crowded we ladies were permitted, at the entreaty of "Far away Moses" of Mark Twain, to go into the yard of a Harem and look in the window, with the native ladies—a very preferable position to being inside, where the atmosphere was so bad—and thus saw the ladies and their children at the same time. The weather was very fine. I got a seat on a tombstone; the rest sat on the ground, as is the custom here.

The children are very handsome; such eyes, but so odd-looking, long wadded wrappers on, and make you wonder how they can run and play; but they do, and are like all other children.

I am notified to bring this to a close, so must stop; but not until I tell you how I rejoice with each member of the family at the additions. But with Mary and Dan., perhaps, the most. Remember us most affectionately all around your circles. I do not think any of our friends and relatives at home are forgotten; nay, perhaps they are more frequently before us, and trust we will be permitted to meet again on earth. Surely we have reason to be thankful for past mercies, and trust for the future.

We shall leave here next week for Vienna, and our route takes us to Milan again for a day, which *we* do not regret, as we have a sort of a home feeling there, besides its own attractions. I must say *farewell*. With so much love to *all* and *each*. I can't write any more, so let this serve for each. I am sorry for Mary Gibson and family. Is. must help them for us. I should if at home.

     Yours most affecty.
                A. C. MORRIS.

I had intended writing to little Annie. Also to brother Galloway; but he and Margaret must take our love this time. Love also to them at Cedar Park and Ridge. I do hope James is much in Baltimore. He can in that way benefit himself and cheer them.

           3.30 P. M., Thursday, April 18, 1872.

My Dear Children:

I have just returned from a ride on horse-back and which has satisfied me that I have not exaggerated the virtue of the horses here. I never more enjoyed a seat. A beautiful sorrel, with curved neck, and fine eyes, and the most *perfect little ears* you ever saw, and a trot which would not shake the water from a wine-glass of a good rider on his back, sure-footed and steady-going, carried me across to Stamboul, and beneath the arches of the ancient aqueduct, which, with its two stories, one above the other, still spans the streets and overlooks the houses, and conveys its life-giving streams to the various fountains by the wayside, which are fitted up and maintained as a work of merit by pious Moslems, though it was constructed centuries ago by some of the Roman Emperors of the East. I went in search of a special obelisk and column, which I did not find; but did what I should not otherwise have done, saw the remains of old Constantinople; and much of the miserable wretchedness of the present Stamboul amid it all. Near the old aqueduct and in the heart of the Turkish town I saw a sign, "Coleman's Starch No. 1," like a "new patch on an old garment" certainly.

I crossed the Golden Horn by a bridge of boats, from which the two quarters could be well studied. On the one side mosques and domes and minarets told its own story; on the other European blocks of houses in straight lines and of solid masonry invaded ancient cemeteries, taking the place of tombs with Arabic inscriptions, and dark pyramidal Cypress trees. With no respect for the sacred dust, the dead are made to give place to the living. Shall any higher regard be paid to them in their turn?

Your mother has gone with the rest of the party to the Bazaar and the Howling Dervishes. Your uncle was sufficient care-taker, and as I did not care to wast time on either, which it would have been on my part, I trusted her with him.

In the middle of this sentence I was most delightfully interrupted by the arrival of dear Galloway's most acceptable letter of the 29th of last month. You will find in mine the most entire frankness of communication on every point, and you know your mother and myself have always acted on the principle that this is the true mode of promoting the happiness, by securing the confidence, of those who are separated. I have not entered into expression of our sympathy with you all in your trials ; nor enumerated those to whom we would send messages of affectionate regard, *only* because time, strength, paper and postage are all exhausted by the writing which is necessary to keep you "*au Courant*" with our progress; and I feel that we can all trust each other, and, each praying for the other to Him, who seeing in secret rewards openly, I trust that we shall be kept in unity of spirit and the bond of peace and in righteousness of life. I am thankful that Galloway can assist a "neighbour" in the way to which he refers in the case of the youngster, his fellow-lodger. It is the only way to perform the duties of our stewardship, and fulfill the ministry of the state of life to which God hath called us ; and it is not by great efforts, but the daily discharge of little duties, this is accomplished. What a comfort it will be if hereafter we can find that we have thus served Christ while really promoting our own happiness now ! I had arrived at the same conclusion about the stage and movements of the microscope, and will gladly select for him such glasses as he writes for, either in London or Paris.

You will find our time for return is just what you suggest. It is a trial to your dear mother and myself to remain away so long. But the same reasons which prevail with us to remain, influence also our determination to continue with your uncle and aunts, so that we shall probably not see Switzerland. Our present plan is to leave here on Tuesday next, cross the Black Sea to Varna and thence by railroad to the Danube ; reaching Pesth, the capital of Hungary, on Saturday, April 27th, and remain there till Monday. Then to Vienna for a week or ten days, and thence to Trieste and Milan, and so across Italy again to Genoa and Nice and Paris, where we shall probably be about the last of May. From there Mr. Longstreth will leave for England and home; and the others for Strasburg and Germany, and so to England the last of June. This plan may be altered, but such is your uncle's present arrangement.

You will have learned from my letters how much we enjoyed the Holy City. I love to call it so; and feel as the Jews do who stand at the wall and utter the lament, "It pitieth us to see her in the dust." The difficulties we were safely carried over and preserved through enhance the richness of the treasure of recollection, and we prize it as among the most important parts of our voyage. Those substructions of the temple grow in importance to my mind whenever I recur to them, and I am glad that our visit was made after they were laid open. I believe they belong to Solomon's temple. So the Moabite Stone and Urn and tessera, which had only arrived during our visit, are most important things. Some day I hope some of you may make a pilgrimage, and that in the meanwhile fresh developments may be made from year to year adding to the interest, and if only the *debris of superstition* piled so heavily above the true objects of interest can be carted away with the material rubbish, Zion will once more be the "joy of the whole earth."

I have mailed a letter to West River at the same time with this, and shall now resume again my regular course of correspondence, addressing my letters to each in turn and designing each equally for all. You must not be uneasy about your mother because she does not write often. Her time and strength are fully occupied, and I will keep you posted about her health. We are all favoured to be doing well, and the little attacks I have had, and of which you will have heard from others, need give you no anxiety on my account; and are a part of the Divine ordering for our good, which I gladly welcome.

I will now lay aside again the personality and betake myself again to my notes of what is passing around us. My late attack brought me acquainted with the medical man here, and he has promised to put me in some communication with the friends of Dr. Goodell. I saw Mr. Boker and am indebted to him for his kindness in getting permits for us to visit the Mosque of St. Sophia and Ahmet and the Museum; in which I expect to find more to interest me than in any Dervishes or Bazaars. At Mr. Boker's this morning I met Col. Grant and Gen. Sherman, to whom I mentioned Dr. Murray, when the General said: "What, Bob! do you know him?" and seemed very cordial, but they were just on their way to the Palace and in haste, so I could not go further into the matter.

I have mentioned the horses of Constantinople. The children will like to hear about the dogs. They are the scavengers of the place and keep it perfectly clean from everything offensive. To accomplish this they must of course be *countless*. One may see two or more *scores* at any time. They do not pay the least regard to any one; lying about when not at work. But let any one pass leading a handsome dog with a collar and by a chain or ribband, then there is an outburst. Every cur within sight and hearing lets out on him in full burst. I have seen this so often repeated as I have walked that there is no question about it. Sleeping curs start as if roused by magnetic telegraph to express their disgust at the servile dignitary. Fat puppies abound at almost every corner. The dogs are never killed, but when they die their skins are cured and make fur linings for the coats of the people.

It is now 5 P. M., and your mother has not yet returned; I am afraid she will be greatly fatigued. They left at 10½ A. M. and were to have a Turkish Lunch somewhere. They are under the guidance of "Far-away Moses" of Mark Twain's book. He has this printed on his card.

Love to Mrs. Buckley and Mrs. Ellis. A special kiss for Willie Stuart Morris.

The enclosed letter is from a poor Mrs. Alley, one of the Jaffa Colonists. Enclose it in one from yourself and ask for an acknowledgment of its receipt to you; and let me know what it is. You can say she has a nice boy about 8 or 10 years old, and she and he are living in a small tent without any means of support. She thinks her letters have not reached her friends.

    Your loving father,

                Caspar Morris.

          Constantinople, April 19, 1872.

My Dear Children:

We have just mailed letters to Harry and Galloway, and are now waiting the arrival of carriages to take us to see the Sultan go in state to the Mosque, which is the moth to consume the morning, as nothing can be accomplished before, and nothing done afterward, before dinner. The day is a delightful one; the trees are pushing out their leaves into the sunshine; the horse-chestnuts ready to expand their colored spikes; and everything spring-like; so that this afternoon it is proposed to go to the Valley of Sweet Waters by kaïk.

There is a strange collection of Americans here just now. Col. Grant, Gen. Sherman, Gov. Curtin and ourselves. Your Aunt Mary and Miss Harris are delighted to have the Governor within reach, as he is an old friend and neighbour at Bellefonte. He is now our Minister to St. Petersburg and comes to conduct the son of the President to Russia, where they will have a grand time of course, after the reception of Alexis in U. S. A.

I find the aqueduct I saw yesterday was erected by the Emperors Hadrian and Valens. So that it has poured sweet waters into the capital of the Eastern Empire, and that of Turkey, at least 1200 years. Its venerable arches are adorned with hanging vines and look most benignantly imposing as they stretch over the hovels which now cover the area once filled with the magnificent porticoes of splendid palaces and towers. The column I saw was erected to support on its top a statue of Marcian; at each corner of the capital one may still see the eagle of Rome. This morning the Sultan went according to custom (this being the Mohammedan Sabbath) to the Mosque, in state. It is not known to which of the many Mosques he will go until the very morning. This morning it was to one situate on the Bosphorus; and the procession was by water in kaïk. About 11½ A. M. we were summoned to the carriages. Your mother had passed a poor night, having suffered from the fatigue of yesterday, so that both she and I doubted whether it were best she should incur the toil; and when we reached the street, finding the demand for carriages had rendered it impossible to secure enough room for all, we gladly availed ourselves of the excuse to remain.

Very soon after the others had left, a city guide came to assure us he could take *me* there if I would go with him, and at your mother's request, I left her. I was carried hastily down the steep street by which we had ascended on our first arrival, and, on reaching the foot, found the tramway and a car just about to start. He motioned me to run, and put me in. It was two-storied, and I would gladly have taken the upper floor, which is used by those who pay less price, but much to be preferred by one who wishes to see. That was closely filled, so that I was obliged to rest satisfied to be packed below in a very comfortable car (better than our own street-cars) with some twenty others, mostly supplied with cigarettes. Every Turk carries with him a package of gummed papers and a box of tobacco with which he makes cigarettes for himself. The tramway is well laid, but only with single track, with turn-outs at given distances, where cars going either way wait for those coming the opposite. More time was consumed in waiting than in travelling. But it was all taken with Moslem patience. After about half an hour, just before we reached the palace, the roar of a salute announced that the Sultan had embarked. My guide told me it was of no account, we should reach the Mosque in time to see him land. Stopping-place after stopping-place arrested our progress, and just as we approached the Mosque, a second salute announced that His Highness was landing. All the vessels in the Bosphorus were gaily decorated with flags, and manned yards as the Sultan passed. This we could see, but not the kaïkes of His Majesty. The car stopped in front of the Mosque, and I found myself in the midst of carriages, horses, and people, a perfect jam. The guide elbowed his way, and made room for me to advance, and then induced the guard to allow me to pass through; and, just as I was about to turn around, I met your uncle and aunts on their return. They had reached the landing in time, and had seen His Majesty arrive. I was perfectly content with an inspection of the gorgeous boats, covered with gilding and surmounted by canopies of the richest purple velvet, hanging in heavy festoons, edged by gold lace. They are carpeted with Persian rugs, and the well-stuffed cushions of purple velvet are embroidered with gold. They were certainly very rich. The Sultan went in one, his family in the other, and the ministers of his cabinet attended in others without canopies or hangings or cushions, but carved, and heavily gilded. Each of the royal kaïkes was propelled by twenty-four oarsmen in livery. The guide wished me to remain and witness the re-embarkation of His Majesty. I told him I had this morning seen the son of the President of the United States of America, and the greatest American General, and I thought them as much worth seeing as the Sultan, that here were the plumes of the bird, and I thought the carcass was much like that of others; so I returned in the carriages by the route over the hills, which afforded fine views of the country and sea.

Yesterday, your mother, on her way to the Howling Dervishes, saw Scutari, the seat of the hospital made so celebrated as the scene of the labours of Florence Nightingale; and the Cemetery in which repose the remains of the English victims of the Crimean war. She says it is kept with exquisite neatness and adorned with attractive monuments. There is also a very exclusive Moslem Cemetery, miles in extent, each grave marked by a stone surmounted by a sculptured turban, or fez, and covered with Arabic inscriptions. It is a great grove of the dark green cypress, with which the Moslems always plant their places of interment. Your mother tells me that the fezzes and turbans on the stones are coloured and gilded, and those of children are proportioned in size to their ages, some being very small.

She was sadly disgusted and disappointed in the Howling Dervishes. They had postponed the hour of commencing their service, waiting for the arrival of the Grand Duke Mecklenburg-Schweringen. This gave our party opportunity for driving around Scutari. When the performance did commence, it consisted only in the bowing, backward and forward, and from side to side, of forty dirty-looking men and boys of all ages, from six years to extreme old age, each howling out the name of Allah and the Prophet in monotonous tones, beginning in a very slow time, gradually increasing in rapidity of utterance until it was impossible to follow it, keeping time with the motions of their body till they became perfectly exhausted. This is maintained an hour or two each Thursday. Two or three of them stood or walked about, tying knots in sashes or kissing each knot as it was tied, and drawing the sashes tightly around their waists. These accompanied the howling of the others by deep grunts. These rites are conducted in the tomb of a Saint, surrounded by a gallery for visitors, the atmosphere of which is said to be terribly foul. Happily the Duke monopolized this privilege, and your aunts and mother were allowed to witness the performance from a court for Moslem ladies where they had fresh air. They are not willing to repeat the experience, and will not visit the dancing Dervishes who perform to-day.

It is now dusk, and the party has not yet returned from the valley of sweet waters, to which they drove, instead of going by kaïk, as they had proposed. Your mother and I did not accompany them. We are glad to be resting quietly, preparatory for our visits to-morrow to St. Sophia.

The cries of the venders of various articles arouse us daily as the sun rises, and both yesterday and to-day we have waked to behold a beautiful morning. The hills of Bithynia glow brightly in its light as they did in those days when Pliny the younger was pro-consul, and wrote to Trajan that letter which has made his name even more widely known than his studies in Natural History, or his greatness as a ruler have rendered that of his uncle.

Little did he think, when he allowed the feelings of this heart to dictate a simple letter to his Imperial master, describing the character and sufferings of a sect whom both despised, that in long distant ages there should come from an unknown region those who, much as they had admired his genius and sympathized in the delight he had known in the beauties of his birth-place and residence amid the mountains of Como and on the shores of its deep and transparent lake, would regard him with a feeling akin to reverence for the humanity which shrunk from inflicting suffering even on those whom he despised as foolish enthusiasts, or simple dissenters from popular belief, and who honored the courage which ventured on an appeal in their behalf, which, in all probability, excited a sneer at his weakness among his friends, the philosophers and statesmen of Imperial Rome, who would think an interest in such people beneath the dignity of the Governor, as far as it was beneath the range of thought of the naturalist and general.

As my eyes range over these hills, stripped of trees and destitute of dwellings, except as the last few years have begun to re-people their heights, my mind runs back over the ages in which they swarmed with a busy and highly cultivated population; and, when passing from the state of a persecuted sect, Christianity became a dominant religion, and, combining with political factions, waged suicidal conflicts between differing sects when councils of the church met under the wings of imperial protection, and spent years in debating points of variance, and moulding formularies of expression of belief in modes of faith. Nicea, Ephesus, Chalcedon and Constantinople have each been the place of such assemblies of bishops. But except that first named none are recognized by Protestants, and in the creed composed by that, we are now asked to make a change.

Evening.

We have spent the morning among the Mosques, which now occupy the sites of ancient Christian churches, or are those sacred structures desecrated by Moslem conquerors. Our first visit was to the Sulumant or Mosque of Sultan Suleiman, with its six beautiful minarets, built A. D. 1550. Nearly all the materials were taken from a Christian church at Chalcedon, immediately across the Bosphorus. The dome, which is very beautiful, rests on four porphyry columns, sixty feet high, the spoil of the ancient Greek temple at Baalbec. The proportions are so admirably adjusted that your Uncle Wistar could not be satisfied that these columns were over forty feet, till, by standing beside one, I convinced him they are ten times my height. It is thought by the Turks themselves the perfection of architecture. The interior is covered with arabesque painting and lined with beautiful glazed tiles arranged in neat patterns, the floor with fine carpets, and the chanting of the Koran by worshippers was quite imposing. A saint was comfortably ensconced in a sacred recess beneath the stairs of the pulpit.

From this we drove to the celebrated mosque of St. Sophia. Constantine, on embracing Christianity, erected a temple to "Heavenly

Wisdom," which he designed to be the greatest ornament of his new capital, and collected in it the most magnificent columns and marbles from heathen temples, and every part of the Empire. The church was burned in some of the riots which disgraced the population of Constantinople so frequently during the dissensions about the manner of the existence of the inconceivable Diety. It is said to have been burned by the adherents of Chrysostom. Another erected instead by Theodosius was again the prey of the flames of civil discord at a time when 36,000 people perished in the strife, so intense and furious were the passions of those Greeks.

The present was built, I believe, by Justinian. The exterior has no grandeur, except of extent; the numberless smaller domes which surround the grand central dome and the loftiness of the four minarets abate the apparent size, externally, of that which is found to be so lofty and grand when seen from within. I shall not attempt any detail of its structure, which could not be interesting without a plan. You enter, first, into a lofty and wide enclosed space, like the portico of the Grecian temple, into which Catechumens were received, and beyond which they were not allowed to advance till baptized. From this, by one lofty entrance and eight smaller, but still grand, doorways (four on either side of the central one), you enter the body of the church. The first impression is very imposing. The lofty dome swells above, supported by four semi-domes, each of which is thirty yards in diameter, while light galleries extend across the front of these semi-domes, which rest on exquisitely-proportioned columns of variegated marbles brought from celebrated temples of pagan gods. The walls are lined with many coloured marbles, some of great beauty, others of great rarity and strangely variegated. Needle-work from Mecca and illuminated texts from the Koran hang against the pillars in some places.

There is one column with a shaft, the stone of which has the property of condensing moisture from the air. It is covered with brazen plates through which a hole is left to allow the faithful to insert their fingers and moisten them with "the sweat of the stone." The brightly polished, irregular margin, worn by repeated touches, betrays the superstition of ignorant worshippers.

The doors by which you enter the church are of bronze, from the plates which once covered the stone shaft or pyramid still standing in the ancient hippodrome or race course, which was before the church. The central dome rises nearly 200 feet from the ground, and has a diameter of more than 100 feet. There are 107 columns of marble of various kinds, placed with great regularity to support the various galleries in the arches above. The capitals of these columns and the front of the galleries are of very elaborate white arabesque work, either marble or stucco, I could not decide which. One of the four angels beneath the dome is still remaining, a colossal representation of the four Seraphim, according to the description given by the prophet Ezekiel. They are in the proportions of human figures, but no feature or limb is perceptible; composed entirely of wings, "with twain they covered their faces, with twain they covered their feet and with twain they did fly." It is a wonderful idealization of active devotion combined with self-abnegating humility—mighty power in earnest action and yet concealing itself. Below each is suspended, in beautiful golden characters on green ground, the Arabic names of one of the archangels, recognized by the Moslem faith. While around the centre of the cupola, in similar letters, each *ten yards long*, is the sentence, "God is the light of the Heavens and the earth." These letters are so perfectly proportioned, though so large, that from the floor they look but little larger than common size. During the feast of Ramadan this inscription is lighted brilliantly by lamps suspended beneath. The report of the splendour of the original church is fabulous; and superstition adorned the story of its construction with wondrous tales, such as that an angel brought 400 cwt. of gold to the emperor to meet the expenses, etc., etc., all which may be found in Murray's guide-book by those who are curious.

We also visited the library, which contains some Arabic books; and the *treasure*-room in the ancient palace of the Sultan. We there saw cushions and carpets worked in patterns with genuine pearls, varying in size from seed-pearls to that of the end of my thumb; saddle-cloths and pistol-holsters embroidered with diamonds, rubies, carbuncles and turquoises; *great bowls* full of emeralds; and swords, and guns, and pistols, and daggers with priceless gems set in the handles and stocks; a *golden cradle*, studded with precious stones, and countless other articles rendered absolutely useless by their costliness, which served to amuse a crowd of European travelers, and to occupy the time of a body of guards, stationed for their protection from robbery at the door and at every turn among the cases in which they are exhibited, but might else have well rested in the shells of oysters in the deep, unfathomed beds of ocean, or blushed unseen in the bowels of the earth. A toilet table, with hanging glass, the entire frame covered with diamonds, was catalogued as worth an immense price, but we agreed that if the stones were genuine they might as well be paste, as we think it not unlikely they are. Some of the emeralds and rubies we saw were certainly of great size and purity, but our eyes have been so often dazzled by such splendor in the treasures of the saints, that they have become familiar sights, and give rise to no covetous desire of possession.

The area of the Hippodrome is still open, and in it stands the obelisk of Egyptian granite brought by the Emperor Theodosius about 1300 years ago from Heliopolis. It is here erected on a marble base, the four sides of which bear sculptures of a rude style, designed to represent the manner in which it was erected here, and the crowning of the Emperor and his reception of captives. Inscriptions in Greek and Latin extol the might and wisdom of Theodosius exhibited in the transportation and erection here of the obelisk. Near stands what, to the uninitiated eye, appears to be merely a special column of some twenty feet in height and two feet in diameter, composed of three tubes, the top broken. Yet few works of man have greater value in the eye of one well read in classic history. It once stood in the temple of Apollo at Delphi, and inscriptions still legible on it prove it to be the support of the golden vase in that temple of which Herodotus makes mention. "The Greeks after the victory of Platæa, having collected all the money, put aside one tenth for the god at Delphi. With this they made a tripod of gold which they offered to the god. It was placed upon the three-headed copper serpent which was near to the altar." Other historians allude to it.

It was in this Hippodrome also once stood the bronze horses which were carried from here to Venice and thence to Paris, by Napoleon, and which he was obliged to return, and now stand on the church of St. Mark. We first hear of them at Corinth, from whence the conquering Romans carried them to the Imperial city, where they stood on the arch of Trajan or Nero and also in the temple of the Sun. Constantine brought them here to adorn the new capital.

The palace of Belisarius was also near the Hippodrome, in which the legends of the lower empire represent him, old, blind and poor, to have solicited alms from those whom, by his military genius, he had delivered from the invasion of the Huns, and whose African empire he had rescued from the Vandals.

If I am not mistaken, Effingham's favourite general, Hannibal, closed his career in this city. But you must all read Gibbon's Decline of the Roman Empire, and if you wish to trace still further, into the obscure mists of history the varied facts which have rendered it famous, you can turn to the Persian invasion of Greece, and still further in the dimness you will find the expedition in search of the Golden Fleece, with Jason and Medea and their associates. Wm. Morris has poured out volumes of modern rhymes on these ancient stories in his "Earthly Paradise," which I may possibly be able to read hereafter, though I could not persevere before I left home.

I have been able to get some good photographs of the Mosque of Sophia, but have not gone so largely into that line as your Uncle Wistar does. Some of the views of the town and neighbourhood are very fine.

Evening, April 22.

Our hearts were delighted and our souls filled with thankful emotions by the reception at dinner table of a packet of letters dated the last of March and 2d of April. So near are we brought together in time. Just three weeks since your hands impressed on those sheets the loving expressions of affection, and now they greet our eyes and cheer our hearts. The only alloy to this perfect enjoyment was found in dear Mary's account of your Aunt Margaret and Uncle Galloway and Miss Alice; all which grieves us sorely. If nothing but pleasure interfered we should, without a day's delay, put ourselves on the route home and travel nearly as rapidly as this letter. Indeed we find it difficult to resist the desire. So far as we are ourselves concerned, we have nothing to gain by longer absence, and there is now nothing we desire to see. Vienna, Paris, London, may have charms for youth; and the science and literature and art of those great emporia may have interest for active minds. All our attraction is now centred in our loved ones at home, and all our desire limited to seeing and doing that which would promote their happiness and welfare.

I have spent this afternoon in visiting the building erecting for the Bible Society. Our grandchildren will remember having contributed toward it some two years ago, and I was gratified in being able to go through it. It stands in a commanding position, with fine views from the windows over the town and harbour and adjacent country. It adjoins a large mosque and overlooks the residence of a wealthy Turk, formerly in high authority, though now in disgrace. He did everything in his power to oppose the building, and demanded that iron screens be placed before the windows to prevent them overlooking his buildings and grounds. They consider the building fire-proof; but though very substantial, it has wooden floors and stairs laid on brick arches. I trust it may be spared from fire or any other destructive agency to disseminate glad tidings of great joy to many generations yet unborn.

We shall leave to-morrow by the Black Sea for Varna, and are sorry to find by the evening papers we are to have the company of the Prince William of Denmark, etc. We have been unfortunately interfered with by Emperors, Princes, and Dukes and Duchesses. Thank Miss Dunlap and Miss Cowpland for their most acceptable letters, Miss Julia Dunlap especially.

Love to all from your mother and myself.

CASPAR MORRIS.

CONSTANTINOPLE, April 22, 1872.

My Dear Brother (Galloway Cheston, Esq.):

We were very glad on reaching here this day week to find two letters from you in our package which had been accumulating here. They were dated about the middle of March, and although dear Margaret had been suffering from one of those bad colds, as she was then rather better, we quite hope ere long to hear again, and that she is able to ride and enjoy the spring weather. We were glad to hear you had engaged Miss Townsend to be with you for the summer, for, from what I have heard of her, I think she will be a comfort to you both, and I think it will be a relief to Mary Ellen also, whom we are sorry to find is again so poorly. She will, however, give the water cure a better trial this year, and I hope much from it for her. Tell her with my love I hope to find her *well* on our return next October.

I suppose ere this you have learned our passages are taken on the "Scotia" for the 12th of that month. Of course, if anything should occur to make us alter our plans, they can easily be given up.

I can hardly tell you how glad, nay, how thankful, *we*, the Dr. and I, are to be back on European soil. You know we went into Syria very reluctantly. It was a month of torture to me, but it is over and never to be repeated, and I can now look back on some things we saw with pleasure. The Dr. had much enjoyment, but the truth is, *old*, infirm people like ourselves ought not to undertake what youth could accomplish with ease.

I am not without cares and anxieties. The Dr. has had three sudden and alarming attacks of illness; the two first, one on the Nile, one at Cairo (our second visit there), and the third this day week, just after writing to you. In the two first he lost consciousness, but the last was of a different character, and he was entirely himself, and able to direct what should be done for him, while waiting for a physician, though his suffering from difficulty of breathing was very great. He calls it an attack of Angina, and we cannot be too thankful it did not occur on the roadside between Jaffa and Jerusalem. He had been to take a bath, and Friezier, the Courier, had piloted him and then sat down to read the newspapers, and was walking back with him to the hotel, when he was seized on the street, and certainly could not have got back here without assistance. He just reached the bedside and fell on it, unable to raise either hand or foot again for an hour or more. Brandy, mustard and a hypodermic after a while afforded relief, and a nice old English physician came to us, to whom I talked freely the next day as to whether he did not think we had better get to our home. He did not advise a change in our plans on the Doctor's account, but wishes him to live more freely. He is exhausted, he thinks, and as our return would take *all* home, which we see is not best for the others, we have concluded to be quiet for the present, and unless we have further reason, we will not unsettle Wistar's plans. They were all much alarmed, and are not only willing, but anxious to do everything they can for us, and we intend from this time to take things more quietly. I know we two cannot endure as the others can, and they are now aware of that fact and will not insist on our going incessantly, and thus I am hoping we will be able to keep together. To-morrow we are to leave here for Vienna, cross the Black Sea to Varna, and thence by rail and steamboat up the Danube, occupying a week between this and Vienna.

We have most satisfactory accounts from our children up to the 4th of this month, and hope they will continue. Mary keeps me informed of the condition of the different branches of the family at West River, from which I learn James, Sally and Sam have all at different times been ailing through the winter. Fanny will quite revel in her *grandchildren*. Is it not funny to think of Fanny being a grandmother? You and I must be *very old*.

I must refer you to the Doctor's letters to the children for descriptions of this place. The views are beautiful, the drives around the city so fine, having the Sea of Marmora, Golden Horn or Bosphorus at every turn, with a great deal of shipping and many fine buildings, contrasting strongly with the mud houses of Egypt. The weather corresponds with ours of this season, delightful out of doors, but as there are no fires, cool and damp within. The Oriental costumes are very queer, and I think the loose pantaloons, or rather a petticoat on each leg, gathered into the ankle on the men, must be as inconvenient as the veiled and loose cloak dress of the poor women, occupying both hands to keep them in place. Then the streets are steep, very rough and difficult to walk on, and they all have a shuffling gait, but through their veils, for here they are very thin, you see the most beautiful women I ever saw. The Doctor says he thinks the color is artificial, but the children too are uncommonly handsome; a homely face is rarely seen.

I wish you could see the horses. They are elegant. Are not used for burden, only for riding and carriages, but are splendidly kept, and so graceful in their movements.

Men perform the labour of transporting on their backs goods of all kinds, and great distances up these steep, long hills. A saddle is placed on the back, and we constantly meet them with their heavy loads. A "hogshead," two or even three barrels lashed together, long pieces of timber for building, etc. The head is bent forward and down even more than "old Uncle Ben's" used to be as he walked.

We were flattering ourselves we were getting out of the region of fleas, not being quite so tormented, until we went to see the Howling Dervishes, a most disgusting sight, and were it not for the beautiful drive it gave us, should think that trip a dead loss; some of the party now tell me, however, they are going to see the dancing ones before we leave.

Give much love to Margaret. We think and talk often of you both, and suppose about the time this reaches you, you will go to Walbrook.

We are eating green peas and have had fresh tomatoes ever since we left the continent last August. Farewell. The Doctor joins me in much love to you both.

Your affectionate sister,

A. C. MORRIS.

I find I will not be able to write to Mary by this week's mail, so will you please let her read this, as I know she will be glad to hear her father is quite well again?

CONSTANTINOPLE, April 22, 1872.

My Dear Brother (Galloway Cheston, Esq.):

I was glad on coming in from a visit to the new Bible House here this afternoon to find Anne had done what I had designed doing, written to you to repeat the expression of our near sympathy to you in the sore trial caused by the long confinement of dear Margaret to her bed, which we learn from our letter from Mary. I wish most heartily we were with you now, or felt at liberty to turn our steps rapidly homeward. No desire for personal gratification, nor even the pursuit of our own benefit or health would hinder us. Indeed nothing but a sense of duty keeps us now, and we beg you to let us know even by telegraph if we can by returning afford you any relief or comfort. We have now returned to the track of regular mails, and I know a friend did last year receive a telegraph at Vienna and reached Philadelphia in a fortnight after. So that we shall be anxiously looking by each mail at least for accounts from you, and should feel that a summons from you would justify our leaving our present position, though we do believe our present duty lies here. This note is designed for your own information only and need not be communicated to any one. Only do believe our hearts are wholly with you, though we are favoured to enjoy the privilege of travel.

   Your loving brother,

            CASPAR MORRIS.

Much love to James and Sally and Samuel, and all our friends.

           CONSTANTINOPLE, April 21, 1872.

My Dear Children:

I know you will look anxiously for further accounts from us, after hearing of your father's indisposition the day we reached here, which will be a week to-morrow morning, and I am very glad to tell you he not only has had no return, but seems quite well and able to enjoy the various objects of interest here which we have been visiting, and I have no doubt he will give you a particular account of most of them. There would be no use in my attempting it even if he did not. I shall content myself by getting a few " Carte de Visite," just to show the costumes and habits, and aid me in recalling much that I want to tell you when I get home, for you may expect me to talk a great deal then, to make up for all this long pent-up time.

Oh it is so trying not to be able to talk or understand those around you. Even the servants in the Hotels are worried, as well as ourselves often, and the morning your father was ill it was both trying and touching, as by ringing the bell I got both a man and woman, but could not make them understand my wants, though they were so interested that they would gladly have done anything for me.

This morning your father and I wandered off to find where there was an English service and were led to a nice chapel where an old English gentleman officiated to a large congregation. We enjoyed the service *much*, and on coming out found a young gentleman waiting to greet us, whom we had met on board the "Hungaria" from Jaffa. It is very pleasant I assure you in this strange land to have one's hand shaken even if it is only by a transient acquaintance, but we have made many very pleasant ones in this way. "Cook's Excursion Party" of fifty were on board the same vessel, and we found some of them, both ladies and gentlemen, very intelligent pleasant people, and he certainly understands the management of such companies nicely.

Yesterday we visited three mosques, each of us taking our slippers, as no shoes are allowed within them, although the marble floors are all completely covered with Turkey carpets. The interior of these buildings are *very fine*, very beautiful, the ceiling of Byzantine Mosaic, beautiful porphyry and Verde Antique marble pillars; and precious stones and pearls abound in many parts. In the Mosque of St. Sophia there is a well which is called the "Holy Well." I gladly took a drink of the water as it was both good and cold, though I have no further faith in it than quenching my thirst for the moment. The chanting we listened to while walking through this building was the finest we have heard since we have been listening to such things.

We have had many very beautiful drives around the city. The views are very fine and very extensive; you have both sea and land all the time before you, and the buildings are picturesque. Either the sea of Marmora, Golden Horn, or Bosphorus, are ever before you. The riding through the streets is very uncomfortable, as they are very narrow, steep, and very rough. It is astounding that any springs can stand them, and the horses are slipping. As two of our carriages have been broken, perhaps they don't. The Palanquins are used here, carried by men, but I have had enough of that way of locomotion, and shan't try one. Your father likes the horses very much, and so he takes a saddle in preference to the carriages. They certainly are very handsome animals. I am tempted to covet them.

I fully expected if I reached this place to indulge myself with a Turkey carpet, but shall leave without it or anything else, as the prices are far beyond our means, and then we know the duties would be heavy. I often regret that we are all ignorant on this latter subject, and it is an obstacle all the time in our way, and I think most likely would not be as great in reality as we imagine.

We are to-day to prepare for a move to-morrow by steamer; are to go aboard again from small rowboats, called the "Kaïk" (you can scarcely imagine my feelings at the prospect of that climb, but as I have been favoured several times to accomplish it, I will try to trust I shall again, though it is so painful). Sixteen hours we will be in crossing the Black Sea to Varna, and we may expect it to be rough. From thence, partly by steamboat and partly rail, along the Danube to Vienna occupying a week, where we expect our next letters to meet us. You see how unreasonable we are, a package of near forty now lying on our table, many unacknowledged, and we longing for more. These had been accumulating while we were in Syria; now we will be able to receive regularly as well as let you hear weekly.

Your father occupies every moment in writing that he can, as he is anxious to communicate and show you all that he sees, and fears to trust his memory to tell you hereafter, and I am sure it is the best way, as so much is crowded in that all can't be remembered, and, indeed, it is impossible to convey an idea of these scenes; perhaps some of you may witness it all for yourselves. I shall never think anything impossible after my experience, for surely there never was any one to whom all this was more improbable.

April 22nd.

We have just received another package of letters, and are quite elated; the last date is the 4th of this month; they are from Ches., Annie and Mary, written on Easter Sunday, one from Miss Dunlap, A. Cowpland, and Mrs. Cope; all truly welcome, I assure you. I only wish, my dear children, I could write to you separately, but I know you will excuse that. We are so thankful for good news of you all, and for just the little home details you give us.

The weather here is now quite spring-like, and I have no doubt those of you who have gardens to look to, are becoming quite busy. Yesterday, in our walk through the palace grounds to church, we saw violets, wall-flowers, pansies, wisteria, and lilacs, all in full bloom, looking very homelike.

We are sure from Annie's account of the photographs and olive articles received that they are just ours, and there has been no mistake or mingling of Uncle Wistar's with ours; so do what you choose with them, as that is the case. We only did not wish Uncle Wistar's to be scattered around. Mary can have them sent to her if she desires it. I do begin to be a little anxious about the little table for Mrs. Cope from Florence; it is a long time since it was ordered.

Unless Dr. and Mrs. Harris (Mary Morris's aunt and uncle) will meet us in Milan, and spend a few days there, we shall go to Venice again to see them. He is an old man, and very feeble, and his nieces wish to bid him farewell.

Ches. asks if we are using wine. We are daily, and have been for four or five months. Up to that time I alone resisted, but find I was wrong, and I am better for it.

Your father has just brought to show me an ear-ring of pearls and a gold coin that were found on a corpse. The latter was under the tongue, the idea being to pay his way, and 'twas from a Greek grave before the Christian era.

I ought to have acknowledged the girls' photographs long since. They are very good, and it is a pleasure to me to have them. All my sixteen grandchildren will have grown so that I will scarce recognize them.

With much love to you all, I am, as ever,
        Your devoted mother,

                                            A. C. M.

[*Note by Caspar Morris probably written in 1874 or 1875.*]

One or more of the letters from Constantinople must have miscarried or been mislaid, and it is difficult now to recall the incidents which were probably narrated.

At Smyrna among the passengers that joined us was a young man of most attractive form and features, who made himself specially acceptable to all his fellow-passengers by the simple unaffected manner with which he moved among them and the readiness with which he entered into their interests in the objects around. We soon found he was a native of Constantinople, of English ancestry and had been brought up there, and was now returning from a visit to a sister, who had married and was settled at Smyrna. Our own party was large, and we found within ourselves all we needed, so that our personal intercourse with him was slight, though we were much attracted to him by his manners and would gladly have seen more of him.

The approach to Constantinople is very imposing. As the sea of Marmora contracts toward the Bosphorus, many rocky islands lie scattered around the shores, and the approaching headlands of Asia and Europe stand crowned with the residences of the population of the city of Constantine. No one can hesitate to accord to that emperor the credit of wisdom displayed in the selection of the site for the imperial residence, the place from which should issue the power controlling the destinies of the world, Europe, Asia and Africa ! There is no position on the surface of the globe so central to them all. The Euxine opened a way to Eastern Europe and Western and Northern Asia. The great rivers emptying into it brought to its shores the products of the interior. Caravans starting from it penetrated to the farthest India, and Alexandria at the mouth of the Nile was as easy of access from this port as from Rome itself. The selection of such a position for his capital vindicates the claim of Constantine to his imperial position. Chalcedon and Byzantium were merged in the royal city, and now as we approached in the early morning it lay before us, shorn, it is true, of much of its grandeur, but like a royal robe of purple still exhibiting, though in decay, the texture, color and embroidery which once challenged admiration. To our left lay Stamboul with its domes and minarets clustering on the heights and enclosed by the ruined wall which once surrounded its palaces and theatres in the day of its glory. Beyond the Golden Horn rose the heights of Galata with its ancient tower, surrounded by modern buildings half concealed in the dark spires of the Oriental Cypress which are planted in the cemeteries, while to the right Scutari, on the Asiatic shore, rises on corresponding hills. Between these opens the Bosphorus, and a crowd of vessels of all nations covers the intervening waters.

We expected to be met on our arrival by some representative of the keeper of the principal hotel, to whom Friezier had telegraphed for rooms, and carriages to convey us to them, but were disappointed and obliged to land as best we might and find our way under the guidance of a porter. This was effected without difficulty, and our trunks, examined, were piled upon the backs of porters to be conveyed to the hotel. It was a strange sight. Each porter (Hamal?) was provided with a saddle, girt around his loins and resting on his hips, and bending forward with hands and arms depending like the forelegs of an animal, trunks and bags were piled as they would be on a cart, till one unaccustomed to such sights would suppose the porter would be crushed beneath the load. As our carriages were not at the landing place we followed the porters, who ascended by a shorter way, which led directly up the height. It was literally so steep that it was with some difficulty we climbed it without any burden, yet they mounted without any complaint. When we reached the hotel we found vehicles had been sent to bring us by the circuitous road, which was necessary to be taken by carriages, and some demonstrations of annoyance on Friezier's part led to explanations on that of the host, which were quite satisfactory, and we were received in a large hall comfortably furnished, and having a table supplied with recent copies of the *London Times* and other indications that we had arrived again on the confines of modern civilization. Royalty on its travels of course claimed precedence, and German Princes must be accommodated before American Sovereign people. So we were obliged to look for accommodations elsewhere, and were glad to find quite comfortable quarters under the patronage of mine host of the Hotel Mezieres near at hand.

Among my earliest inquiries, stimulated by the poetical descriptions of the luxury of Eastern baths, was for the best establishment where I could enjoy the delight of which we had so long been deprived, and having learned where we should find that frequented by the European residents, I took Friezier with me and sallied out to seek it. Our route lay along the principal street of Galata, the quarter in Constantinople occupied by Europeans, and on which open the courtyards in which are the residences of the Ambassadors to the Sublime Porte from European Governments. These are palatial residences, surrounded by extensive gardens; and the royal arms of the several sovereigns are sculptured over the gateways. They all look out over the Bosphorus, and possess the advantages of sea air and extensive views. Passing thence along streets lined with shops filled with European goods, and amid the ruins of the last fire and the yet unfinished and more solid new structures which are rising among them, we reached an establishment, which combines the attractions of a restaurant, smoking-rooms and gambling saloons, with those of the bath. In none of these respects are its arrangements and equipments in any way different from that in our own cities. The attendants speak Italian and French, so that Friezier soon made the arrangements for my comfort, and he took himself to the reading-room, while I enjoyed the luxury of a simple warm bath, with very much the accompaniments to which I am accustomed at home.

While dressing I was seized with a peculiar sensation, which at first scarce claimed my attention, and was not painful, merely a sense of constriction in expanding my chest. I dressed without any serious difficulty, though it continued to increase. I did not mention it to Friezier, till as we drew near to the hotel I found it necessary to seek the support of his arm in walking; and by the time we reached my room I was glad to throw myself on the bed, though anxious if possible to avoid giving any alarm to your mother or aunts and uncle. Mustard cataplasms and foot-bath failing to relieve the constriction, which became constantly greater till it threatened suffocation, I injected, by means of the hypodermic syringe which happily I had at hand, one-fourth of a grain of morphia, which very promptly gave relief; so that by the next morning I was as well as usual in my own feelings, though unable ever to relieve myself from the anxiety which the attack, added to my spell on the Nile, excited in your mother and the family. For a time I had thought myself in peril; and when that thought was subdued still apprehended it was the beginning of a series which would progressively increase. But I am thankful now at the end of more than two years to record no recurrence.

During our stay in Constantinople we drove in the suburbs every afternoon; and beautiful indeed are the views from the hills. But it is the beauty of desolation. There is no culture, and one wonders whence the immense population of the city, said to be certainly more than 500,000 of the various nationalities subject to Turkish rule, draws its supplies. One sees vegetables and fruits hawked for sale about the streets on men's shoulders and donkey's backs; but there are no enclosures, and the fields lie waste or grazed by sheep and goats; and, when we could alight from our carriages to walk, we found them covered by the most diminutive flowers, giving color to the surface, but so small that you must stoop to see them. There was a great profusion of a miniature clover of a pink hue, and fragrant as that of our own fields.

I never learned accurately the localities of the divisions of the city with the names of which every one is familiar; Galata, Para and Tophaneh, but Stamboul proper is divided from these by the Golden Horn, which is crossed by a bridge of boats; and Scutari lies on the opposite side of the Bosphorus. My drives were all on the European side, and led past the various military establishments and schools in which the Sultan trains the officers of the army, and civil government. They are very extensive and well-built structures, and are said to be well conducted to accomplish the purpose designed.

We passed frequently the walls of some of the palaces which contain the harems of the Sultan and his high officials. Some of these buildings are very extensive, and one, on the shores of the Bosphorus, built of white marble most elaborately sculptured, is very beautiful. The entrance to it is by the most graceful gateway, through a screen of white marble.

I enjoyed much the riding on horseback. Beautiful animals with their grooms are to be found on the streets at special places, as carriages are with us, waiting for hire. When you mount one the groom runs beside or before you at whatever pace you may prefer. I was happy in always procuring a pleasant-gaited beast. Our hotel was on the height and overlooked the harbour and the houses which covered the steep slope to it. The carriage made a wide circuit, passing through an abandoned Mohammedan cemetery, which was being covered with modern residences very rapidly. But in addition to the very steep ascent by which we first arrived, there was another leading to the bridge by which Galata is connected with Stamboul, which could be traversed on horseback, though it was literally laid in steps with a rise of some six inches each, and a tread wide enough for the horse to stand on it with all feet before ascending the next. This was the great thoroughfare for pedestrians also, and was constantly thronged by men, women and children. At its foot was the one end of the bridge from either side of which steamboats were constantly passing to and fro to the various quarters of the town accessible by water. The bridge itself presented a motley show of people of all classes and costumes, Oriental and European.

But it was at the Stamboul end of the bridge the crowd was greatest, as there the post office and the various other departments of municipal and general government drew many; and the entrance to the bazaars and market places more. I never rode or walked over it without amazement at the throng, nor without a feeling akin to a want of the sense of security, due to our early association of ferocity with the term Turk, though certainly there was nothing in the countenances or deportment of the people to justify this. Great, indeed, is the change within a short period. Our intelligent young friend, enthusiastic as he was about the present delights of the place as a residence, told us his grandmother, still living, narrated stories of the insults to which Christian women had been subject when she first came here to reside, and found it absolutely impossible to venture on the street ; so that they were compelled to occupy houses with doors opening directly from the one to the other, as they dared not walk any distance. I rode unattended, except by the groom, without molestation wherever I pleased, right into the heart of the Turkish quarter, and to places not commonly frequented by Christians.

Several wide avenues lead from the bridge to the Imperial Palace and offices, but I turned off from these, desirous, if possible, to find some relics of the ancient grandeur of the Imperial period. I found only a dense mass of closely-packed houses, covering, doubtless, the fragments of the ruins of past glory fallen to decay.

One morning was spent by the entire party in witnessing a grand military review, which was held for the benefit of one of the German princes. Though I always held war and all its concomitants in utter abhorrence, and was in a frame of feeling absolutely incompatible with even its music and display, I was induced to be of the party from the hope of seeing fine horses and good horsemanship, and though not disappointed in this respect, even that did not compensate for the weariness of waiting for the several parts of the display nor for the sickening horror of the sight of so much human energy and such masses of human beings devoted to the work of destruction. There were grand flourishes of trumpets and inspiriting sounds from the military bands of music, and much driving to and fro of stately equipages and gorgeous liveries, and prancing of horses backed by skillful riders, but it had no charms to my eye sufficient to conceal the hideous skeleton beneath, nor did the fact that it was all a Moslem, and not a so-called Christian pageant, soften, to my mind, the harsh features of the show. The display was on the grand parade, in front of the office of the Minister of War, which stands on the very top of the highest eminence in Stamboul proper. I sat much of the time outside the gates watching the exhibitions of human nature on the part of the crowd of spectators, which were just the same as would be displayed under similar circumstances at home.

The view over the town and harbour and neighboring hills and sea was very grand, and I could not but think how often such displays had been repeated in the days before "Decline and Fall" were connected, even in distant possibility, with that Roman Empire which had here its capital, and of all the fearful atrocities perpetrated by military power during the conflicts which marked the progress and hastened the consummation of decay.

I also rode, one morning, through the Bazaar, which is an immense congeries of little stalls for the sale of every variety of goods. It is divided into sections, each devoted to one particular kind. Thus at one part you will find only slippers of every quality of material and workmanship, from the simple morocco shoe without heel or shape merely a covering to the toes and a loose sole (in which the foot can be retained while walking only by one rendered expert by practice) to those covered with embroidery and silk and gold thread, and rendered so costly as to be beyond the means of common purchasers. This part of the bazaar was very showy, and so was that devoted to the elaborately-worked jackets, which were thrust at the visitor with earnest entreaties to buy. One part is devoted to Damascus wares, and contains the showy silk articles made in that oldest city upon earth. Are the patterns of its shawls and bracelets now in any way different from those which Eliezer carried from Abraham to "the daughter of Bethuel, the son of Milcah, which she bare unto Nahor?"

Another part is appropriated to jewels and precious stones; into this I did not penetrate. We had seen in the treasury of the Sultan the incomparable collection of precious stones of every variety, and I had no disposition to come down to the petty display which could only be elicited by at least the pretense of purchase. In that part devoted to Egyptian merchants your mother was recognized by one of them, who bowed to her and said, "two Piastres, Madam;" thus recalling himself to her notice. While at Cairo "Far Away Moses" had brought him to Shepheard's Hotel, where he had made some sales of fancy articles to your aunts. Your mother had admired one table-cover of very elaborate workmanship, but the price he demanded was too great to permit her indulging herself in the purchase, and she declined, saying it was too much. He urged her strongly to make an offer, and in order to get rid of him she said, "Two Piastres." With perfect gravity and inimitable politeness he folded it up and laid it on her lap saying, "It is yours, Madam." Of course your mother knew she had no claim to such a gift, for such it would have been, as it was intrinsically worth a large sum, and she would have felt bound to return him its value in some way, and positively refused the offer, which was persistently repeated. We little thought ever to meet him again and should not have recognized him, but for his personal renewal of the acquaintance and inquiry in broken English if we did not think he could sell such goods in America if he should come here.

We visited also the museum, which is collected in the armory, in an old building once a Christian church, and since then a Mosque. There is a vast collection of instruments of warfare of every age down to the present. Many of them trophies of the victory over the Christian power in the days when the name of *Turk* sounded alarm in the ears of Spain and France as well as Germany. Relics of the Crusaders were also there. But the objects which attract most attention are the figures dressed in the peculiar costumes of their office representing Oriental manners. They are rudely made, and the dresses are dusty and dirty, but they bring before us Janissaries with all their ferocity, and Sultans and all their splendor, and Dervishes in their squalor, and all the various grades of rank and peculiarities of occupation.

The streets themselves afforded continually new objects of interest. Among them not the least attractive were the gardeners loaded with plants, till they looked like walking terraces themselves. The love for flowers is an Oriental taste, and the gardens of the various residences of the ambassadors were always attractive to us.

There are two English chapels. That attached to the Embassy is in the extensive and beautiful grounds of the Ambassador's palace, and the chaplain attached to the Embassy is an earnest Evangelical man, with whose service we were especially pleased; and we met there our attractive young friend from Smyrna, who came up to us cordially and welcomed us to the privilege of Christian fellowship in worship with a cordiality which confirmed our estimate of his worth.

IMPERIAL MAIL STEAMER,
ON THE DANUBE BETWEEN RUSTSCHUCK AND BASIAS,
April 25, 1872.

My Dear Children :

Again we have cause for adoring thankfulness for the mercy which has spared us, though I write in the cabin watching beside your mother suffering greatly with a badly sprained ankle. That it was not a broken leg; and that it had not occurred before our final debarkation at Varna, where the open harbour *often* makes the passing to or from the boat *most perilous*, are both present in our minds and give intensity to the gratitude. Suffer she must, but happily we have a light airy cabin on the forward deck entirely to our two selves; so that I can apply the lotions of lead-water and laudanum, and give morphia for her comfort, without interruption except by the passing to and fro of fellow-passengers outside the door; and your Uncle Wistar and Aunt Mary and Holly have the corresponding room, opening on the opposite side of the deck, only divided from us by a thin partition, so that we hear their voices and can by knocking summon them if we require. Your aunts and mother were to have had one room, and we gentlemen the other, but we were obliged to make some changes, as no one could have *slept* in your mother's room, except *myself;* and the wakefulness of others on her account would, *you know*, have exasperated her own sufferings immensely. Happily, though Prince William Charles is on board, there are spare rooms, so that others could be procured for your aunts, where they report themselves to have been more comfortable than they would have been even if your mother had not met with the injury.

Our passage across the Euxine from Constantinople to Varna had been very propitious. A full moon and light breeze made the water smooth and the sailing pleasant. We reached Varna soon after daylight and landed without difficulty. We found first-class, elegant and comfortable cars, run down to the pier waiting for us; and took our places all in one compartment for an eight hours' ride from the Euxine to the Danube.

There were many stopping places, at some of which the detention was for five minutes only, and at others for twenty; the time being announced as we stopped at each place by the very polite officer who unlocked the door. At the twenty minutes station we thought it best to alight and get some relief if only of position. There was a long platform with stone steps at each end, narrow and with a turn in them. The ladies had descended from the platform in a body, your mother among them; I was standing at the top and looking at the other end of the platform when they were returning. Your mother was among the last, and the skirts of an English lady immediately above her shut off the sight of the turn; and I was shocked by an exclamation from some one, and looking round found your mother had missed the step and fallen.

It was a *great mercy* that no more serious injury resulted—painful this is, it is true—but a broken bone would have made it *impossible* to travel, and the interior of Bulgaria would be a sad place to be detained, even at an English railroad station, till union should be perfect. We managed to get her into the car. For some time she was able to disguise her suffering by knitting; but in two hours she was compelled to lay this aside, and there were two hours more before we reached the Danube. I procured porters and a chair to carry her on board, and we shall not be compelled to move until to-morrow afternoon, when we have a railroad ride of some hours to Pesth, where we had designed to tarry over the Lord's day. So you see our traveling arrangements are as well adapted to the accident as we could have made them, unless it had been possible to continue our course by rail all the way to Vienna.

I had hoped this boat was to go on, but find there would be more changes from boat to boat than there are from boat to railroad car, and that the comfort of the boats probably diminishes as we get higher up the river and their size diminishes. So we must make the best arrangements we can to promote her comfort during the ride, and when we reach Vienna she can rest perfectly till she is able to travel. It will, however, effectually prevent her visiting objects of interest for a month at least. Now I have given you a *correct* detailed statement, and you must not aggravate your own suffering by supposing anything is withheld.

The Austrian Lloyd's line of steamers is as perfect in its boats and the equipments as possible. They ply on the Mediterranean and Black Sea, and are large and well equipped. That from Constantinople to Varna was large, *elegant* and commodious, and the meals furnished were all that the most fastidious could desire. We were detained some time in the harbour of Constantinople, and, therefore, had ample opportunity to see its wondrous capacity for commerce and to admire the unequalled beauty of the surrounding country. It is perfectly adapted to be again, as it once was, the emporium of a great people. I was astonished at the number and size of vessels lying in the harbour, even under its present wretched government, and when, as it soon must, it falls into the hands of Russia or Austria (especially the former as the more powerful nation), it will eclipse the glory of the Roman period. Even the treeless hills by which the port is encompassed are beautiful. What will they be when crowned by the residences of merchant princes, as they once were by those of tyrannical oppressors whose luxury enervated them mentally and bodily and made them an easy prey to the ruthless invader, attracted by a proud display of an affluence which the owners could not protect and were unworthy to enjoy?

History has no page more foul than that occupied by the Lower Greek Empire, unless it may be that of the Moslem which succeeded it, and is now kept from dissolution only by the absurd jealousy of so-called Christian powers.

The voyage through the Bosphorus was soon made, and to our great regret we were obliged to go into the cabin to a dinner of courses (we had fasted from early breakfast till 5.30 P. M.), soon after getting under way. We thus missed many points of great natural beauty, as well as the sight of eight or ten palaces of the Sultan, scattered at various points on the European and Asiatic shores. Some of them are said to be elegant buildings gorgeously furnished. A fellow-voyager (a Mr. Lowery, of Washington, D. C., son-in-law of Levi Woodbury), told me he had breakfasted at one of them (I suppose in the suite of Mr. Grant and Gen. Sherman), where coffee was served in cups held in gold cases set with diamonds. Mr. Boker did not honour us, his fellow-townsmen, with an invitation, so that we must put that in the same chapter of missed spectacles with the Arab dinner; and you may rest satisfied that we regret this one as little as the other.

At 9 P. M., your mother and I sought our couches, but not till we had witnessed a glorious sunset. Your mother's patriotism challenges superiority in this grandeur for our own country at large; and I am obliged to acknowledge the glory and beauty of those seen from Ivy Neck, beyond comparison. But this was very rich. The shores of the Euxine remind me of those of the Chesapeake, perhaps rather higher in some points, but evidently alluvial. About daylight I was again on deck watching our progress, which was near enough to the shore to enable me to see that the hillsides are covered with scrub trees.

Varna, for which we were bound, was one of the points occupied by the English, French and Turkish forces during the Crimean War, and from which sick and wounded were shipped to Constantinople. One of our fellow-voyagers told us his brother had been colonel of a regiment encamped here. Out of the one thousand men who left England only thirty returned. We went up to the place of encampment, where we could still trace the circles occupied by the tents.

From Varna our route lay northwest about one hundred and forty miles to the Danube. The whole distance is evidently alluvial with low hills of hard marl. The wheat-fields were of *limitless* extent. There are no division lines, and from our car we frequently looked out over an extent of the country which is like the ocean, or like that grand view over the level plain, stretching to the horizon, from your Uncle Murray's, at Melrose, in Virginia; which it resembles much.

The whole extent was varied only by low swelling hills scarce rising from the plain, covered with the richest green wheat-fields, darker spots recently ploughed and preparing for maze, and intervening pastures, on which great herds of cattle, and horses and flocks of sheep were tended by horsemen. Some hillsides were covered by scrubby forests, but the pastures and cultivated fields were thickly dotted by pear-trees, or apple or cherry just in blossom. So wondrous was the beauty that even your mother, notwithstanding her great suffering, would frequently exclaim with delight. This was not an occasional view only, but without exception the whole distance. Here and there villages of one-storied hovels, constructed of wattled boughs daubed with mud and covered with thatch or tiles, exhibited the poverty of the peasantry of Bulgaria; while at vast distances large square houses indicated that there were nobles, possessors of vast domains, for whose benefit they were cultivated. The entire distance was apparently a grand plateau, intersected by deep ravines in most of which streams flowed, turning mills, whose busy wheels brought back associations of home and childhood very foreign to those through which we have lately passed.

At Rustschuck we struck the Danube, flowing majestically by a sinuous course through the same formation of country as that we had just passed, which reminded us, in all its features, of West River. The same rich, friable, loamy soil, and the same productions; mulleins dandelions, and periwinkles, and blue bottles, were mingled profusely with other and stranger flowers amid the wheat fields; while red-bud was sufficiently abundant to give a pink tinge to the pale-green colour of the young leaves of the wooded hills.

The dress of the peasantry was very peculiar. The temperature, what we call *warm* spring weather. Yet they wear very heavy turbans of many-colored stuff wrapped around their heads, with close-fitting jackets (embroidered with black), of some brown cloth as heavy as our own blankets, a large green or red shawl rolled around the body, and lower garments of the same material as the jackets, and of immense width, gathered in at the waist, hanging very full behind, and sloped from the knees down to fit the leg accurately. Thick moccasins on the feet are carried up to the calf of the leg, to which they are bound by cords passing around and around. It is more strange than graceful, especially as many of the people are short and squatty in their persons.

We saw, in many places, large collections of wagons, some like our farm wagons, some with canvas tops and some without, and others again with permanent tops and the sides painted green and ornamented with yellow flowers. Such, I suppose, were the wagons in which their Scythian predecessors dwelt.

You must pardon the imperfection of my descriptions; my heart was preoccupied by your mother's sufferings. This same cause prevented my clearly taking in the position of affairs where we took the steamer. There were two towns; one in Bulgaria, on the south bank of the Danube under Turkish rule, though the inhabitants are Christians, as proved by the spires of some twenty churches; the other on the Wallachian side, under the rule now of a prince of the family of Emperor William of Germany.

I had always, heretofore, thought very lightly of the question of Roumanian and Wallachian and Bulgarian and Servian dominion. I shall not do so hereafter. These territories should be independent, and the people able to say, with their Scythian ancestors, to the ambassador (of Cyrus?) "If your master wants earth and water he must come and take it." Caspar or Effingham can tell you when and why this reply was given.

It was from these great plains issued the "barbarian hordes"—so the effeminate Greeks and the degenerate Romans called them—who overran their empires when wealth and luxury had enfeebled them, and who, under the humanizing influence of the same causes, became themselves the potent governors of the then known world. It was from these nations the legions were recruited, which often furnished Imperators and Cæsars from their own ranks. It is a great expanse of fertile soil under genial skies.

The Romans once thought the Servian Alps, whose snow-crowned ranges stretch away in the Southern distance, afforded an insuperable barrier to the Northern frontier of their Eastern provinces, and first stigmatized as barbarians the hardy inhabitants of these plains, whom they were afterwards glad to subsidize as protectors of their own civilization in its weakness, and then to admit as participants of the privileges of citizenship, after they had alternately conquered and been subdued by them during centuries of warfare. Till I saw these great and fertile plains with their noble streams, I could never understand the value of the prize for which they contended, and thought only of narrow districts of wooded territory in which men were as savage as the beasts of the forests and the rocks of the mountain passes. The *flats* of the Danube alone are an empire worth striving for. As we pursue our course, and flocks and herds, and meadows on which they range, and immense barges (towed by scores), each larger than our largest coal-barges, lie along the shore, taking in their freight of wheat and maize, or are drawn by steam tugs against the current of the stream, while countless strange-looking masted vessels, with both ends rising high out of the water represent the older navies of the region, and towns containing thousands of inhabitants are seen along the shore. Each such town represents, of course, an inland territory of more or less fertility and greater or smaller extent, dependent on it for foreign supplies and supporting its population by the products of the soil.

We need not boast of our fertile prairies as though they were singular. They are not without their parallel even in these territories once famous in story, now so sunken under the heel of despotism. Nor should we fail to profit by the lesson their history furnishes. Neither natural advantages nor human skill and courage can render any people independent of those laws which the Creator has established for the government of the world and its inhabitants, who rise, "wax fat and kick," and fall, race after race following in the same cycles of growth and decay.

I go out for occasional glimpses, though not willing to leave your mother long at one time. Ruined Roman arches and distant tumuli skirting the horizon tell the story of the past, while my eye feasts on the unchanging features of the landscape, the beauty of which testifies of the wisdom and goodness of the Creator and Redeemer, and gives promise of future products to His glory.

I would not have missed the visit to these regions on any account; even in their present state they are our rivals in the production of cereals. What would they not be were the impulse of proprietorship once given to the toiling masses, and modern improvements in labour-saving machinery brought to bear on developments? Steam navigation on the river, and the occasional tall chimney of some stationary engine on the banks give token of the advancing influence.

Just at this time the boat stopped to land a passenger and some sealed packages of corn, and as barges were lying between the steamer and the shores taking in cargo of wheat, I stepped out to examine the grain. It is very dirty, and is fanned by our old Dutch "wheat fans" as it is delivered into the hold. There is much cockle seed, but I neither saw nor smelt onion. It is evidently threshed on earthen floors. The grain is hard and heavy and red.

We have on board the Pasha of the Sultan, whose duty it is to collect the taxes of Bulgaria, and as we stop at the towns the governor of each comes on board and brings samples of the crop which is now going to market, which are taken by the Pasha, and the tax of this year on all products is levied by this sample of last year's grain. The entire revenue is collected in grain, which often obliges the poor people to buy for their own use some cheap bread stuff, as the wheat crop does not always yield enough to pay the tax on all products.

At 5 P.M. we reached the frontier town; well fortified. A crowd was collected filling every point from which the great man could be seen. A military band poured out gratulatory strains, and a regiment was paraded in his honour.

After being more than five months in the dominions of the Grand Turk, we feel as though we breathe easier on Christian soil, even though it be the despotic government of Austria Soon after passing the frontier between Bulgaria and Servia, we saw on the northern shore an extensive fortress and town belonging to Wallachia. I could not catch the name of either.

The Danube is a noble stream; we are now at least three hundred miles above its mouth, and it is at least as wide as the Delaware at Chester. The shores vary greatly. At times the river spreads out in wide flats with large islands in it, and then again they are rounded hills sloping in varied angles to the water.

IRON GATES OF THE DANUBE, April 26th, 8 A. M.

I can with difficulty tear myself away from the wondrous beauty by which we are surrounded, varying each moment with the changing light and shade, as well as from our progress through the mountain ranges, even long enough to record that your mother is sufficiently relieved to permit the window of our cabin to be open that she may catch passing glimpses of what is indescribably grand, imposing and beautiful. About midnight the boat stopped at Orsova and lay by until 4 A.M, when, the sounds indicating we were about to move, I went out on the deck. Square stone houses surrounding Christian churches with bell-towers, instead of minarets, were the first objects which arrested my notice. Then men restored to the bifid garments we are wont to recognize as the most commodious dress, were moving about on the pier with no intermingling of turbaned, petticoated forms, scarce showing feet at all, waddling and rolling, rather than walking; which, picturesque as they may be, may have applied to them the remark of the English peasant to the enthusiastic lady who was sketching with rapture, a moss-grown thatched cottage, " very pretty on paper, but not so nice to live in." Then the large signs on the front of houses, " Gasthoff," " Dampshiff Gessellschaft," " Apotheke," and such like, told in letters as plainly as the other signs had done, that we had passed wholly into the region of "Vaterland," the final witness appearing in the shape of a sign, "Bier Halle," covering the front of a house.

We soon left, and found ourselves entering a mountain pass, so like those on the Juniata or upper Susquehanna or Delaware, that one might almost fancy oneself transported during the night from one continent to the other; the chief difference being in the absence of the dark-green of the pine and hemlock. The hill sides were all clothed with deciduous trees (no longer scrub), whose delicate green, the first hue of spring, was varied in shade, till the view was like that of some colossal parterre. Gradually the mountains encroached more and more on the bed of the river, which became deeper and more contracted as the cliffs became more precipitious, till these last rose like towering walls of grey rock, with here and there a ledge affording root-hold for some hardy trees, while the contracted channel was filled deeply with a rushing torrent of water pouring over the rocks far sunken below, boiling and seething and churning in ever-repeated whirls, so strong and fierce that, as the vessel forced her way through them under the influence of the powerful impulse of her noble engines, they gave one the sensation of grinding through rocks. I might have thought this a stretch of imagination, if your mother, who of course could not see the water, had not supposed we were aground. Finally we passed through the Iron Gates,—a not inappropriate term. On either side the smooth grey rocks rose to the height of many hundred feet, leaving but narrow room for the river to wind between.

In the solid stone on the south side, just above the surface of the river, now swollen to its fullest flow, are still very plainly seen the square holes on which the Romans had supported their military road, by which the Emperor, Trajan, had carried his victorious arms into the Dacian territories, while, on the northern side, galleries blasted through the rocks convey the modern military road of Austria by which she would fain pour her conquering armies into the Danubian province of Turkey if Russian jealousy did not oppose a barrier more insuperable than mountain ranges. We wound our way mile after mile through this cleft in the rocks, sometimes perfectly perpendicular from the water's edge, sometimes receding a short distance on the one side or the other, leaving nooks in which nestled snug villages, sometimes turning soft green slopes to the newly risen sun, sometimes showing their strata twisted and coiled over each other, like the thread wound on a ball, sometimes covered with noble trees, and very frequently embroidered with great patches of purple lilac in full flower; viburnum, with its countless heads of purest white, and interspersed among them horse-chestnut, with their spikes white in the distant view we had of them, rising like chenille work above the deep green of the trees, which spread like a bed of ferns the soft carpet beneath. Every instant some change in beauty—no abatement, but only variation—filled our souls with ever-fresh delight, which has not subsided, till now, at 9½ A. M., we find ourselves emerging through the range of mountains, and the roar of the rushing waters calls me to look whether this can be an actual cataract. Indeed I have found it almost impossible to take time from looking to jot down the passing impression, knowing that it must be done now or the living colour will fade away.

HOTEL KRINGLER, PESTH, April 27, 1872.

We feel as though we had slept with Diedrich Knickerbocker, and awaked after years of absence in a world wondrously like that in which we had fallen asleep, yet wondrously changed and improved, too. This is a grand city. I had thought of it only as I had learned of it in my geography book as opposite to Buda, on the Danube. I knew it was the ancient capital of Hungary, and had given Maria Theresa to the Austrian empire, and thought it had slept ever since, till, as the result of the revolution of 1848, it had been aroused. We have yet seen nothing beyond the railroad depot, and the long drive thence to this hotel through a street, wider than Broad Street, lined on either side with great storehouses with names on the signs as familiar as those which greet our eyes at home (German, of course). Well-paved streets, noble draught-horses and active business. Tall chimneys, throwing out sooty vapour to the skies, telling of cotton and woolen mills and machine-shops, and everything betokens affluence, energy and skill. Cars, numbered over twenty thousand, some empty, some filled with sheep, and oxen, and wheat, are crowded on the sidings at the depot, and an immense stock of coal tells the story of active business. All this you must accept as the mere "place at which the letter is given"—*the date*—and now I will give the first information about ourselves, which you are doubtless anxious to receive, and am happy to say that your mother's ankle is *doing* well—painful, of course—but less swollen. We carry her whenever it is necessary to move her. She does not leave the bed or couch for any purpose.

I was obliged to stop writing on the Danube before we reached Bazias, which is the place at which we took railroad for this place. It is a mere railroad station; and we were compelled to wait there *eight* hours, as the train for this place leaves there only twice a week in connection with the steamboat from Rustschuck, but does not depart immediately on arrival of the boat, which is somewhat dependent on the weather. It cannot run the narrows during dark nights, and strong head-winds retard her progress. On this trip it blew a perfect hurricane for a short time; and after our arrival we had every indication of a heavy rain, which blew over after refreshing us greatly by the reduction of temperature. We sat patiently in the waiting-saloon, happily able to secure a lounge for your mother; but of course were obliged to discontinue the saturnine applications. A magnificent bright-edged, black-faced cloud hung on the horizon, giving us the lesson of there being two sides to everything. Happily no one of the company which filled the room had manifested any unreasonable discontent; and on one of our fellow-passengers speaking of a cloud, as the most beautiful thing we had seen at Bazias, I could not omit reference to the patience of the company as more beautiful still. Your uncle had instructed Friezier to secure a sleeping compartment for your mother and myself, so that we felt no anxiety about her comfort; but on making application for it we were told we could not have it, as it was wanted for Prince William Charles. He is a hardy, rough-looking Dutchman; short, muscular, sandy complexioned, and I thought certainly had endured greater hardships in the war with France, in which he acquired such great fame for his masterly movements and courage, and we therefore insisted that as we had paid for it we should have it, and after much Dutch discussion we were allowed to get into it. The Prince, I believe, knew nothing about it himself. We found it a very comfortable arrangement. The seats were most commodious, well stuffed and with good springs, and immediately in front of each a cushioned rest for the legs let down from the front of the compartment. Happily we had with us the large air-pillow, more than a yard long, which I had bought at Cairo, and this placed on the stool made a very nice rest for the leg and foot, so that she slept most of the night.

We started at 9 P. M., and reached this place at 7 A. M. It was a fine moonlight night, the road lay over an immense plain without any hills; and during the first part I thought the Hungarians must be at least amphibious and possess some specific against malaria or the country would be without inhabitant. This we found was not the case, as we stopped at numberless villages, and could see that the whole surface of the country which was not under water is an unbroken grainfield. The green surface is limitless; only broken by ploughed patches prepared for maize. As the day dawned we saw the people on their way from the villages to the fields; and herds of cattle and horses, and flocks of sheep, tended by shepherds watching by night, were gathered in groups here and there. The rising sun exhibited the rich green of the growing grain, and the beautiful blossoms of the apple and cherry-trees, and we found that much of the water we had seen during the night was in reservoirs for the cattle, as there were no running streams anywhere.

As we drew near to Pesth the extensive kitchen gardens indicated our approach to a large centre of population requiring ample supplies of vegetable food. The gardens were laid out in oblong squares, divided by gutters, with depressions and wide places at regular distances. Water is raised from the wells by horse power and runs along the gutters, and is thrown by a shovel from those dipping places over the entire bed. This struck me as a more efficient and less laborious process than carrying the water. Vines were planted in trenches and watered also.

The land is owned by large proprietors, nobles, and held in immense tracts. The peasantry are mere labourers and live in small houses of only one room. The walls are of brick about four feet high, with a thatched roof of high pitch; with only one window, a door, and a chimney.

I had forgotten to mention an amusing episode which contributed to the good humour of the party at Bazias. Our luggage had been booked through to Vienna, but the custon house officer there refused to allow it to be put into the car without examinaton. This was most thorough, turning out photographs on the counter by some hundred or more belonging to T. K. Longstreth and Miss Harris (small ones); opening your mother's cap and bonnet boxes, and your aunt's private bundles; and seizing as liable to duty a half bottle of ink in your uncle's trunk, a broken package of tea in my bag, and two small pieces of silk your aunt Mary had bought at Constantinople. All was done with the utmost politeness, but most seriously and determinately. Some of our fellow travellers were obliged to pay duty on their small stocks of tobacco for smoking *en route*. One gentleman told me had more than 100 cigars among his clothes which escaped notice. I do not know how they could have been stowed to escape the searching investigation of ours.

Your uncle and aunts are now visiting the Museum and a Picture gallery of Prince Esterhazy said to possess some unrivalled Spanish paintings. I am satisfied that I cannot see everything in the world and may as well allow these things to be among the vast majority I cannot see, and have not left your mother; who is now sleeping sweetly. Our window overlooks the Danube beyond which rises the garden clad hill on which stands a vast pile " The old palace of Buda."

    Your loving father,

              CASPAR MORRIS.

        PESTH, HUNGARY, April 28, 1872.

My Dear Child:

I find I can't remember when I last wrote to you but rather think it was from Constantinople, where we last mailed letters. Since then I believe your father has written. We sailed from there for Varna, across the Black Sea, on the 22d. Had nice accommodations and a smooth sea, and in fifteen hours had to disembark in one of those little boats again; that trying ordeal to me. But we were quite comforted at finding this was to be our *last* experience in this way, and took a railroad ride of nine hours to Rustchuck, and during that time there were several opportunities given for us to leave the car and gather flowers or get refreshments. Repeatedly I remained in but at last yielded to entreaties and walked with them, to my pain and sorrow, lor. not seeing we had reached the platform, I raised my foot to ascend another step and came down four or five feet, my whole weight on the one foot. which turned ; and consequently I have a very bad sprained foot and ankle. I may say the whole limb is very uncomfortable, but we have so much cause for thankfulness that the bones are not broken. I suffered very much in the rest of the ride and the two days and night on the Danube. I can say with truth I did not see it (the Danube) at all as I never raised my head from the time two men laid me down, until the two sailors came to carry me ashore, to be put in the cars for an eight hours' ride at *night* to this place. We were much favoured with nice accommodations, both in steamboat and on the cars, and *every body* was as kind as possible. The Captain unhesitatingly made arrangements to let us have the stateroom to ourselves instead of putting all five of us ladies in it, and the gentlemen elsewhere, as in that way there could have been no rest for any of us. My groans would have disturbed them, and their sympathy and desire to do for me would have driven me wild, and of course your father would have staid on the deck at the door. Both he and Wistar made the inquiry as to whether I could not be taken directly to Vienna by boat, but learned that the boat we were on board of did not go further up the river, and it would involve more changes with less comfort to try that route, and so I was brought ashore at Bazias, attracting more attention from the crowd gathered to welcome " Prince William Frederick," who was our fellow passenger, than he did. Here in a crowded station we had to wait several hours for the cars, making it nine at night when Friezier and Tom Longstreth lifted me in a chair up to the car door, and your father and uncle placed me on a most luxurious lounge well supported with air cushions. If I had been a Princess I could not have had more done to alleviate pain, but on the other hand if a Princess had the same misfortune she would have to bear the pain, and so had I. We reached here in eight hours. Then I was to be lifted into a carriage and a mile and a half over the streets. But all was done to make it as easy as possible, and when I was carried upstairs and on a delightful bed, I felt thankful and fell asleep. To-day my maimed limb is better, that is less painful, but I have no more use of it than if it was broken.

This is a fine old town. I admired it as we drove through and hear much from the others about it. Very wide streets with fine buildings on each side. My room overlooks the Danube, where I see the boats incessantly sailing and rowing, and have a fine view of an old palace.

Some amusement was afforded the other night at Bazias by the examination of the luggage of about fifty passengers. They all agreed it was the most thorough they had ever known. Every trunk bag and bundle was not only opened but searched, greatly to the indignation of many ; and some things confiscated. They took from our bag a package of tea, from uncle Wistar's a part of a bottle of ink, aunt Mary's two pieces of silk, about eight yards each, which she got in Constantinople to make a down spread of, so as to have it Oriental. My tin cap box was eagerly pounced on, but dismay filled their faces on seeing caps, etc. instead of tobacco. From R. Harris they took a tin box also, but on opening it was filled with "*cartes de visites*" from various places, hers and Tom's (over 400); all of which they spread out, but concluded to let them pass. Now to-morrow as we enter Vienna, the same thing is to be gone through and poor me can't repack but must let your father do the best he can.

VIENNA, 29th.

You will see we have made the move to-day and it was accomplished satisfactorily. The same luxurious accommodations being provided for me and my lame foot, and as my chamber is adjoining our parlour, my chair can be rolled in, and take my meals in the room with them all, tho' I can't sit up to the table. We found here letters from home to the seventh of April; from Is., Mary, and little Sally Murray and Mrs. Cope; for all of which receive our thanks. They are most acceptable and I will try to acknowledge some of the children's now while I am shut in the house.

Of course there will be much here to be seen by the party and your father intends going to the hospitals, one of which we passed as we came from the depot; an immense building, and they are celebrated here. I do not expect to leave this floor until we leave the city. It is a disappointment as I intended to have seen some of the things here, but I will try to content myself with "Murray's Guide Book" and my needle.

We are much concerned to hear, through Mrs. Valentine, that Margaret is still so *very* poorly and I often wish we could be with them, tho' just at this moment I would not, even if in Philadelphia, be of any use, as my foot cannot touch the floor. We do feel *very much* for Galloway and Margaret, and if they at all desire it, would return to them at once, if a telegram would reach us. I do hope your uncle James will stay as much as he can there. I am very sorry to hear he is so poorly too. Remember me to him and Sallie; also to Sam. and tell aunt Sallie I should be delighted to have a letter from her. I was very glad to hear of your getting up to the Ridge and a little about during the holidays, and now I am rejoicing over the prospect of Mary Gibson getting to you. Poor thing she has had a hard time and I am sure must need rest, and a visit to you can be that for her. Let Israel settle with her, and keep her when you get her as long as you can, and let her do up all your things for you, and it is a great comfort to hear Hannah Shuster will do for R. Do not hesitate about having the wardrobes moved; they are not essential to the furnishing of those rooms, as one of those in my room can be put in there in the place of one, and that will be sufficient. Israel thinks he can get another tenant when the Parrishes leave.

You will have to let Annie shop for you, and Is. will furnish the means. She will do it nicely and judiciously, I am sure. I am only sorry to add to her labour which I know is incessant, but I know there is a willing mind.

Tell Harry we regret his being on the Jury, but it is so much better than having him there last Fall (which we feared to hear all the time), that I won't say anything. I hope Jimmy Neal and your German will go ahead with your gardening in his absence.

Here we are again among the Germans. We came yesterday for six hours through a most extensive plain, highly cultivated, everything is most beautiful both in the country and towns, or villages where the peasantry live. These consisted of one story, square houses, each having a nice little garden and well in it, only the one class of inhabitants dwell in these. Romish Chapels, of course, and shrines again everywhere. But the soil is tilled by men, women, and children. Women perform all kinds of work with the men. We saw gangs, sometimes at least 100 people, planting corn. Ploughing is done by oxen; in one place there were ten ploughs each having a pair of oxen—noble fellows too. I am quite fascinated with the German labourers; only wish I could talk to them.

Friezier has just come to say let him have this, so farewell, with much love to all.

Yours most truly and affecty,

A. C. MORRIS.

Here's your father who says plenty of time for love to one and all. I can't tell you how glad I am if this misfortune was to fall on any, that I was the one, and that we had got where we were, instead of its being two or three weeks earlier in our journey. No ships now to climb.

PESTH, April 28, 1872.

My Dear Children:

I find I was not so far wrong in my ideas about this place as I thought I was. In twenty years it has increased in population 30,000 to 201,000, of this number 70,000 are Jews. The large manufactories are flour mills, grinding and exporting the grain the growth of the immense fields over which we passed, and to which the city returns manures of various kinds which we saw being applied to the already productive soil, which is without a stone and easy of culture and thoroughly worked. The new buildings are very imposing; private dwellings, banking houses, offices of business, theatres; all are built of very fine stone by good architects. We have nothing equal to them in our city.

Your uncle and aunts are very much excited over the attractiveness of their drive this afternoon in the environs and to the Joseph Platz or Park. I left your mother and walked out for an hour in the town and saw a public garden planted with lilac and laburnum and horse chestnut and buckeye, all in full flower, and crowded with happy people sitting on benches, standing and walking, with children sporting with those red balloons which float about Chestnut Street; and thought I had never been among a population which gave stronger evidence of prosperity.

The store windows are all filled with attractive goods, well displayed; silks, furs, jewelry, furniture; each speaking of a flourishing condition; more beautiful than any similar display in Philadelphia. Omnibuses and railroad cars are crowded with passengers and the side walks are thronged with pedestrians.

I strayed into the Jews' synagogue said to be the finest in the world. It is large, somewhat resembling in style the new one on Broad above Green, but much larger. The sanctuary at the end is richly carved and gilded, and the veil of purple velvet elaborately embroidered with gold. I witnessed the opening of the doors of the Holy Place and bringing out the rolls, wrapped in costly coverings. It was carried in procession with chanting by very powerful voices, and when portions had been read was replaced with the same ceremony. It was in strong contrast with the wailing at the wall of the temple we had so lately seen. This synagogue was of reformed Jews who, I believe, have abandoned the hope of a Messiah. The size of the building may have deceived me, but I thought there was but a small number to represent so large a population.

PESTH, Lord's Day, April 29, 1872.

No one can imagine, it must be experienced personally to be appreciated properly, the delight of waking, not to confused cries in an incomprehensible language, an utter Babel of sounds, but to the rolling of wheel carriages over stone pavements, and the stir and animation of life to which one has been accustomed during earlier years. Such was our gratification this morning; and now it has all subsided into the semi-repose of an orderly Christian community, with bells announcing public worship, which do not interest us as we could not unite with the congregation assembling even if we understood the language, as there is, we presume, none but Latin services. We were told there would be English service in French; but learn that the clergyman is absent. Your mother and I have enjoyed our own service together, and she is now resting.

Her foot is still very much swollen and discoloured and painful, but *improving*. She can convey some motion to the toes. She does not move except from the bed to a large chair, placing the leg and foot on another. They are very large and comfortable; indeed our suite of apartments is commodious, even grand, and our window commands a fine view of the Danube with its passing boats, and the palace and gardens on the opposite shore.

During the night my mind got muddled with thoughts of Huns and Dacians, Attila and Germanicus, and Hadrian and Valens. Your uncle had described the contents of the museum and the magnificence of the Hungarian crown jewels, and your aunts had been delighted by standing on the mound, formed of earth brought from all the dependant provinces, on which the Emperor annually rides a horse, shod with silver shoes, and stands with bare head and waves his sabre toward the cardinal points successively; in token of his extended sway. This I suppose had given the current to my imagination, and as I roused from my reverie I found myself reaching the conclusion on which I rest, that the world is a *small* planet, has endured but a short period of eternity; its mightiest events, concerns of but little importance in the great concerns of the universe; ourselves of none whatever except to our little selves, and the microcosm composed of those united to us in the blessed bonds of family connection. I thank God truly for the goodness which has established and sanctified the family, and given us to each other as children and parents, husbands and wives, and has concentrated there all the joys and privileges of our being. Upon the faithful discharge of our duties to Him and to each other in these relations, which He has established, depends our unending condition when the records of all the past of the earth shall be forever obliterated by that fire for which it is reserved, and which shall cause " all things to be dissolved."

Yet I cannot withhold my admiration of the grandeur of the civilization which here greets my eye whenever I raise it, whichever way I may turn. Egyptian Grecian and Roman temples and palaces were more massive and imposing and enduring, but the elegance and comfort of private residences and places at which merchants transact their everyday business bespeak here a more wide diffusion of affluence elegance and comfort among the masses of mankind.

2 P. M.

I left your mother to rest awhile and took a quiet walk, from which I have returned more deeply impressed with the greatness of this town. Everywhere one sees large, well-built, substantial houses, stores well filled with goods, and tokens of enterprise and success. The men look as though they had just stepped out of John Wanamaker's, and the women from Homer & Colladay's. The costumes are the same as with us, and the features so similar that one feels as though one must exchange salutations. Flower stores are filled with beautiful plants, and the atmosphere is loaded with the fragrance of the lily-of-the-valley—bunches of which are seen in the hats of the boys, the buttonholes of the elders, and carried by the ladies in their hands. The streets are perfectly clean, and happiness and contentment is the prevailing expression. Hotels afford some indication of the prosperity of the city. We have a suite of five rooms for our party, each of which is more than twenty feet square, carpeted with the softest and most beautiful carpets, and the walls hung with the finest paper; lounges, sofas, arm-chairs of all convenient forms, richly covered, abounding. Yet I find there is nearby another newer hotel, to which the Continental at Ninth and Chestnut is a pigmy affair.

7 P. M. Monday, April 29th, 1872.

We left Pesth at 7½ A. M., and reached Vienna at 2 P. M., and are now rested from the journey, which was accomplished without difficulty in a sleeping-car. We received dear Mary's and little Sally's letters and Israel W.'s of the 7th. Later dates from Mrs. Valentine and sister Mary give us great anxiety about your uncle Galloway and aunt Margaret. Telegraph to us through Brown, Shipley & Co. if our immediate return is desirable, and we will not allow anything to detain us.

We shall remain here until this day week, the 6th of May. We then propose leaving for Milan via Adelsberg and Padua, and so to Genoa and by the Corniche road to Nice, Lyons and Paris, and thence to some of the German Baths and Berlin. You thus see our course will be carrying us daily westward till we reach Paris.

My anxiety about your aunt and uncle in Baltimore is very great, and my desire to do everything in our power to alleviate their sufferings, which seem to be immitigable. No mere pursuit of pleasure would detain me one hour.

Your mother is of necessity carried whenever we move, and keeps her foot elevated, and thus far enveloped in wet compresses whenever practicable. At present, 9 P. M., she sits near the table writing. We are at the Hotel Cour d'Autriche. Our saloon is a good one; the chambers not much—appear especially narrow and dark after those we occupied at Pesth, which were sumptuous.

To-morrow the party commence the tour of Galleries and Churches. Your mother, of course, will not be able to leave the saloon and her chamber, which adjoin. I shall devote myself to hospitals, which will render me independent in my movements, and enable me to be more with her than I could be if I went with them; without interfering with their hours. You all know me well enough to be sure that, much as I admire pictures and fine buildings, this course will be no cross to me.

Our ride to-day from Pesth of six hours was very interesting. At first the road lay through a semi-mountainous region devoted to grape culture. The scene was a very busy one. Spring was actively pushing forth the buds of trees and flowers, and the peasants were very busy driving the stakes and tilling the ground among the vines, which were planted to the top of the hills. The culture is entirely different from any that we have yet seen. The vines are planted about two feet apart, and kept trimmed down to about six inches above the ground. The stakes are about four feet high, and are taken out of the ground when the growth of the last year is cut off. The fruit is sent from here as far as St. Petersburg. After passing through this ridge, the entire distance was a level plain, such as that beyond Pesth, cultivated very highly in wheat and maize.

The peasantry all live in villages of small one-storied houses, at intervals of some miles. The cattle and flocks are herded, as there are no fences of any kind. Some portions of the plain are very rich, and the wide expanse of deep green wheat is very beautiful. We saw in one place twelve ploughs, each drawn by a yoke of white oxen, preparing for corn, and several times as many as a hundred women in a straight line, each following one row and keeping side by side. In other places we would see dozens of people in groups, weeding the tares out of the wheat. They all looked healthy and happy. Each village has its fine church, and the larger towns were filled with busy people. Presburg was the largest, and has an imposing castle.

We have yet seen nothing here but the outside of the Arsenal and Belvidere Gallery, and some wide streets with grand buildings in the newer part of Vienna. This hotel is in the oldest part, not far from the Cathedral, which has a fine spire and a venerable aspect. The stores are attractive-looking and the people very busy, and the roar of carriages and omnibuses almost deafening. As we came to the hotel we passed the grand opera house, said to be the finest in the world.

With all love to one and all,
Your devoted father,
CASPAR MORRIS.

VIENNA, April 30, 1872.
My Dear Brother: (*Galloway Cheston.*—EDS.)

On reaching here yesterday we found letters from home but none from you, which we greatly regret especially as in one from Julia Valentine, she speaks of increased indisposition in dear Margaret, and I fear that accounts for your silence. We do feel *much, very much*, for you both and not only regret our absence deeply but would unhesitatingly go to you at any moment if you think we would be any comfort to you. Indeed our first impulse was to go at any rate, but my helpless condition just at this moment is a serious obstacle.

Perhaps you will have learned from our children of my having sprained my foot and ankle *badly*, the day after we left Constantinople. I have suffered very much with it and am still unable to put it to the floor, and am obliged to be carried whenever we move, so that just now I would only be an encumberance. We had two long railroad rides, one of a night, and after a day and night's rest at Pesth, a day to this place; but such luxurious accommodations were secured for me in a seeping car that the ride did not increase the pain. But don't let this prevent your calling us by telegram, if we can give the smallest relief.

To-morrow is the first of May, when Miss T. is to go to you; I hope she will prove acceptable to you both, and I shall be pleased to hear Mary Yarnall is with you again. Mary Murray mentions her uncle James was with you, for which I was glad. You see I must watch you all. Altho' so widely separated my heart is with you.

We will gladly execute your commission when we reach the right point. I only hope we will be able to get something right handsome. I do often wish I knew what to pick up for dear Margaret from this part of the world, tho' I know she requires no assurance of that kind from me of our remembrance. No indeed, upwards of forty years of uninterrupted and strong attachment to each other requires no outward token of love. I am so glad to tell you the Dr. is quite well, and so are all of our party. They are much occupied in sight seeing, picture galleries, churches etc., it is no trial to me to be deprived of all this; I am only sorry the Dr. will not see so much as he would have done, if I were not so helpless.

(*Not signed, but in handwriting of A. C. M.*—Eds.)

VIENNA, May 1, 1872.

My Dear Brother: (*Galloway Cheston.*—Eds.)

Anne has just laid aside her pen, wearied by the effort to write in the constrained posture which is inevitable from the necessity there is to keep the foot elevated. I do not know what she has said about herself, and may therefore merely repeat the same account. It will be the testimony of two witnesses.

She finds the necessity of assistance about everything very trying to her independent disposition, but I impose absolute rest as the only condition. It is necessary. Any motion of the injured part is not only painful at the present but retards greatly the progress of amendment and also involves the risk of more serious injury. The discolouration extends from the sole under the instep half way to the knee; and about the ankle joint and arch of the foot it is black, and very much swollen. The heat has entirely subsided under use of lead water and laudanum and I am now rubbing it gently with soap liniment and supporting it by a bandage very moderately applied. I roll her from the bed to the window, and as here our chamber adjoins the saloon of the party, she is rolled there in the evening to participate in the reports each one makes of the impression produced on them by the sights of the day, which is interesting, when they are not too wearied by the pleasure seeking to keep it when found.

This is a great holiday here and I suppose we shall not see any of them before late this evening as they spend the morning in some galleries of art and the afternoon at the Prater or Public drive. When once one gets into the ring there is no escape; carriage after carriage sweeps on and one must go with the current. I should find it very irksome even if there was no other reason to stay away. They are all anxious to have Anne put into a carriage and accompany them, but I am sure it would do her harm and shall stay with her myself. With much love to dear Margaret who does not need our experience to add to her knowledge that there are pains and penalties in travel as well as delights.

We shall be in Paris three weeks from date.

Your loving brother
CASPAR MORRIS.

VIENNA; HOTEL OESTERREICHISCHER HOF, April 30, 1872.
My Dear Children:

While your uncle and aunts have gone to visit the sights of this great city I have passed an hour or two in visiting the hospital, and am again with your mother, having secured some soap liniment and bathed her foot and enveloped it in nice bandages. The cold lotions had ceased to afford her relief and there is no longer any more heat than natural. It is still very much swollen and discoloured from the sole under the instep to at least a foot above the ankle bone. She is, as you will know she would naturally be, most unwilling to detain me from visiting the many objects of interest here.

But I have elsewhere seen some museums of natural history, and a few pictures, and can form some imagination of the scale on which they are likely to be here from that of the private residences, public buildings, and hospitals. The streets around the hotel are narrow and occupied by shops; jewellers, clothing, dry goods, etc. A short distance only brings one to the Franz Joseph Park, a boulevard running along an arm of the Danube. There we reach a wide avenue with the walks adorned with lilacs and other shrubs, on the one side, and on the other range after range of great blocks of houses of a light yellow colour five and six stories high with handsomely ornamented fronts, the basement story occupied by shops and banks and offices, the upper as dwellings.

A new hall for the Bourse or Exchange has been recently built; not yet open for use. I wonder somewhat at the delicate sarcasm of the architect, and the stolidity of the good burghers by whom it is built, that they permit it to stand for the amusement of the wits who must take it up sooner or later if they have not already done so. He has placed a figure of Mercury that *accomplished thief* on each corner of the facade. They are good copies of the celebrated bronze, standing on the toe, as it seems to prosaic spectators; "balanced perfectly in ether," say the admiring connoisseurs who think it the perfection of art. According to my judgment of stock operations he is very appropriately placed, balanced on nothing and ready to disappear.

I had taken a seat in the tram way car which led me past this and the very graceful and costly " Votif Kirck " not yet completed. It is very light with lofty spires elaborately carved, many flying buttresses and a large proportion of windows, which will, when filled with good stained glass, have a superb effect. It is I think the most elegant modern church I have yet seen and is erected to commemorate the virtues of one of the Royal Dukes. That part of the town is rapidly filling up with buildings of great solidity, and what was heretofore the parade ground is to be covered with Imperial Parliament houses and new Municipal buildings. I am afraid when I get home I shall think even Pennsylvania Railroad buildings small affairs; and be tempted to advocate new municipal buildings even though they cost millions. One gets sadly demoralized by the constant association with grandeur. Our most costly new houses and buildings are small concerns when placed besides those of Europe.

After passing by these we reached the hospital. It is a town within its own walls. They divide it into *streets*. There are not less than five thousand patients. I delivered Dr. Strawbridge's card of introduction to Dr. Artl and followed his eye service in the ward. He was very polite to me, placed me under the charge of his first assistant who speaks English and knew Dr. W. F. Norris. Dr. A. insisted that I should occupy the best position to witness several operations he did. Three extractions of the lens for cataract and one excision of the skin of the eye lid after detaching it from the cartilege; for the cure of entropion. They were all beautifully done. He operates as readily with the left hand as the right. The perfectly tranquil manner of Dr. A. and the readiness of his assistants, who appeared to act as though they were impelled by impulses from his brain rather than in response to the very quiet utterance of his request, are very impressive. He has not a handsome face nor courtly manner, yet he commands respect by his appearance. Not willing to be long absent from your mother I left so soon as he went into his reception room where a hundred cases at least were waiting his advice. The lens was extracted by incision at the junction of the cornea and sclerotica and the eye looked perfectly undisturbed when he invited me to look at each, and holding objects before the patient tested the power of vision before applying the bandage. They do not use anæsthetics in operations for cataract.

I was pleased with the neatness of the mode of administering the chloroform diluted with absolute alcohol, in the other case. Flannel is stretched on a wire frame with a bridge running from the one side to the other causing it to project above the nose, and a handle at the one side by which the assistant who stands at the head may hold it over the mouth and face with one hand while in the other he holds a bottle of the anæsthetic fluid with projecting tubes, almost capillary, from which he waters the upper surface of the flannel. It is a very neat, economical, and efficient arrangement, much more convenient than our barbarous mode of enveloping mouth and nose in napkin cones or sponges. If this little apparatus has not been introduced with us it should be for convenience and economy. The handle projects towards the forehead of the patient and the projecting bridge runs transversely across the end of the nose. The bottle has tubes through the cork like an inhaler.

After leaving Artl's clinic I stepped a moment into a surgical clinic of one of the most distinguished professors whose name is perfectly familiar but has escaped my memory. I found a patient on the table already under the influence of chloroform. The surgeon was quietly seated at one side and the first assistant at the other, the arrangements being made by the other assistants. When these announced that all was prepared the surgeon still kept his seat while the first assistant disarticulated the great toe, with the metatarsal bone from the tarsus. Just as it was completed the surgeon, who had watched every step in silence, rose and went to the patient and without saying a word satisfied himself that all was right and took his seat. Not a word passed from any one.

The report of the day's action on the part of your uncle and aunts did not excite any regret on my part that I had not gone with them. The entire morning was passed in the Belvidere picture gallery among Durers and Matsys and Rubens and Titians, until they were perfectly wearied. Your mother decided that the pain of her ankle was easier to endure and that I had profited more by what I saw. In the afternoon I went to Neuhoffer's, the opticians, and filled Israel's commission and would gladly have done so for Galloway but his list has not reached us. Your uncle and I will go there again before leaving and we hope for another mail here which may bring it; if not I must wait till I reach Paris. Your mother's lameness puts it out of her power to make any purchases and I have no disposition to do so.

The other members of the party visited the two churches in one of which lie the bodies of the Imperial family, each enclosed in a silver or bronze coffin in a large airy lighted hall, with which some of them were highly gratified. In the other church they peeped through a small grated window in an iron door at the silver and gold urns containing the hearts of those same deceased monarchs. I tell them I am in greater danger of being captivated by the vanity of grand dwellings and noble buildings for the living than by mausolia or sarcophogi for the dead.

Your loving father,

CASPAR MORRIS.

VIENNA, May 2, 1872.

My Dear Children:

I am thankful to be able still to report satisfactory improvement in your mother's ankle. She slept better last night and is now dressing while I wait on her and write at intervals. Your uncle and aunts yesterday visited the arsenal with its collection of ancient armor, which they thought very fine. Better even than that at the Tower, London; or at Constantinople. The hall of statues of Emperors and great statesmen and generals they also found impressive. They were amused by the drive on the Prater, and then went shopping. For myself, soon after they left in the morning I went to an "*apotheke*" to procure an article we generally find at Hubbell's or James Shinn's and was referred to a "*Bandagiste*" corresponding to our surgeon's instrument maker. I wandered along Stephen's Strasse and Kohl Market and Graben, and I know not how many other streets passing shop after shop of every variety of wares except what I needed; elegant and attractive, drawing crowds of people to look from among the greater crowds pressing on in every direction, the throngs as great as those on Chestnut Street on a fine holiday. At last I found another apothecary and made inquiry for a bandagiste in French (be sure you all cultivate French and German, I am shamed of my ignorance). The apothecary answered me in English saying he knew from my accent I was an American. He very kindly wrote on paper for me Schlecht; Bandagiste, Schotten Hof; and I started off.

After seeking the Schottenhof vainly I saw a sign "American Exchange" strangely staring out among the German names, and there I found a forbidding looking countryman of Col. James Fiske, Jr., who told me to go ahead and I would find it. So on I went and turned into a dry goods store to ask again. The storekeeper was about to go to the door to show me when a pretty looking young lady making a purchase said "*je vais le meme Chemin, si'l plait, Mons. pouvait m'accompagner.*" Of course I could do no less than take off my hat with "*tres grands remerciment*"; and wait till she had completed her purchases. She soon ran me aground in conversation, but after going some distance she said "*Mons. attenderat ici un moment*" and darted around a corner and left her purchases, and then joined me again watching for me the carriages, which have no objection to running over foot passengers, and there are no divisions between the carriage and footways, laying her hand gently on my arm with "*Arretez s'il vous plait,*" and then "*Avancez,*" she led me on through carriage stands, past police stations, through markets, on, on till I began to wonder where she would carry me and at last turning into a nook I should not have ventured into she said "*voila, Mons. le bandagiste*" and I read the name of Schlecht and saw the surgical instruments in the window. She very politely offered to go in for me and interpret saying she was a German, but with many thanks I bowed her off.

On my return I went shopping for your mother to purchase some stuff to make a cover for our large air cushion, whose delicate colour was getting smirched by the cinders as it lays under her foot in the cars. Despite my imperfect French I managed to get her a piece of *linen* of mixed colors, which she says puts her in mind of Cousins Martha and Sarah P. Morris, so delicate and pretty is it, and which just suits her. She has already made the cover and says it is very nice.

All this tour of duty brought with it the pleasure of seeing much of this great town, its palaces and squares and stores. There are many monuments in bronze but none manifest much taste. One is a hideous deformity; a pile of clouds in stone towering tier above tier diminishing to a point on which stands a figure of the Virgin; strange idea. It is erected to the honour of the Creator. It starts in three divisions one bearing a Latin inscription "*In Honorem Dei Creatoris,*" another "*In Honorem Dei Redemptoris,*" and the third "*In Honorem Dei Spiritus Sancti,*" these run into each other and are combined in the mass above. All the statues, pillars and monuments I have seen are equally grotesque or abortive.

The old town was encircled with walls and moats which have been levelled and filled up and the space occupied by public gardens and public buildings.

Yesterday afternoon just about the time I supposed your uncle and aunts would return, I left your mother and fell into the stream of human beings of all ages and in every variety of conveyance, railroad cars, omnibusses, hired carriages, and on foot. The current set irresistibly across the bridge over the arm of the Danube and I soon saw before me the trees of the Prater. At short distances were stationed soldiers or police officers mounted on noble horses and beautifully seated, evidently maintaining order. From all points the streams converged at the entrance of the Prater, and I wandered on to take a position as one among the multitude, which in rows of three deep extended beyond the range of vision on either side the drive, standing to look at the carriages. Outside the *standing* spectators were rushing streams pressing on into the more remote parts of the grounds. The road which is four miles long was lined by double rows on each side of Horse Chestnut trees in full flower. On either side of the way was an uninterrupted line of vehicles of every kind, that on the left passing in, and on the right passing out. There were coroneted chariots, with richly liveried servants, drawn by six to two horses each, but unoccupied ; and there were registered carriages for hire crowded by as many occupants as could be seated in them. There were fast women, gaudily attired, driving vulgar looking men ; and their were gentlemen driving their servants. There were fat dowagers, and gouty old gentlemen, and modest girls, and good-looking boys, reposing quietly in their coaches ; and there were hard-working people riding in vehicles, which on common days served to carry their wares to customers or to the market places. Every element of society was mingled and all in perfect order and silence. I saw the policemen order three several vehicles out of the line at different times, but at neither time could I see any reason. Yet the order was obeyed without any remonstrance. No one was allowed to leave the line, and each was required to keep the same gait, a smart trot. There were some fine horses. No miserable worn-out hackneyed beasts. Indeed I have not seen one here. The society for the prevention of cruelty would have no duty to perform. In the carriages I saw heaps of muslin and silks and laces and feathers, with much pearl powder starch and carmine, but no beauty male or female. There are other parts of the Prater frequented by the humbler classes where they find amusements quite as rational as that derived from sitting in carriages and being drawn along to look at and be seen by each other. I was content with what I saw and turned my steps hotelward while the display was at its height, jostled at every foot of the way as I retraced my steps by the advancing crowd of those still entering the charmed ring.

VIENNA, May 4, 1872.

My Dear Children :

I am thankful to be able to report a steady tho' not very great improvement in your mother's ankle. It no longer pains her constantly and the swelling is diminishing. She is able to sleep as well as she does in common, the blackness is now yielding to the usual green and yellow shades and the redness, which at one time threatened erythema and forbid the use of the soap liniment, is abated. She sits with it elevated on a soft chair all day. I ventured to leave her this morning while I went with your uncle and aunts to the Treasury and Library and leaving them to visit the palace and other objects. Thus far their report of what they have seen has not caused me any regret that I have missed the fatigue. Schonbrun, where they spent yesterday is a grand park but very formal in its detail. The afternoon they spent in shopping and that I always avoid.

The riches seen this morning were very imposing but one gets so *blasé* among royal treasuries in every place, that I am not moved now by such spectacles. They seem very commonplace. Crowns, set with uncut gems worn by Charlemagne, sound very imposing to unsophisticated Republicans; and Austrian Regalia require to be guarded by soldiers, who certainly have a richer use of them than the royal owners, who perhaps never see them, except on the day of coronation, while the custodian must keep them constantly in view. When I have a coronet formed of a belt of diamonds, two inches wide rolled on itself, long enough to encircle my brow; with a necklace to match, with ear-rings and brooch and hair pins and cincture or girdle, I will not mingle large rubies at every turn of the scroll and at intervals of a few inches at other parts. The ruby pales among the diamonds and these last lose the ruby light which gives them the lustre. In the Austrian regalia this error has been committed. It is compensated in some other loops and bows and brooches in which emeralds take the place of the rubies, but the most enticing are those in which the diamond is lustrous with its own beauty, "When unadorned adorned the most." Crowns and globes and crosses, covered with gems, are all arranged in cases and well guarded; while for a consideration you and I, and who ever pleases, may enjoy the sight of them, and that is all the enjoyment they can give the royal proprietors.

In this treasury are several apartments lined with cases containing *crystal vases*, and dishes, and goblets, and table ornaments, all graved with cunning art and cut into fanciful shapes and some enriched by settings of gems around the edges. There are clocks and watches, whose worth is fabulous in gems, but yet valueless compared with the moments they are designed to chronicle. One watch is seen enclosed in an emerald which has been excavated to receive it. The crown with which Napoleon's brow was indued is also exhibited; but we are told its splendor is fictitious, its diamonds paste. Is this so, or is it in accord with his well known fondness for sham? The cradle of his son, the Duke of Reichstadt, stands a melancholy looking memorial of the emptiness of human glory.

After I left your uncle and aunts they went to the collection of gems and coins, in which they were much interested and some of which I would gladly have seen. They brought me a photograph of an onyx eighteen centimetres high and twenty-two broad, cut in intaglio, having on it more than twenty full length figures representing the Apotheosis of Augustus. The figures are all perfectly proportioned and the faces genuine portraits of Augustus and his family. It is considered one of the most valuable relics of Roman art in existence. I wished very much to see it but was not willing to be so long absent lest your mother should want aid.

There was also a gold dish having on it over 100 medallion portraits, the central one being that of Cleopatra. Such were the services of plate from which she fed her guests, and then presented them with the dishes from which they had eaten.

Your uncle Wistar was particularly impressed by the perfect workmanship of the dies for coinage and the bold relief of the figures of the coins themselves. One gentleman has a collection of more than 100 coins of one Emperor issued from different towns in the empire during his reign. Certainly the art of stone and gem and metal engraving had reached perfection under the patronage of these Emperors. The collections of gems and coins in the various cities of Europe must have an aggregate value which it is hard to estimate, and many more are scattered in private hands, and many more buried in the earth. It is useless for any but those of great affluence to attempt to make such collections, as Princes and Kings are always ready to buy what are genuine at large prices, and the number of counterfeits which are imposed on inexperienced virtuosi is great indeed.

I occasionally stroll out. The contrast between the stately grandeur of the modern structures, erected on the site of the old fortifications, and the solid close packed buildings of the central parts, is very strong. But the poor people who occupy the tall houses and narrow streets have free access to the beautiful parks and shrubberies in front of the palatial houses. These central parts are solidity itself piled up story upon story, and there is also a venerable grandeur about them.

The streets are *thronged* to repletion with men and women and vehicles and horses. The Kohl mart and Graben and Stevansplatz, are as thronged as the lower part of New York; and the roar of passing carriages is literally unceasing.

The blankets and shawls displayed in the shop windows are very gorgeous, and the display of jewelry and leather ware and smoking apparatus very beautiful. The people are all busy looking, and there is a general appearance of prosperity and its attendant pleasure, for which I was not prepared. There are no beggars in the streets and no appearance of poverty. I have not seen any part of the town that has the squalid aspect of the lower parts of Philadelphia. I have not seen the slightest approach to intoxication nor heard any indecorous or loud talking as I pass the crowded "*restaurations*," which abound, and strange to say there is little or no smoking in the cars or on the streets and none in the shops and offices in which I have been. The streets are kept perfectly swept, the pavements are good, and no one chews and spits.

We were disappointed in not receiving any letters of later date than the seventh of April from Ivy Neck and one still older from Israel, but hope to be feasted at Milan this day week. Your uncle has written to secure carriages; those we had before (if they can be got) to carry us over the Corniche road to Nice, and in three weeks we hope to be in Paris which will be next door to home.

I find your uncle designs to return from there by Strasburg to Munich and so to Salzburgh and Ischl. It will require some effort for your mother and myself to turn our faces from you again.

I find the box from Cairo has reached Liverpool and will therefore probably soon be with you. You must not be disgusted with its worthless contents; it is the best we could do with them. They are not worth cost I know. Send Carson the senna. He might have acknowledged my two letters.

Your loving father,

CASPAR MORRIS.

ADELSBERG, May 7, 1872.

My Dear Children:

A ride of fourteen hours in the cars brought us from Vienna here, through scenes of unrivalled beauty; but before entering on any attempt to describe them I will perform the easier and more pleasant duty of assuring you that wearisome as it was your dear mother got through it better than some of the others of the party, and as we sat down to our *first* meal from 5.30 A. M. to 10 P. M., laughed and said she believed rail road travel was good for her ankle as it really felt much better than yesterday; and now while she is completing her toilet I can add to her assertion my assurance that it is less swollen, and less sensitive; and she is able to communicate some motion to the toes without suffering.

We had a very good night here in comfortable beds in this perfectly clean though plain inn, kept by two maiden ladies. We shall leave your mother under their care while we visit the cave, which brought us here, though they speak the language of Carniolia which is Sclavic and therefore more allied to Russian than German. Signs of eye and hand serve as a medium of communication, and are much cultivated by Europeans as well as Asiatics to help out the imperfection of language, and we are becoming somewhat *au fait* in them. But I shall never cease urging on the young to cultivate the knowledge of other languages than their own, just in the proportion in which I am humiliated by my own deficiency.

In our drive from the hotel in Vienna to the R. R. depot your mother had an opportunity to see a little of the imperial splendor of that splendid city. We drove by great ranges of lofty buildings, erected in what where once the suburbs; outside the city walls and and moat, which have been levelled and transformed into gardens and walks planted with exquisite taste and kept in perfect order at the expense of the government. Thus that which afforded protection from enemies in those days when Turks invaded Europe and threatened Christendom with subjugation, and were then absolutely essential to the safety of the people, now in these days, in which the progress in arts and science have carried the art of war forward with others, so that castles and moats and walls are powerless as means of defence, furnishes wide breathing spaces and opportunities for pleasant exercise and refreshment to those whose necessities still confine them within the narrow limits those defences once encircled. The affluent, no longer requiring walls for their protection, transfer their dwellings to wider spaces beyond; and the poor citizen has *at his door*, without cost to himself, all the enjoyments which gardens and flowers and lakes and lawns afford to Princes, and rich landed proprietors. Nothing so beautifully and impressively speaks the advance of humanity. It should be one object ever kept before the community at home, where the increase of our towns, carrying increased value to the adjacent territory, is likely to render such provision for the health and improvement of the people more difficult with each advancing year. Our great towns will become great *foci* of disease, worse than those of the middle ages shut in by walls, just as they are of greater extent and population.

I blush for my native city when I contrast its foulness with the perfect cleanliness of Vienna; and its utter absence of any effort at elegance in its few public squares, with the lovliness and attractiveness of these numerous and widely diffused resorts of the common people, for whose use *comfortable* seats are abundantly provided where they can hear the birds sing, inhale the odor of wide spread flower borders, and saunter at will among lawns and groves, planted within easy walking distance from every habitation.

2 P. M.

Your mother and I have enjoyed such a treat. Just as I had closed the last sentence I heard Friezier announce that if your mother would consent to be carried in a chair by four men, she could visit the caves, and was made perfectly happy by her reply that nothing would give her equal pleasure. So the arrangement was made at once and we left at 10 A. M. and have only now returned.

The two hours spent in exploring the recesses of the interior of the mountain passed without note of its duration. It was pleasurable excitement every moment renewed, and every moment at the highest point of enjoyment. The arrangement was for 1800 candles to *illuminate* the cavern. That number was *lost*, scattered as they were from point to point in our progress. Five miles have been explored, and as we walked on at a moderate pace we must have advanced at least half that distance, returning by a different passage. Every foot of our way led through wonders, which, as they are unique, words have not been invented to express them. There are great halls of hundreds of feet in length and breadth and varying in height from 60 to 180 feet, and connected by passages of width and height equally differing but none so narrow that many persons may not walk abreast, nor so low as to require stooping for the tallest man.

For some distance you feel some sense of disappointment. It is a grand cavern in the limestone rock, majestic in its proportions and filling you with that sense of awe which is inspired by grandeur and vastness. The glimmering lights in diminishing perspective add to this by the idea of distance. After advancing some distance the roof and walls are found covered with the calcareous deposit, assuming strange forms of pilasters, caryatides, drapery, and many grotesque shapes. The smoke of the torches of successive visitors for centuries has so discolored them that you can scarcely distinguish them from the rock except by their shape. Presently as you advance you find the sense of awe increased by the sound of rushing waters; and find yourself standing on a natural bridge spanning a gulf lighted up by some hundreds of candles arranged far below you, which cast a little glimmer on the rushing river which frets its way between the yawning jaws of the opening depth.

After passing this spot the cavern spreads more and more in width, and opens in height. The columns of stalagmite assume wondrous resemblance to water falls and fountains, instantaneously solidified as they burst into curving falls or break into the lightest foam.

Chandeliers depends from the roof, and the drapery hangs from the walls in folds so graceful and easy that the most accomplished upholsterer would stand with hands fallen by his side, and admit that he could not rival them. Lace in its light and delicate grace, brocade in its rich and heavy folds hang in every variety of drapery ; while a light suspended behind them exhibits fringes and borders and tracery-like figures all duly proportioned and distributed with as much elegance as the shades in color on the petals of the Heart's Ease in the beds of your gardens.

Palm trees shoot up their stalagmitic trunks to be crowned by stalactitic foliage ; banyan trees spread themselves widely and send their stalactitic roots to be inserted into hillocks of stalagmite rising from below to receive them; pulpits with sounding boards, each richly hung with drapery and fringes, appear only to wait a human form with angel tongue to give a meet utterance to a homily on the text " How marvellous are Thy works O God ; in wisdom hast thou made them all. The earth is full of Thy glory."

In perfect accord with such a discourse is the rich harmony of the rock organ brought out by striking with stick, stone hammer or hand, on various pendant stalactites, giving out every note in the octave as they are more or less delicate in their structure and hang with differing lengths and breadth. To attempt to describe the sizes and shapes of the various halls and chambers would be a useless expenditure of time and paper on bare statistics, which could convey no idea of size and shape. Miles of railroad are being laid, and there is one large hall hung with drapery and chandeliers and ornamental fountains and grotesque shapes innumerable, the deposit from the still dripping water, all white, or variegated, or red or yellow, according as one or another mineral was held in solution with the lime whose deposit, from the ceaseless percolation of the water through the superincumbent rocks, causes these marvellous records of the innumerable ages of the past.

In this hall on Whit-Monday there is an annual ball attended by thousands from Vienna, Gratz, and surrounding country, with a grand orchestra ; and the space is wide enough not only for the numberless dances, but to give accommodations for booths and stalls for the sale of the refreshments necessary. Penetrating far beyond this we found ourselves in vaulted halls and passages equally grand. One filled with stalagmites taking the forms of sarcophagi and tombs and grave stones some four or five feet high, while the stalactites, from which the water has dropped, hang far overhead. This presents the appearance of a vast cemetery. Another has numberless stalactites hanging in great white sheets, as though waving in the wind, and has been named very appropriately the Laundry. Cascades and fountains and *jettes d' Eau* abound every where, and tabernacled niches with figures of virgins and saints as though the work of the cunning sculptor. There was one wide arch which was covered with cherub heads and fluttering wings just such as Perugio and Murillo painted in cloudy perspective around their Assumptions and other Celestial conceptions. Monkeys and birds and heathen gods and goddesses were also there. In truth every conceivable form waits only the imagination of the spectator to give it a name, and are so perfect that you utter it before the guide can say it is " so or so."

I said in one of my late letters that I was *blasé* with diamonds and gems. I had not then been in this cavern of wondrous gems. As I mentioned in describing the first impression I was disappointed, and accused the author of the essay from which I derived my first idea of a cavern and a desire to visit one, which has never been gratified in the half century which has gone since I read it in Lindley Murray's reading book—the description of the grotto. of Antiparos—of gross exaggeration. As we penetrated further I changed my criticism for the expressions of the Queen of Sheba and gazing on the glory of Solomon's gems and purple, "The half was not told me." Hangings of salmon, and brown, and purple, and white velvet, literally dazzled ones eyes, so richly are they set with glittering gems of purest ray serene. I could not tell the half ; you would not believe the half I do attempt to tell. So I will only add that we would gladly have possessed strength to spend twice the time we did devote to this wondrous scene of enchantment.

Your mother was uneasy lest the strength of her porters (four men carrying her in a chair on poles, changing two and two) should become exhausted. Those who walked were fatigued by the length of the way, not wearied by the wondrous sight, so we turned our steps toward the upper day and emerged to the glory of the outer world, with its emerald meads embossed by the flowers of the spring, which lay spread at our feet as we left the cave. Just below we saw the river rush into the deep abyss in which it enters the lower cavern through which it travels in darkness five miles before it emerges again into the day.

The next morning as we left Adelsberg we passed another stream whose name is familiar to the boys as sung by Virgil and Horace, the Timavus, which has an out-door course of only two furlongs between the spot at which it issues from a cave like that we had visited and that at which it pours its tribute to the Adriatic Sea. It has an underground course of more than twenty miles from the place at which it sinks under the mountain. These are wild limestone regions. The hills great masses of grey and whitish-grey stones, with but little earth ; on which a few shrubs and a little grass and a few flowers plant themselves to relieve the monotonous sterility.

The railroad runs along the edge of the hills, while below at first a narrow green meadow, gradually widening into a limitless green plain, intervenes between the mountain ranges and the waters of the Adriatic Sea which expands itself to the south. The level plain is dotted with the campaniles of churches which mark the sites of villages where once stood the great "oppida" of the Romans, among them Aquileia, often the favorite resort of Augustus ; and the northeastern frontier of Italy. That town then boasted of 100,000 inhabitants. Now malarious pestilential marshes usurp the place of fertile Campagnia, and the population has dwindled to a few thousands. The railroad through this district was constructed by the Austrian Government as a military avenue to Italy and, like the carriage road by which we crossed the Stelvio, is perfect in its construction and equipment. The ride was one of wondrous beauty and variety. Snow clad mountains, vine clad hills and smiling green meadows, each perfect in beauty and all in sight at the same moment. Hedges of Laburnum, in *full* flower, extended for miles ; while lilacs of every hue from a reddish purple to the palest pink and purest white were clustered at every turn. At some places we passed precipitous cliffs, their fronts perforated by strange looking cavernous openings which in Egypt we should have thought might have been tombs, but which we believe to be ancient mining works, as the Romans procured silver and lead from this district and the quick-silver mine of Istria is not far away.

We lodged at Nabresina a point at which the railroads from Trieste, Venice and Milan all converge. There is a grand depot and *excellent* restaurant, but no hotel. The proprietor of the restaurant, having been telegraphed, had procured for us very nice lodging in a house about half a mile distant. In the morning we were waked by the soft melody of the nightingale, to which was soon joined the rich tones of a very sweet chime of bells in the neighbouring village. The sun rose brightly on our chamber and we were speedily dressed, and, returning to the restaurant, had an excellent breakfast and started at 8 A. M. on our way to Padua, where Dr. and Mrs. Harris are to meet Wistar and Mary.

I have tested a glass I got at Vienna for Israel W. and find it so good I fear I shall take all the look out of it.

Your loving father,

CASPER MORRIS.

May 7, 1872, PADUA, Italy.
My Birth Day, 62 years old.

My Dear Children:

So old, the alloted time for man nearly gone and Oh, such a waste as my life has been! But I dare not allow myself go on in this strain so will stop short or I shall not be fit for what is before us for the day. You will all conclude that my foot is doing well when I tell you we have been unceasingly on the go since Monday morning. We left Vienna at 6 in the morning (having been called at 4.30) and reached Adelsberg at 10.

The next morning we all went to see the cave which is said to be the largest in the world. I was glad to be carried by four men in a chair. It to me was more interesting than picture galleries, etc. That occupied four hours, and after lunch we had five or six hours' ride in cars; but it being a saloon one, I was very comfortably fixed and would gladly have remained in it all night, if we could have made the arrangement, so as to avoid the moving of me twice, which still has to be done by Friezier and T. Longstreth. I cannot put the foot down and you can all understand this is trying to me, but there is no help for it I believe, unless I could use a crutch.

Yesterday we came here to meet Dr. and Mrs. Harris, who will now be with us for a week or two. The poor old gentlemen is very feeble. They have now gone to a botanical garden, etc. At 11 o'clock we are to meet them with Wistar and Mary at the depot to go to Milan. Do you not think *we* will remember Milan. This is our third visit.

Well we have such pleasant recollections of the others, that I am quite pleased at the prospect of resting there for a few days; which to me it will be. But I have no doubt a plenty of objects of interest will be presented to keep all our friends fully occupied (the amusing part to me, is to hear them say they are taking things quietly now). Your father gets *very weary* by night, but sleep starts him pretty fresh again. The waiting on me, which he does *all* himself of choice, of course adds to his fatigue.

We enjoyed extremely the rides through Austria—the country so beautiful and the cultivation so fine; the towns and houses everywhere so comfortable, and the people looking thriving. But you no sooner cross the line into Italy than you are struck with the contrast. Oppression is evident in everything—wretched-looking people, miserable houses and towns, squalid and dirty; shrines again in every direction, on the hill-tops and by the roadside; and we again encounter beggars, and I don't wonder at it—they look as if they wanted bread.

I suppose we shall meet spring now from this time. Peas, asparagus, and here most delicious strawberries, are served us. *Very small*, like our wild ones, but very high flavored and no acidity. Unless the size can be increased by cultivation, we would find them too troublesome in our country to gather. Here labour is so cheap it is no object.

MILAN, May 10th.

We reached here to a six o'clock dinner. (I am not a convert to them, I assure you, and am thankful that we usually dine at two; it suits us all better.) Now all are off to see, first, *the cathedral*, and do some shopping. Your father writes at my side, and I am very willing to let the poor foot rest as it does on a nice lounge. It is so much better that I can move the ankle, and so hope before long it will bear some weight on it. I can get from our room to the parlour with one knee on a chair and pushing it along, and am very proud of that much liberty, and hope by Monday, 13th, when we have to leave for Genoa, to be more advanced.

We found letters here from you all, for which many thanks, and we were surprised to see one from cousin Emily, but rejoiced at her safe arrival at home, and have no doubt she is a busy woman. I only hope she won't do too much. Thanks to Mrs. Buckley for her nice letter. It was highly appreciated.

May 12th.

I have been thinking very much of you all to-day, and imagining you each able to get to your different places of worship. Gall. and Han. are, I suppose, in Germantown, and I hope will enjoy their home there. Gardening time has come, strawberries blooming, etc, and before long

Ches. and Mellie will be thinking of Fernbank; but I hope not too soon, as stone houses are cool at this time of the year. I shall not know where to look for Israel and Annie. I fear he is too busy to be settled anywhere except in Philadelphia, and I often feel troubled that he should have all our concerns to look after in addition to his own; but he may feel thus far easy in that we shall be entirely satisfied with whatever arrangements he can make. I hardly expect he will be able to rent 1428 this summer, as most persons will be wanting country residences. Cheston's little note in Mrs. Cope's envelope, written there, gave us the only intelligence from Baltimore, and was particularly acceptable, as I was feeling very anxious about Aunt M. It will now be a satisfaction to hear Abby Townsend is with her.

We have had a very pleasant visit here of three days. Dr. and Mrs. Harris are quite adding to our pleasure. To-morrow we shall separate again; they to Venice, we to Genoa. It will be a trial to the old people and their nieces, as it is not likely they will ever see their uncle again, he is so feeble.

By this day week we shall be at Nice, and then to Paris. I do hope by that time I shall be able to walk. Would it not be too bad to have to sit all the time on a sofa in Paris and *see nothing?* You will laugh at my *wanting* to see, I am sure; but now that I am here, I might as well.

We will not be able to write by this mail to cousin Emily, but of course she will be willing to come in with you children if back in Philadelphia, and read what we send you. We feel a little concerned about her, lest she should be doing too much.

(Not signed, but in handwriting of A. C. M.—EDS.)

MILAN, May 10th, 1872.

My Dear Child:

You will see we are here in this nice old city again and at the same hotel, delightfully fixed. I do not at all regret paying a third visit here; should not if I were able to be about, as I have a sort of *home* feeling, besides there being so much to see that is beautiful. But I expect to spend the time on the lounge, with the foot up, hoping to promote its recovery, for which I am anxious, as I do not like at all to be carried about, and I cannot stand on it at all. Yet it is two weeks since I hurt it; but your father tells me I must be patient.

We expect to leave here on Monday for Genoa, thence to Nice and then to Paris; expecting to be in Paris on the 6th or 7th of June; and, strange as it may seem to you, I begin to feel so much nearer you all. Dr. and Mrs. Harris are now travelling with us. He is our consul at Venice. They are uncle and aunt of your Aunt Mary Morris. He is a very feeble old gentleman, but pleasant company and one we feel much for. She is a bright, pleasant woman, not young but much his junior, and they quite enliven our circle. She speaks both Italian and French fluently, and so is a great assistance to our ladies in shopping, which, I assure you, we find very difficult to do through the courier, and I am constantly deterred by the various obstacles from getting what I would like. But this shall not interfere with the purchases of the watches ; and tell Robbie even he shan't be overlooked. He must keep on trying to do his part of the proposition. We do not expect to get to Geneva, but there are agents here, and we are told they are entirely reliable.

On reaching here last night we were cheered by a nice package of letters. Oh, you don't know how much good they do us, me especially, I think, for I am often very down and they brighten me up. I have two from you 14th and 21st of April; Cornelia and Mary, Ches., Is., Annie, Mrs. Buckley, Gally; and your father several others, so you see we have quite a treat. I only regret we cannot acknowledge all, but I do assure you when we are travelling we are all too tired at night to write. But I love to hear from each of you just what you are about in the different families. It comes nearer to visiting you than anything else. I was very glad to hear of the pleasant "sheet and pillow case party" at Cedar Park as I do think a little cheerful enjoyment is good for both old and young, and when I get home I must fix some of you in Arab costume by way of variety, or Turkish either, tho' perhaps it will not disguise them as completely as the sheet.

I am very glad to find you are all reconciled to our prolonged stay. October does seem a good way off, but I expect it is better than getting home in mid-summer, and I hope also that by prolonging your father's absence it will have fixed his patients with Cheston and Murray and he will not be annoyed by their entreaties. He is not able to practice, and I hope will not think of it. I cannot say what is the matter, but he is not strong, and very little exertion exhausts him very much at times. We intend from this time to avoid such long railroad rides, tho' we do it in saloon cars in which we move about and can recline, as sometimes we have three sofas in the main car and a retiring room in which there is another. Friezier is an ample provider ; we seldom move without our lunch basket being well filled with cold meat, bread, wine, water, eggs and plenty of fruit.

I did think of having our Planaquin photographed, but there was no place after leaving Jerusalem that it could be done, so I had to content myself with buying one in Constantinople somewhat like mine. But I have no particular fancy for the vehicles especially when mounted up on mules backs. Carried as I was in a Sedan chair the other day for four hours by men, through a most wonderfully beautiful cave at Adlesberg, is much better. Your father has written a description of that cave so I will not repeat.

(*Not signed but in handwriting of A. C. M.*—Eds.)

MILAN, May 11, 1872.

Your mother is busy with her needle on the couch doing some sewing which it is necessary should be accomplished and I have promised to fill her sheet for her. The weather is most delightful and everything around is wearing the fresh and beautiful garb of spring and strawberries and cherries as well as flowers adorning our tables and perfuming our room as well as pleasing our taste. Miss Harris and Mr. Longstreth mounted to the spire of the cathedral before breakfast this morning and report having seen Mt. Blanc and Monte Rosa and the passes of the Alps.

They are of course all covered with snow as even the Alpine ranges nearer here are perfectly white with it. There has been an unusual duration of wet weather in this part of Italy which is ruinous to the people, who depend on their silk worms for support and the weather is so damp that they dare not hatch the eggs and yet the leaves of the mulberry grow and will become too coarse and hard. The naked trees, entirely stripped of leaves look in sad contrast with the beautiful green wheat fields in which they stand, festooned by grape vines trained from the one to the other about twenty feet apart; in rows with twice that distance between them. The crimson clover fields afford another contrast and so do the scarlet poppies which are plentiful as any farmer can desire weeds to be. As we passed the very extensive fortifications of Verona we saw the entire length of the embankments, the most extensive in Europe, literally sanguine with the poppies. It was better so than with the blood of defenders. This part of Italy is a vast plain wholly devoted to silk, grape and wheat culture; the three crops growing simultaneously on the soil. The mulberry trees are kept cut down to about eight or ten feet. Thus the new shoots spring out annually with succulent leaves. These are gathered in bags and chopped by a machine like our hay cutters and so fed to the worms, which are kept in the chambers of the people; and as they grow become most offensive not only to the eye but to the smell. It is from such sources our ladies derive their exquisite silks. I do not wish to see the culture introduced with us. I was very sorry to hear that small pox had invaded your neighborhood and pray that you all may be favoured to escape. Make my best regards to Dr. Waters whose active Christian faith claims our highest regard. Love to all including Miss Alice.

    Your loving father,

           CASPAR MORRIS.

MILAN, ITALY, May 10, 1872.

My Dear Grandchildren:

You must allow me to take you all in "a lump" and address a family letter to Ivy Neck as I have not time nor strength to say to each one separately how great is the pleasure your grandmother and I have derived from the very nice letters we have received from Cornelia, Mary, Emily, Robert, Sally, and Anne at several times. They have all come safely and each has filled our hearts with thankfulness to our Heavenly father that he has blessed us with children and grandchildren who love us, love each other and we hope, love the Lord Jesus.

We are looking forward with great hope to the pleasure of seeing you all in October, and now are enjoying the sight of the many beautiful and grand things around us more for your sake than our own. We are here to-day amid plains of very many miles extent to the south and east and west, hundreds of miles all as flat as Long Neck, and all planted with mulberry trees in long rows about twenty feet distant with grape vines stretched from tree to tree, and the intervening space green as the field your dear mother says looks so beautiful from your south door in wheat and grass.

The clover has tops as red as the lines on this paper making a strong contrast with the green wheat fields. To the north are huge mountains in long ranges perfectly white with snow. I have formerly described the majesty of the Cathedral and the beauty of the town so I will not repeat that.

Your grandmother and I enjoyed a great treat two days ago in our visit to the wondrous cave at Adelsberg near Trieste in Austria (find it on the map at the head of the Adriatic sea). The entire extent of the cave has never been explored; I think we must have gone not less than four miles. Your grandmother was carried in an arm chair hung on long poles by four men. There were 1800 large stearine candles burning to illuminate parts of it, while the guides carried lamps with them to light us from one hall to another. Some of these halls were 180 feet high and many acres in extent and halls and passages were all ceiled and covered with the crystallized lime deposited from the water which percolates slowly through the rock. Some is white as the purest snow, some salmon coloured, some green, some purple, and all, miles after miles, glittering and sparkling as the crystals reflect the light of the candles and torches. Then from the ceiling hang deposits of this same spar in an infinite variety of form. As the first drop oozed out of the rock it left its mineral, and each successive drop added to it, till in the long ages it has grown down forming strange shapes called stalactites. Some of the water falling to the floor deposits its mineral there below the stalactite and that is called stalagmite. In the long ages these have grown till they meet, forming trees and fountains and statues all grouped as though by design. There are hundred of forms which look precisely as though they were cascades or fountains or *jettes d'eau* which had been by some miraculous power changed into stone at the moment the water was turning in graceful curves, or breaking into the lightest foam. Then at every turn you are met by some new form of beauty. At one place there is a succession of drapery hanging in the most graceful folds, and so thin and transparent that when a light is placed behind them they look some like lace, others like satin damask, or rich brocade. If you were to form an arch higher than the house all the way to the quarter, and hang it with curtains across from side to side every few feet, all the way, and each curtain hanging full and loose and differing in colour and all spangling with diamonds, you would not equal the glory of the cave. Then you must extend that for miles. There was at one place a perfect pulpit with drapery of the richest kind and trimmed with fringes, all stone; and around an arch above were thousands of cherub heads and wings in white marble sculpture, all like the frost work on the window panes, and so perfectly graceful, I thought if we only had an angel there to speak in heavenly tones of the wondrous work of Redeeming love! By striking on the hanging stalactites we brought out all the notes of the musical scale. But I must refer you to my letter for further account as I have only room to express my hearty love for you all and beg you to remember me to Miss Alice and Uncle James; Sam., and Dr. Murray, and Dr. Waters, and cousin Sally, and aunt Sally, and all our West River friends; and to believe me

Your most loving grandfather.

CASPER MORRIS.

MILAN, May 11, 1872.

My Dear Children:

This place does not lose by repeated visits. I have just returned from a drive with Dr. Harris around its grand boulevards, bordered with double rows of noble horse chestnut trees, now in full flower and foliage, and of course still more attractive than they were last October with their sere leaves and falling nuts. The gardens are equally attractive and the shops and the people are fully stocked and as busily occupied.

I have strolled into the cathedral several times for short visits, but have not been willing to leave your mother quite alone, and the ladies are all busy shopping.

As we drove this morning the glory of the snow clad Alps in the distance was most impressive. The white summits lighted by the sun, rose beyond the long outline of the blue mountains which skirted the plain. It was an elevating as well as an attractive view. I shall always remember it in association with the cathedral and church of St. Ambrose and picture of Leonardo da Vinci, each sublime in simple grandeur. As I drove around taking in delight from them all my heart expanded under the influence with a loftier sense of the majesty and power and love of the Creator of so much beauty and Redeemer from so much ruin, and I thought with rapturous delight on the inconceivable glory of the renewed creation. If while the creature groaneth in bondage it is all so fair and grand, what may we not anticipate as the exhibition of the undisputed and undisturbed possession of the ransomed inheritance of the sinless people of God.

We passed also the great Lazaretto of St. Carlo Borromeo with all its mingled associations of human sorrow and suffering and Christian charity, still standing in its simple dignity *vis-a-vis* to the splendid structure of modern grandeur, and recalling associations of self-denial, love for Christ, and those for whom Christ died, which cluster around that name; one of the most honored in the calendar.

May 12th.

This is the coldest and most cheerless day we have known since we left Rome. In the Vaudois church this morning prayers were offered that God would open the eyes of the people of Italy to see the chastisement. The weather is most disastrous to the silk worms and already the price of silk has been affected by it. They keep fires in the room but that is but an imperfect substitute for warm sunshine. The worms that are hatched sicken and they fear to hatch more, and meanwhile the mulberry leaves become old and hardened. The snow which you have not had is lying deep on the mountains about Lake Como, greatly to the discomfort of Royal as well as other visitors. The Prince and Princess of Wales and some of the Royal family of Denmark have been driven here. We understand they wished to have come to this house but we are happily allowed to keep our rooms.

Your mother still improves. The swelling of the limb is decidely less and she now has little or no pain when it is kept perfectly at rest. She is most beautifully patient though the trial of being dependant on others to carry her to and from the carriage is very great. Our chamber adjoins the saloon of the family and she is able by placing her knee on a light chair to hobble with the other foot from the one room to the other, and has a small table at the sofa. She thus enjoys the pleasure of your aunts' company at meals and when they are within. They were very busy shopping yesterday and she enjoyed their purchases more than she would have done the making them. Her inability to move of course prevents her from doing anything in that way, and I am quite disgusted with my own inefficiency in that line, as in all others.

Last year we followed the fruits of summer, having had strawberries from the time we landed in Liverpool till we reached this place and now we follow the advance of the spring, having commenced with the same fruit at Constantinople and shall probably keep in the region of it till we reach England again in July. I enclose a paper on which I dried a few berries which had the most luscious odour and taste, we all agreed, we had ever known. Galloway will please plant the seeds and try what they will produce. I sent some last fall but these are very superior in size and flavour to those.

We are quite troubled to find that he and Hannah have both suffered from miasmatic disease. If it had been Galloway only I should have laid it to the charge of Ivy Neck. There we know it does prevail and dear Mary's account of Miss Alice is very sad. I often grieve greatly over them and frequently reproach myself for having planted them there. I do not just now see any way of escape for them but pray that God will provide. His mercy is our only refuge and that is as sure when clouds lower as when the skies are bright and clear, and we know not what shall prosper. It is only important that we should endeavour to take each step of our lives under the guidance of His love and care, and in such honest desire to do what is right that we may be able to look back without condemnation of our own state of heart and feeling.

We have not only no plans for our own course on our return, but really do not think about what it will be, leaving it to be directed by the circumstances in which we shall then find ourselves. The death of Dr. Jackson, and Mrs. Jackson's removal, will create a great change for cousin Hannah. She has so long been accustomed to their society and to render them assistance and cheer them and comfort them that the change will be a serious loss to her.

I have not attempted to visit any of the churches or galleries here this time but have enjoyed greatly this morning the service of our church and shall go again this evening.

Cheston will please apologize for me to Mrs. Cope as I have given her hour to-day to Miss Julia Dunlap and do not feel strong enough to write another letter this afternoon. I had also one from Miss Helen Griffitts which I wish to answer. Her sad suffering calls for much sympathy; I feel much for her and her sister Rebecca also, who is one of my great favourites and am specially thankful for the recovery of their father. I had thought much and anxiously about his health. I do not feel as though I should be able to take up the duties of professional life on my return (should God be pleased to spare us to reach our earthly home again) but I retain all my interest in the healing art and desire for the growth of the science and am quite as much attached to my former patients as I ever was.

I already feel that we are again getting into the current of old influences as we have approached so much nearer, and the idea that in case of necessity we could reach you in three weeks from any point that we are likely now to visit, is very satisfactory. It is time to close this, take tea and go to evening service. I was very near you all this morning and hope to be so again in spirit this evening.

Your loving father,

CASPAR MORRIS.

VELVETOPOLIS (GENOA), May 13, 1872.

My Dear Children:

Had you heard so much discussion on the colour, width, duty, durability, and value of the staple manufacture of Genoa as has passed, and is now passing, in currents as conflicting as those which escaped from the bags in the cave of Eolus, before that controller of the winds whipped them into obedience and tied them up again, you would not wonder at the title I have given this old city, once known as Genoa Superba.

While I write the contrast has become as painful as that in the cave, for your aunts have summoned Friezier and Mr. Longstreth and carried your mother, against her earnest protestations, to see a Filagree silver shop, which is kept in one of the rooms of the hotel. This has effected a diversion from the controversy on the "field of velvet," but whether it will result in "chains or liberty" is still doubtful to my mind, though you all know I can trust your mother in the midst of heavier temptation than such light things as silver butterflies and fans.

We left Milan this morning, having risen at 5 A. M., and breakfasted at 6. The first part of the road led through the least attractive and most unhealthy of all agricultural scenes, vast extents of flat land devoted to the culture of rice, which requires to be flooded at certain stages of its growth. Nearly one-half of the surface of the country was under water. The mountains lay far away to the north, with their blue irregular outline skirting the horizon, beyond which the more distant Alps raised their loftier summits clothed with the dazzling whiteness of everlasting snow. Northern Italy is a vast plain, stretching from the foot of the Alps to that of the mountains of Calabria; skirted at the west by the Appenine range, through which we penetrated on our way hither.

After crossing the Ticino we entered again the mulberry, silk, and grain-growing regions, and from it, as we approached the eastern slope of the Appenines, the more rugged hills covered with terraces and planted with grapes. Through these mountains the railroad is carried by no less than eleven tunnels of various length. One being over a mile, and another requiring seven minutes to pass through it, being about two miles in length. As we emerged from this we found ourselves in a beautiful wild mountain valley, the hill-sides clothed with chestnut trees, and the narrow glades having fig trees again. The very tops of the cliffs and the highest peaks of the mountains were crowned by monasteries and castles, and the hillsides with large houses of affluent proprietors. The towns were crowded and dirty-looking.

About 12.30 we caught sight of the blue expanse of the Mediterranean and the vast citadel, which commands the town and harbour of the Gulf of Genoa. At Alessandria we had passed through the extensive fortifications which have made it celebrated. It was built in the middle ages by the Ghibelline party to be a fortress, and peopled by colonists from the various cities which formed that faction, and has been from that time to more modern periods the centre of military manœuvres.

The history of Genoa is not without much interest of the same kind. I think you will find in Allison's history of Europe a most thrilling description of a siege by the French, some time toward the close of the last century or early in the present. The incidents then narrated were brought forcibly to my memory as I looked upon the heights enclosed in the line of fortifications, and passed through the narrow, crooked streets running among houses of seven and eight lofty stories in height. This hotel looks out directly on the harbour, which is densely packed with masts, thick as a forest. Between us and the shore runs a line of railroad, over which, supported by arches, is a wide marble-paved promenade, guarded by marble balustrades, on which our windows look and where we see children sporting, and gentlemen and ladies walking for air and exercise, neither of which can be had on the hillsides crowded with houses, the access to which is often by squares of stairs and steps. The shops are small, like those in eastern bazaars, and without any light except what reaches them from the fronts which are all door and window. In the middle ages the Republic of Genoa was the rival of Venice, not only in traffic, but in military power. But great as is its historical glory on that account, as the birth-place of Christopher Columbus it has a more enduring fame. As we left the railroad depot the first object that met our eyes is the statue of the great discoverer, the wise philosopher and the devout Christian, erected by "his country." Two figures—one emblematic of the New World and the other the effigy of the discoverer of the New World—stand on a lofty column, the corners of the pedestal of which are occupied by representatives of religion, justice, navigation and geography. I have seen but little else.

I started with your uncle and aunts after dinner, but by the time we had looked into the Church of Annunciation I found myself too weary to persevere in sight-seeing and returned to your mother. The dome and ceiling of the nave and transepts of that church are brilliant with gilding and frescoes. I could not avoid expressing my opinion that it looked like a huge porcelain church, like Sèvres china. It was first gilded with gold from Peru, presented by Ferdinand, the Catholic, but has been renewed of late.

From there the others went to the palace and were specially delighted by a piece of modern statuary representing some noble matron and her child, the draping of which they thought very beautiful and graceful.

Tuesday, P. M.

Your mother and I have passed the morning in unpacking our trunks and rearranging them preparatory to passing the custom examination on leaving Italy for France. This afternoon your uncle and aunts and I will submit ourselves to the yoke and go sight-seeing. Your mother's foot is better, but she will remain at home, as we are both wearied by the morning's exertion. Your uncle has secured the same carriages and drivers as they had in Switzerland to take us to Nice, where we hope to be on Saturday afternoon.

>Your loving father,
>
>>CASPAR MORRIS.

SAVONA, May 16, 1872.

My Dear Children:

This is an old town, on the Corniche road from Genoa to Nice, in what is known as the Riviera and was once Liguria, of which province it was the capital. We left Genoa yesterday morning in carriages and stopped, about eight miles from that place, for our mid-day meal at Pegli; near which is the palace of the Marquis of Pallavacini, one of the most beautiful achievements of taste, art, affluence and benevolence. The Marquis determined it was better to recompense toil than to encourage idleness, and has employed more than 500 labourers at least ten years in converting a sterile, rocky hill into a paradise. The soil has been carried and deposited in the spots where it was required, and the climate being perfectly equable and adapted to the growth of tropical plants, as well as those of temperate latitudes, every variety of beauty is introduced and cultivated in the open air. Camphor, cinnamon, pepper, palm, are side by side with cedars of Lebanon and cypress from the Levant; and the Araucaria of Brazil stands by the Eucalyptus of Australia and the Magnolia Grandiflora of our own country. The arts of sculpture and landscape gardening have been called into requisition, and certainly were never more worthily or successfully employed. Lakes, grottoes, lawns and shrubberies, all kept in the most exquisite order, beguile the visitor from point to point over a vast extent of mountain, presenting ever-varying views of sea and forest, and rock and valley. Statuary of great beauty, and ornamental temples and towers crown the heights, and while they add picturesque effect to the whole, afford places of rest from which to enjoy fine prospects. Your uncle and aunts were more than two hours in going rapidly to the most prominent objects of interest. Your mother sat quietly in the saloon, looking out on the glorious sea; I was obliged to be content with a short tour through the most accessible parts. While I was resting in a grove on a seat overlooking a lovely little lake, on which were sailing the most *superbly* plumaged water-fowl I have yet seen, the chimes of the church which gives sanctity to the whole establishment, rang out their melody, soft and sweet; floating through the groves as angel harps might have sounded in Eden. And I did not envy the enjoyment of the more vigorous, though they did climb to the loftier heights and gaze over more widely-expanded stretches of sea and land, and forest and city, all which are combined in the views from this villa of villas.

From there to this place the road follows the sinuosities of the winding shore; now crossing a lofty promontory which projects into the sea, now turning along the side of another up a wild valley overhung by wooded heights, and then rounding the head of the valley and returning by the other side to the sea. Ruined castles stood gaunt and grim on the savage rocks, to guard vine covered hillsides; while the waves broke into foam at the base of cliffs, and the broad bosom of the sea was rendered animated by the numerous white sails which dotted its surface. Town after town lay sheltered in the nooks on the shore or climbed the sides of the mountains.

The road often lay directly on the beach, where I saw more shipbuilding than we have known in our country since the days of my boyhood. Dozens of large square-rigged vessels were on the stocks, some just ready for launching (which is not done till they are masted and have all their spars and rigging ready to sail), and they are launched bow on instead of stern foremost, as with us. At one of the villages we passed through, the carriages drew up before a house bearing the following inscription, which Effingham and Caspar may construe for the benefit of my other readers:

HOSPES, SISTE GRADUM, FUIT HIC LUX PRIMA COLUMBO;
ORBE VIRO MAJORI HEU NIMIS ARCTA DOMUS!
UNUS ERAT MUNDUS. "DUO SUNT" AIT ILLE. FUERE.

The honour of being his birthplace is disputed between this village and the city of Genoa, where his father had a house; he always called himself a Genoese, and we saw there the original letter in which he says his heart is always in Genoa, though his body is in the New World, and sends them one-tenth of a year's income; and the volume in which he inscribed the various patents of nobility bestowed on him by Ferdinand and Isabella, which is still shown in the bag of Cordova leather in which it was originally enclosed by the great navigator. Some absurd Yankee woman cut off a fragment of the paper on which the letter is written, and getting that which did not in the least enrich her has impoverished succeeding travellers by rendering it more difficult to get sight of these relics.

Friday, 17th.

While your mother is dressing, I will occupy the interval in waiting on her with a report. She is *doing well*, the swelling daily abates, and though the instep is still very painful on touch or pressure, the progress of restoration is positive.

Our ride yesterday was through perpetual changing scenes of exquisite loveliness. Sea and mountains and plains are thrown into a monster kaleidoscope, with trees from every climate and flowers from every land, mingling their various hues and delicate forms in the ever-changing combinations, affords the best illustration which presents itself to my imagination, stimulated by the perpetually renewed appeals to its activity. If you take a map and look at the gulf of Genoa, and follow the sea line with its absolutely innumerable sinuosities, and remember that these are due to mountain spurs projecting into the water and that the road follows the line of beach, you will be able to form some idea of our course. Occasionally we penetrate some promontory through a tunnel, and now and then cross one at an elevation, but the greater part of the time the road lies along a shelf in the edge of the cliff, some 100 or 200 feet above the level of the sea, as it rounds the promontories and then runs along the glades or valleys till it reaches another spur.

The hillsides are terraced to the highest summits, wherever there is room for a man to stand and build a wall from four to eight feet high. This wall supports a level space of about the same width, on which olive trees are planted as thick as they can stand, with here and there fig trees. The olive trees are now just in blossom, and smiling with the fresh verdure of the new-budding leaves which tip the ends of the boughs, still covered with those of last year. You can form no idea of the fantastic shapes of the trunks, some of which are excavated till they are the merest shell to support the bark, and gnarled and twisted till they give you the impression of having been tortured. The olive is not a handsome tree either in form or color of the foliage, but, clothing the mountain sides as we look up from below, they give a general appearance of cultivation which is pleasant. We are living amid scenes which recall Dr. Watts' lines :

> "There everlasting spring abides,"
> "And never-fading flowers."

Each day we find new beauties mingling with old favourites. Oleander, pomegranate, cactus, aloe, palm, oriental cypress, and elm and locust. Among the trees are scattered profusely white gladiolus, iris, broom, valerian, yellow immortelles, sweet briar ; and wild roses are gathered in clusters on the hillsides, and scarlet poppies and yellow flags and all the profusion of vernal beauties adorn the meadows.

BORDIGHERA, 7 P. M., May 17th.

If you wish to have an idea of our position and its beauties turn to Dr. Antonio, by Ruffini. Chapter X. gives a description of the prospect from the balcony of the Osteria, to which Lucy has been confined with her broken leg. The scene is laid just here, and the description is not in any degree over-coloured. As we rode just now round the bay of Spedaletti, I thought I had never had *an idea of the beauty of the sea.* The ultra-marine gradually shading into blue and purple ; and the white foam of the breakers at the rocky shore, winding in graceful curves, made contrasts and harmony of color, while the mountains seemed pressing around as though to guard in their strong, yet loving embrace, the soft and delicate form which wooed them by its kisses. The palm groves waving their feathery crowns, and the *dark* green spires of the cypress shooting up from the midst of the pale, ashy, foliage of the olive, (which literally covered the mountain sides) served only to enhance the attractiveness of the surroundings. Ancient castles, built in the ninth and tenth centuries for protection from the Turks, reared their ruined, skeleton-like, forms from the rocky peaks; and beautiful modern villas peered out from them amid the groves and pretty-looking villages, with grand churches, dotted along the ridges, crowned the whole view. The profusion of flowers exceeds conception. The sides of the cliffs, often apparently perpendicular, would be entirely clothed by them grouped in great bunches, of yellow genista, and purple valerian, and yellow immortelle, and pink convolvulus, all mingled with an innumerable variety of smaller flowers.

I think I have found the place for invalids to spend the winter months. St. Remo is surrounded by villa residences with beautiful gardens, and has several large hotels and "Maison à Pension," which afford excellent accommodations. At Alassio, where we lodged, there is a very great hotel, and here this Hotel d'Angleterre is a pattern of nicety and elegance without display, and is kept by a worthy Swiss who devotes himself to the good of the surrounding country, as well as the comfort of his guests. The houses all look out on the sea.

We have frequently, as we passed, seen the fishermen catching sardines, which abound in these bays. Their nets are very long, and of very fine twine and small meshes. The fish are first dried from water by being laid in the sun on the stony beach, and then plunged into boiling oil. From this they are dipped out and drained before being packed again in oil for keeping. The surface of the bays is often dotted with the boats, and the shores animated with the crowds of women and men drawing the nets and gathering the fish.

The hill-sides yield the olives to be pressed for oil, which, of course, is fresh and sweet. The entire district through which we have ridden since leaving Genoa is one great olive yard.

We drove this afternoon through St. Remo, an old town with very narrow streets and very high houses within the old walls, but surrounded by beautiful villas, with gardens surrounded by hedges of aloes, with the tall stems of last year's flowers still lifting their candelabra-like form. Some have low walls covered with the mesembryanthemum, its rich green hangings gemmed with large flowers, some white, others pale-yellow or pink; roses in profusion give colour, but their odour is lost in that of the lemon and orange trees which abound on every side. The fruit is very inferior to that of Jaffa. Palm trees flourish here, but the fruit does not ripen.

There is one family which enjoyed a monopoly of the supply of palm branches to the churches in Rome under the Papal government on Palm Sundays. When Sixtus V., in the year 1588, transferred the Egyptian obelisk from the circus of Nero to the place in front of St. Peter's, in order to maintain order in the assembled crowd, it was ordered that no one should speak under penalty of death. There were forty levers worked by 800 men and 140 horses. In some part of the process the whole was brought to a stop by some part of the rope being a few inches too long. Every one was in an agony of suspense, when a sailor in the crowd called out, "Wet the ropes." You know this caused them to contract, and the result was to accomplish what could in no other way have been done. The success caused the Pope to pardon the violation of his edict, and on the solicitation of the happy sailor the right to supply these branches annually forever was bestowed on him and his descendants. He was a native and resident of St. Remo.

NICE, 8 P. M., May 18, 1872.

We arrived here safely, having had one of the most delightful drives the world can offer; sea and land, mountain and valley, tree and flower, fruit and grain, olive, citron and orange and fig, all combining to make the picture perfect. The drive down the mountain to the valley in which the old town lies, at the mouth of a small river on the coast of the Mediterranean, is surpassingly beautiful.

Letters from Is. and Annie, and Mary, and Cousin Emily, of the 28th of April, brought us pleasant accounts; and also two very nice letters from Cheston and Henry.

That God may bless and keep you one and all is our earnest prayer.

Yours lovingly,

CASPAR MORRIS.

SAVONA; ON THE CORNICHE ROAD,
ITALY, May 16, 1872.

My Dear Children:

We left Genoa yesterday for this place after having spent three days there very pleasantly. All except myself visited some places of interest; some very handsome palaces were there on some very highly improved grounds; and quite a pattern almshouse, with which they were all so delighted they can't tell me too much of the comforts and happiness of the inmates of all ages; all occupied, various trades taught, and brought to a state of great perfection. The women and children sewing; very attractive and beautiful; both plain and fancy work, embroidery very nice; but it was rather tantalizing not to be able to purchase from them. It was night, and the store was closed, and we left at 7 Monday morning. We were all very glad to be able to get at Genoa the men, horses and carriages that we had had last summer for the Swiss mountain travel, to take us as far as Nice on this Corniche road, which is considered, if not the most beautiful one in the world, extremely so, and it will occupy us three and a half days, and if it is all as attractive as what we have seen it is preferable to the railroad; and with the air-cushions my foot bore it very well yesterday. The trip could have been made in less time, but on my account they take it easily. We halted yesterday, midday, four hours at Pegli. Your father and I rested. We went with them awhile to visit a palace of uncommon beauty. It kept them between two and three hours, but it was so beautiful that they were not aware of the time it was taking. The building itself was not so remarkable a building, but the grounds and the views! It is on a rock, and the whole thing is artificial, having given employment to five hundred workmen on the spot for ten years, besides all the beautiful statuary, which has been made elsewhere. They had a row on a lake of considerable size; then a ride on horseback, then in certain parts of the grounds there are pipes so arranged that practical jokes may be played of giving a slight sprinkle or a good shower bath. One of them is over a very fine swing. Some young people might like this part, but I would not at all, though our party seem to have been greatly amused at it. At every turn they say there are very fine views and beautiful shrubbery, and trees from every part of the world. Then remember all the soil even had been brought, as this was a barren rocky mountain overhanging the Mediterranean.

NICE, May 19th.

The four days' ride now over. All of it was very grand, and we had much enjoyment, "Corniche," means Cornice, and the road is a shelf cut out of the rough mountain, which in many places overhangs the sea. But for the whole distance of two hundred miles you have sea on your left and right at or under your feet. High mountains on the right; covered with olive-trees wherever there was soil enough to hold one. In the valleys lemon orchards, and the roadsides thickly strewn with flowers. Oh! how Aunt Sally would have enjoyed it if she could be transported into their midst without the perils of travel, for I think she would suffer from them even more than I do, if that were possible. My comfort, however, in those four days was greatly increased by having the driver whom I knew. I had a great liking for him from first sight. He was so extremely like Murray Cheston that it was a great satisfaction to have him right before me. His face, manner, walk, voice all were Murray's, only he speaks Italian. His attentions to our comfort were very touching, and I really regret parting with him, as we do now finally, for from here we go by rail to Marseilles; then to Lyons and on to Paris.

I forgot to tell you that there has been a railroad constructed from Genoa here, which we crossed in our drive over two hundred times, and there are two hundred tunnels. Of course much of the scenery is lost to travelers; in fact almost all, to travelers who take that route.

I am still entirely unable to take a step, so of course see nothing of these cities except as we drive in and out again; I have to be carried to and from the carriage, and always up two flights of stairs, so when I reach our suite of rooms am a fixture till we travel; I rather regret it now, for I am sure if out I could pick us some things that I can't even commission any one to get for me. On reaching here last night I found letters from you, Is., Annie, Ches. and Hen., Cousin E. and Mrs. Cope; all truly welcome. I do feel very thankful to hear of dear little Harry's improved condition, for when we left he was forlorn. I hope he will keep well through the summer. I begin now to feel that October will soon be here, and then hope we will all be reunited, in health.

We are very glad Uncle Galloway remembered and attended to the hams. We had forgotten them. I wish I could think of them at Wallbrook as more comfortable, but I fear they have even less than in the few last seasons, and Julia will be a great loss to them if her marriage takes her from them, which I fear it will; but perhaps not this summer. Poor Uncle G. has a very depressing life, and I think it is well for the family to cheer him whenever they can. James's visits certainly do, and they like to have Sally too, and feel the want of society more at Wallbrook than in town where their friends can step in. I sometimes regret we are so far from them, and am almost tempted to say, "Let us go back," but again find it very difficult to say just what is best for all round; but it would not take much to turn us homeward. We do want to do the right thing.

Yesterday we heard Will and Sallie Morris had arrived, but we are not likely to meet at once, as they take England and Scotland first, while we are in France and Germany; and they return home in September. They have come on his account; he has been quite an invalid for eighteen months. Cousin Emily writes us Mr. and Mrs. S. Hollingsworth and daughters are coming over for a year; so I suppose we shall meet somewhere.

Give much love to Miss Alice; we are sorry to hear she is not well; tell her to take care of herself and try to be robust before we get back. Your father says I must ask you if you would like to have the girls have another little trip this summer, and we would be glad if Miss Alice would make one of the little party. If we were at home we would take them, but as we are not, can you not make some arrangement with Is. and Annie to join them as they did last summer? All seem to have enjoyed it then so much. You can think it all over, and do as you think best. You know we would like to give them all the advantages in our power.

We have been somewhat troubled about the small-pox, as from both public and private accounts there has been so much of it at home, and feel very thankful all our immediate friends have thus far escaped; and we hope it did not spread with you.

I am often reminded of Harry in his truck patch as I ride along. I hope he will be as successful with vegetables as last year. Here everything is so luxuriant and beautiful; they have had peas and asparagus all winter. Now great abundance of strawberries and tomatoes; we have scarcely been without the last all the winter ourselves.

Tell the girls the hillsides are very beautiful, covered with scarlet poppies and gladiolus, and many other equally gay flowers; then the pink and white horse-chestnut trees side by side, oleanders growing out of doors, and the geraniums are small trees. Don't think I exaggerate; perhaps some day they may come and see. But the odour from the lemon and orange orchards is beyond description; and the profusion of fruit on them at the same time with the bloom.

But I must say farewell; with much love to all, in which your father joins me. I wish I could say he was well; he is not sick, but is not well, and every little exertion exhausts him so much.

Yours truly and most affectionately,

A. C. MORRIS.

MARSEILLES, 23d.

I am sorry this was mislaid; and thus accounts for its old date. But it shall go, and not be as one I wrote you from Jerusalem, I thought too old and so tore up.

We reached here last night after a very long and tiresome railroad ride, and to-day I am resting my foot, and your father himself in general, while the others are off sight-seeing. We can't keep up with them. To-morrow we will have thirteen hours in the car.

This is a large and very nice-looking place. I wish I was able to go out a little, but I will try to be patient, and maybe I will get to see something of Paris. My foot is so much better that to-day I have on a cloth overshoe or sock that your father got for me in Rome, and they have been a great comfort in cold weather. But you will know I am longing for the time to be able to walk. I have no one to do any shopping for me but your father, and he knows so little about it. We were all shut in a day at Nice by pouring rain, the first day of the kind we have had since we left home. Aunt Jane read the Lady of the Lake while we all sewed, and we enjoyed it very much.

Here we have such elegant apartments that I feel out of place in my room, but as the windows open on to the balcony which looks out on to a very wide street where there is an increasing stream of passers both on foot and in showy carriages, some very odd-looking ones; I will look out instead of in. It is adjoining an elegant saloon, where we have a private table. There are people here from every quarter of the globe and in every variety of costume. I wish I could sketch some for you. I am tempted to cross this, notwithstanding Harry's feelings on that subject, as we find postage is double in France what we have paid anywhere else; but, no matter, you shan't suffer on that account.

NICE, May 19, 1872.

My Dear Sister (Emily Hollingsworth.—EDS.) :

Your letter without a date as to time, but from Miss Turner's, was cordially welcomed last evening, on our arrival. We have been so long used to the sound of the name, and it is so closely associated with the residence of friends and acquaintances here in quest of mild climate, that there is quite a familiar, almost home-like, feeling attached to it. Our experience confirms the opinion I had formed from all I had heard. This day near the last of May is cool and damp. If that be so now, during the winter there must be many cold ones. Yet it is a most attractive spot. Nothing can excel the beauty of the drive down the mountains by the Corniche road from Genoa to this place. The entire route of about one hundred and fifty miles is through scenes each of which, if alone, would be said to possess surpassing beauty. You will find some descriptions in "Doctor Antonio" (the scene of which is laid on the road between those two cities), which are not overdrawn, and are very attractive pieces of word-painting.

If you ever feel disposed to cross the ocean in search of perfect winter-quarters, I should name Bordighera, about fifty miles from this place. It is directly on the sea, in a sheltered nook screened by lofty mountains covered with olive trees; while palms, orange and lemon and other tropical plants grow abundantly about it. The house is a pattern of cleanliness, and is kept by a religious Swiss, who maintains at his own cost a school for the education of boys, and has built a church for the service of the Church of England, and there is, I believe, generally a resident chaplain. There are also lodging-houses in the vicinity.

Bordighera itself is an old Italian walled town, with fortresses about it for the defence of the inhabitants against the Turks in those long-gone days when the Barbary corsairs descended on the coast and carried off the people, giving occasion for the introduction into Christian liturgies of the prayer for all prisoners and captives. Its narrow streets, high houses, and foul smells serve only as a foil to the sweet odors of orange groves, and the beautiful gardens and lawns of the modern villas about it. St. Remo, a few miles distant, is still more frequented, but I should prefer Bordighera under the management of its present proprietor. It is as easy to reach as St. Croix. From London there by railroad is easily done in a few days.

But I trust when we reach home we may be favoured to rest there the few remaining days of our earthly pilgrimage, and while we do not desire to influence your movements in the least, we can only reiterate our expression in our last letters, that home will be much more home-like with your presence to bless it wherever it may be.

Your summer is arranged before this, we doubt not. Our arrangements for the winter must remain unsettled until we reach Philadelphia in October. Then if our house is unoccupied, we shall, of course, return to it. If it is in any way disposed of, we must seek another. We are not of "anxious mind" on that subject, but willing to trust that if our lives are spared, some dwelling will be provided, and we shall hope it may be where you may find comfort with us.

We were glad to learn from your reference to them that our letters from Jerusalem had been received, thus relieving your anxiety on our account. I felt ashamed of my want of courage, but really dreaded the fatigue and exposure of that part of the trip, not only on account of Anne and myself, but for the other females of the party, younger and older. We were not only favoured to get through safely, but all look back upon it as the most interesting and important stage of our journey. The deadly pall of superstition is spread over it, as it were over the remains of honoured goodness and greatness committed to the tomb, in the sure and certain hope of resurrection. He that once wept over its children, and pronounced the doom which has fallen upon it, "shall come and will not tarry." Then Jerusalem shall "arise and shine because her light is come," and the glory of God and the holy angels shall beam upon her.

Since our return to Europe our route has lain amid evidences of temporal grandeur and prosperity, well adapted to promote the feeling of infidel confidence that since the fathers fell on sleep all things continue as they were since the foundation of the world; and to produce doubt about the promise of His coming. We have need to live constantly in earnest struggle to hold fast the beginning of our confidence steadfast to the end, lest we be beguiled into the feeling, "My Lord delayeth His coming," and go to eating and drinking, "for to-morrow we die," and fall asleep as the fathers have done. It is only by fighting the good fight of faith that we can be saved, and, whatever others may find, my experience is that it is a sore conflict with an unwearied enemy, and one in which the victory is sure *only* because He that is for us is greater than he that is against us.

P. M.

I went to church this morning, leaving Anne (who is unable to walk on her foot), and the others having gone to the Scotch Church. We had a very simple, but unexceptionable sermon appropriate to the day—Whit-Sunday—and the announcement of a meeting on Wednesday to intercede for the outpouring of the Holy Ghost on all churches, in all lands. The hymn was a very sweet one, asking for more love as the best of all the gifts of the Spirit.

Please give ours to all the circle in which you are, whether in West 19th St. New York, or in Philadelphia. We are greatly interested for Mr. Montgomery, and hope ere this he has met with some business engagement which will suit him.

I observe by letters from Cheston, and also from Miss Helen Griffitts, that Miss Margaretta Robertson is confined to her bed. Her's has been a life of active self-denying daily devotion to the comfort of others. I have seen and known her more than most, and have a warm affection and profound respect for her. Please remember me especially to her. Most earnestly do I pray that He "who is not unrighteous to forget the work of faith and labour of love," of those who thus serve Him may supply all her needs from the abundant stores of *His grace*, and that in her hours of weakness and suffering she may realize the blessed peace which passes understanding which Jesus gives to those who love Him. She has passed through many and sore trials, ever looking to Jesus as the finisher as well as the author of her faith; there is laid up for her a crown of righteousness which the Lord shall *bestow* on all them who look for His appearing. Anne unites in dear love, with

   Yours truly,

               CASPAR MORRIS.

              NICE, May 20, 1872.

My Dear Children:

 I yesterday mailed a letter giving a hasty sketch of our progress to this place, which we had designed leaving to-morrow morning for Marseilles and Lyons, en route for Paris. Friezier received here a telegram announcing that Miss Grant has possession of the suite of rooms he had applied for for our service, and that all Paris is full. He has been telegraphing backward and forward, and has now (at 10 P. M.), just heard that we can have the apartments now occupied by the Prince and Princess of Wales, when they leave Paris on the 31st, and meanwhile can be taken in on Saturday, the 25th, in some other part of the same Hotel. We therefore shall leave here day after to-morrow, Wednesday, and hurry on to Paris Saturday night. We cannot aspire to any better accommodations than that which satisfies the heir of the throne of Great Britain, though we should not have thought so much of our present apartments had they not been gilded by that honour a few days since.

 Nice is a great collection of vast hotels and boarding-houses, very grand and imposing in architectural character, but has a very deserted aspect at this season. They are all closed, and the shops are empty, and signs "*à Louer*" stare you in the face at every turn. The public gardens alone have any cheerful aspect. The drives in the neighbourhood must of necessity be attractive, and the report of those who spent the day in the carriages is one of great enjoyment. Mountain heights, rich valleys, wide sea views. This, being Whit-Monday, is a holiday, and they saw the common people gaily dressed disporting themselves in merry songs and dances in the public gardens.

 I thought it better to avoid the fatigue of long drives and was content with sauntering about the public walks and streets, which looked much as Long Branch or Newport would do in the winter; this place being to Germany and England, for the winter months, what those places are to the United States for the summer.

Among other places visited by your uncle and aunts this morning was a grotto, of small dimensions, in which flows a stream holding lime in solution, which belongs to some one who makes a living from the silent work of the mighty agent, chemical affinity, which causes the lime to combine with the carbonic acid and desert the water so soon as it reaches the air. Moulds of celebrated works of art are disposed on shelves so that the water flows slowly across them and deposits the lime in infinitesimal portions moment by moment till a perfect cast is made. Your Aunt Hannah kindly brought your mother a beautiful cast of the celebrated Helvetian Lion, of Thorwaldsen.

Tuesday Morning.

A damp chilly day with occasional showers quite reconciled your mother and myself to our quiet enjoyment of the scent of orange-blossoms and the twitter of birds. Carriages had been engaged yesterday for a drive to Villefranche over the heights of Mt. Boron, which we shall enjoy more in the reports of others than by our own giddiness, even if the day were bright, and the decided improvement in your mother's foot approves the course I have taken in enjoining perfect rest. I hope by the time we reach Paris I may be able to have a boot made which she can put her foot into, and then shall encourage her to walk *some*. It will be four weeks to-morrow since the injury. How rapidly time flies!

(Noon.)

Steady pouring rain has confined the whole party to the house, and I have beguiled two hours for them and myself over the fascinating pages of Doctor Antonio. The descriptions of scenery about Bordighera and Taggia in the chapters narrating the trip to the sanctuary of St. Maria de Lampidusa are perfect, and quite worth your perusal as paintings of what we enjoyed in our ride along the Corniche road.

Speaking of pictures recalls to my mind that I have repeatedly forgotten to request that Israel will have any photographs which may arrive *unmounted* put on good Bristol board. Cheston will probably be able to inform him how he can get access to Henry Smith, son of Stevenson Smith, and nephew of Clifford, and give him the benefit of the job. He was once a photographer, and will know how to do it nicely, and will, I suppose, be glad of the compensation. There are many duplicates among the Egyptian collection; mount both.

I suppose the Cairo box may have reached home about this time, and often amuse myself at the blank disappointment the *miscellaneous* contents will cause, and at the fun the customs officers will have over them. You know your mother's principle against throwing anything away. The only thing she has left, voluntarily or involuntarily, or destroyed, is the old boots with which she left home, which I prevailed with her to leave at Vienna, as she certainly *could* never wear them again. To my horror I heard her expressing to your aunts her deep regret, as she was sure if she had them now she could attach one of the soles to the black shawl in which I envelop her foot, and thus walk a *little* on it.

MARSEILLES, May 23d.

At 10 A. M. yesterday we left Nice by railroad in a saloon car, and reached this place about 7 P. M. without having left it. The distance is about one hundred and seventy miles. At first the road followed the coast, giving us a continued repetition of beautiful bays and inlets and mountain promontories. The blue of the Mediterranean is unique and indescribable, and so are the purple hues which vary in it. At one place these were contrasted strongly with the muddy current of the Aar, which is seen like a long sand-bar running out into the stainless blue. For some hour or more we had grand snow-clad mountain ranges in the distance, while olive, and fig and palm trees proved that winter never scattered even hoar frost in the valleys.

Some of the bays, by which we skirted, have celebrity. In one Napoleon Bonaparte landed on his return from Egypt when he had been defeated by the English in his attempt to invade India by that route. He was then only a General of the French Republic. From the same place he embarked for Elba when he had been subdued and abdicated the throne of Emperor, and retired to Elba, a small island on the Italian coast; and in another he had landed again in 1815 when he astonished and startled Europe by his return, and during one hundred days kept every heart beating wildly with apprehension, till he was finally defeated at Waterloo.

There was great diversity of soil and surface. A long distance we ran directly across a level plain surrounded by mountains, and smiling with abundance; olives, and grain, and grass. Then we passed into mountain ranges with pine, and then into valleys with mulberry and silk culture, and then were carried by tunnels (one two miles long) through savage-looking rocky ranges bristling with ruined castles, guarding old towns. It was the Provençal region so celebrated for its songs, its troubadours, and its minnesingers. The weather was most genial, and flowers and fruits were abundant. We passed through Toulon, the great fortified harbour of the French Navy in the Mediterranean.

Your loving father,

CASPAR MORRIS.

MARSEILLES, May 23, 1872.

My Dear Children:

We have arrived safely at this point en route to Paris, where we hope to receive late accounts of you all. Our ride yesterday in a saloon car, occupied by our own party exclusively, was pleasant in every respect; and we find ourselves here in quarters so gorgeous and commodious, and at tables so sumptuously spread with the delicacies of the sea, the garden, and the field, that one whose heart was set on such things might be permitted to look with apprehension to any further progress.

An old and celebrated Roman colony, Massilia, it may have offered similar temptations to degenerate sons of the mistress of the world when her senators had learned to despise "the spare feast, a radish and an egg," and squander fortunes on a single meal. It was with no little regret we exchanged carriages, with good horses and accomplished drivers, for the elegance and commodiousness of the saloon car of the railroad, involving as it does the loss of the wondrous attractions of the Corniche road, so smooth, so well graded, and running through scenes of such alternating and commingling grandeur and beauty; sea, mountain, valley, rock, castle and garden. No one has ever driven over it, since it was first made by the people of the country to enable the king of Savoy to return to his capital without encountering the perils of the sea, without a blessing on those who made it, and a desire to experience again the unrivalled enjoyment. The railroad, however, enabled us to come yesterday in one stage (from 10 A. M. to 7 P. M.), a distance equal to that we had required four days to accomplish, from Genoa to Nice; and as that distance and time were intervening between you and ourselves, we were enabled to balance the one gratification against the other.

You must, one and all, read Dr. Antonio; the scene of which is laid in the "Riviera di Ponente," as that district is called. Nice could not be more deserted when we turned our backs on its orange and palm groves, than it was when we entered and all the time we were there.

The heavy rain of Monday gave way to a most beautiful morning on Tuesday. So that everything laughed and sang as we rolled rapidly in the car through its beautiful environs. The road lay for some distance along the shore, or at least within sight of the sea, whose blue and purple waters were divided by the muddy stream of Aar, which rushes down from the mountains thick with the soil which it carries far out into the ocean without mingling with it. I was obliged to take Israel's glass to satisfy myself that it was not a spit of land; and a vessel near the end, a lighthouse.

Again and again as we rushed past openings in the mountains, here clothed with olive and fig trees and other sun-loving tropical plants which perish if a cold breath reaches them, we caught glimpses of vast snow-capped peaks, and long ridges of pure white snow-clad heights. We soon reached Cannes, a little nook filled with ornamental residences surrounded by beautiful gardens and shrubberies, the resort of English people of rank and fortune. It is also celebrated for the manufacture of *eau de fleur d'orange*, and we saw the people busily occupied in picking the bloom from the groves as fast as the buds expanded. We therefore missed the odor which scented the gales for miles at Jaffa, but which here, committed to the keeping of the bottled waters, may be transported even to you.

As far as Fréjus the road lay generally along the shore, giving us full opportunity to enjoy the wondrous and unique beauty of the blue sea. At Fréjus, which was an old Roman colony, we saw the ivy-covered ruined arches of an amphitheatre and an aqueduct.

On our way we passed several points which possess more modern associations. One at which Napoleon landed on his return from his expedition to Egypt in the latter part of the last century, when he (then only a general of a French army) assumed all the pomp of a great conqueror, and attempted to beguile the people by adopting the tone of speaking of a Mussulman, and had stained his name by the horrible massacre of his own sick soldiers at Jaffa. Another from which he sailed for Elba in 1814, after he had been forced to abandon his usurped empire. Another still at which he landed in his attempt to recover it, which agitated the world from March to June, 1815, when he was finally overthrown at the battle of Waterloo. These are all quiet-looking little bays, surrounded by mountains, retaining no vestiges of the passage of the great events.

There are many little islands dotting the shore, some supporting castles, some towers, some convents. One of the islands we saw was long the prison of the celebrated unknown prisoner of state so celebrated as "The Man with the Iron Mask;" another was the residence of some monk who uttered the absurd definition of what is truth, which has been flaunted in the faces of all dissentients as so oracular, "*Quod semper, quod omnibus, quod ubique,*" which, stripped of its scholastic gilding, means nothing but "what has been believed at all times and in all places and by everybody." Who is to decide what that is? Yet our high-church friends fall back on it as though it afforded an unanswerable argument to all cavillers.

The distance between Nice and this place is put down at 225 kilometres. The French system starts with the metre as the unit and makes the 1000 metres (kilo. being 1000) serve for one mile. It is, I think, about ⅔ of a mile, which would give the distance as about 180 miles. The scenery varies greatly. Part of it is wild and barren rocks, sometimes entirely naked and at others covered with the peculiar pine known as umbrella pine from its squat shape and rounded dome-like top. From the heights you would fancy you were looking down on an immense multitude of men, each holding a green umbrella overhead. Other mountains were terraced and planted with grey-leaved olives; and some of the plains were cultivated for the olive also. This tree *requires* cultivation. We see them all dug round, and they are manured freely with animal matter. They are now in full blossom, but the fruit does not ripen till next January, and is likely to suffer greatly from the drought of summer or from the cold of early winter, and the crop is therefore very uncertain. But the extent of territory devoted to the culture proves that it must be profitable. Greece, Italy, Southern France and Spain, and all the borders of the Mediterranean Sea, are planted with this tree. Where wheat can be raised, the spaces between the trees are sometimes sown with it. Its fruit, and the oil expressed from it, is not only largely exported, but the oil enters into almost all the cooking of all classes of people, from the highest to the poorest, and when nice is very preferable to either butter or lard for frying and making sauces. Some of the plantations of the olive trees through which we passed were evidently very old. One could imagine them of any age, they looked so gnarled and twisted, and had trunks either hollowed and kept clean or of solid girth. Yet even these were full of young leaves and the delicate bloom.

There is some consumption of the oil in the curing of sardines; but that is trifling compared to other uses. I watched the hauling of a net one evening. A crowd of lookers-on was collected; among them lots of boys. The moment the net is landed the tiny fish escape through the meshes, and it is the privilege of the boys to catch as many as possible of these for their own benefit, while the fishermen are emptying the masses of them into the baskets. With the picturesque dresses of all, and the monkey-like agility of the boys, the scene is attractive. There were but few other fish taken in the haul I saw, and they were nice-looking. But in the market here this morning I saw such a collection of the products of the sea, exposed for sale and to be *eaten*, as would astonish any of our seine-haulers. Some were red-colored, some black, some yellow; the least repulsive-looking were huge "*Millers' Thumbs*." Some were squids and some cuttle-fish. (The West River family may turn to Brooke's natural history and see what ugly-looking, long-legged, long-armed fellows these are). Rays, and diminutive devil-fish, with their squinting eyes, and eels (black and yellow) were curled up in baskets like hideous worms, and many unformed objects lay like masses of sea-nettles. Then there were some with immense heads and tapering bodies and long horny fins. It seemed as though all the deformities of the dwellers of the "waters under the earth" had been collected on the stalls among the dirty women who sold and bought them.

In very beautiful contrast with this was the display of the flower market, an open square shaded by nice trees, among which were stalls raised above our heads covered with handsomely-ornamented canopies. Under these sat pretty women, with nicely-starched and plaited white caps, surrounded by heaps of flowers which they were busily tying in bouquets of varied size and disposing of them to the crowd of eager purchasers. Fruits and vegetables were also abundant and neatly displayed.

I made this survey this morning while your aunts and uncle were driving, and I could leave your mother seated at the window knitting and watching the passing crowd. At the same time I visited the dock in which lie the ships, and saw them discharging cargo. Though the docks have great celebrity, the mode of discharging cargo is very bad. Wheat and grain in bulk, as well as all other goods, are thrown out on the jetty, or walk, which is nicely paved, but without any cover. A shower came on at the time I was there, of course damaging everything. There was much variety. Peanuts from Senegal; palm-nuts from Africa; wheat from Algiers and Alexandria; cotton-seed from India; sesame from Egypt. Each was being discharged in heaps, from which it was being weighed or measured (under the inspection of sworn officers), into bags to be carted to the warehouses. The peanuts and cotton-seed and palm-nuts (I was told on the spot) are to be pressed for the oil. Is it to adulterate the olive oil? I strongly suspect so. The peanuts are very inferior to ours, and in a very dirty condition; and they as well as the wheat are all sifted on the wharf by the means of large round sieves suspended on tripods and worked about by men; one throwing the nuts or grain on to the sieve with a shovel, and another agitating the sieve and tossing them into another heap, from which they are measured or weighed. It makes a busy spectacle. The products of the western world were also represented by a cargo of sugar from Guadaloupe.

As I passed to and from the docks I turned each time into the Bourse and Merchants' Exchange, a large handsome hall, the façade ornamented by two figures intended to represent early Massilian navigators, whose names I have forgotten already, but to one of whom we owe the first notice of the length of days in the northern latitudes, and the rise and fall of the ocean tides. (You know there is no tide in the Mediterranean sea.) When I was there first it presented the same scene of excitement as our own stock-room, a part of it being railed about for the brokers, who bought and sold with much wild gesticulation and loud cries. At my second visit it was crowded with merchants; and the reverberation of the talk from the vaulted ceiling was as loud as the noise of a train of railroad cars.

The streets of the older parts of the town are narrow, and the houses high. The main street is wide, well-paved, and lined with shops whose windows are filled with an elegant display of goods by day, and brilliantly lighted by night.

Your uncle and aunts report an interesting visit to a church which crowns the summit of a lofty conical mount rising above the harbour, consecrated to the Madonna de la Guarda, who is the special dependence of sailors. It is filled with *votive* offerings of models of ships and pictures representing storms and wrecks; presented by those who have sought the intercession of the Virgin in time of danger or sickness or accident at sea. They report also having seen the keel and ribs of a Roman Galley, dug up at a distance of sixty metres from the seashore; thus proving that the coast has risen and the sea receded that distance. There were stones also which had been used as projectiles from catapults, and many urns, and sarcophagi, and statues and sculptures exhumed in the neighbourhood, and some Phenician remains and glass of very ancient date.

Friday Morning, May 24th.

I had written thus far yesterday when dinner claimed my service, after which a nap. Then I went to the office to mail a letter for West River (which contains the commencement of this). While doing so the hotel carriage arrived from the railroad depot, and I could not be satisfied that the two rotundities who rolled out were the really familiar forms I thought them, till my eye caught the long, lank shape of Ellerslie Wallace doubling itself up in the effort to get through the door. I gave them the hearty greeting familiar faces are sure to meet on foreign soil, and Wallace raised his hand, in which hung a red Russia leather bag, and said with his perfectly homely, bluff manner, "Look there, do you see that? it is a perfect comfort; just fills up a lacuna; your son and daughter sent it to me the day before I started." So Cheston and Mellie will be held in pleasant association with the comfort of travel during the enjoyments of its delights. It was a gratification to us to see those who had left home more recently than our latest dates, though they had nothing new to communicate. We are preparing this morning to leave this about 10 A. M., and shall continue without stoppage to Dijon, where we hope to arrive at 10 P. M., and lodge; and to-morrow leave early for Paris.

My letter sent to West River and this are most disjointed and discursive and I have left unsaid very much that interested me. I have only room to add that your mother and I are amused by the quaint collars on the draft horses. They have a point at least fifteen inches high, rising above the hames, and these project on either side, like the long horns of an ox. They are often hung with bells. I saw one little donkey pass who seemed almost lost in collar.

DIJON, May 24, 1872.

My Dear Children:

Leaving Marseilles at 10½ yesterday we rode all day through the rain, reaching here about midnight, having skirted the shore of the gulf of Lyons from Marseilles to Arles, where we struck the Rhone and followed its swollen, muddy stream to Lyons; which we reached just in time to be able to form some idea of the beauty of the vicinity and the extent of its manufacturing establishments.

From that place here the journey was made by night; and we of course know nothing of what we passed through. A few hours' sleep here in a chamber on a level with the pavement has not refreshed us much; and a cheerless rainy morning makes no promise of much comfort during the two hours we shall be confined here before we start on the two hundred and fifty miles, or more, we shall traverse to-day; hoping to reach Paris about 6 P. M. We have left the region of orange, olive and palm; and are now to find our pleasure, as we did yesterday, in tracing the growing resemblance to our own trees and shrubs.

The historic associations of the entire route, and of this place also, are all horrible. Marseilles and Lyons were the scenes of the most horrid atrocities which render the French Revolution the darkest spot in human history. Perhaps other ages may challenge pre-eminence in cruelty ; Rome had its conscriptions, and Egypt its butcheries, but these scenes are so associated with our own history, and so near our own times, that they have the freshness of recent transactions. I could not but think of the guillotine, and then of the *noyades* and *mitraillades*, which literally choked the stream with the bodies of the dead.

This is a quaint old town, formerly the capital of Burgundy, so celebrated for its connection with English history and Shakespeare's plays, and has one glorious bright spot illustrated by some artist in a sculpture representing the then governor of the province standing with great calmness, behind him a company of females and children ; while before him are the military officers (presenting his orders from Charles IX. for the massacre of the Protestants), and a prelate holding out the crucifix as the sign of the authority of the church ; not to be resisted under penalty of excommunication. The officer refused to execute the atrocious edict. He thus at his own peril saved the lives of thousands.

Sunday Morning, PARIS, May 26th.

The rapidity of our transit across France (it cannot be called our journey through) has not permitted any notes by the way and has scarcely allowed opportunities for observation. We are quiet enough this calm Lord's Day morning in our own chamber, which, though it looks out on the Rue St. Honoré, is undisturbed by any sound except that of the venders of radishes and lettuce at an early hour, and the occasional roll of a coupé or chaise, since. We are at the Hotel de Bristol, in the Place Vendome, fellow-lodgers with the Prince and Princess of Wales, who act as splendid foils, diverting attention from ourselves. Your mother is of course obliged to stay in our room ; so that which opens on the street has been allotted to our service. The party occupies two suites, so that there is a parlour, which also opens on the street, and another which looks upon the court of the building, in which we take our meals. The only discomfort is that there is no access to either of the sitting-rooms but through either your aunt's chamber or ours. Your dear old grandfather had a remark often on his lips that "Love makes room," and it is equally true that it makes a way. I shall go to the American Episcopal Church this morning. The others have selected the Wesleyan Chapel and the Scotch Church. Friezier's wife joined the party yesterday, so that we are in large force.

This is all I can yet report of Paris, beyond our arrival here at 6 P. M., and that in driving from the railroad we passed the walls of the Tuilleries and other public buildings, scarred by the shells of the

Germans and blackened by the fire of domestic sedition. All else is as "*gay as Paris.*" We saw one column around which scaffolding indicated the repair which is in progress, and just in front of the hotel is the pedestal from which the Colonne Vendome, on which stood the bronze statue of Napoleon I., was thrown down with such difficulty by the Commune. I find my nearest route to church will lie across the Champs Elysées and through the Place de la Concorde, so that I shall see more before dinner.

We left Marseilles in the rain, and it fell heavily and without intermission until we crossed the Jura Mountains, which form the water-shed dividing between the streams flowing into the Mediterranean Sea and those which run to the Atlantic Ocean. The Rhone and its tributaries were much swollen and very muddy. The character of the country was of course very varied; and at one point we passed through the longest railroad tunnel in France, occupying 7 minutes in passing and being more than 2 miles long. Vienne is beautifully situated on a rocky eminence in a narrow valley on the Rhone. A tunnel passes under it, on emerging from which we looked back on its mediæval church and castle. It was a Roman town in Gaul, and was the scene of terrible persecution in the earlier centuries of our era, and as such was impressed on my mind, though I cannot recall the names of the distinguished martyrs who gave it celebrity. It was here also, so the guide-book tells us, that Pontius Pilate spent the later years of his life, the book says an exile; and not far distant from it lies the route by which Hannibal led his Carthaginians to Italy.

Orange is another town whose name is familiar as giving its title to the famous Prince who so distinguished himself as the champion of religious truth in Holland, and also to him who afterwards became husband of the daughter of James II. of England and, in her right, king of Great Britain. But before reaching these places we passed through Avignon, for nearly 100 years the seat of the Papacy when the city of Rome was in the power of the Ghibilline party.

Before breakfast, Tuesday morning,

PARIS, May 28, 1872.

We have now been two days in this wonderful city, and though I feel much like one of the large trees in the Bois de Bologne, which have been transplanted by machinery within a few weeks and now stand well stayed by wires stretching out on every side and fastened to the earth, and only now putting out their buds, while all around other trees are in full leaf, I yet begin to understand how those whose wishes, and views, and hopes, and aspirations, are all limited to the life that now is, should think Paris is heaven. Every one here may follow the bent of one's own inclination, and find satisfaction for the devices of his own heart and have no one to interfere with him, so long as he does not interfere with another.

Through the neglect of the porter at the hotel at Nice we are yet without our letters. Friezier had a telegram from the inn-keeper telling him that two letters had been found after we left. one of which must have been that to Brown, Shipley & Co., requesting them to send letters here.

I have done nothing yet beyond going to church on the Lord's Day, and to the *banker's* yesterday morning, and a GRAND DRIVE in the Bois de Bologne yesterday afternoon. To-day we commence life here. I should be content to spend the whole fortnight in the Bois de Bologne.

Your loving father,
CASPAR MORRIS.

DIJON, FRANCE, May 25, 1872.

My Dear Children:

We left Marseilles yesterday morning. Had a long trip, and notwithstanding all the luxury of the saloon-car, containing three apartments and elegantly fitted with easy arm-chairs and three sofas, and not to omit an abundantly supplied lunch basket, a ride of thirteen hours without leaving the car *is tiresome*. It was past twelve last night when we reached here. A hot supper and good beds have refreshed us, however, and now, having left me to chat in my own way to you all, they have all gone to see what is considered a good museum; to return in an hour for our start to the depot for Paris. We have two hundred and seventy-five miles to go to-day, and so, of course, a little additional fatigue, but to-morrow is a day of rest. Not that it is universally so here, far from it, but we make it so, and just now I must forego still the pleasure of getting to church with them. I do occasionally try to hop a few steps at a time, but it is very little that I can do, so there is no probability of my seeing any more of Paris than I have done for the last five weeks of other places. Only imagine a lady coming to Paris and not *shopping*. Well, I shall be singular at any rate; perhaps it will be economical. Here comes Friezier with our lunch basket to empty and replenish for to-day. That you may see we do not suffer in this way, I will give you the "Bill of Fare," for once: Tenderloin of beef, pair of nice-looking roast chickens, sliced ham and tongue, two dozen eggs, beautiful rolls and a little pot of butter, pepper, salt, wine and water; as fine strawberries and cherries as I ever saw, and some kind of preserve, and if we needed more when we stopped at the stations we could replenish. But that has never been required; he is a good provider.

I was sorry to see nothing more of Lyons than just to pass in the cars, but it was thought the best arrangement of our time. It is a very large town and a busy, thriving manufacturing place of silks and velvets.

PARIS, May 26th.

Yes, my dear children, we are here actually in Paris; but don't be alarmed, I am not going to inflict any descriptions. I could not if I would, as we only reached here last night, and *all* or the most I shall see will be from my window. We are on the third floor, and the street is about as wide as Chestnut Street, so it will require some effort to see even what passes there. They tell us Paris is *very full*, that is all the hotels; the street here is not at all so, so I scarce believe that; it is only to put us off with anything in the way of accommodations. We hear the Prince and Princess of Wales are here in this house, but as it is an immense affair, there is little probability of our stumbling on them; none of mine. It will not trouble me, however. Aunt Mary is very anxious to do so, and I think most likely will accomplish it in some way.

May 28th.

Dear Cheston's birthday. I can see him just as he looked that day; a little black-headed precious thing. I wonder if he will take a holiday and spend to-day at Fernbank. He may not be able. And Israel's is the first of June. I shan't forget that too, and will be with you all, though I am shut in *in Paris*. But stay, I shan't be so shut up now, for I must tell you I actually got into the carriage yesterday before any one knew what we were about, with only your father and a cane. We took a nice long drive which we enjoyed much, and I saw a little of this great city, for surely it is a great place.

Your father is trying most industriously to get a dress made for me, or rather finished; it was got at Milan, that silk, and I am now in great need. But every one wants weeks to consider about it, and we are to leave on Monday a week, so I fear I shan't even get a dress in Paris. I wish I had one of you girls to get me a bonnet, for with only one foot I can do nothing, and your father's efforts to help me are amusing, and the prices are enormous, of everything. The truth is we don't know how to manage in this great place; but I am not troubled, I see people wear all sorts of things here.

Oh such a nice package of letters; good accounts from you all. I am glad to tell you your father is well. Has had no trouble except weariness since we left Constantinople. Love to Uncle Galloway and Aunt Margaret. So glad to hear they are at Wallbrook and she more comfortable. The mail is about to close. Much love to each of you. Galloway's telegram was in time. No microscope had been bought, though some had been looked at.

(*Not signed, but in handwriting of A. C. M.*—EDS.)

PARIS, May 29, 1872.

My Dear Brother and Sister:

We have had two nice letters from you and feel truly thankful to find you are getting along more comfortably; dear Margaret down stairs, and I hope in your next to hear she is enjoying the "Garden Chair." I shall imagine you at her side going around that elegant circle, and stopping to admire the view and examine the trees alternately. I do hope your evergreens have not suffered as they have done in the neighbourhood of Philadelphia. I shall be anxious to hear how she likes the chair and if you take that walk every afternoon. I hardly expect to see it this summer, as after much thought on the subject we have concluded it is best under present circumstances to be still. About the time that I wrote of the doctor's alarming attack in Constantinople I did think very seriously of trying to get home, but he recovered very promptly; and then at once followed my sprained ankle, which at first was extremely painful, but now is not at all so, except when used; and that is diminishing daily, so that although we are not an able-bodied couple by any means, we are able to care for each other, and the doctor certainly does enjoy *much;* and as I am very sure he ought not to attempt practice again, I am the more willing to keep him out of sight and call a little longer, as well as avoid our summer, for although both Wallbrook and Ivy Neck halls are very cool, the atmosphere here is not so debilitating as with us; no warm nights for instance. I am glad to have your views on the subject, and admit mine coincide very much with them, but I have given you our decision for the present. I am sure we shall have more pleasure after we get home, in reflecting on all this, than now, while enduring the fatigue and petty annoyances.

I do feel much for poor Sallie H. as regards our taking Tulip Hill. I am very much afraid to think of such a thing; we know full well West River lands do not pay, and have we not enough of that sort of property already; and yet must the "Old Home" go out of the family? Is it impossible for her to keep it during her life?

I here had to lay aside the pen to take a drive, and a most delightful one it has been. Such roads or streets, and through a beautiful park, and I am so pleased to find I can to-day walk alone with a cane. But I must say farewell; with much love to Margaret. Tell her I have had her beautiful example of patience much before me for the last five weeks, and hope I have profited by it. It did go pretty hard with me to be so helpless.

Your affectionate sister,

A. C. MORRIS.

PARIS, May 28, 1872, 1 P. M.

My Dear Children:

Just as we were making our arrangements for the day the longed-for letters arrived, and your mother and I have just finished reading them, with hearts overflowing with gratitude for all the mercy we have received. Each precious letter seemed of itself enough, and each successive one only added to the perfect joy. Our only regret arises from the thought that you should have suffered any anxiety on our account. Your mother's ankle is decidedly better, so that she now walks about using an umbrella for a cane. I do all in my power to spare her, and she does not attempt any sight-seeing or shopping. Indeed none of the party have undertaken either until this morning, and then we were content to be left behind with our letters. This afternoon we shall probably drive with them, as that suits us both better than the fatigue of sight-seeing.

You have no occasion for any anxiety on my account. My only trouble has arisen from the alarm your mother and uncle felt. I can *not* account for the attacks by any mental anxiety or indigestion; and Mrs. Roosevelt, who met us on the Nile and is now here, says I have gained greatly. And I think your mother has also. She certainly sleeps better than she has done for a long time. The whirl and excitement of Paris would fatigue us if we allowed ourselves to be drawn into it; but we shall not attempt to do as much as the others do, though I will confess I feel a little ashamed of myself to be here and doing so little.

I cannot go abroad from this hotel without seeing the ruins of the Tuilleries and the public buildings, which are the only tokens remaining to indicate the terrible ordeal through which the city passed so recently. The avenues and boulevards are crowded with people, the shops filled with attractive goods, and the gardens of the Tuilleries and Champs Elysées literally swarm.

The latter part of our journey from the south was rapid, and we began to think we had come faster than the season, but to-day the weather is warm enough, and the beauty of the trees and shrubs is very great.

Among our letters was one from William and Sally Morris, from London. We fear greatly we shall not cross each other's orbits this summer, as both bodies have somewhat of the comet in their composition, and the paths are so uncertain that the places of crossing cannot be calculated.

Mr. Longstreth will leave us next Monday; we shall miss him greatly, and regret that he cannot go with us to the end.

The numerous deaths mentioned in the various letters, of those more or less dear to some of us, impresses us all with the uncertainty of life. May we one and all live each day as it were our last. It is the *only way of life*. Let Faith embrace our own sinfulness, the perfect sacrifice and constant intercession of our Redeemer and the simple *honesty* of living as becomes those " who are not their own, but bought with a price," and then all is well. Life is one state of being only, *changing* by the *changing* of the common earthly body for the glorious body, like unto our Lord's. Death is but this change. But how sad if, when we lose this mortal body, we find we have not any house eternal in the heavens! I pray those I so love, children and children's children, to use diligence to make sure their calling and election to eternal life.

I am glad to hear good accounts of each, from Tyson (the oldest) down to the large flock of little ones. God bless them one and all, prays

Your loving father,
CASPAR MORRIS.

G. C. M.'s telegram received. I am relieved, as I almost feared to venture on a purchase.

PARIS, May 29, 1872, 8 A. M.
My Dear Brother (*Galloway Cheston.*—EDS.):

It was not until yesterday we received your two last letters, and I scarcely know which subject of congratulation and thanksgiving is uppermost in our hearts; that you should have been able to accomplish the removal to Wallbrook with dear Margaret, or the great improvement in Anne's ankle. Our anxiety about you has been very great, and we know full well that yours has not been less on our account.

We shall hope to learn that dear Margaret enjoys her garden chair. Ever since I wrote you about it last summer from Ragatz I have wished I were in a region from which I could send you one, and am delighted to learn they may be had in New York. We shall think of her passing among the lovely evergreens of your lawn and enjoying the view; so fine that we would select that spot for scenery even after all our enjoyment of what we have visited. Our climate does not permit the high culture which clothes everything here with attractiveness. We hope your trees have not suffered as the evergreens about Philadelphia have done, where some individuals calculate their losses by thousands of dollars.

Anne is now dressing by my side, able to move about without my assistance. The last two days she has walked to the parlour with a cane only, and also gone up and down the stairs to drive; and this morning reports it less painful on motion that it was yesterday. I believe the time has now come for moderate use; but shall proceed carefully.

As regards our return, I think we shall find it best to continue with brother and sisters to the end, unless some imperative duty at home calls us away. Brother Wistar's kindness, and his anxious interest for us, are unbounded; and any suggestion of change involves so many other considerations, and would be productive of so great disturbance, that Anne and I have decided it is better we should accompany them. They are all improving, and when once the toil of Paris is over we shall enjoy the return to the Tyrol and Salzburgh, and the tour through Scotland and Wales. The necessity for long and fatiguing day's journeys has passed ; and as Anne cannot visit picture galleries and general sights, *our* going about in the towns is dispensed with, while the afternoon drives are very pleasant to us. We should, however, gladly forego these pleasures should there be any cause for our return which we could present as imperative, and which would involve no discussion.

My own health is very much as it has been. I have not a large stock of reserve force, and am often stiffened in motion. The two or three sudden seizures, which have alarmed Anne and brother and sisters, have been quite unaccountable. That at Constantinople especially so ; and I did feel, myself, that if it were not subdued by hypodermic application of morphia it might be serious. It was not painful, but a sense of contraction of the diaphragm, which rendered it almost impossible to expand the chest. It came on very soon after a very comfortable tepid bath. Happily the courier was with me or I should certainly not have been able to reach the hotel, which I did accomplish just in time to save myself from falling. Mustard and the morphia relieved the spasm, and I have had no return. I have no doubt it was rheumatism. I have entered thus into particular detail in order to quiet your apprehensions. I do not pretend to accompany Wistar and Mary and my sisters in their visits to the many objects of interest which claim their attention.

It is now 2 P. M., and I have taken up this sheet where it was interrupted by being called to breakfast. I have visited the wards of the Hotel Dieu and the Blind Institution. They dropped me at the Hospital about 11 A. M., and have been spending the morning among churches and picture-galleries, I presume. They will not return till 4 for dinner. I wish very much Mr. King were here ; he and I could inspect hospital buildings and arrangements to our mutual advantage.

I am embarrassed by want of command of the language, and cannot enter into the detail of either sufficiently to derive benefit, but have arrived at the conclusion that hospitals and educational buildings should not have more than two stories, and those should not be so high as we have been making them ; and hospital windows should open to the floor.

The blind school is maintained at the expense of the state. The Principal received me with great politeness, and entered freely into the discussion of the great question now at issue as to the use of signs ; and also as to the best occupations. He at once laid down the principle that mental occupations were to be preferred, as the class in which the blind were more nearly on an equality with the seeing ; and music the occupation in which they were able to enter into competition with the seeing with most hope of success. I was delighted with the earnest kindly manner of the gentleman in charge ; and the healthy, happy appearance of the pupils.

Evening.

We have been driven up and down the Champ Elysées and the entrance to the Bois de Bologne, and have seen the display of fashion. My chief gratification was in the fine horses. Noble animals admirably trained and gaited, driven with two pairs of reins to each horse; one snaffle and one curb. It has rather an odd look to see a pair of reins in each hand of the driver.

Your account of S**** H***** is very distressing. I do wish she could make any arrangement to secure a residence at Tulip Hill during her life. If no prudential considerations influenced us, the mere feeling of sympathy for her would embarrass any purchase during her life.

I do not know what Anne and I will do with ourselves on our return, should it be consistent with God's purpose to permit us once more to see our children and yourself. I *must* not allow myself to be drawn into any circumstances involving *professional* responsibility. At the same time I must have some occupation for my time and thoughts. We must have a home of our own where we can welcome our children and friends; but where we can also enjoy the privilege of quiet and retirement at our own discretion. Whether it would contribute most to the happiness and advantage of the family for us to continue in Philadelphia, where we can offer the benefit of city education to Mary's children, or go to the country, where we can afford a retreat from the temptations of the town to our other grandchildren, is a question we often agitate. So far as we see at present, we are likely to have our house on hand on our return. We have not learned what Emily's plans are. You thus see we are in a condition to ask your counsel about our own plans rather than to offer advice to you. You know my views about Tulip Hill. I cannot but believe, entirely, that with proper management the orchards now planted there ought to yield a fair return, and that, with economy and attention, we might be able to live on our income from other sources. Our only desire is to settle where we can best serve our Master till He comes, and we pray that He will order our going.

With sincere love to Margaret and the kindest message possible to Mary Ellen. Much love to James and Sally and all our friends. I will gladly attend to your commissions and any others you may favour us with.

    Your loving brother,

        CASPAR MORRIS.

PARIS, June 2, 1872.

My Dear Brother:

We were thinking of looking here at bronzes for you, and suddenly remembered that we are not posted as to requisite colour, whether copper or green, and we can't agree at all about your clock and the little ornament which stands on the top, so I write to beg you will let us hear *at once*, as there will just be time for a letter to reach us at Berlin. And do you think those you have seen were bought there, or in London, or here? If you could ascertain it would be well, and *where*. We intend to visit a manufactory here to-morrow, and we will look for the Partridges, but in this dilemma about colour will be afraid to purchase.

I am very glad to be able to give you more favourable accounts of ourselves. I have just walked across the room *without* the cane; no longer suffer except in going up or down stairs, and the doctor is decidedly better. Yesterday we drove to Versailles; 10 miles; spent the day; he going through the palace and grounds, enjoying it very much, and was not as much fatigued as he often is; slept well and is comfortable to-day, so we all feel quite encouraged about him. Wistar is as kind as possible and very anxious we should only do what we see is right, and if we do find it desirable we will stop and rest. We now expect to leave here on the 11th for Brussels, and most likely this time will see Van Houtte's establishment; so our next will tell you of that. We will not pay in advance for anything there, I assure you. From there to Antwerp, Hamburg, and thence not decided. Wistar is certainly much better himself, and all the rest are quite well, and we are getting along nicely.

We shall miss Tom. Longstreth very much; he has been kind and attentive, and especially helpful to us since my accident. His leave of absence expires, and he leaves us with reluctance for England. Expects to sail on the 2nd of July on the "Algeria;" will see the family on getting to Philadelphia and report all about us. With much love to Margaret and yourself, in which the doctor joins. He would write, but will not have time to-night.

    Yours truly and affectionately,
            A. C. MORRIS.

                    May 30, 1872.

My Dear Children, Cheston and Mellie:

I must not make this over weight, so will be very concise. I suppose you are at Fernbank. I hope it will not be too great a tax on the former's strength, but, mother-like, have my fears. It is very nice to hear from you and have such good accounts of each child. I am in earnest when I enjoin on each of you not to try to write; I know full well how fully you are occupied, and we don't expect it.

We are getting along now pretty well. Father is certainly better again, though he is not strong, and would be and *is* obliged to save himself. He enjoys much what he sees; but the more quiet he is the better, and I do not intend to let him write as much as he has been doing, as I am sure it exhausts him, though he don't think so. He has had no return of unpleasant attacks since Constantinople. I am sorry he has had so much waiting on me to do, as I have been so helpless; but that is over now. We would not let him carry me, but he did all the rest of the waiting on me. T. Longstreth and Friezier did the lifting generally. The former leaves us in a day or two for England, and then home; we shall miss him very much. A good-tempered, willing, obliging boy he has been.

I think you would all be amused to see your father's efforts to get me a dress here in Paris, and I really believe he is going to succeed, with the assistance of Mrs. Roosevelt, of New York. The difficulty is, it is the height of the season, and everybody is too busy. Also I had bought the silk in Milan, and many only make up their own materials.

Farewell, with ever so much love to each and all. Tell Mrs. Cope her letters do your father good. I am glad she is pleased with the table.

Your affectionate mother,

A. C. MORRIS.

PARIS, May 30, 1872.

My Dear Son:

I enclose to your care a letter to my dear friend, Miss Margaret Robertson. I wish I were where I could in any way minister to her comfort. We have passed together through many heavy trials, in which I have not only admired her firmness and gentle patience combined, but have sympathized in her griefs. I thought it was well to send it by your hand.

We are sorry to learn that dear Mellie has many domestic perplexities, and is still delicate, but would fain hope Fernbank may afford her renovation. I was very sorry to hear also of Caspar's sufferings. I know how terrible it is in some cases, and hope it may not prove inflammation of the inner ear. I am always fearful about those early baths, and know that the boys are tempted to remain too long in the water. I made the original teacher promise he would never permit any one to exceed twenty minutes as a condition of my recommendation of the establishment.

Your mother's ankle is steadily improving, though still much swollen. She now moves from room to room, and goes down stairs to drive, when the weather invites, in the afternoon. Galleries, etc., are of course out of the question. To-day it is raining. I wish you would do me the favour to convey my kindest regards to Mrs. Clark. I hope to find her as well as I left her. You may give her my dear love, and my kindest regards to Ephraim also. I cannot mention by name my numerous friends, but you know how gladly I would send a message to each. Thank the Coates family, if you see them, for their cards; the Lockes, etc. I have heard nothing of Mrs. Humphreys; if it falls in your way let her know how often I think of her, and would have written, had my strength permitted any other than the letters to the family. Give my dear love to Tyson and all the boys. I cannot convey to you or them any idea of the place they hold in my heart. We are delighted with the name of dear little William Stewart. With dear love to Mellie, in all which your mother joins.

Your loving father,

CASPAR MORRIS.

PARIS, June 1, 1872.

My Dear Children:

The lesson of our Lord to gather up the fragments that nothing be lost, is especially applicable to our present condition. Fragmentary opportunities are all that are available to us, as we never know at any moment what we are to do the next. I therefore keep the paper lying on the table and take up a letter to one or the other as a moment offers without demand on it. Yesterday was allotted to Versailles, but the morning was so rainy that the plan was changed and the day given by the ladies to shopping. Thus far it is our plans to-day to drive to Versailles, but some obstacle has presented which I do not understand, and while waiting for Brother Wistar and Friezier to arrange it, Anne takes her knitting and I turn to you.

That knitting is as important to her as was the web of Penelope to that pattern of conjugal fidelity and perseverance. I hope she may not be obliged to undo anything she has wrought; but suppose there is little fear of it as the shop-keeper at Milan looked astonished at the quantity of cotton I bought for her on our first visit in October last; and was still more surprised when, being there recently, I asked for more than he had on hand. I hope, therefore, there may be no necessity to undo what has been done, as she may still produce new stripes and squares.

Before I had quite completed the last sentence we were suddenly summoned to the carriages and drove by the right bank of the Seine to Versailles, which lies about ten miles southwest of Paris. The road led through some poor suburbs by the bank of the river.

About five miles from the fortified works, by which Paris is encircled, our attention was arrested by a long range of old buildings which we found to be the old manufactory of Sévres porcelain. We had not time to stop, as it would have been interesting to visit the collection of pottery and porcelain of every age, and from every quarter of the world which is collected in the museum there. The wooded heights around were all clothed in the delicate foliage of early summer, and though the houses skirting the roadside were poor and often squalid, we could see beautiful residences nestled among the trees on the hill-sides.

The approach to Versailles was through a grand avenue of elms, two rows of lofty trees on each side of a wide, well-paved road, some miles in extent in a direct line. The trees are all trimmed and trained below, so as to form an uninterrupted line of green drapery on either side, while the towering heads above meet over each sidewalk forming verdant side aisles with vaulted roofs. This approaches the rear of the palace, which presents an irregular appearance of extensive masses of building, without any symmetry or order, in advance of the centre of which stands an enormous equestrian bronze statue of Louis XIV., and on the pediment of a Corinthian pavilion is the motto, "To all the glory of France."

We drove back to a restaurant and ordered our dinner, and then passed into the park and enjoyed all the advantages of royalty without sharing its cares or participating in its perils. These parks cover an area of not less than *ninety mile circuit*. This is all laid out in avenues and planted with trees, under which well-constructed carriage drives lead in every direction. The trees are noble elms, horse-chestnuts and other large trees, and the ground is covered with fine turf. Thirty thousand men were employed at once at various periods, and for long years in the ornamentation of these grounds; and the cost was not less than 1,000,000,000 francs. The front of the palace is on a uniform plan, and a terrace runs along its entire length, from which steps descend to the plain below, over which the eye wanders till its powers fail to discern the objects lost in the distant perspective, lakes and canals and fountains and plantations; every part of which is beautiful, and each part beautiful, as it is in itself lost in the combined beauty of the whole.

After driving some two hours in the grounds we dined and repaired to the palace. Part of it is now occupied by the present government, and the chambers of parliament were in session. We visited the stables; affording stalls for one thousand horses; and the coach-house in which are kept the grand carriages of successive dynasties which have vied with each other in display. At present they still bear the insignia of the late Emperor, who turned them all out in his procession at the baptism of the Prince Imperial. One of them cost $300,000, and certainly cannot be moved by less than eight of even the noble horses we see here. The costliness depends on the carving and gilding and painting. Each panel has a painting by some distinguished artist. The harness corresponds with the vehicle, and the whole cost of the eight carriages is enormous. There were also the beautiful sedan chair of Marie Antoinette, and sleighs of various monarchs and princes which dazzle and amuse the curious visitors, but which are as well understood from the engravings with which we are all familiar.

I attempted to accompany the party in their visit to the galleries of the palace, but was compelled to leave them after being satisfied by a few rooms of portraits of former kings and queens and princesses, which hang here in quiet companionship, as the dead bodies of the originals lie in the dust of the earth. Portraits of Bourbons, Orleans, Bonapartes, each executed with consummate skill by the most skillful artists of their several periods, are hung in successive chambers. The Princess Lamballe, Charlotte Corday, Marat, Danton and Robespierre, some side by side, some vis-a-vis. There are hideous caricatures of some of our statesmen and presidents.

Leaving the interior I rested my wearied mind and body with a quiet stroll along the main avenue with its cypress and beach trees, cut and trimmed into pyramids and cones, and saw the grand fountains. Large placards announce that they will be flowing to-day—Sunday—when Paris will empty itself into these grounds. It has been raining all the afternoon steadily, however.

The contrast between the crowd I saw last Lord's day as I went to church, and the almost deserted condition of the Champs Elysées to-day as I crossed them was very remarkable. Those who had sought their pleasure in them last week must have gone to Versailles this morning. Our party has passed a very quiet day. I did not get to the hotel from morning service till 3 P. M., and have not gone out since. Your mother and I are greatly indebted to T. T. L., who has assisted Friezier in carrying her ever since her accident, and has always been kind and attentive. I hope he will call and report us to you. He carries this letter to England and mails it there.

I had begun this letter yesterday, and finish it to send by Mr. Longstreth, who leaves us in the morning.

    Your loving father,
                 CASPAR MORRIS.

                PARIS, June 2, 1872.
My Dear Cousin (*Emily Hollingsworth.*—EDS.):

It is so nice to think of you at home again, among those we both love, for it is a lonely feeling to be jostled by crowds of strange faces. I don't become reconciled to it at all; but the time is passing, and it will not be very long ere, if our lives are spared, we will be reunited. Of course, dear cousin, you will not hesitate to make any use you wish of 1428. Indeed, I will be glad if you will at any rate look in at Isabella occasionally, and remind, and reprove if need be, as you know her defects.

I am very glad to think of your going to pay Mary a visit, and do hope you will have a pleasant time there; they all seem to be in good health and spirits. The girls write very frequently to us, and occasionally we have acknowledged; but we cannot write regularly even to their mother except in connection with her brothers.

I know you will all be anxious about the doctor until you know he has had no return of that unpleasant attack since we left Constantinople, and is gaining strength. We think it is best for us to remain with the party, not only on their account, but our own, unless there is some reason for our return. We would like to avoid our summer, if possible, and we are getting along very comfortably here, and very luxuriously; much more so than I would choose, but you know we have nothing to do with that in any way, though I do occasionally venture to remonstrate, as it is so different from our habits that it quite troubles me.

Wistar is decidedly better; indeed, I think, well, and looks well; he is as kind as possible to us, and has been concerned much both for the doctor and me in my lame condition. The whole limb is still very much swollen to the knee, but I can hobble with a cane on a level floor very well. The stairs I still find very troublesome and painful, but I hope it will soon be well. It has been a most inconvenient foot, and I (oh, so often) wished for home.

You have not given us the least idea of your plans for the summer. I should be glad to think you would stay with Mary if it will suit you, but don't wish it if you find it does not. I should love to see little Harry; Mary writes me he is so hearty and lovely-looking. I fear Miss Alice is very delicate, and wish I could hear of her being braced up in some way, not only for her own sake, but for Mary's too, for she is very important to them.

We rejoice with Mr. and Mrs. Montgomery in the prospect he has, and do hope his health will permit him to engage in business.

It is a great comfort to us to find Gall. and Han. at home and enjoying the place again. Will you not try to be with them as much as you can when in Philadelphia? They love to have you, and it will be nice both for you and Han. to be together.

Remember us to them both at 8th St. and Germantown. I quite want to know what Is., Annie and Mrs. B. are going to do this summer; they are very good about writing to us. I do feel ashamed that I can't do more in return, but I really cannot, and I am sure the doctor *ought* not.

Farewell, dear cousin. Sister H. joins me in much love. I am looking with much pleasure to the many long talks we will have next winter.

    Yours most affectionately,
          A. C. MORRIS.

PARIS, June 2, 1872.
My Dear Children:

I know you will not think you are hearing too often from us, and yet it seems that we are all the time hurrying off letters; I am told again they must go to-night. Well, I will begin with the best intelligence I can send you, which is that we are "all well." Your father is certainly better, in fact, has no disease, and with moderate exertion is able to enjoy everything, and I hope with care he will continue to do so.

We wrote some of you by the last mail, I cannot remember who or which, that *we had thought well over* our plans and had come to the conclusion to remain on this side of the ocean until October, unless we see further reason (either here or there) for some change. Our travels from this time will be deliberate, and we will forego the galleries, etc.,

etc., very much, and thus diminish the fatigue; and if we find it desirable will *stop* and *rest*, letting the others go on; so I think all anxiety on our account can be dismissed.

I do think your father will have to write less also, for, although he is fond of it and does it with great ease to himself, I am sure it is exhausting, especially when one is already very weary. It will be a trial to him, too, for he is anxious to tell you all he sees at the time, for he knows his memory will not retain near all.

Yesterday we drove to Versailles, about ten miles, and spent the day. He will give you a description of what they all saw there. They were all much pleased with palaces, grounds, carriages, etc. etc. I went with them for the ride and what I could see by the way, but of course could not go the round with them. I did see some very beautiful grounds in very beautiful order, and I also saw where there had been great destruction by the two armies. The town of St. Cloud just destroyed, palace included; and repairing (or in fact rebuilding) whole blocks. Much has been done of this in every direction. I am astonished at the population, and feel most tempted to doubt so many lives having been lost so recently. There is surely no lack of men, labourers of all sorts, and a great many soldiers, too.

I know you will all rejoice with me when I tell you my foot is getting so much better that I can get about quite tolerably on a level. Up and down stairs is painful still, but that will come right before long. I enjoy the afternoon rides very much. The streets and roads are so very fine that there is scarce any motion, and it don't incommode me at all. The Prince and Princess of Wales left here yesterday, and on our return from Versailles we found all our luggage had been moved to the apartments they had occupied. It is a very fine drawing-room at the corner of the house, with windows opening on a verandah on each side and overlooking three streets, and a wide space in front; all of which is very brilliantly lighted at night. But I suppose we must be willing to pay for the honor of the thing. It was so noisy last night that I wished myself back in my own little quiet corner; it was elegant enough I assure you. I sometimes fear we will be spoiled and not know how to live at home at all. I do admire the horses here, both carriage and draught ones. Tell the little ones that the latter are very large, fine animals, and generally wear as an ornament a very large sheep-skin (dyed blue) on their shoulders. It is a large fur cape; it will be rather warm in mid-summer, but now I quite envy them, and am almost tempted to get one for myself. It is really cold here to-day, and we are all in our winter clothing and talking of fire.

Your father met Miss Haven on the street, and she promised to come see me; perhaps some of you will remember her; she is residing here, I believe. We are sorry to learn from her that Dr. Carson is so poorly. If any of you see him remember us to him.

Farewell; with much love to each and all.

        Yours truly and affectionately,

                                   A. C. MORRIS.

Uncle W. quite approves of your taking the microscope; is sure you can't have gone amiss. T. Longstreth takes these letters to England for us. We shall miss him very much; he is to sail July 2nd, on the "Algeria." Will see some of you in Eighth street.

PARIS, June 8, 1872.

My Dear Child:

On the principle that half a loaf is better than no bread, I am going to scratch in the greatest possible haste a few lines to give you good account of ourselves. We are both well and enjoying ourselves; I am able to get across the floor without support of even the umbrella. We are busy trying to see a little here. The drives are very beautiful, but I don't want to live in Paris. T. Longstreth leaves us this morning for London, and will mail this package for us. We shall miss him very much, indeed; he will see the boys in Philadelphia, and give them the intelligence of our condition when he gets there about the middle of July.

From here we go to Brussels, Antwerp, etc., and where thence I do not know, but before long to the salt mines. Then back through Holland, and so to England, and we look to the 12th of October to sailing. The time will soon slip around, and then I hope to meet you all; in the meantime take care of yourselves. I want to hear what you will do about the girls, let them go, or use the amount for something else? I am scratching just as I got out of bed determined, we both were, you should have a line, especially as this goes in this way for a fourth one by mail from here would. Don't be uneasy about us; we will be as careful as possible, and my foot is a good excuse to be quiet part of the time. Farewell; with oh, so much love to everybody!

Yours truly and affectionately,

A. C. MORRIS.

I have written to Uncle G.; poor fellow, I do feel for him! His is a very distressing life, and it must be a great trial to have a new set about them. They don't speak of Sarah, Mary Ellen's cousin; I hope she is with them; and what has become of Rachel? I knew they were very unsettled last year, and feared this.

It is impossible for people to be more anxious to contribute to our comfort than your uncle and aunts are; too much so, especially the latter. W. is kind as possible, and we are living so luxuriously; sadly, so I think; it troubles me, but I have no control, or nothing to do with it.

PARIS, JUNE 2, 1872.

My Dear Son:

Your letter of the 11th of May reached us here day before yesterday. You may feel quite at ease as to the possibility of our misunderstanding your advice that we should remain abroad until October; we highly appreciate the kindness which dictates both lines of counsel, your Uncle Galloway and that of yourself and brothers. Our affections would carry our bodies where our hearts are, and we have sometimes hesitated as to the line of duty. We are very anxious about your uncle and aunt, and should find more satisfaction in efforts for their comfort than any sights, whether of nature or of art, which gratify the eye and amuse the mind, but do not feed the soul or fill the affections. There is much to interest and amuse us here. If I could lay aside the aspirations after what eye hath not seen nor ear heard, the joys of that Father's house, mansions in which are allotted to every child of God, to prepare a place for whom Jesus has gone for a little while, and to welcome them to which He will come again in power and great glory; if I were willing to forego all the peace which passes understanding which He gives to those who love Him, even in this life, as an earnest of the joy to come, an anteport of the fullness of the joy in His presence forevermore, I should be content with a very humble lodging in Paris and an opportunity to spend my days in the gardens of the Petit Trianon at Versailles. In such a course of life one might forget the world and be forgotten by it. Might eat and drink and forget the terrible thought that to-morrow we die, and all these joys cease forever. What a contrast between such a life, and that of Mr. Charles E. Lex, every moment of which was devoted to the relief of the sufferings around him; the instruction of the ignorant; the training of immortal souls for the inheritance incorruptible, undefiled, and that fadeth not away, which is reserved in heaven for those that love and serve God! Inviting, enticing, alluring the young to seek their Creator in the days of their vigor. I had hoped his life might have been prolonged, and that some of my grandsons might have felt the power of the influence by which he won young souls for Christ. I see by a Baltimore paper that he was at his post in the convention one day, the next among those whose place on earth shall know them no more; among those who, having washed their robes and made them white in the blood of the Lamb, cast their crowns at His feet, and join the song, Salvation to our God which sitteth upon the throne and to the Lamb, who shall serve Him day and night in the temple, whom the Lamb shall feed and lead unto living fountains of waters, and from whose eyes all tears are wiped away. His is an honorable record, that of the faithful servant who used diligently his Lord's money. What a contrast to the fearful and unfaithful one who slothfully hid that committed to him, fearing to use it! If we use it as our own we may fear, but if we bear ever in mind that whatever powers we have are the Lord's and that He has promised to crown with His blessing on our toil every effort we make to His glory, if we look only to His glory and are willing ourselves to suffer shame for His name's sake, instead of thinking His cause is to be advanced by the honor in which we may be held or injured by the shame which may arise from being falsely accused for His name's sake; then, and then only, we should be found good and faithful servants.

Everything one sees here is stained and corrupted by the historic associations which cluster around them. Palaces, gardens, galleries of art, triumphal arches, columns and monuments, are all connected with some record of blood or shame which tarnishes its glory. Yet notwithstanding the shudder which frequently passes over me as I look at them, they are gravely beautiful. Starting from the Tuilleries, whose naked skeleton stands across the great space through which flows the Seine, one is never out of immediate connection with some object of art till you reach the great triumphal *Arc de l'Etoile*, through which you pass out to the Bois de Bologne. The gilded dome of the Invalides on the opposite side of the river towers above the halls of Legislation on the left, and on the right the façade of the church of the Madeleine rises with its imposing colonnade and richly sculptured pediment and architrave. The obelisk from Luxor, raised by Louis Philippe on a lofty pedestal, stands central to groups of colossal statues and flanked by a fountain with numerous bronze figures, all veiled in the silvery curtain of lace-like water which rises from its centre and falls around in living beauty a perfect triumph of this application of art. Noble trees, beautiful shrubberies, rich flower borders, smoothly shorn grass plats, neatly swept paths and wider carriage-ways, lined by thousands of chairs and seats, and thronged by thousands and thousands of pedestrians, equestrians, and carriage-drivers, troops of cavalry and infantry, all combined to form a picture presented nowhere else in the world.

I have wandered into the wards of the Hospitals, Hotel Dieu, and looked at the museum of Ecole d' Medicine; have glanced at some of the miles of pictures and statuary in the Louvre and three galleries at Versailles; have driven each afternoon in the Bois de Bologne and much about the various Boulevards, so that I have a pretty good idea of Paris, but nothing has so captivated me as the garden of the Little Trianon with its majestic firs and wondrous variety of trees grouped with a taste which certainly can never be excelled. Even the miles on miles of avenues of trees at Versailles itself, and the palace built to commemorate "all the glories of France" did not impress me so pleasantly. I felt as though I might be like one of the little birds carolling amid its grandeur and enjoy it without the thought about the dazzling grandeur of Louis XV. or Mad. Du Barré, or even of the harmless sports of Marie Antoinette, who delighted here to lay aside the trammels of royalty and amuse herself and her ladies with the ideal representations of shepherdesses and dairy maids. I enclose a few seeds your Uncle Wistar plucked from a tree, somewhat resembling the Laburnum, and which he shared with me.

    Your loving father,

                  CASPAR MORRIS.

PARIS, June 4, 1872.
My Dear Children:

A great waste of time in finding what we can do and how to do it in Paris is inevitable. We are just now, after having been here more than a week, learning our way, and after having been over the same ground daily, begin to form some faint idea of the grandeur which has been destroyed by the mad fury of the Commune. The lofty walls of public granaries, the Hotel d'Ville (a masterpiece of architecture), the Palace of the Tuilleries, and the Ministry of Finance, are all within easy walking distance of our hotel; and the palace of St. Cloud and the beautiful private residences in its neighborhood, which we drove past on our return from Versailles, all reduced to masses of ruin by the fire of the French themselves, to dislodge the German forces, are so many strong illustrations of the terrible influence of War. They stand like so many gaunt skeletons among the revelling masses, as the sword over the head of Damocles at the feast. The feelings of the people are like the constrained power of a slumbering volcano, ready at any moment to burst out into active eruption. The hatred of the Germans is intense; and they make no hesitation in avowing their determination to be avenged so soon as opportunity offers, and it is probable that the reaction in favour of Napoleon is substantial though the partisans of the legitimate heirs—the Bourbons—and the intermediate power—the Orleanists—are watching their respective interests with anxious observation.

As we drive through those parts of Paris occupied by the labouring classes we cannot but be struck with the power they must wield, and can see that Paris is like an immense mass of ponderous matter, which must crush whatever it falls upon or against in the rocking of revolutionary earthquakes. The tendency of the loose population of the Empire to concentrate in one of the three great cities—Paris, Lyons and Marseilles—is very great. All the young men and women who are not absolutely required in the provinces gravitate to one or the other of these centres, and remain there generally without the elevating influence of domestic association, collected together in masses during the day-time in the various "ateliers" or workshops; and in the evening in the places of amusement, or the cafés or restaurants. They are thus left the prey of passion without the control of a sense of responsibility, and ready for any excitement which may be presented.

There is one very prominent token of the present unsettled state of society. In those parts of the town occupied by the lower classes, one sees a large number of vacant houses, shops and apartments, the former occupants of which are said to be either killed in the disturbances, shot by the orders of the powers that are, or in prison. In the quarters occupied by the affluent and higher orders, very many "Hotels" bear bill of "for sale or for let;" and many are closely shut up, giving evidence that the feeling of insecurity has caused their occupants to desert them for less exposed residences, either in some other part of France or as exiles. The shopkeepers complain greatly that this interferes with their sales, and that, many strangers as there are now, there are fewer than in former years.

June 5th.

We yesterday visited the "Halles," or vast market arrangement for the supply of Paris, which is one of the many permanent substantial evidences of his great wisdom and administrative ability left by Napoleon III. It is the huge first stomach or maw of the monster, into which is gathered all the produce for the nourishment of the "*corpus vastum horrendum.*" Each of the 10 pavilions is 120 feet by 100. There are 3 halls for wholesale and 57 for retail. The wholesale is effected by the public auction or "cry," as they call it here. The various kinds of provisions are sold in special halls. Fish in one, vegetables in another, poultry in a third, etc., etc., and there is one central dome, called "Halle au Blé," which is the corn market. The space on the level with the street is all covered with lofty glass walls and roof, and divided into stalls. Most of the transactions are conducted by women, whose neat attire contrasts strangely with the rough appearance of our hucksters. Each stall above has a corresponding vault below, well lighted and airy. This under-space communicates by a tunnel under the Boulevard Sebastopol with the great railroad depot of Strasbourg, which is connected by the railroad "*de Ceinture,*" which runs entirely around Paris, with all the other railroads which come to the city. The design was to have the cars which bring all the supplies of every kind from all parts to the city run along this tunnel to this central depot, at which they should be sold wholesale, and from which they should be distributed to the several markets, one of which is erected in each of the *arrondissements* or quarters, into which the city is divided, and the same channel should be used to convey away all the *débris* which accumulates about such places and return it as a source of fertility to the places from which the supplies are derived. The German war arrested the progress of this work before its completion. It is a grand design, and, so far as it is executed, well done. The display of fish is very fine, and a stream of water passes through marble channels in the vault underneath, divided by wire frames into compartments, one allotted to each dealer. Huge carts, capable of carrying many tons, were gathering up the refuse material as fast as it fell, and drawing it away. We met them in our drives in the suburbs among the vegetable gardens. The size of the carts is very astonishing. We have seen an entire rick or shock of hay or straw or wheat, on wheels, drawn by immense horses; each ornamented by a blue sheep-skin thrown over his shoulders, like a fur tippet. One cart which was carrying bags of meal was so long and large that they ran trucks in it to move the bags on.

Yesterday afternoon we visited the garden of Acclimatization in the Bois de Bologne. There are glass-covered spaces planted with tropical trees and shrubs from New Holland, Brazil, Borneo, etc., and great aviaries in which birds from all quarters of the world find the temperature they require, with freedom of motion. The animals have large paddocks and nice huts, and everything is in exquisite order. The arrangement for fish is very fine. Large pools are arranged on a level with the eye of the visitor, the bottom covered with sand or gravel and rocky projections, to which they may attach themselves, or under which they may take refuge. Sea anemones and serpulas were in full blow, and lobsters and crabs were crawling about with all the pleasure they could have found in their native haunts. While we were looking, each pool was suddenly rendered opaque, as though by a snow-storm. This was caused by the injection of air finely divided like powder, which is done at stated intervals.

You must excuse fragmentary letters. Have just seen Thomas and Mrs. Hockley.

Your loving father,

CASPAR MORRIS.

PARIS, June 6, 1872.

My Dear Children:

Your mother has driven with your uncle and aunt to visit the Pere la Chaise, and I remain behind in order to avail myself of the only opportunity to write by this week's mail. Her foot is much better. There is no longer any pain, though the entire leg from the knee to the toes is still much swollen. She really enjoys driving out and seeing what presents in that way.

This morning we drove to Sevres and saw the splendid display of porcelain. Paintings equal to oil pictures; copies of the best works of Raphael and Tintoretti and Vandyke. Three copies of Raphaels are valued at $5000 each. Then there are vases, and sets of dishes and plates, each of which is an exquisite work of art. One large piece of fruit and flowers with three peaches in it and some chestnut burrs and ears of corn, which would cost two or three peach crops. The museum of chinaware and pottery of all ages and from all parts of the world was very interesting.

The picture galleries have disappointed me. There are some of wondrous beauty and priceless value, but countless numbers worth no more than those in our own galleries, which is very little.

The more I watch the course of affairs here, so far as I can understand them, the less confidence I feel in the permanence of the present government. The debates at Versailles are angry and personal. An ordinance requiring the greatest vigilance in suppressing the circulation of inflammatory pamphlets, printed in England and Belgium, tells plainly enough the uneasiness of the authorities. Houses for sale and to let stand thickly in all parts of Paris, while the scarred remains of burned buildings testify of the length to which popular feeling goes when once freed from control. The government is rapidly demolishing these gaunt memorials of the madness of the people and selling the materials.

The weather is cold and damp; I am wearing all my thick under-flannel and an entire heavy winter suit. Your mother rides in her water-proof cloak and camel's hair shawl with a blanket shawl over it, besides two sacks over her dress, and one of our friends has fire. Italy, you will see by the papers, is suffering from deluge. The lakes where we were so happy last summer have overflowed the very houses we staid in. Thus your drought is balanced by the floods here.

Please give our love to all our many friends. I shall write as much and as often as I can, but find my time and strength both fully occupied. Thank your Uncles Henry and Israel for the kind letters which are most grateful to us and acceptable. We are all getting on nicely, and I hope and pray we will reach our homes with thankful hearts, and find you all glad to welcome us.

The grandchildren must not think we forget them or are regardless of their pleasure. I can scarcely refrain from the enumeration of each one by name, a message to each; but must include them all in the common prayer that God may bless and keep them from all evil and bestow upon them the choicest good.

Much love, especially to Mrs. Buckley and Cousin Emily.

Ever your loving father,

CASPAR MORRIS.

PARIS, June 6, 1872.

*My Dear Brother (Galloway Cheston.—*EDS.):

Your kind letter of the 20th ult., is just received, for which both Anne and I heartily thank you. We are able to report myself quite well, and her foot so much improved that she no longer suffers and is able, with the help of a cane, to walk on level surface. This morning she ventured with us to visit the Sévres porcelain works, and enjoyed it much. I write now hastily in order to relieve your anxiety. We have thought much and carefully over the question of our return; and as you will have learned by our late letters, have decided to remain, unless something at home should require our attention; and each day confirms us in the wisdom of that conclusion. Every member of the party is improving, and our separation would be inexpedient. Our greatest solicitude is on your account and dear Margaret's; and we trust we may be spared to each other till October, and be able to rejoice together in thankful adoration for the goodness and mercy which have followed us all our days.

Coming here by Northern Italy we propose to return to Germany, and shall stop at Van Houtte's on our way. Your drought has been balanced by the excessive rains in Italy and Switzerland, causing most destructive floods and interrupting railroad travel in the very districts over which we have recently passed.

A notice to all police magistrates to exercise the greatest care and diligence to suppress the circulation here of tracts designed to undermine the authority and bring contempt on the power of the present government, affords proof of the correctness of the impression entertained of the tendency here to disturbance. I shall breathe more freely beyond the boundaries, until I reach our own soil, where I apprehend the elements of discord predominate almost as much as here.

We were much interested by your account of your efforts to procure a portrait of your honoured father. I am quite sure you will not be able to find satisfaction yourself, or give it to any of us, but hope to find something we can unite in adopting as having some resemblance to his most expressive countenance. Our curiosity and interest are both stimulated. Give much love to dear Margaret, with the assurance of our prayers for large spiritual gifts, such as our Father in Heaven knows are best suited. For the ordering of temporal affairs, we are ready to trust His wisdom and love.

Love also to James, Sally and Samuel.

Yours most affectionately,
CASPAR MORRIS.

P. S.—Anne has ridden with the party to Pere la Chaise. I remain to finish and mail letters.

My Dear Brother (Galloway Cheston.—EDS.):

I will do a little towards filling the doctor's sheet while he takes a few minutes' sleep, and assure you of our improved condition; able now to enjoy in moderation the objects presented. We leave here next Monday for Brussels, and from there will go to Van Houtte's. I am anticipating much pleasure in that trip. We were amazed to hear of your attempt to get a portrait of dear father; of course will be very glad indeed if it is successful. But how can it be? It does seem impossible, and almost incredible, that any one would undertake it. It is a little singular that within a week Wistar had asked if we had any likeness of him, and I of course expressed my regret that there was none of either him or mother. Do report from time to time your success. I should have thought James Farr would have been of great assistance. I am sorry to hear from West River that the Cedar Park Smoke House has been robbed; quite a loss to Fan. and the doctor.

But I must close, with much love to dear Margaret; and be ready for the afternoon ride. Please don't be troubled about us.

Yours most affectionately,
A. C. MORRIS.

PARIS, June 8, 1872.

My Dear Children:

The time of our sojourn here is rapidly drawing to a close, and I feel that there remains very much unseen. Yet I am more impressed daily by the peculiarities of the character of its people. Not only in the vacant places around the ruined walls of its once grand structures, converted into advertising boards regularly rented out to speculators (the government, I understand, deriving a rental from them); but while they have found it necessary to issue orders to use the utmost vigilance to suppress the circulation of inflammatory pamphlets printed in England and Belgium, and designed to incite to the overthrow of the present government, and the day after this fact was announced in the papers to declare that such a statement is *apocryphe* (not untrue), the most perfect order and decorum stamps everything that meets the eye of the most inquisitive visitor. I should say Paris is, of all places I ever visited, the most decorous in its outward deportment. But little conversation with its residents is needed to prove that the satire of the epigrammatist is perfectly applicable: "A hag, repaired with vice complexion-paint." There appears to be no moral tone; it would be wrong to call it a *low* tone. It appears to be dead or absent.

I have sauntered in the evening around the galleries and arcades of the Palais Royal, with its splended lighted shops and cafés and restaurants, and have waited on Mrs. Curtin and her daughter, along the Rue de la Paix, from the Place Vendome to their residence, at 11 P. M., and order reigned alike in both. I did not mount the stairs at the Palais to see what was being done in the saloons above the shops, nor have I entered into any of the places of amusement; I speak only of the thoroughfares and streets. The boulevards are thronged with quiet people, and the chairs in front of the restaurants, as well as the saloons of those resorts, of all classes, are all occupied by sober-looking people taking some light refreshment or reading the papers, while the *garcons* or waiters are as quiet, orderly and respectable in their appearance and deportment as the most reputable people at home. In all my wanderings I have seen but one intoxicated person, and he was being quietly led along by one of the *Sergents de Ville*. In the Champs Elysées, and other places of public resort, they walk quietly or drive. Crowds collect around the objects of interest, gratify their curiosity, and pass on. One day they poured in a steady stream, not a rushing torrent, to the Palais d'Industrie, which was open without a fee; on another afternoon a military band was performing under the trees in the garden of the Tuilleries. Crowds were walking around in the most orderly manner, while many hundreds of well-dressed men and women were seated on chairs (for the use of which they paid $\frac{15}{100}$ of a franc) listening to the sweet melody. I could not but feel happy that the poor soldiers have such a resource, and the people of Paris such a diversion. The ladies had their embroidery or *tâteing*, at which they worked constantly during the performances, and the gentlemen their newspapers or books, to which they resorted in the intermission. There was no crowding or wrangling about places, and a very fine-faced woman, in a perfectly plain brown worsted dress and a neat white cap, passed around collecting the payment for each chair as the occupant took the seat.

We see no gaudy dress on either man or woman, and questions about buildings or inquiries about the way are always sure of a respectful answer. Great numbers of people, often of the labouring classes, frequent the *Jardin des Plantes* each time that I have been there; and I am as much astonished as at anything, that, while public buildings stand in ruins, and vast sums are being paid the Germans as indemnity for the war, during which the animals in these and the *Jardin d'Acclimatisation* were consumed as food by the starving population—nay, while there are still thousands of communists untried, and the courts are sentencing them (daily) to death and carrying those sentences into execution, the government has procured fresh specimens of all the foreign birds, beasts and reptiles; and the borders of the gardens are all as beautifully cultivated and as well stocked with plants as though the peace and order of Paris had never been interrupted for a moment.

I have walked as well as driven through the smaller parks; very elegant they are, through the garden of the Tuilleries and the Champs Élysées. Almost every bench was occupied by women with their embroidery, or knitting, or other such work. These public benches are very substantial, and, at the same time comfortable seats, and are found not only in the gardens and parks, but, at short intervals, along most of the boulevards, which are all planted with good shade trees.

It may be objected that this public accommodation renders unnecessary the provision of private comfort, and interferes with the domestic ties. Perhaps it does; but I cannot but look with gratification on the pleasant faces of the contented-looking people and hope that they may find peace and happiness in their way as we seek it in ours. One may serve the Lord in spirit and in truth on the public highway, and one may serve themselves only in the retirement of that home of which we think the Frenchmen know nothing. There are many things in which the general opinion here is all sadly wrong. The great race, for example, is to be to-day (the Lord's day). This is only one of the great logs on the stream, indicating the course of the current. There are inumerable straws floating in the same direction, and even the stillness of the deep pools is not without significant tokens of the strong set below the surface. It is unhappily true that it is almost impossible to stem the flow when once you get upon it. There is no one about the places of resort of travellers to turn them into any other way.

It was not until last evening that I learned by a London paper that the Synod of the French Protestant Church is now in session here. I would gladly have availed myself of the opportunity to see the faces of men whose names are familiar. But shops and shows and drives are all ready arranged, and one has nothing to do but take one's place in the carriage and *go*.

We spent some hours yesterday in the Louvre, entering it by the gate over which Catharine Medici sat to enjoy the spectacle of the massacre of the Huguenots, the signal for which was given from the tower of the church of St. Germain Auxerois, directly opposite, whose bell was chiming sweetly as we entered the gateway. So indiscriminate was the slaughter that it included at this very spot one of the artists in the employ of the king in the adornment of the palace, Jean Goujon, two of whose massive sculptures still stand and give name to one of the halls—the Salle d'Caryatides. These statues support a gallery which contains some very superb bronzes of the celebrated Benvenuto Cellini, whose genius displayed itself in the exquisite delicacy of design and perfection of minute detail of all his works, from the finest stone engraving to the colossal bronze figures which are here seen.

One often feels at a loss whether to admire the *power* of the artist or mourn over the tokens of depravity and corruption displayed by the art in his hands. Certainly it is true that the strongest evidence of the fallen and corrupt character of man may be found in the perversion of his highest gifts. Literature and painting and sculpture agree in their evidence, and unite in our condemnation, and it is sad to think that it has chiefly been in the service of superstition, that these most precious gifts have been disenthralled from the tyranny of vice. In one of the galleries of the Louvre hangs the most beautiful production of human art—the Madonna of Murillo—before which I have sat again and again, each time saddened by the thought that it was probably the last opportunity to drink in delight from such loveliness and purity. Yet the same art which could thus exhibit the positive evidence that we know what purity was in itself, and how it could adorn the human form, almost restoring its pristine glory, is often degraded to the expression of the most corrupt tendencies of our nature, and in the same saloon (though happily not side by side) may be found the pure ideals of Murillo and the equally celebrated productions of Rubens. Of the art of the painter one may say, as St. James does of the human mouth, "Out of the same mouth proceedeth blessing and cursing. My brother, these things ought not so to be."

I spent much time in the Egyptian and Etruscan and Pompeian galleries. They are rich collections of all that can illustrate the habits and manners of those nations. I regret greatly that the Assyrian and Mexican and Peruvian collections are not open. It would have been not only interesting, but instructive, to compare the character of the remains of ancient peoples so widely separated territorially, and who could have had no communication with each other. I had looked forward with great expectation to the opportunity which is offered nowhere else than here. The sarcophagus of Rameses II., the great warrior, who overran the world so many centuries ago, stands empty here, in the halls appropriated to it by the great warrior of modern times, whose remains have been brought here from the distant rock in the ocean on which he perished—a melancholy exile—and within sight of the gilded dome which covers the tomb to which were brought his remains by the "*nephew of my uncle*,"—himself an exile, sheltered in the palaces of that very power by which the uncle was overthrown and held a prisoner. Such vicissitudes mark the history of man.

Paris is empty to-day. As I returned from church I met "toute le monde" *en route* to the race course. To-morrow we leave for Brussels. A few hours will find us beyond the boundaries of the nation which has kept the world in agitation during centuries, and whose escutcheon is tarnished by the dark spots of St. Bartholomew's and the French Revolution. I feel as though I had seen nothing here.

BRUSSELS, June 11, 1872.

We arrived here safe about 11 P. M., having left Paris at 3.45 P. M., a beautiful ride.
Your loving father,
CASPAR MORRIS.

PARIS, June 9, 1872.

My Dear Child:

We have letters from you up to the 20th of May, and good accounts, and I hope before this you have all been relieved about us. Your father is well, and I am walking about without umbrella, though I cannot do much of it, and not at all on the street, of course. So I suppose I am to leave Paris, which we are to do to-morrow, without shopping, the most unusual thing for a lady to do. I did hobble from the carriage into two stores more as a matter of curiosity than anything else, and am glad I did. Each covered a square and was four stories high. I did try to move about with the cane and an arm, but the floors were so highly polished and slippery that I could not. Then the crowd of people was very great; it was like a small fair, and the display of goods very fine.

I must not forget to tell you your father at last, with the assistance of Mrs. Roosevelt, has succeeded in getting my black silk dress made, and I am fixed up in it—"a Paris dress." I feel very fine, I assure you, and am wearing it to-day to take the new off, as I can't hang it in the wardrobe now for a year! I am shocked at it, and threatened to strip off some of the lace trimmings (an overskirt and basque trimmed with it). You would have pitied both me and the dressmaker had you seen us when she came to take the order. She could not speak a word of English, and I not one of French; so we tried signs. At last she, in despair, rushed to the bell; the waiter came, and he could not aid us. I asked for Friezier, then for his wife, but all were out, so I had to let her do just as she pleased. So you will know I have been quite anxious to know my fate. Well, it is a success, except too stylish for me. You would not know me. And now what am I to do about a bonnet? You will be surprised to hear I am getting a velvet one.

You talk of warm weather! We have not known anything of the kind. We are wearing all our winter clothing, and when I ride of an afternoon (remember the carriages are all open), I start in two sacks (wool) under my cashmere shawl and scarf, well pinned over the chest. We take both your father's and my blanket shawls. One soon goes over the camel's hair round my shoulders, and the other on our laps, and I put the hood over my bonnet. So I have concluded a velvet is best, and I see many are wearing them here. I would have liked very much to have shopped here. Indeed it is quite a trial to me not to. Your aunts are willing to do for me, but that did not suit me, and I found their choice was not mine, so I must wait for London. I am glad we had got the watches, for I could not have looked here.

Do thank the girls for their letters, and tell them they must consider themselves answered in this and write me. Poor little Emily and her poisoned face! Give my love to her. Tell them and the little ones that my eye constantly follows children of their sizes, and often I see little boys who resemble Robbie.

All of our drives of an afternoon take us through streets double the width of Broad Street, and several miles long. It is delightfully smooth and filled with elegant equipages dashing up and down; the ladies and gentlemen many of them in full dress. The women are very handsome; but the horses are, too. On these wide streets there is as ample accommodation for foot passengers—not only very wide, smooth pavements, kept perfectly clean, but seats. You will see fifty chairs here and there, besides benches, and many occupying them; of all grades in life. Then the public squares or gardens are curiosities, so filled with children of all ages, with their nurses, all nicely dressed and enjoying themselves, having swings and other sources of enjoyment of different descriptions. One kind is a dozen hobby-horses suspended in a circle. Children get on them and they go round and round as on a threshing floor. Each child is provided with a stick, and he or she is to endeavor to take a ring from a post as they go swiftly by. Occasionally they succeed.

BRUSSELS, 11th June.

Well, here we are back again. I did not expect to see this place again when we left it last year, but do not regret it. It is a very attractive place, and I think I shall quite enjoy being here a few days, especially as we are all now well. The ride yesterday afternoon from Paris was a pleasant one. Here is a rainy day, so as all have gone to picture galleries. I am quietly enjoying my own room, which overlooks a most beautiful garden which is much frequented, and a fine band of music entertains us from there every afternoon and evening.

All our accounts from home speak of your wanting rain, so that we fear you are really suffering. There is nothing like it here; everything is as luxuriant as possible and a great abundance of vegetables and fruit—splendid apricots, and I never (even at Wallbrook) saw finer strawberries than we have had three times a day for the last three weeks; and while I think of the warm weather you are all suffering with now, I contrast it with the temperature we have. Less than two blankets would not do at all. It is just delightful! I only wish I had some of you with me. I do so often feel lonely; and yet I know I ought not, and dare say I shall not, now that I shall be getting about a little.

I can't tell you how pleased I was to be able to get into and out of the cars yesterday with only the assistance of your father and uncle. No child was ever more tickled at walking than I am. We are cheered again to-day by the letters from Gall., and from Annie and Mrs. Cope. It is the next thing to seeing you all, and we do not feel so very far off now. Annie has been as faithful a weekly correspondent as yourself. Occasionally Is. has been prevented. They tell all about Philadelphia concerns, etc., and I fear Mrs. B. has had rather a poorly winter on the whole, tho' Annie did not dwell on it.

I gather from some of them that Murray will be married in September. Where will they settle? In Sixteenth Street? She will have to be a mighty nice girl to be equal to Murray.

I think perhaps cousin Emily will be with you when this reaches you; if so, share it with her, as I cannot write another by this mail. I hope she will have a nice visit to you, and that the air will suit her. Tell her I am too sorry to hear Mr. W——— has made his appearance in Philadelphia. Perhaps she will be surprised that we all turned our backs on Paris with some regret, and thought if the arrangements (rooms taken, etc.) had not been made, we could have occupied another week pleasantly and profitably there, tho' I admit we all felt it is in a very unsettled condition, and many of the inhabitants unhesitatingly say so. In fact, it is less settled than six months ago, and there may be trouble there any day. But it is a grand city, and I wanted to see more than I was able.

Give much love to all around you and take a large share for yourself. I hope Miss Alice will soon be better. Tell her your Father wants her to try a change of air, and he hopes she will gratify him by doing it in some way, whether with or without the girls. We are too far off to help make plans, but you all know we have your interest at heart whether here or there. Four months will soon roll by and then we will be together, I trust.

Yours most truly and affectionately,

A. C. MORRIS.

BRUSSELS, June 11, 1872.

My Dear Children:

We were blessed with a very delightful ride from Paris to this place yesterday afternoon and evening; arriving about 11 P. M. at our old quarters in the Bellevue Hotel; and as I now look out on the old park which lies before our chamber windows, I am delighted to find I was not too enthusiastic in my praise of its beauty when I wrote from here last summer; and can refer you to my letters then for an idea of the impression it makes now; and the sculpture which crowns the gate posts is quite equal to any we have seen.

My last morning in Paris was more interesting than any day I had passed there. Your mother's ankle is so far restored that she determined to go with your aunts to a place called "Bon Marché," equivalent to our "cheap store," at which is sold every article a lady can require, at prices below those of other shops generally. It is a village of shops itself. I therefore determined as the Louvre was closed and no other place of interest accessible in the two hours at my command, to visit the tomb of the First Napoleon under the gilded dome of the church of the Hotel des Invalides, whose beautiful proportions and rich ornamentation had attracted my attention every day, as it is one of the most prominent objects in view from almost every part of the city, especially from those around the places most frequented. We were to dine at 1.30 P. M. preparatory to our long ride, and the entrance to the hotel was not open until 11 A. M. The distance is considerable. My route lay through the Place de la Concord; carrying me by the Obelisk from Luxor, which commemorates the glory of Sesostris, the great conqueror of his day; and over the Pont de la Concorde, built in part with the materials of the Bastille soon after the demolition of that fearful dungeon; which has been doomed to eternal infamy as the type of oppressive tyranny.

The legislative halls spread their classic front immediately before the passenger over the bridge. They are now closed and carefully guarded, as the present government does not venture to hold the sittings of the assembly within the walls of Paris. Palaces and public buildings and the University are all grouped together here, giving a most imposing aspect to the front of the river, from which a wide open space extends to the hotel.

When I reached there I found no part was yet open to visitors; so I sauntered about in the very beautiful little garden which surrounds the entrance; from which I could see the interior, subdivided into small lots, one of which is appropriated to each of the pensioners (if he choose), and many of which are neatly cultivated by them. While loitering I was addressed by a stranger who enquired if I could speak English, and announced himself as a South Carolinian, waiting like myself to find the entrance to the tomb of the great warrior. I gave him the information he sought and we walked together, talking over affairs at home, past, present and future, and found we could do so without serious difference.

When the hour arrived we went into the great hotel and saw the arrangements for the comfort of the pensioners of the nation. The buildings and grounds cover nearly thirty acres of ground and have been gradually increased and improved ever since the commencement of the establishment, on a comparatively small scale, by Henry IV. Nothing which can conduce to their comfort is neglected; from the service of plate, for the table of the officers, given by the Empress Marie Louise, during the short period she was the wife of Napoleon *Le Grand*, to the humble arrangements for the common soldier. The accommodations are sufficient for 5000, though at present there are only 700. We occupied ourselves in looking at them, and the collection of cannon and mortars in the museum of artillery, till the time at which the church covering the tomb of Napoleon is opened. To reach the entrance we were obliged to make the entire circuit of the building. While doing this, engaged in an earnest discussion on our own war, its causes and results, we were hailed with the inquiry whether we could indicate the entrance to the tomb and invited the inquirer to join us, and found that he was a Virginian. So we had it two to one against me. But whether it was southern chivalry which disdained to avail itself of the advantage, or northern indomitable sense of right which would not yield, I found I was left in possession of the field. We agreed we had but one duty common to our country which was to bury passion, and cultivate affection, and each to do all in his power to promote the harmony and welfare of the whole. Just as we had reached the happy conclusion we found ourselves at the entrance of the most imposing structure in the world. My southern friends agreed that language is absolutely inadequate to convey any idea of the impression it makes on the beholder. We were in the midst of an animated argument on a subject on which we differed, but which each held of vital importance. But simultaneously we all stopped and stood still, spell-bound. There is a perfection in the proportions of the parts and an adaptation to the purpose to which it is devoted, and a simple grandeur in the whole, which places it without a rival in the line of architecture.

There is the imposing effect of vast extent and elaborate detail in Milan cathedral; vastness in St. Peter's, Rome; sacredness in many of the English cathedrals, a sense of religious awe, which is wholly absent about the church of the Invalids, and yet you can but admit it is grandly imposing. The lofty dome rises as you enter; on either side extend the arms of a Greek cross into chapels, each containing a massive black marble sarcophagus and marble busts and statues; and you take it all in at one glance, while at the same time your attention is riveted by the shrine opposite; composed of a baldachin or canopy, with four twisted columns of black veined marble, bathed in a golden light which suffuses the whole, admitted through concealed windows filled with amber colored glass. The entire intervening space, beneath the dome is open, surrounded by a balustrade of white marble, elaborately carved, within which you realize must rest the mortal remains of him at whose name kings turned pale and peoples trembled.

Approaching the balustrade you look down upon a massive sarcophagus of red porphyry of exquisite proportions and shape, highly polished, and crowned with a simple bouquet of Immortelles. My thoughts went quickly to the hall of the Louvre where only a day or two before I had stood beside the vacant Sarcophagus of Rameses II, that other troubler of the world, and I realized the truth at which Napoleon himself arrived when he said in a melancholy moment to one of his friends during his exile at St. Helena, "I am thinking of how small a spot I will fill on the page of history." I am no worshipper of glory, and if I were, Napoleon would not be my idol. He was a powerful force, not a great man. He was thoroughly selfish—a heartless egotist. Even the glory of France was of no account if it was not the glory of Napoleon, and none of the false dispatches which he so often dictated and justified, and for failing to equal his audacity in which he reproved the only one of his brothers whose opinion he valued,—Joseph—was more destitute of truth than the sentence inscribed on the entrance to the tomb, "I wish my ashes to repose on the banks of the Seine among the people of that France I have so loved." The term love is profaned by its utterance from lips which could sacrifice Josephine to his ambition ; and love for man could not dwell in a heart beating under a brow so strongly stamped with selfish pride ; and love for France was only for the France of which Napoleon was Emperor. But I have said enough; you must read Alison's history, and you may temper it by that of Thiers ; and then you may gather trophies if you please from the flowers scattered around his path by his worshippers.

I walked back with my newly found friends. We exchanged cards of friendly recognition. I prescribed for one of them and advised another where to seek relief from a ball he carries in his leg and we parted good friends.

About 3.45 P. M. we left Paris, not without regret. There was much I wished to see I had not seen, and I am sure I could spend some months there profitably in its hospitals. But I am flitting like a butterfly from flower to flower, rather than like a bee gathering stores. Our journey here was across most fertile and highly cultivated plains, rich in all the luxurious green of wheat and rye and grass ; relieved at intervals by large fields of beets, cultivated for the manufacture of sugar, and by orchards of apple trees just putting forth their bloom. The farmers were busily engaged cutting and curing hay and cultivating the beet crops. Every inch of surface is in culture and without division or fence or hedge of any kind ; while the labourers all live in villages, so that often there is no house in sight far as the eye can range.

The Continent of Europe seems to be made up of a series of vast plains ; not like the Atlantic slope of America, with its rolling broken and hilly surface. The beautiful monotony of green fields was broken yesterday by some towns of historic interest, such for instance as Compeigne the scene of the wonderfully interesting and exciting drama of Joan of Arc, who was there betrayed by the cowardly jealousy of the Governor; who caused the portcullis to be dropped behind her when she was leading in sally against Burgundians who besieged it ; and the Burgundians and English must share or divide between them the shame of her Martyrdom, as neither can cast it wholly on the other. St. Quentin lies on the route also, near which was fought one of the finally decisive battles of the late war between France and Germany, and the fortress of Ham lies on the way, in which Louis Napoleon was imprisoned when he made his first descent on France, and from which he escaped in the disguise of a carpenter carrying a plank. We also passed through the forest of Compeigne, a favorite resort of all the French monarchs, especially Louis Napoleon. It was very late when we arrived here and we have not yet recovered from the fatigue of the journey.

This morning I left your mother and went to see a collection of pictures painted by Wierz a few years since. I felt all the time I was in the room which contains them, much as I suppose I should do in a fine music hall filled with perfect instruments on which some dozens of good performers were each displaying his skill by perfectly distinct and unconnected pieces and on discordant instruments and keys. It was raining but I was compelled to go outside and walk up and down while the others inspected the detail. They are the wildest conceptions of the most unchecked genius. Each illustrative of his views of the tendencies of the human passions. The perfect representations on canvas of the most horrid imaginations of delirium ; the work of a life time of an ill-directed power ; some so hideous that I feel as I used when a child waking from a horrid dream, afraid to sleep again less it would be repeated.

From there we went to the Hall of State and saw the various apartments appropriated to the Legislative body ; which are very neat. One of the lobbies is ornamented by figures representing several clauses in the Belgian Constitution. One ensuring Freedom of the Press ; another General Education ; another Liberty of Conscience in Religion, etc., etc.

The figures *adopted* are all those of a shrew—and if I wished to illustrate the license of the press I would select that placed here as my model. Strange to say they have allowed another set of figures, which were proposed by another artist, to stand in an adjacent lobby. They are very fine; calm, dignified, loving beauty, being the characteristic of the countenance and attitude of each. From there we went to the gallery in the Ducal Palace in which are two or three superb cattle pieces by Robbe, and some domestic scenes by Block which are worth whole collections of Battle Scenes, and Martyrdoms and Mythological legends, and absurdities of imagination of artists who have no just claim to merit, in my judgment at least.

I have been a little fearful lest the enthusiam of my feeling here a year ago might have betrayed me into too strong expression about the beauty of the park and the style of architecture of Brussels. But your uncle agrees with me that it is quite equal to any place we have visited. In Paris the shops are scattered every where, occupying the *Rez de Chaussée*, as they term it, or of every house; that is the floor on the level of the pavement. In Brussels the more modern part of the town is occupied by the more affluent citizens, as with us. The houses are of uniform colour and architecture and all neat and home like. The streets in these parts are very quiet. In the business parts all is bustle and activity, and last night we were roused and disturbed by an immense procession of men celebrating the success of one of the parties in an election held yesterday. They sang and shouted much like we shall find our own countrymen doing soon after we reach home.

The rain limits us to picture galleries for enjoyment and prevents the ladies from shopping.

Your mother avails herself of the opportunity to repair old dresses; and your aunt Mary is making a bonnet for her.

To-morrow your uncle and I propose an excursion to Van Houtte's gardens at Ghent, if the weather permits. Then the ladies will revel at will in shawls, laces, and other shops. On Friday we leave for Antwerp; and on Saturday for Rotterdam, where we propose to spend the Lord's day, and thence to The Hague and so South again.

Your mother's ankle is gaining daily though still swollen. Remember me to all our cousins and friends, and Dr. Hodge among the number. I hope George's wife will be a comfort to him as well as a joy to her husband.

      Your loving father,

            CASPAR MORRIS.

            BRUSSELS, June 11, 1872.

Our course of travel has brought us back once more to this beautiful city. I wrote so enthusiastically about it when here last summer that I felt a little fearful of coming here again, lest I should find I had been carried away by the excitement of novelty. I find however that even under the disadvantages of our coming here direct from Paris it proves itself worthy of any commendation I may then have bestowed.

The grand trees in the noble park, which meet my sight as I raise my eyes while thus sitting in my room writing to you, are as attractive now as they were then ; and though the streets appear deserted when compared with the crowded ways of that capital of the world, and the park itself is small when compared with the gardens of the Tuilleries, the Place de la Concorde, the Champs Elysee, and the Bois de Bologne, opening the one from the other in almost endless stretch of extent and beauty of culture, there is sufficient grandeur to satisfy any moderate desire.

In the heart of Paris the "*rez de Chaussée*" is always a shop of some kind. Here the shops are in one quarter and the dwellings in another. At Paris "*toute le monde*" lives out of doors, eats, drinks, meets friends (everything but sleep) at the Restaurants, or on the Pave or in driving. Here the people live within doors in modest houses on quiet streets. At Paris there are many grand Obelisks, and columns and fountains. Here there are a very few choice marbles and bronzes.

I spent the morning in a small private picture gallery, and though I was not enraptured by a Murillo I was delighted by some nice pictures of cattle by Robbe and some very good ones by Block. One of these represented a scripture reading in the family of a Fisherman. The venerable father read, while sons and daughters and their children were grouped around him, each one being the representative of some form of devotional attention. Another was a sick mother propped in bed to listen to the sweet words of truth flowing through the sweet channels of a daughter's lips. I would rather possess one such than a whole gallery of powerful battle scenes or mythological allegories, or frightful martyrdoms, even though gilded by the name of the highest masters of art.

Telegrams from America keep us posted in the daily course of events with you. Political conventions are not much less disturbing than labour organizations, and the necessity to protect by police power the establishments of those employers who refuse to submit to the demands of their employees. One trembles at the thought to what these things may grow, and the stark walls of the burned buildings at Paris (the work of Communal madness), are not sights calculated to assure one's heart. The arms of Omnipotence, which invite all so lovingly to take refuge in them, offer our only refuge from storms without and distrust within. May we and ours be kept steadfast in Faith !

BRUSSELS, June 12, 1872.

My Dear Children :

After a two days' rain the sun is now (7.30 P. M.) lighting up beautifully the grand elms in the park planted by Maria Theresa when the "Low Countries," of Belgium, formed a part of the kingdom now the Austrian empire. We have just returned from a drive around the shady Boulevards and spent the morning in visiting its museums of painting and natural history, and some of the municipal buildings. The Hotel d'Ville is one of those quaint old structures with which we have all been made familiar by engravings and photographs; and in the space before it we stopped and did homage to the memory of Egmont and Van Horn who were executed here; the Duke of Alva gratifying his cruel taste by standing in a window to view the martyrdom. A great monument, crowned by statues of the noble pair, marks the spot; and in one of the Courts of Justice is a fine modern painting, representing the signing of the agreement to resist the power of the Inquisition by the Nobles, executed by a good artist at the expense of the present government. The personages represented as participating are all portraits and the heads and faces are the appropriate shrines of the minds that could conceive and the wills that could accomplish great things. I have always shrunk from the perusal of Motley's History and the same feeling fills me with sadness as I move among the places made sacred by the noble devotion of the actors in their history.

In the same room is also a fine historical picture of the abdication of Charles V. which took place here. The faces are also portraits and the artist has admirably represented the glowing superstition of the actors by the awful solemnity of every countenance, though some of the females are beautiful.

In one of the squares is a fine monument erected to the memory of those who fell in defence of the liberty of Belgium in 1830. The pedestal has on each face a panel of marble containing very fine bas-reliefs representing various incidents in the conflict, so life-like that I turned from them as I would have done from the spectacle itself.

There is however one gallery here, that belonging to the Duke of Aremberg, which is worth all the other galleries I have visited. Every picture in it is a gem. There is not one that can offend the most fastidious taste or shock the nicest sense of delicacy, and not one that is not a trophy of art. There are only about 200 pictures, and none of great size. There are portraits by Rubens and Rembrandt and Vandyke, and cattle pieces by Paul Potter; and interiors by Van Eyck and I cannot tell who all, besides a portrait of himself by Gerard Douw, etc. The subjects of the compositions are all good and the execution perfect. The Duke has been offered two hundred thousand francs for one picture and equally large sums for others. There is a fine portrait of Jean Calvin and one of Jansenius.

But of all the portraits there is *one* claims the regard of every visitor, not so much for its artistic merit as for the sacredness of the subject. It is a small picture of Marie Antoinette, painted by a man who had been an artist in the employ of the royal family but found himself as one of the *Garde Nationale*, mounting guard over her, a prisoner in the temple, just before she was removed to the Conciergerie. It is the sweet face of an elderly looking woman in a plain mourning cap and white muslin handkerchief folded over the bosom. Just such a picture as any one would love to possess of a mother; no expression of agony or even sorrow on the beautiful features, but a placid subdued look of resignation such as could be presented by no one whose soul was not at peace. The frightful pictures of theatric excitement which we sometimes see are disgusting—the mere portraits of a beautiful woman in regal attire are not attractive to me except as works of art—this sweet picture is calculated to bring before one the woman for whom in the eloquent language of Burke "one would have thought a thousand swords would have started from their scabbards." An inscription on the back signed by the former Duke of Aremberg certifies to his having purchased it from the artist himself.

The house is a modest one, a part of it still just as it was when occupied by Egmont; such a house as any modest gentleman might wish to live in. The room occupied by the gallery is small but well lighted, and there is another used as a library which contains 38,000 choice volumes arranged in cases, all accessible, the doors of large glass plates, each bearing on it a beautiful painting illustrative of the subjects treated of by the authors whose works are within. There is also here a cast from the head of Laocoon, found under a bridge at Florence. The original antique marble is prized so highly that it is kept in a private apartment and not allowed to be exhibited. The cast is a perfect model, and opposite it is placed another cast taken from the same portion of the Laocoon of Michael Angelo, at Rome. The contrast is very strong. Not only does the entire features of the work of the modern artist fall short of the utter agony of the work of the Grecian, but the head looks as though it were stuck on the neck of some other body, while the muscles of the neck of the ancient head are as instinct with expression as those of the face and eye itself. The various objects of interest were shown to us and described by a servant of great intelligence, and with a courtesy as though we had been personal friends of his master. The family is at some other residence, but the Duke himself in this on the day of our visit.

After enjoying our pleasure in looking at the pictures, the guide told us if we could walk softly and without speaking, he would shew us some parts of the collections which are not generally seen. We followed him through some rooms hung with ancient tapestry, but when we reached the door of the room to which he was leading us, he opened it cautiously and motioned us back, as the Duke was there. I believe it was only some fine china. In the library there is a good collection of Etruscan and other ancient vases and bronzes, copied after those of Pompeii. The present Duke is a descendant of one of those who combined against the Inquisition.

After our enjoyment of the place, we went yesterday to Ghent to visit the gardens of Van Houtte. The entire route lay through those thickly cultivated fields which I wrote you about last summer, now heavily laden with grass and flax and wheat and rye. Not a square inch which is not occupied, and all so evenly and perfectly good that you can discern no difference. It is a smoothly shaven lawn laid out in beds, all the growth of equal height, and only differing in the variety of shades of green. Some of the meadows have enough of yellow buttercups and white ox-eyed daisy to prove that here the farmer has to contend with the same enemies as with us. How they secure such uniformly high culture I cannot conceive. The houses of the peasantry are all of one story, and apparently of only one room and an attic, and generally grouped in villages. But few cattle grazing ; all fed.

BRUSSELS, June 13, 1872.

My Dear Brother (Galloway Cheston.—Eds.):

I have just returned from a day's excursion to Ghent, made for the purpose of visiting the horticultural *establishment* of Van Houtte. No other term is appropriate, so much does it embrace; and at the risk of the danger of the forfeiture of your confidence in my judgment, I must assume the position of his advocate. Wistar says he was never more agreeably surprised. Everything is in the most perfect order. Not a pot less clean than a lady's breakfast service ; not a sickly-looking plant, much less a fallen or dead leaf, anywhere on the entire area ; and range after range of hot and green-houses, and acre after acre of borders and nursery, all in equally good condition. One hundred and thirty gardeners are occupied in the cultivation of plants, and sixty artists in preparing and colouring the plates for his serial. The eighteenth volume is the last issued ; the plates for the nineteenth are now preparing. We saw the artists busily occupied on them. They are all seated in a long hall, each having a mirror so suspended that the superintendent can see from his seat exactly what each is doing.

Wistar and I spent several hours going about the grounds and admiring the plants, accompanied by some one appointed for the purpose. I did not feel authorized to order the forthcoming volume in your name, but did so in my own for you. I also got catalogues in connection with Wistar, and shall order some bulbs, of which I hope you will accept a part. The rhododendrons are out of bloom, but the plants are not larger than your own. They are all screened by evergreen hedges. His larkspurs and pyrethrums and violets and potentillas were in blow, and inconceivably fine, and so were the calceolarias. I found he substitutes baskets for pots in large plants standing out in the sun, such as your oleanders and pomegranates. You must forgive him.

Anne is doing nicely, and we are all getting on happily and profitably, so that we shall continue to travel with brother and sisters unless something at home renders our return proper. Friezier waits for my letter, so that I have only time to utter what you know we feel—the assurance of unbounded affection, and our trust that we may be spared to meet in October with thankful and joyful hearts.

I am solicitous about the state of public affairs, which appear to me to become more and more troubled.

Anne unites in love to you and dear Margaret, and both desire to be remembered to Mary Ellen (when you write), with the assurance of our deep sympathy in her sore afflictions, and a prayer that she may be kept through them all by that power which has been so mercifully vouchsafed to her in the past, and know more and more of the experience of that love which is unchangeable, manifested in Jesus, and still bestowed on every member of the body of Christ.

Yours sincerely,

CASPAR MORRIS.

ROTTERDAM, June 16, 1872.

My Dear Children:

Leaving Brussels with all its charms, and expecting to be there again on our return from Germany, we went the afternoon of Thursday to Antwerp, once the great commercial metropolis of northern Europe, and the seat of that great struggle which marks the era of the Reformation.

These low countries, as they were then called, had been annexed to the Empire of Austria by the marriage of one of the female heirs of Brabant to the Emperor. The activity of mind which had developed the commerce and manufactures of the country, and the energy which had reclaimed so much of it from the sea (thus at the same time recovering from the waves the very land on which to erect cities from which to send forth fleets to convert its waters into a highway for bringing to its shores the wealth of other lands), rendered its population peculiarly fitted to receive the impression of the awakening of the Fifteenth Century. Erasmus was a native of Rotterdam and the struggles in Antwerp were marked by the violence which led to the beheading of Van Horn and Egmont.

Yesterday we passed the place at which the attempt was made (without success) to ensure uniformity of belief among the Protestants—Dort;—and to-day we find ourselves in a place where the Dutch church has predominance, for which its members claim the merit of being the mother of churches having fostered and nourished and protected the refugees from England in the Marian persecution. Tyndale found refuge in these Low Countries for a time and perfected and issued here that translation of the word of God which forms the basis of our own "authorized version"; and here, between Brussels and Antwerp, he suffered the pain of burning and obtained the crown of Martyrdom for the truth. Such are the thoughts and associations that rise uppermost as one is driven over the level plains or along the sluggish waters we have traversed the last two days.

The whole country is a triumph of human energy over obstacles and of human perseverance under difficulties. About Ghent and Antwerp the culture is of the highest order. Between Antwerp and this place there is much land which is naturally as barren as that in New Jersey on the way to Atlantic City. Vineland there is only a repetition of the experience of the past generations here. You may get from any soil a return for well directed and properly applied labor and manure. I do not dispair of seeing the pines of New Jersey as productive as Holland.

The cathedral at Antwerp has a grand spire, lofty, and elaborate, and light. The great attraction for travellers is found in the pictures of Rubens. I have yet to see one production of that artist which affords me any pleasure. The subjects are all repulsive either from their horror or their sensuality, and there is no manifestation of the slightest trace of soul, much less of any devout feeling in any of them. The drawing is good and some of the colouring, but they all have the appearance of want of delicacy and are rough, as though the hasty production of one who was striving to turn off as many pictures as possible; "to make hay while the sun shines." There are many Vandykes and Jordaens in the several churches and one has a life size representation, in wooden figures, of the calling of Andrew and Peter by our Lord, which is really impressive and admirably carved. The net hangs over a rock, as flexible as though woven, and the fish are perfect, while the attitude and expression of our Lord and the apostles prove that the artist entered into the spirit of the act. It is a modern work and proves that there is the same power yet in the human family to produce works of art as there was of old and that the patronage is all that is needed to elicit the same great results as charm us in the works of the masters.

We saw one collection here of modern pictures which affords full proof of this. I purchased a catalogue and marked those which gave me special delight. There were two by Arey Schaeffer—Margaret seated on her chair with her wheel beside her; and the Annunciation to the Shepherds; which were especially impressive. The artist has made the canvas and brush express the varied feelings of the soul as clearly, deeply, strongly and as impressively as could the presence and words of the parties themselves. You hear the melody of angels' songs as you gaze on the rapt expression of the faces of the shepherds, and the whole soul of sympathy is drawn out by the returning of the soul of Margaret to the love of virtue, with the feeling that there was in the world no hope, mingled with a scarce encouraged longing for a hope beyond, which contrasts strongly with the companion picture of Faust in his study, where there is no expression of anything but abstract and deep thought, without feeling or emotion. There is in the same collection a picture of age (by Arey Shaffer also), illustrative of a ballad of Goethe, describing a man drinking his last draught from a cup given him years before by a dying wife, which is wondrously expressive. Shaeffer among moderns stands in my estimate beside Da Vinci and Murillo among the painters of former times.

It would be a useless effort on my part and an unprofitable consumption of your time for me to attempt any description of the treasures of art in the galleries at Antwerp which are so celebrated. I was much delighted with one little incident. My pencil had become useless by some derangement of the works by which the point is projected. I had found it was getting out of order and endeavored to find some one who could repair it in Paris and Brussels. At Antwerp it got so that I could not shut it and I went into several shops but they all shook their heads. At last I found one small shop with a man and his wife in it, who said he could try. When I went for it he expressed great regret and was particularly pleasant admiring the pencil, which was of a construction new to him. I mentioned incidentally that I used it chiefly to make notes in the galleries of art. He then asked if I were fond of pictures and whether I could climb some stairs and offered to show me his collection. The house was not more than sixteen feet front, the only entrance through the shop. We mounted three stories to the parlor by a very narrow stair. It was without carpet; in the middle a piano, and the walls hung with a very pretty collection of good pictures. Thus a poor working jeweller found his gratification in the indulgence of his taste for the beautiful and sweet, without grudging the larger enjoyment of the rich and great. He had some very beautiful little pictures. I saw also in a window a very pretty one of a child catching a bottle fly, which was waiting a purchaser.

Cheston will remember the man born without arms who supports himself by painting; using his feet and toes as hands and fingers. He took quite a fancy to your mother and sent her one of his photographs. His pictures are valuable as evidences of the power of man to overcome difficulties. It is very interesting to see how perfectly he has converted his legs and feet into arms and hands. He cannot use them for both simultaneously however. He must sit down before he can wipe his face.

        Yours truly,

                      CASPAR MORRIS.

ROTTERDAM, June 17, 1872.

My Dear Children:

We have at length overtaken the summer. I sit now at six A. M. with window raised listeneng to the chiming of the bells of the Cathedral while writing to you before dressing. Only three days ago we were wearing our entire winter suits, with overcoats. These chimes, as well as those at Antwerp, are very sweet and mark with their melody each quarter of the hour. Can the recording angel sing with joy as he notes our passing moments? That would be melody indeed. We have got among singing birds too. At Ghent attention was arrested by the strong sweet liquid note of a bird in the garden of Van Houtte and was told it was the black bird; and here the varied notes of the Thrush are quite equal to our mocking bird.

We spent yesterday quietly in this old town made up of immense brick houses with perfectly plain fronts, venerable with age, facing the wide canal, which brings the largest vessels directly to the doors of their owners to discharge their cargoes from Batavia, Sumatra and the other Dutch colonies especially, but also from our own country, and a first-class ship with our flag lies almost in front of the hotel. Fine Quays lined with elms, lie along the banks of the canal; thus giving a pleasant shade in which the vessels are loaded and discharged.

I walked the entire distance along this canal to the park last evening after tea. When I got beyond the business part of the town the houses were encircled with pretty little gardens but also surrounded by ditches. They are all built on piles and lie some eight or ten feet below the level of the embankment along which the road is carried. I saw a pool in which piles were being driven on which to build a large house.

Arriving here late on Saturday evening we have seen nothing but what I have thus mentioned. We shall drive by carriage from this to the Hague starting soon after breakfast and stopping by the way at Delft, which has given its name to a peculiar ware, though it is no longer made there. My grandmother had a choice tea service of it which impressed my childish imagination as something very good and was certainly very beautiful. The place has historical interest as that at which the assassin, hired by the priests, killed William of Orange, called "the silent," the great leader of the Protestant league.

HAGUE, HOLLAND, Evening, June 17th.

We have had a delightful drive to this place this afternoon, leaving Rotterdam about 3 P. M. and passing an hour at Delft. The entire distance is a vast plain redeemed from the water, intersected by canals, and cultivated chiefly in grass and used for grazing immense herds of beautiful cattle of large size and all spotted, black and white. The road the entire distance is paved with hard brick set on edge and is kept in perfect order. The weather is warm but a fine breeze refreshed us, and there is a light hazy cloud constantly prevailing which diminished the intensity of the heat and light of the sun.

Every step brought more forcibly into view the wonderful energy and perseverance of the Hollanders. We are too apt to adopt the bias of English writers, and look with jealous eyes on those nations which have been the rivals of our mother country, and among them the "Ambitious Hollander." I remember my childish delight in reading the defeat of "The Insolent Van Tromp," who dared to carry a broom at his mast head as a token he had swept the channel of all rivals. But I might perhaps feel different now if I were to read these pages again. Here I find it recorded that he had been victor on thirty-one sea engagements and perished in the thirty-second.

We stopped at Delft as I wrote we designed, and went into the church and saw the monument erected by the States General of Holland to commemorate the founder of the Republic, William of Nassau, Prince of Orange, called The Silent; who was assassinated by a Burgundian who was soon after arrested and cruelly put to death. The crime is supposed to have been instigated and rewarded by the Spanish king; certainly the denunciations of him by that government were adapted to produce such a result.

The monument is a fine one, consisting of a well executed effigy in white marble, recumbent, a dog lying at his feet as a memorial of a faithful animal who had saved him from a previous attempt at assassination. Around the white marble recumbent figures stand life sized bronze figures of Justice, Religion, Liberty, and Prudence. They are all fine expressive figures. Some of the party visited also the spot on which the murder was committed.

Delft is a dear quaint old town, as nice as possible; not often disturbed by two carriage loads of inquisitive Yankee sight-seers, I think; at least we attracted some attention as we drove through. Whether honorable distinction or ignominous notoriety we could not decide. We are probably forgotten ere this even by the boys who ran after us and the older people who stood staring at us. The costumes of some of the women there, here, and at Rotterdam, are very peculiar, and to us very funny looking. We bought a few photographs for your amusement. Everything at Rotterdam, Delft and here is gay with the display of bunting, an immense flag, of orange white and blue, floats from every house in honor of the birth day of the queen of Holland, and now at 10 P. M. all the youthful members of our party have gone into the park to see the fireworks which are to be displayed on the same account. Our hotel faces the park which is very large and the exhibition is at the other extremity, a thick double row of large trees intervening between us and the fire works.

We hear the sweets strains of the distant music and find it pleasanter to sit here and acknowledge with our hearts full of gratitude to our loving Heavenly Father the pleasure we have derived from the receipt of letters from Coz. Emily, Mary, Cheston, and Galloway, of the last of May. Our hearts respond to all your loving expressions and we daily seek a continuance of the blessing. Letters from Cornelia and Mary and Robert were very nice. We wonder what they would think if they could see the wonderful Flemish horses we have been looking at the last week. They are more like elephants. Those of Paris were large and had the most graceful actions and were admirably groomed, and made a most attractive spectacle as they were driven on the fashionable parade. But these Flemish beasts exceed all my ideas of the possible size of horses and are as fat and sleek as well-fed oxen. Then they draw great wagons or trucks with very low wheels, loaded with tons of merchandise. At Rotterdam they gave them a bath every morning. The grooms ride them down an inclined plain into the water and curry and brush them there.

This is a grass and grain country. The butter is the best I ever tasted and your mother and myself are enjoying it very much. We also have strawberries at every meal, and have had ever since we returned to Europe from Palestine, and probably shall have them all summer as we follow their ripening in our journey. Those we have had lately have been very large and very luscious. I have found two or three berries as many as I wished; holding them by the stem and eating them as I would a pear.

As I write our attention is diverted by some magnificient rockets which rise above the trees, while the sweet strains of the band come to us softened by the distance and we rejoice with the privilege of age to stay here instead of standing out on the ground. Just as I had written this sentence brother and sister came in and agreed that we had the best of it. They were very wearied; we could not see the wheels and fountains, and red and blue lights, but there were very many showers and finally a grand display of many coloured rockets sent up simultaneously.

Morning, Tuesday.

We retired about 11.30 P. M., and now I seat myself, while your mother occupies the wash stand, both quite *well*. O for songs of praise adequate to the expression of all the mercies and blessings. Our chamber is not large but has three windows, opening to the floor, which overlook the park with its noble trees and a fine herd of deer lying lazily before us, and crows and little birds hopping gaily about among them and a soft summer breeze fanning us. The town is not yet awake. Very few persons on the streets though it is 7 A. M. You are all we trust sleeping sweetly under the guardianship of those holy angels who are sent forth to minister to them that are heirs of salvation. May you each know that holy keeping during the day as you attend to its duties, as well as while you are sleeping. One of the terrible pictures which drove me out of Wierz gallery at Brussels, represented a young man with ministering spirits, one of good and one of evil, each expressing the appropriate feeling at his self distruction. "From all evil and mischief, from sin, from the craft and assaults of the devil, from thy wrath and everlasting damnation, Good Lord deliver us."

This, "The Hague," must be a very beautiful place. Driving here from Delft we passed some very fine country residences and the part of the town through which we passed before reaching here is filled with large houses, each having windows reaching from the floor to the ceiling, with plate-glass. Like all the other Dutch towns (Low countries), the houses present an appearance of comfort and cleanliness which is very attractive. Even those which have but one story are scrupulously neat, well painted, and with clean curtains at the windows; while those of more affluent occupants are wide fronted, large windowed, solid walled, and handsomely furnished. At Rotterdam (being built on piles) they have settled, but it is so regularly that there are no cracks in the walls which are none of them quite perpendicular. So that the houses have the appearance of a crowd of people of dignity, some holding back and some bowing and desiring an introduction but all grand and eloquent. Some of them bear on their fronts the date of erection running back to 1524 and all intervening years. In the churches lie tombstones with corresponding dates. They once had on them the armorial bearings in solid bronze of those who sleep below. Those were taken away by the French under the old Republic leaving the bare stones, with the rude cavity occupied by the bronze, having a ragged appearance. Have some of the descendants of those rich merchants and nobles come to rags also?

Not only are the country and towns alike intersected with canals, but there are ditches dividing the fields which for countless miles (day's journeys by rail road) are as level as the meadows between Philadelphia and Chester; or the swamp at West River. These ditches are all covered by a thick coating of green "*duck weed*," having a repulsive appearance, but really beneficial as it is a vegetable growth and purifies the water. We saw at one place an immence flock of geese, and very often ducks, swimming about and dividing the green surface which was so thick that it closed behind them leaving no trace of their passage. The gentlemen's parks have lakes and serpentine waters among the shrubberies but they have generally the same coating of green, which is not pleasant to an unaccustomed eye.

The curious old windmills are another striking feature in the Dutch landscape. Sometimes there will be a dozen or more in sight; huge oddly shaped masses covered with thatch; with old hoods on their tops (as odd looking as the head gear of the women) and great arms swinging lazily around.

HAGUE, 2 P. M., June 18th.

While waiting for your uncle and aunts to come in to dinner I will occupy a few moments in describing our morning occupation. We left the hotel door and drove along a street, one side lined by very fine residences and the other by the park which gradually lost its appearance of culture until you might readily imagine yourself in the deepest wilds of an American forest. Lofty trees, of great age, covered some hundreds of acres through which we could trace winding drives till suddenly we brought up at a modest looking country house, before which servants in royal livery stood to help us to alight, and we found we were at what is known as the "House in the Woods," built by the widow of a former Prince of Orange, and now occupied by the Queen of Holland. The king is not worthy of her and she lives here in the retirement of simple elegance. Plain carpets covered the floors, and simple tables and chairs afford rest and refreshment, while a few choice pictures hanging on white walls prove the purity of the taste of the occupant. One room is furnished with most costly Japanese silk embroidered hangings, and chairs with seats to match; said to have been presented by a Mikado or Tycoon to an Orange Prince some 200 years ago. Whether before Japan was closed to Christan nations and native Christians were compelled to trample on the cross, or during the time the Dutch retained the privilege granted to no other nation of annually two ships to trade at one of the ports, we were not told. One of the Royal family came suddenly upon us as we were gazing at the fine old china (not better than some other I have seen) and we were obliged to hasten on.

We drove from there through the deep dark woods amid the songs of birds and emerged at a different side from that by which we had entered the park; and then through streets of beautiful houses to the city palace. Friezier sought entrance for us, but returned saying His majesty was at home but declined seeing visitors; for which two of the party most heartily thanked him, and we all drove away (without leaving cards) to a Bazaar where there is exhibited for sale an immense collection of things we did not want and could do without. The only thing I saw that attracted my attention was a life size and life like picture of *a cow*. Some of your aunts (not those that had had practical experience) had expressed a desire to enjoy the occupation of Dairy Maids since visiting the "*Vacherie*" of Marie Antoinette at the Petit Trianon and I suggested that as the most admirable beginning of stock for the establishment.

This afternoon we drive to the fashionable resort by the sea side, and as the carriages are announced I must once more bid you adieu with all the fondness of a parent's affection and the earnestness of a parent's prayers for your preservation and happiness.

Your mother's foot is greatly better; she walks without suffering, but it is still swollen, so that she can not yet put on her own shoe. I am quite well.

     Your loving father,
          CASPAR MORRIS.

       7 A. M., Wednesday morning.

All well and enjoying a fine fresh summer morning. Thanks to the merciful providence of a loving Father.

         HAGUE, June 19, 1872.

My Dear Children:

Without knowing at all what your father has written I take my place at the little table in our room, before breakfast, to bid you all a good morning and tell you, in the midst of our enjoyment, we are not forgetful of you, each and all, down to the youngest, in fact; and more frequently than morning and evening are you carried to the Throne of Grace for the best gifts. I know you will all be glad to hear we are both well again.

Your father like himself, and enjoying much. I am walking, and without suffering, and quite hope ere long to be able to get on a boot. All the rest of the party are well and we are getting along nicely. We are quite enjoying Holland. Both Rotterdam and this are very old towns and fine, with many handsome houses and wide clean streets, and such an air of comfort pervades the whole place and people that we love to look upon it. Those of you who have been here will remember the extraordinary head dress of the women. Gold or silver bands around the head with spiral wires projecting several inches front, by the eyes, and from them dangling ornaments; and over this a lace cap. Then the hats are as odd; an open carriage has passed in which four women are seated, their hats literally forming a canopy, so that it looked like a carriage of hats. Don't understand me that these are universal for many still wear a piece of lace and a flower or something as small.

These towns are intersected in every direction by canals, and yet they tell us they do not interfere with the health. There is an ample provision for fresh air in parks, walks, drives beautifully planted with trees, and the people do enjoy them; daily walking and often taking their tea or *beer* in them. Called to breakfast and must close.

   (*Not signed but in handwriting of A. C. M.*—EDS.)

         HAGUE, June 17, 1872.

My Dear Children and Grandchildren:

We reached here about two hours ago and found a package of most welcome letters, one from West River containing yours, Cornelia's,

Mary's and Robbie's, one from Gall. Cheston, and Cousin E. All were eagerly read and re-read, and before I had quite finished we were summoned to tea and, as we were all much refreshed by it, they have all gone to the park except your father and myself, to listen to music and see the fireworks, this being the birth-day of the Queen of Holland. I suppose the display will be handsome; the whole town was much decorated with flags, and preparations for illuminations were being made as we drove thro' this afternoon.

I do feel much self condemnation when I receive letters from home, that I do not write to you all more frequently and tell you more of what we are seeing and doing, and wish I could use the pen more freely. Do, my dear grandchildren, cultivate it; it is the only way to have the power. I think my last to you was from Paris. From there we went to Brussels. It is a nice place; there is much more appearance of real comfort than in Paris, and the people are different too; more solidity. We enjoyed the drives here too; they were very delightful, and I wished I had known where the Maxcys had lived. From there we came to Antwerp. It is a very nice old town; some parts very handsome, and here I was able to walk a little and actually went to a picture gallery, at Friezier's earnest entreaty; assuring me it was a small one, and each was a gem, and so I found it. It was a private collection and the whole thing was in elegant taste, and I enjoyed it; and the next day was persuaded to visit another where there were paintings by a man who has no arms but uses his toes. Well we saw not only his pictures but he, himself, at work painting a beautiful little picture. It is wonderful the dexterity and neatness with which he works. He gave me his photograph and autograph, and is to copy a picture for Wistar. While talking to us he took his handkerchief from his pocket, with his toes, used it, wiping the perspiration from his forehead and neck, and replaced it. Took a small vial from his box, removed the cork put a little paint on his board, and then replaced cork and vial. So you see he uses both feet, and with as much dexterity as we do our hands. He invited us to his house but I could not go with them; the walk was too long; but Mary and Wistar were highly gratified. He lives with, and now supports, his mother. Everything beautifully nice about them. Does it not show that much can be accomplished by patience and perseverance even under great difficulties? He never had any arms. Your father examined his foot; it was a perfectly natural one. The knee was very supple to enable him to take things from his pocket.

From Antwerp we came to Rotterdam. This is a city built on piles; the whole has been reclaimed from the sea, and there were canals in every direction thro' the town, as at Venice. You step out of the doors into boats on one side of the houses, while on the other there are wide streets and very many very fine, indeed elegant, houses. These canals are filled with boats. There is a great deal of shipping from here and many of them very large vessels. It is a perfectly clean town, and all these canals have draw bridges every five hundred yards over them, but the whole town being on piles, some of which have settled, the houses are all leaning a little either one side or the other and I should feel insecure, tho' they say none have ever come down and some have stood there since 1549.

I went with your father yesterday to church, rode of course; but took a short walk with him after service while waiting for the carriage. It is eight weeks since we did such a thing. We quite enjoyed it. Indeed I cannot tell you how delighted I am to be able to move about (altho' my gait is a limping one) with tolerable comfort.

June 18th.

We came here yesterday from Rotterdam in carriages; a ride of fourteen miles. It was very delightful, tho' thro' a perfectly level country intersected by canals in every direction. Between them such a growth of grass as I never saw. They were hay-making, and the wheat rye and flax very fine. Some beautiful cattle, and where ever they were milking (which was quite frequently), the hind legs of the cow were tied together. The butter in Holland is the best we have had. Altogether we are much pleased with Dutchland. But oh! the costumes of the women are too funny, and such caps and hats! I have got some photographs to show you. This town is also built on piles and is very large and handsome. We came thro' a very large part of it yesterday.

This hotel is in front of a most beautiful park; our windows open on it. There are several hundred deer grazing there, and last night your father and I had the full benefit of the fireworks and music (without leaving the rooms) both of which were very fine and were kept up until 12 o'clock, for I must tell you it is light enough to read at nine, so the exhibition did not begin before ten.

I must not neglect telling the children that the canal boats are towed along by men, boys, women or dogs (often the last), and all kinds of produce are moved on them. We saw several that looked like flower gardens, on their way to market. They looked very beautiful, and the vegetables are very fine.

I am so glad to hear from you, particularly of all the branches of the family, and that all were well. I do hope that you will be favored with health this summer, and I was glad to hear James had gone to Baltimore. We had no letter from there this time, but know his visit will be acceptable to Galloway and Margaret. We are now feeling the first warm weather, and yet I cannot say it is oppressive except in the sun at midday.

From here we go on the 20th to Amsterdam; stay two or three days, thence to Berlin. From there nothing is decided. We shall be there a week. We may go to Copenhagen to see Miss Dunant, cousin

Emily's friend, while the rest are there. I am very glad to give you a good account of our health now. Your father is certainly much better; indeed is quite like himself, and is able to enjoy everything and we are doing so moderately, and do not intend to allow ourselves to be enticed into excess in any way; so I think you may all dismiss anxiety on our account.

I am really feeling better than I have done since leaving home, and the lameness and weakness of my foot is a good excuse for not doing too much. So you see it will work all right, tho' I was deprived for sometime of seeing and doing what I would have liked.

Give much love to all round, not omitting the family at the Park, Ridge, etc. I often think of you all and believe me as ever your devoted mother,

A. C. MORRIS.

We are getting on nicely. Much love to cousin E., if with you.

THE HAGUE, June 18, 1872.

My Dear Grandchildren:

Shall I name either of you? No, you may spare me the labor of writing and consider one and all equally addressed, and each assert a joint partnership in the letter as you do in my affection; and consider it an acknowledgement of yours to me, which always afford great pleasure to your grandmother and myself, who follow the indications of the various enjoyments whether in "planting your rows of peas in your little gardens," the "visits to the little mule in Long Neck," the "rides to our neighbours," or "the parties of pleasure"; hoping and praying that amid them all you will not forget your Creator in the days of your youth, but ever remember from whose love all your blessings come and who says "my son give me thy heart." You will never find your pleasure less for loving the Lord your God with all your heart and soul and strength; and knowing that Jesus has bought you with his own blood, and that you are bound to serve him with your bodies and your spirits which are His. I often think of the question "Know ye not that your bodies are temples of the Holy Ghost?"

Your dear grandmother and I are sitting writing with our windows looking out on the wide spreading park with its beautiful lawns, with a herd of deer grazing peacefully, and great flocks of crows making a clamor in noble elm trees, whose tops are shaken by a brisk breeze which fans ourselves also, so that we forget how warm it is in the sun. We are in Holland; the land of meadows and ditches, and beautiful green grass, and splendid herds of cattle, and women with strange antiquated costumes. They milk the cows in the fields and always strap the two hind legs together so as to make it impossible for the cow to kick or move. The strap or rope is buckled round each leg just above the heel. That you know is high up, as cows and horses walk upon the points of their toes and the knee is in the large muscles of the body. The horses here are enormous beasts. I should like to know how much some of them weigh. More than half a dozen such as those your father drives in the carriage ; and the wagons are large in proportion, with very low wheels. I have seen hay enough for a good rick drawn by one horse. They are like elephants but kept elegantly groomed and fat and glossy. We tried to procure a photograph of some but could not. Your grandmother has photographs of the women and their head gear. I think I have mentioned before the curious harness of the horses in South France. Here they are harnessed like our own.

This is a very grandly beautiful town with a *magnificent* park and wild wood, with great trees like those in our forest, in the midst of which there is a quiet homelike house in which the Queen lives like any wealthy lady. We went through it. There is no splendor; only real comfort. One room is hung all around with silk on which birds and flowers are embroidered, and the chairs are covered with the same. These were presented by the Emperor of Japan some two hundred years ago. The house itself is not much larger than Ivy Neck and the drives through the deep wild woods, with the sweet birds, make it a pleasant home. But—there are buts about everything—the King does not love his wife and is not worthy of her love, so here she seeks peace in retirement. While driving for miles among the noble trees we could scarcely believe it is immediately adjoining a large town. Yet the moment we emerged from the edge we saw our hotel.

Your loving grandfather,

CASPAR MORRIS.

HAGUE, June 18, 1872.

My Dear Children:

At 9.30 P. M. yesterday I sat reading the paper without any lamp, and 3.30 this morning the sun was shining on the Park before our chamber windows. We thus realize that we have nearly reached summer solstice and are in a more northern latitude than you. Yesterday was warm. We drove in the afternoon to the shore of the German Ocean at a point which is much resorted to, not only by the citizens of this place, but from all parts of Europe. We found very large hotel accommodations, and a great paved courtyard opening to the sea. There is in the midst of this yard a pavillion with music stand, in which the band performs every evening; while crowds of people sit at little tables and drink tea, coffee, and beer. I never saw a more decorous assembly—we staid a short time only. The more we drive about the Hague the more we are impressed with the quiet, dignified grandeur which marks its dwellings and garden and park.

We have seen several very fine private collections of pictures containing gems by Teniers, Gerard Dow, Backhuysen, Van Ostade and others. In one we recognized a fine picture by Bougeaureau. Arey and Henry Schaffer catch my eye as soon as I enter a room in which they hang. There is a lofty purity of conception about them which is peculiar. In the museum there are some grand pictures, Potter's famous Bull, standing, with a cow lying beside some sheep beneath an aged tree. There is great power in the figure of the bull, and the sheep are perfectly painted. I think the whole group is the most perfect representation on canvas of animal life. A peasant leans against the tree, whose moss covered trunk stands out from the surface of the picture as though one might carve one's name upon it, as Paul Potter has placed his on the rail of a fence with the date of 1524 (I believe) attached.

It is now 7.30 P. M., and the sun yet quite an hour above the horizon. Your mother drove with the other members of the party after dinner, and they have not yet returned. When I had rested from the morning, I sauntered along the street to the wood I have mentioned before, and turned into one of its broad ways winding among its venerable trees; such as I have never before seen for size and vigor and age. I was soon lost in what, but for the wide neatly made ways, I would have been supposed a wilderness " far from the haunts of the sorrows of men," with birds carolling sweetly overhead. I came at last upon a space enclosed with light railing within which was a house surrounded by hundreds of small tables each with four chairs, and walking around the enclosure I saw piled upon each other as many metal vessels, like our coal scuttles, as there were tables; each containing a furnace for coals. Beside these were arranged an equal number of copper kettles for hot water. Liveried servants were moving quietly about and a pavillion with music stands proved that it is one of the places of evening resort frequented by the people here. A notice on the gate excluded all but subscribers from the reserved space within the railing; while numerous chairs and benches outside afforded opportunity for others to partake of the pleasure. As I returned I found many places filled both within and without and met, between there and the highway, a crowd of well-dressed gentlemen and ladies with familes, all hastening to the spot; each lady carried on her arm, neatly folded, a nice blanket, or Scotch plaid, or Vienna shawl; and each gentleman his overcoat. The hours of business were over, they had dined and would take their tea while listening to the music, provided by subscription, seated amid the grand old beech and maple trees, till bed-time. It is light until 10 P. M. at this season. There was no display of extravagance in dress, nor of excitement of manner. It appeared like a regular arrangement for the enjoyment of the evening after the duties of the day were done. Acquaintances exchange visits and converse between the pieces.

June 20th, evening.

We have just returned from a day's excursion to Leyden, the scene of the fearful seige by the Spaniards about 1524, with which we have all been made familiar by history and painting. One of the grand but fearful incidents is commemorated in a picture, which we saw, representing a crowd of citizens of all ranks and ages from the highest to the lowest and the oldest to infancy, all exhibiting the traces of starvation, entreating the Burgomaster to surrender. He drew his sword and offered it to them with the remark they might take his life to satisfy their hunger with his body, but he never would surrender. The admiral of the fleet, sent to their relief, cut the dykes and flooded the country, thus dislodging the Spaniards ; and a providential wind drove the water to the town carrying with it the vessels containing food.

This fact is recorded by an inscription over one of the doors of the Hotel d'Ville. To stand in the chamber which had witnessed the gallant deed of the Burgomaster and wander amid the houses in which the brave and Christian people had dwelt, was a source of great gratification. Old as are those houses they look as fresh and bright and clean as though they had been recently erected and the tenants now had but lately taken possession, and proved what care can do. I wandered through the smaller as well as the larger streets and found the same testimony applicable to all alike.

We visited with great interest the museum of Egyptian, Assyrian, Greek, and Roman remains. A choice collection in either department; and also that collected by Dr. Siebold in Japan, Sumatra and other parts of the East Indies, which is very rich in articles the products of those countries.

But I was specially interested in the halls and lecture rooms of the old University ; so celebrated as the mother of modern medical schools; our own University of Pennsylvania deriving from it through that of Edinburgh. It stands as it did when Tulpius taught anatomy, and Boerhave the practice of medicine, while he added dignity to his unrivalled position as the greatest physician after Hippocrates, by his Christian faith. We walked about its Botanic Garden where he had instructed his pupils in that science before he was advanced to the chair of Practice. It is now very beautifully and scientifically arranged.

Some wag of a student has inscribed over the door of the room in which examinations are held the celebrated lines which Dante places over the gate of Purgatory " Who enter here leaves hope behind," and sketched upon the walls, very ably, two figures; one "Penseroso," seated at the one side ; and the other " Allegro," dancing off at the other ; thus proving that joy may be found within, even if hope does not enter with the aspirant. There are other "charcoal sketches" illustrative of student experiences to which attention is invited by a hand holding the label " Gradus ad Parnassum" and pointing to a slouchy-looking lad departing, with a father's blessing, and a mother's tears, from home and taken by the hand by Minerva who introduces him to Truth and Labour as the object to be sought and the guide to her. They are cleverly done.

We went into the hall around which hung the portraits of all the professors from its foundation to the present. An honorable company.

*(Apparently a sheet or more of manuscript is missing here.—*EDS.)

HAGUE, June 20, 1896.

*My Dear Sister (Emily Hollingsworth.—*EDS.) :

We are here in this beautiful court residence ; for it is nothing else; has neither commerce nor manufactures, and is occupied only by the retainers of royalty and maintained by their expenditure. It is a very attractive spot. There is an air of quiet gentility pervading the houses; the gardens are beautiful, and the park grand. The scene of some of the most important events in European history and the residence of the descendants of those who were faithful unto death in witnessing for Jesus, the associations with the past are as imposing as the present elegance. William the Silent stands in effigy in bronze, in the most imposing attitude, with his chosen symbol sculptured on the pedestal, an ark amid the waves, with the motto in Latin ; "*safe amid peril*" ; and a grateful posterity has placed at his feet, here, as well as at Delft where he was finally assissanated by a hireling of Spanish bigotry, the form of a faithful dog which saved him from a previous attempt.

The churches at Rotterdam, Delft, and here, are all of Reformed principles and destitute of the attraction which draws lovers of art and seekers of the amusement to look at the pictures. But they are noble piles with all the dignity of venerable years. It is much more agreeable to my feelings to look at, and comment on, works of art in public museums or private galleries. There are some very celebrated works in the museum here, beautiful as well as great; while here as elsewhere we find much to prove the corruption of human nature, which prostitutes the noblest gift of God to the lowest purpose, and much to offend our feelings in the horrible subjects chosen by the artist in order to exhibit his power to represent things as they are.

We were all enchanted with a visit to the residence of the Queen of Holland. It stands in the midst of a dense forest of venerable and majestic trees, which stretches out for miles (almost imperceptibly thickening and growing darker), from the Park, which is skirted with elegant private dwellings, on the one side and on the other reaches to the heart of the city. When we drove up to the door we should have taken it for the residence of some very modest citizen but for the royal livery on the servant who assisted us to alight from our carriage ; and we entered a room with the floor carpeted more inexpensively than those of our own apartments at the hotel, and passed by a passage with a white wall, on which hung simple but beautiful pictures of home life, to a room furnished with chairs of white wood and plain green rep cushions ; the walls covered with beautiful Chinese paper, with a few simple pictures hanging there ; then to her majesty's private boudoir with a grand bouquet of fresh flowers, filling it with the fresh perfume of nature.

The object of visitors is to see in an octogonial room built by the widow of a former Prince of Orange and ornamented with paintings by the pupils of Rubens, which exhibit all the vice of that school. There is another room hung with silk embroidery of the most gorgeous pattern ; presented by an emporer of Japan some two hundred years ago.

These belong to the establishment ; but everything about the rooms occupied by the Queen betoken the most refined and chastened taste, and its surroundings of noble trees are such as I did not suppose Europe to possess. We are told this wood extends to Leyden, ten miles distant, and I write now to fill up the time while the family is assembling to start for a drive there and return this evening. This will enable us to visit the scenes made famous by the celebrated seige by the Spaniards in 1574, and the University, in which taught that most eminent Medical Professor and earnest servant of the Lord Jesus, Herman Boerhave ; and also some pictures and a museum of antiquities, Egyptian and others.

I am happy to be able to make a good report of the health and happiness of all our party. Anne's foot and leg still swollen greatly, and she is unable to get her own boot on ; but her general health is better than it has been for years, and she is really enjoying her travels and is undoubtedly the most useful member of the party. The weather is delightful ; just that degree of heat which is comfortable, relieved by a fine air ; and our journeys at present are not over fatiguing.

We derive comfort from the conviction that " *our Father's* " love and care are over our dear children and those we love at home ; but our affections run thither steadily and we pray that our lives may be spared, and you all kept in comfort ; that we may assemble once again to offer united thanks for the goodness which has watched over you and ourselves in our voyaging, so signally interposed for the deliverance and restoration of dear Mellie and Hannah, and kept the others in health.

We shall never see anything sweeter or more imposing than the park and woods which here stretch out before out window, with the herd of deer grazing, and the winding canal running through it. In the distance we see the passing forms of masses of troops, which are reviewed every morning.

The quaint costumes of the peasant women and servants which float before us frequently, give piquancy to the spectacle. You can conceive of nothing more grotesque. Yet, like everything Dutch, they are patterns of cleanliness and purity. Nothing can exceed this proverbial ¡characteristic of this race. The smallest houses have an attractive air from this cause, and large ones are such as any one might desire to possess. The windows are all larger in proportion to the fronts than with us, and rise to the ceiling and descend to the floor in every story. They use large glass—in the better houses the largest sized plate glass—which is kept scrupulously clean and bright, and all the wood work is freshly painted and purely white, with the exception of the doors, which are dark coloured, often green. Houses having inscribed on their fronts the date of building, proving them to be not less than two hundred years old, look as fresh as though they had never been occupied till the present year; and pretty lace curtains and blooming plants in pots as clean as grandmother could have wished, or "Betsy Baker" exhibited, adorn the window sills.

We have just returned from Leyden, and these remarks are as applicable to that city as to this and Delft. It was especially interesting to me to sit on the benches in the lecture-rooms where Boerhave and Tulpius and Albinus taught, and to walk in the Botanical garden where they studied the beauties and wonders of nature, and looked through them to the wisdom which made them all. The University there was founded by William the Silent, who, desiring to testify his sense of the patient patriotism of its citizens in enduring the horrors of the siege, offered them their choice of a dispensation of taxes or a University, and they chose the latter. A wise choice. Six hundred students still frequent it annually.

Remember me lovingly to brother Henry and Caroline and all my friends.

    Your loving brother,

              CASPAR MORRIS.

          ROTTERDAM, June 22, 1872.

My Dear Brother (Galloway Cheston.—EDS.):

We have Margaret and yourself always in our hearts, and literally "at each remove" further from you (as we are now making daily), "drag a lengthening chain." But each day satisfies me more posi-lively that we are (so far as I am able to see what is right and wrong) in our proper place. Dear Anne's ankle is decidedly mending, so that she walks about on it freely, though she is still unable to put on the foot her own shoe, and the limb is swollen from the knee down. Her health in other respects is good. She generally sleeps better than she has done at home, and any attempt to separate from the party would interfere with the comfort of all. A few weeks more and we shall turn our face decidedly and permanently westward; and even now there is a feeling of satisfaction in receiving letters in one day from London, and fourteen from home.

From the references made to you in those of our children, we infer that you are as usual; and are glad to find you have Mary Yarnall with you, and that James has been staying with you during Convention. Our greatest trouble is the thought of your sufferings. Had we no other association to bring you frequently to our minds, it would be impossible to avoid having you frequently on our tongues, as we have sat down three times daily ever since the beginning of May to fine dishes of strawberries; some very diminutive but of an aroma so high and fragrant as to perfume the room, and others so large that I take them by the stem and eat them as I would a pear. Of course there is much variety of flavor and flesh, but generally they are luscious and tender. I enclose a few seeds of some we thought very fine in both respects.

We are now in the region of gardens. I wrote you after having visited Van Houtte's establishment. We procured his catalogues, and brother Wistar has marked some orders for himself; but I am so uncertain about my own future plans and abode that I have abstained for the present. Yesterday we stopped near Haarlaem, at a large establishment, and got catalogues of bulbs and strawberries. Of the latter they have over two hundred varieties, all of which they recommend. I think it probable that we shall order some plants, or venture on some seeds of choice kinds, and I design without doubt to order some bulbs either from Van Houtte or from some garden at Haarlaem, where they ask less than he does, and will, I have no doubt, furnish bulbs which will produce flowers beautiful enough to gladden the heart and please the eye of any who is humble and willing to be pleased.

We see *grand masses* of rhododendrons as we drive through the parks and pass by the lawns in all parts of Northern Europe, which must be very beautiful in the season; but they, as well as the hyacinths and tulips, are out of bloom this year.

The park and forest at the Hague are grand and imposing. I never saw finer trees in our aboriginal forest than those beeches and elms, and the extent is sufficient to afford days' drives. I thought the trees at Versailles were unrivalled; these surpass them.

The cleanliness of these Dutch towns cannot be described, and they wear an aspect of refinement and gentility which is most attractive. These remarks do not apply to Amsterdam, however, so far as we have yet seen it. We drove through it last evening, the hotel being very remote from the railroad depot ; and whether it is from the contrast with the Hague, Leyden and Haarlaem, or that it is really dirty and foul, it made a very unfavourable impression on our nostrils ; while the crowded, bustling streets (narrow and lined by stores filled with various commodities for daily service) were less attractive to mere travellers than the wide, well-paved ways of Paris and these other towns, and the dazzling brightness and splendor of the shops filled with dress and jewelry and fancy goods of the great metropolis of folly, or the genteel residence of affluence and refinement which are collected at the Hague ; or the staid, well-brushed, carefully-dressed aspect of retired competency which characterizes Holland generally.

The country residences are as attractive looking as careful gardening and skillful planting can produce in a perfect plain. The illimitable stretch of green meadows dotted with herds of fine cattle, and with the monotone broken only by strange looking windmills, by the dozen, and the spires of churches in the distance. There appears to be but little culture of cereals. Pasturage and dairies are everywhere the same, and the only occupation of the rural population appears to be haymaking and milking. The butter is delicious, really ; and to us who have been nearly a year without any that is fit to eat, is very attractive. Palaces, picture galleries, museums and gardens are the only objects of interest to travellers except the historical associations, and the evidences of patient industry of a sober diligent people. The University at Leyden (which was the Lugdunum Batavorum of Drusus) interested me as the Mother of Medical Schools in America ; and the director of the museum at the Hague took pleasure in showing us a series of medals struck by the Dutch Republic in commemoration of a naval engagement in which the Dutch ships beat the English during the war of our Revolution and thus as he said aided us in securing our Independence.

I have now written out the time at my command, as we shall soon be called to the labour of the day. To what it will be devoted I have no idea. When summoned we put on our harness and follow our leader.

The atmosphere of Holland is nowhere free from the influence of its ditches, but this town is just now peculiarly offensive in consequence of the damming *up* of some streams and damming *off* others, in order to facilitate the great work in which they are engaged in opening a shorter channel of communication with the German Ocean. We shall be glad to escape from its influence and return once more to fast land leaving the meadows and ditches to the Beaver-like inhabitants.

Our letters received here are all gratifying. Our next will be at Berlin, where I shall look for your bronzes. We see many imitations in zinc; cast and galvanized with copper which sell at low prices.

The Presidental election and labour strikes at home make an ugly appearance in the telegraphic summaries in the daily papers here; and papal letters; synodical controversies; German complications, into which Ultramontane aggression enters so largely, produce an impression of unsettlement in public affairs generally, well adapted to convince us that man has not changed his character since the begining of the sixteenth Century. Thank God that He changes not, and as we have advanced since that period in science, art, and soul comfort, He will cause all the present excitement to result equally in progress. His heaven remains open alike to us and them.

With love to Margaret; and kind regards to all around you.

Yours truly,

CASPAR MORRIS.

AMSTERDAM, June 23, 1872.

My Dear Children:

We do not find this busy place as agreeable to travellers as the more elegant gentility of Antwerp and the Hague, or the literary and scientific dignity of Leyden. The last week or ten days has been passed in Belgium and Holland, the old Low Countries or Netherlands; so celebrated in the history of the struggles for liberty of conscience as well as political freedom in the sixteenth century, and as the rival of Great Britian in Commerce and for the control of the empire of the Ocean. Her Van Tromps and Dewitts and Vanesses are as distinguished as the Drakes and Blakes and Cooks of our mother country, and we have been shown their tombs and monuments, and portraits of themselves and their wives, with the same feeling of patriotic pride as England exhibits those of her Nelsons and Wellingtons.

The feeling with which one passes day after day in crossing plains as level as the floor, all lying many feet below the level of the water, whether river, canal or ocean, the encroachment of which is prevented by great dykes running along their banks, while wide ditches covered with duck weed intersect those plains and divide the fields, which are dotted with great herds of very beautiful cattle grazing on the verdant grass, which is the only product of the soil, is one of ever increasing admiration of the patient industry which achieved such a conquest and the perseverance which maintains its possession during so many centuries.

We reached here yesterday morning and were sadly disappointed by finding, instead of the wide clean streets of Antwerp the Hague and even Rotterdam, a bustling crowded place with high houses and narrow streets and narrower alleys, and wide canals of stagnant water black, red or yellow, and so offensive that I suggested at once that it could not be a healthy atmosphere and that nothing it had to exhibit could compensate for the discomfort and risk of even one day's detention, much less two or three, which is the time allotted to it. We are told that this foul condition of the water, and consequent fetid state of the air, is due to some temporary damming up of the canals, which is necessary to the completion of a new outlet to the German Ocean. It is so offensive to the population, however, that there was some riotous exhibitions of their dislike last night, and that the windows of the residence of the Burgomaster, or chief official of the place, were broken by a mob. Your uncle decided to carry out his program and remain till Sunday, and to-day has been spent in visiting various picture galleries, rich in paintings by Dutch artists, some of them very beautiful, some very imposing, and some very grotesque. Paul Potter's animals; Wouverman's horses; Tennier's village festivals; Steen's vulgar merriment and drunkenness; and the exquisitely furnished interiors of Gerard Douw and Van Mieris, have all contributed to our pleasure; while the portraits by Rembrandt and Hals, introduced into historic pictures and groups of old burgomasters, feasting, and conferring on affairs of State, have gratified us.

There are also some beautiful works of living artists which prove that the present age is not deficient in ability, and that the power of the artist is expended on subjects more in accordance with the feeling and taste than those of the older masters. Arey Shaffer's "Christ the Consoler" is a better conception of the character of our Lord and Master in his human nature than that of most others, and I rejoiced yesterday on seeing the original picture in the gallery here. "Himself bear our sorrows." He is "touched with a feeling for our infirmities." He is our Loving Master who bids us love each other "even as He hath loved us." The expression of the face of our Lord is not equal to that of Da Vinci's Last Supper, but is very winning, and the exhibition of human grief and suffering He came to sympathize with, and bear away, is very perfect. That is within the experience of the artist, and may be expressed on canvas.

On Saturday afternoon we visited the Zoological Garden, which certainly deserves the reputation it has of being the best supplied and arranged establishment of the kind in the world. The garden is well arranged, and the houses for the animals are airy, large and clean. There are all the usual animals, from the elephant and rhinoceros to white mice, among quadrupeds. Monkeys in abundance in a large house with a bell in it; which they ring most mischievously. One of the attendants motioned to us to follow him, and he took us to the cages of bears, of which he had charge. He led us first to that of the immense grizzly fellow from the Rocky Mountains, which I informed him by pantomime was a fellow-countryman of mine. He held up his hand and showed us how he had lost a piece of it by the jaws of the beast, who had caught him unawares. He then made him open his mouth, into which he thrust a piece of bread, for which the unwieldly brute grunted his thanks, bowing his head and scraping his paw most servilely. In the next cage was a yellow bear, who expressed his thanks for his bread by hugging his arms together and slobbering on them, while he shook his head as if saying, "Oh, how good"; which he repeated as often as the bread was given. In the next was a black bear, who kissed the man and hugged him around the neck while he was being fed. Then came the arctic white bear, who snarled and snapped at the slightest attempt of familiarity, and took his bread, returning nothing but growls of ferocious hate and defiance.

The birds were largely and beautifully represented. The weaver finch from Africa had ornamented the cage by interlacing many colored threads across the wires on both sides of the cage, and spreading a hammock of the same from one side to the other, as gorgeous as a Turkey carpet. Ant-eaters, chameleons, and serpents were all represented.

I forgot to mention, at Paris we saw, in the Jardin des Plantes, the boa who swallowed the blanket and kept it three weeks. It is now rolled just as he made a gulp of it, and hangs in the room near the cage.

We are all urgently desirous to get away from this disgusting place, and shall therefore not stay long enough to go to Broeck, which need not be so very clean to present a strong contrast to it. It is occupied by retired merchants, who have made fortunes in this foul atmosphere.

Monday morning, June 24th.

Many odd-looking sights attract our attention as we drive through the streets or ways of this singular country. There being no stone, the roads are everywhere constructed of small very hard, yellow-colored, brick set on edge. In this town they have imported stone; but all the country roads we have seen from Antwerp here are brick-paved. The signs are often curious, as are the customs. We saw one yesterday. "Hier (pronounced here) mangled men," meaning mangling done here, and "Fire and water store" is a common sign. People in warm weather make no fire in their own rooms, but take their tea or coffee pot, with their tea or coffee in it, to one of these shops and pay for boiling water. No asking for second cups at table in such families.

The peculiarities of female cap and head dress among the peasantry are great, and present something new to us very frequently. They have been transmitted from mother to daughter for generations. One sees a well-dressed man in modern costume walking with his wife in gold helmet covered by a cap of white muslin, sometimes plaited closely to the forehead and down the cheeks, and at others with a wide-covered border, or a long full veil hanging down the shoulders. In this town the children of the orphans' and foundling schools are retained in them till they acquire some trade for their support, and have, each school, a distinctive dress. One will meet a flock of girls of all ages; all attired in black gowns with square white muslin kerchiefs folded neatly across the shoulders and bosom, such as the old Quaker ladies once wore with us, and white caps with a border stiffened and standing up from the head; boys and young men with jackets having one red sleeve. Every pupil is numbered, and a heavy fine is laid upon any one selling liquor to such a child or youth.

How any one can live in the foul atmosphere of this place is quite inconceivable. Friezier says it is not always so bad, and the fact of a riotous disturbance caused by it confirms his statements, but a poor woman who talks English and hobbled after us from church, where she had sat at the door asking an alms, inquired how we liked the place and hoped we would return, but admitted it was always foul-smelling.

This place is celebrated for diamond-cutting, and that branch of art gives occupation to many thousands of artists, all Jews. When the Queen of England became possessed of the celebrated "Mountain of Light," they were obliged to employ a workman from here to cut it. They would not trust the gem out of the kingdom, and the machinery necessary was all taken from here for the purpose. If it were not for the offensive air, we should remain here and visit the workshops, though I do not think there could be any interest about them. We have seen a few diamonds in our own country and treasuries filled with them in various places in Europe, and quantities of imitation stones, which pass for genuine both there and here. The process of polishing and cutting has no special interest, except that the stone is so valuable.

Your uncle has also decided that Broeck shall not be defiled with our shoes treading its streets, so that we shall miss that wonder of our childhood. If cleaner than Leyden and Haarlem and The Hague, it must be a curiosity in its way. Friezier tells us that he visited it with the Misses Stevens, of Princeton, N. J., who found to their delight the names of their ancestors inscribed with a diamond on a window-pane of the house in which they had lived. They knew they came from somewhere in the neighbourhood, but visited the house by chance.

The people are just stirring with sounds as strange to our ears as the sights to our eyes. A very noisy fellow now under our window is calling the maids to bring out their dirt and dust, while bakers' boys ring wooden rattles to call them to take in the bread.

(*Nothing missing here, but not signed.*—EDS.)

AMSTERDAM, June 23, 1872.

My Dear Children:

We have been for the last ten days in Holland, and have enjoyed exceedingly the entire nicety of everything—houses, people, farms, towns; although it is as flat as possible, and the streams and many of the canals higher than the country, and the towns and farms intersected in every direction with canals or wide ditches, many of which are very repulsive-looking, being covered with a green vegetable growth, but we are assured it is not unhealthy. In no place have we found it offensive until we reached this place, and here it is in some places intolerable; consequently, we shall not tarry here to see much. We are told it is not usually so, but is owing to some alterations that the supply of water is being cut off, and the inhabitants are making great complaint. They think the work could have been completed more promptly, and like some of the demonstrations in our own land, last night the burgomaster's house was attacked and windows demolished; but the disturbance went no further, and we heard nothing of it until to day.

In order to see the country, especially gardens, we are moving now a good deal in carriages instead of cars, and are able to procure very comfortable open ones, and we all prefer that mode, though I expect it is rather more expensive. Our luggage is sent ahead by rail, so we are now in hand-bags, a few days at a time, and I find it very nice; saving all the time and trouble packing and unpacking, as no dressing can then be expected. So you see I am lazy. There is no reason for it, for I am well and am glad to tell you your father is, too; and we are really taking more pleasure in the trip than we have done at all before. Sometimes we are with them in picture galleries visiting, and see some very pretty ones. There are many of them by modern artists.

At Haarlem, which is a beautifully nice old town, we visited a palace formerly the residence of Napoleon. We entered by the basement, and were taken through the kitchen, the first royal one we have seen, and I wanted to stop and admire it; but our guide would not understand and did not seem at all willing, so I had to follow, though I would have taken quite as much pleasure there as in the pictures and furniture upstairs. I did see a good deal, and that everything was extremely nice. The floors and walls were covered with tiles: the floor, alternate black and white; the walls, small white; the hall and stairway, blue and white figures. The fire-place was not less than twenty feet long, with cooking-range having numberless little holes to place the most beautifully bright copper vessels on, for you must know scarce any other are used here for cooking in, and they are kept very bright, and the food is very good, and we have every variety furnished us. The only complaint I can make is, too many good things, and the wish that some one who is not so highly favoured had a part, but I don't feel as if we can interfere; it is not our business.

Sunday morning.

Your father and I have just returned from church, having found it was very near—about as far as the Epiphany; of course, we walked, and have had a very satisfactory time, a most excellent sermon from a young Englishman, and I think we will go again this evening. You can hardly understand what a treat it is in this far-off land, and where you are hearing an unknown language all the time, to get to your own church and hear there a sound discourse. These churches are supported by the Church of England. The small congregation, and mostly composed of visitors, could not do it.

We went yesterday afternoon to a zoological garden; said to be the first in the world, and it is certainly the finest we have seen. I was sorry I could not walk about it as I would have liked, but all the rest were highly gratified. Your father was particularly pleased with both plants and animals. He saw many of each that he never saw before, and the animals were in fine order and well provided for with abundant space.

The fruits and vegetables here are very fine and very abundant. We are eating very fine strawberries, three times a day, and have been since the first of May, and yet are not tired. The cauliflower is very fine. We see fields of them; for market, of course, and some of the gardeners tell us they have two hundred and fifty varieties of strawberries. One can scarce credit it, and some so large and heavy that they have crinoline supports for the plants so as to keep them from the ground.

We have your letters up to the second of June, and were very thankful for such satisfactory accounts of health and happiness, and do hope you will be able to continue such reports. We are very glad you called on Israel for the money, and thought both he and you understood that was our wish. Ere this, unless our letters are miscarried, you will have seen we had thought of some summer excursion for Miss Alice, as well as the girls, and we are very glad to find she has one in contemplation. I am afraid from Israel's extra work this summer he will not be able to take the girls, but perhaps Effie will pay you a visit instead. I have heard nothing about this summer's plans; so, of course, must leave it all to you at home to arrange among yourselves. All that we can do is to find means, and if you choose to use it in some other way, do so without hesitation. Also call on Israel for money to pay for your sewing; you know I should have paid Mary G. had she gone to you.

Your father met with the "Sunday at Home" in Paris—the five numbers for this year, and I was very glad to get them; they are home-like. Do you get them and the children's papers this year? It has been very thoughtless in me not to ask before. If not, do let Annie send them to you.

I did receive the girls' photographs, and was much surprised at the size and age of them; thought they were very good. I am afraid the children will have grown so I shall hardly know them.

We have a letter from Cousin E., and find most likely she will postpone her visit for a few weeks. She seems well, and I hope she will continue so, and it is well for her to keep out of Philadelphia in the summer, for you know if she is there she will be at work. I fear we shall not be able to get to Copenhagen, it will give us five very hard days' travel, and we are a little afraid of the fatigue. I think if they would let us off alone to go, we'd try it, but I don't believe they will. I shall be sorry, as I think Cousin would have liked us to have seen Miss Dunant, and I wished to have done it also. If we go at all, it will be from Berlin, a week hence; we go from here to Osnaburg, Hanover, and Berlin, and expect to be there a week, as there is much to see in and around.

Evening.

I cannot give you a stronger proof of our being well than to tell you we have just returned from the second service, which we enjoyed as much as the one this morning. The afternoon is very fine. We talked of the dear ones at home, by the way, and hope you are all enjoying it as much.

With a great deal of love to all from us both.
> Believe me, as ever, your devoted mother,
> A. C. MORRIS.

ARNHEIM, Monday P. M., June 24, 1872.

Greatly to the delight of the whole party we escaped from the disgusting canals and foul smells of Amsterdam at 4 P. M., and after a two hours' railroad ride found ourselves breathing a delightful atmosphere in this dear old town surrounded by beautiful quiet residences of retired gentlemen. The transition is beyond expression delightful. The first hour in Amsterdam convinced me that we ought not to tarry over night, and I have been astonished that your uncle, who suffered greatly himself from the depressing influence, allowed himself to be overruled by Friezier and remain. There are some good pictures in De Hoop's collection and some in the Museum, but nothing to compensate for the stench and abomination of the foul canals.

From that place on our way here we gradually emerge from the flat lands and cross a wide barren moor, without habitation or tree. I suppose it is irreclaimable, as nothing is done with it, and the energy which has recovered so many square miles from the waves would not allow this to lie waste if it were susceptible of cultivation.

We passed through Utrecht, an old Roman station, and still a large flourishing city; the scene of important events in the history of Europe, one of the epochs of which is marked by the peace, the treaty for which was negotiated here early in the eighteenth century, I believe, closing the wars which were connected so intimately with the struggles between Romish power and Protestant liberty.

We find ourselves in a good hotel, with a nice garden, having a large strawberry bed and many fine raspberry bushes laden with fruit ; and walking out after tea under an avenue of young linden trees, filling the air with their sweet perfume, while neat, rather elegant houses skirt the streets, we could not but regret the three days spent amid the discomfort of Amsterdam still more than even on our first arrival.

Before leaving Amsterdam, we visited the large establishment of Mr. Coster, the diamond cutter, and saw hundreds of men and boys diligently engaged on these precious and beautiful gems. Before being dressed they look very rough and unlikely to yield such exquisite beauty. The skill of the artist detects the character of the gem under the rough exterior, and subjects it to the friction which develops the beautiful facets from which the colored rays of light are reflected back upon the eye of the beholder. The process is very simple. The uncut gem is fastened in cement to a handle, and two are rubbed violently against each other. When the rough exterior has thus been chafed away, each is set firmly in a ball of molten lead to which a handle is attached, and held to the surface of a polished steel desk on which diamond dust is sprinkled and which is made to revolve with very great rapidity. In each room are some half dozen drums turned by steam power, around which run numerous bands, each one passing to one of these metal plates beside which sits a man or a boy with the diamond. We saw beautiful little sparklers of pure water, and were shown crystal models of all the distinguished gems in the world.

We were carried also to the synagogue of the Portuguese Jews, which has nothing attractive about it, although it is one of the recognized "objects" at Amsterdam. A crowd of beggars literally besieged the door as we came out, after seeing the shawls with which the readers cover their shoulders and some other soiled pieces of embroidery. The building is dingy and unattractive.

There is also a huge palace built on some thirty thousand piles, and having a hall in it 100 feet high. It has nothing interesting either in its paintings or sculpture except some imitations of bas-relief of little cupids whose little heads stand out, inviting some one to wring their necks, until he gets below them and then he finds that they are all sham, as is also some of the lining of the walls, which are supposed to be marble till the touch proves some of them to be plaster, and the rolling of the edges and corners betrays the fact that the lofty arches have been filled in with canvas and papered. This palace was built by the State and presented to Napoleon Bonaparte and was, I believe, occupied by Louis Bonaparte when king of Holland. Certainly royalty should not visit Amsterdam, and plebeian travellers will miss but little by seeking Teniers and Dows elsewhere.

In the Great Kirk are some monuments to the great naval commanders. One erected by his descendants of the present day to the memory of an ancestor, is a beautiful recumbent figure of a man with one of the finest heads and one of the most benevolent faces. That of De Ruyter has Fame flying over his head and sea gods blowing his praises out of conch shells, while turgid Latin verses record his many victories, and the whole is summed up in the assertion that he was "the dread of the deep sea."

We saw also a very fine modern painting representing the famous self-sacrifice of Van Speke, who was one of the orphans of Amsterdam, and having risen to the command of a gun-boat which was overpowered by numbers of the foe who crowded upon it, fired his pistol into the magazine, thus sacrificing his own life in the destruction he carried into the ranks of the foe. The black and red of the orphan uniform became at once the favorite color in which everything was clothed, and the name of Van Speke was attached to everything that could bear it. "He had his reward." Be it ours with equal self-sacrifice to seek one more glorious and more enduring. Looking to the witnesses by whom he was surrounded and the government he served, he did well, died nobly, and deserved the crown he aspired to.

We have a nobler assembly, and look to a higher reward from the hand of God, our Saviour. Let us not hesitate to sacrifice ourselves, "not counting our lives dear unto ourselves, so that we may finish our course with joy." So, says an apostle—he did.

HANOVER, 9 P. M., June 25th.

Leaving that gem of a place, Arnheim, this morning, after having driven around its elegant park and seen the neatness of its streets and the elegance of its suburban residences, we reached this place about 7 P. M. Soon after leaving Arnheim we fell again upon a tract of barren moor, utterly irreclaimable. Neither habitation nor animal gave any token of its ever having been, or of its susceptibility to become, a portion of the *habitable* globe. Nothing but the railroad and the stations. After passing over leagues which were so like the barrens of New Jersey that I thought of the story told of the traveller who stopped and looked compassionately on a man leaning on his spade who was looking terribly disconsolate ; when he saw the sympathizing look of the stranger the man said, "You need not pity me, I do not own a foot of land." So of this I thought kings would be rather justified in contending how to get rid of it than for its possession.

Toward the latter part of the day we passed through a range of hills, containing coal and iron, and then into the Kingdom of Hanover. The land became better, and was devoted to the culture of rye almost exclusively ; with some beans, and flax, and sugar beets.

The valley in which this old town stands appears to be fertile and well cultivated. But I do not wonder that the pride of Great Britain found it hard to submit to the rule of the Hanoverian dynasty. We have not seen anything but the outside of the place yet, and shall only remain to-morrow morning, leaving in the afternoon for Potsdam, where we shall spend two days amid the memorials of the majesty and tyranny of Frederic the Great ; of whom you may find all you want to know in last summer's *Harpers*'. We are all well and desire our dearest love to all.

HANOVER, June 25, 1872.

My Dear Children:

Our stay at Amsterdam was cut short by the offensive condition of the canals, though not until Friezier had carried us to several picture galleries and the palace of Napoleon, which he had condescended to accept in 1808. Having been led to expect much we were all greatly disappointed; it is a large building, built on thirty thousand piles, and we are told it is very elegantly furnished; if so, it is so covered that we saw nothing, and we concluded that it was a great humbug and not at all worth going into. From there we went to see the diamond cutting, and, taking a hurried lunch or dinner, took cars for Arnheim; and I can hardly give you an idea of the relief it was to us all to breathe the fresh air as soon as we got away from Amsterdam, and we concluded if it is always in this condition it is wrong for travellers to stop there.

We had a delightful ride to Arnheim—it is on the way here—and found it an uncommonly attractive place; perfectly clean, every part of it, and the new part of the town beautiful. I only wished they would stop there a week, but our rooms here were engaged; so, after riding around the dear little town, we took the cars and came here.

Having only been here long enough to get our suppers I can only tell you the impression received in coming from the depot; which is, it is a dingy, smoky place, though having some fine houses and wide streets.

The peasantry, as we came here, were busy in their hay fields; and abundant crops they have; and their harvest is approaching, the grain ripening. The women were attired, generally, in red flannel petticoats, some plain, some embroidered; black bodies, with full, white sleeves; and a sort of black skull cap on their heads. Imagine them working in the field dressed so. The costumes of the Holland and German women are so extraordinary, and I would so like to show them to you, that your father says if I were to take home all that I would like to have we might open a museum. So it ends in my getting none. In Holland many of the women wear a band of silver or gold around the head, and over it a thin cap. I quite wanted one of them, if the plated could have been had, but I was not willing yet to pay the price for the real of either.

Our present expectation is to leave here to-morrow, after riding around here a little, for Potsdam. It is a suburb of Berlin. There we shall be two days and then into Berlin, where our letters are to meet us. The weather is now warm here, and makes me think much of you all; you must be feeling it much more than we; our nights are always cool, and it is only uncomfortably hot when exposed to the sun. We have not seen Sally and Will Morris yet, and it is hardly likely we shall now. They are moving, and so are we. If we go to Stuttgart we shall certainly endeavor to find Mrs. Johnson, and hope she will not have left before we get there, as I would like so to meet her. We will also try to see R. and Julia Tyson, if we stay long enough.

(*Not signed, but in hand-writing of A. C. M.*—EDS.)

POTSDAM, June 27, 1872.

We have passed rapidly across Northern Germany. While faint and indistinct visions of Varus and his legions, and Arminius and the innumerable legions of ever-increasing Hermans, who, generation after generation, pay homage to the valor and strategy and skill of the patriot, who, by the overthrow of those legions, arrested the progress, north and east, of the Roman power, filled the air, the earth over which we passed was much of it not worth contending for. I have never been so disappointed by the reality where my ideas had been so firmly rooted. A very large proportion of the territory consists of bogs, destitute of tree or any sign of culture; with here and there some peat laid out to dry; and of sandy plains only a shade less desolate than those of Egypt. Where attempts to cultivate have been made the results are so trifling I wondered how any man could summon energy and courage enough to drive a plough, or hope enough to scatter the seed.

There was one district, just before we reached Magdeburg, which was rich; not in contrast only, but in real fertility. For leagues we passed through one field of grain, wheat, rye, and oats; only varied by some potatoes and sugar beets. Far as the eye could reach it was like a great, green sea, not a tree or hedge, nor even a house in which the laborer, who had planted and would reap such crops, could dwell. They are all collected in towns.

Near Hanover there was much grass culture, and there the people were at work gathering the hay, and houses and barns were scattered on the farms as with us. From whence do the immigrants to our country come, and how are the armies of the German Empire reinforced?

The Elbe seems to be a dividing line between the fertility and the desolation, which stretches from there to this place with but little variation.

As we drove from the railroad station to our hotel through palaces and palatial structures I could but remark that it appeared almost as extraordinary a triumph of human enterprise and energy as the meadows and pile-founded palaces of Holland. There is certainly nothing here which is not the effect of force. Frederick determined it should be done, and it was accomplished. How he acquired the influence he wielded is inconceivable, and equally so how Prussia has risen to the position of head of the German Empire. I am told the entire country around Berlin is as barren as that through which we have passed.

We have not yet been out this morning, and when we do go we shall visit, first, Sans Souci, said to have been built by Frederick at the close of the seven-years' war, to exhibit the fact that his resources had not been exhausted by it.

Potsdam and Magdeburg are familiar names to all youthful readers as the places of the imprisonment and scenes of the marvellous escapes of that wonderful hero of our youthful imagination, Baron

Trenck; and I think our own Lafayette was immured for a time at Magdeburg, which is still very strongly fortified. We are told that after having endured the horror of a siege by the French forces during many months 30,000 of the inhabitants were butchered by order of the French commander. This occurred in the reign of Louis XIV.

We yesterday passed near the birthplace of Martin Luther, and at Magdeburg they exhibited many relics of the great reformer. At Hanover we visited the museum collected by John Kemble, which is in the old palace of George I. of England, and contains some very terrible relics of the barbarous cruelty of the age of the Reformation, in the shape of racks and wheels and instruments of torture, with which one of the chambers is filled. I turned from them with loathing. Human nature changes not; will it ever again resort to such means to procure the possession of power? We saw there also a cage with two compartments of open work, into which two quarrelsome people were put, separated only by a light frame-work which prevented them striking each other, and kept there fastened together until they became reconciled. There was also a good collection of armor, etc., of the period of the Crusades.

The botanical garden attached to the royal residence at Hanover is surely worth visiting. The palm-house contains the greatest variety and largest-sized specimens we have yet seen. They were nearly as large and quite as healthy-looking as in their native climes. There were specimens from various parts of the tropics, east and west. As they grew too tall for the houses, pits were sunk beneath the tubs in which they are planted. The royal carriages were greatly inferior to those at Versailles, though rich and costly; but the horses, which are all either purely white or dun-colored, are very splendid animals. The tail of one was shown thirty-two feet long which had required four men to carry it for the poor beast to which it belonged when he was paraded on state occasions.

Thursday afternoon.

We have spent the morning in visiting the various palaces and gardens. Though Berlin is the capital of Prussia and now of the German Empire, Potsdam is the royal residence, as Versailles was that of Paris. Our first drive was to Babelsburg, a beautiful castle in highly-decorated grounds lying on a lake-like expansion of the river Havel. A steam-engine in an ornamental house on the water's edge is employed in raising water for the fountains, and it is also freely distributed on the lawns, the verdure of which is exquisite. The terraces and parterres were gaily planted with many-colored flowers in patterns of various devices, and everything around betoken good taste. Your mother and I did not enter the house, which has been occupied lately by the Crown Prince, who married the daughter of Victoria of Great Britain, and is now being fitted up for the Empress, who is to come next week. Those who did walk through were charmed with the refined elegance which marked all the domestic detail. We were satisfied with the grounds, which were perfectly homelike.

From there we drove to another palace which took much time and contained nothing but faded and tattered finery within, and is neglected without. Thence to Sans Souci, a magnificent pile of terraces and colonnades, belvideres and orangeries and fountains and statues. Within are exhibited various relics of Frederick the Great, Voltaire, and Madame Pompadour: The clock which stopped at the moment of Frederick's death, and has never been wound-up since; the graves of his dogs, near which he was carried in his chair when dying and uttered what is said to have been the last words: "That he should soon be still nearer to them." He had directed in his will that he should be buried among them. This wish was not complied with. The terror of his temper and his cane had ceased.

Just across the road from the gate of entrance stands the mill, so celebrated; and called the Historical Mill. Frederick wished to buy it and add the ground it occupies to his gardens. The owner refused to sell at any price. The King applied to the courts of law by some process which was decided against the royal suitor, and the mill was permitted to swing its sails at the very entrance of the palace. The King manifested his royal satisfaction at the majesty of law and his pleasure at finding one of his subjects as obstinate as himself by giving the miller means to enlarge his building, which stands as majestic among mills as Sans Souci among palaces. The base on which it is built is very large and high, and quite covered with ivy and ampelopsis. Recently a descendant of the valorous owner became embarrassed in pecuniary circumstances and offered to sell it to the Emperor, who declined the purchase; but bestowed on the miller such an amount as enabled him still to retain the possession of what his Majesty was pleased to call the "Historic Mill."

30th, evening.

From Sans Souci we drove to the new palace built (as I believe I said by mistake Sans Souci had been), to exhibit the unembarrassed state of his finances at the end of what is known as the seven years' war. It is an immense pile of ornamental brick-work, containing grand rooms opening out to magnificent views of parks and gardens.

It is here that they exhibit a copy of the works of Frederick, who, it is well-known, aspired to be as distinguished in philosophy and literature as he was in arms, "published by authority of Apollo." This copy contains the marginal notes of Voltaire, sometimes sarcastic, sometimes servile in the adulation. As for instance when he anticipates the celebrated expression of Van Buren about General Jackson and says: "It is sufficient glory to have served such a master." His royal master was even with him, having ornamented a chamber with pictures of animals and birds illustrating the habits and manners and appearance of the philosopher. One *monkey* being a portrait of him, and parrots being introduced as a satire on his volubility. When one sees here the busts and statues of the prince of pedants, and the leader of those fools who says there is no God, one can readily conceive that such a face and form might have been the typical illustration of the absurd theory under which a more modern philosopher covers an equally atheistical system. I am willing to acknowledge that I find within the passions and principles which originate with him of whom the lips of truth assert, "I beheld Satan as lightning fall from heaven;" but I do not consent to admit that I find the lineaments of form or feature which prove my ascent from a monkey. I leave that honor for Darwin and his disciples, and am willing they should accept as the highest type of their development the poor creature who spent his summers here with Frederick, and his winters with Louis XIV. and Madame Pompodour at Versailles. The fantastic tricks of the monkeys in the great cages of the Zoological Gardens afford us no inapt parallel.

June 28th.

A hail storm at Berlin last evening has cooled the atmosphere here, and we shall drive this morning around the gardens, and in the afternoon go to Berlin. Our journey from Hanover here was made through heavy rain. In this vicinity everything was parched and brown as though there had been no rain this summer.

I P. M.

We have returned from our drive. Potsdam is a forlorn place. The people look as though they had never fitted their clothes, which were poor to start with, and have been worn without brushing or washing till they are ragged, and houses and grounds all corresponding. The only attractive-looking places we have seen during our stay are the grounds and castle of Babelsburgh; and the residence of Prince William Charles, the ornamental entrance to which has been newly gilded, and, like the grounds at Babelsburgh, the lawns are neat and smiling, and the one view from either place has a tiny frigate moored in the lake, with a castle beyond it as the end of the vista.

In the old palace at Potsdam the apartments occupied by Frederick the Great remain as they were in his lifetime. We were shown his writing table and dining table, so arranged that the centre of it could be made to descend to the room below to have the various courses changed, while the margin remained stationary, around which his majesty and his guests sat without being observed by living waiters. They must have been content without any damask cloth on the table, though they may have had napkins on their knees. His hat and boots and flute and toothbrush, etc., are exhibited under a glass cover. Napoleon carried away the sword, which has been mislaid, and also cut a piece out of the velvet cover of the writing table. In one of the apartments hangs a portrait of Napoleon as first consul, sent by himself at some time as a present, the guide tells us in 1814, which must be an error.

Some of the chambers are occupied by the prince and princess royal when they visit Potsdam, and they are plainly furnished, even to rudeness. In fact the entire aspect of the palaces and environs, as well as the town, is one of rude want and finish. It has not the respectability of venerable antiquity nor the elegance of modern polish, but the appearance of a violent effort to be great, abandoned to decay. I neglected to mention when alluding to relics of Frederick that we saw on the shelves of his library the three or four quarto volumes of "Oeuvres de Philosophe d'Sans Souci," as well as the works of Voltaire, and in the music room were notes of the music he "composed" lying on the spinnet or piano at which he played. It is a small instrument, shaped like a grand piano, and as I touched the keys with one hand they gave out the air, "Shed not a tear," quite softly. A clock which he bought of Mad. Pompadour still keeps perfect time. Some of the party visited the tomb, and it is as simple as though he had, according to his wish, been buried with the dogs. I stop my writing to pack up for Berlin, to which we go for dinner.

BERLIN, June 20, 1872.

The journey from Potsdam to this place occupied less than one hour and was without interest. The evidence that we were approaching a great city was given in the improvement of the crops, owing to manure from the town. Even this does not raise the fertility beyond a very low grade, and within sight of the railroad were great uncultivated plains. On the dinner table was a dish of most diminutive strawberries which the waiter informed us were gathered in "the forest," and on your Aunt Hannah expressing surprise he said there is plenty of it everywhere. The berries are the smallest I ever saw, but very pleasant-tasted. Children bring them to town and sell them at about 1 cent for a teacupful. One would think a day might be spent in filling a cup, though they are said to be very abundant.

We are at the St. Petersburg Hotel of the Unter Linden, which is the great street of Berlin, being about double the width of Broad street, having a wide footway in the middle bordered on either side by linden trees, but very poor specimens after the noble ones which perfumed the air at Arnheim and many other places we have visited. A wide carriage way lies on either side of this central avenue, and good-paved footways pass before the houses, most of which have stores, in the windows of which are displayed rich shows of jewelry, silverware, engravings, amber articles, Berlin iron filigree work, and fancy goods generally.

I walked out immediately after dinner to look for bronzes, that I might get some birds your Uncle Galloway wrote for and which I could not find at Paris. I saw much that is beautiful, but none such as he described, and was referred to Paris as the only place to get them. They told me they kept no stock, but each customer must take what pleased his taste of what was displayed on the counters and shelves.

On my return I found all the party except your mother had gone to an aquarium, to which I followed them. It is an interesting exhibition on a large scale of the usual sea anemones, serpulas, and fishes. The cases containing the anemones are very beautiful. Some I literally thought were lemons and oranges thrown into the water till they expanded their mouths and threw out their fibrils like various-colored Queen Marguerites, making a display really like a well-assorted flower border. There were hundreds of them collected on the stones as thickly as they could be placed. In other cases were great lobsters, crawling about like spiders on the tips of their legs, and crabs in the same positions. Both these kinds of shell fish move about more by crawling than swimming. Some of the larger lobsters have been deprived of their claws or they would destroy all their fellow-lodgers and swimmers. Great horse-shoe crabs crawled about, and, attempting to climb the rocks, were tumbled back, falling on the shells below. It was amusing to witness their struggles to right themselves with paddle and tails. They would become so exhausted and lie so quietly that I thought them dead till a frantic effort, more like the convulsive movements of dying, would accomplish the turn and the round shell would move away with no signs of motive power.

The variety of fishes was very great, and some exceedingly beautiful, with tail and fins tinged of a very fine blue; others tipped with crimson and striped with several shades. I was most interested by the tribe of flat fish, which really move in the water like birds in the air, fluttering the margins of their flat bodies as wings; white below and spotted and variegated above. Some floated like buzzards, others flew like eagles or hawks, and one family of little flounders acted very much as flying squirrels, rising to the surface and then floating down to the bottom, just as the squirrels do from the tree tops. There was one serpula with a tall stem like a palm tree, from the top of which it waved its white plumes as much like the crown of foliage of the palm as can be imagined.

The space occupied by the various compartments extend very widely below ground and is adorned by grottoes and stalactites, while in the centre rises a great cage filled with birds from Australia, New Zealand, Africa and South America. A water-fall is introduced into one compartment, on the rocks of which several birds sat and enjoyed the pleasure of the dashing spray. Altogether it is an interesting and instructive exhibition to which I shall be tempted to return if I have a spare hour.

There are a few public buildings, imposing from their size and of Grecian style. The Rath House or Town Hall is a very large structure of red brick, and offers a very fair sample of what may be effected with that material. The ornaments are of terra cotta and are in very good taste.

Lord's Day evening, June 30th.

We spent yesterday in the gallery of paintings, but as I would not go there to-day neither will I allow my mind to dwell upon the effort to recall the recollection of all the beautiful things we saw, but keep the description for another time. The day has been rainy, and your dear mother has remained quietly within doors. I left off the bandage from her foot this morning, and she was able to get her own stocking on, but not her boot. I enjoyed the privilege of worship in a room in an old palace appropriated to the service of the Church of England. It is a privilege to be thankful for, bringing us its lessons from the Word of God and its expressive prayers. We had also a good sermon from an earnest minister.

As I passed the palace, the carriage of the Emperor of Germany drove slowly out, and I saw it standing waiting for him near the door of the church he attends. It was a plain heavy carriage with a pair of good serviceable horses. A smaller and lighter chariot followed; both had evidently been used since they had been washed, possibly to carry the family to church. Except the arms and the livery there was nothing by which they would have been known.

We propose an excursion from this to Wittenburg, the residence of Luther and the place at which he nailed his Thesis to the church door and proposed to defend them; the first open act of the Reformation. How soon we shall see another struggle for the truth it is difficult to determine, but certainly the signs of the times are very decided. The *Times* of yesterday (rather that which reached us here yesterday) contains news from Rome which may almost be considered the throwing down by the Pope of his gauntlet and challenging any one to the combat. In an address to some German societies, who called on him, he asserts the absolute necessity of affiliations, acknowledging no allegiance to any other power than the church and himself as the vicar of Christ and head of the church; and tells them he has sent to the German government to ask it to consider what it is that had made it necessary that "every priest shall be a conspirator against the state." This is very plain talk and cannot be misunderstood. It is his sanction to the interference of the clergy in secular affairs. Now the church in the language of Rome is one. The Pope is its head. He is infallible. There is no longer any mistake about this assumption. It is made a necessary article of faith by the decree of the late council. Therefore, not in Germany or Italy only, but all the world over; in the United States of America as much as in Ireland, it is the duty of the priest to direct their people in their votes. In Ireland it has been done so decidedly that a Roman Catholic judge has set aside an election return on the ground of the interference with their votes by the power of the clergy over the voters. It is, therefore, no longer a covert thing, but an open and avowed assumption of a right of that church to control government.

In this country a bishop had excommunicated two professors because they refused to accept the decree of the council affirming the infallibility of the Pope personally. The government demands the withdrawal of this excommunication as an interference with that liberty of conscience which is guaranteed to them by the government, whose officers they are as professors in an University supported by it, and to which they have been appointed as Catholics. The bishop refuses, and asserts he owes an allegiance to the church which is higher than that of the state. Thus the conflict of power has already begun. How long it will be held in the arena of diplomacy none can foresee.

In Holland the Romanists have had sufficient influence to prevent the celebration of the third centenary of independence of the low countries and are preparing to keep the anniversary of the massacre of St. Bartholomew. At least Friezier tells us he learned that such is the fact while at the Hague and that it is the cause of much anxiety among the people there. He is not a religious man, but assumes the position of a free-thinking liberal philosopher, though his wife is a Romanist. My old formula covers still my faith. The power which created, the love which redeemed, and the wisdom which governs the world can neither be defeated or disappointed. If we are very members incorporate in that mystical body of which Christ is the head, we have his Spirit dwelling in us and must be safe. "If we suffer with him we shall be glorified with Him." This, therefore, need be our only care. "In Christ, on Christ, for Christ." My only cry is, "Lord, I believe! Help thou my unbelief." "He that believeth on Him shall never be confounded." That He may reckon each one of you among His jewels to be made up in the last day, is my earnest prayer for one and all; in which, and in much love, your dear mother joins. We hope for letters to-morrow; our last were to June 4th or 5th.

    Your loving father,

              CASPAR MORRIS.

             BERLIN, June 10, 1872.

My Dear Sister (Emily Hollingsworth.—EDS.):

Until this time Anne and I have never, since we left home, abandoned the expectation of being able to accomplish our desire to visit your friend, Miss Dunant, at Copenhagen. On our first arrival we were pressed for time, and obliged to rush hurriedly through northern Europe in order to reach Switzerland before it got too cold; and from there were equally hurried to reach Cairo in time for the high water on the Nile. We talked over the visit frequently, and it was always one of the points to be touched at; the only question being from what place we should diverge from the regular route. Our experience in the low countries caused us to get out of them as quickly as possible. Wistar suffered from asthma, sister Mary from extreme exhaustion, and sister Jane was very unwell. The atmosphere was very depressing, and the water bad. In the towns all the sewage is in the canals; the level of the country is uniform, so that in some places the only current in the canal is caused by a steam pump, at certain points moving the water. It must, of necessity, be offensive and unhealthy. We found it necessary to get out of the region. If from there we went to Copenhagen it carried us over the same kind of country north, and we should be obliged to return over it again to this place, and, now as we have got here, it does not seem right to carry the party back over the *same character* of country, and they are not willing to allow us to go without them. We have, therefore, determined reluctantly to give up the pleasure we had looked for; we regret it very much. We have always felt a visit from us would be a great gratification to Miss Dunant, an event in a life which is probably monotonous, and, though it would have been a short-lived pleasure to her, it has been a long-continued, pleasant expectation for ourselves, and we hoped it would afford grateful retrospection also; and that it would gratify you. I find it difficult to reconcile myself to it, and, if it was not that it would disarrange all brother Wistar's plans, and disturb the order of harmony of the party, I should persevere and carry out my purpose. Brother Wistar kindly proposed to write to Miss Dunant and offer to bear her expenses to this place to meet us. But both Anne and myself doubted the expediency of this, as she is or has been an invalid (certainly is not used to travel) and might find it very unpleasant. It would also be a constraint on the others.

Thus you have an illustration of the uncertainty of all our movements. It is very delightful to be freed from all the responsibility which attaches to independence, and yet sometimes there is an abatement from the perfect satisfaction in such a shape as that in the present case. Anne and I can say truly we never know one hour what we shall do the next. We get into the carriage with Sisters Hannah and Jane, and it follows that in which Brother Wistar and Sister Mary are, and Friezier with them, on the box. Where he stops, ours draws up, and we enter the building or garden without knowing what we shall find there until we inquire.

You know how rebellious I have been and desirous to be rid of the weight of responsibility. I sometimes feel sinfully so. This is not our rest. We were made to labour in our Master's service, and the command is not only to work while it is called day, remembering that "the night cometh in which no man can work," but with good will to do service, "as to the Lord and not to men; knowing that whatsoever good thing any man doeth, the same shall he receive of the Lord whether he be bond or free." The labour of the slave, therefore, who had no choice of what he should do, is as certain of a recompense of a reward as that of his master, however high or noble he may be. I must forget the things that are behind, leave them all at the foot of the cross, look to Jesus for pardon, and now in this accepted day, after so long a time laying my sins on Jesus, start on a fresh career in His service, as though now for the first time the offer of salvation was presented :

> "Just as I am without one plea,
> But that Thy blood was shed for me,
> And that Thou bidst me come to Thee
> O Lamb of God, I come, I come."

I pray most earnestly that I may be strengthened to look still to Jesus and reach forth to the things that are before.

Travel amid scenes of earthly grandeur, and with all the appliances of luxurious gratification, is not enduring hardness as a good soldier of our Lord Jesus Christ, and while I do not pray for difficulties and trials, I would entreat that when the time of trial comes I may not be found like the Carthaginian soldiers—after the winter-quarters at Capua—enervated and worthless.

I do not think I ever united more heartily in the prayer, composed by John Bradford at the time of the Marian persecution, and ever since retained in our own service and that of the Church of England, than I did this morning. It runs "that those evils which the craft and subtility of the devil or man worketh against us (may) be brought to naught." The atmosphere is troubled; clouds arise, and long murmurings of thunder prelude a storm. The power of the Papacy is aggressive. The Pope has openly avowed that religious secret societies, subject to his authority and not to that of the temporal governments, are essential to the interests of the church, and accuses the German Emperor of making it necessary that every priest shall be a conspirator against the state. His bishops defy the power of the state, and say they owe a higher allegiance, not to God—that we all do—but to the Vicar of Christ. That Vicar is stirring up the priests in Ireland to interfere in the elections; in France, is striving to establish an "ultramontane" party in power; in Spain, is abetting the Carlists, who are the tools of the priests; in Italy, is defying the civil government, and in Germany, is stimulating civil discord. Even in Holland the power of the Papacy is such as to prevent the celebration of the third centenary of the independence of the Low Countries from Spain, because that was inextricably associated with the prevalence of the principles of the Reformation; and, at the same time, the Papists are preparing to commemorate St. Bartholomew's day, with its frightful atrocities, which the apologists for Rome strive to make us believe were civil, and not religious. It is a blessed assurance of our Lord that for the elect's sake the days of persecution are shortened, and we know that His grace is always sufficient for His people's need. We will not "foredate the day of woe"; "sufficient to the day is the evil thereof."

Anne sits beside me quietly reading in this foreign land. You are about going to the House of Worship; may you there enjoy all the blessings of the privilege! It is a delightful service. Our lessons and prayers for the day are all the soul can desire, or needs.

With love to all our dear friends as though named, which I will trust you to distribute in due measure to each, and in which Anne joins me.

     Your loving brother,

                Caspar Morris.

            Berlin, July 2, 1872.

We have been here several days, including one Lord's day, which was devoted exclusively to public worship, and rest in our own rooms. Palaces and gardens and some drives in the park here have been relieved by some shopping, and this morning was passed in the New Museum as Saturday had been among the picture galleries of the Old. In going to and from these places we have passed repeatedly the many imposing monuments and statues which give Berlin a distinctive character. They are numerous and very wonderful exhibitions of the power which can mould and chisel such solid materials as bronze and marble into the display of mental power and give expression, without language it is true, but with great clearness of force to the immaterial. In one case a dead marble body lies as placid on the arm of an angel as though it really were inanimate clay, while the spirit of the warrior animates, almost, the various figures representing the forms and commemorating the deeds of the heroes whom Prussia delights to honor. They are many, and as all the palaces and public buildings are clustered in one quarter of the town they make not only an individual impression, but possess the influence of a multitude.

The University is a large building directly *vis-a-vis* to the palace of the Crown Prince, and nearly opposite that of the Emperor. There the youth, as their character is being moulded, are being daily impressed by the oversight of them by their present and future rulers, and these are daily compelled to look upon the growing strength of the people, and thus each taught to respect and care for the other.

The various stores display splendid works of art for ornament as well as for domestic service, indicative of active prosperity. The men are not fine looking, though some of the women are beautiful. During the business hours all is bustle, but early in the afternoon the entire population, male and female, young and old, appears like a current in full flow; all seeking some garden at which to listen to music and drink tea, coffee or beer; where they sit or promenade all evening. Their deportment there is graceful and decorous.

In the museums we find crowds also all day, not only of strangers and cultivated citizens, but mingled with them large numbers of the labouring class; men and women. These would not have the desire to visit such places if they had not been trained by the Prussian system, which compels the education of every child; and could not gratify that desire, after it was formed, if the industry of the country was not prosperous, affording more than a bare support to the labourers.

I was very much impressed by the deportment of the collegians when I saw a large number walking amid the handsome shrubbery which ornaments the grounds about the building, as though they felt a restraint from individual ownership and consequent interest in the preservation of the beauty, and I cannot but hope that the trustees of the University of Pennsylvania may adorn the ample grounds about the new buildings, and that a sense of honor equally strong may pervade the minds of the students of my Alma Mater, so that trees now planted may shelter and afford delight to future generations of her Alumni. If our political institutions be, as we claim they are, those best suited to the development of the highest and noblest elements of human character and afford the best protection to human interests, we must prove them to be such by their results. As three of my grandchildren will be connected with the first classes to meet in those halls, I shall hope their influence shall be in the right direction. It is a great gratification to me to have them thus associated with its new era, and hope their grandchildren may walk under the shade of the trees they see planted.

The great delight of this morning was derived from the wonderful pictures of Kalbach painted on the hall of entrance to the New Museum. We enter through the Old, in front of which stands a huge basin of polished granite twenty-two feet in diameter, and some ten or twelve feet high, cut from a boulder which lay isolated on the plain thirty miles from here. On the walls supporting the ends of the wide and lofty stairs by which you ascend to the platform stand two very fine bronzes, one representing an Amazon equestrian figure contending with a leopard; all life-size and very fine in attitude. The other, a man on horse-back fighting a lion. There is not far away in the court of the old palace an equally spirited group of St. George and the Dragon, the action of the horse in which is wonderfully exhibited. The wall of the portico of the museum is covered with paintings I did not pause to examine. Within you enter upon a rotunda, around which are hung tapestry copies of the celebrated cartoons of Raphael. They were made for Henry VIII. of Great Britain. I do not know how they came here.

Passing across this rotunda and through a long hall filled with antique marbles and casts, we came to the stairway of the building erected to receive the excess of objects of interest collected by the government. The walls of this are covered by the grand epic poem by Kalbach. It is designed to represent the progress of the human race from the dispersion at Babel to the present time. The conception is grand and the execution worthy. Each picture is of colossal proportions, designed to be looked at from a distance, but each figure is finished with delicacy. In each tableau there are three principal groups in the foreground, while the other parts of the picture are filled up with accessories. In the fore-front of the first is a hideous figure mounted on a buffalo, designed to represent brutal superstition; surrounded by illustrative figures. On the left a group designed to represent the patriarchal dispensation, as attractive by its representations of the softer virtues as the other is repulsive by its hideous deformity. On the right is another group designed to represent the chivalric and martial virtues, as symbolic of the German or Indian race and its destinies. There are many very impressive episodes in the filling up of the picture. The second picture is designed to represent the influence of Greek poetry and letters; the third, the destruction of Jerusalem, in which all the horrors of Divine judgment for the failure to accomplish the mission entrusted to the patriarchal dispensation, are exhibited. The fourth is designed to represent the progress of Europe under the figure of the battle of the Huns. The fifth, the re-introduction of the Christian influence, in the crusaders before Jerusalem. Godfrey offers his crown to our Lord as true King, while Tancred, Rinaldo, Armida, Peter the Hermit, and other admirable figures fill up the three groups. Then comes the epoch of the Reformation as the highest step of progress, with Luther in the fore-centre and my picture of Leonardo da Vinci in the back-ground as the dim germ of light. It would be impossible to do justice to this grand painting by any analysis short of a volume of notes and comments embracing the history of art and science in their influence on civilization and religion.

We are thirsting for the truth of Luther and the cradle of the Reformation.

Yours hastily, but lovingly,

CASPAR MORRIS.

BERLIN, July 4, 1872.

My Dear Children:

We have just returned from our pilgrimage-like excursion to Wittenburg, the cradle of the Reformation; the place at which the monk of Erfurt endured the suffering of the terrors of the law of God; the place at which he heard the first whisper of peace through the Covenant of Grace, in the "New Testament of our Lord Jesus Christ," from the lips of the old monk; and where, in the library of his convent, he found that word of God, which he opened and held up, not to his townsmen or countrymen only, but to the world. (*This is, I believe, an error; he was not here, but at Erfurt.*) This is the place at which, with his characteristic boldness, he attached his Theses against indulgences to the door of the Schloss Kirche, opening on the principal Platz of the town. The place where, with equal boldness, he exhibited his conviction of the false principle which led to vows of celibacy, by his marriage with his Catharine. We were in the room in which he lived, and in it still stands the table at which he sat and talked with

Justus Jonas and Bugenhausen and Melancthon; over which he held earnest discussions with Erasmus; the table which has been made so familiar to childhood as that on which stood the celebrated Christmas tree around which his children were gathered.

There stand in the old window the seats on which he and his Catharine sat; and the stove built of terra cotta, and ornamented by figures of his own devising, representing Geometry, Mathematics, Astronomy, not leaving without a distinguished place of honor his much-loved music. The room which has resounded so often with the rich melody of his powerful voice as it poured out the expression of his faith in his favourite words, "Ein feste burg ist Gott;" the room in which, like Jacob, he wrestled in prayer; struggled in fierce conflict with the adversary of souls, and in which he realized the rich blessing of that peace which passeth understanding, by which his soul was refreshed and strengthened for his conflicts with man.

It was a high privilege to sit at that table and recall the general impression of all those great councils whose influence, though for a time (it may be) have been perverted and seemingly transferred to evil, is yet destined to accomplish grand results. The struggle between light and darkness, and good and evil, God and the devil, is not yet ended. When it is, good will prevail, and evil be forever crushed beyond the possibility of raising any of those hydra-heads which still shoot out from the trunk, more numerous than those which have been cut off. We must not be deterred from ever-repeated blows, however much the evils may apparently be multiplied by the very effort at extermination. Jesus is "the Truth," and even heathen wisdom could discern, "Magna est veritas et prævalebit."

The building had been a convent or monastery, and was appropriated by the Elector to educational purposes. He founded and endowed a university, of which he made Luther one of the professors, and here he and Melancthon closed their lives. We visited the Schloss Kirche, to the door of which he nailed his Theses or propositions in opposition to indulgences; and saw there the graves of the two great reformers, on which some Americans had deposited fresh bouquets of flowers a day or two before our visit. They were still beautiful, and as we saw elsewhere the names of the Rev. Herrick Johnson and Mrs. Johnson, we gave them the credit of this token of respect for the truth and honor to its champions.

The interior of the church remains in appearance as it was at the time of Luther's death, having been restored since it was used as a barrack by the French army, who destroyed much of the woodwork, including the doors of entrance. They have been replaced by bronze doors, on the exterior of which are cast in raised letters the celebrated Theses.

We saw Luther's "Missal" and the frame of the hour-glass by which he regulated the length of his discourses. The old pulpit was destroyed by the French, but it was a pleasure to sit on one of the benches and look at the spot at which the great preacher had stood, and from which he had poured forth those energetic words which accompanied by Divine power, had accomplished such marvellous results.

Full length portraits of Luther and Melancthon and the two electors, "the wise" and "the steady," who had held up his hands by their support, painted by Cranach, are on the walls. The house of Cranach, which was destroyed by fire, is being rebuilt at present. That of Melancthon remains as it was—one of the best in the place. The university is now undergoing repairs, but the room of Luther is left with the same quaint ornaments on the walls and the same windows, floor, and doors, as when he occupied it. The guide gave us each a fragment of the floor of the room occupied by Catharine and the family, which is being renewed, and, as your mother sat in Luther's chair, she observed that some vandal lover of relics had been cutting off a slice and had left a portion hanging, which she appropriated, though certainly she would have been the last to be guilty of the profanation of the relic by cutting it herself.

Wittenburg is a quaint-looking, quiet old place enclosed by strong fortifications, which withstood a siege, by the French, of ten months. I walked around the Rathhouse and Stadt Kirche, which, like the dwelling houses and market place, remain unchanged. Many curious old monuments and monumental inscriptions are on the walls of the church, among them one to a daughter of Bugenhausen.

Just outside the fortifications we were shown a young and vigorous oak tree planted on the same spot where an older tree, now decayed, had stood to mark the spot at which Luther publicly burned the Bull of the Pope excommunicating him as a heretic. I bought small Parian busts of Luther and Melancthon, and some photographs, as memorials of the visit; which was filled with unalloyed satisfaction.

On our way we passed the spot at which the knight, who had purchased indulgence for a sin he designed committing, robbed Tetzel of his box containing the sums he had collected by the sale of indulgences. The box and one of the papers are still shown in a neighboring church. It was a rather forcible and *just* (?) comment on the absurdity and wickedness of the system. We saw notices of *"Plenary indulgence"* in consideration of a certain number of prayers and masses to be said and paid for on *almost every Romish church* we entered in Italy. The doctrine that the priesthood is possessed of the power to give indulgence, or "relief from the penal sufferings of purgatory" is a logical result of the claim that man can merit reward at the hands of God. If I can by my own merits earn my own salvation I can do more than is necessary. If more than is necessary, the surplus is my own, which I can dispose of as I please; and if I am a saint, I may give my merits to the store of the Church, and the Church may sell that treasure to another and use the money for its own purposes.

The entire distance from Wittenburg to Berlin is a wide plain of sand; part of it uncultivated and part planted with pine and birch trees, which never attain any size; and that which is cultivated yielding so little in return for the toil of the husbandman that one can hardly understand why it is tilled. Rye and potatoes are the chief crops; the rye about a foot or eighteen inches high, with small heads, now ready for cutting; and the potatoes very small and covered with blossoms, till half the surface of the entire country looks like a flower bed. There are no partition arrangements of any kind; the only division being into patches of rye, potatoes and barley, with here and there a lupin field in blossom, looking like an immense plantation of dandelions in full bloom. There are *no* houses, so that you wonder by what process the land has been ploughed and the crop put in, and though it is now fully ripe it is only here and there you see any of it harvested.

The towns lie at some distance from the railroad, and often there is literally nothing to meet the eye which gives an idea of the presence of man or beast, except the *dwarfed* crops, looking as though it might be fairy-land. The perfect cleanliness and freedom from weeds and brambles would favor that impression. And yet *this is Brandenburg:* the germ from which has been developed that mighty power which now commands the destinies of so many nations. This fact, under our present observation, may strengthen our faith in the records of sacred history. God does not put down one and lift up another nation because of their greatness and worth, but according to His own purpose; that we may learn that all might and power and wisdom are His, and as each nation fulfills its mission, or fails in the performance of it, He transfers the trust to another.

The more closely I scrutinize the intricate combinations of human interest, the more clearly I see the evidences of divine wisdom controlling and guiding all. The same principle is applicable to the concerns of our individual relations; and I adopt fully the idea of that philosophy which sees "God in all," but it is not (as I fear too many do) as a mere influence pervading everything and all space, but as an omniscient, omnipotent, self-existing God, loving *me* and bringing to bear on myself the wisdom and power which made, and upholds, and governs all.

July 5th.

We yesterday drove to the Royal Berlin Iron Foundry; in which I was disappointed. Of course iron moulding and casting is pretty much the same process everywhere; but I did not find the museum so large as I expected. There are some very long and fine blooms and specimens of pig-iron from various parts of the Kingdom of Prussia, and a few fine castings of works of art, and many implements of industry. There are also good collections of specimens of ores of iron, and lead, and coal. There was one copy of Da Vinci's Last Supper; a fine specimen of delicate casting in iron, the exact counterpart of one your Uncle Stephen imported nearly fifty years ago, and which was borrowed from him by an artist, who never returned it. There were some copies of bronzes, on which the ornaments were very fine and clean-cut; and there were machines for making rifled cannon shot, and for testing the tenacity of iron, and some well-toned bells. You may ask what more could be expected, and I should find it difficult to reply; and yet my imagination had fancied something more regal in its extent and arrangements. I neglected to mention an extensive display of salt in its native condition, and in its various forms of potash and soda produced from it, as well as in its different stages of manufacture.

From there I took your uncle to see the beautiful little Augusta Hospital, and the rest of the day was spent in fruitless efforts to get into the palace, etc. Your mother and I are sick as sea-sickness of them, but we get into the carriages and follow where we are led. Happily for us we could not get into either of them, so the morning was spent driving from one to the other, and finally to a distant private collection of pictures, which did not contain any that were worthy of note.

In the afternoon we had as usual a drive, and in the evening were delighted by a visit from William H. and Sally Morris, both looking in perfect health and as happy and as gay as the most loving bride and groom in the very honeymoon of their first excursion could desire to be, which is saying more than can always be said of what they are.

We had received our letters at dinner time, all so full of causes of thankfulness. While we regret exceedingly that dear Hannah should require such a sacrifice as Galloway must make in leaving his business, that feeling is balanced by gratitude to the Giver of every good gift that he is able, even at a sacrifice, to give her the benefit which we trust she will derive from the voyage and travel; and our pleasure in meeting them will be very great. When and where it will be we cannot say. I shall write to Galloway to meet him on their landing, giving him as nearly as we can our route and the dates at which we shall be at certain places, in order that they may cross over to the Continent and join us if they choose. Brother and sisters all express their wish to have them do so. I think myself they will see more by moving *independently*. Much time and strength are often spent in discussing the plans to accommodate the views and wishes of the various members of the party which could be spent by each individual more advantageously if alone. I would advise them to go up the Rhine, take a short trip through Switzerland, and return to Paris about the time we shall get there, and cross again to England and Wales and Scotland with us. There we can move entirely freely. That will give them about the length of time usually spent by British tourists in a summer trip to Switzerland.

Your mother and myself have made no purchases in any of these capitals, and there will be time for us to execute any commissions you may send to us in England, where we can go to stores in which we can make our wants understood. Friezier's time, of course, is fully occupied with others, and we *never* could do anything when disturbed by crowds of observers in our own shops, much less where there is the additional difficulty of speaking in a language imperfectly understood or by means of an interpreter who could not enter into our reasons or the feelings which govern a choice. Do not hesitate to send us any commissions you may desire executed there.

The weather here is cloudy, sometimes a little rain falls, but it is pleasanter than hot summer suns would be. Friezier has just summoned us to the carriages. I asked him where we were going, to which he replied, I cannot tell. So we must bid you farewell and start out.

Your loving father,
CASPAR MORRIS.

BERLIN, July 5, 1872.

My Dear Child:

Yesterday we received letters from home, and the news, though not entirely unexpected, that Gall. and Han. will sail about this time; we are all *very glad*, and your father and I are strongly tempted to run off and meet them in London. We certainly would do it if we could get off without a great stir in the camp, but I think we will have to exercise some patience and let *them* join us, though it will be hard to do it, especially as we will be going over ground *we* would rather avoid. From here we go to Dresden, thence to Ratisbon, then to Salzburg, and we think they may be able to catch us either there or in Munich.

DRESDEN, 7th.

If you could only see how I have to write, you would make every allowance for the incoherency. It is by snatches, and often in great haste, so as to get my scrawls into your father's envelopes, for you know he is always prompt, and can drop down on all occasions and write while I am taking off bonnet, etc. But enough of all this; I know you do not expect much from me, so I will send the letters.

Afternoon.

I will try again. Yesterday on reaching here we found letters from Gall., and so now we learn they ought to reach Liverpool on Tuesday. I can hardly tell you how impatient we are to see them. Of course we have written to them our whereabouts, and suppose in about two weeks they may join us. I have no doubt it will be a good thing for Hannah, but I know, too, it must have been a great trial for her to leave the children, although the arrangements they have been able to make are most satisfactory. I shall urge Gall. and Han. to go on with their travels entirely independent of us. I am sure they can accomplish more with much less fatigue when there are not so many to consult and accommodate.

We spent rather more than a week at Berlin very pleasantly, making an excursion to Wittenburg one day ; a very quaint old town where Luther and Melancthon lived. We visited their places of residence, also the former's church, which remains pretty much as it was. In it both were interred. It was a pouring rainy day, and no carriages were to be had in that small old place, but the one omnibus, calculated with squeezing to carry six, and as we were nine it was a tight fit, but we took it merrily and enjoyed the day, and were glad to see many things that had been used by Luther, and to visit the spot under an oak tree where he burned the "Papal Bull."

I looked anxiously for an acorn as a relic, but not one could be found, so I have to content myself with a little piece of the floor of his room, a splinter off his chair, and a few photographs. The last we bought, but the former the guide gave us.

In Berlin we were kept busy visiting picture galleries, museums, palaces, iron foundries, botanical and zoological gardens, etc., and drives of an afternoon, and some shopping, but we did but very little of that. It is so difficult to do any when you do not understand the language, though I think I could soon learn German. I found I was learning to read the signs in riding. Ask the children what *Handschuhe* means. You may also tell them I had remembered in Paris to get your aunts (not being able to go myself) to get some gloves. but oh, I am so tried about them ; they are good for nothing ; but as my foot is getting well and we are going back there, I shall try myself on our return.

I walked to church this morning with your father, as the distance was short, and we were scarce seated before Will. and Sally came and sat beside us. They had come on from Berlin last night. Tried to get into the hotel we were in about 1 o'clock, but it was full, and I am sorry we are not to be longer here, as it is so nice to see home people. After service who should speak to them but Miss Wade, Pattie Horning's old pupil ! Mr. and Mrs. Wade have been here a year ; so you see we stumble on acquaintances wherever we go.

We were very glad to get your two letters ; one mentioned Miss Randall's visit and the favourable impression. I do hope she is the right person for Murray. None of you say when they will be married. I hope soon.

In your last letter you tell of Tom Neale having varioloid, and I feel anxious to hear again. It is a great pity to have that disease introduced into your neighborhood ; I very much fear it will spread, for those people will not be careful.

I looked at Berlin, at worsted work cushions, and did get some, but I cannot see that they are any better and prettier than Mrs. Iander's, and certainly will not cost less, if duty is to be paid on them ; I think I shall have to put a few stitches in each to prevent, just as we are told to wear each article we want to take in, even gloves ; twelve pairs being allowed only.

I am so glad to hear from you all that little Harry is so hearty a little fellow ; and such a pet, too. I hope the young gentleman had such a fright that will prevent his running off again. It was well he took the road and not the bank. I suppose you are enjoying the bathing now. It is warm now here, though not oppressive. I have on your barege to-day. I have only worn it three times, however, in the now almost year.

Oh! how badly I felt this time last year; and have we not *much* cause for thankfulness when we look back and see all we have come through, and take courage for the future? Indeed, I do try; and three months will soon be over. We are both well and able to enjoy much, though sometimes we are very tired and reminded we are not young.

We shall be here until Thursday, 11th. Then to Prague; and to Ratisbon on Saturday, 13th, and by the 15th or 17th Salzburg. Then they will be making excursions. I shall avoid being away from the hotel, as G. and H. may join us there. I wish the girls could have come over with G. and H., but such wishes are vain; the expense would have been too great. But I would have loved to have had them. Tell them, with my love, that when I was at their age there was no more probability of my *ever* coming than there is now of theirs; so have patience. But I do enjoin on them to study the languages—the want of that knowledge is a constant stumbling-block—French and German.

I note the favourable account of the wheat, and do hope it is going now to improve. From Berlin here we came through hundreds of acres of wheat—very thin; ripe, and some being cut. The Germans from these parts would not make a mistake by going over to America, except that in all the towns there are most ample provisions made for recreation. Many very large gardens or parks, with abundance of shade and seats for all classes, are frequented by all, for refreshment of mind and body; and every afternoon from 6 o'clock good fine music is in most of them. All are free; those who choose order a cup of tea or a glass of beer. Just see the advantage over any of our cities; and, as it is light until 10 o'clock, they are open until then. Our men and women, too, have not the time, but here they seem to have; they are very many of them mechanics, with their wives and children. I suppose the eight-hour system prevails. Well, I am not surprised at their wanting to be at home.

July 8th.

A bright summer morning finds us all well. William and Sally spent last evening with us, and we are to move off in a body to see most extraordinary things to-day; they having been here before, and are quite a help to us. I must not omit telling you the Queen of Holland vacated the suite of apartments we are now occupying, I hear, before we came in them. They are very fine—a drawing-room, elegantly furnished, and very large; four chambers, two on either side and communicating, each twenty feet square, and sumptuously arranged. But I don't find all the necessaries to our comfort, and shall be quite willing to come down to our own way of living.

I imagine you all in the midst of efforts to get off somewhere. If Cousin Emily is with you, share this with her.

With much love from us both to you all, yours most truly and affectionately.

A. C. MORRIS.

Much love to them all at the Ridge. I do hope they will not take varioloid. We have escaped so often in our house that I hardly think they will. Four times have we had it in our house.

DRESDEN, July 8, 1872.

My Dear Son:

I was annoyed and disturbed this morning by the banker here, after having entered a draft on my letter of credit, discovering it had expired on the 1st of July. Your uncle will let me have what I need, but that is not pleasant, and you will remember that the sum entered on the face of the letter here was cancelled by the banker himself, and not paid to me. Please attend at once to the extension of the letter till the 1st of November. I have only drawn £370 of the £2000. The last was at Paris, June 8, for £40.

The weather now is very warm. We shall remain here some four or five days, and then make our way to the mountains of the Tyrol. I have written to your brother Galloway, inviting him to join us there; and either remain with us or unite with his cousins, William and Sally, who are now going to Vienna, and will meet us at Salzburg.

We have great cause for thankfulness that we escaped safely from the Holy Land. Two parties whom we left there have suffered. One from being overturned in the *diligence* coming from Damascus to Beyroot; a lady had her collar-bone broken and sat eight hours in wet clothing. One of the others had fever. Both were detained six weeks at Beyroot. Our lives are in better hands than our own, and somewhere we must lay them down. May we be found ready whenever, wherever and however it may be.

Thank Effingham for his letter, to which I will reply some day. Just now the incidents of travel are thick. The number of my letter is $\frac{B}{K}$ 1283, date, July 1, 1871; limit, one year; sum, £2000. With love to Annie and Mrs. Buckley.

Your affectionate father,
CASPAR MORRIS.

Evening.

You may judge of my annoyance when I came too late for the mail and found that in enclosing my envelope to you I had omitted the accompanying half sheet, for which only it was sent. You must have been surprised on opening it to find only the pencil note your mother wrote while sitting this morning in the picture gallery. Your Uncle Wistar kindly offers to furnish me any money your mother and I may desire to spend. It is especially unpleasant, as we had designed making some purchases at this place. It is very happy for us that we had not separated from the party, as in that case we should have been in a very ugly position.

In one of his late letters your Uncle Galloway mentions having bought the usual supply of hams and coal for Ivy Neck. I will thank you to pay him for them, and any other charges he may have on my account.

Tuesday morning.

We find the weather very oppressive, but not approaching to that we see reported for you, as the telegram of the 6th speaks of two hundred deaths from one thousand cases of sunstroke in New York. Our anxiety about the family at Ivy Neck is increased by the news of small-pox at the Ridge. But we seek for grace to confide in the Divine protection, and know that our Heavenly Father will not suffer us to be tempted above that we are able to bear, as He supplies the strength as well as orders the trial. With renewed love to Annie and Mrs. Buckley, and all our friends; Cousins Martha and Sarah, and Catherine Brown, especially,

Your loving father,

CASPAR MORRIS.

DRESDEN, July, 1872.

My Dear Harry (Henry M. Murray.—Eds.) :

You asked, some time ago, what was the secret of the fertility I saw everywhere, and I replied that the entire produce of the soil was apparently restored to it, the people who tilled the land living like the animals they drove in the ploughs. During the last fortnight we have been passing over a country which has no token of fertility about it. If you can imagine yourself traveling through the lightest and thinnest part of Locust Point field by railroad hour after hour *for days*, you may form some idea of the country around Berlin, in the kingdom of Prussia. Buckwheat in flower about three inches high, rye not over a foot or eighteen inches, grass-fields which looked as if they had been shaven, and you could scarce see the little hay cocks. Potatoes in flower, showing that they had their full growth of vine, only a few inches high,—these were the crops where the land was tilled; much of it was not; and a mere waste sandy plain or covered with pines, like the *Shades of Death*, as they used to call the Piny Woods between Annapolis and Baltimore. You cannot conceive how any one can live. Indeed, you see no sign of there being any population except the poor crops. There are no houses out of the towns, and these are widely separated. You thus see there are some parts of the world worse than our own.

In Holland and Belgium, where the crops are so luxuriant, they dredge the canals, into which everything drains from the fields and towns, and apply the mud as manure. Their cattle are numerous and very fine; and there are no scorching suns to bake the soil. I have yet to see any country more favored than our own, and your Uncle Wistar says he is much better reconciled to our crops than he was before he saw those of Europe.

The horses of Berlin are very poor creatures; they have neither size, shape nor action, and are badly kept. This strikes one very forcibly after having seen the grace of the Arab at Constantinople, the high breeding and great power, and elegant training of those of Paris, and the immense size and power and fatness of those of Belgium and Holland. The men of Berlin and that vicinity are not imposing in appearance or carriage. Since we reached Saxony we have been better pleased. The valley of the Elbe is richer, and this place gives promise of being very pleasant.

Please remember me to James and Sally and Samuel and your brothers. I feel very sorry to learn that small-pox has reached your neighborhood, and hope that ere this reaches you *all* your family and servants have been re-vaccinated. No matter how recently it was done it should be repeated whenever there is such an epidemic as that now among you.

Tell the children their letters have given us very great pleasure, and we hope to find them all very good and happy when we reach home, when we shall of course soon get to Ivy Neck. We have seen nothing which could surpass it if we had the money to expend on its improvement; which gives such elegance to many of those which attract our notice here. A steam engine to pump up water and distribute it wherever you wish and freely as you need, would make grass and grain grow anywhere.

Your loving father,

CASPAR MORRIS.

DRESDEN, July 8, 1872.

My Dear Cornelia; and from her down to Harry, Jr.:

As I have a few moments unoccupied while waiting to be called to breakfast, I will kiss each of you across this wide continent of Europe and the stormy Atlantic. It would be much sweeter if I could squeeze you in my arms while doing so.

A few days ago your grandmother and I stood beside Luther's table and sat in Luther's chair, beside Luther's stove, in the room occupied by the great Reformer, when he was professor in the college at Wittenberg. I think there is a life of Luther in my library, illustrated, in which you will find an engraving of this very room, which remains now just as it was three hundred years ago. So if you look at that picture you may see the representation of a room and chair in which your dear grandmother sat on the 3d of July, 1872. It is the same table and room which are represented in some of the children's books, with a Christmas tree on it, and Luther's children standing delighted while he invites them to come and help themselves.

In the same town we saw the church against the door of which he nailed his arguments about the folly of selling people pardon for their sins against God. We also passed through the district in which a man who had bought a pardon for a sin he *intended to do*, waylaid Tetzel, the monk, who had sold it to him for the Pope, and who had collected a larger sum by such sales, and robbed him of all his treasure. The box is shown still, and also one of the papers which promised pardon. I have seen several of them ; and even now we see pasted at the doors of the churches a promise of deliverance from purgatory in return for a certain number of prayers or masses said in the church. Every sign about us here convinces me more fully that we shall see a struggle between the Pope and the Jesuits on one side and the people on the other before many years, perhaps before one passes.

Your loving grandfather,

CASPAR MORRIS.

PICTURE GALLERY, BERLIN, July 5, 1872.

My Dear Children :

As I cannot wander around here and halt over picture after picture, although there are some very attractive ones, I will talk to you all at home for a while and must begin with what is uppermost—our pleasure at the prospect of seeing Gall. and Han. so soon. We heard yesterday they will sail to-morrow. Our first impulse was to rush right off and meet them in London or Liverpool, but we have taken a night to think it all over (I did so literally), and we find, all things being considered, it is best not, but give them opportunity to join us if they choose immediately on landing. They will then meet Will. and Sally, and perhaps go off together. I cannot advise their staying with us ; they would lose much time. We are all well and getting along nicely, but cannot even propose separation. They all want Gall. and Han. to come to us.

Since my last to you all, we spent a day delightfully in a visit to Wittenberg (I used to spell it Wurtemberg, but I was wrong). We were in Luther's house, sat in his chair; at his table on which he wrote; were in his church where he and Melanchthon were buried; saw Luther's books, hour-glass, etc., etc. It is a quaint old town. Saw Melanchthon's house also, and the monuments erected to their memory. Then went to the oak tree under which Luther burned the Papal Bull; got a few photographs and relics and returned to Berlin the same day.

Last evening who should surprise us by walking in, but Will. and Sally? It was a real pleasure, I assure you, and just now I raised my eyes and found they were here, without any concert.

THE MUSEUM, DRESDEN, July 8th.

I find I must sit down and let all who wish walk around. I am told there are miles of pictures here, and I believe I have seen many very beautiful ones, and sat and enjoyed Raphael's "Madonna;" it is said to be the finest in the world. We have been this morning to visit the "Green Vault," and see principally the finest collection of jewels in the world; the most exquisite ivory carvings, bronzes, etc.; much silver and gold richly chased; and what I call a princely Baby House, representing "The Grand Mogul" sitting in state on his throne, and two thousand of his subjects surrounding, all in rich attire. Two elephants of precious stones equipped and bearing some grandees to the palace, besides some in beautiful little palanquins.

Will. and Sally are here with us and it adds greatly to our pleasure, although they will move on independently of us, as their time is short. Yesterday your father and I were scarce seated in church, when they came in and sat besides us; they had arrived in the night from Berlin, and we were not aware of their being here at all, but it was very pleasant to have them with us—only sorry they could not get into the same hotel.

I find your father about to mail a letter, so in great haste close, with much love to all. Thank Tyson and Eff. for their letters; both came to hand. We are looking with great pleasure to seeing Gall. and Han.; shall watch for their arrival from to-morrow.

Yours most affectionately,

A. C. MORRIS.

DRESDEN, July 9, 1872.

My Dear Children:

Summer is now on us with a witness, and we wish ourselves out of reach of picture galleries, which are all close, oppressive halls, and shopping, which is a chafing and heating occupation when one does not know what one wants, nor (if they did) how to ask for it. So we are all quite ready to abandon capitals and seek the retirement of private life in some out-of-the-way place. Meanwhile some dresses are being made by a *man* here for your Aunts Hannah and Jane; for which we must remain till to-morrow evening.

This place is much pleasanter than Berlin, and I do not wonder that those who exile themselves should choose it as a winter residence. The picture gallery contains some of the choicest specimens of art; the world-renowned Sistine Madonna of Raphael alone is worth coming here to see, and some Correggios, and Sassoferratas, and Carlo Dolces, and Claude Lorraines, are very beautiful and attractive. Then there is a Madonna of Holbein which is very fine, and I found some portraits of Melanchthon and Luther by their friend Cranach. One of Melanchthon, taken after death, is very impressive. It has also inscribed beneath it, by the same friendly hand that fixed the heavenly expression of the features, the record of his age and cause of his death, an acute fever, in the seventh paroxysm of which he died; his last words being the Latin version of the text, "My sheep shall never perish, for none can ever pluck them from My Father's hands." The galleries are very extensive, and well supply a delightful place of resort for a lover of art, to which one might return day after day. In the evening we drove, stopping at a garden where we heard some music, decidedly the finest I have heard this side the Atlantic, from the Midsummer Night's Dream, a wedding march; an aria from the Magic Flute; and a Rondo of Weber, and a piece from Mozart. Seated under shady trees in our comfortable carriages, it was the height of luxury for a warm afternoon, and we were allowed to remain at a position where distance lent enchantment to that which was attractive anywhere.

One afternoon we went to a curious mechanical exhibition of musical instruments. There were eight or nine large instruments constructed on the same principle as the common musical boxes, with springs and cylinders, on which the airs are arranged in points, but they have flute, and hautboys, and clarionet accompaniments, producing all the effects of an orchestra, and may be arranged to play any number of pieces, as the cylinders are movable. The application of galvanism to the piano was also shown. The music is arranged on a sheet of stiff paper by piercing it with holes corresponding to the keys to be touched. This rolls around a cylinder, which is turned like that in the magnetic telegraph. The communication is cut off as the cylinder rolls around at the points, and you see the keys on the key-board of the piano moving simultaneously. An operator may thus perform on a piano from an adjoining apartment. There was also a magic trumpeter, who sounded his own praises quite melodiously. These perform every afternoon at a given hour, after which visitors have an opportunity to order musical boxes at every price from a child's toy to snuff-boxes with little birds in the lid which spring out, turn around, and shake their wings, while the box warbles sweet notes; or Alaudions or Choralaudions at $1000 each. There is an orchestrion which I should be sorry to live next door to, if the owner were disposed to keep it constantly grinding. It is as good as a band any day.

Among the most celebrated wonders of Dresden are the treasures of the Green Vault. I have already told you I am satiated with jewels, and I should fear to disgust you if I were to attempt to describe the riches here displayed. The silver mines of Saxony made it one of the richest kingdoms of Europe before the discovery of those of America caused the power which gold and silver possessed to be transferred to Spain. The Saxon kings collected rich stores of gems, which are now displayed, and afford some revenue, as the place is crowded with visitors, each of whom pays a fee for the sight of carved ivory, and bronze, and jewels. There are some curious and valuable works of ancient art among them.

We drove around the environs, among the beautiful dwellings occupied by the English and Americans, who live here in sufficient number to sustain two English and a Scotch church, and there is also an American Episcopal congregation. The houses are elegant, and surrounded by neat gardens. Many, however, are divided between two families, and many families live in the town, occupying rooms on the upper floors. Wages are very low, and the general cost of living about two-thirds what the same comfort would cost at home.

Mr. Wade, whom we met and who has been here some months, says it is a very bad place to bring or send boys to be educated, and that American boys have a bad reputation, so that many teachers refuse positively to receive them, as one would spoil a whole school, and others charge double the rates at which they take German boys. The discipline of German families is much more rigid than it is with us. Mr. Wade mentioned that the parents of one boy who occasionally visited at his apartments had prohibited his visits on the score that he was rendered refractory at home by the sight of the greater liberty allowed at Mr. Wade's.

We have got again into a region where the horses are better. Those of Berlin were wretched creatures, misshapen and badly kept. Here they are of better breed and large, and well-groomed and fed, and we have seen some good oxen. As there are no fences or hedges (we see wheat and oat fields lying open to the road directly alongside the most frequented drives so soon as we pass the *thickly* built streets), no cattle graze in or are driven without yokes or halters. I saw a fine ox driven by reins fastened to his forelegs just above the hoofs and passed through a ring attached to a belt passing around his body. By this arrangement he could be tripped by one or both forefeet and brought to his knees in a moment if he manifested any obstinacy.

Both here and at Berlin we have been amused by the peculiar costume of many nurses carrying children. It appears they all come from one place, Altenburg, the women of which have a high reputation as nurses, and devote themselves especially to that service. The head-dress is white and very large; with a scarlet petticoat and black bodice and short, white sleeves. There are so many of them in this peculiar costume, each with a young child under her care, that they do not attract attention except from strangers. The infantile and juvenile population of Germany is in large proportion to the adult, and all are educated. You see troops of children, boys and girls, each with a knapsack strapped to the shoulders carrying their books, marching to school like soldiers to drill; and cab drivers and street messengers read and write well.

At Wittenberg, and also here and at the little towns we passed, we saw many wagons which reminded me of the description given of the Germans in the days of the Roman invasion; mere skeleton or framework of wood with wicker or basket-work sides and ends and seats. Some painted and some not. The country people ride in them without any springs, and generally with one horse harnessed to the one side of a central pole instead of in shafts.

Everything is made strong and durable, and thus prevents the change of fashion. The same article of dress, or furniture, or equipage which was used by the father or mother is transmitted to the son or daughter, and there is no redundancy of means to enable them to lay aside the old, and get new, unnecessarily. Hence the unchangeable habits of the people.

July 10th.

A very heavy storm attended by lightning and thunder passed over us during the night, and has made thick winter clothing to-day as necessary as yesterday it was oppressive. We have spent the day in the pursuit each of his or her own taste; have walked about the town looking at the stores, and then took a final look at the grand pictures by Correggio, Murillo, Holbein, Raphael, Carlo Dolce, Sassaferato, Batano and the Gerard Dows, Ruysdall and Claude Lorraine and Teniers.

This afternoon we are to drive; and start at 4 A.M. for a thirteen hours' railroad ride to Ratisbon, where we stay one day, and then on Saturday go to Gmunden, where we spend the Lord's day quietly, after which to Salzburg, where we hope to hear something of Galloway and Hannah.

The pictures are very attractive to me, though many of them have points which are unpleasant, abating the delight which is caused by the entire conception, and in others the conception is offensive while some of the parts are beautiful. They vary, too, greatly in the style. Some depend for their effectiveness on boldness of conception and strong colors, while others give delight from the perfection with which the most minute detail is finished. In this gallery every taste may find gratification, but I still repeat my remark about Rubens. There are many of his productions here, but they only confirm my opinion. He was a disgrace to art!

Evening.

We have enjoyed this evening the perfect luxury of delight in a drive of some hours through the beautiful Park of Dresden, with its grand old oaks, its charming glades, its moss-grown nooks, its long avenues of trees, and neat shrubberies. It is as attractive as any such place we have seen, and happily free from the nuisance of stagnant pools and ditches miscalled lakes and streams. Since tea I have strolled upon the old ramparts amid a crowd of artisans enjoying the soft air, the moonlight and the music. We are now all packed and preparing to retire for some rest before our morning start. We all agree that Dresden is before Berlin as a place of resort for the traveler. I met Virginia Smith this afternoon; looking well.

With dearest love to all, your affectionate father,

CASPAR MORRIS.

RATISBON, July 11, 1872.

My Dear Children:

After a very hard day's ride of thirteen hours, leaving Dresden at 4 A.M. (having risen before 3), we arrived here after 5 P.M. The rails are laid too wide for the cars, and though the road appears to be in perfect order, the lateral motion was very annoying and fatiguing. The disturbed night made the day seem long, and the heat was oppressive; so that we "came in rather jaded."

The country is rich and fertile and highly cultivated; swelling bosoms spreading their luxuriant fields of wheat, rye, oats, potatoes and hops to the sun. In some places the grass was mowed and being cured; while the grain crop was still green. In others they were reaping the wheat and rye. Some districts are also rich in minerals, iron, silver and copper; others have very large manufacturing establishments of various kinds. There are extensive machine-shops and iron works as well as smelting furnaces; and it is said that the population reaches five hundred per square mile. Much of it is collected in towns and villages lying at short distances from the railroad which appears to run along a ridge, so that we saw the towns at a little distance. Between 5 and 6 A.M. the roads were thronged by labourers going out to their daily work.

The entire absence of hedges or fences, and the universal culture of the varied surface, is very imposing. The *roadsides* are planted with *fruit* trees, on which the fruit hangs unmolested, even near the great towns. The houses are neat and comfortable in appearance; very many of them have peculiarly-formed windows in the tile roofs, looking so like eyes under eyebrows that I am sure it was the intention they should have that effect. They are more picturesque than comfortable, as they can admit but little light, and no air, to the garret rooms, which in summer must be excessively hot. There is some peat bog, by the way, which is cultivated where it is not being cut for firing, and appears to yield a very fair crop, though not at all equal to the upland.

Where the cereals and grasses will not repay labour, firs and pines are planted ; and we passed a royal college for the instruction of pupils in the art of planting and cultivating timber. It is interesting to see the immense plantations in various stages of growth, from a foot high to large trees. When they attain full size they are cut by acres, and every branch and leaf is carefully gathered and tied up in fagots and sold for fire-wood. These plantations are always of fir or pine, and the rich, dark-green patches on the hillsides, surrounded by the various paler green and yellow tints of the grass and grain, add greatly to the beauty of the landscape. The valley of the Danube, in which this town stands, is here wide and fertile and highly cultivated.

We were all too weary to make any observations on the town, which is antiquated but not imposing, so far as we could judge from the streets through which we were driven to the hotel, which is straggling, with huge rooms and thick walls and galleries running outside, around the court-yard, on which the stable opens. There is a total want of comfort in the appearance.

12th.

A good night's rest has refreshed your mother and myself. We have not yet seen any of the party. I sallied out of our chamber to seek for the *Times*, and look in it for news of the "Calabria,"* but found the only newspaper in the English language taken here is Frank Leslie's *Illustrated Journal*. This will do to *brag* on along with the fact of the correspondent of the New York *Herald* having succeeded in interviewing Dr. Livingstone at "Unanamyambigwee," or some such unpronounceable place in the heart of Africa, while geographical societies and government commissions were spending thousands of pounds and much talk and discussion about the possibility of his being still alive.

None of you can read history without meeting with Ratisbon as the seat of the German Diet or Congress of Electors and Princes of the German Empire. Now we should say the greatest noise it makes in the world is with the whips of its drivers, who certainly have a skill in that way exceeding that even of the Neapolitans, though that is terribly annoying.

It was at this place the Crusaders took boats to float down the Danube on their way to the Holy Land. The walls of the room in which we lodge are not less than three feet thick, so that this very house might have been standing then, and occupied—who knows? —by Godfrey of Boulogne, or Henry, or Richard of England. Our thoughts are more given, just now, to Galloway and Hannah, and our hearts to the commemoration of the goodness and mercy which have watched over and preserved us during our pilgrimage to that same

* *It was by the steamer " Calabria " that G. C. and Y. P. M. were at this time crossing the ocean.*—EDS.

Holy Land during the year we have wandered by sea and by land, since this day marked in our "Soul's Enquiries" as that on which we sailed from New York. How can we be thankful enough? No human heart can. May God's good Spirit fill us with more than we can utter, and work in us more entire conformity to His holy will!

As I look at the poor women toiling along the wayside, bowed under the heavy baskets loaded with various goods, or those who are labouring in the harvest-fields, with sons and brothers away in the camp, and liable at any moment to be marched away to the field of slaughter, on account of strifes and struggles for glory and empire in which they have no interest beyond that which belongs to the enthusiasm kindled and nurtured in the camp, I am often humbled under a feeling of condemnation that I should ever have fainted under the burdens I carried and am ashamed of the selfishness which led me to seek an enjoyment so costly as that in which I am now participating and in the midst of which the temptation still presents itself to murmur if all is not unalloyed gratification. I did hope to return wiser, humbler, holier than I left, and more ready to adopt the sentiment:

> "Joy to find in every station,
> Something still to do or bear."

2 P. M.

This has been a very warm morning. We drove through ripe grain-fields to the Valhalla, a magnificent temple, built in imitation of the Parthenon at Athens, on the summit of a lofty hill about six miles from this place, and in a forest of pine and fir growing on rocky cliffs which overhang the valley of the Danube. It is a grand idea of Louis, King of Bavaria. The Valhalla, in Scandinavian mythology, is the hall in which the gods and heroes meet and feast together. The king's idea was to build a temple to the fame of Germany, in which should be placed the busts of those of her sons who had added to the glory of the German race by deeds worthy of fame, whether as statesmen and warriors, or in the more peaceful pursuits by which the knowledge and pleasure and happiness of mankind are promoted. It is a noble conception, and has been carried out grandly and appropriately. Upon the savage heights of rocky grandeur, surrounded by primeval forests, symbolizing the early history of the German people, stands the classic temple, the climax of perfection in art. From its portico the eye ranges far and wide over plains loaded with the fruits of the labour of the husbandman, and embraces in its view the cities which are thronged with artisans pursuing the industrial arts, which have been gradually developed during the ages in which man has advanced from the savage life in the forest to the builder of such shrines. On another cliff beside it frown the ruins of one of the strongholds of mediæval power, which was blown up during the Thirty Years War, which followed the era of the Reformation. Below lie the peaceful plains studded with towns, and at the distance of six miles the towers of the cathedral at Ratisbon, beside which are shown the dungeons and implements of torture which still remain, marked at every corner of the building with the crossed keys, the emblems of the *soi-disant* successors of St. Peter, who have thus transmitted to posterity, under their own seal, the story of their own shame.

But it is time I should return to the portico of the Valhalla, from which all this has been seen. It stands on the highest of three terraces, each 100 feet high, and faced with dressed marble, with flights of stairs winding up at either end, the building 218 feet long, and 100 feet wide and 60 feet high, surrounded by 60 Ionic columns, all of gray dressed marble of a very fine grain. The pediment at either end is adorned by fine sculpture in *alto relievo*, symbolical of the history of the Germans. On the one the victory of Arminius over the Roman Legions under Varus; and the other Germania receiving the tribute of honor from those States which compose the Empire.

The interior is very impressive. An oblong square hall lighted from above is lined with red marble, thickly studded with coralline fossils of a light color, giving sufficient relief to the dark color, and the light is clear and strong. The length of the hall is broken by two projections supported by white marble columns, and the height is relieved by a gallery, from which caryatides richly dressed and gilded support the roof. Each compartment has on either side a figure of Fame, in white marble, varying in attitude and expression, yet each perfectly beautiful, all the designs and execution of Rauch. The floor is paved with polished marble of several colors, in stars and various patterns.

In the floor of the first compartment you enter is inscribed in large letters of black marble inserted in a yellow marble ground with black borders—*Resolved on 1808*. In the second: *Commenced in 1830;* in the third: *Completed in 1842*. Around the walls are arranged white marble chairs of very elegant patterns, from which you may study the busts of those who are admitted to the honor of place in this Temple of Fame. These are all in white Carrara marble of life size. With Herman, Charles the V. and other warriors, are mingled, without any classification, those of Copernicus, and Herschel, and Paracelsus, and Boerhaave, and Gutenberg, and Mozart, and Gluck, and Beethoven, Catharine of Russia, Maria Theresa, and Luther, and Erasmus, and Goethe, and Schelling, and Kant—every one who has achieved for himself a title to a niche in the temple of Glory. We sat and gazed at the familiar features of old friends, as though holding conversation with the giants of mind; and *reluctantly* turned away with the feeling that Louis of Bavaria had erected for himself a Cenotaph which would be the shrine to which will resort pilgrims from every nation under heaven so long as the world endures.

Who is not debtor to these great men? If it were only Boerhaave and Luther and Gutenberg, they were enough. There they stand "alone in their glory;" occasionally visited, but always resplendent like the stars in the canopy above. St. Paul says, "Yet show I unto you a more excellent way," in which we may each become a star in the *Redeemer's crown.*

Your loving father,

CASPAR MORRIS.

RATISBON, July 12, 1872.

My Dear Children:

At the close of a very warm day, while your mother sits knitting, before retiring for the night I will resume my account of the day's observation. I wrote at dinner time a little sketch of the visit to the Valhalla.

After that I turned out to look about me here. On the front of this very house are tablets with bronze figures on them, the subjects of which I cannot decipher, and the date 1523. There are several irregular towers in the front, on one of which is a medallion stone portrait, life size, of the Emperor Charles V., surrounded by several verses in German, which record the fact that he had resided here.

Whichever way I wandered, my eyes lighted on antiquated-looking houses with projecting towers at the corners or in front, each having embrasures or loopholes, or narrow windows, as though they were designed to watch what was passing below, or places from which with crossbow or arquebuss an approaching foe might meet a hostile shot. All these houses are entered by arched ways into court-yards from which the stairs ascend to the parts which are inhabited. On the outside of one of these old towers are colossal figures of Goliath and David, the painting of which has been recently renewed. Indeed most of the houses have been recently painted or color washed, giving them an air of cleanly freshness, which contrasts strangely with their ancient form.

The Cathedral was begun in the 13th century, and in each succeeding century some addition was made, but the scaffolding still stands beside it, and the latest additions were made within the last few years. It is considered equal to any of the German cathedrals. The Protestant church is also a large and imposing structure, and in its cemetery was buried Kepler, the astronomer, who died here in 1630.

One square space in the town is called Heideplatz (*heide* meaning heathen), from the legend that in it a conflict took place between a pagan giant and a Christian champion, and the heathen, who, like Goliath, had hitherto been always victorious, was slain.

Such are the associations of these centres of ancient power, for this was once one of the most important places in Europe, and its bishop-prince wielded a power only second to that of the Emperor himself. In one corner my attention was arrested by a gothic archway over which were two projecting figures, one apparently ready to throw a stone (which he holds in his hands) on the head of any one attempting to enter. On looking around I saw crossed keys sculptured at various places on the front of the building, and consulting the guide-book found it is the Rath-house or the building in which the Diet or Congress of the Roman or German Empire formerly sat. It was built in the 14th century. The windows are filled with small circular panes of glass, and the walls of one of the chambers are hung with tapestry of the 14th century, containing the most grotesque and fantastic figures, with quaint head-dresses, riding on deer; and wild boars and men. The guide who took us around could speak and understand nothing but Dutch, and I was left to my own ability to decipher the story which no doubt beguiled the weary hours of some nunnery.

After looking at these rooms the guide motioned me to wait and left me at a door which was under the stairway. He returned with a lantern, and I followed him down into vaulted chambers below the hall, which were without any means by which light or air could be admitted. One of these was divided longitudinally by a screen of close lattice-work into two apartments of unequal size. The smaller one was provided with an easy chair for one person, and a desk and seat for another. Here were seated the judge and his secretary that without being seen they might hear and record the expressions wrung from the agonized victims of the torture which was applied to the wretched objects of suspicion in the adjoining larger division of this same apartment, thus appropriately placed in darkness below the ground. I was taken into that room where still stand the terrible implements by which the frames of human beings were crushed and mangled and strained, to wring from them confessions of their own guilt or accusations of others. I could wish to obliterate from my memory what I there saw.

From thence we were taken to a vault, so low that I could not stand in it, with an iron ring in the centre to which should be attached the chain to which was fastened the poor wretch who surely was abandoned by hope when he entered there. A small hole in the wall through which his food could be thrust in was the only avenue of communication with the world which remained when once the iron door clanged upon its inmate. As though in this infernal place there could be a deeper pit, I was led to an iron grate in the floor and a paper lighted at the lantern of my guide was thrown in, which illuminated a well twenty feet deep and about six feet in diameter, and I was told the miserable relics of humanity were put living there.

I was then shown an oven-like chamber lined with wood and having a thick wooden door fastened by a bar some ten or twelve inches square sliding into an iron clamp. The chamber was No. 18, and I was told there were more than twenty of them, none more than six by eight feet and about four feet high. In this it is said a Count was confined on suspicion of treason about 1630. He was a friend of the celebrated General Wallenstein, who was assassinated at the same time in one of the places we passed between this and Dresden.

But enough of the horrors of past ages. Let us be thankful that our lot is cast in better times. The people here now do not look as though their ancestors could have been guilty of such atrocities. I never saw two more beautiful boys than a pair I met soon after leaving the Rath-house, engaged in the most earnest and animated discussion of some subject dear to the heart of boys. I could have taken them both into my arms and kissed them for the relief they afforded me. One black-eyed and brown-skinned, with the bloom of a ripe peach on the sunny side; the other fair, with light eyes and gentle look: either might be the model of an angel for the painter of some celestial mission to a suffering, sinful earth. I see them still and hear their soft clear notes ringing in the ears of my heart of hearts and make sweet melody there. There is nothing so moves me as ingenuous, happy boyhood, and these Ratisbon boys will occupy a place in my memory with the cherubs of Raphael, Sassofarata, Carlo Dolce and Battoni. God grant that they may never know the power of sin!

Saturday, July 13, 1872.

Ratisbon certainly deserves the palm for noise. By 3 this morning the cracking of whips and creaking of wagons announced the commencement of the market day; and looking out of our windows, which open on the Heideplatz, which is the corn market, we saw the arrival of wagon after wagon loaded with grain in bags, which were deposited in heaps and the wagons driven off. Soon after 6 I sallied out and wandered around the Cathedral, which is in a large *platz*, which I found filled with country people seated on the pavement, each behind a basket containing some kind of garden or farm produce. One long street was devoted to a pig market. The animals were in large baskets without cover, packed in like herrings in a barrel, each with nose and eyes up. It certainly was a very amusing spectacle. The little eyes sparkling, and the long snouts protruding from the mass of pied red and white fat, which filled the basket. They were all of about the same size and color. The purchasers would lift out a specimen animal and hold him up by the hind legs and discuss the value, the porker making no more resistance than if lifeless. They appeared all to be "good little pigs." When a bargain was struck the buyer would put the purchase, (if a woman,) into a basket strapped upon her shoulders; if a man, into a sack, and tying it up, throw it across his shoulders, with two in front and two behind. They were good, large-sized grunters—nearly half grown. In other parts of the market dead pigs were exposed for sale. They do not scald and scrape them, but singe off the hair with a hot iron, so that each carcass is black as charcoal. The market supply was very abundant. Geese appear to be a favorite article of food, as they are served to ourselves, and we see them, living and dead, in large quantity in the market. With us they are only eaten in cold weather. Here evidently at all seasons. The wheat, rye and oats exposed for sale was of last years' harvest, and I should think was not a fair sample. Much of it was small and in a bad condition, being full of cockle, and poppy and other seeds.

Ratisbon, with its antique dwellings, interesting Rath-house, grand old cathedral and magnificent Valhalla, is well worth the attraction of a tourist seeking for objects of interest, and we left it with the feeling that we have by no means exhausted its treasures.

GMUNDEN, AUSTRIA, July 15, 1872.

Our ride to this place on Saturday brought us through a region of unrivalled fertility and high culture. We have not before seen any crops to surpass the wheat. There was apparently one unbroken sheet of waving corn, just yellowing for the reaper or yielding to his scythe. The district through which we passed is called, and deservedly so, "Granary of Bavaria." Wherever we saw the soil upturned it was a rich light loam of dark color, and the houses of the farmers were large and well-appointed, giving token of wealth. There was no ornament about the buildings, nor any shrubberies or plantations. Evidently they were the residences of an unintellectual but contented class of labourers. The valley is wide and extensive.

In the after part of the day we struck into the mountains and left the grain-growing for the grazing districts, and thence through the higher hills to this place, which is a very beautiful watering place at one end of the lake of Traun; *Traunsee*, they call it. A small and beautiful sheet of water surrounded by lofty mountains, some of them preciptious cliffs of grey rocks rising to the height of five thousand feet; others with more gradual slopes varied by green pine and fir forests and the softest grassy verdure, with gorges and valleys of greater or less depth cutting into them and producing the most beautiful landscapes. The different points are adorned by handsome villas, the country residences of affluent Viennese; and there are many hotels, lodging-houses, and bathing establishments, which give attraction to the place. A steamboat runs from the one end of the lake to the other, only about six miles, and there are numerous little row-boats, of pretty shape and gaily decorated, which are hired to visitors. We found William and Sally had arrived from Vienna some hours before we reached here, and were rowing when a shower drove them to shelter.

We spent the Lord's day quietly in our own rooms. It was a rainy day and afforded us great relief by the change of temperature. The last few days had been very oppressive. It is still cloudy, and Brother Wistar and some of the ladies have gone for a drive this morning. Your mother and I think the drive this afternoon by carriage to Ischl, which will occupy about four hours, is as much as we will find strength for.

William and Sally started by steamboat at 8 A. M. down the lake about five miles, and then by diligence all the way to Salzburg, where we have a faint hope we may meet again on Wednesday. They are well and very happy and gay; traveling with great rapidity and bent on making the most of the Tyrolean and Swiss Alps and passes.

ISCHL, 7 P. M.

We have had a very delightful ride over a perfectly good road around the shore of Traunsee to Ebensee, and thence following the Traun to this place, which is situated at the junction of the Ischl and Traun, two large and rapid mountain streams. The mountains are very grand, some towering to the clouds with naked rocky summits, and others clothed with heavy pine and fir forests. The valleys are beautifully green, and the houses of the peasantry as neat and pretty as whitewash and green paint can make them. Not only at Gmunden and this place, but at intervals on the way between them are very fine villas with elegant grounds and drives. The grandeur of everything one sees here is *fearfully annihilating*. But one has only to look at the lofty hills and spreading sky and realize the sublime truth, "My Father made them all," and walk out unconcerned in the midst of it all.

It is not only the resort of the Viennese nobles, but the Emperor himself has a villa here, and all the arrangements are on an imperial scale. I do not wonder that it has become one of the most fashionable places of resort in Europe. Certainly no spot can present greater attractions in its native beauty. The area covered by the beautiful houses is not large, and is surrounded on every side by mountains divided from each other by green valleys which diverge as from a centre.

When in Italy last summer I was distressed by the state of the Italian peasantry, which I was disposed to attribute to the tyranny of Austrian oppressive rule. But since I have passed through Vienna and other parts of the Empire, and more especially since coming into the mountainous districts, I have suspected that there may be two sides to this as to other questions. There is an air of contentment on the part of the people, of neatness about the houses of the peasantry, and of simple elegance in the homes of the affluent which we have not met with anywhere else in Europe. Education is universal. No one can be married who has not certificates of a certain attendance at school. The opportunities of education are provided by the government, so that not even the poorest can plead inability. It is true that education is conducted wholly under the auspices of the priesthood. Hence the religious character of the people. No where are so many shrines seen by the way side. But they have here this redeeming trait: they are figures of the Saviour, not of the Virgin. As we came to-day we passed scores of them, some larger and others smaller and some elaborately carved and gilded.

ISCHL, July 15, 1872.

My Dear Son:

You may tell Miss Shannon, with my kindest regards, that she did not speak extravagantly when she bade me not omit a visit to this beautiful spot. I sit soothed by the rush of the waters of the Traun, which flows directly under our windows, which look out on a grand panorama of pine-clad mountains, while at our feet lie the beautiful dwellings of this favorite watering place. I do not know whether you have been here and regret, if Galloway and Hannah join us at Salzburg that they should miss so much beauty. We propose remaining here to-morrow, and the next day drive to that place where we shall at least hear what their plans are.

I find I have taken a scrap of paper on which a Paris shop-keeper had given me a direction to find Dr. See, to whom he also gave me an introduction.

Love to dear Mellie and all the boys. Tell Miss Shannon my slippers have been a great comfort and are very beautiful still. Give my dear love to Mrs. Cope and Miss Griffith, and Mrs. Clark, and any other of my friends. I have been obliged to omit my usual letter to Mrs. Cope this week, and take the time for perfect repose. We go from Salzburg to Munich, Nuremburg, Stuttgart and Paris.

Your affectionate father,
CASPAR MORRIS.

ISCHL, July 16, 1872.

My Dear Children:

I dispatched a letter from this place last evening, hoping it might find its way to you one week sooner than if I reserved it, as I shall do this till after I receive your letters, which we hope are lying waiting for us at Salzburg.

This place and Gmunden, where we spent the Lord's day, and Ebensee, through which we passed on our way here, are the centre of the salt manufacture, which is a monopoly of the Austrian government. At Gmunden we saw great piles of loaves, like sugar loaves, lying on the landing ready to be sent off by railroad. And at Ebensee there is a very extensive building with the royal arms on it which contains evaporating pans. The salt mines are twenty-five miles distant, and the brine is brought to Ischl and Ebensee in conduits along mountain sides and on lofty arches more than one hundred feet high across valleys, as there is not wood enough near the mines to heat the pans and evaporate the water. The salt lies in strata in the mountain, in chambers in which water is allowed to flow and kept there till it dissolves the solid salt; when it is allowed to flow out and is carried in pipes these long distances; and fresh water is admitted in place of that which had become saturated. The manufacture of salt is a government monopoly and yields a net return of some eight or ten millions of dollars, being equal to one-seventh of the Austrian revenue.

Nothing can exceed the beauty of this region, which grows in my eyes hourly. Lofty mountains clothed with pine forests, with here and there patches of softer green, where the wood has been cut off, and, grass growing freely, affording pasturage for cattle, are divided from each other by soft grassy valleys, in which nestle the clean, white houses of the thrifty peasantry, while beautiful villas stand perched on prominent points half way up the mountain sides. The town of Ischl is composed of hotels and large lodging-houses, mingled with shops and smaller dwelling-places, all perfectly neat; and it is nestled among the mountains like a nest in a pine tree, while there is the perpetual music of the rushing streams which are strong and clear, rushing rapidly over stony beds. The day is showery, with occasional gleams of sunshine breaking out for a few moments, but not sufficient to justify our making any excursion. The entrance to the imperial residence is very fine, giving the impression of great beauty in the grounds, but as the family is now here there is no admission.

SALZBURG, 1 P. M., July 18.

We are told this morning that the Crown Prince of Prussia, with his wife, the daughter of Victoria, Queen of England, would arrive here at this hour to lunch at this house on their route to Berchtesgaden and Köenigsee, where they are to remain some weeks. Our rooms look directly on to the portal of the railroad station, and we saw them alight. Carriages were drawn up to receive them, but a plain-looking gentleman and lady, with no peculiarity of costume, came down the steps and walked quietly to the hotel. We had returned from a drive just at that moment, so that we had a fine view of the royal state.

This is a grand hotel of great size, and well constructed and appointed; standing in an extensive garden or lawn, beautifully planted. The only objection to be made is the noise of the trains arriving and departing during the night, as well as frequently in the day, and the distance from the town for those who wish to visit shops, etc. Whether both objections would not be equally great in the case of the proposed Mammoth Hotel at the Union Depot for the Western, Southern and Eastern-bound railroads in West Philadelphia, is a subject worthy the consideration of those who propose its erection. It is certainly well to be near the place of arrival and departure, but I have thought it possible to "pay too much *for the whistle*," since we have been annoyed here by its shrill screams.

It is impossible to use language too strong in the effort to express the wondrous beauty of this region. Every element which enters into the ideal of attractive scenery is combined and perpetually renewed. Towering rocky peaks rise to the height of six or seven thousand feet, standing giant warders of the scene; and as such, visible on every side and at every turn with features as varying as the points of observation. Clustered about them are lofty ranges of pine-clad mountains, broken and interrupted by deep fissures on either side, clothed with trees of the richest foliage. Larches, and beeches, and oaks mingle with the dark evergreens; while irregular spots, clothed with the softest green grass, are scattered here and there along the sides, and run, often, to the very top of the ridge. Streams running down the gorges leap from rock to rock in snowy whiteness; and lakes lie in the spaces between the mountains like great plains of polished malachite mingled with lapis lazuli and beryl. Then castle and convent and villa crown the lower heights, while farm buildings and pretty villages nestle in the nooks, surrounded by fields of grass and grain.

These farm-houses here are immense buildings, of small elevation, but great spread of roof. At the one end they are white-washed, and have glazed windows and ornamental gables, with galleries and porches, and are occupied by human beings, while the other end of the same roof covers the crops and herds and stock. The houses are clean and pretty-looking, but the people are small of stature and uncomely in countenance and awkward of gait, and not neat in their personal appearance. The horses are well fed and of large size, and make excellent draft-horses. The oxen are very fine, well-trained and are worked singly or in pairs, drawing by their heads, and attached to the wagons with traces. Often one only is harnessed to the one side of a pole, or put into shafts. They move easily and quickly, and carry their heads up instead of putting them down, as those worked in yokes do. A padded leather collar is passed across the front, below the horns, and a small yoke attached to it behind, to the ends of which the traces are attached and supported by a back-strap.

The shrines at the road-side are numerous, sometimes containing merely a crucifix, sometimes a representation of the dead body of our Lord lying on the lap of the Virgin, and sometimes a picture designed to represent some deliverance from danger experienced on the spot.

The road from Gmunden, through Ebensee and Ischl, to this place, follows the shores of three beautiful lakes in succession, and the course of the streams which supply them, while the mountains rise like walls on either hand, shutting in the soft, green valleys. It is a trip which no lover of natural beauty will ever regret making, especially at this season, when the richness of the harvest-scene is added to the natural beauties.

In every grain-field are placed upright posts with cross-pieces a foot or more long, and about that distance apart, to which are attached the sheaves, two or three standing upright at the foot, and one laid on top, with the heads turned down and the butts projecting at top, all in one direction. The effect is very curious. They look like groups of dancing bears, or long processions of cowled friars.

The streams and lakes abound with noble trout, which are served up at every meal, either boiled or fried. The most fastidious epicure could not desire anything more.

SALZBURG, July 19, 1872.

My Dear Children:

    I am going to make the effort to talk to you all at home, seated directly in front of the railroad depot, and I am watching for the arrival of Gall. and Han.; so is not that trying to do two things at once? Your father and I declined riding this morning with uncle and aunts, as there is a possibility of the train getting in before their return, and now your father has walked out, and I am all alone.

    We came here on the 17th, a most beautiful ride along the valley between mountains and lake, and yesterday we spent in the carriages again around here. We found letters from you all, and I can in truth say that is better than any of these things. Our hearts were full, and I hope we are thankful for the merciful preservation of dear Mellie. Ches.'s letter was written only the day after the upset; we shall have later intelligence by Gall., and hope she continued to do well. I am not surprised to hear they are thinking of a larger house. I had thought it would be almost a necessity, and on some accounts ours I think would suit them very well. But how could they reconcile our neighbors to a family of boys in the yard;—by *cousining* them?—Ches. go in and smoke with them? There was good in them once, and perhaps there is a spark left, and Mellie can find it. I know the house is comfortable for both winter and summer, and I would love to see them in it. If they do not take it, how would it do to rent for the winter again with the furniture, and cousin and we board and fix ourselves deliberately? I really feel it is too much to let you all have that to do for us. It is requiring more of you than *I* would like to undertake for any one. I would be perfectly willing to board either at a hotel or with Maria. Of course I know nothing of her plans or Murray's. He may be going to remain there. Of course on reaching home the last of October, I shall get pretty promptly to West River and Baltimore, as they can't come to us, and would like to feel at liberty to stay as long as I wish, and the truth is we will feel that we have been spoiled and don't want much care of house, etc., and it will take a little time to get broken in. Your father will not think of resuming practice, so we must live within our means, without any addition from that source. You know I have always felt that Chestnut Street property must increase in value. I still think so, and for all your sakes I think it best not to part with it, but fix ourselves in a small house in a more retired situation. I have some times wondered if David Scull intended to keep his town house on Pine Street. Such as that we would like. I know we have but one interest in all these arrangements, and so I suppose will have to leave it to you. We will be entirely satisfied with the most simple accommodations you can make.

    I shall have to stop. Just imagine yourself at the Pennsylvania depot, and watching and listening to the incessant coming and going, and your heart palpitating, and you'll *see you cannot write.*

    Afternoon, 6 o'clock, Gall. and Han. did not come, so we now look for them to-morrow; but we have been cheered again by another package of letters. We have on our table two from Cousin, two from Mary, two from Is. and Annie, one from Ches., two from Mrs. Cope, one from Mary Hutchinson, and one from Mr. Biddle; all of which are most acceptable, I do assure you each and all, and if I thought it would give as much pleasure to you all to hear from us, I should be ashamed to say, "I am too tired to write to-day," which I constantly find myself doing. I never saw any one like your father; he drops down to the writing on all occasions, and it is by taking advantage of the seconds, I tell him, that he accomplishes so much.

We are so glad to have good accounts of you all notwithstanding the heat. It is delightfully cool here, except occasionally at midday in the sun. I sleep under two blankets, and I never ride without waterproof and blanket shawl in the carriage, and often have both on. The foot continues to improve.

I suppose about this time Ches. is off with the boys if Mellie is as well as we hope she is. I am glad he is going to take a trip with them, though I don't expect he will find much in the Virginia lands worth looking after; still I do think some one ought to attend to them. We have rejoiced over Eff.'s trip, and shall now want to hear how he and his companion made out. I suppose by this time they have returned and perhaps he has gone to West River to escort Cousin Emily. You see I am following you all. Indeed I find it a great comfort to be able to do so, thanks to you all for keeping me so well posted.

We are quite relieved to hear the Bohemian glass reached you safely, and wish now very much we had sent the trunk from Genoa home instead of to Liverpool; as we have many fears for it and it is of importance, having all our little valuables; not much, but more than we want to lose, or can now replace, but we hope it will yet turn up. It was to go by sea and we have the receipt.

Give much love to Mrs. Buckley; tell her there is no danger of our wearying of reading letters; it is only that I am too lazy to acknowledge them. But I know writing fatigues her too, and in this hot weather she ought not to do it. I hope to hear she has found a cool spot somewhere to rest in, and that the intense heat is over. How glad we ought to be to escape it!

With a great deal of love to each of you, think of me as a most devoted and affectionate mother,

A. C. MORRIS.

We now have no plans, have no idea when we will leave here, or where we go next, but will write again before we actually get off. I have fixed myself at the window to watch for the dear children, I am so impatient to see them.

Afternoon.—Gally. and Han. are with us now. Would at any rate send messages, but they are resting, and we are told these must go. She looks to me very delicate, but is tired to-day.

SALZBURG, July 18, 1872.

The beauty of the surroundings here, though old as the "everlasting hills," grows daily. The day has been variable, sometimes showery and at others bright with sunshine; and this variation of light and shadow has lent additional and changeful charms. This morning we had a beautiful drive to Hellbrun (clear spring), the former residence of an Archbishop who built the chateau about the year 1600. The stream which runs through the ground may well be called the crystal spring. I never saw water more translucent and pure, and the trout which floated lazily in the pools were provokingly attractive to any one who would not prefer to gratify his eye by seeing them swim and turn up their spotted sides, to the transient pleasure of the sense of taste as the deformed and mangled bodies are transferred to the stomach.

After paying our respects duly to the finny genii of the stream we were introduced to the curious products of the taste of the Archbishop, who amused himself more than two hundred and fifty years ago by constructing fancy grottoes with heathen gods in them, and fountains with imaginary figures pouring out the water in very unnatural and uncomfortable positions. Then jets were arranged so that unexpectedly a guest or visitor might find himself in a shower-bath or subjected to a douche from the mouth of a deer's head hanging against the wall, or some equally unlooked-for source.

The great attraction of the place consists in groups of puppets worked by machinery moved by water-power, turned off or on at will. One represents a woman turning a stone on which her husband grinds a sword. Another a flour-mill, with the miller pouring wheat into the hopper, while the stone revolves and the meal runs out below. Another a potter, seated at his lathe, which is apparently turned round by his feet, which work upon the treadle, and his hands mould a basin before him. Passing these, one sees a representation of a virgin chained, and a great dragon rushes out with open mouth to devour her, but as he approaches the figure of Perseus emerges from a hole in the stone and takes off the monster's head with his sabre.

There is shown a much larger grotto, in which are collected some hundreds of figures in and around houses. The king stands and bows to the people who are dancing on the street before his palace. A house is being built, and all the various artisans and labourers are busy working on it. Coopers, shoemakers, and blacksmiths, ply their trades. Sentinels march to and fro before the palace and salute the officers as they approach. A bear dances and a woman waltzes and shakes her head and hands, till you fear she may have shaking palsy. A man trundles his wife in a wheel-barrow, and all the time the bells of the church steeple are chiming. The whole affair is simple enough, but its venerable age, and the fact of its having been the toy of an archbishop-prince induce one to look and laugh.

The grounds are extensive, and have a very fine outlook from an amphitheatre cut out of the solid rock on a lofty pinnacle, to which I did not ascend.

This afternoon we drove to a convent and church on another lofty eminence, from which the view is very extensive, reaching over two wide and rich valleys bounded by the irregular outline of Alps, enveloped in clouds. When we had gone as far in the carriages as they could mount we climbed still higher by steps. At each landing-place there was a shrine containing life-size figures admirably carved. In the first the agony in the garden, then the scourging of our Lord was most painfully truthful in the representation, with the text in German: "By His wounds we are healed." Then the crowning with thorns, with the text: "My Lord and my God." So with many other scenes; one our Lord fainting under the burden of the cross and Veronica holding up the napkin with which she had wiped the sacred brow, retaining miraculously the impress of His features. On the top was the actual crucifixion, with the thieves on either hand, and the women who had followed him out of Galilee. Before each was *prie Dieu*, at which the devout pilgrims knelt and offered their prayers. Undoubtedly many a loving heart and pious soul has here poured out vows to God, excited by this mode of representation, as we are by reading in God's word the record He hath given us of His Son, here transferred to wooden and stone emblems, instead of letters on paper. There is peril of idolatry, undoubtedly, but God looketh at the heart, and is found of them who worship in spirit and in truth.

The church of the convent is filled with votive representations of miraculous deliverance from sickness and perils of various kinds in answer to prayer to "God and the Virgin." We read several of the inscriptions which were very simple. They are defaced by lead-pencil inscriptions of the names of visitors. All German.

When writing this morning I omitted to mention one of the fountains at Hellbrun, which was especially beautiful and exhibited most decidedly the extreme purity of the water. It was a large bouquet of colored flowers over which the water was made to turn a perfect shade like those of glass which are used to cover artificial flowers. It was perfect in its power to deceive one. I have never before seen water so perfectly free from all impurity.

The most imposing structure about Salzburg is the castle, still the residence of the archbishop, though he is not now, as once, the feudal lord and military leader, as well as spiritual "Lord over God's heritage." I wonder that expression should not have deterred the bishops from assuming such power and state. This castle strongly fortified, stands on a lofty eminence just where the Salza bursts from the mountains and takes its course, rapid and tortuous, through the wide valley at one end of which Salzburg lies. On the opposite side, a little less elevated, a strongly fortified wall runs a long distance around the mountain enclosing the grounds of a convent of Benedictines. The old monks were sometimes skillful warriors and defended the castle and convent against their rebellious peasantry. One great insurrection against their oppression took place as early as 1520, and was not connected with any doctrinal tenets. But about a century later not less than twenty thousand of the dwellers in this region were cruelly driven from their homes on account of their faith. Strong it must have been, and dear to them the "hope of everlasting life in Jesus Christ their Lord," to enable them to abandon these sweet vales and fertile plains and glorious mountains, which they might well think were made for the peculiar abode of the chosen people of God. Yet they went forth not knowing whither they went. Some I believe were received into Protestant districts in Germany, and I have somehow an impression that some of their descendants found their way to America. Very many of them were miners.

Some parts of the mountains contain ores of gold and silver. Our term Dollar is a corruption or modification of the German *thaler*, which was the oldest silver coinage, and being made in the valleys, or Thals, where the ore was smelted, received the name of "Thaler" or "valley piece." It is said that the expatriation of the Protestant miners caused the abandonment of the mines.

July 19th.

As we sat last evening enjoying the wild radiance of the moon, nearly full, as she rose above the crest of the mountain covered with snow and converted the clouds which sailed through the blue expanse into mimic snow-wreaths, we anticipated a fine day. This morning it is settled rain, though a gorgeous bow spanned the valley just before sunset; brilliant and clear as that which greeted the earth's old sire as the sun's rays burst through the final rains of the deluge, when God chose its beauty as the seal of His promise that the earth should no more be utterly overflowed.

SALZBURG, July 19, 1872.

My Dear Sister (Emily Hollingsworth.—EDS.):

Your most kindly affectionate letter of the last week in June was among the latest we have had, and we as heartily welcomed on our arrival here day before yesterday. We are sure there are later dates which we ought to receive; and are anxious for Dear Galloway and Hannah who wrote us from Brussels last Sunday, and will be here, we hope, either to-day or to-morrow, and spend at least the Lord's day with us. What course they will then take we do not know. If they had been able to reach here in time it would have been very nice for them to join William and Sally who left here yesterday for the Swiss mountains, which I know Galloway desires much to pass over. I think they will be more independent in their movements, and see more they desire to examine if they move about independently of us, and fear they will suffer inconvenience from coming here to meet us. It is true they will find here every element of beauty and grandeur, but less that is curious and strange. Mountains, valleys, lakes, streams, snow-clad peaks, cascades and green meadows are the groundwork of pictures which vary with the changing light and shade of morning and evening and sunshine and cloud; continually changing. The roads are perfect and the carriages comfortable, so that drives which we take daily to some object of interest afford us all healthful excitement and pleasure.

The entrance of the river Salza into the wide valley, in which the town with its 18,000 inhabitants lies, amid smiling meadows encircled by lofty mountains, clothed with dark green fir trees and overlooked by snow-capped peaks, is through a narrow defile. The cliff on one side is crowned by the castle of the archbishop, whose frowning battlements and numerous loopholes and embrasures, speak more of the militant than the spiritual power, and in consonance with this the hill on the other side is encircled by a wall, with towers at short distances, running along the edge of the cliffs; which wall encloses a convent of Benedictine monks. All this savours of the same spirit still lingering here which caused a former archbishop, Prince of the Empire, to exile some 20,000 of his subjects on account of their Protestant faith. I never realized more fully how much faith would be necessary to sustain one under such a trial. They must have had a full confidence of faith in the promise of Jesus that he had gone to prepare a place for them and would come again and take them to himself, and must have realized the beauty of that better land, to enable them to turn their backs on this which is like the garden of the Lord.

As I raise my eyes they fall on sloping mountain sides dressed in living green, with beautiful villas standing picturesquely amid groves of trees of majestic growth.

"If then these lower worlds are fair,
How glorious must the mansion be
Where Thy redeemed shall dwell with Thee?"

Present trials surely are small in comparison, and yet how we shrink from them.

We yesterday drove to a convent situate on the summit of a lofty hill and commanding a glorious view of two richly cultivated and fertile valleys. We were obliged to climb the latter step by step, at each turn of which were shrines containing life-sized statues representing the Passion of our Lord in its various stages, from the agony of Gethsemane to the dying cry "It is finished."

It was an instructive and impressive lesson, and as I read beneath the scourging, "By His stripes we are healed"; and beneath the crowning with thorns "My Lord and my God"; I prayed for an increase of the faith which would enable me to become a participant in the blessings thus purchased. O my dear sister, travel does not feed the flame of heavenly desire, nor nourish the life which is hid with Christ in God. The same sinful nature cleaves to us, change our skies as we may, and the same enemy of souls spreads his snares around our path and beguiles our feet. Thanks be to God that He ever is at hand and will keep that which we commit to Him, whether we journey or labour in our calling in our several homes.

The weeks are speeding rapidly by and soon we shall begin to count by days the interval before the period at which we hope to meet. May God grant us a happy reunion on earth or a happier one in Heaven. I hope I have done right in sundering the ties of professional obligation, and that I may find power to serve Jesus in some little sphere while I wait the call which is ever sounding more near to me. My great dread is that I may be found to have been an idle and slothful servant failing to use my Lord's money. An unprofitable one I know I am.

Anne sits beside me quietly knitting. The other members of our party are driving. The day is showery and we thought it better to remain within even *if* we had not hoped for the arrival of our children. Love—dear love to sister Caroline and Brother Henry. We are glad you are with them. Please remember us also to Isabella and Sarah and Richard and Lizzy when you see either of them.

I enclose a slip I cut from a Paris paper which will show you how your *cousins* are estimated abroad and do things at home.

Your loving brother,

CASPAR MORRIS.

SALZBURG, July 21, 1872.

My Dear Child:

Just think of me seated opposite to Han, writing to you. Gall., and your father out. Well you can hardly understand *what* a treat it is to get hold of them away off in this distant place. They joined us here yesterday, we having been here two days had a nice room adjoining ours ready for them, looking out on a most beautiful mountain prospect; and uncle Wistar insists on their being his guests for the time they are here, and all seem very glad to have them. I only regret I don't get quite as much of them to myself as I want, but you see I am greedy for home people and home things especially *my children*. In a few days we shall separate and then meet again in England. They will be visiting places we have been in. Hannah is thin and looks very delicate and is far from strong. I feel quite concerned for her, but think they are pursuing the right course and do hope she will be renovated. They are not going to join Sally and Will as it is best for them to avoid much that the former want to do, and go quietly; and if alone when weary stop without incommoding anyone. It is the wisest course and they find they can manage with their knowledge of French to get along.

I have two letters from you on the table, one has a page from Cornelia, the last of July 1st; and one from Annie tells me Effie has gone down, so I imagine the young people having a nice time notwithstanding the heat, which from all accounts must be intense. All we experience of it is a hot sun at midday.

Gall. and Han. met Lizzie Murray a few days ago in a railroad depot. She had just been put under the care of Dr. Agnew, of Philadelphia, an entire stranger; so I have no doubt was glad to meet friends. They travelled together two or three days and were quite sorry then to be obliged to leave her alone at Mayence. She was well and happy. I shall hardly now meet her as we are going in opposite directions.

Tell the children one of the rides we have taken was to see the Chateau of Hellbrun, which has an artificial garden and water-works. Water is made to accomplish every variety of purpose. Several grottos very beautiful and curious, having strange figures in them and most unexpectedly a thousand little streams of water rise up from the floor. Then there is a town represented in full bustle of life. Every trade you can think of; *all* busily at work, and a band of music playing at one moment. Then in the cathedral there is sacred music, and all this is done by water, and these little puppets are three hundred years old, but they don't look so. It was all built by an Archbishop but it now belongs to the Emperor. There are many places through the garden where you are in danger of a shower bath, either from above or below. I think I shall go there with Aunt Han.

Yesterday the Crown Prince and Princess lunched here at this house. They *walked* over from the depot and we stood on our veranda to look at them. They were, I have no doubt, sumptuously entertained. After they left we went into *their* parlor, which was adjoining ours, to see the beautiful flowers, etc., but I had the opportunity of seeing the two little children, a boy of two years and baby of three months in short clothes; looked very small, not unlike other nice children. They and suite left in four handsome carriages for a watering place a short distance from here.

July 24th.

Since writing the above we have been having a very nice time. Gall. and Han. are still with us, but we will separate to-morrow. I shall miss them very much, but have the prospect of meeting them again soon. The only drawback to our pleasure with them is to see more and more plainly her critical condition. Your father says this trip was the best thing for her and this was the time to do it, if anything was to be gained by it. We all went together on an excursion the day before yesterday, occupying the whole day. A ride of about forty miles, and stopped at the salt mine. All descended except Aunt Hannah, your father and myself. They were dressed in white pantaloons, fancy cloth caps; each held a lantern in the left hand and used the right to steady themselves as they slid or coasted down the inclined planes on a plank. Some said it paid, but I don't think Han. felt it did. It was almost too much for her. The day was a delightful one, and the ride very grand; and then we had a row on the lake (in a fancy covered boat) of six miles. Dinner, and then were rowed back by two girls and three men in fancy costumes. Again took the carriages and drove eighteen miles to the hotel in Salzburg; a tired party I assure you, and we have not yet recovered from it, so have allowed them all to go off on a long trip to-day without us. So now just see what a treat we are enjoying, Gall. and Han., your father and I, to *ourselves*, for altho' each one is occupied with the pen, it is so nice just to see and feel we are together unrestrained. I find from Gall. that Mary Kirk is in Brussels at a school. They are under the impression it is a convent. I am very sorry I did not know it when we were there. I should certainly have gone to see her, and if we should return that way, will. Oh, it is such a mistake for parents to send their children to these Romish institutions. No one can question Dr. Kirk's having done it without feeling the separation very keenly, but he thinks no impression of a religious character can be made on her. I greatly fear he will find he is mistaken when it is too late.

Han. and Gall. join me in much love to you all.

Yours most affectionately,

A. C. M.

SALZBURG, July 23, 1872.

My Dear Children:

We have been enjoying greatly the privilege of the company of the dear Galloway and Hannah in this sweet place, and though the weather is warmer than we have felt for two years, they tell us is so much less hot than it was at home when they left that we may be thankful. To-morrow we separate; they for Ischl and Vienna and we for Munich. They to go to Italy and Switzerland and we to Baden and Paris, hoping to meet again in England in about four weeks and then to meet frequently till we finally sail for home together in October.

Yesterday we drove together to visit Königssee; stopping on the way at Berchtesgaden, where all except your Aunt Hannah, your mother and myself, descended into the salt mine. We saw them all equipped in suits of miners' clothing, white pantaloons, dark jackets, jaunty caps and black leather aprons fastened behind for them to sit on. Thus equipped, each with a lantern in hand, they came out of the robing room, crossed the road, and disappeared through an archway in the side of the mountain into which ran a narrow gauge railroad. They were absent rather more than an hour, at the end of which time we heard the rattling of cars on a railroad in the bowels of the mountain; soon after which several benches mounted longitudinally on the rails, shot out of the door in the arch and across the road, on which they were seated astride, one behind the other, as closely as they could be packed. Some parties rushed up to the *atelier* of a photographer and were photographed. Our party was content with buying pictures of others, as the time would not permit them to wait for their own.

They were highly gratified by their visit to the chambers, from some of which the salt has been quarried in great blocks like stone. It is of a dark color and contains many impurities. You have probably all seen specimens in the blocks, which are sold with us to place in the fields for cattle to lick at. It is crystalline in structure and sparkles when the light is thrown on it; requiring to be dissolved and evaporated to fit it for domestic use. The plan pursued is to open cavities in the strata of salt and admit water to them, puddling them with clay or earth, so that the water shall not run out till it is perfectly saturated when it is allowed to run through pipes to those places where the fuel can be had for the purpose of boiling and evaporation. In some places it is carried twenty or thirty miles; being pumped by machinery to such a height as enables them to carry it across ravines and even over low mountains.

In visiting the mine they are ferried across one of these ponds or small lakes of water, the walls around it having lights suspended on them so as to illuminate it all round. The workings are on different levels, to which the visitors descend by a succession of slides, being seated upon rails down which they glide like coasting down hill on snow or ice.

When they had changed their clothing, we all drove on through the narrow valley, skirted on either side by mountains, rising many thousands of feet, some clothed with dark green pines, some with majestic firs, some with soft grass, and some bold and bare rocks. Beautiful villas and houses for the accommodation of visitors, stand clustered in small groups, lending the charm of ornament to the wild scene.

The Königssee itself is a lake about six miles long and but little more than half a mile in width, but five hundred feet or more in depth, shut in on every side by lofty mountains which rise directly from its margin. Snow lies on the sides and in the clefts in some places all the year, while the water itself has an *intensity of depth of green color* which cannot be described. We left our carriages and took our seats in a flat-bottomed boat, sharp at both ends, and covered over the middle with a wooden canopy, and two women at the forward end and three men at the stern rowed us to the other end of the lake, firing a pistol on the way to amuse us with the ringing, sharp, echoes sent back by the hills. It was a delightful excursion, the temperature on the water requiring warm wraps, though on shore in the sun the heat had been oppressive.

We had a good meal of fried trout under shade of trees, at the restaurant at St. Bartholomew's, directly under one of the high snow capped peaks, and then were rowed back. The sun descended below the caps of the mountains and the serrated edges divided the skies with lines of alternate light and shade ; while the condensing vapours were driven from the points like smoke from so many chimneys. All was tranquility. The numerous parties of visitors floating like ourselves were all silent. The surroundings were too majestically grand to permit idle mirth.

The drive along the valley on our return was very delightful. One after another the mountain tops were cast into shade but still the lofty peaks of soft gray stone caught the rays of the sun and raised their brows, bathed in the rosy light, above the dark green pine forests on the lower ranges. One transverse valley stirred every one with admiration as we passed the opening. A *deep dark rich blue* mist filled it. The sides were partly covered with forest, and partly cultivated ; and were all in shade while at the remote end a perfectly bald projecting mass of rock, towering *far above* all others, and extending on either side entirely across the valley, was lighted up by the ruddy rays of the setting sun. It was wondrously imposing in its unrivalled grandeur. Our road lay the entire distance along a rushing stream with numerous falls ; while mills for grinding hydraulic cement and for rolling toy marbles, gave evidence that the water power is not wasted in idle frolic with the many colored stones which show through the perfectly clear volumes which roll over them.

We had left the hotel at 8 A. M. and did not reach it till 9 P. M. ; wearied it is true but voting the day one of unalloyed delight. This day has been devoted to rest praparatory for our start to-morrow.

Wednesday, July 24th.

Gall. and Han. have decided to stay here with us to-day, and your uncle and aunts go off for a day's excursion so that we shall have a quiet time together. The weather is delightful.

Last evening Mr. Borie and Mr. John T. Lewis, Jr., spent an hour or more with us. Mr. Lewis is the image of my dear old friend (and patron) his grandfather, Dr. James, and makes the impression of being a very fine, intelligent, modest worthy young man. It is a comfort to think such are rising up for the service of succeeding generations. May he glorify God as his grandfather did.

Yesterday afternoon Hannah and Galloway and your mother drove to Hellbrun. They were as much pleased as we had been and in speaking of the purity of the water gave an illustration which escaped my notice. There was a painting of an Alpine view over which the water passed as a thin sheet like glass and was quite as transparent as the finest glass. It is now nearly midday and, though pleasant in the house, the sun shines very bright and hot, yet I have just called Hannah to look at the snow lying directly before us on the slopes of the mountain with the full glow of the sun upon it.

All unite in love with

Your loving father,

CASPAR MORRIS.

SALZBURG, July 23, 1872.

My Dear Brother (Galloway Cheston Ed.):

It is a long time since we heard from you personally and feel as though it has been a long time since I wrote to you. We have been comforted by the company of Galloway and Hannah, though we cannot look at her without seeing the plainest evidence of the commencement of the work of the destroyer. I am convinced the best thing that could have been done to arrest the progress is this excursion, but I do not look with any hope to the issue. It is a great effort for Galloway, but not too great for the stake. She is very lovely and most important to him and the boys. Anne has driven with them this evening while I write to you, and to-morrow we separate; they to go into Switzerland and Northern Italy, and we to make our way gradually north to England and Scotland, where we hope they may again cross our way. Passages are taken for the entire party on board the "Scotia."

This meeting has been a pleasant episode in our journey and this place is one of the most delightful we have visited. The mountains are lofty and grand, the peaks snow-capped, and glaciers lie enclosed in the higher slopes. The meadows are covered with the softest verdure, and the mountain streams are rapid and run over beds of stones of various hues; while lakes of surpassing loveliness lie embosomed among heights clothed with dark fir trees, or reflect still loftier peaks, with bald and scarred front, too precipitous to permit the snow to rest upon them.

Castles and convents and villas adorn the tops and sides of the lower ranges of mountains, while immense farm-houses stand in the midst of ripening grain fields and green meadows. The residences of the Austrian peasantry are far more comfortable than those of Northern Germany or Italy; their horses are noble animals and their working oxen the most perfectly docile, well-broken beasts. They are harnessed with traces and back-straps and draw by their heads, having padded leather cushions over their fronts. I should think from their free movement they felt much less constrained than when yoked and bearing the weight upon their necks.

Austria took the lead in *compulsory* universal education; every child is obliged to go to school and all her citizens, male and female, read and write well. The education is under the control of the priesthood and is of course confined to such topics as Rome sanctions. The result is an undisputed submission to the authority of the Church, and an universal display of symbols of religion. Churches and chapels are not so numerous as in Italy; but shrines by the roadside supply the want. So far as the traveller who does not speak the language and cannot mingle with the people can form a correct judgment, it would appear that the people are happy. There is nothing picturesque about their costume to atone for its poverty, and therefore the people do not appear neat and attractive in their persons, though the liberal use of whitewash and green paint about their houses, on the walls and window-shutters, and the pretty flowers about the doors make the homesteads very attractive.

This district with its mountains and lakes and valleys is a favorite resort of nobility and gentry during the summer months, and crowds of English and American tourists now rush through it during the few weeks of summer. The money thus spent enriches the people. The hotel at which we are is a very grand one and the proprietor, entirely the gentleman, receiving his guests. The Crown Prince of Prussia with the Princess, the eldest daughter of Victoria, was our fellow lodger on the first day of our arrival. Baron Erlanger has been here since and now we have *Miss Nellie Grant* and our fellow townsman, the Hon. Adolph E. Borie. Thus we sail on the same stream with the apples.

But the beauty of the scenery, the balmy character of the air, the delight of the senses, and the dignity of these fellow travellers are only passing incidents of the way by which we are travelling rapidly to the end of our earthly pilgrimage, and all passes away and perishes. The one great question forces itself more and more on my notice "What then?" I came away from home to sunder my bonds to professional duty because I felt that I could not any longer continue to receive the confidence of patients who would be better treated by younger and more energetic and better instructed minds. Now as the time for my return approaches and I realize that I can no longer follow the lead of another and depend upon the kindness of my brother to provide the place where I shall lay my head at night, and the means of enjoyment by day, I am obliged to ask myself what shall I do with myself that I may not be a burden to my children and friends? Something for the Lord "that bought me with His own precious blood" I *must do* and must do cheerfully with good will; not grudgingly nor of necessity. Neither Anne nor I can determine what is best *for us* or what will best promote the interests of our children. Their temporal and eternal interests are so inextricably interwoven that they cannot be separated, and so are ours. The question therefore is one of infinite importance and I will commit the decision of it to that Lord who has been so wonderfully gracious to us in the past and changes not.

Our anxiety for dear Margaret and yourself is very great. We fear the intense heat of which we see daily reports in the telegraphic news may exhaust her and know that both she and yourself are suffering from it. We could not mitigate its violence if we were with you and perhaps our absence may be a relief to you, as you know we are not suffering in the same way. I sometimes think it is one of our Heavenly Father's mercies to us that Anne is not exposed to it. She is wonderfully well, but a little exposure to the sun prostrates her very much. She now walks with but little limp, but her foot is still too much swollen to permit her to put her common boot on. She is compelled to wear a cloth overshoe which I bought for her last autumn to wear over her shoes on the cold marble floors of the Italian inns and picture galleries. The company of Galloway and Hannah has been a great blessing to her, and I shall be glad if she does not become depressed when they leave us.

The accounts of political matters in the United States are not encouraging and the conflict in Germany and Italy is surely rapidly approaching. The open challenge by Manning in England, who avows that the Jesuits are the great power which are to govern human affairs—the attempt to assassinate the king of Spain—and the direction of the Pope to the people of Europe to seek to conquer at the ballot—are all tokens of a fierce struggle in the not very remote future —while the faintheartedness of most, and the treachery of many, and the dissensions among Protestants, all indicate plainly that our help must come from the Lord and our trust be in Him and not in man.

With best love to Margaret, and kindest regards to Miss Carey and all our friends around you and also to Mary Ellen for whose sufferings we are deeply distressed.

Your afft. brother,

CASPAR MORRIS.

MUNICH, BAVARIA, July 25, 1872.

My Dear Children:

A Gracious Providence has watched over and protected us in our goings out and comings in, travelling by land, by water, and now after the lapse of a year (within a week or ten days) we find ourselves comfortably returned to our old quarters in this magnificent town. It is after 11 P. M., but as your mother is not quite ready for bed I will fill up a few minutes with you. We left Salzburg about 6 P. M. and had a delightful railroad ride here. The first three hours our route lay amid the lakes and valleys and mountains which made Salzburg so attractive. Our sojourn there was one of the pleasantest experiences of our tour. First William and Sally and then Galloway and Hannah gave us some of the pleasures of home associations. No place at which we have been could have been better adapted to such joys. We took our last look at the snow and skirted the foot of the range of mountains, along valleys which laughed and sang with the rich crops of wheat, oats, flax, hops, and clover, which repaid the toil of the husbandman. The Chiemsee and another smaller lake lay at the base of the mountains; the slopes of which are covered with forest, supplying timber for lumber, which is piled in large quantities at various points on the railroad line, and also wood for evaporating salt water which is brought in pipes a distance of forty miles for the purpose. Quantities of scrap iron at some of the stations gave the idea that rolling mills for working it up were not far away and everything betokened the wealth and prosperity of this Kingdom, Bavaria, the boundary of which we passed over a short distance from Salzburg. The custom house for examination of baggage is in the railroad depot at Salzburg.

As we drove from that place for short excursions we were liable to have our bags examined twice in one afternoon as we passed out of and into Austria as often. Such are the annoyances to which secession would subject us at home if it had been successful. What is before our country now? Mr. Borie laughs at any doubt about the re-election of General Grant. I cannot place any reliance on such an unprincipled combination as that of Greeley and the Democracy, and yet I am jealous of the effect of a continuance of the present system. God is our refuge in America, and in Europe there is everything to cause anxious foreboding if we look at human agencies. But here and there we daily see more to confirm the truth of the teaching of His Holy Word—" In vain do the heathen rage and the people imagine a vain thing "—" Yet have I set my king on the Holy hill of Zion."

Friday morning, July 26th.

A good night's rest has refreshed us, and while your mother makes her arrangements for the breakfast table I will continue my letter. Yesterday morning I wandered about the streets of Salzburg, looking at the shop windows, and penniless as Dickens' character, like him feasting my affections with selecting the most beautiful; and thinking how much pleasure it would afford me to present it to "the dearest girl on the earth," but like Traddles I was obliged to turn away satisfied with the will for the deed. Beautiful carvings in wood, ivory and bone, made by the dwellers among the mountains in the Tyrol and Switzerland, were very tempting. I met also Orientals in full costume, sitting at the church doors or walking near them, offering to the people beads and carved shells and pressed flowers from Jerusalem and Bethlehem.

The streets were crowded with country people who had come in on pilgrimage to the church on the mountain side which I mentioned in one of my former letters. They are not well looking, though they may be and, I doubt not, are good. They were in their best attire, which is *not* so picturesque as some of the Netherland or Swiss costumes. The women wear a black silk kerchief folded around their heads with the ends turned out above the ears. On their throats they put an ornament about the size and shape of a ladies' belt or shoe-buckle, which is set with beads or stones, according to the ability of the owner, and is held around the neck by some twenty or more strands of silver chains. In these days of electroplating I suspect most of those we saw for sale in the shop windows were merely silver washed, but when the fashion was adopted they were doubtless all pure metal worked out of the mines of the neighbourhood. A short jacket, full skirt, and an apron, full and long, of some color strongly contrasted with the skirt (often green or crimson) completed the attire.

The men wear tight fitting jackets and small clothes, and ornament them with silver coins or balls as buttons, in great numbers. They have also an embroidered belt of patent leather, and each one carries in a pocket on the right hip of the breeches a knife, fork, and spoon of bone, often richly carved. These are the best. As we see both men and women at their work one would think they *put* their clothes *on* and *wear* them *off*.

The contrast between the neatness of their houses and the untidiness of their persons is very strong. The men at work wear leather breeches pretty much after the pattern of those worn at swimming school, leaving the knees bare. On their legs they wear stockings of woolen yarn, knit in patterns of various colors, but without feet, covering only the calves and ankles. These leggings of the women are often made of white angora yarn, looking as though they were of white rabbit skins.

The Hotel del Europe, at which we staid, is not only very large, but admirably arranged and very well kept. We had grand apartments and your Aunts Hannah and Jane gave up their room, which was next ours, that we might have Galloway and Hannah near us; and your Uncle Wistar most liberally and kindly invited them to take their meals at our table at his expense. Indeed nothing can exceed his lavish generosity in providing everything for our comfort which the most luxurious taste could desire. We did enjoy the privilege of having them with us and I believe your uncle and aunts all participated most pleasantly in our joy.

Hannah and Galloway left us in a carriage to drive through the beauty of the Salz Kammergut. We hope they did not suffer from the heat. Here we find it very oppressive out of doors, though the evening and nights are cool and pleasant. We all regret that our time is occupied now with city sights and galleries instead of valleys and mountains, and are desirous of moving by trains which run early and late, and avoid the midday exposure.

27th.

We still find the heat oppressive for sight seeing and shopping, which appears to be a chronic malady, recurring in violence at every opportunity. The eruption varies as much as do those of Zymotic diseases, sometimes *Picta*, sometimes *Stuckerei*, sometimes *Pelz*, and sometimes *Innominata*. Monday we leave for Nuremberg. With much love to all,

Your affectionate father,

CASPAR MORRIS.

MUNICH, July 28, 1872.

My Dear Children:

My last to you all was from Salzburg where we had the pleasure of having Gall. and Han. with us for a few days, and I cannot tell you what a treat it was to us all, but especially to your father and myself. We had a very quiet time while they were with us, for altho' we took some delightful rides, we had a resting period between and that was so home-like—to knit and talk or be read to by your father. We all left on the same day; they in the morning for that beautiful drive to Ischl; and so on to Vienna, which they expected to reach last evening. We took the cars for this point, choosing the evening train as preferable in the warm spell of weather, which we are now enduring. I cannot give the degree by thermometer, but I know by our *feelings*. The midday is extremely warm, the sun most exhausting, though the nights are of a delightful temperature, so I do not mean to complain, especially when I think of what suffering from heat all at home have been experiencing for a month. It is really cause for thankfulness that we have been spared that, but we do sympathize with you and look with anxiety for accounts. Feel now quite sorry that by some mistake we shall not get last week's mail for ten or twelve days, then we will have a double supply, but that don't make amends for the long wait. Well it is the *oft* repeated and now *oft* required lesson to be patient and forebearing; but I am such a dull scholar that at my advanced age I almost despair of learning.

When we were here last summer it was only for a day and we saw but little, so now there are galleries to be visited, and notwithstanding all my protestations against them I find myself there. To be sure I take my knitting bag, and when head and foot give out find a seat and occupy myself until all the rest are satisfied; which is never less than two hours. My brain gives out very soon, though some of them are very beautiful (and I would be sorry to miss seeing them) yet I do feel often that to me it is a very dear sight, even the little that I do.

July 29th.

All are off again this morning sight-seeing, except Aunt Mary and myself. She would have been with them as she is always foremost in these things, but little Holly has quite a cold and she is to be kept quiet to-day. The child is rejoicing at not having to visit museums and picture galleries, both of which being no longer novelties are extremely wearisome to her. We are now looking to leaving here to-morrow for Nuremberg; thence to Baden Baden. For what we are going there, as none of us "*Play*," I cannot tell; but so it is. Thence to Paris again, and then to England. But all this may be entirely changed before night. It is very certain to my mind that unless Holly is much better we shan't leave here so soon as to-morrow. We had a gust last night which has cooled the air very much, and we all feel as if we could now "do up" Munich.

We suppose Gall. and Han. are in Vienna to-day, but knowing they would have as much writing to do to America as they could well accomplish we told them not to write to us unless something of importance was to be said.

Your father watches for the *Times* at all the Hotels until I tell him the waiters will call him "*Times*" and then for telegraphic intelligence from America. He cannot often get American papers and when he does I tell him it is only to be disgusted, as it is *Herald*, or *Frank Leslie*. I am glad to tell you he is getting along pretty well, heat and all things considered, for you know he always feels the warm weather very much as well as myself; but we do what we can to keep cool. Sometimes I hear a proposition from Uncle Wistar to run back to Switzerland for mountain air, but I don't think they will do it. It is not the road home, and they are all beginning, I am glad to see, wanting to go there.

I am very anxious you should not give yourselves any more trouble to fix us than is absolutely necessary. We shall be so glad (and thankful too) that anything will satisfy. Only *very inexpensive*. *The cheapest arrangement* you can make is what would suit us best. I am in earnest and mean every word of this.

With much love to each and all of you,
Your affectionate mother,
A. C. MORRIS.

MUNICH, BAVARIA, July 27, 1872.

My Dear Children:

We have now been here two days, both intensely hot. Notwithstanding which we have enjoyed our visits to the grand galleries of pictures collected here by Louis of Bavaria; the same monarch who erected the Valhalla. It is one of the strong illustrations of the corruption of human nature that this same Louis allowed himself and his kingdom to be governed by the infamous Lola Montez, and among the pictures collected is a gallery of portraits of beautiful women (very beautiful they are) collected with reference only to their personal form without regard to their moral deformity.

The gallery of ancient masters contains many beautiful pictures; representations of the several schools. Among them are few more celebrated or more worthy of admiration than Murillo's "Beggar Boys" and "Fruit Sellers." Nothing can exceed the truthfulness of these pictures, or the happy freedom from care and thoughtless enjoyment of the young vagabonds, shared by them with their dog who sits with them in each picture. The photographs of them are fine, but want the color, which adds greatly to the life of the pictures. Raphael's "St. Cecilia" is a fine picture of rapt absorption in heavenly meditation. This is however almost the only example of the school of painting which represents the higher and holier emotions of our nature. The Dutch school, with its interiors and exteriors of rollicking festivity, by Teniers and Brower, with monkeys and cats feasting and holding concerts, appears to have been a special favorite, and there are some very beautiful pictures with the exquisite minute finish and purity of subject and conception of Gerard Dow. One very beautiful one represent a woman asking a blessing on her meal.

There are two or three very fine pictures of animals. One by the object of my detestation P. P. Rubens. It required some struggle in my mind to bring me to admit it could be good when I found he was the artist. For a wonder it has nothing about it to offend. It is the most perfect representation of "energy in action," to quote the author of "Rab and His Friends." A lion and wolf and men and horses are grouped, attacking and being attacked, and all tied up in the confusion of a struggle for life, and yet it is not inextricable confusion. You can assign each part to its proprietor without an instant's hesitation, and each is perfectly appropriate to its place in the whole group as well as to the individual. You are fascinated by the horror of the suffering of man and beast and the admiration of the action of each for attack or defense. There is in the same saloon another picture of animals exactly the opposite in all its features. A group composed of three cub lions and a roebuck in sport.

One of the great efforts of art is a singular exhibition of the absurdity of Romish superstitions. It represents the death of the

Virgin, who, though the church has decreed that her "conception was immaculate" and that she was without sin, of course, for having a sinless nature she could know no sin, is represented surrounded by apostles, one of whom places in her hand a blessed candle and another bestows upon her the peculiar benediction of that church. There are not many fine pictures and if all were eliminated except those of real merit, great expense in the erection of the Pinacothek might have been spared, and if we think of the aggregate of fatigue of the tens of thousands of visitors who are wearied with the inspection of pictures, which they decide have no merit, while they seek for the few which have, we cannot but wish the expenditure of King Louis had been less both in building and purchasing. The Murillos alone would be worth coming to Munich to see them.

The modern school of Munich has a well-deserved reputation. We spent many hours in the galleries of Wimmer, a dealer who has a fine collection of pictures, by living artists, for sale. There is one representing the inauguration of the order of Jesuits which like the portrait of Ignatius Loyola, which I saw when we were in England nearly forty years ago, is calculated to make a favourable impression of the earnestness and self dedication of the founders of that society. I shall never forget the impression that portrait produced on me. One could scarcely resist its appeal in behalf of the wonderful man. So this picture is instinct with the spirit of self immolation. Every face is a portrait of one of the original founders, and every attitude is that of devoted consecration. If I were a Jesuit I should wish to see it well engraved and widely circulated as the most powerful appeal in their behalf just at this juncture, when they are the leaders on the side of Rome in the great struggle which is about to agitate the world. How subtle is the adversary of souls thus enlisting on his side the greatest intellects and loftiest passions of human nature.

In contrast with this picture in the same galleries are many beautiful mountain and lake views of the scenes through which we have lately passed ; recalling their glorious and beautiful features so vividly as to make one long to be able to carry them home, that you might participate in our pleasure. But we must be content with the picture defined in our memories and you must comfort yourselves, as I have so many years, with the confident belief that if I did not see them during my mortal life I should, when that short span was passed, see not only these but more glorious tokens of the wisdom and power of God. When these things, "the earth and all things therein are burned up," it is only that we may have a "new heaven and a new earth wherein dwelleth righteousness." Shall that be less grand and beautiful and glorious than this ruined earth, the dwelling of sinful man? I trow not.

This Munich school owes its origin to the collection of old and new paintings made by Louis of Bavaria in the Pinacothek. Those in the galleries devoted to modern art are very fine. Portraits of Louis himself, painted by Kaulbach and also the colossal model of Bavaria in a car drawn by four lions, a very fine group cast in bronze, which now adorns the top of the triumphal arch here. It would be impossible to enumerate let alone attempt to describe the many beautiful paintings collected here, all belonging to the royal family. The building in which they are was erected at the personal expense of the king and cost nearly 250,000 florins.

There is one most impressive picture representing the assassinated body of Count Wallenstein, the great General of the German forces in the seventeenth century. I alluded to the crime in one of my late letters written at the place at which it occurred. He kept with him an astrologer who is said to have warned him of impending danger. He is represented standing over the body of his master with an expression of mingled awe and grief at the crime and his loss of an employer, and satisfaction at the confirmation of his art. A celestial globe marked with the constellations and a bell lying on the floor tell that part of the story. I never saw a more perfect representation of death's triumph than in the perfectly inanimate body as it lies, attired in a white silk quilted doublet; having fallen beside a table and caught in falling the satin cover which is dragged beside him, while a rich Persian rug on the floor is thrown into folds by the struggle. Rich velvet hangings conceal the bed, and the astrologer is clothed in black velvet. One can scarcely decide which part is most perfect; the attitudes of the living and dead men; the natural folds of the rug and drapery and table-cover; the *lustre* of the diamond, the ring on the finger of the murdered man, which literally sparkles in the picture as though it were real; or the rich sheen of the silk and satin and velvet. I have often wondered how the artist, when he lays his colors on the canvas, in *rough* masses, can conceive of the delicacy of the effect they will produce to the eyes of the beholder at the proper distance. At the appropriate point of view this picture has the appearance of the delicacy of miniature finish—standing close one would think it was finished with a mason's trowel.

In the same apartment are two views of the interior of Westminster Abbey, London, which are wonderfully perfect. There is also in this collection an oil painting by Kaulbach of the destruction of Jerusalem, a copy of that on the wall at Berlin. I have already described it. It is a grand painting and I should like to possess a good photograph of it, were it not for the painful nature of the principal group in the foreground—the self-destruction of the high priest, with his family gathered around him. On one side is a beautiful group, symbolical of Christianity protected by Angels, emerging in peace and safety from the ruin of Judaism; on the other the wandering Jew is driven away by avenging furies. The body and background of the picture are occupied by Roman soldiers and scenes of conflagration and destruction, over which avenging angels hover.

In another room is a very large picture, left unfinished at the death of the artist, representing the Deluge. The various passions of our corrupt nature are exhibited in the multitude crowded on the last peak uncovered by the flood. Idols are invoked or despised, love is exhibited and selfish greed displayed. It is a forcible illustration from which one turns with a shudder, and thoughts of that time when "waves of ire again the world shall fill"; and longing to be found safe in the ark which "rides the sea of fire and rests on Zion's hill."

The remark I made on the collection of old pictures is equally applicable to this, there are too many of inferior merit. But the number of *good*—real good—pictures is very great. Cattle pieces, in which you can fancy the lowing of the herds and bleating of the flocks. (There is one picture at Wimmers for sale which is very fine. A storm is approaching and a flock of sheep running from it come suddenly on a scare-crow thrown down, they stop and consult over it, one very young lamb pressing closely to the side of the ewe, looks as wise as infancy often does.)

The landscapes are also fine, and so are some of the pictures of character. One represents two boys at a cigar shop making a first purchase. They are not sick yet, have only just made the few first triumphant puffs while the old dealer looks on, happy in the prospect of future customers.

But it is a vain attempt to convey to readers the pleasure the visitor finds in looking at these beautiful works. A love for art is deeply implanted in our nature; and our own artists will soon supply us with pictures quite as good if we encourage them. Americans are the best patrons of living artists in Europe now. We must cultivate our indigenous productions more liberally.

Monday evening.

Little Mary has taken cold and is quite unwell. I shall be very happy if she is not seriously ill. She coughs, breathes very quickly, has fever and some congestion of the left lung. It *may* prove to be typhoid fever. Yesterday I was quite anxious about her. We have been quiet here to-day on her account, and this afternoon she appears livelier and coughs less, but is yet far from well; if she is well enough to-morrow we shall make a short journey to Augsburg on our way to Stuttgart the next day, and so to Baden Baden, which will be a pleasanter place to be detained at than this is. The weather is very hot and we have visited most of the objects of interest and your uncle and aunts have made their various purchases here. The time will consequently drag heavily till we move. The stimulus of novelty is exhausted and there is no Swiss tour nor Nile voyage before us. I believe most of us would gladly shorten the interval till we reach home, though England and Scotland are not without attractions if we could only get *there*, or *somewhere*, out of the heat.

We met one of our fellow voyagers on the Nile who had just returned from "Cape North." He says he never saw glaciers or snow-clad mountains to approach those of Norway, and finds the heat here more oppressive even than we, by the contrast.

We are longer than usual without letters and shall not receive any before Saturday, and not then unless we can get to Baden, where they are ordered to meet us.

Tuesday morning.

Little Mary is better, though still so unwell that we have decided to stay here to-day and allow her to recruit. A storm last night has cooled the temperature and improved the air, but I shall be glad to get nearer home. On mentioning to Friezier my anxiety about the child lest it should prove typhoid fever, he expressed much alarm and said he had been with an English party who had lost a daughter at Berchtesgaden a few years since with that disease, named Lloyd; a banker of Birmingham. He was one of the Braithwaite connection. I hope we may be spared the anxiety and sorrow. Your mother and I did a little shopping this morning and one of the shop girls had a head which shewed she was convalescent from an attack of typhoid.

Your mother is obliged to lay aside again her own shoe and return to the large cloth one which is rather warm for this season. Your uncle and I will leave the ladies within doors and visit some of the museums. There is also a fair in operation with its whirligigs and wax works and (double-headed negro girls and Aztec children among them)—human nature is the same here as at home. Lotteries take the place of dollar stores. The customer pays his Kreutzer and takes whatever he gets in return. The counter is crowded with people getting all sorts of things, but chiefly very cheap pressed glassware. The children enjoy greatly the swinging round on wooden horses.

Your loving father,

CASPAR MORRIS.

MUNICH, July 28, 1872.

*My Dear Sister (Emily Hollingsworth.—*Eds.):

I know how anxiously your heart beats in sympathy with us and how you yearn for information about dear Hannah and Galloway, and therefore avail myself of a few minutes while waiting for dinner between services to say how delighted we were to have them spend a day or two with us at Salzburg last week. To-day we hope they are in Vienna and that they may enjoy the same privileges on this blessed

Lord's day as have refreshed us here. The provision made for the refreshment of the souls of travellers by the Continental Society maintaining chaplains at the most important places in the current of travel is worthy of all commendation; and as I listened to a most instructive sermon on the text "That Rock was Christ," most ably illustrated by ample quotations from the word of God, commencing with the caution given by Isaiah not to put confidence in *man*, followed by the quotation from the same prophet "A *man* shall be for a refuge" and thus exhibiting the adaptation of Christ; perfect God, and perfect man; to be a "shadow," a "cleft rock," and a "smitten rock," from which spiritual waters flow for the refreshment of His people in this wilderness journey, I could not but be thankful that we had such blessed teaching.

The weather is *intensely hot*, enabling us to appreciate the force of the figure that "a man shall be as the shadow of a great rock." The heat is not so great as it has been with you, but I quite agreed with Anne that it is too great for her to venture out, as the church is at some distance from the Hotel.

We imagine you as still at Ivy Neck and pray that you as well as dear Mary and Harry and their children may escape disease and that we may be permitted to meet in October in health and peace. But who can tell what a day may bring forth;

Little Mary has been rather drooping for some days past—I thought only from fatigue and perhaps some cold. This morning she was so drooping that I advised she should keep her bed; she now appears brighter. Should she be sick I shall feel the responsibility a very oppressive burden, and shall need grace to enable me to cast it on Him who careth for us and who has certainly dealt very mercifully with us thus far, and deserves our gratitude, which should manifest itself, among other ways, by continued unwavering *trust*. Mary has grown very much during our journey, but her appetite is very capricious and she looks pale and is easily fatigued. Picture galleries and sights can have but little attraction for a child of her age, and yet it is very surprising to hear her refer to things we have seen and places at which we have been which you would not suppose could interest her.

Evening.

On my return from afternoon service I find little Mary much better, sitting at the piano going over some hymn tunes with her mother. So that I hope my anxiety is without foundation. We are all trying to keep as quiet as possible. A great fair has been opened here *to-day* and though Bavaria is the most intensely Romish of the German peoples, we see but little manifestation of religious feeling or sentiment in any way.

We desire our dear love to brother Henry and sister Caroline and their children. We saw Henry G's name yesterday on the books of Wimmer, the picture dealer, who has some very tempting pictures now for sale.

Your loving brother,

CASPAR MORRIS.

AUGSBURG, August 1, 1872.

My Dear Children:

We have slept under the roof covering the house in which the Emperor Charles V has sojourned ; and stood by side the fire-place on the hearth of which Fugger kindled the flame of quills of cinnamon whose odours have diffused themselves and transported his name to regions more remote than the Taprobane, in which grew the trees which furnished the fuel for that flame, in which he consumed the bond which told only of the wealth he had acquired by honest industry, which he sacrificed to the fame of nobility for himself and his posterity. This hotel is said to be the oldest house devoted to that purpose in the world, having been thus occupied three centuries, during which period it has received within its doors scores of guests whose names are illustrious in history. How many unpretending pilgrims like ourselves ? Immediately adjoining stands the house of Fugger, the entire front of which extending more than 100 feet is covered by modern frescoes, designed to illustrate the events of his life ; from the little boy starting off with his bag on his shoulder to the gorgeously apparelled citizen standing before the throne of the Emperor, while his porters bring in the treasure box whose contents are to supply the means by which Charles is to carry on his war with the Pope and strive to secure the Papal crown for the head, as well as the Imperial Sceptre for the hand, of his descendants forever, and at the same time crush out and extinguish the Protestant spirit which dared to oppose the royal command that they should submit their consciences to the control of priests at the head of whom were Borgias and Leos.

Augsburg has been the scene of many important events. Many Diets of the German Empire have sat here. No less than five during the reign of Charles V. Was it not to a Diet here that Luther was summoned, and to attend which he received the Imperial safeguard and to which his friends urged him not to go and received the reply that if there were as many devils there to confront him as there were tiles on the roofs of the houses he would go in despite of them all ? And was it not from here that he was carried off by Ulric von Hutton to the castle of Wurzburg ? I am not positive about it. Certainly it was to another Diet held here that the Confession of Faith, which is still the formula of the doctrine of the Lutheran Church, was presented.

It is a grand old town with a very wide main street and fine old houses. We were there but a few hours in the evening and left at 7 A. M. this morning quite favourably impressed by its dignified respectability. I was amused by the sight of an immense stork's nest built on the top the chimney of one of the tallest houses.

Five or six long-legged storks were very busy house-cleaning and kept up an unceasing flutter as they stood on their long legs and tossed their long necks about throwing out refuse matter.

The rooms we occupied in the Hotel Drie Mohren were of great size ; our chamber not less than 30 feet square, and the apartment in which Fugger burned the bond is forty-five feet square and said to be just as it was then, except that the ornamental painting of the wall has been renewed after the old figures, which are not very elegant. The ceiling is of cedar, in panels, with carved mouldings. The windows are lattice with small panes set in leaden frames. We left at an early hour in the morning, not doubting that if we had tarried longer we could have found houses and corners which would recall to the memory of those whose minds are stored with the history of the Reformation many of the stirring incidents of that wonderful epoch, and would serve as stimulants of wavering faith and help the true believer to gird up the loins of his mind and be sober and vigilant, not knowing at what time the Son of Man cometh again, not with an offering for sin, but to judge the world which has so despised and rejected him. I find constant need of the quickening and strengthening power of the Holy Ghost to keep me like one who waiteth for the coming of his Lord, that he may enter with him with lamp trimmed and burning and oil in the vessel with the lamp.

The more I see of the fearful trials endured in those days for the truth's sake the more ashamed I feel of my own weakness of faith and the more firmly convinced that if any man will be the disciple of Jesus he must deny himself, take up his cross daily and follow Him. And the more I see of the hurly-burly of the world, and its political and commercial affairs and the vanity and hollowness of its pretensions in its personal affectation of pleasure in sin, the more earnestly do I pray that its chains may be stricken off of me and mine, and we may be made free indeed by Him, the Son who only can make us free.

STUTTGART, August 2d.

Our trip to this place from Augsburg was a very pleasant one of about five hours by rail. The earlier part of the route lay across one of those wide plateaux which are so peculiar a characteristic of this continent. In some places there were peat bogs, but even the surface of these is cultivated and appears to yield a fair return of wheat, barley and oats which were ripe and either being reaped with sickles or waiting for the slow progress in harvesting with the primitive hook. It was curious to see the square cut margins of the places from which the peat had been taken with growing crops on the fresh edge, and ploughs and harrows preparing the *dark brown* soil to receive fresh crops immediately alongside of the white harvest or stubble, and on the next lot the black brick-shaped turf piled up to dry for winter use. In some places there were large open-work receptacles on which it is stored, and in others long buildings in which it is kept for fuel for the locomotives.

From this plateau we passed into a very beautiful rolling district with green crops of beet and flax and oats distributed in parallel patches, some in long and some in square divisions and some arranged concentrically, thus giving variety to the otherwise unchanging repetition of shades of green and yellow. Clover patches and potatoes now were added to the other elements of beauty and finally maize cheered us with its familiar green coat and yellow tassel.

We next passed through a mountainous district, not the towering rocky peaks and snowy ridges we have been so delighted with, but lofty hills, clothed with pine and fir, intersected by deep valleys of smiling grassy slopes, dotted with hamlets. We passed over the ridge forming the water-shed between the sources of the streams flowing on the one side to the Black Sea and on the other to the North Sea, and at Ulm took our leave of the king of European rivers, the majestic Danube, which we have sailed upon and crossed so frequently within the last year, touching so many points from its source, in these German forests and mountains, to its mighty rush through *the gates*, as they are called, at which it emerges into the vast plain through which it flows to the Euxine. When we entered Wurtemberg we found ourselves again in the region of vines, which cover the slopes of the hills.

BADEN BADEN, August 3d.

We enjoyed greatly the drive to this place. The road lay through a region resembling our Chester County with the mountains skirting it. Immense potato fields were added to the cereal crops which were fully ripe and about half harvested. There was also a very abundant poppy culture. We passed through Carlsruhe, the capital of the territory of the Duchy of Baden, and Rastadt (a highly fortified place). A heavy gust had just passed over the country, giving freshness to everything and reducing the temperature so that we found it very pleasant to travel.

This is a narrow valley winding among high hills. It is filled with villas, lodging houses and hotels of every size and shape. A rapid but small mountain stream runs through it, which is confined by stone walls about ten or twelve feet high which limit its largest flow, and are hung for a mile or more by beautiful drapery of Ampelopsis, planted along the top and hanging, the graceful branches in irregular festoons, to the bottom. The bed is about fifty feet wide, paved with flat stones, while the actual flow of the stream is limited at present by curbs which restrain it in a channel about four feet wide, running down the centre. Along the top of the walls are walks and drives, while the hillsides are planted with shrubbery and evergreen trees, many of which are covered with the Ampelopsis, which grows most luxuriantly, and falls in the richest folds from tree to tree like green drapery, revealing the form and varying size of the supports which it covers. Walks are laid out with much skill and flower beds planted, so that one is tempted to wander illimitably.

We were too wearied last evening to go far and everything was saturated by the rain which had fallen heavily. I only sauntered out a little while just before tea. As I wandered up stream my attention was arrested by brilliant lights glancing through the foliage before me and approaching them I was instantly reminded of Bunyan's description of Vanity Fair, with its rows and booths, on which were displayed all the merchandise of the world. Certainly nowhere else can be found so many shops splendidly lighted and filled with all manner of wares to attract the eye of taste. Passing along in front of them I arrived at a grand promenade, in the centre of which stood a pavilion filled by a band of musicians, while, like so many moths around the flame, flitted thousands of men and women *en grand toilette*, talking French, English and German. Along one side of the promenade stretched the columns of a portico, some two hundred feet long, on which was seated a dense mass of men and women, while at either end crowds were flocking into the brilliantly lighted hall, whose open front displayed the gorgeous arrangements within.

I mingled in the crowd at one end and as I reached the point at which the streams met, found your uncle Wistar, who had gone out before me and had taken an entirely diverging course at the start, in the other. A grand chandelier hung in the middle of the hall under which stood a table, around it a standing crowd of men and women, while at it sat as many persons of both sexes as could find places. In the centre of the table was a gilded bowl around which revolved some inexplicable arrangement of balls, on which all eyes were fixed ; while the spaces of the table were marked out by lines crossing at right angles and numbered, and some marked with words in French, *Par, Impar, Manque,* etc., the application of which appeared to be well understood. Pieces of money were placed on particular points of intersection or numbers, some gold and some silver, and at irregular intervals persons placed toward the centre of the table raked them off, and they disappeared ; I could not see how nor where. A pile of pieces of gold and silver and bank notes lay before one person at the centre of the table who every now and then distributed some on either side.

The whole process was conducted in perfect silence and except for the dress of the parties one would have supposed themselves at a banking establishment at which receipts of deposits was going on. There seemed few or no payments of demands. Your uncle and I stood a few minutes and knowing your mother and aunts would be waiting for us at the more congenial table spread with the tea equipage, and surrounded by loving hearts and smiling faces and cheerful words, we turned our backs on the pool of chance in the revolving vortex of which fools were sinking money and drowning souls, and walked back to our inn. The air resonant with the bewitching melody of the band playing the music of the opera of Oberon, as we were informed by a transparency in front of the stage. The weather this morning is cool and pleasant and the sky overcast. We shall remain here a few days and then return to Paris.

We received letters last evening from dear Mary of the 8th of July, and one from cousin Emily of the 11th, and from brother Galloway of the 16th, none from Cheston or Israel and none from Galloway and Hannah. We shall probably get none now till we reach Paris next week, as the direction to Brown, Shipley & Co. was not to send anything here later than the 2d. Cheston we suppose was absent in Virginia, Annie at Atlantic City and Israel very busy; as Mr. Longstreth reports he found him when he called at the office.

I was sorry to leave Munich the day we came away as the crowd was already collecting for a grand celebration of the tricentenary anniversary of the foundation of the University at that place, and though we could not appreciate the sentiments of the orations we could have enjoyed the excitement of processions and music and military display and torchlight gatherings, all which were to enter into the ceremonies

At Stuttgart we called on Mr. R. W. Tyson and were edified by the assurance that we shall yet see the *Stars* and *Bars* take the place of the Stars and Stripes; and that Ulysses S. Grant is aspiring to the position of *king ;* to which I responded by the expression of my inability to find the principle which could lie at the bottom of the combination between the Democrats and Horace Greeley. I am digusted at the exhibition we make of ourselves. I am satisfied the South is wronged by the unprincipled hordes of Northern speculators who are inflaming the passions of the two races, and yet I cannot feel anything but disgust at the combination which is made in opposition. It is with no fanatical fatalism, but a faith, feeble it is true from my own weakness, yet fixed and immovable, that God does reign and will restrain the evil passions of sinful men and cause light to shine out of darkness, that I leave all to His ordering.

Your mother waits for me to walk out.

Your loving father,

CASPAR MORRIS.

BADEN BADEN, August 4, 1872.

My Dear Child:

We came here from Stuttgart two days ago; having left Munich two days previous. Were almost driven from the latter place by intense heat. Oh, it was so oppressive and exhausting, but when we read the accounts from home, both in the papers and our letters, I feel as though we should not allow ourselves to say a word. Yours has been so prolonged and there has been so much suffering with it. *Here* we are delightfully cool and it is a very beautiful spot naturally. Surrounded by the Black Forest, which only means a forest of the deepest shade of evergreens you can imagine, extending for miles. Everything has been done to make this place attractive in the way of drives, walks, etc., and it is a place of great resort. Forty thousand visitors here now, and this is the "season"; so of course we see it in its glory. "The Billiard Saloon" is to be broken up at the close of this year, so perhaps the lovers of that kind of *amusement* (shall I call it?) may be more eager than usual to make the most of these few weeks. Don't be too much startled when I tell you I walked through the building, with your father and aunts yesterday and saw at least six long tables *crowded* with eager players, men, women and children; many in elegant attire, but oh, such countenances! It made my heart ache for them, and of course a few minutes were sufficient for us. We understood nothing, but saw piles of gold and silver staked and swept off; the changing countenances of those who were playing. It was perfectly quiet, not a loud word, scarcely an audible one. From there we walked around to look into some most beautiful shop windows, but as the articles are held high we are not likely to be purchasers. Then we went into the "Drinking Saloon," which sounds badly but is only to drink *hot* (yes, too hot to drink,) water from the natural fountain. Most walk up there before breakfast, but I don't think any of us will be energetic enough for that. We took a beautiful drive up the mountain to an "old castle," for the view, in the afternoon; and now I feel as if we had done here and would be glad to push on, which I believe we are to do the day after to-morrow, to Strasburg and then to Paris; as they all seem to think they did not finish it.

We have letters from you up to the 8th of July and feel very thankful all was well with you; also heard Cousin Emily had gone down (which I was very glad to hear) this morning.

We have a letter from Gall, from Vienna, they were getting along pretty well. Had been invited by Mr. Borie to dine with their party of nine (Miss Grant included) at the hotel. Found them all pleasant people; two young men, Mr. Keating and Mr. Lewis, acquaintances of Gall's, are travelling with them. Americans greet each other cordially when they meet.

In Stuttgart we had a most warm reception from R. W. and Julia Tyson; they came to the hotel and spent the evening. She was fascinating to all around, very bright; and gave us some directions for Paris which we hope will be helpful. Poor R. is I fear not improved; it was sad indeed to see his condition. Nannie was sick, so I did not see her.

Then your father and I went to see the four little Gepp children who are at Stuttgart with a sister of their father's (Annie Cowpland's nephews and nieces). We were very glad we did, as they too were so glad to see any one from America, altho' strangers. You know a motherless child goes right to my heart, and it did warm up to these. We found them living in an attic with a very fine view, and very comfortable apartments, kindly cared for I have no doubt; and they look well and happy. It is customary here for persons to rent a floor. Their aunt is a widow, taking boarders, but very nice looking person.

We left them a few books and they were highly delighted. Please don't anybody congratulate me on having a Paris dress. I have it on now; absolute necessity makes me wear it, but I don't feel like myself, nor do I know how to alter it or I would. All tell me, except your father, it is handsome. He, poor man, like myself, has to bear it. But give me Mary Gibson; tell her so with my love. I am so glad she is with you, and think it was so kind in Mr. McMurtrie to send all those girls' dresses. My dress is a black silk trimmed with Guipure lace. An overskirt. But oh, so stuck up do I feel! I am hoping I will find something of a bonnet in England. There is nothing but jaunty hats here.

Our time is shortening. Next Saturday nine weeks we will sail. What will you do? Meet us in Philadelphia or wait for us to go to you; which we will certainly do as promptly as possible.

I find your aunt Mary intends getting an Irish poplin for you if we go to Dublin. What colour shall I choose, blue, purple, or some grave colour? and as I *must* cut the breadths, or pay duty, will you have it a short skirt or with train. All street dresses here are made short; that is no trains. Tell me the number of inches at once, so that I may get it in time.

We have been quite anxious about little Holly; she has been a right sick child for ten or twelve days; quite threatened with typhoid fever; but, child-like, fights against laying by, and we now think she will escape. She looks very badly and, altho' they don't know it, your father has been quite troubled about her. Yesterday she tried a donkey ride, but reports the animal very obstinate; not at all like the Egyptian ones. To-morrow she will try a donkey carriage ride as we see them here.

Give much love to all. Dear little Sally; I hope her boils are over. Effingham can sympathize with her for he had a great many bad ones.

It does give us so much pleasure to hear of the young people having a nice time together. Ere this Eff. has left you, I expect, but I hardly expect from what we hear of Israel's pressing engagements that he can take the young people away this summer.

We do feel very anxious about Han. She is a very sick woman, we think, but if anything was to be done to arrest the disease this trip was the thing, and just at this period of it—the beginning. I do hope her children will keep well.

Your father is pretty well, and we are all getting on well.

Love to cousin and share this with her.

Yours most affec.,

A. C. M.

BADEN BADEN, August 5, 1872.

My Dear Children:

I mailed a letter here on our arrival and now shall endeavor to take up the broken thread of my narrative—inextricably tangled I fear—and worth but little when drawn out. I had forgotten Stuttgart till we reached there the second time, and I found the sight of its colonades and fine buildings and the drive through the beautiful park revived my former enthusiasm, and I felt ready still to endorse all I then said about its grandeur and the beauty of its surroundings. The railroad depot is worth the imitation of any of our chief lines at their principal terminus, and they are now building a hotel in connection with it. The order which pervades all the arrangements and the size and cleanliness of its waiting-rooms and restaurants are very attractive and imposing. The panels of the doors are of oak carved most elaborately and artistically and the third class accommodation there is far better than the best I ever saw in England or America. Your aunts walked, ignorantly, into one of the apartments, the door of which was open and a man at work planing the floor, who at once sprang to his feet and with great earnestness implored them to go out. I met them at the door quite disconcerted and looking at the inscription overhead found to my amusement it was The Royal Waiting Apartment. I did not see how it looked inside, as the man shut himself in, but do not know how it could have been made more elegant than that in which we poor republicans were invited to make ourselves at ease. The building is not less than 200 feet long and I should think as wide. I suggested to your uncle that it would absorb some extra stock dividends.

I walked and drove through the town several times. Once with your uncle and aunts to explore its beauties, and through the park and out to a suburb where there is an alkaline and gaseous spring, much frequented. The water is so highly charged with carbonic acid gas that when you look into it in the deep fountain it has a milky appearance; though it is perfectly clear when held up to the light. The grounds around it are laid out beautifully and provided with seats. The mountains lie all around the town and are covered with terraces and cultivated with vines.

I sought out the grandchildren of my friend Mr. Cowpland, who live here with a widowed aunt, a sister of the father. She is a lovely looking woman and they nice, sweet well behaved children. They live in the upper flat or story of a house having eight rooms on each floor, so that they are quite above the world which rolls and bustles below them, and from every window have a grand view of the mountains and enjoy the pure fresh air. But then there is no such thing as "just running out a minute" or "taking a play in the yard." Your mother went with me but was unable to climb so high, but the children made her a visit as she sat in the carriage, and she sent me out early the next morning to hunt the book stores for something which would please them, and you never saw more delight than from a few volumes I gave them. The apartments were very pleasant. But think of wood, coal, water—everything wanted—being carried up to the fifth story. It makes one ashamed to complain of any trifling inconvenience. We also saw Mr. and Mrs. R. W. Tyson. I sent my card and they very politely called on us. Mordecai had returned to school in Switzerland.

Every one I talk with here says parents do not know what they are about when they send their children to Germany for education, and all we have seen justifies the observation. It is but too common for men and women when they leave home to reason that they may do as others do, and thus justify the violation of God's universally applicable law by "following a multitude to do evil." What is to be expected from the inexperience of youth thus misled by age? And yet we have returned to the region in which I was so deeply impressed last summer by the majesty of law. Gardens and vines and fruits all lay exposed and unrifled. Great lines of fruit trees, cherries, apples, plums and pears hanging on them unmolested, are planted along the common roadway. The orchards themselves are large and healthy looking, and bear freely, so that I suspect cider is in demand to adulterate wine. We passed several sugar making establishments also, and saw much land occupied with beet culture.

We have been in Baden Baden now two days and are enjoying ourselves much. The house we are in is a good and quiet one and our table well supplied. The parlour has a balcony with the windows opening down to the floor and looking out across the rapid stream of the Oös to a lofty hillside planted with ornamental trees; and about half way up the gilded dome of the Russian or Greek church crops out above the foliage.

I think I mentioned in my last how nicely the bed of the river is paved and its margin walled up and covered with the drapery of green vines which hangs so thickly as to cover the stones. This wall is some 12 feet high and the stream rises in Spring so as to fill the space between the walls and would if it were not thus restrained spread over the valley, every part of which not occupied with hotels and villas for the accommodation of visitors, is now laid out in beautiful grounds with clean nice walks, and planted with ornamental trees and shrubberry and flower beds. Comfortable seats are placed at short distances so that every inducement is afforded to visitors to resort here during the warm season. There have been frequent showers so that all nature wears a rich green hue and we find the temperature most genial. The drives are also very attractive.

Your uncle Wistar who does everything to promote our pleasure regardless of expense, yesterday afternoon had carriages and drove to the old castle on the top of the mountains above the town. It was a beautiful drive along perfect roads zigzagging the mountain, which is clothed to the top with noble firs and pines and oaks and beeches. At intervals we caught views of the valley below, opening into that of the Rhine. Wide and green with the shining river meandering through the fertile plains as though reluctant to leave them. From the castle at the top the view is very extensive said to reach even to Strasburg.

Your mother and I sat in the carriage while the young folks (your aunt Hannah at the lead) mounted the many stairs to the top of the tower. It was a grand view from where we sat and we drank in a sufficiency of delight without the extra labour. It was too hazy to catch the tower of the cathedral.

After tea I went again to the great place of concourse and passed once more around the saloons, crowded by the votaries of chance and doubtless many who, like myself, were mere spectators drawn by curiosity. It is a sadly solemn spectacle. Men and women made in the image of God with souls capable of the highest and loftiest conceptions, who might find delight in the works of nature so grandly and beautifully spread around them ; or, happiness in the service of their Creator and Redeemer ; spending hour after hour in silent wrapt attention to the revolutions of a gilded bowl and the gyrations of a little ball rolling around its margin, and watching, as for the decree of fate, the moment when the neutralization of forces shall cause it to drop into a cell, the number inscribed on which decides who shall lose and who win the gold and silver pieces deposited before them. Such at least appeared to be the solution of the game. Not a word uttered by anyone. Pieces of money thrown down as you would throw out crumbs to birds or corn to pigeons, to be raked off at the moment the ball falls, and replaced again by others.

From 11 A.M. to 11 P.M. daily, there are six or eight tables, each twenty feet long, surrounded by crowds standing around those who sit closely around it. There are certain men in charge who are changed every hour, while liveried servants are perpetually moving about—I could not see for what. Young men, with the soft, rich tint of opening manhood blooming on their still unfurrowed, unbearded cheeks, and the lofty bearing of a noble nature, not yet obliterated, were thoughtlessly pressing into the stream that was to bear them onward and downward, and convert them into the bowed and brutalized shapes which sat around the board; while, saddest sight of all, thoughtless and heartless mothers led their daughters by the hand, and tempted them to try their yet-untested luck.

When I was a child I used to turn often to the pages of a huge quarto volume of geography, in which is described the Maelstrom on the coast of Norway, and I have often shuddered as I figured to myself the horrors of the great vortex, whirling round and round the noble ship which was driven by winds within the fatal sweep of its outer current; the diameter ever diminishing until it was engulfed. The gilded bowl, with its mysterious revolutions, brought it all back to my imagination after half a century.

There were other modes of gambling being pursued at other tables, all in perfect silence. Neither visitors nor players uttered a word, except the master of the game, who counted the cards or announced the number of the cell into which the ball fell. The proprietor of the establishment pays £12,000 for the privilege. When to this $60,000 is added to the cost of keeping up all the elegance around, and the salaries of skilled and qualified assistants, sufficiently numerous to relieve each other every hour, and all the minor expenses, and to this the sum he must make for his own profit, some idea may be formed of the amount *lost* here annually to supply the little that is won. Yet such is the fascination that the crowd of visitors flows in year after year.

There is no apology for the resort to the gaming table for amusement. I cannot conceive of any place presenting greater attractions. The valley itself is naturally one of great beauty, the mountains around are very fine, though not lofty, and are clothed with majestic forests of fir and pine. Old castles crown the crags, which jut out through the dark-green foliage, and modern villas are scattered everywhere, surrounded by pleasure grounds. The Oös meanders through the valley, which is planted with ornamental trees and laid out in walks and drives, kept in perfect repair, and carried for miles along the mountain sides and across their tops, giving endless variety of views. Shops in the town, and booths on the promenade, display fancy and other goods in profusion. Book stores offer variety of literature. The tables are abundantly supplied with every luxury. It is an old Roman station. *That* people certainly had a taste for the beautiful. They fixed themselves and built villas wherever thermal springs burst out of the earth, in every land over which they carried their eagles.

There are but few French people here now; perhaps none. We hear the language occasionally, but it is probably from the lips of Russians and Italians. Germans predominate, with many English and Americans. A Mrs. Ware of Boston, died here last week, and a young Bickersteth, the son of the Bishop of Ripon, one of the best men on the Episcopal Bench, was cut off in the flower of his youth by a sudden hemorrhage. He was travelling with a tutor, and died in this hotel.

August 9th.

We have been detained here longer than we designed by the sickness of your Uncle Wistar's little girl. She has not been well since we left Salzburg, and before we arrived here was quite sick with a suffocative catarrh. She had ear-ache added to it on Monday and considerable fever. Yesterday she was much better, and took quinine and slept well last night, so that we hope to leave here to-morrow for Strasbourg and go to Paris on Saturday.

We shall remain there till the middle or last of the next week, and then cross to Dover, and so to London. We shall feel as though we were then but a step from home, though that is a long one and across a stormy sea. But we desire to commit ourselves to the guidance and protection of the great mercy and love which have been with us thus far, not only on our journey, but all our pilgrimage of life.

I had a very kind letter from Mrs. Betts, the widow of the gentleman who died at Assouan, inviting your mother and myself to make our home with her while your uncle and aunts travel over England and Scotland. She lives only twenty minutes out of London, and suggests that I could go there and see all I wish, and your mother stay quietly with her. It is very kind, and shows how well she appreciates your mother's character. We shall not think of accepting the offer, grateful as we are for it.

Canon Lysons, whom we met in Jerusalem, gives us the same invitation to his house near Gloucester for the whole party. He knows well the representatives of the Cheston family still living near him. I shall make an effort to *call* on him as we pass in his neighborhood.

Mrs. Betts writes us that a Mr. Richardson, who was with us all the way up and down the Nile in a boat like our own, and owned by the same party, died at Pesth a few weeks since. We saw each other very often, and your Aunt Mary was very desirous to join them at Cairo, and go to Jerusalem across the Desert of Sinai. He and Mrs. Richardson were very nice people, and they had a son with them about twenty years of age. Mrs. Richardson and Mrs. Betts had been intimate before marriage, and they sympathized deeply with her in her trial. Mr. Richardson was in perfect health when we parted. It was a great mercy they should have got fairly back to Europe before he was taken ill; and Pesth is a very fine city, with everything a traveller could desire. Thus you see two of our Nile acquaintances are already gone. The wife of Norman McLeod, the great Scotch minister and writer, was also an intimate friend of Mrs. Betts and Mrs. Richardson, so that the three friends are left widows almost simultaneously.

I received a letter here from Galloway, at Vienna. He and Hannah appeared then to be well and enjoying themselves. They had dined with Miss Grant by invitation of Mr. Borie. We are anxious about them, and almost fear to receive letters. They are now, we hope, in Switzerland or Northern Italy. They could not join William and Sallie, which we regret very much, as it would have given them companionship and diminished the cost to both. William and Sallie had got too far ahead before Gall. and Han. arrived.

With much love to all the family and our various friends, as though named. Cheston will think of this whenever he sees any of my old patients, to whom I am greatly attached, and also my medical associates, Dr. Hodge at the top of all the lists.

Your loving father,

CASPAR MORRIS.

BADEN BADEN, August 5, 1872.
My Dear Brother (Galloway Cheston.—EDS.):

We were somewhat relieved of our anxiety about you by your letter of July 14th, received here yesterday, as we had heard that yourself and Miss Townsend had both been ill. The report of the great and prolonged heat keeps us still uneasy, knowing as we do know how much dear Margaret suffers from its exhausting influence. We must endeavor to seek for each other and ourselves grace that we may follow the bright example of Mary Ellen, and daily depend with simple, childlike confidence on the wise and loving care of our merciful and compassionate God, the Father of our Lord Jesus Christ.

You will be surprised to find us still on the Continent, and may perhaps smile at learning we are here. It is a very beautiful and attractive place, and there is no apology for evil where there is so much that is good and beautiful to delight the eye and cheer the heart and occupy the time. I have not yet felt any temptation to indulge in the besetting sin of the place, though I have ventured repeatedly within the charmed circle as a study. I cannot understand the principle of the games, and I can see that a man must be a worshipper of chance to venture at all, where he must see that chance so favours the proprietor of the establishment as to enable him to pay $60,000 annual rent for the privilege of taking his chance at the pockets of the 40,000 visitors who annually come here, and expend probably as much more in salaries and various outlays in addition, and yet find the profit sufficient to justify the employment of so large a capital. The whole affair is conducted as quietly and decorously as a bank of deposit and payment.

The actors are tranquil, the officers polite and decorous gentlemen; the spectators stand silently by. What passions are caged and curbed—what hopes and fears flutter and are convulsed—what remorses rage—what envy gnaws the heart of those who look as unmoved as the green surface of the beautiful valley around!

Boys with the soft smile which you know is so bewitching in its influence on me, and the delicate glow of yet unsullied innocence on their rounded cheeks, lay their sovereigns on the magic table;—and mothers lead their daughters, three in hand, to the sacrificial bowl revolving in gilded brilliance, while the little ball of fate makes its counter gyrations along the margin, and teach them to venture within the current of the vortex which is to engulf them—neither sex deterred by the sight of the haggard and withered automatons who sit before them at the table—the older devotees, whose powers seem to have become dwarfed to the mere ability to deposit their coins, handle the rake, and make a note on the card which lies before them.

How many generations have followed each other in the same career? This year is the last of the lease here. Where will the demon set up his altar next? I suppose Saratoga and Newport have shrines perhaps as much frequented.

I am not relieved from the dark and anxious forebodings about the future destiny of our country (for which my friends chide me) by the nomination of Greeley and Brown, which will doubtless result in placing Brown in the presidential chair with such politicians as the Blairs to manipulate the wires by which the country is to be governed. Jefferson's utterance as to the future was like that of Balaam in the case of Israel of old: " There is no attribute in the divine character to which the white race can appeal in its struggle with the negro."

I had written thus far when I was summoned to see Wistar's daughter, who has been complaining for a fortnight. I hope she is not seriously ill, but feel anxious about her. We may be detained here some time. At present it is ear-ache.

August 7th.

Wistar's little girl is much better. We shall remain here over to-day, and then start, hoping to reach Paris on Saturday evening, and London about the last of the following week. I have sent an order for bulbs to Van Houtte.

I wish you would write us your views about the question what we may and may not carry in with us through the custom house. I do not know what the law permits, and while we wish to pay what is honest and right in the sight of God and man, we do not wish to do more. What others think and do is nothing. I know very great laxity of morals on this subject is admitted by some whom we respect. We have nothing but trifling things of little cost.

We are enjoying our rest here and profiting by it. I shall make it a point to visit A. Waterer's nursery.

Your loving brother,

CASPAR MORRIS.

BADEN BADEN, August 8, 1872, Friday.
My Dear Children:

We are still detained here by little Mary's indisposition, which appears to have resolved itself into sore throat. This morning she is better—quite bright—but we shall not move before Monday at the earliest, and have ordered our letters sent here, and hope for them to-morrow. I walked this morning along the beautiful grounds lying on either side of the Oös ;—amid the charming villas with their shrubberies and gardens, and the grand mountains overlooking them. I was absent quite two hours, all the time amid attractive scenes, stopping a half hour to enjoy the morning service in the nice little church. I was sorely tempted to impertinent intrusion as I saw the name Wissahickon in large letters on the gate of one of the villas. Who can have brought here a fond recollection of the beauty there?

I am occupying the hours with Motley's History of the Rise of the Dutch Republic. The terrible and disgusting details of human ferocity and duplicity, of which I had some faint conception which has hitherto deterred me from reading it, are rendered still more painfully impressive by our having so recently passed through the scenes in which the tragic transactions were performed. I am astonished that the people should preserve and *exhibit* as they do in the town halls and museums of the low countries, and in various towns of Germany, the terrible implements of torture, and dungeons of darkness, just as they were three centuries ago. And not only so, but in the exhibitions at the fairs, wax figures representing those horrid atrocities are constantly exhibited. I never heard any one attempt to describe them, or explain the circumstances under which they were employed, as I have no knowledge of the language, and did not think it best to ask through interpreters. At Hanover, at Ratisbon, and at Nuremburg are large collections of racks and other instruments of torture which stand dumb, yet expressive, witnesses of the truth of pages of human history which, as fellow-men, we would wish blotted out ; and which one would think the immediate descendants and inheritors of the name and honors, or dishonor, of the actors would certainly obliterate so far as to destroy the terrible testimony afforded by the walls of dungeons and implements of cruelty. When one reads of the atrocities perpetrated by the associates of William the Silent and the followers of the great Reformation, who disgraced the cause of truth by their distortions of its doctrine ; and who, driven to bay by the crushing tyranny of Charles, and Philip, and the Guises. and Medici, turned in the ferocity of despair and retaliated the unendurable and unutterable wrongs they had suffered, one must blush for our common nature which is capable of such acts under any circumstances of wrong even: and one is unable to palliate them even by the darker shades of the ground on which they lie, much less to justify them, though they were merely the natural reaction, and often the just avenging of intolerable oppression. For years I have refused to read what I knew would harrow my soul and agitate my judgment, and, if I could, I would obliterate forever all traces of such crimes. But they are the awful accompaniments of the display of the loftiest and holiest features in human character, and which could never have been brought out but for them; and they give more value to the unspeakable gift of the Son of God to redeem such a race as man, who could thus misapply even the love which died for sinners into the occasion for such a display of corruption, for it is fearful to be obliged to acknowledge that the most atrocious of all crimes were committed in the name, and professedly for the advancement of the Kingdom of Christ, by both parties. This is only, however, carrying on the work begun by Caiaphas and the Sanhedrim who condemned our Lord Himself to be crucified for the glory of God, assuming that He had committed blasphemy when He made Himself equal with God.

STRASBOURG, August 12th, 1872.

Leaving Baden this morning, we passed along the valley of the Rhine, which is here miles in width, to this place celebrated not only in the history of past ages, but for the siege it endured during the Franco-Prussian war, recently.

Last evening we were surprised by a pleasant visit from Morris Patterson and Miss Blanchard and Mr. and Miss Rosengarten. It was very refreshing, with its home associations, and we left Baden with regret only softened by the knowledge that our progress now is designed to be steadily homeward. The Cathedral of Strasbourg (or rather its spire) is visible to a great distance, rising over 400 feet, being a little loftier than the Great Pyramid. It looks like an immense structure of *cards*, the reverse of the pyramid. Each story is composed of open work in stone through which one sees the light in every direction, giving it an air of lightness very widely different from the massive solidity of the work of the Cheops. The original design of the structure embraced *two* spires. One only is completed; the other ends abruptly just above the roof and is surmounted by a dwelling for watchmen whose duty it is to notify the people of danger from fire. The other is piled up in square open work, tier over tier, gradually diminishing till the point is surmounted by a cross.

The Cathedral is some 400 feet long, consisting of nave, aisles and chancel with transepts. It was built not less than 400 years ago. The architect by whom it was designed having died, the work was continued by his son and completed by his daughter: of whom a beautiful statue stands in the south portal. This opens into a transept which contains the clock which is as celebrated as the Cathedral itself. The present one is of modern workmanship, having been placed here in the present century by a Swiss clock-maker as a substitute for one which had become worn out and stopped in 1796, after having defied the ravages of the destroyer, whose passage it noted, two centuries. The old works of wrought iron still stand in an apartment in the house built and once occupied by the architect of the Cathedral, close by. It has in it a very beautiful spiral stone stairway. We timed our visit, together with a crowd of "Jews, Turks, Infidels and Heretics," so as to witness the evolutions of the machinery at noon. There were some hundreds of us; literally including just what I have enumerated, —several Turks, with their familiar scarlet Fez with the long black silk tassel dangling behind, towering majestically above the crowd of squat Germans and English, and the irreverent remarks of other spectators proving that they regarded neither the sacredness of the place nor the value of the time whose flight was being chronicled so impressively before them.

At the base of the structure which encloses the machinery stands a large globe fixed properly on the axis around which it revolves. Behind this is a map of the earth on a revolving dial-plate, like that on the Yankee clock in our dining-room, which shows the true time, the part of the world at which it is noon being always uppermost, and the corresponding hour at Paris, London, New York, etc., being noted on the periphery. Above this a plane rolls round, throwing out daily the figure of some mythological representative of the day. That for this, Monday, is Diana seated on a car. Above this is a large face on which the position of the planets is exhibited, and on a ledge, at the top, two cherubs sit, the one striking the quarter on a bell, and the other turning an hour-glass at each hour. Still higher is a clock-face with the mean time, which here differs about three minutes from the true. Above this stands a figure of Time, symbolized as usual by a skeleton with scythe in one hand and baton in the other, with which he strikes the hours on a bell beside him; and as each is thus noted a series of figures, beginning with infancy and terminating with age, hobbling on a crutch, passes in review before him.

At noon a similar series representing the twelve apostles passes on a stage, still higher up, before a figure of our Lord, each bowing as he passes and receiving a benediction from the uplifted hand of their Master. As they complete their evolutions a figure of a cock, which stands still higher, flaps his wings repeatedly and crows, so that the echo of his "clarion shrill" reverberates among the groined arches of the nave and aisles.

There are other more elaborate parts of the machinery which exhibit, *e.g.*, the various feasts and fasts of the church of Rome for nine hundred years. It is a most elaborate specimen of human skill and nicety of calculation.

If we stand astonished at the power which can make such delicate combinations, able to display the wonders which human observation has discovered in the order of the seasons and movements of the planets, how passing wonderful and overwhelming is the thought of that wisdom and power which contrived the whole; by whom "things which are, were not made of things which do appear." "Who spake and it was done, commanded and it stood fast forever!" Who would not say, "Thou fool" to the babbler, who, standing before the clock, should venture to express his belief that it came together in its various complex parts, perfectly adapted to work and exhibit regular irregularities during nine hundred years, fortuitously, or by natural selection, or *developed itself* out of a "Nuremburg Egg?" That it was developed from a Nuremburg egg is certain; but the immaterial mind of man, that spark of divinity which inhabits these mortal bodies, was the agent by which that development was effected, and that it does "inform our clay" and produce such wonders, is, to my mind, a sufficient answer to the science, falsely so called, which would degrade man into a developed ape.

The beauty of some of the old glass windows is very great. Some of them were injured by the Prussian shot and shell during the siege. Great holes in the roof penetrating the stone lining still gape at the visitor; and the verger takes great satisfaction in showing these traces of the destruction effected by the hated Germans; and smiles grimly as pointing to a hideous black figure representing one of the Three Kings in an old window, he says, "*Bismarck!*" thus salving the contumely by the tribute to his wisdom as one of the "wise men."

The ruins of the library building, in the burning of which no less than 200,000 volumes were destroyed, many of them such as can never be replaced, and other roofless walls which stand like gaunt skeletons by the way along which war marched to victory, are so many tokens of the relentless power of the demon, which excites the maledictions of the people, who (though originally German and annexed to France by conquest two centuries ago), have become French in their feeling, and have an intense abhorrence of their new masters. The injury done was not voluntary, and the German government is contributing to the restoration of the comfort of the citizens by paying the cost of reconstruction of all buildings as fast as they advance. So that we may hope under the fostering influences of peace Alsace and Lorraine may become reconciled to Germany.

There are several statues in various parts of Strasbourg generally of French dignitaries; and in one of the churches is a very elaborate marble monument erected by Louis XV. to Maurice of Saxony. It represents that great military hero descending to the tomb, the lid of which is held open to receive him by Death, while France interposes herself in the form of a beautiful female figure with one hand pushing back Death, and with the other restraining the descent of her hero. On the one side are banners captured, and on the other the Austrian eagle, the Dutch Bear, and the British Lion, lie overturned, or skulk beaten away. Does it comfort the hearts of the people in their present sense of subjugation to look at the vainglorious monument to the pride of Louis? It is nothing else, since he styles himself "Auctor et Dux Ipse Victoriarum," even on the stone professedly raised to the general of his armies.

There is no respect for Louis Napoleon. In one of the stores sister Hannah bought a folded paper so arranged that when closed it had a human face, and when opened it was developed into a herd of swine, feeding. The storekeeper drew her attention to it, and said: "It is Louis Napoleon." Thus vanity and spleen find various means of expression.

The occupants of the apartments adjoining ours in the hotel are the King and Queen of Portugal, who arrived soon after in a hotel voiture, looking like respectable people of any rank. Two large bouquets, which had been given them at the hotel they had left, and the marked obsequiousness of the waiters as the carriage drove up were the only marks of distinction. They had neither courier nor servants.

We appear to have got through the rainy spell, which has prevailed for a week past, not only at Baden, but throughout the country. We shall be glad if it has not interfered with the pleasure and comfort of dear Hannah and Galloway, from whom we hope to hear at Paris. I did not order their letters (which were to be directed to the bankers) there to be forwarded after the 5th, as we did not design remaining so long at Baden.

13th.

A fine morning finds us thankful for a good night and a clear day for our ride to Nancy, where we shall rest till to-morrow at 2 P. M., and then "On to Paris," hoping to get there about 9 P. M. Little Mary is better, but I fear the long day's ride for her.

The Germans are building new fortifications at a little distance, designed undoubtedly like those of Paris to control the town, as well as to defend it from foreign foes. When they are completed those which have so long made it a stronghold against Germany will be destroyed.

The Rhine as it passes here is a noble, rushing stream, and the country around very fertile and highly cultivated. It is also a great manufacturing place. The French government had a very large tobacco establishment here, which is now converted into barracks for the German troops.

Your loving father,

CASPAR MORRIS.

BADEN BADEN, August 11, 1872.

My Dear Child:

I wrote to you from this place this day week. Then we expected ere this to have moved on and been to-day in Paris; but here we have been detained by the indisposition (I may almost say illness) of little Holly. She had taken cold. It did not amount to pneumonia quite, but she was in a very prostrated condition for several days. I am glad to say it is entirely relieved, and she is gaining daily, though much reduced and looking badly. Of course this has been cause of great anxiety to your father, and he is feeling the effect of it most decidedly, but I hope it will soon pass off, with him. Our present expectation is to leave here to-morrow for Strasbourg, where we shall rest a day, and then take two more to reach Paris. So you see we will take it easily. We have all rejoiced, as we had to "lay by," that we were in such nice quarters—a most beautiful spot, fine mountain air, no heat, nice walks and drives, and hotel accommodations perfect, and a good English apothecary.

We received our package of letters from home last night, some of which were up to the 26th of July, yours of the 21st. I suppose by this time your large family has somewhat diminished; that is, if Israel has been able to get off from the office. I do hope the girls will have a nice trip with them, and think the addition of Miss Alice and Flora *very nice*.

1.30 o'clock.

Since writing the above we have been to church, and not only enjoyed the service, but heard an excellent sermon, and we feel greatly refreshed. I hope all our dear children, although so scattered, have been able to have similar refreshment. Galloway and Hannah are somewhere in Switzerland, we suppose; also Will and Sally, though hardly together, and we are not able to keep each other apprised of our exact position, notwithstanding that it is a great comfort to me, especially when I get a little "down," to feel that I have two children on this side the "*Big Water*," and the railroad would soon bring us together if needed. But I hope that will not be. There is no prospect now.

Only think this day nine weeks we will be on the ocean. Sometimes I feel very impatient and would gladly forego seeing anything more, and then again I think I would like to see Scotland and Ireland; as we were not there 35 years ago. But I believe uncle's plan leaves them last and goes over Wales and England; so I fear we shall be hurried at the close. But the prospect of home will reconcile to much,—almost anything. On thinking over our plans on reaching home, of course I want to get to Baltimore and West River as soon as I can. But I hardly think I can wait until the necessary unpacking and arranging at home is done before seeing you, so how would it do for you to meet us in Philadelphia, and then pay a little visit and I would go home with you? I don't want you to come to New York; it is a useless expense and very unsatisfactory. Of course we will not tarry there, only just long enough to get through the custom house.

Among our letters yesterday we have one from Cousin Emily giving us an account of Mrs. Old's death: it really seemed wisely ordered that cousin should have reached Philadelphia when she did, as she will be a great comfort to Caroline, and I am so glad she will be with her now for some weeks. I was also very glad to hear Rachel and her children are staying at Henry's in Newport with Patty.

As regards our housekeeping arrangements I believe I shall have to leave it pretty much with Cousin Emily and Annie to start us, as we are too far off for much consultation. If Isabella and Sarah will work in together again I don't know that I can do better. Of course I would like Sarah Brian *very much*, but I doubt her coming back, and if she did she would want to keep the child; and do you not think both will be somewhat spoiled by Providence life? But I am lazy enough to be willing to throw all this on any of you that will take it. You will see us *very much spoiled*. I do often feel sorry and troubled at Israel and Annie having had so much to do for us, but it was unavoidable.

STRASBOURG, Monday, 12th.

We came here this morning, and although some of us were very tired, after washing and refreshing, with bread butter and beer, we went to the Cathedral in time to see the old clock perform at twelve. Notwithstanding it's being a daily thing (and has been for 300 years) the place was crowded. To be sure this is the season when there are many travellers passing through.

The Cathedral itself is a most grand old building and justly highly prized by both the French and Germans, and in the late war, when this city was bombarded, the Germans took great pains to avoid the destruction of this church. Still it was struck several times and marvelously escaped. As I fear I could not give you much of an idea of the clock I am almost afraid to attempt description on paper, but with the aid of a photograph perhaps can do more with the tongue. I find your father is more courageous and I dare say he will succeed.

This is a very fine old town, and perhaps we take the more interest in it as we have read, with Holly, a nice little book, "Max Kromer." The scene was here, and during the late war, and it is said to be founded on facts, so that she has been particularly anxious to come here. Of course there are many traces of bombardment and great destruction. Much repairing is going on. The house opposite my window has nine marks on its front, and the roof has been repaired.

I must now say farewell, with love to all, in which your father joins me.

    Yours truly and affectionately,

              A. C. MORRIS.

The King and Queen of Spain (*Portugal.*—EDS.) have just arrived at this house. We saw them alight from an elegant carriage. We were on the verandah over the door, and then they had to pass our parlour door, as theirs is adjoining. She is a very fine-looking woman, but he very commonplace. How often have we been thrown with nobility! Sometimes I wish we could get a little nearer and talk with them.

13th.

We leave to-day for Nancy, and to Paris to-morrow. All well and happy.

NANCY, August 13th, 1872.

My Dear Children :

I this morning mailed letters to Phila. and Ivy Neck from Strasbourg. Soon after, we left that city, whose name has been rendered so familiar to our ears by the prominence it has had in the history of Europe from a very early period, and its important position on the highroad between France and Germany. To the younger of the children it sounds natural as the residence of Max Kromer. Some of our party were very anxious to know if his grandmother still lives, and which was the house she occupied among the number with stories of little windows in the high-pitched roofs from one of which he witnessed the bombardment.

The surrounding country is very flat, and we passed for leagues through fields of the highest fertility laden with the shocks of wheat ready for carrying, and oats ready for the sickle. All the grain is cut with sickles and reaping hooks, unless it is so desperately tangled as to require the scythe.

There appears to be no rotation of crops. It is often all wheat as far as the eye reaches, with only small strips of clover, which is fed green to the cattle. The cows are used for ploughing and hauling, and look as well as though they did nothing. It is indeed necessary to their health, as the absence of fences and hedges forbids the turning them out to pasture. We are all struck with the very small force of labourers by which the fields are worked.

About half way between this and Strasbourg we passed through a mountainous range; the railroad cutting through by tunnels, one of which is a mile and a half long, and is attended by a canal, which is carried through the same excavation. At the new line of frontier we passed the custom-house inspection, and were required to exhibit our passports for the first time since we left Alexandria. Happily I carry mine always about my person in case it should be needed.

This is a part of France still held by German troops as a guarantee for the payment of the indemnity. The feeling of irritation is therefore great, though curbed. It is a quiet, old town, with wide streets and very plain-fronted buildings ; and, if one may judge from the number of shops filled with embroidery, must be the centre of that trade. Handkerchiefs, cuffs and collars, in every shape and quality and with every variety of embroidery, are piled up in the windows ; dirty-looking enough to make any one hesitate at touching it, and proving that it is done in the habitations of poverty. It is from here the Paris dealers get their supplies. How it is possible that life should be sustained with the small compensation for the time the embroidery requires, I cannot conceive. There can be no indulgence of the appetite beyond the amount of food absolutely requisite to keep the body alive. Like the lace of Belgium, it is beautiful.

August 15th.

"*Nous voyez vous une autre fois a Paris. Cest une affaire etonnant:*" such was the exclamation as the lights of the capital of France burst upon our sight, about half-past nine in the evening; and as we drove through the streets, light as day, from the cafes, restaurants, *magazins des modes*, and of everything one can conceive, from "*chaussures*" for the feet to "*châles*" and "*dentelles*" for the adornment of the head and shoulders, each on a scale of extent and magnificence of which Paris only can boast. We realized how the French can glory in Paris, even after having admired all the grandeur of every other capital of Europe. We find ourselves in our old apartments at Hotel Bristol, our occupancy of which astonished Mrs R. W. Tyson, and have cause for great thankfulness in the mercy which has watched over our dear children, as well as ourselves, amid the perils by land and sea, since we left here.

Our letters from home, down to the end of July, are all pleasant. We should have been glad of accounts of dear Hannah and Galloway, but found none.

Evening.

Soon after I had thus written I sallied out to Monroe & Co., and there found a letter from Galloway, giving very satisfactory accounts of their great enjoyment up to the 8th of August. We found this to be a fete day: the bankers and all the shops and places of business are closed.

On my return I found your mother and aunts, not knowing this, had taken a carriage and gone to the Bon Marché, an immense establishment like Stewart's, in New York, only vastly larger. They did not make their appearance till nearly two o'clock, when I was greatly relieved by their return. They had found some place they wished to go to, and had occupied the morning there. This afternoon we have driven once again along the crowded avenue of the Champs Elysees, by the Arc d'Etoile to the Bois de Boulogne. Certainly Paris deserves the epithet given to it by the *coiffeur* who trimmed my hair this morning, "*Une Ville Grandiose.*" Its bourgeoisie were all out for the enjoyment of the holiday in *cabriolets* and *voitures* and private equipages; and the Bois de Boulogne, with its magnificent avenues, and secluded walks, and lakes, and waterfalls, and cafes, offers pleasure in the form he values it most to every seeker. Some were walking, some driving, some riding, some seated under the trees in little groups, with their provisions spread before them, some seated about the cafes, drinking iced water and eating ices and confectionery and coffee. Every grade of society appeared to be represented, and all wearing the aspect of enjoyment. The trees planted this spring, to replace those which were destroyed during the siege, are growing, and where the stumps of those cut have been allowed to remain, they are putting up vigorous shoots; so that, in a few years, the traces of war will be supplanted by new beauty. The arrangements for watering the grass and shrubs are novel and excellent. Hose, jointed and fixed on little wheels, so that it can be easily moved from place to place, terminates in a vertical section, supported by a tripod, on the summit of which is a revolving rose, which scatters the divided water over a considerable space, perfectly imitating the natural shower. A similar arrangement of jointed hose on castors is used for watering the streets, which is thoroughly done even while crowded with vehicles, and without the slightest inconvenience to the travelers. This afternoon the avenue was perfectly thronged, and we were amused, as well as amazed, to see gentlemen on bicycles running among the horses and carriages, with folded arms, quite at ease on their seats, and winding in and out of the crowd with perfect facility. I saw an account, in one of the papers, of a trial between a skilled velocipedist and a pedestrian, on a six days' trip. The pedestrian arrived several hours before the machine.

16th.

Last evening Mr. and Mrs. Henry Wharton and Dr. Tyson called, so that we had quite a Philadelphia conclave. Mr. and Mrs. Wharton are making only a six weeks' trip, and feel that it is a tantalizing affair. They can only dip and go away, with the desire for more unsatisfied.

17th.

Your uncle and I called on James T. Morris yesterday morning, and he spent an hour with us last evening. He looks badly and coughed a good deal. Mr. Castner called also, with a letter he had received from Galloway, at Bellagio, on the 10th. They hope to join us in England in about two weeks. We received dear Mellie's letter yesterday. Could not they buy Mr. Waln's house and use the parlours for offices?

Your loving father,

CASPAR MORRIS.

BOULOGNE-SUR-MER, August 20, 1872.

My Dear Children:

While your mother changes her dress, preparatory to the *discomfort* of "crossing the Channel," I will occupy a few minutes with you. We left Paris yesterday about noon, and had a pleasant journey through a beautiful country, with a rich harvest lying on the fields, partly cut and partly waiting for the sickle. The surface was more undulating than most we had previously crossed, until we passed Amiens. Between that place and this the road led through marshes and peat bogs, between chalk cliffs and sand hills, which serve as a barrier to the sea. We had come through the Normandy so celebrated in mediæval history, and saw old castles and chateaux, which have celebrated names.

Boulogne is a much-frequented sea-bathing place, to which many English people come, as it gives them the opportunity to say they have been to France,—to see the costumes of the peasantry and fisherwomen (which are picturesque), at the same time that they get the benefit of invigorating sea breezes, and also, as *they think*, the *good* of being seasick.

This morning your mother and I started out, immediately after breakfast, for a stroll through the town. Our attention was soon drawn by the crowd of women with the peculiar, deep-bordered, stiffly starched, perfectly white cap of the Norman peasant, attended by priests in costume, and we found they had come from the country to attend special services connected with a miracle-working picture of the Virgin, which are held during the month of August, in the Cathedral of Notre Dame. We returned to the hotel and gave the information, and your uncle and aunts took carriages and drove to see the services.

Boulogne is divided into upper and lower, the latter being the bathing place on the shore, and the former the old town; enclosed by a wall on the heights above. We entered through the gates and climbed to the church, which was thronged with priests in costume, acolytes, and worshippers in every kind of dress. The music was most impressive and solemn; and following in the current of people we found ourselves before an image of the Virgin and Infant Saviour placed in a ship, with the sea and shore painted on canvas behind and around it, in a niche above the chancel. Votive tributes record the miraculous interposition of the Virgin in their behalf.

LONDON, August 21, 1872.

I have only time now to announce our safe arrival here. We feel *so* happy! As our eyes rested on the green shores of England, and our feet planted themselves on her rocky cliffs we realized, in a feeble degree, something of the emotion with which we shall stand on those shining shores toward which we trust our pilgrim feet are turned. To hear our own tongue, to see houses like our own, and fields enclosed by hedge rows giving the idea of ownership, the houses standing isolated, and not huddled together for mutual protection; and above all, far above all, to feel that we were in a Christian land, where Jesus is recognized as king and people wait for His coming again in power, and meanwhile rely upon His righteousness—His atonement—His intercession—as their only dependence; all this is joy indeed.

We have no letters from any one except dear Cousin Emily, who mentions Cheston's return from Virginia in health, but says nothing of Israel or Mary's family. I have letters from Galloway. He and Hannah are doing nicely and enjoying Bellagio as your mother and I did.

Your loving father,

CASPAR MORRIS.

BOULOGNE SUR-MER, August 20, 1872.

My Dear Brother (Galloway Cheston.—EDS.):

I am sure your spirit unites with ours in devout thankfulness that we have been preserved in our goings out and comings in to this point, and that we can gaze once more on the white cliffs of Britain, and this time with the feeling that it is the last step between us and you. Our own experiences of preservation were sufficient to call for loudest notes of praise, but when by that picture we place the obverse, that two parties who started from Cairo with us in company at the same moment and kept our company all the way up and down, thus having almost daily intercourse, returned mourning each the death of the husband and father,—Mr. Richardson, of Glasgow, and Mr. Betts, of London,—the latter under my care at Assouan, and the former at Pesth, after having passed through the Desert of Sinai, the Holy Land, and Syria, our sense of the goodness and mercy which have followed us is quickened.

We feel as though it had been long since we heard from you, and that during a period of especial trial for dear Margaret and yourself, on account of the heat of July and August, and we humbly trust we may find pleasant accounts of you when we reach London to-night. Your accounts at last dates were as good as we could have reasonably hoped for. We do not know what to do about Mary Ellen. It is very sad to think of her prolonged suffering, but very consolatory to learn that she finds " peace and joy in believing," knowing that her Redeemer liveth and that He will keep that which she has committed to Him. We heard an excellent sermon a few Lord's days since from a clergyman of the church of England at Baden Baden on the process by which the Lord is fitting the living stones of which His spiritual temple is to be built hereafter. There will be in heaven no sound of hammer or chisel. The dressing and fitting of each is to be perfected here. The great " builder and maker " knows how to adapt each to the purposed place, and we may not say, " Why hast thou formed me thus?" Better anything than to be left unhewn in the quarry or to be rejected as unfit for any position, a rude and *spally* block which can be fitted to no position. Well may we pray, From *this*, " good Lord, deliver us."

The few weeks which now remain to us on this side the Atlantic will be fully occupied, and we shall be compelled to leave much unvisited to the sight of which we had looked forward with pleasant anticipation, and I fear I shall be cut off of some visits to Hospitals and Blind Institutions, from which I hoped to derive lessons for our own management. I do wish I could have joined F. King in visiting some of them. The last notice of them which met my eye was in Switzerland, so that there is but little probability of our meeting until we do so in your parlour. There is quite a disposition here to condemn costly buildings, and to adopt temporary structures, which can be erected at comparatively small cost, and removed when changing circumstances render it expedient. I certainly would be more strongly opposed than I always have been to expensive buildings and lofty ones. Where space can be had it is better on every account to lay out the money on ground and build one-storied pavilions.

Wistar and I walked a whole day in Paris in search of bronze birds, and saw more of the town in that way than we should otherwise have done, and I was rewarded by seeing him go largely into the purchase of some very beautiful ones. I had some partridges sent to the hotel for Anne to decide about the color and finish. I have no doubt they are the same of which you speak, but our description of others at the manufactory caused her to think there might be some more beautiful, so we put her into a carriage and drove next day to the manufactory. It was difficult to select where all were so attractive. *But we went and did it*, and shall tremble till we learn how you approve our aste.

LONDON, August 20th.

We arrived here safely about 7 P. M., having left Boulogne at 2.30. I cannot find language to express our delight. It seemed to me as though it might be *a faint shadow* of the feeling we shall know when we pass over that narrow sea which divides us from the better country. To be once again in a Christian land, where our language is understood and our affections reciprocated, is like getting home. The weather is warm, but we are well. Much love to dear Margaret and kindest regards to Mary Ellen, and also to Miss Carey. Give our love to James and Samuel and the West River family. The last we heard of them was from Uncle Samuel at Stanton, where Cheston met him on his way to Virginia Springs.

We are without any advices from Cheston and Israel by this mail. Galloway writes us from Bellagio. He says Hannah is doing well, but unable to encounter the terrors of Swiss mountain passes.

Oh, how blessed it will be to meet once more!

Your loving brother,

CASPAR MORRIS.

LONDON, August 21, 1872.

My Dear Children :

I mailed a letter this morning, written partly at Boulogne and hastily here, just to announce our safe arrival and the pleasure we derive from being, *as it were*, within *sight* of you all.

You cannot understand the intensity of this feeling. We have been so long running round, or further and further away—among people of barbarous tongues and usages foreign to our own—if Christian, professing a form of faith very diverse from that we confess, and with modes of worship as different as the forms of faith ;—that to set our feet among fellow-believers, to hear the pleasant sound of familiar words, and see names like our own—the same family names—gives us a homelike feeling we have not known for now thirteen months. Then we know our faces are now *set* homeward, and that only a few weeks intervene before we take the final step on board the steamer which is to bear us across the ocean. That, it is true, is a wide and uncertain step. But, however much we may have doubted previous steps, that we *know* is in the right direction, taking us back to paths of duty and works of love. We know you will welcome us if it be the will of our Heavenly Father to carry us safe to you ; and if His will be different, shall we gainsay His will? It must be right; be it done.

September 1st, 1872.

We have been so busily occupied ever since our arrival that this sheet has lain on my table challenging attention now ten days, and I have not found time to take up my pen. And yet I have done nothing to report. Each day has been spent as days in London must be in wearisome pursuit of distant objects. It may well claim for itself the title of Metropolis of the World. The interests of all people on the face of the earth are discussed in its press, and most of them are represented here; and it is the great heart which throbs with sympathy with them all in their social, political and religious relations. Its Bible and Tract and Missionary operations reach to the most remote regions. In the affairs of every-day life its warehouses and shops are stored with the productions of them all, and we have amused ourselves by seeing how we might have spared the trouble of carrying with us many things which have been vexatious in the transit, and bought them here.

I have spent some time with old friends and renewed the pleasure of former years in their society, and have found some new ones. One day was given to the Blind Asylum, which has been greatly enlarged and improved since I was here thirty-six years ago. One day I gave to the Assyrian and Egyptian Halls of the British Museum. They are both very interesting and contain wonderful specimens of the work and illustrations of the habits and manners and customs and religious rites of those old peoples. As I stood before some of the sculptured slabs brought from Nineveh I could almost fancy they were Egyptian, so closely do they resemble them in many particulars, and yet there is sufficient diversity to give each its natural characteristic. Both are records of the triumphs of conquerors, with battering down walls and assaulting fortresses, and the signs of rivers, lakes and mountains are the same in both. In both, captives and suppliants throng the way of the conqueror and present their tribute of the animals and productions of the conquered lands. The obelisks are smaller than those of Egypt, and the collection of implements of agriculture and domestic life less numerous and not so well preserved.

The collection of terra cotta tiles, bricks and cylinders, containing inscriptions and records in cuneiform character, is very interesting. No one could see them without being at once impressed with the conviction that these marks had been made for some purpose. But I should never have thought it possible to decipher them. They are in very perfect preservation, of various shapes and size, and by the assistance of bilingual inscriptions Sir Henry Rawlinson has been able to read them and finds they contain records of events noticed in the Bible, and thus afford confirmation of the truth of its historic books. There are many seals engraved on precious stones; one I remember was that of Darius Hystaspes. The great colossal winged bulls and human-headed lions stand majestically at the entrance of one of the halls, and must have presented a very imposing aspect when they guarded the temple of Konynjik.

The Rosetta Stone which is placed prominently in the Egyptian Hall is in very fine preservation and has rendered most important service to humanity, though it records only the idolatrous proceedings of a Ptolemy.

There has been received recently the first instalment of marbles from the excavations at Ephesus. They are very grand and prove satisfactorily that the explorers have discovered the remains of the magnificent temple of that "Diana whom all Asia and the world worshippeth." One fragment is a portion of a pillar ten feet in diameter and covered with figures of life size in the very highest style of alto relievo. Though the more delicate tracery has disappeared under the corrosion of time, the proportions and attitudes and expression remain and prove it to have been equal to any other sculpture of the best Grecian art, far before the Elgin marbles from the Parthenon. Your uncle Wistar and I spent an entire day in going to and visiting the nursery of Waterer, about twenty-five miles from London. What do you think of an acre or more of Lillium Auratum; all in flower, some of the plants having from twenty to thirty flowers? The atmosphere was perfumed with the odor. Then there were sixty acres in rhododendrons of the choicest varieties, which had all flowered. They covered the ground entirely with their foliage. Then there were standard plants of twenty and thirty feet head; and holly and cedars, and conifers of great variety and beauty. Three hundred acres are devoted to this culture. There is a hedge of holly fifty years old and at least twenty feet high, green, and polished, and straight clipped. Everything in perfect order, and the plants perfectly healthy.

Your mother and I were obliged to give one day to poor Mrs. Betts. She lives in a sweet spot, with every comfort and very great elegance, we should say. But when she showed us photographs of her former residence, which was palatial in its grandeur, we could realize that what to us appeared so attractive, must in her eyes be very simple indeed. I had heard the splendor of the establishment spoken of by others, but had formed no conception of the size and grandeur of the house, and the extent and beauty of the grounds. One of the halls was ornamented by a picture, painted especially for Mr. Betts, and designed to occupy that particular position, by Sir Edward Landseer. We see engravings of it. A noble stag, standing on a lofty rock, while three does are grouped around the base. After Mr. Betts' reverses it was sold for some 3,000 guineas. They have brought with them to the present dwelling two beautiful, life-size marble groups, representing the children of the family at play. These relics of past grandeur must have painful associations for the older members of the family, while to the younger they will present nothing but their present beauty. We were most pleasantly impressed by them all. The oldest is pursuing his father's business as an engineer, and at present engaged in mining operations in Cornwall. The second, a most attractive youth, is preparing for holy orders at Cambridge. Two very nice lads are at Harrow Public School, taking honors. They are noble specimens of highly cultivated, intelligent boys, who promise to be a comfort to their widowed mother and do honor to the memory of their father. Can boys have a higher ambition ? The nice little gardens of each proved that the story books do not misguide us by their pictures of English home life, and the interest with which they listened to serious conversation, and carried me to see the church, in the erection of which their father had been very greatly instrumental, was relieved by the very genteel pleasantry of their conversation with each other and their sisters.

I found my friend, Isaac Braithewaite's family, in the deepest mourning, and very much depressed on account of the death of one of the sons. He was married about a year since, was absent on his bridal tour when we were here last summer, and died a few months since. His mother seems as though she could not rally from the shock, though she is evidently a Christian woman. My friend is calm and peaceful, but very feeble. We did not venture on leave-takings.

I find two of my dear old India friends still living. One is at present on the Continent, so that I shall not see him, though he wrote me a most affectionate letter. The other I shall see probably this week at or near Litchfield.

At Isaac Braithewaite's I met the son of Bevan Braithewaite, a nice lad, who had come to bring his uncle letters from Dr. Livingstone, in whom they are much interested, and are trustees of a fund for the benefit of his family. There was not time for me to do more than look at them, and they are very much the same as those that have been published in the New York *Herald* and London *Times.*

Mr. Stanley is the lion of the day, and must be made of good material if he be not spoiled by the adulation of the press and the perpetual fêting with which John Bull is given to manifesting his approval. The Queen has just presented him with a gold box set in brilliants as a token of her gratitude for his service in seeking and carrying relief "To one of her subjects so dear to herself and her people." It was a grand conception of Mr. Bennett, most admirably executed by Stanley. Is he an American?

I also met a daughter of our old friend, Mrs. Savory (*née* Braithewaite), the most beautiful woman in England, at her uncle Isaac's, and waited on her to town. She is a sweet girl, full of Christian zeal, and was on her way to a meeting for religious improvement at the house of Lord somebody—I could not catch the name—who conducts these meetings in his own house. I had a nice note from her a day or two since, pressing me to go to their house, Buckhurst Park, opening on Windsor Park, with the privilege of driving in the Royal Grounds. They wish us to spend a week with them, but we must decline. The father and mother are absent in Wales. I saw one of the sons, who is as splendid a specimen of a man as the mother is of a woman, and bears in the expression of his countenance the confirmation of his mother's statement, that "Four of her children have been found of the Good Shepherd." She also wrote begging us to visit their establishment and give their children our company. It certainly would be more pleasant to us all than all the sight-seeing and traveling—gratifying though these are.

To-day your mother and I attended divine service at Westminster Abbey. It was worship truly. I never had a deeper sense of the privilege of public prayer, and am quite as enthusiastic about it as I was about the service at Chester a year ago. It was grandly solemn, yet beautifully simple. The perfect harmony accorded well with the language of the service, and the deportment of clerical and choral participants was just what one would desire. I sat immediately beside the clerical reader in one of the stalls. The choir and chancel of the Abbey were filled with worshippers, and the sermon was one so adapted to my own condition that your mother remarked it. If I had made full confession to the preacher, and he had prepared his sermon for my benefit, it could not have been more appropriate. It was from the text, "It is I; be not afraid." This afternoon I attended service again in St. George's, Hanover Square, close by our hotel, and was again edified by an excellent discourse from the language of Jeremiah: "For my people have committed two evils; they have forsaken me, the fountain of living waters, and hewed them out cisterns, broken cisterns, that can hold no water." Thus a merciful and loving Father provides for us nourishment for our souls, as well as pleasure for our bodies, in this tour. What shall I render to the Lord? may well be the inquiry of my soul. We are now counting the days till we meet.

To morrow we leave for Bristol, Chepstow, Ross, Tintern Abbey, etc. This is our old ground. We hope, before we leave, to hear from your brother and sister, who will probably soon leave the Continent. The weather has been very fine, but it is raining to-day, and we must expect that from this time. I have been obliged to draw heavily, which I regret greatly.

Your loving father,

CASPAR MORRIS.

Fischer's Hotel, 11 Clifford Street, Bond Street,
LONDON, August 23, 1872.

My Dear Son:

By the time this reaches you, you will have returned to the city, with its toils and anxieties. I am sorry to add to them in any way, but we have reached the shopping place and will be compelled to refit our wardrobes, which is always an expensive and troublesome affair. I have already drawn on you for £80 in two days, and shall want £100 more before we leave London. I mention this in order that you may be prepared to meet these drafts. After leaving here we shall not be likely to spend much. Pounds and guineas fly here at the same rate of disappearance as dollars do at home. Your mother and I are limiting ourselves to the articles we shall require so soon as we return, and shall be thankful to get into a quiet corner, where we can help our children and serve our God in the station to which He hath called us. Part of these late drafts is on your Uncle Galloway's account, for bronzes and engravings he commissioned me to procure for him, which he will repay of course. I should be glad to have some idea of how my funds are holding out, but it will be too late for you to give me any information after the receipt of this.

Thus far we have done nothing here but go to shops and tailoring establishments; neither visited our friends nor exhibitions, and I am doubtful of our being able to do either, as after having finished purchases everything must be packed for the voyage before we leave London. This is almost as large an undertaking as it was to prepare for leaving home, but it is done with sweeter hope. May God give us grace to keep our souls in peace, and strength to support the bodily fatigue.

We are now well and happy, and though the mid-days are warm and exhausting, the nights are cool and refreshing. This hotel is a perfectly quiet house, in a good location, at the West End, near the shops and parks and places of resort, and your uncle has provided us with delightful apartments. Indeed, his whole arrangements for our accommodation have been on the most liberal scale in every way and during the whole tour. We shall find ourselves obliged to come down considerably when we are left to our own resources.

We have no accounts from Galloway and Hannah since they left Bellagio, nor of William and Sally for a longer period. We saw Mr. Castner in Paris and thought we should find him here, as we gave him the address of this hotel. We should not know there is any one in it but ourselves. It is a private house apparently. Stultz, the fashionable tailor, is next door. I have not been there nor to Poole's, which is close at hand. With much love to dear Annie and Mrs. Buckley, and Mrs. Ellis and our cousins in Spruce Street, and all our friends.

I have ordered a case of bulbous roots. If they arrive before we do, let your Uncle Galloway have it at once.

Your loving father,

CASPAR MORRIS.

LONDON, August 25, 1872.

*My Dear Sister (Emily Hollingsworth.—*EDS.*)* :

We are indebted to your kind letter of the 5th for our latest information.

CLIFTON DOWNS HOTEL, September 3, 1872.

You see you are more frequently in our thoughts than the letters you receive would indicate. That you are always in our hearts I know you rest assured. We are now once again on *our* old track, and would gladly have you to retrace it with us. Bristol, with its dirty streets and old churches, and Clifton, with its magnificent views and beautiful dwellings, and Bath, with its Crescents and Quadrangles, rising tier above tier on the hillsides, all present familiar objects, though mingled with novel ones and great growth.

Anne and I enjoyed this morning a stroll among the cliffs overlooking the Avon, and this afternoon a visit to the Orphan Asylums of George Muller. You are, I believe, familiar with his history : A profligate youth, converted by the grace of God, devoting himself to the service of Jesus, and with no personal influence—a stranger from Germany—setting on foot an effort for the relief of poor orphan children. With no money of his own, asking means only from God in private prayer, he has been honoured as the agent in accomplishing the erection of fine large solid buildings in which to-day there are two thousand orphan children fed, clothed and educated under Christian influences. You have read his annual accounts, I am sure, and his statements are amply confirmed by our own observation. The average cost of support during the past year was not over $60 for each child.

They are taken very young and kept till they are sixteen, during which time they are taught to read and write, etc., and trained in habits of industry, so as to render them suitable servants and apprentices. They are taken without regard to denominational diversity, from every part of the kingdom, including India and Australia, as vacancies occur. The accommodations are very simple and perfectly neat. The employees are all professedly Christian men and women, but are all paid salaries for their services, Mr. Muller only superintending and directing. Would not Wilberforce and Miss Hannah More and John Wesley and Mr. Jay and Mr. Reynolds and the other eminent Christian philanthropists, who have each been associated with efforts for the relief of the suffering and the instruction of the ignorant of Bristol, have rejoiced to anticipate such blessings in store? My favourite idea even finds confirmation. The generation of God's children does not cease, but every age finds one and another rise up in the place of those who depart to be with Christ in glory. Our own dear, venerable Muhlenberg is a noble specimen of the same family.

I have not seen as much as I could have wished of our old Braithewaite friends. Isaac is living in great splendour in a grand establishment at Epsom, and gave us a most cordial welcome. But he and his wife are plunged into deep distress by the death of a son, who had been but a few months married. Caroline sent us a sweet note begging us to go to their house, which is called Buckhurst Park, and adjoins Windsor Park, and has the privilege of driving in it. It is also a grand establishment. We could not avail ourselves of her kindness, however. She and her husband are absent in Wales. I saw two of her children, a son and daughter, noble specimens of lovely Christian young people. I should have loved to see more of them.

I found my dear friend Latham still living, and now a Canon of Litchfield Cathedral. He invited us to come and stay with him there, and we did design to visit him, but find that the Cathedral is closed for repair, and shall therefore go to his residence near Derby. You remember we stayed some time with them at Barton under Neidwood.

Another of my India friends is also living, but obliged to reside at Nice for his health. It is tantalizing to know that we spent two days so near him, when we would have been glad to have seen a friend, and much more such an one as he. He is dependent on a reader and amanuensis on account of impaired vision, for which he has submitted to an operation unsuccessfully, and his wife has also had cataract extracted from both eyes.

MATLOCK BATHS, September 9, 1872.

You will see by the above, dear Emily, that you have not been out of our memory and attention, though you have not received any token of our love for some weeks. But indeed the days are too short for the labours and the nights for the needful repose to renew our strength.

Since leaving London Anne and I have been passing over the scenes you visited with us thirty-six years ago—Bristol, Chepstow, Tintern Abbey, Ross, Gloucester, etc.—and find they are correctly imaged on our memory, having still a beauty and interest at least as great as their first attractions. Yesterday, however, was one of those times of refreshment which we do most truly wish you could have shared with us, and by sharing have increased our joy. You remember dear Mr. and Mrs. Latham and Barton under Neidwood, where we spent a week in lodgings. I little thought they could be still living; but, seeing his name in a clergy list as vicar of Little Eaton near Derby, wrote him, and found he is also Canon of Litchfield, where he invited us to visit him, as he was obliged to be resident there nine weeks every year. The Cathedral was closed for some repair, however, about a week ago, and he wrote again to invite us to his vicarage, where Mrs. Latham is confined to her chamber by age and disease. We contrived to get there on Saturday afternoon, and met a most hearty welcome to as beautiful a Christian home as earth can show. Everything about the house was simple and inexpensive, proving that they have set their affections on the home in heaven, and yet neat and elegant as becomes refined and cultivated character. But the indescribable tone of Christian love and faith and hope which gave a charm to everything cannot be communicated by language. We could say as truly as the patriarch on his stone pillow: "This is none other than the house of God and gate of heaven;" and when I tell you that my first participation in the bread and wine with which we "do show forth the Lord's death till he come," forty-five years ago, in the first warmth of new-born faith and love, was with Mr. Latham leaning on my arm as we went up to the table of the Lord, you will enter somewhat into my feelings as she, and Anne, and Mr. Latham and their daughter and son-in-law and I gathered here around the table of the same Lord, and partook together once more of the emblems of the broken body and shed blood, through which only we obtain remission of our sins and all other benefits of His passion. It was indeed a blessed day, a day long to be remembered, and for the privilege of which we must give account at the last day. You will unite with us in devout thanksgiving for the blessing, I am sure.

We have to-day rejoined brother and sisters. All well and happy. Much love to Brother Henry and sister Caroline.

Your loving brother,

CASPAR MORRIS.

LONDON, August 26, 1872.

My Dear Children:

London occupation leaves little time for writing and produces no result to record. We rise and go out and wander among the wilderness of houses and shops and spend the time and money and come in with no profit to set down as the counter entry.

Yesterday we were thankful for a *Sabbath* on the Lord's day. It was truly rest. Your mother and I went to the nearest Church of England place of worship in the morning, a chapel within a square of the hotel; and in the afternoon I went only a square further to St. George's, Hanover Square, on both occasions realizing the advantage of a Liturgy, with lessons from the word of God, and listening to plain, simple instruction in paths of every-day duty.

This morning your uncle and I arose at 4.30 and drove to the great cattle market, where we saw good accommodations for the sale of the herds and flocks on which this great metropolis of the world depends for its support. The yards surround a central octagonal building in which the *bankers* and officials are accommodated, and I saw a bulletin announcing that there were to-day for sale 2300 head of cattle and 15,700 sheep. They were all arranged in paved yards; the sheep in pens containing about ten, each opening into each other, and divided into blocks by passages running through from one wide way to another. They were driven in, in flocks, by men assisted by trained dogs, who would spring on the backs of the sheep and run over a large flock so as to head them off at the command of the master; or work themselves among them biting at the legs of the sheep to control their movements. There was not only *no profane* swearing, but no loud talking and no crying to the animals. A light stick was occasionally laid on a refractory beast, but never with sufficient force to hurt. One would hesitate about its being felt through the fleece.

The cattle were all drawn up in rows standing as closely as they could be packed, each one fastened by a rope to a rail in front. They were prime animals, very equal in size and condition. Different breeds were arranged in different ranges; Short horns, Herefordshires, each by themselves. One lot of some hundred or more was very beautiful. They were all of a dun color with very long and widely spreading horns, and the only answer we could get was that they were Spanish. They certainly cannot have been imported from Spain in the fine condition they are now in. They are short-legged, round-bodied, very compact animals, and I should suppose would be favorites for beef. I inquired the value of a lot of very fine pure Southdown sheep, and was told seventy shillings a head.

The dryness and comfort of the Paris arrangement, which places the animals all under cover, is superior to that of London. It was raining this morning, enough to make cover desirable, but in a heavy rain the exposure must be very unpleasant to the dealers. The clean well-drained pavement is a vast improvement on our arrangement with mud knee-deep; and the tying the beasts in rows enables the dealer to judge their points without inconvenience as he goes from one to another.

In Paris they were not only thus placed, but had space to lie down and were provided with straw, so that they were kept free from any disturbance up to the moment of slaughter. I am not sure that I found time to describe our visit there to the abattoir, which is, I suppose, the most perfect establishment for that purpose in the world. Here the animals are driven in flocks and herds on foot. There a railroad connecting with all the various roads leading to Paris collects the beasts and carries them to the stables of the abattoir where they are lodged, the owners being charged so much per diem so long as they remain unsold; and provender is furnished by a licensed purveyor at regular rates. We did not visit the slaughter-houses here, but they are in long pavilions divided into many compartments, each one rented out to an individual at fixed rates. We there saw the different meats hanging in carcasses. It was very fine. Calves are allowed to attain a much greater size than with us or here; and there are arrangements for the preparation of the feet of sheep as well as calves by scalding them and stripping off the hoofs and hair. The sheep's feet are a large article of consumption and quite as nice as those of the calves. There are also at Paris extensive arrangements for preparing the fat for market and for utilizing all the refuse matter. There as well as here I was much impressed by the order that prevailed and also by the sobriety and respectable, decorous, deportment of all we met with. The Parisian butcher who gave us information was a portly man with a fine benevolent expression of face, seated at the door of his apartment with his pipe in his mouth; the very impersonation of contentment. Some dozen carcasses of calves of great size and oxen of prime quality hung behind him, ready for distribution to his customers. Here the men who drove the sheep and cattle watched them, to preserve order, and well might any one of them be chosen to represent the interests of a society for prevention of cruelty to animals. Some of the younger ones had faces which were attractive in despite of their occupation, and dress appropriate to it.

The potato disease has commenced its ravages and is causing consternation. Large tracts are abandoned as utterly ruined. This is a most serious affair, as it must cause an advance in the value of other food material. In addition to this there is a large population which *depends* on the potato, and is too ignorant to understand the substitution of any other article.

Fruits here are very beautiful, but also high-priced. We have been accustomed on the Continent to have peaches, plums, pears and grapes on our table twice daily. On Saturday as we passed a fruiterers your mother and I paused at the window attracted by the beauty of the fruits. You never saw such peaches unless in pictures. The price is only eighteen pence each, or twelve shillings a dozen, equal to thirty cents for one. I cannot report on the taste, as it certainly is too metallic to suit me. I would rather provide some for others' mouths.

We are disappointed at not having letters this morning. It seems now a long time since we heard. God grant we may hear nothing but what is comfortable when they do reach us, and bring us safely where we shall see each other and speak and hear.

We are well, though very wearied. Your mother and I go this morning to see poor Mrs. Betts. Her son called on us this morning;

a noble and also lovely-looking youth, preparing at Trinity College, Cambridge, for the ministry of the Established Church.

Our latest dates are the 5th.

Your loving father,

CASPAR MORRIS.

LONDON, August 25, 1872.

My Dear Child:

I know I have allowed a longer time than usual to elapse without writing. I hope you have not been troubled about it, and I will try to do better hereafter. You will see from the date that we are moving now towards home, and indeed it feels so. And oh, it is so nice to hear English spoken again! We had been so long without it that I found myself (the few first days) forgetting that I could make my wants known. This day week we were in Paris, took our leave of it finally last Monday, and with some regret too, for it is certainly a grand place, and we were beginning to feel quite at home. Well, we took two days to come here and were glad we did, for oh! *that Channel* is enough for one, although we were only two hours in crossing. The little boat was crowded, and so many were so sick, even if we had desired it (but no one did), there was no room to move about, and the waves washed over all the time. I do assure you it was with thankful hearts we came ashore on British soil, and two hours more by rail we were nicely fixed here in a hotel that has a very homelike feeling. It is kept now by Cervetto. He was our courier when we left here, and he is particularly desirous to make us comfortable, but we feel that our time is getting short, and we will not tarry here as long as we would wish, as there is much that they all want to see in Scotland and Wales, as well as England.

We have been working very hard since we came here trying to finish up our shopping, which is a most laborious piece of business. I, for one, am much tempted just to stop short, as your father and I are both feeling much exhausted by it.

To-morrow we have a painful duty in prospect. We are to spend the day with Mrs. Betts and her family. You will remember the name. Her husband died at Assouan last winter, and your father was much with them both before and after his death, and, I have no doubt, a great comfort to them. The remains arrived here the day we did, and were interred in a little church which he had built near his own residence, a few years ago. Then he was affluent. Since then he has lost very heavily, and been obliged to sell that estate, and they are indebted to the present proprietor for this privilege. They very much feared, when on the Nile, it could not be done. There was another boat on the Nile that kept with us, and we saw them frequently—Mr. Richardson and his wife. We were sorry to learn from Mrs. Betts that Mr. Richardson died on his return from Palestine. You know me well enough to know how I dread this visiting, but I have also to spend a day at Mr. Isaac Braithewaite's, in the country too, this week. They live in great style. They have just lost a married son, so you see we will be thrown with friends in affliction.

27th.

Yesterday your father and I went a short distance into the country to pay the visit to Mrs. Betts. One son came for us; another met us at the station with their carriage, and a most hearty welcome did we receive, on arriving, from Mrs. Betts' sons and daughters, nine in number. They are in a beautiful, small establishment, surrounded by everything nice. We lunched with them, and returned by five o'clock, feeling that, by the effort, we had both given and taken pleasure.

Here is the 29th, and this must go, and yet, if I am as often interrupted as I have been, I fear it will be cut short. Oh! we are so busy trying to finish up shopping, etc., etc., and pack for home ! All well and happy, and that is cause for thankfulness; and yesterday we had such nice letters from you all—Annie's was the latest—telling of their prospect of getting off in a few days to Lake George, with the young people. I hope they will all enjoy it. I let your father go, yesterday, to Mr. Braithewaite's without me, having several reasons for so doing, and now quite regret I did not overcome some obstacles and go with him. In the afternoon I went with your aunts, Hannah and Jane, to see a Miss Casson, the daughter of an old lady who, years ago, gave your father the plaid shawl that Margaret took such a fancy to. I never was in such a neat little pill-box of a house ; your parlor would more than take in the whole thing. She lives alone with one servant; just now has an Irish friend staying with her. We spent two hours ; staying with her most delightfully. A lovely woman she seems to be. We were soon invited to her tea room, just large enough to accommodate the five, and there had a nice tea, although it was only six o'clock. Should she ever visit America I must find her out. She is an intimate friend of Cousin Sarah Morris, and when Sarah was here they travelled together.

September 1.

Such a press of work, in and out of doors, has just made it impossible for me to write, and I hardly expect to be able now. Here we have had to *pack* for *home* as well as conclude the shopping. Well, both have been hard work, but it is now done, and the trunks, fifteen in number, left yesterday for Liverpool. Now we will take a little breathing time, and start to-morrow for Bristol, Tintern Abbey, Chepstow, etc., etc., but to see England, Wales, Scotland and Ireland in six weeks will, of course, not admit of much tarrying anywhere.

Your father and I have just returned from Westminster Abbey, where we enjoyed the services exceedingly, and heard one of the best sermons I ever listened to. You know we have been prejudiced against choral services, but this was an exception to any I ever before listened to. It was so solemn and undoubtedly great devotion, which we did not think there was when we attended them thirty-six years ago. Your father has been having some correspondence with some of his old friends here: a Mr. Elliott, whom he knew intimately in India; and both regret very much he is just now in Switzerland, so they cannot *meet;* Mr. Latham with whom (and his wife) we were much, thirty-six years ago—another India friend. Them we will make an effort to see near Derby, but regret much not seeing Caroline Braithewaite (that was), now Mrs. Savory; she is in Wales. She speaks of you and wishes, if you ever cross the ocean, you would let her see you. Her residence is near Windsor Castle.

Since writing the above, Willie and Sally looked in on us; they left Gall. and Han. in Geneva—comfortable—and I fear they will get here about the time we shall leave, and I do not know that we shall meet until about to sail from Liverpool. Gall. thinks Han. is improving, and they are judiciously taking things quietly.

But I must say farewell; with so much love for all, not only for you, but all around. Only think, eight weeks and we will be at home; or, if the house is rented, with some of you. Your father sends *much love*. We are all well and happy, but very tired. Some sight-seeing and excursions, and the British and other museums.

Last night I took your father to Madame Tussaud's wax-works and he thought it paid. Saw Dr. Livingstone; he is like Andrew Ridgeley.

Yours, most affectionately,

A. C. MORRIS.

LONDON, August 31, 1872.

Dear Brother (Galloway Cheston.—EDS.):

We are about closing our visit to London, and it feels like the end of one of the chapters of life. Our time has been very fully occupied with but little result. One feels as though one should be much wiser and better after a fortnight's sojourn in the Metropolis of the World. It well deserves the honor, in whatever light we regard it, in commerce or in religious influence. Peoples of every nation and realm congregate in its marts, and it extends the arms of its charity, and hands filled with munificence, to the most remote quarters of the globe. It has been greatly stirred by the results of Stanley's search after Livingstone; and American energy is the proverb of the day. I see by to-day's "Times" that the Queen has presented Stanley with a gold snuff-box set with brilliants. I saw a day or two since a lot of letters from Dr. Livingstone to Mr. Braithewaite. Bevan has just left on a Bible Society

Mission to Berlin, Vienna, Constantinople, Athens, and Rome. At the latter place the theatres are crowded by highly-excited audiences to witness plays in which Jesuits are objects of derision, and in one representation the horrors of the Inquisition are brought prominently forward for the purpose of condemnation. The Pope may well feel disquieted. But where will the re-action against the expulsion of the Jesuits from Germany, and this opposition to the Papacy in Italy, carry us hereafter. In our own country, and here, Romanism is gaining ground faster than it loses it elsewhere. In this country it is openly challenging hostility.

Wistar and I spent a day in going to Waterer's nursery. What would you give to see sixty acres thickly planted with choice rhododendrons at the time of bloom? We saw that area of fine, healthy shrubs, and three hundred acres devoted to the culture of rhododendrons and azaleas. Mr. Waterer told us Spring was the proper time to ship them. I therefore did not order any for you, but send you by mail a copy of his catalogue, ticking in the margin those he recommends as *hardy*. He has also some very beautiful conifera and ornamental trees, though his specialty is azaleas and rhododendrons. I thought it better to allow you to avail of the descriptive catalogue and order for yourself. The nursery is twenty-five miles from London and three miles from the nearest railroad station, in the midst of a barren moor, very much like the pine barrens between Philadelphia and Atlantic City. It covers a peat bog, and the nursery is all underdrained. He makes an artificial soil not less than two to three feet for all his plants. They look perfectly vigorous. He has many hundred seedlings yet untested. There were two acres of lilium auratum in flower. One plant had *thirty-one* flower buds. There is a compact holly hedge thirty feet high, fifty years old.

These coming eight weeks will fly sluggishly.

With love to Margaret and all our friends. Anne is well, and our letters from Galloway and Hannah are satisfactory.

      Yours affectionately,

          CASPAR MORRIS.

         BRISTOL, September 2d, 1872.
My Dear Children :

We left London at 11.45 this morning and were whirled along so rapidly that everything presented the appearance of a blurred, green coloured photograph; making but one stoppage and reaching the station here by 2.30, having run the entire distance at the rate of about fifty miles an hour running time. The speed was wearisome, and the plate glass which formed the immovable sides of the saloon car rattled terribly, while the roughness of the road shook us considerably. Conversation, even at the highest key, was impossible; and heads and eyes and backs all ached. It was very tantalizing to be whisked through meadows—by hamlets—past churches and gentlemen's seats,—flying away, before you could decide what they are like. The grass was beautifully green, and the meadows dotted with fine flocks and herds peacefully reposing or grazing lazily. The hedge rows were planted with elms and oaks so thickly that the distance everywhere presented the appearance of forest. The first part of the course was through the valley of the Thames, passing Windsor Castle, Eton, Runnymede, the scene of the meeting between King John and his Barons, when they extorted from him the signature of Magna Charta, the foundation of British liberty—developed into our constitutional freedom in the Declaration of Independence,—which is only the necessary growth of that germ. Henley-on-Thames, and other pretty towns we left, as John Gilpin did Edmonton, flying through. Happier than John, your mother flew with me instead of crying "stop" and sending a post boy after me.

The latter part of the road was through a hilly region very closely resembling Chester County near Fernbank. A long tunnel (nearly two miles) carried us through a range of hills, and we soon reached Bath, the celebrated watering-place, whose springs have been frequented by pleasure-seekers, as well as invalids, ever since the days of the Romans, whose fondness for bathing led them to form sanitary establishments wherever the waters were warm or saline. Your mother and I recognized its familiar crescents and ranges of lodging-houses, which are built of a free-stone, which is soft when quarried and easily worked, but becomes hard on exposure to the action of the atmosphere. These ranges of buildings rise terrace above terrace on the hillsides, which are steep.

Twelve miles from Bath we reached Bristol, an old, dirty, dingy-looking place, with narrow streets, running very crooked, over the hillsides and along the streams of the Avon and Trome which unite here, and their waters are used to supply an artificial harbour or dock which accommodates a large amount of shipping.

The steamers Great Britain and Great Western were built here, and I think, by a singular oversight of the builder, the Great Britain, which was first built, was so large that they were compelled to break away the gates of the dock to get her out.

The old parts of the town look just as they did thirty-six years ago. One might think one had been sleeping a night only, and waked again in the morning.

Near the railroad station is the fair ground, which was thronged with holiday-seekers, this being the time of the annual fair. We were particularly interested in the large number of animals for sale,—cattle, horses and sheep. Of the latter we saw four Oxford Downs of immense size. They were said to weigh each twenty stone; which would be 280 pounds each.

Clifton is a beautiful suburb of Bristol, lying high, as its name implies, on the cliffs which overlook the Avon, which here runs in a narrow cleft between lofty precipices and steep banks, clothed with noble trees. The buildings of Clifton, public and private, are large and elegant, and there are numberless parks and squares and public promenades, which render it a favorite resort of persons, who wish some change and leave their inland homes for a few weeks' vacation.

I have visited the Blind Asylum, which is a well-conducted institution for the education of blind children, containing only thirty inmates, though designed for sixty. Each pays three shillings a week, and they are taught very much the same arts and mental instruction, and musical, as at ours. Their basket work is beautiful. I saw a nice class of girls learning to read under the teaching of a sweet-looking blind lady. The museum is a very good one. Conybeare was born here, and many fine specimens of fossils were presented by him. The entire collection is well arranged and nicely displayed.

After visiting these objects I sauntered along the higher parts of the town revelling in the glories of the widespread view, glowing under the rays of a setting sun. As I passed a church-yard my eye caught a costly monument to Legh Richmond, Esq., son of the Rev. Legh Richmond, rector of Turvey, so well known and much loved; and near it one to some one whose name was of no moment. It was wreathed with garlands of fresh-cut flowers, though the date of the interment was some ten years past. The motto on it, which some of our young collegians will please render into plain English, was "*Jesu esto mihi Jesus.*" Bristol is one of the oldest sea-ports of Great Britain, and was long a richer place than London. Mr. Cornish had large transactions here, as testified on his trial, and your mother's grandfather was member of the firm of Randolph Stevenson & Cheston, of this place, the others being his half-brothers, and the Mr. Conynges, who married the last survivor of the name of Cheston here is the descendant of a wealthy Alderman, who, some four hundred years since, built the church of St. Mary's, Redclyffe, here; an old church, in the tower of which the unhappy poet Chatterton asserted he found the manuscript poems, which he wrote, and published, as ancient works, discovered there. The literary world was for a long time deceived, so clever was the imitation. He was but a boy, not sixteen years old I believe, and all his talent did not preserve him from the crime of suicide to which he was impelled by poverty and mortified pride and disappointed ambition. Southey, the poet, if not a native, was a resident of the neighborhood, and I think Coleridge lived here. Certainly the publisher, Amos Cottle, rendered celebrated by his connection with them and Byron's sarcastic criticism, "O Amos Cottle! Phœbus! what a name," was a Bristol bookseller. Barley Wood, Hannah More's residence, was in the neighborhood. Your mother and I visited it thirty-six years ago. Richard Reynolds, the wealthy Quaker philanthropist, was a Bristol man, and so were several highly-eminent clergymen. Even now the parishes are supplied by a most evangelical ministry.

September 3d.

This morning your mother and I walked on the cliffs and admired the grandeur of the scenery. This afternoon we all drove to the Müller Orphan Asylum in the neighborhood. On our way we had full opportunity to admire the beauty of this part of Bristol, which is made up of villa residences of larger and smaller size, but all surrounded by handsomely ornamented grounds and neat shrubberies and flower borders. The Orphanage is comprised of five well-built but very simple structures, each capable of accommodating 500 children. The institution is one with whose history we are all familiar. Thirty-five years ago Mr. Müller received a few orphans into a private house, depending for their support on assistance which he sought from God by prayer. He assures us he has never asked anything from any man, yet it has in that comparatively short period grown to the size indicated. All the funds needful for the daily support of the large household, and all required to meet the purchase of the land and the erection of the buildings, have been contributed by voluntary donors, moved only by the Spirit of God operating directly, without any instigation from Mr. Müller beyond the annual publication of his reports of what he had done with those already received. Everything is perfectly plain, but very substantial. The stairways are of slate and iron, so as to guard against danger from fire. Though perfectly plain, the proportions of the buildings are such that they are really attractive. Neither in the furniture nor ornamental grounds is there any unnecessary expenditure. The cots are arranged in rows, without chairs or stools, in the dormitories, and benches are provided in the refectory and schoolrooms. Elsewhere they are expected to sit on the floor. Their meals are amply abundant: oatmeal porridge in good milk for breakfast always; meat, of various kinds and in various forms, five days in the week for dinner, and bread and butter and milk for supper. In the playrooms each has a little compartment in which to keep personal property, and in rooms adjoining the dormitories a similar one for clothing. The dress is uniform and as inexpensive as possible. They must be orphans who have lost both parents, and care is taken to prevent the abuse of charity by the reception of those whose friends are able to provide for them. They are generally received in infancy or early childhood, and kept till they are sixteen, when they are placed out in families as servants or as apprentices, care being taken to secure good Christian homes. The object being to train them up as Christian children, prayer is offered without ceasing to God for the gift of His Spirit, and Mr. Müller reports special outpouring of grace in answer to prayer. The cost varies from year to year with the price of food. The last year's average was about £13 per child. Certainly a very small sum. The assistants are all required to be professing Christians; but no preference is allowed to any denomination. Mr. Müller is himself a Baptist, but has views which are peculiarly his own. The teachers attend their own places of worship in the town of Bristol, and services for the children on the Lord's Day are conducted by clergymen and laymen of different denominations in the several houses. There are weekly meetings of the teachers and servants for prayer conducted by Mr. Müller.

While this orphanage is the central work, he has other arrangements for the circulation of the Word of God and maintenance of missionaries and support of schools in various parts of the world, contributors designating the object to which they desire their gifts may be appropriated. His success is a wonderful illustration of what may be accomplished through a feeble agency by the Divine power bringing a strong will into subjection to the control of the Spirit, which works by that agency to accomplish its own purposes.

Certainly no one can restrain the expression, "What hath God wrought?" The gift bestowed on George Müller and Dr. Muhlenberg is not given to every one. But to every one the self-same Spirit distributes the power to aid according to his several ability in feeding the hungry, clothing the naked, giving sight to the blind and healing the sick, and God asks of each according to that he hath, and not according to that he hath not, and He knows what He has given. Only let each one seek for grace to do with his might what his hand findeth to do,—knowing that there is neither device nor knowledge in the grave, whither we go.

LEAMINGTON, September 7th.

We have been spending several days in driving from Clifton to Chepstow Castle, and thence, along the valley of the river Wye, to Tintern Abbey and Ross, and so to Gloucester, where we again took rail to this place. It has been a very delightful trip, through scenes of unrivalled loveliness of natural formation, to which is added all the grace of culture, which gives such a charm to England.

At Gloucester we made a morning call on Canon Lysons, whom we met at Jerusalem. We found him living in the house his forefathers had dwelt in for over 300 years—a plain, low-ceiled, extensive pile of buildings, surrounded by beautiful gardens and commanding an extensive view over meadow and valley; terminating in ranges of cultivated hills and embracing the town of Gloucester, with its magnificent cathedral tower, and reaching as far as Cheltenham ; one of the most celebrated of English watering places. He gave us a most cordial welcome, only diminished by his regret that we declined his invitation to stay longer. He had invited your mother's relatives, the Gordon Canynges, to meet us at dinner if we should remain long enough. They live seven miles away. Mrs. Gordon Canynges was a Miss Cheston, her father having been one of the canons of Gloucester Cathedral and the last of the name.

Just at the foot of the hill on which stands Hempstead Park, the residence of Canon Lysons, runs a ship canal which connects with the Bristol Channel; and it was a curious sight to see large ships and brigs passing through the meadows, bearing timber from Russia and Norway to the large lumber yards and workshops of Gloucester. These are on the land of our friend, and have given great value to his estate. He has built at his own charge and (endowed) a chapel, and does not permit a public house, as they call taverns here, to be built on his estate. He is a fine specimen of an English country gentleman and clergyman, and his youngest son, who is also a clergyman and has a family living about twenty miles off, is a very good exemplar of what a clergyman should be. He and his family are at present with his father while a rectory is being built for him. They carried us to their fruit houses and plucked a supply of beautiful peaches and grapes, and insisted on your aunt and uncle accepting them. The peach and plum trees are trained against walls, and only the finest fruit allowed to remain on the boughs. They thus have a smaller number of them, but every one is of the very finest quality.

Tintern Abbey is one of the best preserved ruins in Great Britain. It was one of the wealthiest and oldest monastic establishments. Built in the eleventh and twelfth century, lying in a quiet vale surrounded on every side by high hills covered with underwood, dotted with huge yew trees, standing out very distinctly on account of the deep green of the foliage, and studded thickly with the pretty berries, looking like little cups of rose coral. The buildings, which covered many acres, have all disappeared except the walls of the great church with its stone-mullioned windows and wide transepts, and the refectory. These are roofless and mantled with ivy, and where were once the floor and stalls for the monks, nothing is now found but soft green turf. The monks were grass and their glory as the flower of grass. Little did your mother and I, thirty-six years ago, think we should again enjoy the great delight of visiting the remains of their grandeur—so beautiful in its decay. It was so unchanged in those years that we could almost imagine it was but yesterday and that we had passed the night in the beautiful little inn, just by, and walked out in the morning to take a farewell glimpse. At Ivy Neck you will find lithographic views of the ruin we then bought. Photography was unknown, and we now added some stereoscopic pictures which will prove how little change there has been.

From Tintern we drove up the Wye to Ross; a beautiful drive through highly cultivated farms. Ross is celebrated not only for being a fine old town but enjoys the renown of being the birth-place and residence of John Kyrle, a philanthropist of the last century, celebrated by Pope as the "Man of Ross" in one of his poems. Churches alms-houses and public walks, built and endowed by Kyrle, still attest the truth of the character given him by the poet. His is a fame far more noble than that of many whose effigied tombs cumber the space in the churches which should be occupied by living worshippers instead of stone memorials of the pride of survivors or descendants. I honor the statesman whose wisdom serves and saves his country, and the warrior whose courage defends her from the attacks of enemies; but the more humble worth of the peaceful citizen who labors to acquire wealth to be expended for the good of his fellows, is also worthy of all praise; and there were few things in London itself more interesting than the houses erected by George Peabody, on which I happened one day in my wanderings about the streets in the heart of the city. We are about starting. I find it out of my power to write.

Yours truly and lovingly,

CASPAR MORRIS.

We quite approve of Israel's views about Cheston's house. Hope the telegram reached you safely. A *small* house will suit us on every account. We are about to spend a day with my dear friend, Latham, at Derby. We are glad to hear the Jerusalem trunk has arrived. We have sent none other. I think our Rome articles went in your uncle's box, but am not sure.

LITTLE EATON, NEAR DERBY,
September 8, 1872.

My Dear Child:

Your father and I separated from the party yesterday and came here to spend a day and two nights with Mr. and Mrs. Latham, and are enjoying it very much. We find them quite advanced in life—she a great invalid, confined to her room, and has been for a year. He has charge of the little parish church close to his house, and his son-in-law is his curate, residing as near on the other side. As Mr. Latham is canon of Litchfield Cathedral, he can only be here a part of the year. They are the same lovely Christian people we knew thirty-six years ago. The wife of the curate, Mr. Garland, was then about eight or nine years old; now she is the mother of nine children, their only daughter and four sons all away; two in India. This is a nice specimen of an English parsonage, beautifully situated. The view from the window where I write reminds me of the inland view from the Neck house, before it was so shut out by the trees; only that the green of these fields far surpasses ours, as they have no hot suns to burn them. Your father and Mr. Latham are having a very nice time together. We expect to join uncle and aunts to-morrow at Matlock Baths; from thence to York, and reach Edinburgh by next Saturday.

Since writing we have been to Kenilworth, Warwick and Warwick Castle, and to Stratford-on-Avon—to Shakespeare's house, where he was born,—also to the church where he was interred. These two last we did not visit when here before, but the others looked precisely as we saw them then, no more ivy even on the ruins at Kenilworth, as they trim it away constantly. In Shakespeare's house many curious things are shown of his, and the house itself is very quaint.

Since writing the above we have been to church with Mr. Latham and a Miss Johnson, who is here as companion to Mrs. Latham, and Mr. Latham gave us a very good sermon. His curate read service. Then he and his wife walked back here with us, as Mrs. Latham wished to have the Holy Communion administered to her while your father was with them. You may not remember these are friends whom he was much with in Calcutta.

We have thought and felt much for you all since hearing of Frank's (*F. K. Murray.*—EDS.) death. He was as an elder brother to all those girls, and his loss must be much felt for a long time. Remember me affectionately to Sally and Carrie as well as their parents. I fear they will not be able to spare them to you this winter, and you will all miss them.

YORK, September 11th.

We took leave of Mr. and Mrs. Latham and joined the party at Matlock Baths on the 9th; visited the wells there, saw the very one your father took the "Crows' Nest" from, and very much the same collection of things are now being encrusted as then. Then visited the spots where Derbyshire spar in every variety and shape is offered for sale, but as of old they command such high prices and are so fragile that we resisted the temptation to purchase, notwithstanding your uncle's offer to send them home in his box for us. They *did* all buy. We then drove to "Haddon Hall,"—ten miles in the rain—to see an "old castle," kept in its original state, not only the building itself, but the furniture. I do not think they understood comfort as we do, though it was curious, and yesterday came by rail here, and now have passed the morning in "Yorkminster Cathedral." It is a fine old specimen, but we have seen so many that I cannot say this is No. 1.

We, your father and I, left them at a museum and have come in to write, as I cannot imagine there can be anything in it that will be novel to us, after a year's occupation in this way, and so I will rest my foot, for it does not relish being dragged about. From here we go to Ripon, and thence to Fountains Abbey, and thence to the lakes and Kendal. Then we shall be at home again for a day or two.

We have just received a letter from Cousin Emily, mentioning the death of Mifflin Wistar. We had heard by the previous mail of his illness, and so rather expected this. I know she will feel this keenly, as it was an attachment of long standing. They lived next door to each other as children, and the intimacy then formed has been uninterrupted. I am glad to find she will go and stay with Mrs. Wistar for a month, as I have no doubt it is a good arrangement for them both.

We are having good accounts from Gall. and Han.; they are now in Paris, and she has improved. We may meet in Wales, but it is doubtful; and I am sure it is best for them to move independently of us, even if we don't meet until we go aboard ship at Liverpool.

RIPON, September 12th.

Before leaving this morning we were cheered by letters from home, one from you with them. I am very glad the girls returned to you. I am sure it was best for them, and I hope all will keep well. It was quite a relief to me to hear from Annie that Mary Gibson was making a Hernani dress for you, as I so regretted my having yours, and had intended giving you one in its place on my return. We find we cannot take home dress materials in the *piece*, so that I cannot carry you anything of the sort, but you'll have to be content with goods bought in Philadelphia, and, indeed, everything can be had there that is here; and, as you meet us in Chestnut Street, we will see to all that. The house has not been disposed of, so, of course, we will go to it, though we prefer a much smaller one, and were even willing to board, if one did not present promptly.

Of course you cannot bring all on with you, and I shall want to see all, so we will pay you a visit, and stop in Baltimore before settling down for the winter.

Your father will not have the strength to resume practice. He cannot bear much fatigue, though he is pretty well. You must expect to see us *old people*. I take cold very easily, and am lame, can walk but little; but I am sure of a hearty welcome, let our condition be what it may.

Yours, truly, with love. Carriages at the door to go to an abbey, etc., etc. Oh! I am so tired.

A. C. M.

MATLOCK BATHS, September 10, 1872.

My Dear Children:

We have found so many home-like and familiar associations in this blessed Christian country that they have sadly interfered with the regularity of my communications to you, though not interrupting the flow of our affections toward you, or our interest in all that concerns you and desire to promote your happiness. I feel as I sit down this morning to write to you as though there had been an immense chasm in my letters which I know not how to "bridge over." Where was the thread broken? I remember nothing I have written, and whether my last account of our seeings and doings was up to London and down to Bristol, or whether I ever got fairly out of France I cannot tell.

The last few days have been so full of enjoyment both to your mother and myself in the renewal of our intimacy with dear old friends, that leaving them is like another transplantation, and we cannot avoid some sensations of regret, though the sweet odor of our pleasure still lingers around us, and the faith that our separation will be but for a little while, and our reunion *eternal* in the Father's house, under a Saviour's protection, comforts us. You know how warmly I love my old English Christian friends, and I have found new cause for this feeling in my recent intercourse with them. We have nothing which is like it with us. The frank, earnest, honest way in which they express their views and feelings on religious subjects is unknown so far as my observation extends in our country.

We spent Saturday afternoon and the Lord's day at the vicarage of the Rev. Mr. Latham, who is also Canon of Derby. This office of Canon is one of the appendages of cathedrals, and the duties consist in conducting the daily service and preaching on the Lord's day without any parochial or personal care of individual souls. There are several attached to each cathedral, receiving an income from the cathedral endowment. Each is obliged to reside three months only in each year. The remainder of the year they devote, if they please, to other duties, and many of them hold also parochial livings in which they employ curates who perform the services during their absence at the cathedral. The office is bestowed as a reward for faithful services,—in theory,—and in the case of Mr. Latham was given as an acknowledgment of the importance of a training-school for teachers which he had instituted and conducted for many years, in Derby.

He wished us to have visited him at Litchfield in order that he might have shown us the very fine building, but your mother and I were glad we were not able to get there till it was closed for repairs and he returned to his home, as that enabled us also to see our old friend, his wife,—who is so infirm through age and disease that she is confined to her chamber and an adjoining room, and of course unable to attend upon him. No splendors of architecture—and I would not under-estimate the grandeur of Litchfield, nor the touching impressive beauty of Chantrey's monument to the children, which attracted us so forcibly on our former visit that I wished much to see it again ourselves and that your aunts should see it also—no human work could have been so impressive and full of glory as the Divine workmanship and living building of God we found in the little parsonage.

We drove out from Derby in a cab, about three miles, in a beautiful hilly district with its green pastures divided by irregular hedge-rows and dotted with fine trees. We stopped at the little "public" in the village, designing to leave our bags and take lodgings there. In this we were disappointed as they had no accommodations they were willing to shew us, even. We were therefore compelled either to forego our anticipated pleasure and return to Derby or intrude upon our friends and see if they could receive us. Driving past a neat little church we entered through a gate into a small enclosure planted neatly with clumps of Laurestinus, just bursting into full blow, the white bloom relieving the deep rich glossy foliage; while Holly, Mahonia and Rhododendrons were set against the wall, and the edges of the border were planted with Queen Marguerites and Nasturtiums. The house was entered through a little stone porch into a small hall with a study at one side, the stairway at the other, and before us the two doors entering, the one into the drawing-room, and the other to the dining room. Was not that a homelike entrance to Ivy Neck folk? But then it was all on a nice diminished scale.

In the drawing room, to which we were carried by Mr. Latham, who gave us no opportunity to send in a card or inquire if he were at home, we found a nice collection of books and two couches and a few chairs which filled all the wall space except two bay windows opening to the ground, one looking out on a short, steep slope, below which lay a nice little pasture lot, in which a cow and horse were quietly enjoying the green grass. There is nothing gives so great a sense of comfort as the herds of cattle in the rich green pastures, more often quietly ruminating than grazing. They are perfect pictures of animal content, with abundance.

In the centre, covering one-third of the entire floor space, was a table on which lay the usual books of polite literature. It was about 5.30 P. M. and the first question was: Would we have tea or a substantial meal? Having dined at 2 we could very honestly say we preferred the tea. Mr. Latham then introduced to us a lady who stays with Mrs. Latham during his residence at Lichfield, who took your mother up stairs, where I soon followed and found her in a snug little room, the floor not wholly covered, and that which was covered being done with drugget and ingrain carpet of three different kinds, while the chairs, bureau and washstand all showed they had seen the family service during many years. We were soon summoned to see Mrs. Latham, an aged and infirm but lovely woman, to whose comfort they are obliged to devote the two principal rooms on the second floor, and there are but the two stories. One she occupies in the day and the other as a bedroom.

Now do not you one, and all, realize how happily your dear mother and I spent that evening. We were soon called down to that simple *English family tea*, a tea-pot and a few cups on the table and a plate of thin buttered bread and a rack of toast and a plate of cake. This did not detain us long; after which your mother went to Mrs. Latham, and Mr. Latham and I paced the gravel walk among his little shrubbery until late. Then a good hearty supper of chicken and ham, etc., and then to bed. The next morning found us refreshed, and prayers done at the breakfast table by 8 A. M. Then Mr. Latham left us while he went to open his Sunday School.

We followed to church at the hour of service and enjoyed the delight of a country congregation, a well trained choir, and well rendered service, followed by a most excellent discourse. On our return to the house we participated in the communion of the body and blood of our Lord in Mrs. Latham's room. It was an extraordinary privilege. My first participation in this privilege was with Mr. Latham leaning on my arm as we walked to the table of the Lord in *Old Mission Church*, Calcutta, in the month of Jannary, 1827. How wonderful that we should be once again permitted to unite in this most solemn sacrament on earth, after the lapes, of so nearly half a century, in this quiet nook of Old England. Neither had supposed the other still on earth till a few days ago I took up the clergy list and found my friend's name and residence.

An afternoon's service was followed by a very good sermon from Mr. Garland, son-in-law of Mr. Latham, and curate who lives in the village. Himself and wife joined us at tea, and his wife and two eldest children stayed to supper. It would be impossible to give any idea of the delight we enjoyed. Our converse flowed uninterruptedly in the channel into which thought and feeding alike tend under such circumstances, and we retired again to refresh our bodies for the travel of the Monday.

At 8 A. M. we met at the breakfast table the second son of our friend, who is a clergyman and head master of Repton school, which is about three miles distant. His father had sent word of our being here, but three full services had occupied him all the Lord's day, and he had walked over to meet us at breakfast before we should leave. You know how fastidious I am about those to whom shall be entrusted the training of our children ; an office which I regard as the most important filled by man. Mr. Latham fills my idea of a *typical* character as teacher. A noble expansive brow crowns a face, every line of which is inwrought with intelligence, while the eye beams with the warmest and holiest affection, and his well turned limbs and graceful movements tell of active habits. Everything about him was cheerful and attractive. We enjoyed the little time we were together—too little to permit more than the interchange of those few expressions by which one is able to acquire and give an insight into character and establish the relations of friendship or its opposite. We parted with regret that our intercourse had been so limited and a mutual regard which would lead us to look forward with pleasant anticipation of that future union which is the hope of the Christian.

I have been frequently interrupted, and just as I had reached the bottom of the last page we were startled by the demand for our luggage—our departure being hastened by the arrival of a party waiting for our rooms. We were obliged to vacate, and after after waiting a little while at the station, had a pleasant ride of two hours to this place; "Ripon" from which we visit Fountains Abbey, the most imposing ruin, it is said, in England. It is now nearly dinner time and we shall be occupied all the afternoon in visiting it.

My letters are so disjointed that you will infer from them the way in which we are "*jumping* about." Yesterday was spent at York in visiting the *Minster*, the grandest ecclesiastical building in England. York itself is a fine old town, having been a Roman station and is enclosed yet by a wall, a part of which is said to have been built very early in the Christian era. Constantine the Great was born here and if I am not deceived by memory it was here that the legions declared him Emperor. Of this I am not however quite sure; some of you young folks can look into Gibbon and fix it properly in your own minds. We saw the part of the wall which is unmistakably Roman.

I visited the Blind Institution which was endowed by subscriptions for a memorial to Wilberforce, who represented this place and the county during so many years. It is in an old building rented for the purpose from the Crown, having been the palace of the Kings when they came into the northern counties, and the residence of the Governor of the North. It is very antiquated in appearance and adorned with the armorial bearings of many sovereigns. Among them Wentworth, Earl of Stafford, had placed his own very conspicuously, and this was one of the circumstances alleged against him on his trial as a sign of his criminal ambition, which led to his being beheaded in the days of Charles the First.

I was much pleased with the manner in which it is conducted, and enjoyed especially being permitted to unite in their prayers in the evening, which were chanted most feelingly as well as harmoniously.

The cathedral service which we attended before visiting its objects of interest was also very well done, but there was no attendance on it except by those who, like ourselves, were drawn by a desire to visit the building. This is very imposing with its massive columns, lofty Norman arches, and great windows filled with glass of the eleventh and twelfth century. A lofty tower rises at the junction of the nave, choir and transept, supported by very massive pillars. You will all remember that an insane fanatic fired the building some thirty years ago. The draught to the tower, which rose as a chimney in the centre, saved the glass windows by carrying the heat from them, so that though the roof and all the wood-work of the interior was burned the windows escaped injury. In the crypt we saw columns which had been built in the day of William the Conqueror; very massive and richly wrought for that period; and walls and arches of a still earlier date supposed to be the seventh century.

There are also many Roman stone coffins and fragments of altars and tombs. In the cathedral itself are many monumental effigies of

Earls and Nobles and Archbishops of various dates, from the Conquest down. Among the later one which pleased me, is erected to commemorate the virtues of Beckwith M. D., who, living, served the people, and, dying, left his fortune thus honorably earned to various religious and benevolent purposes.

In the church at Little Eaton, immediately in front of the pew in which we sat, is a tablet to the memory of Dr. Baker, whose "Scriptural faith was the source of a holy and consistent life, during which he devoted himself to the relief of the sickness of the people of Derby." It always does me good to recognize such characters in the profession I so love and honor.

From York to this place we have passed over a very fertile and beautiful country. There is still much grain, wheat, barley and oats standing, and a larger quantity cut and waiting to be carted. The weather is wet and it is sad to see the shocks of corn standing in great ponds of water—rising half way up the sheaves in some places.

We visited the very fine nurseries of Backhouse, near York, and on asking if they ever sent anything to America was told they had an old correspondent, a Mr. Alt, in Baltimore, to whom they had just sent half a ton of cabbage seeds.

We are again called to the carriages, so must say farewell.

YORK, September 11, 1872.

My Dear Sister (Miss Emily Hollingsworth.—EDS.):

Though I mailed a letter to you only yesterday morning, which will probably reach you by the same mail as this does, I cannot allow the morning to pass without indulging my own feelings, and I trust contributing toward the comfort of yours, by expressing the deep sympathy *Anne and I* (and I may safely add all our party) feel with you in your affliction, and dear Mrs. Wistar in her almost unparalleled bereavement. I should say quite unparalleled, so unusually tender and intimate were the relations between dear Mifflin and herself, had I not in my observation known a few other cases in which a similar peculiarity of circumstances had produced a similar result; concentrating on each other all the affections of two loving souls. The very observation of similar cases enables me to understand more fully and entirely the length and depth of the overwhelming calamity. Faith will enable the bereaved survivor to dwell upon the glory and honor and immortality which is the reward of those who through faith and patience are inheritors of the promises; and, looking back on the trials through which the sufferer has passed, to rejoice that he has "entered into rest;" but that does not remove the sting of the terrible wound in our own souls, nor diminish the sorrow which our loss involves in it for ourselves.

The everlasting arms bear up the sufferer who believes in Jesus, but still the suffering is felt. Jesus himself wept with his friends in their distress, even though he knew all the glory on which the departed entered; and knew also what he should do in the restoration to their arms in this life, of the brother whom they mourned, thinking only of the resurrection of the just in the last day. How heartless, therefore, in any one to chide the sorrow of those who mourn, even though they do not sorrow as those without hope, but know that "them also which sleep in Jesus, will God bring with Him."

For yourself you have lost a brother, and we do feel for you as knowing how near and dear he was to you, and feel not only that we have ourselves lost a highly valued friend, but that being as near to your soul as Jonathan was to David's, you must be sorrowing as did the Royal mourner. How high is the office with which God clothes you in making you the minister of consolation to those whom he chastens. You cannot take away the smart, you cannot ward off the blow, but you are commissioned and empowered to carry balm to the wound, and to pour the wine of the gospel into the fainting soul. The angels who were sent to Jesus in the garden did not take away His suffering; they only strengthened Him in His agony. You may not be able to take away the terrible sense of loss from the soul of dear Mrs. Wistar, but I trust you will be enabled, by the grace of God strengthening you, to help to bear her up; and in doing so, will find that the promise is sure that is expressed in the language "They that water shall be watered upon," and sharing with another the comfort wherewith you are comforted of God, you will find your own strength increased.

We had not received the letter to which you refer. Our only note of preparation had been sounded by sister Mary Ann, who in a letter to sister Hannah, alluded to a note she had received from you, written at the request of Mrs. Wistar to inform her of Mifflin's illness.

We received last evening, together with yours, a letter from Galloway, dated at Paris on the 6th, giving very pleasant accounts of dear Hannah's improvement. I doubt whether we shall meet again till we embark.

I must now close. We were summoned to breakfast and as it is decided to go to the Minster in time to be present during the service, which commences at 10 A. M. daily, and I wish to write to Galloway before going there, I must bid you good-bye. Please remember us most affectionately to dear Mrs. Wistar and Miss Smith with the assurance of our deep sympathy in their distress and our prayer that they may find refuge in the loving arms of a compassionate elder brother and Lord.

Yours most truly,

CASPAR MORRIS.

Love also to Caroline and Henry. We are driving through everything here as rapidly as possible. We hope to reach Kendal on Saturday and rush around the lakes and so to Edinburgh.

RIPON, YORKSHIRE, September 12, 1872.

My Dear Children:

I do not know how it happens; but where I would fain write the most and have the most to write about, I accomplish the least. You know my fondness for England and English scenes, and English people, has been always great; and so far from suffering diminution, it has been enhanced by the objects and incidents which I meet with now. And yet I feel as though I had utterly failed to give you any impression whatever, much more to give you one adequate to the expression of my feelings. To-day we left York and had a charming ride to this place by railroad through a fertile country, partly plain and partly beautifully undulating, without any of the towering chimneys vomiting out volumes of black smoke, and obscuring the entire scene, such as we passed through on our way from Matlock Baths to York. The trees and hedges and meadows are all beautifully green; and the cattle and sheep are all too well fed to be said to *revel* in their pasture. They take a *quieter* joy in eating and *ruminating*. I am surprised at the *paucity* of the stock in numbers, but they are all lying down as though perfectly satisfied. The grain fields look sadly, about half the crop yet standing or lying cut on the fields, soaking in water and deluged by rain. The landlord of the inn here says the crops of these northern counties is a failure and the potato crop is acknowledged to be such all over the Island. So that the people are looking forward to a winter of high priced provision and coals and therefore of sufferings.

This afternoon we have enjoyed a great gratification in a visit to Studley Park, the seat of the Marquis of Ripon, one of the cabinet at present, and one of the commissioners to negotiate the Washington Treaty. In this park stands the celebrated ruin of Fountains Abbey, the largest and grandest ruin in England. It is truly a grand building, even in its decay; and gives an idea of the riches of the old monastic establishments as well as of the corruption which preceded their overthrow, which not even Tintern and Vale Crucis Abbey do.

A few monks, desiring to escape the *laxity* of discipline of the monastery to which they belonged, are said to have retired to this valley, then wild and rude, and to have lived in caves and under trees. The fame of their sanctity drew favour toward them; and large gifts of money and land led to the erection of massive and splendid buildings, which still stand, though roofless, to exhibit how naturally man yields to the temptation to use wealth to gratify his taste and promote his ease.

But grand as are the ruins of the Abbey they are insignificant when considered in connection with the magnificence of the park in which they stand. A stream of some size meandering through a narrow valley is dammed and used to form lakes and canals and waterfalls, while the slopes on either side are planted with shrubbery and groves and woods; and intersected by well kept roads, winding for miles among these varied beauties, each turn revealing some new beauty of prospect or of foliage, or of water, or of tree, till one feels absolutely lost in admiration. The most noble firs, and hemlock spruce trees I have ever seen, are here. I stepped the circuit of the branches of one Norway Fir as they laid on the ground and found it more than ninety paces, nearly 300 feet, while it rose straight as a spire over 130 feet, green from the ground to the summit. There is also one enormous hemlock spruce, with its deep dark green foliage. Beeches, Oaks, Chestnuts, Limes, and Elms, were scattered about profusely, each rivalling the other in grandeur; while long avenues of horse chestnuts and elms and beeches recalled those of Versailles. Indeed this park excels any royal domain we have seen. There are walks shut in by great hedges of yew of the blackest of green and the most compact foliage, from behind which one hears the music of rushing and falling waters; while at intervals natural openings afford glimpses of the lakes with their sloping margins, or the dashing of the water over rocky ledges, while the heights on either side are clothed with masses of wood.

At the end of a mile or more of such beauty, varied by widespread mossy banks, and great clusters of evergreen bushes, the great skeleton walls of the abbey burst on the eye, as you turn a corner, with a grandeur which is indescribably imposing. Your mother was not able to walk further, and of course it would be improper to permit indiscriminate use of the exquisitely fine drives which, winding through the park and its beauties, lead to the ruins.

These roads are kept in as much neatness as the foot-walks in any gentleman's garden. Old men were busy with brushes and baskets gathering off the falling leaves from the wide carriage-way with its mile and more of length. Your mother took her seat on some stone steps so soon as she had got a good distant view of the abbey, and I walked further, but felt convinced I could not explore them without undue fatigue, and was therefore content with the general view of the lofty tower, great stone mullioned windows, receding arches of the nave of the church, (all in fine preservation), and the ivy-clad ruinous walls of the other parts of the structure, which in its integrity must have been very solemnly impressive.

Your uncle and aunts wandered around and identified the kitchen with its enormous chimney, like the stack of a modern iron furnace; the refectory with its traces not only of the hospitality for which such institutions were originally established, but the revelry into which that virtue degenerated; like other virtues becoming vices and involving of necessity their overthrow.

I walked among the yew and laurel hedges and paused to admire the beauty of the views and listen to the rush of the waterfalls or admire the graceful borders of the lakes and the long line of canal with the islands and statuary, and Gothic and Grecian temples which crown the heights, bosomed in deep woods, or stand majestically on open glades by the borders of the stream. Every element of natural and artificial beauty is combined, and we were of the unanimous opinion that we had seen nothing more worthy of a visit. As we drove away we met a relative of the marquis driving in the park in a very quiet gentlemanly manner; and the Bishop of Ripon, a very dignified and worthy representative of his order, with craped hat (having lost a lovely son lately at Baden) accompanied by a younger son, both on horse-back.

KESWICK, September 15, 1872.

My Dear Child :

Since my last to you we have paid our little visit to Kendal. The approach by railroad was very different from ours by carriage thirty-six years ago, but the beauty of the surroundings cannot be spoiled. There are but two members of the Braithwaite family residing there, each a short distance out of town, in very beautiful residences, and both the heads, Charles and Forster, are engaged in the same business their father carried on when we were here before—"Woollen Manufactory." We arrived late in the afternoon, having had a fatiguing day, and so let your uncle Wistar and Aunt Mary, and sisters Hannah and Jane go without us out to Charles Braithwaite's after tea, and we rested. They were most cordially received and strongly urged to *stay* with them, and a proposition to send in for us, *bag and baggage*. All this was however declined, as we wanted to move on next day. Your father and I feeling refreshed by a night's rest, took a carriage early, and drove out to call on each of the families, leaving the others to start, and we would join them, as it was to be a drive over here of thirty miles, and a most beautiful one it was, and the weather delightful. We all enjoyed it exceedingly. The whole distance among mountains and lakes Windermere, Ambleside, Grassmere, and so on to Keswick, where we have now stopped for a couple of days to rest. The views here are extremely beautiful and the country highly cultivated. But, poor farmers, they have had so much wet weather that the wheat is all out, some not cut, and it is thought it will be more than half lost. So you will see others have their troubles as well as you, and as the potatoes are rotting, it is a sad condition, and as so many depend on them the prices must go up, and those who have will be the gainers. We are much struck by the healthy appearance of the inhabitants in this region. They are florid, and the children robust looking, which we have not thought in the southern counties and cities.

Between York and Kendal we stopped at Ripon to visit Fountains Abbey and Studley Park, both of which are justly considered remarkably fine. It is certainly the finest park I have ever seen, and they tell me much about the Abbey. *We* were too tired by the time we reached it to explore it, but are quite content to listen to the description of the others, and I think can imagine it.

We expect to leave here the day after to-morrow for Edinburgh direct. We find we shall be much pressed for time. Now I would omit some things, but they are disposed to drive ahead; won't admit they are *tired*, but I see they are.

EDINBURGH, September 19th.

We reached here two days ago comfortably, and the next morning all started in carriages to the castle and grounds around. Thence to Holyrood of which, however, we could not see much, as more walking was necessary than I could accomplish, and the weather was so cold and searching that we left them and went shopping for warm clothing, and without difficulty was soon comfortable. So yesterday we drove pretty near all day in pouring rain. We took the Queen's drive; a beautiful one it is, stopping at Roslyn Castle and then around a long distance to see several other places of interest, and on our way back went to Roslyn chapel. All got back very weary, and concluded to rest to-day, and this morning your letters were brought in, giving good accounts of you all. I was quite amused to find our choice of your dress, which is in Liverpool packed for shipping, is just what you wanted it to be. I told your aunt and is she much pleased. I did not cut all the breadths, but hope they will be right as [well as the color.

As 1428 is not rented you will of course come there and bring whoever you choose. Oh, I do want to see you all so much! Cousin will be there by that time also. She is with Mrs. Wistar now.

As we got out of the cars here on our arrival we recognized Miss Williams, the Doctor's oldest daughter, Maria. As she was only sixteen days from Spruce Street, where she had seen Cheston and the children, we got from her very direct accounts. She has come for the winter to visit a friend. She has called on us and your father has returned the visit and apologized for me. She is looking badly.

To-morrow we are to go to Melrose and Abbotsford, and leave here the day after for Sterling and thence to the Lakes. So you see we keep moving. Won't I be glad to settle down in Chestnut Street and put my clothes in drawers and wardrobes!

We have good accounts from Gall. and Han.; they are now in London and will, I think, join us in Wales on our return from Ireland, about ten days before we sail.

We thought of Murray on the 5th; wishing him much happiness. I suppose by this time they are returning from their little trip to settle down in Sixteenth Street. Murray is such a nice fellow that much will be expected of her. Will Bob remain with them? I suppose so, though I have not heard it.

It is mail time, so with much love to you, one and all,

Yours most truly and affectionately, in haste,

A. C. MORRIS.

KESWICK, September 15, 1872.

From Ripon we crossed by rail through Darlington, Castle Bernard, so to Kendal in Westmoreland. It was an irregular and tedious route, involving long stoppages to make the connections, but carrying us through scenes of varied interest, partly agricultural, with fine pastures and rolling fields and beautiful hedges; partly wild moors, without trees or hedges, and used as sheep pastures and grouse preserves. So numerous are these birds that the Newcastle paper which we purchased, mentioned the fact of one sportsman who had shot eight hundred in one day. It must have been *hard sport* to pull the trigger and load the breech sufficiently rapidly to do this.

As we entered Westmoreland the hills became higher and ruder and the valleys embosomed among them more and more beautiful, till we felt as though one need not go from here to find enough to enable them to praise the wondrous skill and power of Him who made all so fair. We entered the familiar vale of Kendal, passing the ruins of the Castle of Parr, the father of one of the unfortunate Queens of the Eighth Henry, which stands without any progress of decay, just as we left it thirty-six years ago, and reached Kendal Station by rail. That *was* a change! But when getting into carriages we were drawn through the narrow streets of old one-story stone cottages, and heard the clatter of the wooden-soled and iron-bound shoes of the children, and heard the broad dialect in which they addressed each other, the old feelings of your mother and myself were worked up into strong emotions of affection and gratitude to those we had so loved who had once welcomed us here; and kindliness toward the survivors who, then youth, are now the honored and worthy representatives of goodly ancestors.

After tea your uncle and aunts went to Mr. Charles Braithwaite's and spent the evening. Your mother and I were too wearied by the York and Ripon exertion, and the day's travel, to give or receive pleasure even with such incitement, and staid quietly at the Kings Arms,—the very inn to which we had gone formerly and from which our friends had carried us to their home. When your uncle and aunts came in they reported the cordial welcome they had received, only tempered by the disappointment of Mr. and Mrs. Braithwaite, that they would not accept the hospitality of the house and stay some days with them.

In the morning, directly after breakfast, your mother and I took a carriage and drove to Charles Braithwaite's, a beautiful home on the height above the town, surrounded by neat garden and shrubbery; the interior made attractive by art in various modes of expression, and the view from the drawing-room windows very wide and beautiful. Mr. Braithwaite was not married when we were here before, and now, among other ornaments, were objects brought from the Holy Land by one of his sons; and another has just gone to join his uncle (Bevan Braithwaite) in a visit to Constantinople, Athens and Rome. Mr. Braithwaite had left for his place of business before we got to the house, but Mrs. Braithwaite gave us a most genial welcome and entered into our feelings for his mother and father and sister as warmly as though she had known us as well as them.

From there we went to Foster Braithwaite's, another equally beautiful home, where we met his wife and her sister, whose brother is the husband of Foster's sister, Caroline Savory. There we met your uncle and aunts by appointment and had an equally pleasant visit. The daughter of Lord Macaulay, the historian, had left as they entered the house, having been making them a visit of some time. Mr. and Mrs. Braithwaite remembered Cheston and Hannah's visit, and asked kindly for him and the boys, whose ages they had not forgotten, though I suppose Tyson and Caspar retain no remembrance of their visit.

KESWICK, September 15, 1872.

My Dear Children:

Certainly your father's privileges have been greater than those commonly conferred on man. Who has been more kindly provided for in temporal blessings? Who has enjoyed more of the good things of this life? Seen more of the beautiful and grand, or been more carefully protected in travel by land and by sea? I will not enumerate the private blessings and mercies which have been renewed to me with every returning morning; nor lift the veil which God has graciously spread over the pardoned sins and iniquities which have abounded. Thanks to him that *grace* did much more abound.

But you will ask what does all this mean. Well it was not enough that I should be permitted to find pleasure and refreshment to my animal and intellectual nature amid these beautiful lakes and rivers and mountains, with their ever varying light and shade, but going this evening to church, I listened to an excellent discourse on the text, "Come, for all things are ready." There was communion after it. As I had communed last Lord's Day with the Lathams (with whom I had *first* partaken of this privilege) I hesitated somewhat about remaining. But the thought how long it might be before the privilege would again offer (as we go to-morrow to Scotland where it is only a quarterly service) led me to stay. Losing my way in returning I enquired it of a poor woman who had also been to church, and from her learned the preacher was J. C. Ryle. What name is more honored? Thus from my earliest years have I been warmed and fed and guided, and entreated by eminent ministers of Christ. There is scarcely a distinguished preacher of any denomination in our own or foreign lands whom I have not heard. What shall I render to my God for all His gifts to me may well be a searching question. I can only answer in the language of the hymn.

>   Just as I am, and waiting not
>   To rid my soul of one dark blot,
>   To thee, Whose blood can cleanse each spot,
>   O Lamb of God I come.

for after it all in me dwelleth *no good thing*.

EDINBURGH, September 10, 1872.

We have just arrived here at 5 P. M. from Keswick this morning. As we alighted on the platform I said to your mother, "There is Maria Williams." "Now do behave yourself, and don't be rushing up to everybody and claiming acquaintance," was the prompt reply. Every look confirmed me in my conviction, and at last I burst over the restraint and was recompensed by learning that it is only sixteen days since she saw dear Cheston and Mellie, and reports them quite well. As we stopped this morning at a little way station in Cumberland, for a moment, we caught a glimpse of William and Sally Morris looking charmingly. We had no time to do more than change salutations, as we were coming north and they on their return south. They have been two pleasant incidents of a cold, raw, rainy day.

It is very sad to see the wheat, oats, and hay crop of the northern counties of England and South Scotland still unharvested and much of it ruined. The potato crop is generally spoiled, and I saw an estimate in a Newcastle paper within a few days, that the deficiency would require not less than £37,000,000 in the value of foreign grain.

I was troubled a day or two since to see the report of the robbery of the Third National Bank of Baltimore. We hope it is not the Old Farmers' and Planters'. I was shocked on Saturday by the telegraphic report of five failures there for $3,000,000 of liabilities. Such a calamity must effect the community.

We are now travelling with great rapidity and seeing everything hastily. Our visit to Kendal was a very pleasant renewal of old affections. Our friends there are nicely settled. Your mother and I were too wearied to call on either of them in the evening, but in the morning went to both Charles and Foster Braithwaite's, and had cordial welcome at each. The latter is very like his father, not only in personal appearance, but in the very gracious ease of his manner ; making every little incident a hook on which to hang a pleasant remark.

Those of you who have been among the English lakes will understand how useless is the attempt to give any description of the wondrous beauty. After leaving Mr. Foster Braithwaite's, we drove in open carriages along the shore of Windermere and Grassmere, and Rydal Water, passing the house where your mother and I had formerly enjoyed the privilege of visiting Wordsworth with an introduction from Miss Anna Braithwaite. It is now owned by a Mr. Crewdson, a relative of the Braithwaite family also ; but we did not stop. This morning we stopped at Penrith, where are the ruins of a castle once occupied by Richard, Duke of Gloucester ; Shakespeare's hunchback, afterward Richard III of England. We found the walls used to support cattle sheds ; and the only living tenants were poultry.

At Carlisle we were detained long enough to dine, and drive to the castle, now enclosed by a dry moat and used as a part of the barracks of Her Majesty. There is also a good modern cathedral. Soon after leaving it we crossed the *Solway*, and passed the once celebrated Gretna Green ; and so on through finely cultivated farms at first, then perfectly wild moors and barren hills, along the ridge dividing the waters of the Clyde and Tweed, to this place.

Our hotel faces a green deep vale, on the opposite side of which rise lofty Gothic buildings ; while the summit is crowned by an ancient looking fortress. We have been too wearied to wander out, but have enjoyed the beauty of the moon—nearly full—rising over these buildings and shedding her light on the green lying between us and them. A little to the left is a Gothic structure which we supposed to be the monument of Walter Scott, but some one tells us it is that to Christopher North (Professor Wilson), quite as worthy of such honor. Each was endowed with a lofty intellect and fine imagination, but there is something more elvated in the tone of Wilson which attracted me even more than the Wizard of the North, whose poems your Aunt Jane reads to the party every evening while the others work. They are all at this moment absorbed in " Marmion."

With love to one and all,

Your affectionate father,

CASPAR MORRIS.

EDINBURGH, September 17, 1872.

My Dear Children :

When I endorse the usual expression of opinion that this is a *grand* town I do not design to compare it with Vienna, though next to that it may well deserve to be so called. Our hotel stands on a wide street. Before our window lies an open park, and directly across it rises a hill crowned by an old castle of large dimensions, and away along the crest of the hill rise ranges of Gothic structure with fine spires, rising above churches; and the statues to John Wilson, and the Gothic monument to Walter Scott are in our view as we look to the left.

The weather is cold and gloomy and when we started this morning we found it so cold on Calton hill that your mother and I left the party at Holyrood in order to procure some warmer dress for her than any we have brought with us. We thus missed the interior of the palace and will be obliged to refer you to the books of history and story for the description of Mary's chamber and Rizzio's blood-stain on the floor, as well as for the long line of imaginary portraits or imaginary Scottish Kings and other legendary wonders of the palace. We saw the ruined abbey which must have been very beautiful. The murky atmosphere prevented our having any view from the hill, but we can well understand it must be very grand as well as extensive on a clearer day. A strictly clear day I believe they cannot boast.

The lamentation over the harvest is universal. We are told the wetness and cold of the summer has never had a parallel. The potatoes are all rotted and the grain growing where it has been cut and shocked, and much has not ripened at all.

Wednesday morning, 18th.

The clear notes of the animating bugle call, resounding from the Castle which crowns the craggy heights across the ravine by which the old and new town are separated, stirred the dwellers in the town as well as the two thousand men in garrison, and caused me to rise and open our shutter and admit the bright light of a clear day, which must bring hope and joy to many a heart crushed with a sense of the loss of the potato crop and serious injury to the harvest; so dire a calamity, not to the cultivator only, but to the consumer also. Throwing up the sash I admitted the invigorating breeze which shook the tops of the trees on the grassy slope which forms this side of the ravine, while the other is rocky and precipitous. The air has all the crisp freshness of an October morning at home, making us rejoice with the farmer who will go forth to his fields with merry heart and open his sheaves to the ventilation. The sun rose over the heights of Arthur's seat with golden glow on a cloudless sky and the animating bustle of the street below bade us be moving also.

Yesterday I walked along the Canongate and by the Tolbooth and over the bridges and got some idea of Old Edinburgh, with its streets running along the ridges, and Wynds and Stairs and Closes diverging from these down the steep sides of the hills. These passages are only a few feet wide and run down, down, down ; either winding slopes or by stairs between houses seven, eight, nine, and ten stories high, covering the entire area, and all swarming. I have never seen so many *boys*. I wonder where the women and girls are. Men and boys crowd the streets, all bustling with business or sport, while ever and anon a stalwart Highlander, belonging to the regiment at the Castle, stalks by with his tartan plaid and bare knees and great mass of black feathers on his head. The firm gait and sinewy thews are very imposing even if not set off by the showy costume, which is so familiar to us in pictures and associated with the romance of Scottish history.

We were here interrupted by a package of letters from home and other friends, all calling for thankfulness on our part for the abounding mercies vouchsafed to us. Thank Eff, especially for his. We suppose he and Tyson and Caspar are among those who are making themselves heard in the new building, and while doing so are laying deep foundations on which to build a fair superstructure of usefulness during their lives on earth, and striving to discharge their duty in the station of life to which God hath called them, and be found like men waiting for the coming of the Lord, that they may be found of him in peace. The lesson of Frank Murray's early call cannot be wasted. It must either be of service or it must add to condemnation.

10 A. M. Wednesday.

We are now about starting for a drive to Roslyn Chapel, etc. ; said to be very beautiful. Have just had letters from Galloway and Hannah, who are now, we hope, safe in London and we are looking forward to a pleasant meeting with them. We left here for Roslyn with a bright sunshine and promise of a fine day. Our drive lay around Arthur's seat and Salisbury Crag, from which we had splendid views not only of the country but of Leith and the Firth of Forth. Clouds soon gathered, driven by a furious gale, and rain fell almost unceasingly, only lifting a little occasionally, and shewing immense fields of grain cut and standing, and a large acreage of potatoes as black as though fire had passed over them. The result of this entire loss of potatoes and great injury to the grain, added to the price of coals, which is double what it was last winter, must be great suffering, not only to the destitute poor, but to all persons of only moderate means.

We stopped at Dalkeith and saw the splendid park of the Duke of Buccleugh ; some of the party going through the house, which is a large plain edifice with retiring front and projecting wings. The grounds are very extensive (one thousand acres) and well planted and kept.

From there we drove through a beautiful rolling country, watered by the Esk to Roslyn ; a curious little chapel built some three hundred years ago, but falling far below my expectations in beauty. Its merit is rather its oddity. The stone work is not of a high order and the style is nondescript. It is still used for worship. I ventured to look into the service book and found it Anglican and not Scotch.

19th.

Auld Reekie forever! Edinburgh is a very *nice* place now. Once it was anything else. Dr. Chapman's account of its dwellings and inhabitants when he was a student here, is strongly in contrast with anything that meets one's eye and nose to-day. Not only the private dwellings and public buildings in the newer parts, but the various parts of the old town are kept clean. In walking about I have found myself in the Tolbooth and other places familiar in name, and find them all crowded with antiquated dwellings, many stories high. The progress of modern science is marked, however, by the demolition of these old buildings and the erection of others more convenient and comfortable, though less substantial in their construction. We never walk out that I am not impressed by the grandeur of the unfinished national monument, whose massive marble columns and architrave crown the summit of Calton Hill, and are all the more imposing from their unfinished condition, allowing the light to fall through the colonnade.

The Scott monument is certainly the best architectural monument in Great Britain. Its proportions are perfect and the detail and finish equally so. It is so well known by the engravings and photographs that it would be useless to describe it. It is like a cathedral spire, with a sitting statue of the great *unknown* admirably executed; the likeness unmistakable.

Near by is a monument to Scotland's greatest poet, James Thompson, a very fine life-sized marble full-length statue on a pedestal.

Burns—poor Burns!—has also a monument; which gave occasion for the cutting sarcasm "He asked for bread, and they gave him a stone." He and his admirers are unmindful of the sad truth that his sorrows were all like those of other men of genius, the ripened harvest of the seed of his own follies and sins. We are all too ready to censure Divine Providence, or chide our friends, for the consequences of our own errors and perversenesses.

There is a great diversity of architecture in the various public buildings here, some Gothic and others classic. The building stone employed is light colored, but soon acquires a very sooty coat. The private houses have wide fronts and low elevations, which is made more magnificent by the width of the streets. There is a very pleasant homelike appearance about the crowds of honest looking men, women and children who throng the streets. There is a great display in the windows of very beautiful agate, onyx, and cairngorm pins and brooches, and amethest, and topaz, and pebble gems. I do not trust myself within the doors, nor venture to ask prices, but am content to admire them where they are instead of putting them where they would lose their beauty, or at least have it greatly dimmed by the thought of how much it cost and how inappropriate to our means ; and am thankful to be free from the working of envy of those who can wear them without. On the persons of such I admire them just as I do in the shop windows, as beautiful works of Divine creation and human art.

Your uncle and aunts have made an excursion to-day to Melrose and Dryburgh Abbeys and Abbotsford. Your mother and I have thought it wiser to remain here, as to-morrow's journey will be a long one, and we find over-fatigue is injurious to us in every way. We have seen so many impressive ruins that we can appreciate the loss in missing these, and yet can understand how they do look sufficiently well to have some knowledge of their appearance. The surroundings vary, but abbey ruins are all very much alike. The genius of Abbotsford is departed and we do not care to wander through deserted halls whose lights are fled.

2 P. M.

I have just returned from an interesting visit to the college library of two-hundred thousand volumes with some manuscripts. It is a noble hall, well arranged, and with shelves weighted with the works of great minds. A few busts of familiar worthies ; Playfair, a most noble head and brow, with a fine benignant face ; Cullen, to whose great works I was set down just fifty years ago as the first step in medical study by my worthy preceptor, Parrish, whose ability as well as moral worth I estimate more highly the larger is my own sphere of observation. Monro, Primus, Secundus and Tertius, Duncan, etc. Christison's is a very fine head.

A full length life-size statue of Sir David Brewster stands opposite the entrance into the Quadrangle, surrounded by these halls devoted to the lecture and recitation rooms of Theology, Law and Medicine, in all which the school of Edinburgh holds so high a position. Being the source from which we of the University of Pennsylvania derive our collegiate life this must ever be honored by us.

From the college I went to the Museum, where there is a miserable collection of specimens of animals and birds, scanty in number, badly mounted, and in bad preservation. A giant Gorilla, however, repaid me for the trouble of going. A lion may well shrink from the encounter with such a monster in size and ferocity of expression. I do not know what is the measurement or what may have been the weight of the beast, but he is at least three feet across the shoulders, with long muscular arms and great paws. A grizzly bear would suffer in an embrace. I do not envy the *muscular* philosophy which accepts even this as a type of our nature as it came from the hands of an omnipotent as well as wise Creator, who could as easily create man upright and in His own image (as He said He did when He pronounced His work good) as throw off an imperfect being to be improved by "*selection*," or in any other mode which seems better to the finite judgment of the man who glories in having reached by such processes the highest stage of which he is capable, and is willing to rot with the beasts, whom he chooses as his companions, rather than *believing* what God has said, and accepting what He has offered, to commit His body to the dust in the sure and certain hope of a joyful resurrection to *eternal* life. As I passed through the college I saw a drinking fountain with an inscription on it; erected to the memory of Prof. Hope by his son.

In going to the college I passed St. Giles, the Cathedral of Edinburgh, in which John Knox preached, to the great discomfort of many and in which some stalwart Scotland woman manifested her zeal *against Popery* in the most unseemly manner by throwing her stool at the head of the Archbishop whom James or Charles (I forget which) had sent to replace the Kirk and Presbytery, by the establishment of the Anglican Episcopacy. As I was gazing about, some liveried flunkey addressed me with the remark that Mary did not like Knox; to which I replied that Mary would certainly have handed Scotland over to French and Popish control, so though Knox may have been as rough and rude in his line as the woman was in hers, the cause they so improperly advocated was the cause of Truth.

We are now looking cheerfully toward the rapidly approaching time for our embarkation. We shall in all probability not meet Gall. and Han. till we reach Liverpool, as I think there is more to attract them in what we have already seen than in what is before us. The mountains and lakes of Scotland and Ireland will occupy over two weeks, so that we shall only have a few days for Wales, as three at shortest (and if possible four) must be given to final arrangements at Liverpool.

I spent an hour or more yesterday with Miss Williams at her friend's, Miss Scott's, who was governess to the family of the Prime Minister, Mr. Gladstone. She is a sensible, pleasant woman.

Give much love to your uncles, Israel and Henry, and thank them for their very kind letters, so full of brotherly affection.

I shall reply to both, if possible, before we sail. If I do not they must not think my not doing so is from neglect or want of appreciation of their kindness. I am constantly busy.

Your loving father,

CASPAR MORRIS.

EDINBURGH, September 18, 1872.

*My Dear Sister (Emily Hollingsworth.—*EDS.):

The consumption of time and strength in sight-seeing leaves but little of either for higher and holier and pleasanter duties. You see I have taken a small sheet on which to address you, not as the measure of my love for you or as capable of conveying all I feel and wish to utter, but as the pattern of ability. If I were to take a larger it would be like the great buildings of St. Thomas' Hospital, in which the sick are like the little kernel in a thick shelled and thicker hulled hickory nut. I wish what little I have to say were less sadly distressing. I enclose a melancholy letter just received which needs but little comment. While riding in the cars a few days ago I found we were passing through Harrowgate and as a gentleman who sat near me had been very agreeably communicative about persons and things in the neighborhood, I inquired if he knew anything of Dr. Bennett. "Oh, yes," was his reply, "he has been utterly ruined by the extravagance of his sons and is broken down and obliged to leave." Notwithstanding this information I wrote him a note at our next resting place, inquiring for Miss Dunant, with the hope that the account might be erroneous, and the desire at least to know what he had to say about her. I, of course, made no illusion to what I had heard of his own affairs and only expressed my regret at having failed to see her while on the Continent and my desire to learn something about her. He does not say to what extent he has been accustomed to contribute toward her support.

For that you must depend upon her, and if you find it necessary to enlarge your remittances do it, not at the cost of further self-denial in your own comfort, but remember what Ann and I have said. You shall be a partaker of ours whatever it may be without your being bound to any definite share of the expense.

We find the house in Chestnut Street is as yet on our hands, and if it be so when we arrive we shall go there till it can be more profitably disposed of, and we can find a more moderate establishment, which will suit us better on every account. I believe the time has come, if we are permitted to return safely, for us to try to live very simply and quietly the rest of our days on earth. Something I must do to "redeem the time," but it must be in very simple way, involving no responsibility. If God has any work for me he will graciously indicate the path in which I shall walk.

We think much of you and the sad surroundings which cluster about you. It is your privilege to be his minister to soothe the sorrows and relieve the distress of many. Give our dear love to Mrs. Wistar and mine to Miss Smith also. We do pray that He who alone has the power may heal their bruised and crushed affections and cause their present sore distress to be the means of preparing them for greater glory.

Yours most lovingly,

CASPAR MORRIS.

TROSACH'S HOTEL, September 23, 1872.

My Dear Children:

To fail to write you from the "Land of Cakes" over which the genius of Burns and the magic power of the "Wizard of the North" have cast such a halo of glory, and which has been rendered so famous by the mighty minds of Chalmers and Stuart and Hamilton and McCosh, would certainly be treason to taste and manifest a want of power to estimate the value of human intelligence. Yet I shall do but little and that hastily. It is cold and wet, and in this very charming little hotel, so appropriate to the spot, our chamber is too small to have a fire and is also destitute of the necessary accommodations for writing, and the sitting room is a little gem of itself, but it does not permit so large a party to scintillate in it. We can just pack ourselves each in his own *sedilium*, as did the old monks in their refectories; be content with the glimpses caught through the high narrow windows which look out on the heath and moss-covered sides of the low mountains, which rise from the soft shores of Loch Achray, a beautiful little sheet of water which lies calmly cradled amid their sheltering heights. This morning I am sole possessor for a little while and embrace the opportunity to write a few lines.

We yesterday attended worship in the little Kirk which stands on a headland running out into the lake and heard an excellent as well as eloquent discourse from the minister, whose prettily little manse stands just across the road. These are almost the only habitations of man we saw on our way from Callander here, certainly the only ones after leaving the borders of Loch Vennachar, which, larger than Achray, lies in a more populous and fertile vale. Soon after we reached here, on Saturday afternoon, I walked along the only road which passes from Callander by Vennachar and Achray to Loch Katrine, and as each turn of the way carried me more and more into the heart of the gorge, through which flows the water from one loch to the other, I thought I had rarely seen more beautiful wildness. The head of Ben-A'an, a bald and scarred rock, towers above the rounded shoulders of the several ranges of lower mountains covered with varied bracken and purple heather, while the lower sides are covered with shades of soft green moss brown birch and ash and aspen and holly and oak; from among which masses of rock protrude and little waterfalls glance among the green boughs. Swans have become naturalized and float on the lakes, while burrows of foxes tell that the savage is not entirely ousted by the crowding civilization which has brought a steamboat to ply on the waters of Loch Katrine instead of the barge of Rhoderick with the ever green pine and song of the rower.

I have formed a higher estimate of the powers of Scott since I have been amid the scenes he has rendered so familiar to all possesssing literary taste, and as I think of his literally giant powers I am led to the more consecrated talents of Chalmers and those who, like him, have been stars in the great northern constellation of intellect. Scott's powers were all creations of his own mind, and it is not a little amusing to see how perfectly he has beguiled the world into the belief in the real existence of Douglasses and Rhodericks and Rob Roys and Jeannie Deans. I heard a lady at Sterling ask the guide for Rhoderick's dungeon. He was a fine, bright looking old soldier, who had been amusing the company by story after story about the helmet and visor and casque, winding up by showing the hat of Oliver Cromwell (which outweighs the casque and morion and *all* of other heroes, and would take into its capacious cavern head, neck and almost shoulders of common men), he replied, "That's all *hum*." "Do you know the origin? A lazy fellow was hard up, and wishing for a drink asked the keeper of a bar to suggest some way in which he should be apt to raise the wind; and you know," said the guide, "we Scots are all canny, so the bar-keeper suggested that he should shew an old wine vault to the first visitor as Rhoderick's dungeon." From similar made material Scott has woven the countless pages which beguile our young imagination and delude us even in more mature years, and have a sad tendency to dim our moral perception and make us look with more leniency on the *crimes and sins* of Douglasses and Jamesses, and almost betray us into the adoption of the superstitions of Ellen and Allan and Brian.

GLASGOW, 24th.

The opportunities for writing now are few and inconvenient. The weather is cold, nor even if it were warm enough, do these hotels provide tables or room for them in our chambers. The parlours, or sitting rooms are small also, and though I might write in a commercial, or coffee room, undisturbed by conversation around me in which I take no interest, I cannot be so abstracted in the small space of our sitting room with your uncle and aunts chatting. So you will be obliged to rest satisfied with my very meagre descriptions of scenes and incidents full of beauty and interest. What is more sad still I find they make only superficial impressions, so that I fear even the stimulus of your interest in them will fail to recall them so vividly as I should desire when we meet face to face.

We yesterday rode in an omnibus through the Trosachs, only about a mile, to the pier ; where we took the steamer on Loch Katrine. The pass is truly beautifully wild with its rocky cliffs and deep wooded dells, and great beds of bracken, and soft *clothing* of moss, and delicate coloring of pink heather. The little boat glided noiselessly, as was beseeming such scenes, over the lake, past Ellen's Isle and the Silver Strand of the secluded nook. I had sent my field glasses in my trunk, thoughtlessly, to Glasgow, so that small as is the lake I was dependent on the more convenient and portable lenses of imagination, aided by which I pointed out Ellen standing waiting in a *birchen* shade ; and not long after saw a "gallant gray" quietly pasturing on the hillside. Soon after which all romance was dissipated by the pipes and air tubes which indicate the route of a tunnel opening out of the lake by which the *canny bailies* and *burghers* of this commercal capital of North Britain indicate their thrift by carrying the water of the lake of Scott to the supplying of the various necessities of its mills and dwellings and manufactories. They need it all, for it is a dirty place. Those of you who have been here need no description of mine to recall the witchery of the scenes through which we passed from Callander along Vennachar and Achray, through the wild pines of the Trosachs and across the bosom of Loch Katrine, and so by coach to Loch Lomond, and upon its dark bosom, amid castellated halls and beautiful villas, to Balloch, where the car and locomotive took us up and hurried us past Dumbarton's craggy rock, standing like an outpost advanced far into the lowlands. It is a curious mass of rock, crowned with a castle, standing entirely disconnected from any hill, in the midst of the fertile valley watered by the Clyde.

The sad sight of shocks of wheat and oats with their tops as green as the grass which covers the intervening ground, proves that the wail of the agriculturist is not uncalled for. This, however, is better than the "harries" of the highlanders, which have been sung by the bards and celebrated by the romance writers who have given such interest to the dark pages of Scotia's history. To live at all in the glens and fells and mosses and moors of the highlands they must have preyed on the labor of the lowlands. Even now only a few straggling sheep, or cattle with long hair like wool, scattered here and there on the houseless moors, tell that somewhere a few hardy fellow-beings make shift to maintain a precarious existence. They are no longer as ferocious as Helen McGregor, nor as *predatory* as Rob Roy ; and the universal diffusion of education gives them a—

(*Evidently interrupted here and unable to resume.*—EDS.)

DUMFRIES, September 26, 1872.

We have been bustling about Glasgow since I commenced this letter. The weather has been cold and penetrating. Snow and ice are reported on the Grampian Hills. Yesterday we left Glasgow for this place, designing to lodge here and then cross over to Belfast, leaving here at 7 A. M. The cold and stormy aspect caused brother Wistar to determine to change our route and omit Ireland. So that we shall retrace our steps by Carlisle to New Castle and so into the midland counties and Wales. I am convinced it is best.

Your mother and I had decided to remain on this side even if the others had crossed. We heard yesterday from Galloway and Hannah, not comfortable accounts. In a few days we shall be able to join parties.

The route to this place from Glasgow led us first through the celebrated iron districts, bristling with the tall chimneys and furnaces, whose blazing tops spoke of the molten stream of riches they were pouring out below. But we learn the irregularity of the demands of the operatives, who strike constantly for advancing wages with advancing prices of iron, renders the profit so uncertain that the masters have determined to stop operations.

After leaving the iron districts we passed through a beautifully rich agricultural district with large flocks of sheep. The paper of the morning reports snow three feet deep and the thermometer down to zero in the Highlands and snow and ice in Yorkshire; with very sad accounts of the ruined harvest and rotted potatoes.

This is a very pretty and very prosperous town, supported by the manufacture of tweeds. Yesterday as we approached we met numerous trains crowded with people returning from the fair which is just closed. Some sad illustrations that the temperance of the people now is not more decided than it was in the days of Tam O'Shanter and Robert Burns.

NEWCASTLE ON TYNE, September 26th, Evening.

We arrived here this afternoon after a ride of about five hours from Dumfries, by way of Carlisle, where we stopped an hour for luncheon. The country about Dumfries, and between that and Carlisle, is very beautiful, highly cultivated and well stocked with sheep. Between Carlisle and this place it varies greatly; passing through collieries and iron furnaces and coke ovens, which in some parts fill the atmosphere for miles with sooty fumes. Other parts are purely agricultural, chiefly devoted to sheep pastures, while here and there were naked hills, peat-bogs, and forests. The latter half of the distance the road followed the course of the river Tyne, and carried us past Hexham and other large towns, and some ruined ancient castles, as well as grand modern residences. It was a ride through varied scenes of great beauty.

This place certainly may challenge for itself the palm for blackness. It has some two hundred thousand inhabitants and some fine monuments and churches and public buildings ; and many very handsome stores, well stocked with elegant goods. But all sooty black. Literally the fronts of the buildings are like the backs of chimneys and one feels that he is inhaling carbon (in its most minute state of division it is true), but in appreciable quantities to say nothing of what is swallowed. The entire atmosphere is poisoned by carburetted hydrogen gas, so that my letter must be of an illuminating character or it is unworthy of the inspiration of this great mart of coals. It is quite a descent from Bannockburn, Wallace, and Bruce; and Loch Katrine and Douglass and Walter Scott and Dumfries and Ayrshire and Burns, and the Cotter and Mary, to this smoky foul region. Just before leaving Dumfries we made a pilgrimage to the house in which Burns lived and died, and to the grave in which his ashes repose, marked by a very well executed marble monument standing on a stone dome. The monument, in white marble, representing the poet standing at the plough handle, his face upturned to a female figure floating in the air, representing either the genius of poetry calling him from his labours to higher pursuits (as suggested by sister Hannah), or probably the spirit of "Mary in Heaven," as addressed by him in one of his sweetest lyrics.

I am more enchanted with English scenery than ever before, and quite pleased with English people. There is an air of neatness and comfort about the dwellings and arrangements of these northern counties and a civility, as well as independence, in the deportment of the people which is very attractive. The cottages of the farm labourers are here, as elsewhere in Europe, generally only of one story and apparently only two rooms, and therefore too small for the proper accommodations of the families, but they are in these northern counties neat and white-washed on the outside ; and sometimes have pretty little flower-beds about them.

Snow, hail, wind and cold have induced your uncle to abandon the trip to Ireland and we have turned our faces south and shall spend a day or two at Malvern.

Your loving father,

CASPAR MORRIS.

BIRMINGHAM, September 29th, 1872.

My Dear Children:

A bright and apparently mild morning smiles upon us here in the midst of the din and smoke of this great manufacturing mart. We yesterday rode through half the length of England and if I were asked for a succinct discription of the kingdom I would say it is a great workshop of various trades and arts with some gardens about the houses of its many millions of operatives, and parks about the residences of its capitalists. Grand as are some of the palaces and castles of its hereditary aristocracy the power and glory have been transferred from their possession to that of the mechanic and industrial arts, and for the power to maintain the splendour which the old aristocracy still display they depend very largely, not on their ancestral acres so much, as on those mechanical and industrial arts, which give value to the coal and iron which lie below the surface. It is to his iron and coal interests that the Marquis of Bute owes his great income and the Marquis of Westminster in like manner derives income from the growth of London which is due to similar influences.

Leaving Newcastle and passing through Darlington and York and Sheffield, with all the numberless outlying dependencies on these great centres of coal and iron and other manufacturers, this train of thought is naturally suggested by the crowding masses in these workshops and the comparatively spare population of the agricultural districts. In many places the entire atmosphere for miles is thickened and blackened by the coal smoke poured in volumes from tall chimneys and furnace stacks and coking ovens. The fleece of the sheep are blackened by it in the fields.

We passed yesterday through Burton-on-Trent, the seat of the great brewery of Allsop & Sons. The buildings are very extensive and the barrels are piled up in immense stacks, covering many acres. The product of the huge vats is distributed to every part of the world, as I used to find it in India; we are all familiar with it in the United States, and we saw it exposed for sale in the Greek groceries far up the Nile.

We passed within sight of the sweet little church and dear home of our friends at Little Eaton and recognized the towers of Haddon Hall and also the grand front of Kippex Park, the residence of the mother of Mr. Bland, the husband of Mary Wharton.

September 29th, Malvern.

You will see I write up the minutes as opportunity offers and now sit down, while waiting the coming to breakfast of your uncle and aunts, unable to repress the expression of the delight I find in this most beautiful spot. I sit in a window which opens on a lawn, so closely shaven that it looks like a great spread of green velvet, at the foot of which stands a noble walnut tree, and beyond it parterre after parterre and terrace after terrace stretches off with house top peeping though the clustering foliage of beautiful trees planted in the grounds by which they are surrounded. At the left hand, immediately beside me, stands the grand old Abbey church, built about the twelfth century, from the tower of which the soft notes of the chimes have recorded the flight of every quarter of an hour since we arrived here after nightfall yesterday evening, and whose melody invites us there to worship Him who made all so wondrous fair as the distant landscape, that is simply beyond description; limited only by the horizon, it takes in cultivated plains with hedge-rows planted with trees, the green pastures between them diminishing in apparent breadth under the influence of distance, till they are finally lost in an indistinguishable mass of forest. Here and there hills swell up from the level plain and in one direction gradually rise till they are lost in the blue lines of the mountains of Wales. Church spires, projecting through the trees, tell of villages hidden among them, while the soft sunlight gilds irregular spots, and dark shadows of clouds move slowly across the panorama, giving perpetual change of light and shade.

I was here interrupted by the arrival of a precious packet of letters; some from home and one from dear Galloway and Hannah, who are well, in London, and will join us here or at Capil Curig, about the middle of the week. How can we be sufficiently thankful for all the mercies which have followed us and prevented us during all these fifteen months and brought us safely thus far on our return. "To this Christian land;" that alone is enough, but we will trust that the same fatherly love and care will carry us safely home on earth.

Tell your uncles, Henry and Galloway, we both appreciate all the love which invites us to share with them so freely of their privileges, and only hope we may have wisdom given us to "know how to abound."

Monday, 2 P. M.

Yesterday as I came down the stairs I was saluted by an exclamation, "Dr. Morris, is that you?" from a lovely looking lady dressed in deep mourning who came out of a parlour directly opposite to ours. She advanced promptly and seized my hand with an expression of delight, I was quite at a loss for some little time, when suddenly before she could explain I recognized the likeness to Mrs. Braithwaite, and said so, just as her husband advanced and she introduced him to me. They have been here a week for the benefit of her health. After church your mother and I called on them and found them highly intelligent, cultivated lovely people, delighted to see us, and urging us strongly to turn right about and go to London and spend the time till we sail with their father and mother. This would be very pleasant truly. Late in the evening we received a note from Mrs. Barksworth, inviting us to breakfast with them this morning and thus take an hour for a quiet chat before we leave, which we had told them we should do to-day. We accepted the invitation and passed a very pleasant hour, after which she went to be subjected to a pressure of half an atmosphere more than the usual sixteen pounds per square inch on the surface of the body. This is under the advice of a hydropathic Doctor. I think he should add pneumatic to his titles. I cannot understand the principle on which it is to be of service.

MALVERN, October 1, 1872.

Every days' detention in this home of the beautiful fixes it more and more deeply in my affection. Of all places I have ever seen it possesses the greatest combination of those elements of attraction which in their individuality are charming and when grouped, as they are here, are made a perfect whole. Before me spreads out an expanse of cultivated farms, gentlemen's parks, and villages and hamlets embosomed in trees ; bounded on the opposite side by lofty eminences —mere blue outlines against the sky. While a lofty height, clothed only with gorse and ferns and heather, rises behind me.

The rich level plain was once the arm of the sea, like the channels between England and France and England and Ireland, the boundaries of which were those lofty cliffs. Malvern itself possesses a stately Abbey church, more than seven hundred years old, and is composed of beautiful cottage and villa residences, and large and elegant hotels and lodging houses, each of which is surrounded by lawns of neatly shaven grass and clusters of shrubbery of every variety of lesser tree and plant. The beauty of all may be inferred when I tell you there are certainly miles of hedges of Laurestinus, kept neatly trimmed, and now tipped with the greatest profusion of unexpanded flower buds, now of a light rose-color, soon to be snowy white and with rich odor. It is ever green and retains its blossom all winter. At this moment the distant view is half hidden in a veil of cloud through which here and there the rays of the sun give a golden glory to spots, bringing out clearly their special beauty, while all around is "half concealed."

The houses are built on terraces along the lower slope of the mountain while zig-zag roads invite ambitious climbers, either on their own feet or by the aid of donkeys, to reach the summit, from which the view is said to embrace fifteen counties. This mountain is a narrow ledge dividing the valley which lies before me from another and similar one on the other side. We drove yesterday around it. Every yard we passed over seemed to reveal some new attraction.

On the summit of one portion of the height is the perfectly well traced outline of an ancient encampment, whether British or Roman I am uncertain, and on another a lofty shaft rises as a monument of one of the Lord Somers. A part of our drive was through their park and forest of Eastnor Castle, the residence of that family, an ancient building, but kept in good repair and still inhabited. One part of the road through the grounds was buried in over-hanging yew trees;—some of them of very great size, while open glades and bosky dells and wide-spread lawns, dotted with majestic oaks, spread over thousands of acres pastured by herds of deer, and some flocks of sheep and cattle. We drove more than three hours without retracing our steps, on roads, without any exaggeration as smooth and firm as the floor of a dwelling house.

Several lines of railroads cross these lowlands, passing by tunnels through the intervening heights. The fossils found in these excavations are of great interest to the geologist and I saw a very fine collection of them admirably arranged in the hall of the Townsend house—one of the large hydropathic establishments for which Malvern is so celebrated.

As I came down stairs here the day after our arrival I was recognized and saluted by a lady who proved to be the oldest daughter of our highly valued old friend I. Braithwaite. She is here with her husband under treatment. By their invitation I went to see them this morning take the bath of compressed air. They sat two hours in an iron chamber like a large diving bell, into which the air was forced by a steam pump till there is a pressure of half an atmosphere more than the natural degree. They sat there looking out occasionally through thick plate glass windows and pursued such occupations as they pleased for the occupation of the time. This morning they wrote letters home. Though avowedly a hydropathist, Dr. G. is one of those keen witted men who either deludes himself or deceives others. Every appliance for the comfort and amusement of the inmates of the establishment is amply provided and it is somewhat amusing to hear of the great and the noble who have patronized it. Among his most honored patients he held he said in especial esteem Dr. Alonzo Potter and his wife, who with their children had been here some years ago; and was not a little amazed when, after he had described the boys singing for him "Waiting for the Wagon," I told him one of those boys had acquired the rank of General in our army by his courage and active service during the rebellion. He frankly admitted the English sympathy with the Southern people on the score of their being more aristocratic than the mere shopkeepers and manufacturers of the Northern states. I strove to enlighten him a little on the subject, but I suspect the next American visitor will find him "a relapsed heretic."

LLANGOLLEN, Wednesday evening.

Does the bow of hope forever span with its glorious arch this beautiful valley? Thirty-six years ago it spread its enchantment to our view as we drove down from Capel Curig and now this afternoon, as we entered again, there it hung on the face of the dark cloud, as pink and bright and beauteous as then. What vicissitudes of storms and calm have your mother and I experienced in these years? Yet here we are able still to enjoy the same beauties.

Your brother and sister joined us last evening and we have had a most charming ride from Malvern to this place, skirting Wales and passing through the most beautiful valleys with rich pasturage and enlivened by a larger amount of cattle and sheep than we have seen in any one day since we came to England. It has been one unbroken scene of fertility and richness.

We regret that Galloway and Hannah should have had so little opportunity to enjoy the beauties of England, but are glad that they should be with us.

Thursday morning.

This is a beautiful bright morning. The sun shines into this narrow valley through which the black waters of the Dee rush almost madly from the mountains above toward the beautiful valley below. The ruins of Castle Denas Bran crown the heights across the stream, just in front of our windows. We propose driving in carriages from here to Capel Curig, just reversing the trip we made when here formerly when we came down the same road.

CAPEL CURIG, N. Wales, October 4, 1872.

My Dear Sister:

Do you remember our leaving this place a little more than thirty-six years ago in company with our dear friends, Isaac and Anna Braithwaite? The place retains all the grand beauty with which it has been originally formed and which has been the result of the lapse of ages clothing its rugged heights with the soft color of moss, and fern, and heather, and gorse. Dear Anna has joined the great company who have washed their robes and made them white in the blood of the Lamb, to which our dear and highly valued friend M. W. has more recently been added. Isaac is in feeble health and Galloway and Hannah will tell you how heartily and kindly they welcomed them to their beautiful home near London. A few days since we met with their oldest daughter and her husband, both in delicate health, at Malvern. Very intelligent and Christian young people. What a blessed thing it is to find the generation of God's children continually renewing.

I believe I did write to you from Mr. Latham's, but I fear several of our last letters have miscarried. Certainly they have not gone promptly either to you or dear Mary and the children, to all of whom we wrote promptly on the receipt of the sad letters announcing the removal of our dear friends—*not lost*, only gone before—and gone where we have always desired they should go. Therefore while we mourn over our bereavement let us rejoice in their joy. We sympathize with dear Mrs. Wistar and her sister more deeply than we can express. Who can enter into the inner chambers of her grief—only He who knows our frame and formed our hearts to find their fullest and purest and keenest delight in those relations which He himself established as the highest and holiest of our being—having made man He made woman for man, and gave them to each other that in the union of their hearts He should find the highest glory of His creative power. Though in the future life we shall neither marry nor be given in marriage, and therefore shall not renew the relations which have been sundered by their removal from us, we shall be permitted to be together with them " forever with the Lord." Shall either they or we ask anything more either for each other or ourselves? "I trust not."

Lest my former letters should have entirely miscarried, I will repeat my message of love to Mrs. Wistar and Miss Smith, in which Anne unites.

We note in your letter just received the expression of a shade of doubt of your joining us in our home when we arrive, if it be the will of our Heavenly Father to carry us in safety to the haven where we would be. We shall be sorry on our own account if anything shall prevent; but we do most truthfully and earnestly hope you will act just as you believe will be right. We know assuredly that you desire only to glorify God in your body and spirit which are His, and God forbid that we should place any impediment in the way of perfect freedom of action. We shall desire if you unite with us to allow you entire freedom as we shall take ourselves.

The letters just received gives us some hope that we shall not be obliged to go again into the house 1428 Chestnut Street, or at most only for a little while. Wherever we may be, we shall be thankful to have you with us, either permanently or where and how it suits yourself. Few indeed and short must be the steps remaining to us on earth. With faces Zionward let us strengthen each other and help to steady each other that so as each comes to the bank of Jordan, we part there only to meet above.

We are all (including Dear Galloway and Hannah) gathered here around a fire with rain falling heavily and steadily, and snow on the tops of the mountains above us. It was the design to have gone to Beddgelert and the pass of Llanberis to-day, and to-morrow we shall go to Bangor and spend the Lord's day quietly; and so on Monday to Liverpool, where we shall spend the week in making final arrangements for our sailing. Will you do us the favor to ask prayers for a family gone to sea at the Epiphany?

This will I suppose reach you about the time of our sailing and is the last letter I design writing home. How our hearts yearn over the ideas associated with that blessed word—Home! The home in our fathers house in which are the mansions our great elder brother has "gone to prepare for us." By what method and at what time we shall pass from time to eternity, we may well leave to the wisdom and love which has provided our redemption and created us and carried us thus far on our pilgrimage.

The conversation around is so animated and interesting and our chambers so cold that we cannot retire to them, so I must bid you farewell. Should you see our children or brothers Henry or Israel or their wives give our love to them.

Yours most lovingly,

CASPAR MORRIS.

Give our love also to Mrs. Cope. If we had gone to Belfast we should have sought out the Bickersteths.

CHESTER, October 7, 1872.

My Dear Children:

What a round we have been since in July, 1871, I wrote my first letter to you from this old town. We certainly had no thought we should be here again, much less that I should conclude my series of letters where it began. When I wrote last and said to your mother I shall not write another letter home, she laughed and replied; "I know you better." So if I were absolutely bent on triumph I might restrain the impulse to write to-day, though a furious storm of wind and rain keeps us prisoners within, and throws us on our own resources for occupation.

We left your uncle and aunts at Bangor in North Wales, on Saturday, and came on to this place with Galloway and Hannah, who had arranged to leave here this morning on a visit to Mr. and Mrs Romilly. Your uncle and aunts will pass through here on their way to Liverpool this afternoon, where we are to join them. We have prevailed with Hannah to allow Galloway to go to Mr. Romilly's, as we all think the weather is too stormy for her to undertake two days of fatiguing travel. She is very frail, and had taken cold a day or two since, which she has yet only partially recovered. I am sorry to have her give up a visit from which she had anticipated great pleasure, and which would have given still greater pleasure to Mrs. Romilly, I am sure. But without doubt it is wiser for her, and we must all often submit to have our wishes disappointed. I often think of the reproof my dear friend Mr. Fowles gave to Miss Elwyn, who made herself ill by exposure in keeping an engagement on a very stormy day. She said she had promised, to which he replied, "Was not God wiser than you?" And this naturally leads me to the train of thought which presented itself to my mind as I dated my letter. How wondrous has been the goodness and mercy which has followed and prevented (or gone before us) during all our pilgrimage since we were last here. By land and by sea, amid storm and sunshine, in sickness and in health, God has kept us in the hollow of his hand, and I desire thus to record my sense of His unmerited goodness and call on you to unite with us in ascribing to Him the praise which is so justly due, and seeking for the grace which shall enable us to show forth our gratitude, not only with our lips, but in our lives, by giving up ourselves to His service and walking before Him in righteousness and true holiness all our days.

We left Bangor on Saturday about 4 P. M. We had arrived there about two hours before, and had been received in the same hotel we had occupied thirty-six years ago, and if I had not been wearied and the time too short, I should have endeavored to find the Bible on the blank leaf of which, while waiting breakfast in our parlour, I then wrote the doggerel lines you are all familiar with. It is barely possible the same copy may be still in the same room. Would that I could think the changes which have passed over myself have all been for improvement.

The changes in the country and villages through which we have been travelling the last five days are very great in many respects. The natural beauty of everything is unimpaired, though the change is great in the character of the houses occupied by the peasantry, and there are more large establishments for manufactures of various kinds, and an increase of the number of collieries and iron works.

The drive from Llangollen to Capel Curig was through a valley of great beauty, and there were many charming scenes and pretty waterfalls. One known as the Swallow Fall deserves all the reputation it has. It is like Trenton Falls. The water of the stream, of a deep dark color, stained by the bogs in which the stream has its rise, and as it dashes over the rocks it is converted into snow-white foam which contrasts strongly with the deep color above and below. It is not the incomparable emerald green of the water of the Niagara, but to one who has not seen that it appears very beautiful. The lakes also, though small, are very pretty little nurslings of the lofty mountains which shelter them in their embraces. From the hotel at Capel Curig we looked across one beyond which in the distance rose three lowering peaks, the highest of which is Snowdon, the monarch of British mountains. While we were there snow fell on all the heights around us, adding greatly to the charm of the scene. Your uncle and aunts drove to the pass of Llanberis, designing to visit also Beddgelert, or the grave of the hound, whose story is told so pathetically in the ballad, but they were too late on leaving the hotel and obliged to return without doing homage to the faithful defender of his master's child and victim of fatal impetuosity.

While they were absent I walked, enjoying the combination of soft valley, placid lake, rushing streams, roaring cascades, and snow clad heights. The sheep dotted the hillsides with the white groups of fleecy flocks, while black cattle were being driven in for milking. Some modern cottages were neat looking, while dilapidated thatched or slated hovels laid against the hills. Artists were out with their sketch-books.

In the morning we drove to Bangor, fourteen miles, going first through a pass in the mountains, just below one which is second only to Snowdon. From the pass we drown down through the valley of Nant Ffrancon by the celebrated slate quarries of Penrhyn. There are no less than seven levels worked above the level, and as many below, and three thousand men employed in the quarries. We reached there after 11 A. M. on Saturday. They stop work at twelve on that day, so that we saw them leaving the works. The uniformity of size and form of the men struck me forcibly. I should think they do not vary one inch in height and not many pounds in weight. These quarries belong to Lord Penrhyn and have been worked some two hundred years. It was very interesting to see the process. I was not a little surprised to find they use powder to blast off the rock in large masses, which are afterwards split by hand, and then dressed with shears to the proper size and shape. I should have expected some less destructive process than blasting, which of course, makes many irregular fragments. There is, however, an inexhaustible store in the mountains, and this is the least costly mode of breaking them off.

The surrounding country after we emerged from the mountain valley, is very beautiful, lightly cultivated and adorned by beautiful villas and residences, and near Bangor is the splendid modern Gothic castle of Lord Penryhn, surrounded by a grand park.

From the top of the pass we had a very extensive view, embracing not only these, but the straits of Menai, Beaumaris, the Island of Anglesea, and the Puffin Rocks in the Irish sea. From the hotel windows we looked over the straits to the island, which is very highly cultivated and adorned by very handsome residences. It is connected with Wales by the celebrated suspension bridge of Telford, which allows vessels in full sail to pass below it, and which when we were here, was considered one of the highest achievements of modern engineering. Since then railroad travel has acquired further progress, and an immense tubular iron bridge passes across beside it at a still higher level. A lofty column rises on the heights of Anglesea, bearing on its top a statue of the Marquis of that name, who distinguished himself at Waterloo. The island of Mona, as it is also called, was the last refuge of the aboriginal Britons, and was especially sacred in their superstition.

Bangor itself was the place at which the British Christians took refuge from Saxon paganism in the earlier centuries, and there was a large monastery here with, I think, over eight hundred monks who asserted their entire independence of Rome and refused to recognize the supremacy of the Pope. Mountain districts are the places in which freedom finds its refuge from danger.

Galloway and Hannah and your mother and I came here on Saturday afternoon. The railroad runs directly along the seashore and passes many pretty bathing places. We arrived here late in the evening and yesterday had a fine clear day and went in the morning to the cathedral, which gave your brother and sister a glimpse as we passed at the old "rows" and houses; designing to examine to-day the antiquities which are the attraction here. To-day it is rainy and stormy, so that we shall be obliged to leave without gratifying them and ourselves. We have just sent Galloway off to see Mr. Romilly, leaving Hannah with us. A telegram from your uncle informs us that they will be here at 4 P. M., when we shall take the same train to Liverpool. You will perhaps receive this a few hours before our arrival. I am glad to say that Hannah is better to-day; she and your mother are sitting talking over the fire while I write.

I must stop writing, as I find their conversation is so attractive that I cannot command my thoughts. With earnest prayers for God's blessing on you all,

Your loving father,

CASPAR MORRIS.

INDEX.

Aboo Simbel	442
Abydus	407, 408, 512, 521
Achray, Loch	931, 933
A. C. M. Pneumonia	501
A. C. M. Sprained Ankle	668
Adda, River	127, 129, 136, 175
Adelsberg, Cave at	695, 705
Adler, Pass of	204
Agnamo, Lake	330
Ajalon, Valley of	584, 605
Alexaudria	341
Ali Mourad, Dinner	493, 524
Alost	52
Amsterdam	788, 791
Amunoph, Colossi	413, 428, 504
Anatolia	624
Angina Pectoris, Attacks of	406, 634
Antinoe	392
Antinous	392
Antwerp	17, 48, 769
Appian Way	324
Arab Dinner	493, 524
Arles	728
Arnheim	794
Arona	226
Assos	632
Assouan	421, 425, 441
Asyoot	386, 398
Athenæus	347
Augsburg	94, 862
Austrian Tyrol	112
Baden Baden	864 to 880
Bairam, Festival of	364
Bangor	942, 944
Basias	668
Bassingshaw	36
Bath	903
Belgravia	32
Bellagio	129 to 199, 211, 228, 231
Ben A'an	931
Benisooef	549
Benni Hassan	391, 541, 543
Berchtesgaden	846
Bergamo	247
Berlin	802 to 821
Bethany	593

i

Bethesda, Pool of	618
Beyroot	620
Birkenhead	23, 24
Birmingham	13, 31, 935
Blenheim	31, 32
Bologna	264, 268, 271
Bonn	69, 72
Bordighera	713, 719
Bormio, Baths of	123 to 140, 207
Boulak, Museum	373
Boulogne-Sur-Mer	885, 887
Bow-Bells	36
Brera Gallery	200
Brescia	247
Bristol	894, 896, 902
Bruges	53
Brussels	46 to 58, 756 to 767
Bubastis	571
Cæsar's Palace	315
Cadenabbia	132, 134, 164, 229
Cairo	348 to 360, 551 to 569
Calais	45, 46, 51
Calamy, Dr.	37, 38
Callander	931
Cambyses	441, 446
Campagna Felice	327
Campagna Romana	328
Cannes	724
Canterbury	42
Capel, Curig	939
Capri	329
Caracalla, Baths of	316, 319
Carmel, Mount	621
Cataract of Nile	442
Certosa	234, 237, 248, 266
Chamouni	133, 139
Charlemagne	69
Chartreuse	289
Cheapside	32, 34, 35
Chepstow	896
Cheops, Pyramid of	363
Chester	10 to 32, 942
Chestons & Cannyngs	590, 591, 907
Chiavenna	116, 130, 135, 156, 204, 210
Chiaja, Naples	329, 330
Clifton	894, 903
Coblentz	71, 72
Colico	129, 142, 170, 175, 209
Cologne	61, 64, 65
Colossi, Thebes	413, 428, 504, 508
Como	147, 154, 175
Como, Lake of	129 to 140
Constantinople	634 to 663
Constance, Lake	88 to 96
Coptic Church	463, 498, 506
Copts	401
Cornhill	35
Corniche Road	711 to 724
Cornish, Henry	17, 35 to 38
Cos	624
Crystal Palace, London	38
Cyprus	622

Dahabeyah, America	357, 363, 375
Dalaas	114
Dalatz	204
Damascus Gate	619
Danube	668 to 674
Delft	771, 772
Deuas Bran. Castle	940
Denderah	510, 517
Dendoor	549
Dohm Palm	410, 426
Dijon	728, 731
Diuner, A'l'Arabe	493, 524
Diocletian, Baths of	319
Dort	768
Dover	17, 41 to 51
Drachenfels	72
Dresden	815 to 822
Dumfries	934
Eaton Hall	13
Ebensee	835, 837
Echard	37
Edfoo	422, 436, 474, 475
Edinburgh	920, 923, 924, 930
Egmont & Van Horne, Counts	48, 59
Ehrenbreitstein	72
Ekmin	530
El Aska	598
Elephantine Island	446
El Kab	480
Ephesus	628, 631, 632
Epsom	18, 19
Erment Island	421
Esne	432, 433, 485
Feldkirch	115
Fiesole	276
Finstermuntz	121, 122
Florence	136, 265 to 289
Forum, Rome	316
Fostat	355
Fountains Abbey	917
Franzenshohe	124
Frejus	725
Gebel Aboofayda	394
Geisberg	73, 79, 83, 84
Generoso, Monte	140, 147
Geneva	132 to 139
Genoa	709
Gethsemane	594
Ghent	48, 51, 52, 767
Ghetto, Rome	311
Ghizeh, Pyramids of	374, 377
Glasgow	932
Gloucester	896, 901
Gmunden	833, 837
Gobat, Bishop	601
Golden Horn	647
Guardia, Lake	247
Guildhall	32, 34, 35
Guttenberg	75
Guy's Hospital	16

Haarlem	792
Hadrian	392
Hague	771, 775, 783
Hanover	796
Heidelberg	73 to 82
Helbrunn	840, 845
Heliopolis	359, 373
Herculaneum	331
Hermonthis	421
Herostratus	415
Hezekiah, Pool of	617
Holy Sepulchre, Church of	586, 600
Hospital, Guy's	16
Hospital, St. Thomas'	14
Huss, John	95, 98
Hypolitus	309
Icaria	627
Interlachen	132, 138
Ischl	834, 835, 837
Ismaileh	570, 572
Jaffa, or Joppa	575 to 579, 603, 610
Jeremiah, Cave of	595
Jerusalem	581 to 592, 602, 616
Karnac	413 to 425, 490, 507
Katrine, Loch	931, 933
Kedron, Vale of	593
Kendal	919
Keneh	510, 514
Keswick	919, 921, 922
Kew Gardens	38
Kings, Tombs of	413
Kom-Ombos	440, 460
Konigsthull	84
Konigsee	836, 846, 847
Landau	88
Landeck	112, 122, 206
Lateran Museum	309
Latham's, Visit to	908, 911
Lausanne	134
Laveno	228
Leamington	906
Lecco	173, 175, 176
Lesbos	633
Leyden	782, 787
Liguria	711
Limmat	99
Little Eaton	908
Llangollen	939
Liverpool	11, 23, 24, 30
Lommond, Loch	933
London	30 to 39, 886 to 901
Louvain	68
Lucerne	138
Lugano	212, 213, 216, 227, 228
Luxor	414, 419, 488 to 508
Lyons	731
Lysons, Canon	585, 593, 613, 906

Madgeburg	791
Mæcenas, House of	328
Maggiore, Lake	132, 134, 173, 179
Mals	114
Malvern	936, 938
Manfaloot	394, 395, 538
Mantua	248
Marcus Aurelius, Statue of	312
Marmora, Sea of	634
Marseilles	718, 723, 724
Matlock Baths	895, 910
Mayence	74
Medeenet Haboo	488 to 509
Melzi, Villa	165, 171
Memnomium	414, 491, 494
Memphis	508, 549
Menaggio	203, 228
Meroe	441
Milan	134 to 195, 232 to 240, 701 to 706
Minieh	385, 389, 541, 546
Moabite Stone	603
Morbegno	129, 131
Moriah Mount	596, 597
Mosque of Omar	597
Mount Carmel	621
Mount of Olives	591
Mourad Ali	419, 507
Mourad Ali, Dinner of	493, 524
Munich	851 to 860
Mustapha Aga	414, 418, 490, 507
Mysia	633
Mytilene	627, 632
Nabresina	700
Nancy	883
Naples	327 to 336
Neby Samwil	614
Neckar	73, 71
Nero and Agrippina	312
Nero's Palace, Rome	318
Newcastle on Tyne	934
Nice	715 to 725
Nuremberg	855
Old Jewry	32
Omar, Mosque of	586, 597
On, or Heliopolis	359
Ostend	17, 45, 46, 51
Oxford	13, 31
Padua	263, 700
Paphos	623
Paris	729 to 756, 884
Patmos	624
Pavia	234, 237
Pegli	716
Pergamos	632
Pescheira	248
Pesth	676, 678, 681
Philæ	454
Pinacothek	857
Pisa	284
Pompeii	331

v

Pool of Bethesda	591
Porlezza	213
Port Said	573, 574
Potsdam	AIE
Posilipus, Mount	330
Prague	817
Puteoli, Amphitheatre	335
Pyramids, Gizeh	374, 376, 551, 565
Pyramids, Sakkarah	377
Quarries, Jerusalem	596
Queenstown	7
Ragatz	102 to 139, 205
Ramah	614
Ramesium	504, 508
Ramleh	581, 603, 613
Rapperswyl	105
Ratisbon	826, 830, 832
Rhine	72 79
Rhodes, Island of	624, 625
Ripon	910, 917
Roda	392, 542
Rosetta Stone	373
Ross	8, 9
Rotterdam	768, 771, 785
Rustschuck	668, 671
Sakarrah, Pyramids of	377, 549
Sakkiah	390, 420
Salamo	623
Salzburg	836 to 849
Samos	627
Savona	711, 715
Serapis, Temple of	335
Scio	625
Scutari	652
Shadoof	390, 396
Shaphira	603, 619
Sharon, Plain of	607
Sheik Selim (Santon)	514
Shishak	416, 498
Siloam	594
Silsilis	424, 440, 468, 469
Simplon Pass	132, 134, 138
Siout	398, 513, 528, 534, 537, 541
Smyrna	625, 627, 629
Solfatara	335
Solferino	244
Sondrio	114, 134, 170, 208
Solomon's Temple	594
Soohag	332
Spedalletti	713
Sphynx	567
Splugen Pass	130, 132, 138
Spondinig	121, 135
Sprained Ankle (A. C. M.)	668, 669
Stamboul	647
Staubach	95
Stelvio Pass	123 to 143, 206
Sterling Castle	932
St. Andrews, Holborn	32

vi

St. Cloud	744
St. Lawrence, Jewry	17, 36, 37, 38
St. Mary Magdalen Church	36, 38
St. Thomas, Hospital	14
Stromboli	338
St. Remo	714
Stressa	216, 220, 223
Stuttgart	118, 863
Syene	446
"Talitha Cumi" House	615
Tamina	103, 106, 170
Temple, Solomon's	594
Temple, Substructions of	599
Tenedos	631, 634
Thebaid	395
Thebes	413, 487 to 508
Thinis	406, 408
This	508, 521
Tintern Abbey	896, 907
Tirlemont	65
Tombs of the Kings	413, 491, 501, 504
Trafoi	124
Trasimeno, Lake	293
Traunsee	833
Trieste	705
Troas	631, 632
Trosachs	931, 933
Troy	634
"Two Piastres"	643
Utrecht	794
Valhalla	828
Varna	671
Vatican Picture Gallery	320, 322
Vennachar, Loch	931, 933
Venice	249 to 257
Verona	246, 248
Versailles	740, 744
Vesuvius	328, 335
Via Dolorosa	586
Via Mala	132
Via Sacra, Rome	317
Vienna	680 to 692
Vicenza	248
Wallen See	105, 119
Warwick Castle	13, 31
Waterloo	68
Wittenburg	804, 810, 812
Wolffbrunnen	84
York	915
Zurich	95, 102, 104, 118, 119

www.ingramcontent.com/pod-product-compliance
Lightning Source LLC
Chambersburg PA
CBHW032008300426
44117CB00008B/943